New Progress

to Proficiency

Self-study Student's Book

Leo Jones

CAMBRIDGE
UNIVERSITY PRESS

PUBLISHED BY THE PRESS SYNDICATE OF THE UNIVERSITY OF CAMBRIDGE
The Pitt Building, Trumpington Street, Cambridge, United Kingdom

CAMBRIDGE UNIVERSITY PRESS
The Edinburgh Building, Cambridge CB2 2RU, UK
40 West 20th Street, New York, NY 10011–4211, USA
477 Williamstown Road, Port Melbourne, VIC 3207, Australia
Ruiz de Alarcón 13, 28014 Madrid, Spain
Dock House, The Waterfront, Cape Town 8001, South Africa

http://www.cambridge.org

First published 2002
Reprinted 2002

Printed in the United Kingdom at the University Press, Cambridge

ISBN 0 521 63553 5 Student's Book
ISBN 0 521 00789 5 Self-study Student's Book
ISBN 0 521 63552 7 Teacher's Book
ISBN 0 521 63551 9 Cassette set

Contents

Thanks . . .

to everyone who helped with this book:

Charlotte Adams, Annie Cornford and Alison Silver

The teachers who commented on the first draft of *New Progress to Proficiency*:

Annie Broadhead, Christine Barton, Anne Gutch, Elizabeth Kilbey, Patricia O'Sullivan and Clare West.

The people who kindly agreed to be interviewed:

Shazia Afridi, William Boyd, James Charles, Allison Curbishley, Jayne Evans, Ray Gambell, Tessa Holman, Amanda Hooper, Claudine Kouzel, Karen Lewis, Christine Massey, Alastair Miller, Michael Newman, Simon Russell Beale, Beth Titchener, and Sarah Wilson

The actors who took part in the studio recordings.

Interviews by Susie Fairfax
Recording produced by James Richardson at The Soundhouse studio assisted by Darrin Bowen
Picture research and permissions by Hilary Fletcher
Proof-read by Ruth Carim
Designed by Caroline Spindler at Oxford Designers & Illustrators

From the second edition

I'd like to thank everyone who generously gave their advice and made comments and suggestions which have helped to shape this New Edition of *Progress to Proficiency*.

Heartfelt thanks to Jeanne McCarten, who started the ball rolling and kept the project moving along. Her discerning ideas and wise advice encouraged me to incorporate countless improvements.

Thank you to the teachers who provided feedback on the first edition:

Craig Andrew, Liz Charbit, Anne Cosker, Marina Donald & Margery Sanderson, Shirley Downs, Brian Edmonds, Hilary Glasscock & Jenny Henderson, Cecilia Holcomb, Ian Jasper, Anne Koulourioti & Ourania Petrakis, Sheila Levy, Vicki Lynwoodlast, P.L. Nelson-Xarhoulakou, Steve Norman, Bruce Pye, Michael Roche, Cristina Sanjuan Alvarez, and Jennie Weldon

I'm particularly grateful to everyone who wrote detailed reports on the first edition, and recommended particular improvements and changes:

Margaret Bell, Jennie Henderson, Ruth Jimack, Jill Mountain, and Clare West

The New Edition was greatly enriched with ideas, criticisms and suggestions from:

Ruth Jimack Jenny Johnson Rosie McAndrew Laura Matthews Pam Murphy Jill Neville Madeline Oliphant Alison Silver Bertha Weighill Clare West

And thanks to the following people for their contributions and assistance:

Peter Taylor, who devoted so much time and effort to collecting the authentic interviews, and who produced and edited all the recorded material, with the help of Studio AVP.
The actors who took part in the studio recordings, and who talked about their own experiences and attitudes.
The people who generously agreed to be interviewed.
Lindsay White, Amanda Ogden, Ruth Carim, Nick Newton, and Peter Ducker.
Alison Silver guided the project smoothly, efficiently and cheerfully towards its publication. Her eye for detail and thoroughness enhanced the book enormously. Working with her was, as always, such a pleasure.

Finally, thanks to Sue, Zoë and Thomas for everything.

From the first edition

My special thanks to Christine Cairns and Alison Silver for all their hard work, friendly encouragement and editorial expertise.

Thanks also to all the teachers and students at the following schools and institutes who used the pilot edition of this book and made so many helpful comments and suggestions: The Bell School in Cambridge, the British Council Institute in Barcelona, The British School in Florence, the College of Arts and Technology in Newcastle upon Tyne, the Eurocentre in Cambridge, Godmer House in Oxford, the Hampstead Garden Suburb Institute in London, Inlingua Brighton & Hove, International House in Arezzo, Klubschule Migros in St Gallen, The Moraitis School in Athens, the Moustakis School of English in Athens, the Newnham Language Centre in Cambridge, VHS Aachen, VHS Heidelberg, VHS Karlsruhe, the Wimbledon School of English in London and Ray Thomson in Switzerland. Without their help and reassurance this book could not have taken shape.

Acknowledgements

The author and publishers are grateful to the authors, publishers and others who have given permission for the use of copyright material identified in the text. It has not been possible to identify the sources of all the material used and in such cases the publishers would welcome information from copyright owners.

1.3 ©David Stafford (4.8.91) and *The Guardian*; *The Guardian* for the use of the following articles, all ©*The Guardian*: **1.6** Vivek Chudhary (23.6.99), **3.1** Margaret Horsfield (2.4.91), **5.6** Paul Brown (18.9.97), **8.3** Leader (1.9.97), **9.7** Andrew Northedge (24.9.91), **11.7** Stephen Burgen (28.1.91), **14.6** Anita Chaudhury (14.6.2000), **14.8** Nicholas Bannister (24.7.99), **16.5** Roger Dobson (15.7.97), **18.1** Will Englund (22.6.2000), **18.1** Michael Ellison (22.6.2000), **18.1** Jamie Wilson (22.7.99), **18.1** David Sharrock (18.2.92); *The Observer* for the use of the following articles, all ©*The Observer*: **1.7** John Henderson (27.6.99), **4.5** Alexander Garrett (29.6.97); **2.1** ©Punch (Feb 1984); **2.4** Estate of Peter Fleming for the extract from *Brazilian Adventure* by Peter Fleming; **3.6** Jake Bowers-Burbridge (8.3.2000) and *The Guardian*; **3.8** Estate of James MacGibbon for the poem from *The Collected Poems of Stevie Smith* (Penguin 20th Century Classics) ©1972 Stevie Smith. *"Not Waving But Drowning"* by Stevie Smith, from *Collected Poems of Stevie Smith*, copyright ©1972 by Stevie Smith. Reprinted by permission of New Directions Publishing Corp. **3.8** *'BloodyMen'* from *Serious Concerns* by Wendy Cope. Reprinted with permission of PFD on behalf of Wendy Cope ©1993 Wendy Cope; **4.3** ©The Estate of Anthony Burgess, Artellus Ltd for the extract from *'Language Made Plain'* by Anthony Burgess; **5.2** ©Telegraph Group Limited 1989; **5.3** ©John Henley (10.3.2000) and *The Guardian*; **6.2, CA4, CA16** extract from *Towers of Trebizond* by Rose Macaulay reprinted by permission of the PFD on behalf of The Estate of Rose Macaulay ©Rose Macaulay 1956; **6.5** extract from *'Hunting Mr Heartbreak'* by Jonathan Raban, reprinted with permission of Gillon Aitken Associates ©1991 by Jonathan Raban. Submitted Excerpt, pages 68-69 from *Hunting Mister Heartbreak* by Jonathan Raban. Copyright ©1990 by Jonathan Raban. Reprinted by permission of HarperCollins Publishers, Inc; **6.6** ©Tourism Saskatchewan; **7.2** ©The Economist (2.11.96); **7.3** Dave Hill and The Independent/Syndication; **7.9** ©Telegraph Group Limited 1995; **8.5** Telegraph Group Limited 1998; **8.10, CA8, CA17, CA27** extracts from *'Bad Time For Talking'* by Paul Sussman *'Death by Spaghetti'*, ©1993-6 The Big Issue/©1996 Paul Sussman; **9.3** ©M.A.Uden; **9.9** extract from web page reprinted with permission of the Head Master, Summerhill School. ©Summerhill School. www.summerhill2000.com; **10.3** extract from *Rise And Fall Of The Third Chimpanzee* by Jared Diamond published by Hutchinson. Used by permission of The Random House Group Limited. Submitted extract from *Rise And Fall Of The Third Chimpanzee* by Jared Diamond. Copyright ©1992 by Jared Diamond. Reprinted by permission of HarperCollins Publishers, Inc; **10.5** extract from *The Stationary Ark* by Gerald Durrell. Reproduced with permission of Curtis Brown Ltd, London, on behalf of the Estate of Gerald Durrell, ©Gerald Durrell; **10.7** ©The Economist (13.6.92); **10.10** extract from *Life on Earth* by David Attenborough, reprinted with permission of HarperCollins Publishers Ltd; **10.11** extracts from *'Save the Earth'* by Dorling Kindersley Limited. ©Joe Miller for the use of his poem 'If the Earth were...'; **11.3** extract from *Brazzaville Beach* by William Boyd, published by Sinclair-Stevenson. Used by permission of The Random House Group Ltd. Also used by permission of The Agency Ltd, London; **11.3** extract from *A Dark Adapted Eye* by Barbara Vine used by permission of Penguin Books Ltd; **11.3** extract from *Nice Work* by David Lodge reproduced with permission of Curtis Brown Ltd, London, on behalf of David Lodge. Copyright ©David Lodge 1988; **11.9** extract from *A Farewell to Arms* by Ernest Hemingway ©Hemingway Foreign Rights Trust; **11.9** William Heinemann Ltd and Viking Penguin for the extract from *The Grapes Of Wrath* by John Steinbeck. "Chapter 1", from *The Grapes of Wrath* by John Steinbeck, copyright 1939, renewed ©1967 by John Steinbeck. Used by permission of Viking Penguin, a division of Penguin Putman Inc; **11.9** The Wylie Agency, London for the extract from *The Mosquito Coast* by Paul Theroux; **12.3** ©1998. Extract *Design Flaws* from *Notes From A Big Country*, published by Black Swan, a division of Transworld Publishers. All rights reserved. *Notes From A Big Country* (Published in the U.S. as *I'm A Stranger Her Myself*) by Bill Bryson, reprinted with permission of The Doubleday Broadway Publishing Group; **12.4** ©Telegraph Group Limited 1997; **12.8** From *The Psychology of Everyday Things* by Donald A.Norman. Copyright ©1988 by Donald A.Norman. Reprinted by permission of Basic Books, a member of Perseus Books, L.L.C; **13.3** extract from *My Family And Other Animals* by Gerald Durrell, reproduced with permission of Curtis Brown Ltd, London, on behalf of the Estate of Gerald Durrell. ©Gerald Durrell; **13.3** extract from *The Cement Garden* by Ian McEwan published by Jonathan Cape. Used by permission of The Random House Group Limited. *The Cement Garden*, by Ian McEwan. Copyright ©1978 by Ian McEwan. Reprinted by permission of Georges Borchardt, Inc; **13.3** The Wylie Agency for the extract from *My Secret History* by Paul Theroux; **13.5** extract from *Wilt* by Tom Sharpe published by Secker & Warburg. Used by permission of The Random House Group Limited. Also by permission of Sheil Land Associates Ltd Copyright ©Tom Sharpe 1976; **13.5** Faber and Faber Ltd, Nigel Williams Ltd for the extract from *The Wimbledon Poisoner* by Nigel Williams, also by permission of Gillon Aitken Associates; **13.7** extract from *The Millstone* by Margaret Drabble, published by Weidenfield and Nicolson. Reprinted by permission of The Orion Publishing Group Ltd; **14.5** ©Mark Honigsbaum; **15.1** ©Raj Persaud and *The Guardian*; **15.3** Reproduced from The Art Book ©1994 Phaidon Press Limited; **15.5** extract from *The Shock Of The New* by Robert Hughes reproduced with the permission of BBC Worldwide Limited. Copyright ©Robert Hughes. Alfred Knopf; **15.6, 15.8** extract from web page reproduced with permission of Empireonline.co.uk; **16.9** *Taking The Waters* ©Jane Clarke Author and Nutritionist; **16.11** ©The Economist; **17.1** extract from *Europe A History* by Norman Davies published by Pimlico. Used by permission of The Random House Group Limited. From *Europe: A History* by Norman Davies, copyright ©1993 by Norman Davies. Used by permission of Oxford University Press, Inc; **17.2** the poem *The Soldier* by Rupert Brooke; **17.2** *Futility* by Wilfred Owen is reprinted from *Wilfred Owen, The Complete Poems and Fragments* edited by John Stallworthy and published by Chatto and Windus; **17.2** the poem *The General* by Siegried Sassoon, copyright Siegfried Sassoon by kind permission of George Sassoon. *"The General"*, from *Collected Poems of Siegfried Sassoon* by Siegrfried Sassoon, copyright 1918, 1920 by E.P.Dutton. Copyright 1936, 1946, 1947, 1948 by Siegrfried Sassoon. Used by permission of Viking Penguin, a division of Penguin Putnam Inc; **17.4** extract from *Goodbye To All That* by Robert Graves, reprinted with permission of Carcanet Press Limited; **18.4** ©1998. Extract *Why No One Walks* from *Notes From A Big Country*, published by Black Swan, a division of Transworld Publishers. All rights reserved.

Introduction

New Progress to Proficiency is for students who are preparing for the University of Cambridge Certificate of Proficiency in English examination ('CPE' or 'Proficiency', for short), or for an examination of similar level and scope. Each unit is based on a different topic, and contains sections which will help you to develop and improve your reading, writing, listening and speaking skills in English.

Using *New Progress to Proficiency* . . .
- will make your learning an enjoyable experience
- will be intellectually stimulating and thought-provoking
- will help you do your very best in the exam
- will enable you to perfect your English for professional, academic and social purposes — not just for an exam, but for real life too

The exercises and activities in *New Progress to Proficiency* focus on different aspects of English:
- developing and increasing your vocabulary
- helping you to understand, enjoy and appreciate reading passages
- revising grammar
- studying more advanced grammar points
- improving your writing skills and composition writing
- idioms and phrasal verbs
- improving your listening comprehension
- developing your speaking skills
- Proficiency examination skills

As you work through the units, you'll be building your proficiency in English PROGRESSIVELY. You'll notice a gradual change in the nature and style of the exercises and activities as you progress through the book. At the beginning, they help you to improve your English by giving you guidance, encouraging you to enjoy learning and giving you opportunities to use English creatively. Towards the end, you'll be concentrating more on acquiring and refining the special skills needed for the examination.

Many of the exercises and activities are designed to be done in co-operation with other students, working in pairs or small groups. You'll find that by sharing ideas you can learn a great deal from each other.

Working through *New Progress to Proficiency* will help you to make progress, but it's YOUR TEACHER who can help you to improve the specific aspects of English in which you're weakest, and can guide you towards particular exercises that seem most valuable for you and your class. Your teacher may decide to leave out some exercises if the limited amount of time available can be more profitably devoted to other exercises – you may decide to do some of these omitted exercises as extra homework.

But remember that the most important person in the learning process is YOU! You are the person who is most responsible for your progress: by asking questions, seeking advice and working to expand your vocabulary – and by reading English for pleasure, talking English and listening to English whenever you can.

A lot of this work will need to be done on your own outside class: preparing material for each lesson, regularly reviewing what you have covered in class, learning new vocabulary, and doing all the written tasks that you are set.

You'll need a good English–English dictionary, as well as a comprehensive grammar reference book, because no coursebook can answer all your questions on vocabulary and grammar, and your teacher is only available when you're in class.

Symbols

👤→👤 means 'Join another person to form a pair'

👥 means 'Work in pairs'

👥→👥 means 'Join another pair to form a group'

👥👤 means 'Work in groups of three'

👥👥 means 'Work in groups of three or four'

> Examination advice and study tips are given in notes like this at the side or at the bottom of the page.

Enjoy using New Progress to Proficiency!

Leo Jones

The Proficiency exam

The University of Cambridge Local Examinations Syndicate (UCLES) **Certificate of Proficiency in English (CPE)** examination is held twice a year: in June and in December.

Paper 1 Reading – 1 hour 30 minutes

Part 1   Three short texts (total 375–500 words), each with 6 gaps. There is a choice of four possible answers for each gap.

> You have to choose the best .... to fit in each gap in the text.
> **A** guess   **B** idea   **C** thing   **D** word ✓

Part 2   Four short texts on the same theme (total 600–900 words) with two multiple-choice comprehension questions per text. You have to choose the best answer.

> How many texts are there in Part 2?
> **A** one   **B** two   **C** three   **D** four ✓

Part 3   One long text (800–1100 words) from which seven paragraphs have been removed and placed in jumbled order on the next page. You have to decide from where in the text the paragraphs have been removed. There is one paragraph which doesn't fit anywhere.

Part 4   One long text (700–850 words) with seven multiple-choice comprehension questions.

(Total: 40 questions = 40 marks)

Paper 2 Writing – 2 hours

In both parts of the Writing Paper you have to write 300–350 words. Each part carries equal marks.

Part 1   This part is compulsory. After reading the instructions, you read a short text (maybe a short letter, article or advertisement) and then write an article, essay, letter or proposal. The focus is on presenting and developing arguments, expressing and supporting opinions, and evaluating ideas.

Part 2   There are four questions from which you choose one. One of the choices includes a question on each of the set texts. The following formats are included here: an article, an essay, a letter, a report or a review. The tasks may involve any of the following functions: describing, evaluating, giving information, making recommendations, narrating, persuading, summarising.

(Examiners' marks scaled to 40 marks)

Paper 3 Use of English – 1 hour 30 minutes

Part 1   One text with 15 gaps to fill, testing grammar and vocabulary. You have to think of a suitable word to fill each gap. (15 questions, each worth 1 mark)

Part 2   One text with 10 gaps to fill. Each gap corresponds to a word. The 'stems' of the missing words are given beside the text and you have to transform them to provide the missing word. (10 questions, each worth 1 mark)

> This part tests your KNOWLEDGE of word formation.   **KNOW**

Part 3   Six groups of three sentences, each with a word missing. You have to decide which single word fits into all three gaps. This tests collocation, phrasal verbs, idioms and meanings. (6 questions, each worth 2 marks)

Part 4 Eight key word transformations. You have to rewrite each sentence using the word so that it has a similar meaning. You mustn't change the word given and you must use between three and eight words only. (8 questions, each worth 2 marks)

This is an example of a key word transformation sentence.
kind
This is an example *of the kind of sentence* you may have to transform.

Part 5 Two short texts with two questions on each, and one summary task. The questions focus on the style and tone of the text, and on vocabulary. For the summary you have to select relevant information from both texts and write 50 to 70 words. (4 questions, each worth 2 marks. Summary, worth 14 marks)

(Total: 75 marks, scaled to 40)

Paper 4 Listening – about 40 minutes

Each text is heard twice. You have time to read the questions and to check your answers afterwards.

Part 1 You hear four short extracts, with two multiple-choice questions per extract. You have to choose the best of three alternative answers for each question. (8 questions)

Part 2 You hear a monologue or interview. You have to complete gaps in sentences with information from the recording. Each sentence has to be completed with a word or short phrase. One longer extract with nine sentence completion questions. (9 questions)

Part 3 You hear a discussion or interview. There are five multiple-choice questions. You have to choose the best of four alternative answers for each question. (5 questions)

Part 4 You hear a discussion between two people. You have to match each of a list of six opinions or statements to the names of the speakers, according to who said what. If they agreed about something you write both names. (6 questions)

(Total: 28 marks, scaled to 40)

Paper 5 Speaking – about 20 minutes

There are two candidates and two examiners. One is the assessor (who listens and assesses but doesn't join in) and the other is the interlocutor (who sets up the task, joins in sometimes, and also assesses). The interlocutor also has to make sure that one candidate doesn't dominate the conversations, so that you both have an equal amount of time to show how good you are at speaking English.

Part 1 The interlocutor encourages each candidate in turn to give information about themselves and to express personal opinions. This part involves general interaction and social language. (3 minutes)

Part 2 The candidates are given visual and spoken prompts, which generate a discussion between them. You'll have pictures to talk about (but not actually describe): the interlocutor will tell you what you have to do. This part involves comparing, decision making, evaluating, giving opinions and speculating. The interlocutor only joins in if one candidate is speaking too much. (4 minutes)

Part 3 Each candidate in turn is given a written question to respond to. You have to talk for two minutes on the theme of the question, uninterrupted. After each candidate has spoken, the interlocutor asks you questions to encourage a discussion on the same topic. This part involves organising a larger unit of discourse, developing topics, and expressing and justifying opinions. (12 minutes)

(Assessors' marks scaled to 40 marks)

For more information, visit the UCLES website: www.cambridge-efl.org.uk

1

Time to spare?

A 👥 **Work in pairs. Discuss these questions with your partner:**
- What do you think is going on in the photos? What do the people seem to be doing?
- What's your favourite sport? Why do you enjoy playing or watching it?
- Do you have a hobby? If so, why do you enjoy it? If not, why not?

B 1 👥 **Before you listen to the recording, find out what your partner thinks are the attractions (or otherwise) of these hobbies and interests:**

When you meet someone for the first time (and in the Proficiency Speaking test), you may well be asked about your hobbies and interests. Saying 'I don't have time for any' is a conversation killer. It may be better to pretend that you *are* interested in a couple of sports or hobbies, adding later that you regret how little time you have to pursue them.

2 🔊 **You'll hear Ruth, Bill, Sarah, Emma and Jonathan describing their hobbies or interests. As you listen, note down:**

a the name of each person's hobby or interest
b the reasons why they enjoy it and find it rewarding.

3 👥 **Compare your notes with a partner. Listen to the recording again to settle any points of disagreement, or to fill any gaps in your notes.**

4 Discuss which of the activities sounded most and least attractive.

C 1 👥 **Write down THREE more examples for each of the following lists:**

Hobbies:	*collecting stamps carpentry*
Interests:	*listening to music dancing going to the cinema*
Indoor games:	*chess backgammon*
Team sports:	*soccer rugby*
Individual competitive sports:	*boxing motor-racing tennis*
Non-competitive sports:	*aerobics windsurfing skateboarding*
Outdoor activities:	*bird-watching fishing hunting*

2 👥 → 👥 **Join another pair. Compare your lists and then find out:**

- which of the activities your partners participate in or watch
- which of the activities they dislike or disapprove of – and why
- what hobbies or sports they might take up if they had more time

1.2 Comparing and contrasting   GRAMMAR REVIEW

These **Grammar review** sections will help you to revise the main 'problem areas' of English grammar, giving you a chance to consolidate what you already know and to discover what you still need to learn. The **Advanced grammar** sections will introduce you to more advanced structures.

But they are no substitute for a good, comprehensive grammar reference book, to which you should refer for more detail and further examples.

A 👥 **Match each sentence on the left with the sentence on the right that has the same meaning or implication.**

1 Water-skiing is less difficult than sailing. Both sports are equally hard.
  Sailing is as difficult as water-skiing. Sailing is harder than water-skiing.

2 Like you, I wish I could play the piano. Neither of us can play the piano.
  I wish I could play the piano like you. You can play the piano well, I can't.

3 Your essay was most interesting. Nobody's essay was better than yours.
  Your essay was the most interesting. It was a very interesting essay.

4 The cliff was too hard for us to climb. We were able to climb it.
  The cliff was very hard for us to climb. We were unable to climb it.

5 She is a much better pianist than her brother. They both play quite well.
  Her brother is a much worse pianist than she is. Neither of them plays well.

6 She swims as well as she runs. She is equally good at both sports.
  She swims as well as runs. She takes part in both sports.

7 Bob isn't as bright as his father. Bob is less intelligent than his father.
  Bob's father is bright, but Bob isn't that bright. His father is more intelligent than Bob.
  Bob isn't all that bright, like his father. Neither of them is particularly intelligent.

B **Fill each of the blanks with a suitable word or phrase. Think of TWO different ways of completing each sentence, as in the example:**

1 His sister .... that she can beat everyone in her age group.
  a plays tennis so well   **b** is such a brilliant tennis player
2 Track and field athletics .... jogging.
3 Learning English .... learning to drive a car.
4 On Saturday night .... than stay at home studying.
5 She's a very good runner: she can run ....
6 Fishing .... energetic .... swimming.
7 Collecting antiques is .... that I can think of.

C **Find the mistakes in these sentences, and correct them.**

1 It isn't true to say that London is as large than Tokyo.
2 He's no expert on cars: to him a Mercedes and a BMW are like.
3 Her talk was most enjoyable and much more informative as we expected.
4 Don't you think that the more something is difficult, the less it is enjoyable?
5 Less people watched the last Olympics on TV than watched the soccer World Cup.
6 Who is the less popular political leader of the world?
7 My country is quite other than Britain.
8 She's such a faster runner as I can't keep up with her.

D 👥 Compare and contrast the activities shown here. What are the similarities and differences between them? Look at the example first.

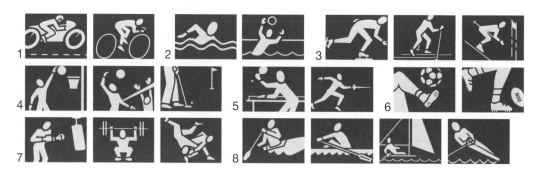

1 *Riding a bike or riding a motorbike both require a good sense of balance. As far as safety is concerned, neither cyclists nor motorcyclists are as safe as people in cars. A new bike costs much less than a motorbike and riding one is good exercise. However, you can go much faster on a motorbike.*

1.3 # Learning a musical instrument

READING

A 👥👥 Work in groups and discuss these questions:

- Do you know anyone who plays any of these instruments?
- Which of them would you like to be able to play? Give your reasons.
- What are the rewards of learning a musical instrument?
- Look at the title of the article opposite: what do you think it's going to be about? Is it likely to be serious or humorous? Why?

B **1** Read the article opposite and note down your answers to these questions. **Highlight** the relevant information in the text.

1 Nine instruments are mentioned: what are they?
2 Three rewards of learning an instrument are mentioned: what are they?
3 Four kinds of pain are mentioned: what are they?
4 What is the difference between the two symptoms of 'Lipchitz's Dilemma'?
5 What reasons does the writer give for advising the reader NOT to take up eight of the nine instruments he mentions?
6 Which of the instruments seems to have the fewest drawbacks?
7 What happened at the end of the imaginary evening out with a drummer?

2 👤→👤 Join a partner. Compare and discuss your answers to the questions.

C **1** Highlight these words in the text – the paragraph number is shown with ¶.

¶1 grudge   ¶5 syndrome   ¶6 maudlin   ¶8 endeavour
¶12 be misled   physical co-ordination   nuance
¶14 unruffled equanimity   ¶17 charisma

2 Match their meanings to these words and phrases, using a dictionary if necessary:

*charm and magnetism   condition   control of one's movements   dislike   effort
get the wrong idea   perfect calmness   self-pitying   subtle variation*

Tinkling the ivories, jangling the nerves

EXCEPT perhaps for learning a foreign language and getting your teeth properly sorted out once and for all, there is nothing more rewarding than learning a musical instrument. It provides a sense of accomplishment, a creative outlet and an absorbing pastime to while away the tedious hours between being born and dying. Musical "At Homes" can be a fine way of entertaining friends, especially if you have a bitter grudge against them. Instrumental tuition is widely available publicly, privately and by post.

Before choosing an instrument to learn you should ask yourself five questions. How much does it cost? How easy is it to play? How much does it weigh? Will playing it make me a more attractive human being? How much does it hurt? All musical instruments, if played properly, hurt.

The least you can expect is low back pain and shoulder strain, in some cases there may also be bleeding and unsightly swelling. Various relaxation methods such as meditation can help.

The most popular instrument for beginners is the piano though I don't know why this should be so. The piano is expensive, it's fiendishly difficult to play, it weighs a ton and it hasn't been sexy since Liszt died. If you sit at the keyboard in the approved position for more than a few minutes, the pain is such that you are liable to break down and betray the secrets of your closest friends. The only good thing you can say about the piano is that it provides you with a bit of extra shelf space around the house.

Being difficult to play means that learning the piano could make you vulnerable to a syndrome known as Lipchitz's Dilemma. Lipchitz was an Austrian behavioural psychologist who observed that setting out to acquire a difficult skill leads to one of just two alternative results.

Either, because of lack of talent or lack of application, you reach only a low to average level of attainment, which leads to general dissatisfaction and maudlin sessions of wandering aimlessly about the house, gently kicking the furniture and muttering, "I'm hopeless at everything."

Or you reach a very high attainment level but, because you spend anything up to 18 hours a day reaching and maintaining this level, other aspects of your personality do not develop properly, which leads to general dissatisfaction and maudlin sessions of wandering aimlessly about the house, gently kicking the furniture and muttering, "Up the Villa."

Having thus established that no good at all can come of any sort of endeavour, Lipchitz himself gave up behavioural psychology and took a job in a Post Office as the person who runs out of things.

The violin is definitely a Lipchitz's Dilemma instrument, but it does have certain advantages over the piano. It is portable and need not be all that expensive to buy. You might not be able to get as good a sound out of a cheap instrument as an expensive one but since it is notoriously difficult to get much of a sound out of any sort of violin your best advice is to forget the whole idea and take up something easier.

The maraca is a hollowed out gourd half filled with beads or dried lentils or some such. Shaken, it makes a rattling sound. Small babies find this mildly entertaining but nobody else is interested.

The harmonica is similar. You buy it. You blow it. You suck it. You put it in a drawer. You lie on the sofa and you turn the telly on.

Some people think that the drums are easy to play and assume it must be fun, thrashing about like that. Do not be misled. Even basic rock'n'roll drumming requires a high level of musical understanding and physical co-ordination. Years of practice are needed to acquire a fluent technique, sufficient stamina and command of rhythmic and dynamic nuance and yet, after all that trouble, people still come up and say, "Must be fun thrashing about like that." This is why drummers often contract some of the more amusing personality disorders from the Encyclopaedia Psychopathics.

An evening out with a drummer can be diverting but be prepared for it to end with lines such as, "Leave it, Terry!" "For God's sake, he was only joking!" and "OH, CHRIST, WHAT A MESS!" Otherwise take my mother's advice and don't have anything to do with drums or drummers.

Brass instruments are much more fun. Professional brass players always wear an expression of bewildered good cheer. This is because they have discovered one of life's most wonderful secrets: you can earn a living making rude noises down a metal pipe. It is a secret that enables them to steer through all life's uncertainties and absurdities with unruffled equanimity.

I have played the guitar for more than 30 years, but I would not advise others to do the same. Far too many other people play the guitar and you will probably find, as I have, that they do it better than you.

A friend once invited me for tea. He had also invited a chap from the pub. The chap from the pub brought his accordion with him. It was an electric accordion which plugged into an amplifier. The living room was small: the amplifier large. He played Lady Of Spain and The Sabre Dance. The International Court of Human Rights has my report on the incident and is considering my recommendations.

For sheer sex appeal you can't do better than a saxophone. Just holding a saxophone gives you a late night charisma, enables you to drink whisky and smoke with authority. But if you wish to maintain credibility, it's as well to have a good stock of excuses ready for when you're asked actually to put the thing to your lips and blow, especially if your best shot is "Oh, The Camptown Ladies Sing This Song, Doo Dah Doo Dah." Otherwise be prepared for maudlin sessions of aimless wandering, gentle furniture kicking, and muttering, "I'm hopeless at everything."

DAVID STAFFORD

D **1** Highlight three sentences which amused you in the text.

2 Discuss your reactions to the humour of the text.

E **1** Look at the six tips given here. There's one word missing from each tip – can you guess the missing words?

2 Discuss which recommendations seem to be most useful for you personally. Highlight the most important pieces of advice given.

Learning new vocabulary

1 If you come across a potentially useful new word or phrase in a text, use a dictionary to look it up. Pay particular _____ to the example sentences given and any information given about collocations*.

2 If a word or phrase seems specialised, obscure or recondite*, you shouldn't necessarily try to remember it – often you can guess its _____ from the context anyway. Make your own choices about whether new words and phrases are 'useful' or not.

3 Highlight useful new words so that they stand out whenever you flip through* the book. Flip through the units you have covered so far at least once a week – you could do this on the bus on your way to or from class, for example. This will help you to assimilate* the words so that eventually you can incorporate them into your own active vocabulary, and use them in your _____ and conversation.

4 Writing new words in a notebook will help you to memorise new words, particularly their _____ . If you put words in categories, rather than making a chronological* list, it will be easier to find them again later. New words can be stored under topic headings: Free time, Sport, Music, Literature, etc. Or you may prefer to build up a 'personal dictionary' where each fresh page lists words beginning with A, B, C, and so on.

5 Use a loose-leaf 'personal organiser' or Filofax as your vocabulary notebook. New pages can be inserted when you run out of _____ in each category. Or use a notebook computer.

6 When writing new words in your notebook, write an _____ of each word in a sentence, as well as a definition. If it's a difficult word to pronounce, make a note of its pronunciation too. Leave a line space between each entry* in case you want to add more information at a later date.

* If you don't understand these words, look them up now. Decide which of them are worth highlighting and remembering.

1.4 'You've got to be selfish' — LISTENING

A **1** Allison Curbishley is a professional athlete. Before listening to the recording, look at the questions and pencil in any information you can guess.

2 Note down your answers to these questions with information from the recording.

1 What are Allison's track events?

	1

2 How long does a typical training session take?

	2

3 Why are her afternoons 'easy-going' and 'lazy'?

	3

4 How did she feel before the relay at the Olympics? [_____ 4]

5 How did she feel after the relay? [_____ 5]

6 Which of these things does she love? Tick (✓) the things she mentions:
winning ☐   flying ☐   training ☐   travelling ☐   socialising ☐
standing on the winners' podium ☐   being applauded by the crowd ☐

7 What is the worst part of her job? [_____ 7]

8 What adjectives does she use to describe herself? [_____ 8]

B   👥 **Compare your answers. Then discuss these questions:**

- What kinds of attributes or qualities does an athlete need to have?
- Which of these adjectives would you use to describe Allison Curbishley?

aggressive	arrogant	brave	charismatic	compassionate	competitive	confident
consistent	dedicated	determined	dignified	disciplined	easy-going	emotional
extrovert	exuberant	fearless	humorous	impetuous	intelligent	introvert
knowledgeable	methodical	modest	persistent	proud	resourceful	ruthless
self-assured	selfish	single-minded	sociable	stubborn	temperamental	

1.5   Adjective + noun collocations

VOCABULARY
DEVELOPMENT

A   👥 **Work in pairs. Look at the odd-looking phrases below: replace the crossed-out adjectives with ones which really do collocate with the nouns.**

a ~~high~~ *great* pleasure   a ~~major~~ *heavy* cold   a ~~profound~~ lake   a ~~nearby~~ friend   a ~~close~~ shop
a ~~loud~~ room overlooking the street   a ~~silent~~ room overlooking the garden
a ~~noisy~~ noise   a ~~quiet~~ silence   an ~~expensive~~ piece of advice   a ~~dear~~ meal   a ~~deep~~ book

B 1   👥 **Decide together which of the adjectives on the left can be used to describe the nouns on the right.**

a/an	absorbing attractive beautiful		adventure animal athlete
	breathtaking catchy close delicious		book boy game interest
	delightful entertaining exciting		meal painting
	ferocious funny gifted great		photographer place
	handsome hard-working naughty		problem song story
	pretty serious slight talented thrilling		student talk view woman

2   👥 **Write down ANOTHER adjective that can be used with each of the nouns above. Use a dictionary if you need to. Look at the examples first:**

a cuddly / wild / furry animal   a fine / readable / long / best-selling book

C   **Here are some adjectives which have similar meanings. Fill the gaps with suitable nouns, using a dictionary from time to time if necessary. Look at the examples first:**

> A good English-to-English dictionary is indispensable when learning new vocabulary. Understanding the basic meaning of unfamiliar new words isn't enough – you have to be able to use them in appropriate contexts and collocations.

1 a light *summer coat*   a pale *face*   a bright *sunny day*   a colourless *liquid*
2 a famous ....   a well-known ....   a notorious ....
an infamous ....   a distinguished ....
3 an extensive ....   a long ....   a wide ....   a broad ....
4 an old ....   an elderly ....   an ancient ....   an old-fashioned ....
5 a new ....   a modern ....   an up-to-date ....
a recent ....   a fresh ....
6 a major ....   a strong ....   an important ....
a significant ....   a vital ....   an essential ....
7 an insignificant ....   a minor ....   a small ....
a little ....   a trivial ....
8 a strange ....   an unusual ....   a rare ....
a peculiar ....   an uncommon ....

1.6 **Tennis stars**

A **1** 👥 **Choose the best word or phrase to fill each gap in this article:**

1	**A** worrying	**B** biggest	**C** large	**D** strange
2	**A** new	**B** recent	**C** unknown	**D** anonymous
3	**A** previous	**B** former	**C** past	**D** n other
4	**A** passionate	**B** emotional	**C** unaccustomed	**D** temperamental
5	**A** large	**B** huge	**C** great	**D** major
6	**A** hard	**B** severe	**C** careful	**D** some
7	**A** following	**B** next	**C** subsequent	**D** successive
8	**A** constant	**B** regular	**C** gentle	**D** familiar
9	**A** most youthful	**B** youngest-ever	**C** most junior	**D** most immature
10	**A** family	**B** educational	**C** sporting	**D** professional

Hingis beaten by girl wonder from down under

Wimbledon witnessed one of the ⬚¹ upsets in its 122-year history after top seed and world number one Martina Hingis was defeated in her opening game by the ⬚² Australian Jelena Dokic, ranked 129th in the world.

A packed court No 1 watched in amazement as Dokic, 16, won 6-2, 6-0, making her the lowest ranked player in modern tennis history to defeat a No 1 seed in a grand slam event.

Dokic, who is of Serbian origin, only made it to Wimbledon by winning a ⬚³ qualifying tournament.

She said after her victory: "I still can't believe I've beaten her. It's a big win for me, especially in the first round, coming from qualifying, but I thought I played quite well and I'm happy that I've won." Moments after her defeat, Hingis revealed she was buckling under the ⬚⁴ strain and pressure faced by young tennis professionals and indicated that she needed a break from the game.

Hingis also revealed that she had decided to attend Wimbledon without her mother and coach Melanie Molitor because the two needed some time apart given the pressures of the last few weeks.

Yesterday's match was the first time that the Swiss player's mother was not present at a ⬚⁵ tournament where her daughter was playing. Ms Molitor has driven her daughter throughout her career.

Hingis, aged 18, who has earned around $10m during her career, said: "I think I need to take some time off. Take a break and recover again."

"I think it has been a great life so far. I mean, I really like it, and I just probably… I need a break. It would really suit me right now." Hingis came to Wimbledon under _____ [6] scrutiny and criticism from the public and fellow professionals following her tantrum at the final of the French Open last month.

When on the verge of losing the match to Steffi Graf she served under-hand twice, entered the crowd and then stormed off court.

She was eventually persuaded to return by her mother, but was criticised for her impetuous, childish outbursts.

Hingis said yesterday that the events at the French Open and the _____ [7] criticism and a temporary separation from her mother had affected her.

She added: "I was probably too nervous, not much believing what I can do or not and didn't really see… I want to try it by myself here [at Wimbledon] and she [my mother] wanted to do more about her private life, to do the things she wanted to do, and the same for me.

"We decided to have a little bit of distance, as I said before, and probably work a bit more on our private lives and see how it is going to go in the future." News of the separation is being seen as a further indicator of Hingis's alleged emotional problems and the severe pressures faced by young women tennis professionals.

Many like Hingis have known little else other than tennis throughout their lives and are under _____ [8] pressure from pushy parents and coaches to compete at tournaments and win.

Hingis began playing tennis at the age of seven and was the _____ [9] player to win a grand slam tournament when she became the Australian Open champion at the age of 16. She won her first major title aged 12 when she won the French Open junior championship in 1993.

Despite the defeat, Hingis denied she wanted to break off all _____ [10] links with her mother and find a new coach. She said: "We are going to talk about it and then we will do some more decisions. But right now, I need a break."

Vivek Chaudhary

2 Find the answers to these questions in the article:

1 Martina Hingis was beaten by Jelena Dokic in . . .
  A the Wimbledon final
  B the final of the Australian Open
  C the first match of Wimbledon
  D the first match in Australia

2 Martina blamed her defeat on the . . .
  A absence of her mother
  B presence of her mother
  C stress of being No 1 seed
  D skill of her opponent

3 Martina was criticised after the French Open for . . .
  A unsporting behaviour
  B shouting at the crowd
  C shouting at the umpire
  D refusing to finish the match

4 Martina seems to have a . . . relationship with her mother.
  A caring   B childish   C stable   D tempestuous

5 After the French Open Martina and her mother agreed to . . .
  A work more closely together
  B focus on their individual private lives
  C end their professional relationship
  D spend more time together socially

6 When Martina won her first adult international tournament she was . . .
  A seven   B twelve   C sixteen   D eighteen

When using a dictionary, remember that the examples given are often more helpful than the definitions. The examples show some of the contexts in which the words occur, and their collocations. If you and your partner have different dictionaries, there are even more examples at your disposal.

"Damn! Trust me to get a seat behind the umpire!"

B Five paragraphs have been removed from this article. Choose the most suitable paragraph from the list A–E for each gap (1–5) in the article.

The ladies' man

Jon Henderson lifts the latch to discover Phil De Picciotto's Advantage in tennis

The big house on the hill overlooking the All England club, where the management company who look after Martina Hingis set up camp for the two weeks of Wimbledon, might not have been a good place to visit last Tuesday after the world No 1 had suffered one of the greatest upsets in a singles match since David loaded up a sling.

1

On the contrary, the front door was ajar and I let myself in to be cheerily greeted by a member of Advantage International's management team, who wondered if I had 'come to talk about Anna'. The queen is dead, long live the queen. In fact my appointment to meet Phil de Picciotto, the president of Advantage's athlete representation operation, had been made before the afternoon's drama to discuss the attractions of a company who have lured such a lustrous line-up. Now, though, a few specific questions about Hingis – and Kournikova – did seem in order.

2

He is sensitive about stories that she and her mother, Melanie Molitor, who was so unexpectedly absent from the Dokic defeat, have fallen out. 'There is no split,' he says. 'Martina's very honest and open with these things. She's a very nice girl who doesn't have any pretences whatsoever, and I think she'll become very much appreciated for this over time. When one doesn't have any pretences in a world where many other people do and when one is young and is the best at one's craft, it's a combination that can lead to instances like this.'

3

Who decided that Molitor should forsake her customary courtside perch? 'Ultimately it's the athlete who makes the final decisions,' says De Picciotto, given an opportunity to discourse on his management techniques. 'We're there to educate, advise and present the options. Whether it's a tennis, business or family decision, we believe that each player is in the best position to make that decision.' But Hingis might have received some guidance from you? 'That's right,' he agrees, guardedly.

4

Dokic, too, comes complete with a ready-made parental problem – 'Damir the Dad from Hell', as one headline described the 16-year-old's father, who had been thrown out of a tournament two weeks ago for supporting his daughter too boisterously. De Picciotto is wary of fanning this one. 'I think there will be no difficulty coping with the father,' he says. 'Everyone is entitled to one bad tournament – on or off the court.'

5

'The point is the media are only interested in anyone over an extended period, and so it is in the interests of the women's tour and each player to eliminate or minimise the distractions so they can extend their careers. They'll all have better stories to tell if they do.'

A

Having recently interviewed Mark McCormack, the autocratic head of International Management Group, Advantage's great competitors (although neither company would admit a rivalry existed), the informality of the big house on the hill was striking. So was the difference between McCormack and De Picciotto. I had interviewed the besuited McCormack in an impressive office overlooking the Thames; I spoke to the casually dressed De Picciotto, a 44-year-old lawyer, under a tree in the garden. He helped to found Advantage in 1983 and, unsurprisingly, he has a different perspective on Hingis than the 'spoilt brat' portrayal in some newspapers.

B

However, in this case they were representing both Goliath and the David of the piece – the Serbian sparrow Jelena Dokic, now an Australian citizen. There were other clients from the company's starry cast list still to be attended to, including Anna Kournikova, Steffi Graf, Jana Novotna, Conchita Martinez and Amanda Coetzer. No drawn curtains, then.

C

Perhaps Advantage's greatest coup was being approached by Kournikova, previously represented by McCormack's IMG. 'We began working with Anna less than a year ago,' says De Picciotto, 'and at that point the tabloid media were creating whatever image of her they wanted. It was the image of the day, completely inconsistent and very difficult to manage. The only way is not just to curtail interviews but eliminate them, except for the obligation, which Anna handles very professionally, to give conferences after her matches.

D

The story of Hingis and her mother provides a classic dilemma for De Picciotto and his Advantage team: the media are invaluable allies in establishing an athlete's name but they can also make life very difficult. 'It is unfortunate that everything is so public,' he says. 'It's always easier to work through any relationship issue if the discussions can remain entirely among the people concerned. At Wimbledon, though, not only is there an open window to these tennis players' lives, but the window has different filters on it depending on who writes the story. What the public decides depends largely on the way the information is presented to them.'

E

Was he, like the rest of us, unaware that Hingis's mother would be missing? 'We wouldn't be doing our job very well and the relationship wouldn't be very good if there were any surprises.'

C **Work in groups. Discuss these questions:**

- Which of the adjectives in **1.4 B** would best describe Martina and Phil?
- What kinds of sacrifices does a top athlete or sportsperson have to make?
- Do you know anyone who is a keen athlete? Describe them.
- What is your attitude to commercial sponsorship of sports events?
- How are professional sportspeople different from amateurs?
- Do you take part in sports for enjoyment, for exercise – or to win? Give your reasons.

1.7 Using participles   ADVANCED GRAMMAR

A **Working in pairs, explain the difference in meaning (or emphasis) between these pairs of sentences:**

1 Standing at the top of the hill, I could see my friends in the distance.
  I could see my friends in the distance standing at the top of the hill.
2 While preparing the meal, he listened to the radio.
  While listening to the radio, he prepared the meal.
3 Finding the window broken, we realised someone had broken into the flat.
  We realised someone had broken into the flat, finding the window broken.
4 Before preparing the meal he consulted a recipe book.
  After consulting a recipe book he prepared the meal.
5 Crawling across the road, I saw a large green snake.
  I saw a large green snake crawling across the road.

B **Study these examples before doing the exercises on the next page:**

I There are two forms of **active participles**:
   You find yourself thinking about what you are going to have for dinner or singing to yourself.
   Having thus established that no good at all can come of any sort of endeavour . . .

and three forms of passive participles:
   Being warned about the approaching storm, they made for the coast.
   Warned about the imminent storm, they prepared for the worst.
   Having been warned about the impending storm, they foolishly pressed on.

2 Participles are used to describe **simultaneous** or **consecutive actions**:
   We sat on the beach watching the windsurfers falling into the water.
   When writing new words in your notebook, write an example in a sentence.
   Dressed in his smartest clothes, he arrived early for the interview.
   Getting to the beach, we looked for an uncrowded spot.
   [BUT NOT: We looked for an uncrowded spot, getting to the beach. ✗]
   Having got to the beach, we found some sunbeds to lie on.
   Having recently interviewed Mark McCormack . . .

and to explain reasons or causes:
   Not being an expert, I can't teach you how to windsurf.
   Being a poor swimmer, I don't go out beyond my depth.

Participles tend to be used more in formal written style than in colloquial English.

3 Participles can also be used after these words:

after   as   before   if   on   once   since   when   whenever   unless   until

After losing the match, she was heart-broken.
All musical instruments, if played properly, hurt.
Once opened, this product should be consumed within 24 hours.
When using a dictionary, remember that the examples given are often more
    helpful than the definitions.

4 Normally the **subject** of a participle is the same as the subject of the main verb:

Waiting for the bus, I saw him in his new car.
(= I was waiting for the bus when I saw him in his new car.)

But in some cases the context makes the meaning clear:

Being difficult to play means that learning the piano could make you vulnerable to a
    syndrome known as Lipchitz's Dilemma.

C Using participles of these verbs, complete the sentences below:

arrange   arrive   complete   finish   lift   reach   require   shake

1 As .... , we'll meet outside the cinema at 8 o'clock.
2 He has been feeling terribly homesick ever since .... in this country.
3 On .... home, I went straight to my room.
4 .... by her indifference, he burst into tears.
5 Having .... the game, they shook hands.
6 Unless .... later, the key should be returned to the reception desk.
7 Remember to use block capitals when .... the application form.
8 Remember to bend your knees, not your back, whenever ....
something heavy.

D Finish these sentences, with each one still meaning the same as the one before it:

1 I haven't got a car, which is why I usually travel by bus.   **Not** ....
2 The demonstrators chanted loudly as they marched into the square.   **Chanting** ....
3 They turned back when they found their way blocked by the police.   **Finding** ....
4 I heard that he collects butterflies and asked him to tell me about it. **Having** ....
5 None of her friends turned up outside the cinema, so she went home. **Finding** ....
6 As I don't know much about art, I can't comment on your painting.   **Not** ....
7 If you drink coffee too quickly, it can give you hiccups.   **Drunk** ....
8 I went to bed early because I felt a bit under the weather.   **Feeling** ....

E Having spotted the mistakes in these sentences, rewrite them correctly:

1 *Looking out of my window, there was a crowd of people in the street.*
2 *Wearing bright yellow trousers, we thought he looked ridiculous.*
3 *Being rather tall for his age, his father treats him like an adult.*
4 *Having been giving such a warm welcome he felt very pleased.*
5 *Sitting together I saw three old men playing cards.*
6 *If washing in hot water this garment will shrink.*

F 1 Using your own ideas, add suitable participles to this story:

On [   ]¹ my eyes, I knew that I was in a strange, dark room. [   ]² that I might
still be dreaming, I pinched myself to see if I was still asleep, but, [   ]³ that I really
was awake I began to feel afraid. I felt my way to the door, but it was locked. I tried to
call for help but, after [   ]⁴ for several minutes, I knew no one could hear me.
[   ]⁵ to the window, and cautiously [   ]⁶ the shutters, I discovered that the
window was barred and, [   ]⁷ outside, all I could see was darkness. My heart sank.
[   ]⁸ with an apparently hopeless situation, I sat down [   ]⁹ what to do. I
remained there [   ]¹⁰ on the bed in silent desperation for several minutes.

Suddenly, [   ]¹¹ a key being turned in the lock, I . . .

2 Add THREE more sentences, continuing the story with your own ideas . . .

A 1 Rearrange these steps into a more sensible order – and decide which of them you would OMIT. If any vital steps are missing, ADD them to the list.

GOLDEN RULES
FOR WRITING A COMPOSITION

Jot down all the points you might make.

Take a break.

Analyse your notes, deciding which points to emphasise and which to omit.

Show your first draft to someone else and get feedback from them.

Edit your first draft, noting any changes you want to make.

Proof-read the first draft: eliminate errors in grammar, spelling and punctuation.

Do any necessary research.

Proof-read your final version, eliminating any mistakes you spot.

Discuss with someone else what you're going to write.

Write a first draft, perhaps in pencil.

Look carefully at the instructions.

Write a plan, rearranging the points in the order you intend to make them.

Use a dictionary to look up suitable words and expressions and write them down.

Think about what you're going to write.

Get feedback from other students on your final version (they are 'your readers').

Look again at the instructions.

Have a rest.

Write your final version.

Try to follow these steps every time you do written work during this course. In the exam, a well-planned, well-thought-out composition is always given better marks than an unplanned one that's dashed off quickly.

2 Decide which of the steps would NOT be feasible when working against the clock under exam conditions.

If you do writing tasks on a computer, decide which of the steps you'd still have to do on paper.

B Choose one of these topics and write an article (300–350 words).

Describe your own favourite hobby or sport, explaining its attractions and drawbacks.

or Write about a sport or hobby that you'd like to take up one day – when you eventually have enough time.

or Write about a hobby or sport you dislike, explaining what it is you don't like about it.

1 Follow the 'Golden rules' you discussed earlier. Before you begin writing, MAKE NOTES of the points you might make. In 320 words, you're unlikely to have enough room to mention them all, so you'll have to select the most important or most interesting ones.

2 Show your finished composition to a partner and ask for feedback.

When writing compositions, leave a wide margin on either side of your work and leave a couple of lines space between each paragraph. This will leave you room to add extra ideas – and even to rewrite complete sentences later, if necessary.

Maybe write on alternate lines of the paper – or print your work out double spaced. . .

. . . and there'll also be more space for your teacher to add comments later too!

2

A sense of adventure

Eight Feet in the Andes TOPIC VOCABULARY AND READING

A **1** 👥👥 **Discuss these questions with your partners:**

- Are you an adventurous person – or do you tend to play safe and avoid risks?
- What kinds of adventures or dangerous activities do you avoid at all costs?
- What kind of people do adventurers or travellers need to be? Which of the following qualities do you think are the ten most important – and why?

arrogance   boldness   charisma   compassion   confidence   courage   curiosity
dedication   determination   dignity   a good sense of direction   enthusiasm   fearlessness
humility   a sense of humour   intelligence   knowledge   linguistic skills   modesty
obstinacy   patience   persistence   resilience   resourcefulness   ruthlessness   stamina
tolerance   willpower

2 **Look at the people in this photo – what kind of people do they look like?**

B **The text below is a review of *Eight Feet in the Andes* by Dervla Murphy. As you read it, find the answers to these questions:**

1 Whose were the eight feet?
2 Who is the heroine of the story?
3 How long was the journey?
4 Where did they sleep?

C **1** **Highlight these words and phrases in the article:**

¶1 saunter   ¶3 madcap schemes   ¶4 frolic   heartening   ¶6 overenthusiastically
day one   ¶7 fretting   coveted   ¶9 homespun   ¶12 sticky moments
¶13 trusting soul

2 **Match their meanings to these words and phrases:**

amusing game   crazy plans   stroll   encouraging   without restraint   the beginning
dangerous incidents   fussing and worrying   envied and wanted   unsophisticated
someone who believes other people are honest

1
ONCE upon a time, with travel writing, the rewards won related to the risks taken. No longer. Travel writers travel by public transport; often they just hop in the car. They travel round British seaside resorts; they saunter up low mountains in the Lake District. Greatly daring, they visit islands off the coast. There is no point in travelling hopefully; far better to arrive as quickly as possible and collect your multinational publisher's advance.

2
Dervla Murphy had never heard of such a thing when she decided, after the death of her invalid mother, to travel from Ireland to India – on a bicycle.

3
Motherhood usually puts paid to such madcap schemes but for Miss Murphy only temporarily. She waited for the child to reach a reasonable age and then took it with her.

4
Rachel was five when they travelled together in South India, six when they went through Baltistan with a pony, and nine when, in this book, she crossed the Peruvian Andes from Cajamarca to Cuzco with her mother and a mule – a 2,000 kilometre journey of which she did 1,500 on foot. This Andean frolic – her mother's term – was to be her last before settling down to school, though it is hard to see what there can be left for her to learn. To read about Rachel is heartening for parents of a generation which seems to be losing the use of its legs.

She is an ideal travelling companion, settling down on a ledge overlooking the world to read Watership Down or write poems after ten hours up one mountain and down the next. "We're seeing clouds being born," she says once. She is thrilled to find a baby scorpion under her sleeping bag. After three months of travelling up and down vertical slopes of

3,300 metres her mother notes almost absently that she never once complained; and she herself only once questions the wisdom of asking a nine-year-old to walk 35 kilometres at an altitude of 4,000 metres on half a tin of sardines.

Rachel confides in her diary: "I got the whole of my upper left arm punctured by lots of slightly poisonous thorns . . . Mummy is in an exceedingly impatient mood . . . I think this is a very pretty place, at least in looks . . . We had to sit down while we thought about what to do next . . . " She has a much better sense of direction and indeed of responsibility than her mother who tends to join overenthusiastically in all religious festivals and who has dreadful blisters from day one in a hopeless pair of walking shoes.

The Murphys clearly see not Rachel but Juana, their beautiful glossy mule, as the heroine of the story. She cost £130 and they fuss over her like a film star, fretting about her diet, her looks, her mood. Juana is coveted by all; as the journey proceeds it is shadowed by the parting from her. There is a terrible moment when she falls over a precipice to certain death but for a divinely placed single eucalyptus tree in her path.

From Cajamarca to Cuzco they follow in the hoofprints of Pizarro and the conquistadores, often camping in the same place, almost always surveying the same timeless unchanging scene.

Miss Murphy's philosophy may be homespun – "I know and always have known that we twentieth-century humans need to escape at intervals from that alien world which has so abruptly replaced the environment that bred us" – but she has an enviable gift for communicating her passion for the road. No heat or cold is too extreme, no drama too intense for her to sit on the edge of some mountain and tell us

about it that evening in her diary. Sometimes the view is too exciting for her to eat her raw potatoes and sardines.

There is very little food; everyone goes hungry. The pair arrive at sizeable towns and find nothing to buy but noodles and stock cubes and bottles of Inca Cola; the restaurant offers hot water to add to your own coffee. There is always worry about alfalfa for the choosy Juana. They are shocked at the poverty they see, and find it mystifying that the Indians can tolerate such a life.

She and Rachel share it wherever possible. They stop, make friends, join in. They accept all invitations, are ready to sleep with hens roosting on their legs, eat anything, drink anything no matter what floats on top of it and they repay hospitality (when permitted) with tins of sardines. She worries that religion is so little comfort to the Peruvian Indian, that the babies chew wads of coca, that the boys Rachel plays football with on their sloping pitches have no future, that she cannot repay kindnesses: the ancient shepherdess who shared her picnic lunch of cold potato stew on a cabbage leaf, the old man who set his dog to guard their tent at night.

There are sticky moments, always near towns. Within a day of Cuzco, Juana is stolen but all ends happily and they reach the Inca city with feelings of anti-climax at journey's end. They took a week less than the conquistadores but then the conquistadores had battles to fight.

The Murphys, mother and daughter, know no fear just as they know no discomfort, and their remarkable journey shows that the trusting soul is still free to wander at will.

Maureen CLEAVE

D Now note down your answers to these questions, referring back to the article as necessary.

1 What is the writer's attitude to most modern travel writers?
2 When was the *reasonable age* that Rachel first got taken on a journey with Dervla?
3 Why was this journey to be their last one together?
4 How did Dervla behave in a less grown-up way than her daughter?
5 When the writer describes Miss Murphy's philosophy as *homespun* (¶9), is this pejorative or complimentary?
6 What did they eat on their journey?
7 What happened to Juana at the end of their journey?
8 What was their worst experience? What was their best experience?

E Looking at the first paragraph again, highlight the words or phrases which show sarcasm or irony. Which of these, if any, do YOU find amusing? (The first is *Once upon a time* – normally used to start a children's story.)

F Discuss your reactions to the text.

- What risks was Dervla Murphy running by taking Rachel on her journey?
- What aspects of their journey would you find most difficult and rewarding?
- Where in the world is it safe for *the trusting soul* to *wander at will*, do you think?

2.2 Articles and determiners GRAMMAR REVIEW

A 👥 **Match the sentences on the left with the ones on the right that mean the same:**

1 What was the mule like? | What is a mule like?
What are mules like? | Could you describe their mule?

2 Do you like tea now? | Is the tea all right for you now?
Do you like the tea now? | Have you overcome your dislike of tea?

3 Some of the difficulties were foreseen. | We expected a certain amount of difficulty.
Some difficulty was foreseen. | We didn't expect any difficulty.
No difficulty was foreseen. | Every difficulty was foreseen.
The difficulty was foreseen. | We expected a particular difficulty.
All the difficulties were foreseen. | Not all of the difficulties were foreseen.

4 Would you like some coffee now? | Would you like a coffee now?
Would you like your coffee now? | Would you like the coffee now?

B 1 Look at these examples:

Some nouns are normally **uncountable**:

advice   applause   behaviour   clothing   fun   information   laughter   luggage
music   news   progress   rain   research   snow   spaghetti   teaching   transport
travel   wealth

Music helps me to relax.   Travel broadens the mind.

But when referring to a **particular** example, a different **countable** word or phrase must be used:

What a pretty song!   What a catchy tune!   What a lovely piece of music!
Did you enjoy your trip?   We had a great journey.

2 Match these countable words or phrases to the uncountable nouns above:

| a/an | action   analysis   article   asset   car   chuckle   class   coat   fact
fortune   game   hint   improvement   joke   journey   laugh   lesson
possession   report   shirt   song   suitcase   tip   train   trip   tune |

| a/an | article   dish   drop   fall   flake   item   means   piece
plate   round | of ...

C 1 Study these examples:

Some nouns are **uncountable** if used with a **general** meaning:

ABSTRACT NOUNS   adventure   atmosphere   business   confidence   death   education
environment   experience   failure   fear   history   imagination
industry   kindness   knowledge   life   love   philosophy
pleasure   success   thought

MASS NOUNS   butter   cheese   coffee   juice   metal   milk   pasta   plastic
poison   soup   sugar   tea   wine   wood

Business is booming.   Do you know much about business?
I have orange juice and coffee with milk for breakfast.

But they are **countable** if they refer to **particular** things or examples:
Some businesses are more profitable than others.
Running a business is a great responsibility.
I'd like an orange juice please.   Lead is a heavier metal than aluminium.

2 Fill the gaps with suitable nouns from the lists above:

1 A thorough .... of English is required.
2 It was an unforgettable ....
3 The journey was a great ....
4 Oak is a harder .... than pine.
5 She had a thrilling ....
6 It was a great .... to meet them.
7 He has a very vivid ....
8 The trip was an utter ....
9 This is a very salty ....
10 Cheddar is a very tasty ....
11 He has a great .... of music.
12 I'd like a strong black .... , please.

The use of articles is often determined by the context, and depends on information given earlier in a text or conversation, as in this example:

Last year I bought a computer from a mail order company. The computer has gone wrong but I can't get it fixed because the company's gone out of business.

D Fill the gaps in these extracts with a, an, the, his, her, their, or ∅ (no article) – in some cases more than one answer is possible. Afterwards, refer back to paragraphs 7 and 11 of the article in 2.1.

The Murphys clearly see not Rachel but Juana, ¹ beautiful glossy mule, as ² heroine of ³ story. She cost £130 and they fuss over her like ⁴ film star, fretting about ⁵ diet, ⁶ looks, ⁷ mood. Juana is coveted by all; as ⁸ journey proceeds it is shadowed by ⁹ parting from her. There is ¹⁰ terrible moment when she falls over ¹¹ precipice to ¹² certain death but for ¹³ divinely placed single eucalyptus tree in ¹⁴ path.

She worries that ¹⁵ religion is so little comfort to ¹⁶ Peruvian Indian, that ¹⁷ babies chew ¹⁸ wads of ¹⁹ coca, that ²⁰ boys Rachel plays ²¹ football with on ²² sloping pitches have no future, that she cannot repay ²³ kindnesses: ²⁴ ancient shepherdess who shared ²⁵ picnic lunch of ²⁶ cold potato stew on ²⁷ cabbage leaf, ²⁸ old man who set ²⁹ dog to guard ³⁰ tent at night.

E Correct the errors in these sentences:

1 *Politics don't interest him, except when election takes place.*
2 *Grapefruits are my favourite fruits, but I don't like the banana.*
3 *The news are depressing today: two aircrafts have crashed.*
4 *There are crossroads at top of hill.*
5 *Mathematics were most difficult subject at the school for me.*
6 *Hague is capital of Netherlands, but Amsterdam is largest city.*
7 *The women are usually safer drivers than the men.*
8 *We missed bus and had to walk all the way home – it was quite adventure!*

F Rewrite these sayings and quotations, inserting the or a, where appropriate:

1 Travel broadens mind.   *Travel broadens the mind.*
2 Love makes world go round.
3 Greatest adventure of all is life itself.
4 Friend in need is friend indeed.
5 Absence makes heart grow fonder.
6 While cat's away, mice will play.
7 Out of sight out of mind – as saying goes.
8 Woman without man is like fish without bicycle.

2.3 | **Words easily confused**   **VOCABULARY DEVELOPMENT**

A 👥 Study the pairs of words below and discuss the difference in meaning between them – putting them in sentences may be helpful. If you're unsure about any, use a dictionary. Look at the example first:

actual = existing as a real fact   Well, I've heard about it but I haven't read the actual article.
current = (most) up to date   Have you seen that article in the current issue of The Economist?

actual · current	in fact · indeed	pretend · intend
advice · opinion	in front of · opposite	propaganda · advertising
control · check	large · wide	remember · remind
editor · publisher	lend · borrow	rob · steal
experience · experiment	lose · miss	savage · wild
fault · mistake	occasion · bargain	sympathise with · like
hear · listen	presently · at the moment	sympathetic · likeable

B 1 👥 **Decide which of the words below fit in the gaps, and which don't. Tick the ones that fit.**

1 The immigration officer .... their passports suspiciously.

  checked ✓   controlled   examined ✓   restrained   stamped

2 Her parents had a big .... and now they're not on speaking terms.

  discussion   argument   debate   fight   quarrel   row   talk

3 Don't take any notice of him, he's just being ....

  sensible   sensitive   difficult   touchy   emotional   moody

4 How many people .... the performance?

  assisted   attended   participated   took part   helped   served

5 Please go away and stop .... me!

  annoying   bothering   disturbing   harassing   pestering   infuriating

6 We arranged to meet at 7.30 and I made a note in my .... to that effect.

  agenda   notebook   exercise book   diary   schedule   timetable

7 Please forgive him for forgetting, he's getting rather .... as he gets older.

  distracted   absent-minded   forgettable   forgetful   preoccupied

8 What are the .... of studying when you could be enjoying yourself?

  benefits   profits   advantages   prizes   rewards   prices

9 It's a(n) .... club to which only members are admitted.

  exclusive   idiomatic   particular   personal   private   secluded

10 They didn't foresee the .... result of their irresponsible behaviour.

  eventual   possible   imminent   feasible   plausible

11 At the end of her .... she had to sit a stiff exam.

  career   course   education   training   upbringing   experience

12 I'm getting tired; how much .... is it to the summit?

  further   furthermore   farther   far   faraway   far away   father

2 Highlight any words in this section that you had difficulty with. Check their meanings in a dictionary. Pay particular attention to the EXAMPLES in the dictionary, not just the definitions. Sometimes the difference is in the context a word is used, rather than its basic meaning.

2.4 / **Brazilian Adventure**   **READING**

In Part 5 of the Use of English paper you'll have to read two texts and write short answers to four questions. Then you have to write a 50–70 word summary, based on the two texts. You should avoid quoting word-for-word and use your own words instead. This is easier said than done, and may require a lot of practice.

In later units, we'll practise some of the techniques you can use to avoid quoting from the text: using synonyms or opposites, using a different grammatical structure, etc.

A **Find the answers to these questions in the following text :**

1 Apart from the writer, how many other people are mentioned in the text?
2 Which of them did the writer trust most – and who did he trust least?
3 How confident was the writer that the expedition would ever leave London?
4 Did Major Pingle really exist?

Outlook Unsettled

THERE are, I suppose, expeditions and expeditions. I must say that during those six weeks in London it looked as if ours was not going to qualify for either category. Our official leader (hereinafter referred to as Bob) had just the right air of intrepidity. Our Organizer, on the other hand, appeared to have been miscast, in spite of his professional-looking beard. A man of great charm, he was nevertheless a little imprecise. He had once done some shooting in Brazil, and we used to gaze with respect at his photographs of unimaginable fish and the corpses (or, as it turned out later, corpse) of the jaguars he had killed. But when pressed for details of our own itinerary he could only refer us to a huge, brightly-coloured, and obsolete map of South America, on which the railway line between Rio and Sao Paulo had been heavily marked in ink. 'From Sao Paulo,' he would say, 'we shall go up-country by lorry. It is cheaper and quicker than the train.' Or, alternatively: 'The railway will take us right into the interior. It costs less than going by road, and we shall save time, too.' It was clear that Bob, for all his intrepidity, viewed our Organizer's vagueness with apprehension.

At the other end – in Brazil, that is to say – the expedition's interests were said to be in capable hands. Captain John Holman, a British resident of Sao Paulo whose knowledge of the interior is equalled by few Europeans, had expressed his willingness to do all in his power to assist us. On our arrival in Brazil, as you will hear, this gentleman proved a powerful, indeed an indispensable ally; but at this early stage of the expedition's history our Organizer hardly made the most of him, and Captain Holman was handicapped by the scanty information which he received with regard to our intentions. In London we were given to understand that the man who really mattered was a Major Pingle – George Lewy Pingle. (That is not his name. You can regard him as an imaginary character, if you like. He is no longer quite real to me.)

Major Pingle is an American citizen, holding – or claiming to hold – a commission in the Peruvian army. He has had an active and a varied career. According to his own story, he ran away from his home in Kentucky at the age of 15; joined a circus which was touring the Southern States: found his way across the Mexican border: worked for some time on a ranch near Monterey: accompanied an archaeological expedition into Yucatan, where he nearly died of fever: went north to convalesce in California: joined the ground staff of an aerodrome there and became (of all things) a professional parachutist: went into partnership with a German, whose ambition it was to start an airline in South America: and since then had travelled widely in Colombia, Peru, Chile, and Brazil. All this, of course, we found out later. All we knew, or thought we knew, in London was that Major Pingle was a man of wide experience and sterling worth who had once accompanied our Organizer on a sporting expedition in Brazil, and who was even now preparing for our arrival in Brazil – buying stores, hiring guides, and doing everything possible to facilitate our journey. A great deal, obviously, was going to depend on Major Pingle. 'This Major Pingle,' I used to tell people, 'is going to be the Key Man.'

It was difficult to visualize Major Pingle, all those miles away. The only thing we knew for certain about him was that he was not very good at answering cables. This, we were told, was because he must have gone up-country already, to get things ready. Whatever the cause, however, very imperfect liaison existed between his headquarters in Sao Paulo and ours in London; and when a letter did at last reach London from Brazil, our Organizer lost it. So it was impossible to find out definitely whether Major Pingle's preparations were being made in the light of our plans, or whether our plans were being made to fit his preparations or neither, or both. It was all rather uncertain.

from Brazilian Adventure by Peter Fleming

B **1** ✎ Write your answers to these questions. Highlight the relevant information in the text, but wherever possible, use YOUR OWN WORDS instead of quoting verbatim from the text.

1 How did Bob, the leader, inspire confidence?
  Quote: *'He had just the right air of intrepidity.'* (line 3)
  Own words: *He looked suitably brave.*
2 How much shooting had the Organizer done on his previous trip to Brazil?
3 What were the Organizer's plans for travel to the interior?
4 How did Bob feel about the Organizer's vagueness?
5 What kind of man does Major Pingle seem to be?
6 Whilst still in London, who did the writer consider their most valuable contact in Brazil?
7 Where, according to the Organizer, was Major Pingle?
8 How had they tried to get in touch with Major Pingle?
9 How many letters from Major Pingle were the party shown?
10 What preparations was Major Pingle believed to be making for the expedition?
11 Judging by what the writer tells us, how is the expedition likely to turn out?

C Find the words in red in the text and highlight them there. Then fill the gaps.

1 Expeditions and expeditions (line 1) means that there are many different ....
2 Miscast (line 3) is normally used when talking about .... , not explorers.
3 A little imprecise (line 4) is an example of ....
4 When pressed (line 6) implies that the Organizer was .... to answer questions.
5 An obsolete map (line 7) is one that is no longer ....
6 An indispensable ally (line 16) is someone whose help ....
7 If you have scanty information (line 18), you have ....
8 According to his own story (line 22) suggests the story is ....

D 👥👥 **Discuss these questions:**

- When do you think the text was written?
- How would you describe the TONE of the writing?
- Does it make you want to read more about the adventure? Why (not)?
- If you had been leader of the expedition, what steps would *you* have taken to ensure that all the necessary preparations were made?
- What do you think the expedition found when they actually did arrive in Brazil?

E ✒ Write a paragraph (about 60 words) summarising the air of uncertainty surrounding the expedition 'during those six weeks in London'.

First of all, highlight the relevant information in the text. Try to use your own words, rather than quoting directly from the text.

2.5 'If something goes wrong . . .' LISTENING

A 👥 **Alastair Miller was a member of an expedition to Everest. Before you listen to the interview, look at the questions he was asked. What answers do you think he gave?**

1 What do you enjoy about climbing mountains?
2 Do you ever find yourself in situations where you're frightened?
3 What is it like taking part in an expedition to climb Everest?

B 🔊 **In the first part of the interview, Alastair deals with the first two points. Note down your answers to these questions.**

1 What are the FOUR things he says he enjoys about climbing – and what are the reasons he gives for enjoying each of them?
2 What are the two kinds of fear he describes?
3 Why did the accident in Yosemite Valley frighten his companion more than Alastair?
4 Why did he have to be *philosophical* during the thunderstorm on the Aiguille du Midi?
5 Why didn't they go back down the mountain when the storm broke?

C 🔊 **The second part of the interview is about the Everest expedition. Fill the gaps in these sentences with information from the interview:**

1 On a large expedition there is a ' .... effect': there are .... people at the bottom of the mountain and .... or .... people trying to reach the summit. This means that .... have to be carried up the mountain.
2 Approaching Everest from the .... , there were no .... to carry their equipment. So it was carried by yaks, and above Camp One, by ....
3 It was exciting for Alastair when he went above .... for the first time, even though he was on .... ropes and was entirely ....
4 Above Camp One they didn't .... or .... , they only cleaned their ....
5 Snow holes are .... but they are .... and ....

D 👥👥 **Compare your reactions to the interview. What impressed you most? What surprised you most? Would you like to be a mountaineer and rock-climber? Give your reasons.**

A Read the composition below on this topic:

Write a letter to a friend describing an exciting or frightening experience you have had (300–350 words).

1 Decide which features of the writing help to keep your interest as a reader, and which features don't. Consider these aspects in particular:

choice of vocabulary   humour   sentence structure

> It had been a long, tiring journey to S_____. The ferry, which should have taken at most five hours, had had engine trouble and didn't arrive till 2 a.m. As the harbour itself was several miles from the main town – the only place where accommodation was available – and much too far to walk even by daylight, we hoped against hope that the local bus service would still be running. Sure enough one tiny, ancient blue bus was waiting on the quayside but imagine our dismay when we saw that about 98 other passengers were also disembarking with the same destination. We fought our way onto the bus and waited for the driver to appear. A man staggered out of the bar nearby and groped his way into the driving seat – presumably he'd been drinking since early evening when the ship was supposed to arrive.
>
> We were very frightened. Most of the passengers hadn't seen the driver come out of the bar. The bus went very slowly up the steep road. On one side the cliffs dropped vertically down to the sea hundreds of metres below. We arrived in the town at 3 a.m., but there was no accommodation. We found a taxi to take us to the other side of the island. We slept on the beach.
>
> As it began to get light and the sun rose over the sea, waking us from our dreams, we realised that it had all really happened and that we were lucky to be alive.

250 words

2 ✎ Although the first paragraph is fairly interesting, the rest is pretty dull – and the letter is too short! Rewrite the second half, incorporating any improvements you think are necessary, so that the total length is 300–350 words.

B **1** Here are some phrases that can be used when telling a story. Complete them in your own words.

1 There was nothing I could do but	7 To my utter amazement ....
2 It was only after .... that I	8 To our surprise ....
3 My big mistake was to	9 Slowly opening the door, I ....
4 All I could do was	10 After a while ....
5 You can imagine how I felt when	11 Without thinking I ....
6 It all started when	12 I held my breath as ....

2 ✎ Write the first two paragraphs (no more than half a page) of a letter to a friend, telling the story of an exciting or frightening experience YOU have had.

3 👥 Read each other's stories and guess what happened next in your partner's story and how the story might have ended.

A 👥 **Discuss the differences in meaning or emphasis in these sentences. How would you complete the last two?**

1 Tricia only wants to help.   Only Peter wants to help.
2 Pam doesn't really feel well.   Jack really doesn't feel well.
   Anne doesn't feel really well.
3 Tony and Jane still aren't married.   Still, Sue and Bob aren't married.
   Olivia and Paul aren't still married, are they?
4 I don't particularly want to see Lisa.   I particularly don't want to see Tim.
5 I enjoy eating normally.   I normally enjoy eating.
   Normally, I enjoy eating.   I enjoy eating – normally!
6 Carefully, I lifted the lid of the box.   I carefully lifted the lid of the box.
   I lifted the lid of the box carefully.
7 Paul just doesn't like flying, he . . .   Olivia doesn't just like flying, she . . .

B Look at the examples and fill the gaps with suitable adverbs or phrases from the lists.

1 Some adverbs are almost always placed **in front of the main verb** in a sentence (or after the verb *to be*) – but not usually at the beginning or end of the sentence:

almost   already   always   ever   hardly ever   just   nearly   never   often
practically   quite   rarely   seldom   utterly   virtually

Have you ever been to South America? ✓✓
Ever have you been to South America? ✗
Have you been ever to South America? ✗

a We have .... finished our work.
b I .... disagree with what you said.
c It is .... as cold as this.

2 Some adverbs are usually placed **in front of the main verb** OR **after the object** – but not normally at the beginning of the sentence:

constantly   continually   perpetually   regularly   sporadically
absolutely   altogether   completely   enormously   entirely
exactly   greatly   more or less   perfectly

He constantly asks questions. ✓✓
He asks questions constantly. ✓✓

a I don't .... agree with her.
b Your work has .... improved.
c He isn't .... brilliant.
d I enjoyed the show ....

3 Adverbs consisting of **more than one word** are usually placed at the **end** of the sentence, or at the **beginning** – but NOT in front of the main verb:

again and again   all the time   every so often   from time to time   many times
most of the time   once a week   once every four years   once in a while   over and over again
several times   twice a day

at the moment   at one time   a fortnight ago   before breakfast   before long
every day   in a moment   in the evening   in the past   the following week
the previous day   within the hour

Most of the time I try to avoid risks. ✓✓
I try to avoid risks most of the time. ✓✓

a The Olympic Games are held ....
b I don't have the information .... , so I'll call you back ....
c .... I agree with what she says, but .... we don't see eye to eye.
d Although she had washed her hair .... , she washed it again ....

Remember that adverbs almost never go between a verb and a direct object:

He ate quickly his sandwiches. ✗
She took gently his hand. ✗
He dropped accidentally the vase. ✗

4 Some very common adverbs can be placed at the **beginning** of the sentence, or **in front of** the main verb, or **after** the main verb or the object:

normally   occasionally   periodically   sometimes   usually
afterwards   at once   clearly   eventually   immediately   later   obviously   presently
shortly   soon   suddenly   probably   presumably

Usually I wash my hair twice a week. ✓   I usually wash my hair twice a week. ✓✓
I wash my hair twice a week usually. ✓

a I can't give you my answer .... , but I'll let you know ....
b Let me know .... what you thought of the film.
c It will .... be time to go home, so you'll have to finish the work ....

5 Most **adverbs of manner**, which describe **how** people act or speak, are commonly placed **after** the main verb or its object – though other positions are often possible:

accidentally   anxiously   apprehensively   automatically   carefully   discreetly   easily
fiercely   fluently   foolishly   frankly   gently   gloomily   gratefully   hurriedly   innocently
instinctively   lovingly   oddly   proudly   reassuringly   reluctantly   sensibly   sincerely
strangely   thoughtfully   violently   warmly

He reacted violently to my comments. ✓✓
He reacted to my comments violently. ✓

a She was behaving very ....
b He held up the prize .... and thanked everyone ....
c She took his hand .... and looked .... into his eyes.
d I raised my hand .... to protect my face.

6 Adverbs which 'comment' on the **whole** sentence are usually placed at the very beginning of a sentence before a comma – though other positions are often possible.

Fortunately   Funnily enough   Hopefully   Luckily   Strangely enough   Surprisingly
Unfortunately

Unfortunately, Elizabeth lost the race. ✓✓   Elizabeth unfortunately lost the race. ✓
Elizabeth lost the race, unfortunately. ✓

a .... , I found my wallet in the car.
b .... , she didn't get the job.
c .... , I'll have finished the work soon.
d .... , they're getting married.

C Find the mistakes in these sentences and correct them:

1 I have seen him seldom so furious and I was shocked absolutely by his reaction.
2 He from time to time loses his temper but he is most of the time in a good mood.
3 Discreetly all enquiries will be handled and you may write in confidence to us.
4 'Don't worry,' she quietly said, taking my hand and squeezing it reassuringly.
5 She many times told them to take care but they ignored repeatedly her advice.
6 The door burst suddenly open and we all looked in surprise up.
7 I do every day my homework and it takes me usually an hour.
8 He just doesn't like ice cream he loves it so much that he eats every day it.

D Rewrite the sentences using the words in red, but without changing the meaning:

1	They eventually replied to my letter.	after a while
2	I'm afraid that's a mistake I frequently make.	again and again
3	There are many occasions when I eat out in the evenings.	often
4	Soon I'll have finished writing this report.	practically
5	They helped me although they seemed unwilling.	reluctantly
6	There's nothing I'd like to do less than go for a walk.	particularly
7	Each branch of the company is a separate operation.	independently
8	I expect that he will be feeling apprehensive.	presumably
9	You should pay constant attention to your spelling.	always
10	She gave me a worried look.	anxiously

Adverb position is a very difficult area of English usage, and it's often best to rely on your *feelings* for what seems right and what seems wrong. Pay special attention to any corrections you are given. There are no hard-and-fast rules, unfortunately.

2.8 Be prepared!

A 1 You'll hear an expert giving some advice. Before you listen to the recording, try to guess or deduce what information seems to be missing here:

Walking in the mountains

TAKE THE RIGHT PRECAUTIONS:

1. DO have at least _____ people in your party. DON'T *go alone* _____.

2. DO be _____. DON'T do anything you're not _____ to do.

3. DO expect the weather to _____. DON'T rely on _____.

4. DO allow yourself plenty of _____. DON'T let _____ catch up with you.

5. DO walk at the _____ of the _____ member of the group.
   DON'T leave anyone _____.

6. DO _____ if fog or low clouds come down.

7. DO find _____ where you can sit and wait for _____.
   DON'T _____ in case you walk over a _____ !

TAKE THE RIGHT EQUIPMENT:

1. *A map* _____ – You must _____ your _____ before setting off.

2. A _____ in case there are no _____ or the sun is obscured,
   and make sure you know _____ – DON'T just follow _____ and rely on your _____.

3. A rucksack, containing _____ and _____ clothing.

4. Footwear: _____ , not _____ or _____.

5. Emergency _____ in your rucksack: _____ , _____ , _____.

6. A _____ in case you get caught in the dark.

7. A _____ or a _____ in case you have to spend the night in the open.

And ...
Before setting out, DO _____ and _____ ,
and DON'T forget to _____ when you get back.

2 🔊 Listen to the recording, filling in the missing information above.

3 👥 After listening to the recording, discuss these questions:

- What important precautions and equipment did the speaker NOT mention?
- Which of his advice do you disagree with?

B 👥 Make a list of your own safety rules for TWO of these activities:

sailing	windsurfing
swimming in the sea	skiing
driving in remote areas	going out at night alone
cycling in heavy traffic	climbing a ladder

C 🖊 Write a letter to a friend, telling the story of a walk in the mountains where you ignored the advice given in the recording but where, despite a number of close shaves, you arrived home safely (300–350 words).

Make notes before you start writing.

(If you prefer, you could write about one of the activities you discussed in B, where you ignored your own safety rules.)

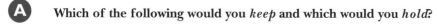

A Which of the following would you *keep* and which would you *hold*?

a diary   a meeting   a promise   a straight face   hands with someone
in touch with someone   quiet   someone company   someone in the dark
someone responsible   your breath   your eyes open   your fingers crossed
your head high   your temper   yourself to yourself

B Find synonyms for the phrases in red, or explain their meaning. Use a dictionary if necessary.

1 She walked so fast that I couldn't keep up with her.
2 There's no point in trying to keep up with the Joneses.
3 You've done a lot of good work this month. I hope you can keep it up.
4 They're getting married next month! Keep it to yourself, though.
5 I'll keep my fingers crossed for you on the day of your interview.
6 I'm sorry for what I did, I hope you won't hold it against me.
7 Their reasoning just didn't hold up.
8 They explained what happened, but I feel they were holding something back.
9 We got held up in the traffic.
10 Hold on a moment, I haven't got a pen. Could you hold the line, please?

C Fill the gaps in these sentences with suitable forms of the phrasal verbs below:

1 The clouds look pretty ominous, I don't .... much hope of sunny weather.
2 Fortunately, their supplies .... till the rescue party got to them.
3 You'd better .... the subject of his first marriage, otherwise he'll get upset.
4 They managed to .... their costs .... by employing part-time workers.
5 It was a private argument, so I thought it best to .... it.
6 She felt that her boss's attitude was .... her .... in her career.
7 If she wants to get on, she'll have to .... her boss, not disagree with him.
8 Tell me exactly what you think – don't .... anything ....
9 They didn't think our offer was high enough, so they .... more.
10 As they climbed up the cliff, the leader told them to .... tight.

hold back   hold back   hold on   hold out   hold out   hold out for
keep down   keep in with   keep off   keep out of

SAY AAARGH

A SENSE OF ADVENTURE

3

Everyone's different!

3.1   Getting away from it all

R E A D I N G

A **1** Read the article opposite, preferably before the lesson. Note down THREE reasons why you might envy the writer and THREE reasons why you wouldn't envy her.

2 👥 Compare the reasons you've noted down. Then discuss these questions:

- Do you like to be alone – or do you feel lonely when you haven't got company?
- Do you enjoy the pace of life in a big city? Or do you find it stressful?
- If you wanted to 'get away from it all' where would you go?

B **1** Make notes on each of the visits to the homestead, in the order the people arrived. Note their name(s), who they were and how they got there. The writer's information is given as an example.

	NAME(S)	WHO THEY WERE	MEANS OF TRANSPORTATION
	Margaret	the writer	float plane
a)			
b)			
c)			
d)			
e)			

2 Who were her friends or acquaintances who *didn't* come to visit? Note down who they were – and the reason why you think she was relieved they didn't come.

	WHO THEY WERE	WHY MARGARET WAS RELIEVED
a)		
b)		
c)		

3 Note down your answers to these questions (¶ shows the paragraph number):

a Who were Don, Bill and Liz?
b Why is the friend described as *heroic* (¶14) and *alarmingly cheerful* (¶24)?
c What were the THREE most rewarding aspects of her stay?

C Highlight the following words and phrases in the article:

¶4 foolproof   ¶6 unassailable   outraged   the bush   ¶8 unsolicited
¶9 positively   ¶13 blissfully   ¶15 egged on   ¶16 abhors a vacuum
¶17 came to nothing   ¶21 flagged   ¶25 tentatively   ¶29 bustle

Then match them to their OPPOSITES below:

calm   civilisation   confidently   continued   did happen   discouraged   invited
loves an empty space   not in the least   precarious   unhappily   unruffled   vulnerable

D 👥👥 Discuss these questions:

- When have you spent time alone? Describe your own experience of solitude, loneliness or isolation. Or imagine what it would be like.
- Have you ever lived in a small community or village? What was it / would it be like?

34

The great escape

LOOKING around the small wooden cabin, I counted seven people. Or it might have been eight. The lighthouse keeper's wife was the last to arrive. She dropped out of the sky, unannounced, courtesy of a Coast Guard helicopter that landed on the gravel beach right in front of the cabin.

"Hi, I'm Lise," she shouted as the chopper disappeared. "I thought I'd drop in for a visit." Looking around, she added: "Hey, I thought you were here on your own!"

I'd stopped thinking that days ago.

"I want to be alone," I had declared on leaving London. I was tired, dog tired, of people and telephones and deadlines and crowds. So I planned a great escape, a Big Sleep, a magnificent foolproof Fortress of Solitude, where for three whole weeks I planned to hibernate like a bear in the middle of nowhere.

Everything seemed perfect. A friend in Canada needed a house-sitter for his remote homestead on the far coast of Vancouver Island, the silvery western edge of Canada. Here, the map ends and the open Pacific begins. Huge silent forests swell in the heavy winter rains, growing dense and impenetrable right down to the water's edge.

I knew I could be entirely alone here. No roads go near this part of the coast. The only way in is by boat or small plane. I would have no telephone, no electricity, no television, no interruptions. I felt unassailable. Friends and family were outraged. "What do you mean, you want to be alone? Out in the bush like that? No one wants to be that alone."

"Oh yeah?" I thought. I said nothing. They kept talking.

And then came the unsolicited offers. No fewer than 15 people offered to come and stay with me. For my own good, of course.

Some of the offers were positively scary. "Is it OK if I bring the boys?" These boys are aged two and four, television junkies from the womb. Their mother has never lived out of range of a washing machine or a dishwasher in her entire life.

"Frank and I will both come – he's much better after his operation."

"I'll bring my guitar."

"I've been really depressed, I need solitude too."

But despite all these offers, when the tiny float plane at last landed in the inlet near the cabin, and I clambered out with my heavy boxes of books and groceries, I was blissfully alone. My first few days were entirely peaceful. A long-dreamed-of silence surrounded me, and vast space. It didn't last long.

The depressed friend arrived first. She was heroically prepared to stay for 10 days. "Don't worry about me – I won't get in your way."

"Oh yeah?" I thought. This friend had been egged on by numerous other friends. "What is that woman doing out there they're all asking? I'm supposed to report back."

It was really very simple. I wasn't doing much at all. I was sleeping and reading and chopping wood and beachcombing and watching the eagles and looking out for other wildlife. The problem for everyone else seemed to be that I was doing it alone. Human nature, I decided, abhors a vacuum. It was clear that I would have to settle for semi-solitude. And in the end I found I didn't really mind. Which is just as well.

No one else arrived from "outside". The threat of "the boys", the guitar and the post-operative Frank came to nothing. But as the days passed I was astonished to find myself meeting more and more people.

My nearest neighbours turned out to be Dave and Diane, living in a deserted Indian village 15 miles up the coast. Diane called me on the marine radio. "Don told us you were there all alone, so we thought we'd check in to see how you're getting on."

"Don?" I thought. I didn't know any Don.

Dave and Diane and their children came to see me in their boat. They told me where to dig for clams and that the herring run had started and that hundreds of sea lions were playing further out in the bay and that the grey whales had arrived on their annual migration.

That was the day Lise from the lighthouse arrived. All day long, the coffee pot spluttered on the woodstove and conversation never flagged. I learned about light-keeping and edible seaweeds and how to smoke mussels and where the gooseneck barnacles grow.

"Here I was worrying about you," said Lise cheerfully. "I never thought you'd have so much company."

Neither did I. But it was good company. On the day of the crowded cabin, we went out in the boat to see the grey whales spouting. Later on, we went all the way to the lighthouse, riding on the huge swells of the open Pacific, in Dave's small boat.

My depressed friend became alarmingly cheerful after all this and thought she might stay even longer. She had, however, to get back to work. As her plane took off from the water, silence returned. The guests had all left.

"Ah, solitude," I thought, tentatively. Just me and the whales and the sea lions and the eagles and the herring. The solitude lasted precisely two more days before a large, friendly person emerged from the forest announcing that he was Bob, from the logging camp down in the next inlet. He'd hiked over to see how I was doing. "Just thought I'd check in. Bill told me you were here all alone." ▶▶

26 "Bill?" I thought, and, "All alone?" Bob stayed and drank a pot of coffee. I learned a lot about trees.

27 A few days later, a strange boat anchored in front of the house and three men made their way to shore. They were from the Department of Fisheries, monitoring the herring run. "Liz told us you were out here on your own. How's it going? Aren't you lonely?"

28 "Liz?" I thought, and, "Lonely?" as I put the coffee pot on. That day I ran out of coffee and learned more about herring.

29 I had visitors on 14 of my 21 days of solitude. I learned a lot, not just about herring and trees and whales, but about solitude and loneliness. In such a remote landscape, people are very aware of each other. The presence of a person – any person – matters. People are assumed to be interesting creatures, and important. In the exhausting bustle of Central London, that doesn't always seem to be the case. I have been lonely in the rush hour at Oxford Circus. I was never lonely in my days of solitude on the far coast of Canada.

30 Next year I've been asked to go back to that coast, to house-sit once again in that green, silent place. I'll go, of course. And I'll know, next time, to take more coffee.

Margaret Horsfield

3.2 Reporting – 1 GRAMMAR REVIEW

A Match these reporting verbs with the verbs with similar meanings below:

emphasise complain confess disclose forecast infer insinuate order
promise reiterate remember suppose yell

*admit gather grumble guarantee guess imply predict recall repeat
reveal shout stress tell*

B 1 Decide which of the endings in blue fit comfortably with these beginnings.
SIX verbs don't fit with any of the endings – which are they?

> It's more interesting for a reader if you use a variety of reporting verbs – not just *he said* or *she asked*.

They ...	accused	admitted	advised	agreed	allowed	... that we had done it.

They ... accused admitted advised agreed allowed
apologised asked blamed couldn't decide
discovered dissuaded didn't expect explained
forbade forgave hoped imagined implied
didn't know learned mentioned persuaded
pretended promised never realised reckoned
refused didn't remember reminded
didn't reveal didn't say shouted suggested
didn't tell threatened wanted warned
wished wondered

... that we had done it.
... that we should do it.
... to do it.
... us to do it.
... when to do it.
... when we should do it.
... if we had done it.

2 🖉 Write sentences using the six verbs that didn't fit with any of the endings and show them to your partner. Highlight the verbs in A and B1 that you want to remember.

C Change each sentence into reported speech, using suitable verbs from the list in B above. Imagine that they were said to you by different people LAST WEEK.

1 'I'll certainly give you a hand tomorrow evening.'
   He promised to help me the next evening. or
   He promised that he would help me the following evening.
2 'I'm not going to help you, you'll have to do it by yourself.'
3 'There's no point in writing it all out in longhand – it'd just be a waste of time.'
4 'It's your fault that we missed the bus, you must have misread the timetable.'
5 'Do you happen to know what time the performance starts?
   I don't want to be late.'
6 'Why don't you phone him up and see if he's free tonight?'
7 'Make sure that you don't start giggling during the interview.'
8 'If you type this letter out for me, I'll buy you a drink, OK? Thanks!'
9 'You're the one who borrowed my dictionary, aren't you?'
10 'If you don't move your car, I'll call the police.'
11 'All right, if you want me to, I don't mind accompanying you.'
12 'I don't really mind about your rudeness – I know you were
   in a bit of a state.'
13 'Haven't you finished writing the report yet?'
14 'I'm very sorry for breaking your sunglasses.
   I didn't mean to sit on them.'

D **1** Note down SIX difficult or personal questions you want to ask your partner.

2 👥 Join a partner and ask each other your questions. Note down the answers.

3 👥 Change partners and report the conversation you had in 2 just now.

> *She asked me … and I told her …*
> *Then I asked her … but she wouldn't tell me whether …*
> *I expected her to tell me … but I found out that …*

When reporting something which was said in another place or a long time ago, place and time phrases may also have to be changed:

'I'll do it tomorrow.' → She told me that she would do it the next day.
'I was here yesterday.' → He said that he had been there the day before.
'Do I have to do it now?' → I wondered if I had to do it then/right away.
'Look at this document.' → She wanted me to look at the document.

3.3 **Punctuation and paragraphs**   **WRITING SKILLS**

A Write down the names of each of these punctuation marks, as in the example:

? question mark ; : ! … - — " " • ¶ * ( ) [ ] / ' .

B Add suitable punctuation in the spaces in this article. Change lower case letters to Capitals where necessary. And decide where to break the text into five paragraphs.

> A rabbit goes into a butcher's shop and asks , " Have you got any lettuce
> The butcher says   We don't sell lettuce here   You need the greengrocer's across the road
> The next day the rabbit comes into the shop and asks for some lettuce again
> The butcher tells him   Look   I told you yesterday   we don't sell lettuce   You need the greengrocer
> The rabbit comes in the next day and asks the butcher again   Have you got any lettuce
> The butcher goes mad   He says   Look   I'm sick of this   How many times do I have to tell you I don't sell lettuce   If you come in here again asking for lettuce I'm going to nail your ears to the floor
> The next day the rabbit comes in and asks the butcher   Have you got any nails
>   Nails   No
> Right   the rabbit says   Have you got any lettuce

C This job reference was typed by someone with good spelling, but poor punctuation. Proof-read it, correct the mistakes, and divide it into paragraphs.

> Clear punctuation helps the reader to follow your meaning. Commas, in particular, are useful for showing the reader where one phrase or clause ends, and the next one begins. A comma can also change the meaning of a sentence. Always proof-read your own written work before handing it in.

> I have known, Jan Hall both professionally and personally, for several years, since 1998 when she first joined my department she has been a reliable, resourceful and conscientious member of my staff with a thoroughly professional attitude to her work; she has cheerfully taken on extra responsibilities and can be relied on, to take over when other staff are absent or unavailable! She particularly enjoys dealing with members of the public: and has a knack of putting people at their ease? She is particularly adept at defusing delicate situations – with an appropriate word and a smile? As her portfolio shows she is also a very, creative and talented person and her work shows great promise during her time with us her attendance has been excellent... She is an intelligent thoughtful, and imaginative person, I have no hesitation in recommending her for the post!!

D Correct the errors in these sentences and then comment on the rules of punctuation that have been broken in each:

1 *Sitting on the beach we watched the windsurfers, falling into the water.*
2 *The aspect of punctuation, which is most tricky, is the use of commas.*
3 *Could you tell me, when to use a semi-colon?*
4 *Feeling completely baffled we tried to solve the problem, with which we were faced.*
5 *He wouldnt dare say boo to a goose hes so shy.*
6 *There were surprisingly no punctuation mistakes in his work.*

3.4 Who's talking?

LISTENING

A You're going to hear five different people talking. In each case it's not immediately obvious what they're talking about or even who they're talking to, so you'll have to pick up 'clues' to get the answers. You'll need to hear the recording more than once to get all of the clues and answers.

FIRST SPEAKER
1 How does the speaker feel and where is she?
2 Who is she talking to?
3 She says: *... they're all over the place ...*   ← Who or what are *they*?
4 She says: *... it's almost time to pick them up ...*   ← Who or what are *they*?
5 She says: *... don't look like that ...*   ← How is the listener looking?
6 Why is the listener silent?

SECOND SPEAKER
7 Who is the speaker talking to?
8 Why has he started talking to her?
9 Who are all the people he refers to?
10 Why is the listener silent?

THIRD SPEAKER
11 Who is the speaker talking to?
12 She says: *... I told her not to include me ...*   ← Who does she mean by *her*?
13 She says: *... I got all the stuff ...*   ← What *stuff* is she referring to?
14 She says: *... I got the bus all the way out there ...* ← What place is *there*?
15 She says: *... they called it off ...*   ← What is *it*?

FOURTH SPEAKER
16 Who is the speaker?
17 Who is he speaking to?
18 He says: *... it couldn't have happened ...*   ← What is *it*?
19 He ends by saying: *Nor is there any likelihood*   ← Complete his sentence.
   in the future of ...

FIFTH SPEAKER
20 What kind of person is the speaker?
21 Who is she talking to?
22 She says: *... you can't put them back ...*   ← What are *they*?
23 Why is the listener silent?
24 She says: *Look, I'm sorry, I didn't mean ...*   ← Complete her sentence.

B 1 👥 **What kind of person do you imagine each of the speakers to be? Make notes of some words you could use to describe them.**

2 👥 → 👥 Describe each speaker to the other pair and ask them to guess which one you're describing.

C 1 🖉 Write five short reports, giving the GIST of what each speaker said in two or three sentences. Try to convey the essence of what they said, not a word-for-word report. Use suitable verbs from 3.2.

2 👥 Compare your reports when you've done this.

A **1** 👥 **Discuss the difference in emphasis between these sentences. One of them sounds funny because the effect is overdone – which one is it?**

1 At no level of society do women have equal rights with men.
Women do not have equal rights with men at any level of society.

2 It occurred to me later that I had made a big mistake.
Not until later did it occur to me that I had made a big mistake.

3 At the top of the hill stood a solitary pine tree.
A solitary pine tree stood at the top of the hill.

4 So lonely did he feel that he went round to see his ex-wife for a chat.
He felt so lonely that he went round to see his ex-wife for a chat.

5 Little did they know that the sheriff was about to draw his revolver.
They didn't know that the sheriff was about to draw his revolver.

6 Bang went the door. In came Fred. On came all the lights. Out went the cat. The door opened with a bang and Fred came in. All the lights went on and the cat ran out.

7 Rarely are shy people taken as seriously as assertive people.
Shy people are rarely taken as seriously as assertive people.

2 **Highlight** the words or grammar that are used to give a special emphasis in the sentences. How have the word order and grammar been changed?

B **Fill the gaps in these sentences with suitable words:**

1 Little .... that she would win the competition.

2 Not only .... the piano brilliantly but she .... too.

3 Never in my life .... so humiliated!

4 No sooner .... the bath than the phone ....

5 Under no circumstances .... the fire doors ....

6 Not until .... finished .... allowed to leave the room.

7 Only after .... the police able to catch the thieves.

8 Not once during her entire .... in trouble with the law.

9 Not only .... rather naive but he also .... very sensitive.

10 No sooner .... our picnic than ....

C **Rewrite these sentences more DRAMATICALLY, using structures from B above:**

Inversion should be used sparingly as over-use can sound ridiculous. It can usually be avoided in conversation altogether. It does tend to come up regularly in the Use of English Paper of the exam, though.

1 We went out in our best clothes. The rain came down.
Out we went in our best clothes, and down came the rain.

2 The thieves drove off with the police in hot pursuit.

3 The umbrellas went up. We went home, wet through.

4 A tall dark stranger was sitting beside her in the train.

5 A fat tabby cat lay under the table, washing itself obliviously.

6 The edge of the cliff gave way and she fell down.

7 There was a ferocious dog behind the wall, barking furiously.

8 Then I realised that I had made a very big mistake.

"Boo!"

Long road to Utopia

A Six paragraphs have been removed from this article. Choose the most suitable paragraph from the list A–F for each gap (1–6) in the article.

Long road to Utopia

JUST 500 miles separates England from Sweden, but if, like me, you're a Romany traveller, the gulf in attitudes is colossal. My wife and I have recently travelled with our horse and caravan between the two countries. On our journey, we experienced not only changes in the physical landscape, but profound differences in attitudes towards many of the issues that lie at the heart of a democratic society – such as race, access to land and respect for a traditional, ecologically friendly nomadic lifestyle.

1 [   ]

In 1998, I went to Sweden with my horse and wagon, in search of Romanestan. Sweden is a large country with a small population and enough living space for thousands of travellers. The roads are empty of traffic. Its law of allemänsrätt (all man's rights) is a model law protecting the "right to roam". Everybody has the right to camp and gather firewood, berries, herbs and mushrooms from the countryside. Romanies are recognised as a distinct ethnic minority by the Swedish government and even have the right to be educated in their own language.

2 [   ]

There is, however, an eeriness about Sweden. The woods are suspiciously silent and empty. The thing that made us come back to England after two years was the total absence of travellers in the rural landscape. Romany communities in Sweden are concentrated in larger towns. Official policy has assimilated travellers entirely through generosity, by giving them all the benefits a well-funded welfare state can muster. It's a far cry from past policy – up until the 1960s, travellers were forcibly sterilised in Sweden – but probably a far smarter strategy.

3 [   ]

Having a lifestyle like mine can give you the annoying status of an eccentric semi-celebrity. A passing tourist once photographed me peeing at 7 o'clock in the morning. Another day, while fetching some water for the horse, I saw a woman walk straight into our home as if it was a tourist attraction. I've probably been photographed and filmed at least once for every mile I've travelled on Swedish roads. The exotic appeal of your life imposes different restrictions on your freedom. But that which makes you a celebrity in Scandinavia defines you as a pariah in England.

4 [   ]

The right to travel is not an issue; all you need is the vehicle. It's the right to stop that is the problem. Most of the old stopping places are gone. Those that haven't had a ditch put through them by local councils have been grabbed by farmers extending their fences or disappeared under the developers' tide of concrete. The commons we once used are gone, the verges made smaller by the widening of roads.

5 [   ]

Since returning to England, I've experienced all these problems. I've met travellers who have been beaten by landowners and refused water by local villagers. At the first county line we crossed, there was a police car waiting, wanting to know our names and destination. The red carpet definitely doesn't stretch to our shores.

6 [   ]

Jake Bowers-Burbridge

A

In short, Sweden is a land where Romanies have rights. It's a long way from Britain's endless fences, criminal justice act and feudal mentality towards land and class. When I first arrived, I felt as if I had found a little piece of Romanestan.

B

In the time of Henry VIII, there was a mandatory death sentence for Romanies. We have survived in an environment that is very hostile to our existence. England is one of the most densely populated countries on earth, with extremely concentrated land-ownership. That's bad news if you're a nomad needing constant access to new land for fuel and food.

C

Travelling in Britain is only possible nowadays with an extremely intimate knowledge of the countryside and a willingness to trespass in defence of the right to live as our ancestors did. We face a stark choice – settle, or engage in daily law breaking. This ongoing struggle has got to be one of the longest running and least recognised campaigns of civil disobedience this country has ever known.

D

Every nation without a homeland has its promised land. For the Kurds, it is Kurdistan; for us, it is Romanestan. But Romanestan is just an ideal, a utopia in time, if not in place. We may originally have come from India but I doubt that many of the world's 8 million Romanies would choose to go back there.

E

If our culture is to survive it must be made possible through political action. By going to Sweden I've seen glimpses of Romanestan in the forests now empty of travellers. By coming home, I hope I can bring a little bit of it back to a country so in need of its promise.

F

If Sweden can be criticised for anything it is that life is too easy. It's so good it's unreal. I've even had free cooked breakfast delivered to my caravan door. The Swedes are a rich nation but many cannot comprehend how anybody would choose to live such a basic life.

B 👥👥👥👥 **Discuss these questions:**

- How much do you sympathise with the writer of the article?
- What kind of discrimination is there in your country against women (sexism), old people (ageism) and members of ethnic minorities (racism)?

3.7 / **Opposites**   VOCABULARY DEVELOPMENT

A Complete these sentences with suitable words:

1 He isn't naive, he's quite _sophisticated_
2 She isn't brave, she's ……………
3 He wasn't sorry, he was ……………
4 Instead of slowing down, he ……………
5 She wasn't guilty, she was ……………
6 They didn't help me, they ……………

7 Instead of spending her money she ……………
8 Instead of pulling the door open he ……………
9 Instead of reassuring me she ……………
10 He didn't get angry, he ……………
11 *Bad* isn't an antonym of *awful*, it's a ……………
12 Instead of slamming the door he ……………

B **1** Decide which of these adjectives form their opposites with **in–** or **un–** :

_un_acceptable	_in_accessible	…advisable	…appropriate	…aware
…bearable	…clearly	…competent	…considerate	…consistent
…conspicuous	…conventional	…convincing	…decided	…decisive
…desirable	…dignified	…discreet	…distinct	…efficient
…eventful	…expected	…explicable	…faithful	…foreseen
…forgettable	…frequent	…grateful	…gratitude	…imaginative
…manageable	…predictable	…rewarding	…sincere	…sincerity
…sociable	…sophisticated	…stability	…stable	…sufficient
…tolerant	…trustworthy	…visible	…wanted	…welcome

2 Decide which of these words form their opposites with **dis–** or **im–, il–** or **ir–** :

_dis_advantage	_il_legal	…agreeable	…approve	…arm
…connect	…contented	…entangle	…legible	…legitimate
…logical	…loyal	…mature	…organised	…patient
…personal	…possible	…rational	…regular	…relevant
…respectful	…responsible	…satisfied	…similar	

3 Here are some slightly trickier ones. Think of a suitable opposite for these adjectives:

thoughtless	_considerate/thoughtful_	clumsy ……………	fearless ……………
neat ……………	noisy ……………	proud ……………	rare ……………
restless ……………	tactful ……………	talkative ……………	trivial ……………

C The adjectives on the left are used pejoratively to describe someone's disposition or behaviour. Choose suitable opposites from among the words on the right.

pejorative

bad-tempered *good-natured*
conceited   deceitful   fussy   lazy
malicious   mean   narrow-minded
neurotic   pretentious   secretive
solitary   sullen   touchy

complimentary

*cheerful   easy-going   frank   generous
good-natured   gregarious   hard-working
imaginative   kindhearted   laid back   liberal
modest   nonchalant   open   perceptive
sociable   talkative   trustworthy   truthful
unassuming*

3.8 **Not waving ...**   **READING**

A Listen to these poems read aloud. Then answer the questions below.

Not Waving but Drowning

NOBODY heard him, the dead man,
But still he lay moaning:
I was much further out than you thought
And not waving but drowning.
Poor chap, he always loved larking   5
And now he's dead
It must have been too cold for him his heart
    gave way,
They said.
Oh, no no no, it was too cold always   10
(Still the dead one lay moaning)
I was much too far out all my life
And not waving but drowning.

Stevie Smith

Bloody Men

Bloody men are like bloody buses –
You wait for about a year
And as soon as one approaches your stop
Two or three others appear.
You look at them flashing their indicators,   5
    Offering you a ride.
You're trying to read the destinations,
    You haven't much time to decide.
If you make a mistake, there is no turning back.
Jump off, and you'll stand there and gaze   10
While the cars and the taxis and lorries go by
And the minutes, the hours, the days.

Wendy Cope

1 How did the man die?
2 Which are the words spoken by the *dead man*?
3 Which words are spoken by his friends?
4 What does *larking* mean in line 5?
5 What was *too cold* in line 7? What was *too cold* in line 10?
6 In what ways was he *too far out* in line 12 and *drowning* in line 13?
7 In what ways was he *not waving* in line 12?
8 What ADJECTIVES could you use to describe the drowning man and his friends?

1 What does the poet think of men?
2 In what ways do the men she meets *flash their indicators*?
3 Why doesn't she have *much time to decide*?
4 Why is there *no turning back*?
5 What will happen if she decides to break up with a man?
6 What are *the cars and the taxis and lorries*?
7 Which words in the poem rhyme? What is the effect of this?
8 What ADJECTIVES could you use to describe the poet and the men she meets?

B 👥 **Discuss these questions:**

• What did you think of the two poems?
• Which one impressed you, or moved you, or amused you more? Why?
• What are the similarities between the two poems?
• What is the effect of expressing the ideas
    In verse,
    Rather than in prose, without
    Any line breaks?
• Are you fond of poetry – or does it leave you cold? Give your reasons.

It takes all sorts ...   SPEAKING AND COMPOSITION

A **1** Note down FIVE adjectives or phrases to describe each of these people. Try to avoid the most obvious or simple words, like *nice*, *young*, *kind*, etc. Use a dictionary if necessary.

2 Follow these guidelines to describe the people in the photos:

- First impression of the person
- Appearance: clothes, age, face, hair
- Their character and the way they might behave

B A friend of yours is going to visit two people you know well*, who are quite different from each other. Your friend is nervous about meeting them for the first time. Write a letter to reassure your friend, describing the two people (300–350 words).

(* They could be two friends or relatives, for example, or someone you admire and someone you detest.)

1 First of all, make notes on the following points:

Appearance: age, clothes, complexion, eyes, face, hair
Personality and character
Family background
Past achievements
Job
Interests and hobbies
Why you like or dislike him/her
Examples of typical behaviour

2 Rearrange the notes in a suitable order. Decide which points should be left out because they are less interesting or less relevant.

3 Discuss your notes with a partner.

4 Refer back to the 'Golden rules' in 1.8. Make any necessary amendments to your notes and then write your descriptions.

5 Show your completed descriptions to a partner, and ask for comments.

4 Let's talk

4.1 Different ways of communicating   TOPIC VOCABULARY

A 1 👥 How would you describe these people's expressions? Imagine they're about to talk to you. What are they going to say – and how will you reply?

2 👥 → 👥 Compare your ideas.

B 1 👥 In these sentences only THREE of the alternatives can be used to complete each sentence correctly:

1 She's going to .... about gestures and body language.
give a lecture ✓   say ✗   speak ✓   talk ✓   tell ✗

2 If you keep on .... I won't be able to understand what you're saying.
grumbling   mumbling   muttering   nagging   whispering

3 During a lecture I try to .... down the main points that are made.
doodle   jot   note   scribble   sketch

4 I'm afraid I've only had time to .... the articles you recommended.
glance at   interpret   scan   skim   study

5 When he told me about his misadventures I couldn't help ....
chuckling   grinning   shrugging   sniggering   stammering

6 He looked at me with a .... on his face when I told him what I had done.
frown   gasp   gulp   scowl   sneer

7 On seeing the body hanging from the apple tree she started to ....
murmur   scream   shriek   squeak   yell

8 She went on to .... that I wasn't working hard enough.
implicate   imply   infer   intimate   suggest

9 She used a(n) .... which I couldn't quite follow.
clause   expression   idiom   phrase   speech

10 And her .... made me feel guilty even though I'd done nothing wrong.
attitude   dialect   expression   idiom   tone

2 👥 Look again at the alternatives that were wrong. Why are they wrong?

4.2 Meanings and translations   LISTENING AND SPEAKING

A **1** Note down some reasons why you might be tempted to buy this product. Then compare your notes with a partner.

2 🔊 You'll hear a broadcast about *The Interpreter*, another electronic translator. Tick the boxes in 1 and fill the gaps in 2–5.

1 Which of these situations are mentioned in the report?
at the airport ☐   at the chemist's ☐   at the railway station ☐   at the bank ☐
business ☐   camping ☐   complaining ☐   emergencies ☐   in the post office ☐
making friends ☐   motoring ☐   restaurants ☐   shopping ☐   sightseeing ☐

2 Which languages does *The Interpreter* speak? ....

3 What 'useful phrase' does *The Interpreter* suggest you might you use if . . .
. . . you want to know the admission charge to a museum or gallery? ....
. . . a building is on fire? ....
. . . you're trying to get a discount? ....
. . . the service in a restaurant is slow? ....

4 What useful phrase is missing from *The Interpreter*'s repertoire? ....

5 You can use *The Interpreter* in privacy, thanks to its ....

6 Its words also appear on the .... as it speaks.

B 🏃🏃 Discuss these questions:

- Which of the products would you like to have? When would you use it?
- Have you ever used a phrasebook when visiting a foreign country? What was your experience?
- Do you always assume people in another country will speak English or do you make an effort to learn some of the language before going there?
- What are the FIVE most useful phrases you'd try to learn if you were visiting another country for the very first time?
- Which do you use more often: an English-to-English dictionary or a bilingual one? Give your reasons.

C **1** 🏃🏃 Student A should look at Activity 14 on page 202, student B at 24 on page 205 and C at 31 on page 207. Each Activity contains definitions of some of these words. Together you should pool your information and discuss which dictionary seems most helpful and clear.

> irony · sarcasm   collocation · cliché · platitude · proverb   slogan · jargon   accent · dialect

You should NOT read your entries out loud – that would take a very long time – but you may wish to read out BRIEF quotations.

2 Now compare the dictionary entries in all three Activities. Suppose you didn't know any of the words above: which of the entries would be most helpful?

4.3 Attitudes to language   READING AND SUMMARY WRITING

A   Ask your partner these questions:

- Where can you hear the 'best English' spoken?
- Where can you hear the 'best accent' of your own language spoken?

B   Read this text and choose the best word or phrase to fill each gap in the text:

A language is a system of communication used within a particular social group. Inevitably, the emotions created by group loyalty get in the way of 1 judgements about language. When we think we are making such a judgement, we are often merely making a statement about our prejudices. It is highly instructive to examine these occasionally. I myself have very _____ 2 prejudices about what I call Americanisms. I see red whenever I read a certain popular woman columnist in a certain popular daily paper. I wait with a kind of fascinated horror for her to use the locution 'I guess', as in 'I guess he really loves you after all' or 'I guess you'd better get yourself a new boyfriend'. I see in this form the essence of Americanism, a _____ 3 to the British Way of Life. But this is obviously nonsense, and I know it. I know that 'I guess' is at least as old as Chaucer, pure British English, something sent over in the *Mayflower*. But, like most of us, I do not really like submitting to reason; I much prefer blind prejudice. And so I stoutly _____ 4 'I guess' as an American importation and its use by a British writer as a betrayal of the traditions of my national group.

Such condemnation can seem virtuous, because patriotism – which means _____ 5 to the national group – is a noble word. While virtue burns in the mind, adrenaline courses round the body and makes us feel good. Reason never has this exhilarating chemical effect. And so patriotic euphoria _____ 6 our contempt of foreign languages and makes us unwilling to learn them properly. Chinese is still regarded in the West as a huge joke – despite what T.S. Eliot calls its 'great intellectual dignity' – and radio comedians can even raise a snigger by speaking mock-Chinese. Russian is, of course, nothing more than a deep vodka-rich rumble bristling with 'vitch' and 'ski'. As for German – that is an ugly language, aggressively guttural. We rarely _____ 7 that it seems ugly because of two painful wars, that it is all a matter of association. Sometimes our automatic sneers at foreign languages are mitigated by _____ 8 memories – warm holidays abroad, trips to the opera. Italian can then seem beautiful, full of blue skies, vino, sexy tenors. Trippers to Paris, on the other hand, furtively visiting the *Folies Bergère*, project their own guilt on to the French language and see it as 'naughty', even 'immoral'.

1	**A** subjective	**B** objectionable	**C** objective	**D** prejudiced
2	**A** powerful	**B** extraordinary	**C** muscular	**D** educated
3	**A** criticism	**B** warning	**C** blame	**D** threat
4	**A** criticise	**B** condemn	**C** welcome	**D** treasure
5	**A** loyalty	**B** antipathy	**C** sympathy	**D** honesty
6	**A** explains	**B** matches	**C** ignores	**D** justifies
7	**A** reveal	**B** discover	**C** admit	**D** suggest
8	**A** nice	**B** pleasant	**C** amusing	**D** worthwhile

C   Now read the continuation of the text and choose the best answer to the questions that follow:

Within the national group, our prejudices tend to be very mixed and, because they operate mainly on an unconscious level, not easily recognisable. We can be natives of great cities and still find a town dialect less pleasant than a country one. And yet, hearing prettiness and quaintness in a Dorset or Devon twang, we can also despise it, because we associate it with rural stupidity or backwardness. The ugly tones of Manchester or Birmingham will, because of their great civic associations, be at the same time somehow admirable. The whole business of ugliness and beauty works strangely. A BBC announcer says 'pay day'; a Cockney says 'pie die'. The former is thought to be beautiful, the latter ugly, and yet the announcer can use the Cockney sounds in a statement like 'Eat that pie and you will die' without anybody's face turning sour. In fact, terms like 'ugly' and 'beautiful' cannot really apply to languages at all. Poets can make beautiful patterns out of words, but there are no standards we can use to formulate aesthetic judgements on the words themselves. We all have our pet hates and loves among words, but these always have to be referred to associations. A person who dislikes beetroot as a vegetable is not likely to love 'beetroot' as a word. A poet who, in childhood, had a panful of hot stewed prunes spilled on him is, if he is a rather stupid poet, quite capable of writing 'And death, terrible as prunes'. We have to watch associations carefully, remembering that language is a public, not a private, medium, and that questions of word-hatred and word-love had best be tackled very coldly and rationally.

We are normally quick to observe regional variations in the use of the national language, but we feel less strongly about these than we do about class divisions in speech. If we speak with a Lancashire accent, we will often be good-humoured and only slightly derisive when we hear the accent of Wolverhampton or Tyneside. Sometimes we will even express a strong admiration of alien forms of English – the speech of the Scottish Highlands, for instance, or Canadian as opposed to American. But we feel very differently about English speech when it seems to be a badge or banner of class. The dialect known variously as the Queen's English or BBC English or Standard English was, originally, a pure regional form – so-called East Midland English, with no claim to any special intrinsic merit. But it was spoken in an area that was, and still is, socially and economically pre-eminent – the area which contains London, Oxford, and Cambridge. Thus it gained a special glamour as the language of the Court and the language of learning. It has ever since – often falsely – been associated with wealth, position, and education – the supra-regional dialect of the masters, while the regional dialects remain the property of the men. In certain industrial areas it can still excite resentment, despite the fact that it no longer necessarily goes along with power or privilege.

from *Language Made Plain* by Anthony Burgess

1 According to the writer, a rural accent may sound attractive, but it may also be . . .
   A admired
   B looked down on
   C funny
   D hard to understand

2 Our judgements on words we like or dislike are often based on a word's . . .
   A sound
   B origins
   C associations
   D beauty or ugliness

3 British accents show which region the person comes from, but may also show their . . .
   A education
   B age
   C gender
   D social class

4 A person with a regional accent may have less power than someone who . . .
   A has been well-educated
   B has no accent
   C uses Standard English
   D lives in London

5 If someone speaks with a Standard English accent (R.P.) they . . .
   A will be admired by everyone
   B show that they have power
   C show that they are well-educated
   D may be disliked in some regions

D **Highlight** these words in the text and match them with the words with similar meanings below:

¶1 *objective   prejudice   instructive*   ¶3 *associations   formulate   aesthetic   pet*
¶2 *exhilarating   euphoria   mitigated*   ¶4 *derisive   badge   intrinsic   the men   excite*

arouse   artistic   bias   connotations   contemptuous   devise   emblem   favourite
happiness   impartial   inherent   moderated   revealing   workers   stimulating

E **Discuss your reactions to the text. Do people in your country share similar prejudices about foreign languages and regional accents?**

F **Write a summary of the British attitudes to regional accents and dialects described by the writer (50–70 words).**

4.4 -ing and to . . .   GRAMMAR REVISION

A **Discuss the difference in meaning between these sentences. Then decide how each one might continue, as in the examples.**

1 **a** They went on running *even though they were tired.*   **b** They went on to run *five more miles.*

2 **a** We stopped to take photos but ......   **b** We stopped taking photos but ......

3 **a** Did you remember to send the fax or ...... ?   **b** Do you remember sending the fax or ...... ?

4 **a** I can't help you to feel better but ......   **b** I can't help feeling better, but ......

5 **a** I'm not used to using a fountain pen but ......   **b** I used to use a fountain pen but ......

6 **a** She heard him scream, but ......   **b** She heard him screaming, but ......

B **1** Match up the verbs and phrases below to make suitable collocations.

to answer	to a letter
to call	a letter / the phone
to contact	someone a letter
to drop	someone a line
to get	someone on the phone
to give	someone by phone / by post
to keep	someone a ring
to reply	someone a story
to tell	through to someone on the phone
to write	in touch with someone

2 Now use the collocations in B1 to complete each of these sentences. Add a suitable PREPOSITION if necessary. In some cases more than one version is possible.

1 I'm sorry _not to have kept_ in touch with you. OR _for not having kept_ OR _that I didn't keep_
2 Is there any point .... by post?
3 I regret .... her my secret. She couldn't help .... all her friends.
4 I forgot .... a birthday card.
5 Have you heard her .... about the penguin and the polar bear?
6 I strongly advise you .... his letter by return of post.
7 He never writes letters because he's so used .... on the phone.
8 Her number was engaged all day but I finally succeeded .... in the evening.
9 It may be worth .... a ring if you ever need any advice.
10 I tried .... on Sunday but there was no answer.
11 And I didn't want .... on your answering machine.
12 I'm not looking forward .... all these letters.

C Complete each sentence with your own ideas, using *-ing* or *to. . .* :

1 To get from the airport to the city centre I don't recommend ....
2 I've never been to America but I hope ....
3 After a heavy meal I can't face ....
4 The night before an important exam it's unwise to risk ....
5 After struggling to follow the first paragraph I gave up ....
6 Some people enjoy .... to Beethoven but I prefer ....
7 The first chapter was so exciting that I kept on ....
8 There was a violent thunderstorm but we carried on ....
9 After a hard day .... at the office I feel like ....
10 If I hear a baby .... I can't bear ....
11 After an enjoyable English class I don't mind ....
12 After .... ill for five days, on the sixth day I began ....
13 She probably wasn't at home when you called earlier. Why not try .... ?
14 I'd love .... a new car, but I can't afford ....
15 Someone started shouting at me but I pretended ....

> Remember that
> *to . . .* is also used to express intentions or plans:
>
> *He did it to help her.*
> *I phoned to warn him.*

4.5 Paragraphs
WRITING SKILLS

A There are no hard-and-fast rules for paragraphs, but here are some guidelines. Highlight the points you want to remember.

> **PARAGRAPHS**
>
> ¶ A new paragraph signifies a new theme, or a change of direction.
> ¶ Paragraphs help the reader to follow your thought processes.
> ¶ Short paragraphs are easier to read than long ones.
> ¶ When there is dialogue, each speaker usually requires a new paragraph.
> ¶ A new paragraph gives prominence to the first sentence, setting the tone for the rest of the paragraph.
> ¶ A strong opening sentence for each paragraph keeps the reader's attention.
> ¶ The last sentence of a paragraph also has prominence and may be the pay-off line.

B 👥 **Before you read the article below, discuss these questions:**

- Do you have a mobile phone? Where do you use it? How much do you use it?
- How aware do mobile phone-users seem to be of other people around them? Have you had any amusing or annoying experiences whilst eavesdropping on them?

C 1 **Read the beginning of this article and look at the analysis of the paragraphs below.**

Why mobiles can be murder on the 8.05

THE MAN in the half-moon glasses was worried. Receivership was looming in a couple of weeks and the main shareholders didn't seem to realise the urgency. ⟨1⟩

'I've got three buyers lined up,' he announced, and proceeded to reel off their names. ⟨2⟩

Nothing particularly unusual about this conversation, you might think; except that it was taking place on a train. The other passengers may not have been very interested in the fate of a small geographical publishing company, but they didn't have much choice; the speaker – whose name we soon learnt – was oblivious to his surroundings as he candidly discussed the most sensitive details for more than an hour on his mobile phone. ⟨3⟩

Once upon a time, mobile phones didn't exist. Then they were used sparingly by those on trains to relay the banal message: 'I've just got on the train, darling.' ⟨4⟩

Nowadays, an increasing number of commuters and business travellers seem to have decided that they can carry out their duties just as successfully from a railway carriage as they can from their office. Appointments are made, files are summoned from secretaries, and political knives are inserted in backs – all from the comfort of an Inter-City window seat. ⟨5⟩

I once spent an hour and a half on a late-night train with one such person. The man spent the entire journey reading the names and salaries of construction workers in the Middle East into his mobile. ⟨6⟩

¶1 *First sentence plunges the reader into the story*
¶2 *Still the same event as first paragraph, but direct speech*
¶3 *Now the writer starts to give his opinion*
¶4 *Change to another time*
¶5 *More precise description — new paragraph gives prominence to first sentence*
¶6 *New paragraph gives prominence to another personal experience*

---

2 **Read the next part of the article and note the reasons WHY the writer chose to start and end each paragraph at the place he does.**

On another occasion, the morning rush hour journey was punctuated by a pushy woman apparently making follow-up sales calls about 'an exciting concept called the One-Stop Shop'. ⟨7⟩ *diff ex*

In the usually quiet atmosphere of a railway carriage, it is difficult for the most uninterested fellow passenger to ignore such conversations, the more so if he is trying to concentrate on his own newspaper or work. ⟨8⟩ *general*

The problem has already prompted one railway company to introduce phone-free zones on its trains. Great Western Trains, which provides services to south Wales, the Cotswolds and the South-West, decided to ban mobile phones in some of its carriages after receiving a barrage of complaints. ⟨9⟩ *solution*

Spokeswoman Louise Wilimot says: 'We did a three-month trial and it proved very popular. First-class passengers then asked for the same.' Great Western does not discourage passengers from working – far from it – but says that most regard a peaceful atmosphere as a prerequisite. The company also discourages passengers from holding loud meetings. ⟨10⟩ *chas*

Other railway companies are reluctant to take steps against those who treat the carriage as their personal office space, preferring to rely upon ostracism by fellow passengers. ⟨11⟩ *other companies*

South West Trains, on one of whose trains the receivership conversation quoted took place, says the commuter-dominated nature of its business would make it difficult to introduce mobile-free zones. ⟨12⟩ *one of them*

South West's Alison Flynn says: 'We expect passengers to consider the feelings of other passengers.' ⟨13⟩ *new pt of view*

For those who work on the move, there is clearly a risk of breaching confidentiality. Boris Starling, of security consultancy Control Risks, spells it out: 'If you are going to sit and talk on the train, you have no idea who else is listening. They might even be journalists. ⟨14⟩ *another pt of view*

'Our advice is to be sensible, and simply not discuss company business on the train, particularly if it is confidential.' He points out that the risk of being overheard on a train, as opposed to another public place, such as a restaurant, is particularly acute: trains tend to be quieter. ⟨15⟩ *final pts. prominence given*

ALEXANDER GARRETT

49

D This is the end of the same article, printed without paragraphs. Decide where to begin each new paragraph.

Mike Platt, commercial director of the business travel agency Hogg Robinson BTI, says: 'Our research among clients shows that they are increasingly using the train as an extension of the office, but they have two main concerns: one is the lack of privacy; the other is the poor signal they often get on their phone on the train.' Platt says he regards the ability to work for three hours as the second key advantage Eurostar has over the plane – the first being the ability to travel directly between city centres. Many companies take the opportunity to hold formal business meetings on Eurostar, calculating that if they book facing seats over a table, they can get away without their conversation being heard. But he adds: 'People are split down the middle about mobile phones. Half want to use them, and the other half regard them as noise pollution and say that they can't do their own work if they are next to somebody who is barking down the phone.' Last week saw the publication of yet another survey demonstrating that the British work longer hours than their European compatriots. Many of us clearly regard a train journey as an opportunity to do more work, rather than to relax and enjoy the journey. Maybe it is time we all let the train take the strain.

A 350-word composition should contain at least four paragraphs, probably more. When planning a composition, decide where each new paragraph will begin. Note down a strong opening sentence for each paragraph before you start writing.

4.6 *Wh–* clauses   **ADVANCED GRAMMAR**

A **1** What you should do is (to) study these examples before doing the exercises.

What annoys me is intolerance.	Intolerance is what annoys me.
What I need is a friend to lend a helping hand.	All I need is a friend to lend a helping hand.
Whatever she does seems to be successful.	Wherever she goes she makes friends easily.
Whoever she meets, they take a liking to her.	
It doesn't really matter whether he gets here in time or not.	
Whether or not he gets here in time doesn't really matter.	

2 Use your own ideas to complete each sentence.

1 What I hate is *people being rude to me.*
2 One thing I like is ....
3 All I want is ....
4 What I feel like doing ....
5 What we need now ....
6 There's nothing I enjoy more than ....
7 I just don't want ....
8 Something that often surprises me is ....
9 What I want to do right now is ....

3 Exchange sentences with another pair. Rewrite their sentences using DIFFERENT structures: *I hate it when people are rude to me.*

B Match the sentences that mean the same as each other:

1 Whatever you do, don't tell everyone.   Tell anyone anything you like.
  Make sure you don't tell everyone.   Tell anyone whatever you want.
2 Say what you like.   Speak to whoever you want.
  Talk to anyone you want to.   Say whatever you want to.
3 Whoever did you give it to?   Who in the world did you give it to?
  To whom did you give it?   Who did you give it to?
4 Why ever don't you phone him?   Why do you never phone him?
  Why don't you ever phone him?   Why on earth don't you phone him?
5 Whenever I mention it he takes offence.   When I mention it he loses his temper.
  He reacts badly every time I mention it.   Each time I mention it he gets angry.

C Rewrite these sentences without changing the meaning:

1 He takes a phrasebook with him everywhere.   Wherever ....
2 It doesn't matter when you arrive.   You can ....
3 I only stuck out my tongue at her.   All ....
4 You did something that was very rude.   What ....
5 She just needs someone to tell her troubles to.   All ....
6 You can put it anywhere you like.   I don't mind ....
7 You can write or phone – as you like.   Whether ....
8 I don't know what time you'll arrive, but get in touch.   Whenever ....
9 He made a very impressive speech.   What ....
10 I was astonished by her confidence.   What ....

4.7 **The English-speaking world**   **SPEAKING, LISTENING AND COMPOSITION**

A   Look at this diagram, which shows some of the differences between various national accents of English. Add two more examples to the key below.

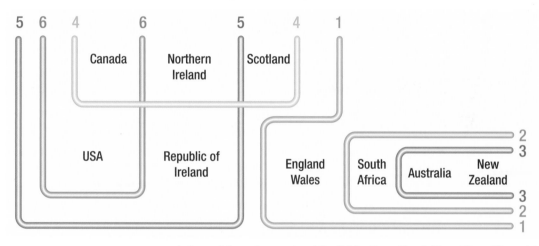

(adapted from *International English* by Peter Trudgill and Jean Hannah)

KEY   **TWO MORE EXAMPLES**

1 /r/ is pronounced at the end of *sure   mirror   far*   ....

2 /e/ instead of /æ/ in *than   thanks   hand   cat*   ....

3 front /aː/ instead of /ɑː/ in *part   farm   car   start*   ....

4 no contrast between /ɒ/ in *cot   knotty   stock*
and /ɔː/ in *caught   naughty   stalk*   ....

5 /r/ is pronounced in words like *firm   bird   word*   ....

6 no contrast between /ɒ/ in *bother* or *doctor*
and /ɑː/ in *father* or *past*   ....

+ /d/ instead of /t/ in *butter   better   hotter   shutter*   ....

+ /æ/ instead of /ɑː/ in *can't   dance   half   banana   fast*   ....

B   You'll hear an American, a Welsh woman and an Australian discussing accents. Decide which person said what by writing USA, W or AUS in the answer boxes.

1 There are two main accents in my country.   **1**

2 A regional accent is not a badge of social class.   **2**

3 People in different parts of my country find each other's accents funny.   **3**

4 Some accents in my country are more pleasant to listen to than others.   **4**

5 Immigration is adding to the variety of accents.   **5**

6 When I was at school some children were encouraged to lose their accents.   **6**

7 We used to laugh at people who spoke with an English RP accent.   **7**

8 When I was at school using incorrect grammar was discouraged.   **8**

C **1** Discuss these questions about your own language. (Some of the questions may be more interesting and provocative than others. Don't discuss the questions that seem irrelevant.)

1 How many people speak your language? Which countries do they live in?

2 How many different languages are spoken in your country? Is there a single 'official language'?

3 What language (and which dialect or variety) is used in schools? Do children speak the same language or dialect at home and at school?

4 Do you use a different dialect or variety of your language when talking with friends or family from the one you use with strangers or people from other parts of the country? What situations are the different varieties used in? What are some of the differences in vocabulary and grammar? Can you give any interesting examples?

5 What are the main regional accents and dialects that most people in your country can recognise? Do people in the capital regard the speakers of any of these as 'funny' or 'uneducated' or vice versa?

6 Do the people in the regions with different languages or dialects have less power than the people in the capital? Do they have TV and radio programmes in their own language or dialect?

7 Do middle-class people and working-class people talk differently? Are there any regional accents which are considered to be less 'educated' or less socially acceptable than others? What is claimed to be the 'best accent' in your language?

> A report is usually for a particular audience, such as your boss or for colleagues.
> A report presents information and interprets it. Reports usually have section headings.

Are there any other points not covered by the questions above that you think would help to give a clearer picture about your country and language?

2 Make notes on your answers to the questions which are most relevant to your language and the questions which are thought-provoking.

3 Rearrange the notes you've made (perhaps using arrows, lines or different colours) to make the sequence of ideas and information as coherent as possible, in preparation for writing a report for foreign visitors to your country (300–350 words):

Write a short report about the different languages, dialects and accents in your country.

4 Decide which points each paragraph of your report will contain. Write down the FIRST SENTENCE of each paragraph. Compare your sentences with a partner's.

5 🖊 Write your report. Include a sketch map or diagram if you wish.

4.8 **Forming adjectives** VOCABULARY DEVELOPMENT

A Form adjectives from these VERBS and add them to the appropriate list below. Be very careful about the spelling of the adjectives you form from the verbs in red.

accept admire advise astonish break communicate convince cooperate
deceive describe distress disturb forgive inform inspire instruct obtain
overwhelm possess predict prevent produce promise recommend upset

-able	*negotiable* *readable* *desirable*
-ing	*moving* *daring* *tempting* *satisfying*
-ive	*repetitive* *acquisitive* *appreciative* *decorative*

B Form adjectives from these NOUNS and add them to the appropriate list.

adventure ambition convention curly hair diplomat education enigma
experience fiction fortnight function religion idealist intention long legs
magnet malice materialist music optimist pale skin person pessimist
profession proportion quarter realist romance season secretary sensation
space week year

-al	*influential* *orchestral* *financial* *practical*
-ic	*poetic* *dramatic* *emphatic* *systematic*
-ous	*cautious* *poisonous* *glamorous*
-ly	*daily* *neighbourly*
-ed	*talented* *red-faced*

C **Fill the gaps in these sentences with suitable words from the list below:**

1 Don't pick those mushrooms – they might be ....
2 She was .... when she was picked for the team.
3 This camera has .... exposure and focusing.
4 People who talk about the 'good old days' have an .... view of the past.
5 He always dresses in a .... way.
6 Small cars are more .... than powerful ones.
7 He was .... when his wife left him.
8 I'm afraid his work is only ....
9 Your signature is barely ....
10 Don't be so .... , someone has to lose – it's only a game!

astonishing • astonished   automatic • automated   childish • childlike
economical • economic   heartbreaking • heartbroken   idealistic • idealised
legible • readable   poisoned • poisonous   satisfactory • satisfying   stylish • stylistic

| 4.9 | *make* and *do* | | VERBS AND IDIOMS |

A **Which of the following would you MAKE and which would you DO?**

an agreement with someone   an appointment with someone   an arrangement   your best
business with someone   certain about something   a comment about something   your duty
an excuse   a good impression   someone a favour   friends with someone   harm to someone
a lot of money   love   a mistake   a profit or a loss   progress   a reservation
sure about something   a good turn   the washing-up   wrong or right   your own thing

B **Find synonyms for the phrases in red, or explain their meaning. Use a dictionary if necessary.**

1 Someone was coming down the hill, but I couldn't make out who it was.
2 Adrift alone in the ocean, they knew that they were done for.
3 I don't see what this has to do with you!
4 It was a three-seater sofa, but they refused to make room for me.
5 None of it is true – I made it all up!
6 I'm sorry you had to do all the work for me, I'll make it up to you, I promise.
7 They were finding it increasingly difficult to make both ends meet.
8 How can I ever make amends for what I've done?
9 It's not very important really, you're making a mountain out of a molehill.
10 Shh, don't make a scene – we can talk about it when we get home.
11 It's a shame we were held up, but now we can make up for lost time.
12 It's a terrible portrait, it really doesn't do justice to him.

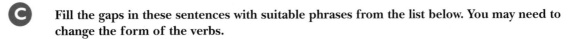

C **Fill the gaps in these sentences with suitable phrases from the list below. You may need to change the form of the verbs.**

1 I left my bike outside the shop and someone has .... it!
2 You've .... this room .... since my last visit. What pretty wallpaper!
3 We went out for a meal together to .... our disappointment.
4 If you're not coming back for lunch I'll .... some sandwiches for you.
5 We collected £48 for her leaving present, so I .... it .... to a round £50.
6 Your shoes need .... , otherwise you'll trip over the laces.
7 Do you agree that all examinations should be .... ?
8 You're heading in the wrong direction if you're .... the station.
9 If too many new staff are taken on, some of us older ones will be .... our jobs.
10 He threw everything on the floor, and then .... without another word.

do away with   do out of   do up
do up   make up   make for   make off
make off with   make up   make up for

"Funny how you soon forget his regional accent."

5

Bon appetit!

To whet your appetite ...   TOPIC VOCABULARY

A 1 Think of the area you live in, or the place you're studying in. Decide what is the best place locally to get the following things, and give your reasons:

> fresh fruit   bread and cakes   a sandwich   a quick snack   a good, inexpensive meal
> a typical local meal

2 Find out your partners' reactions to these photos:

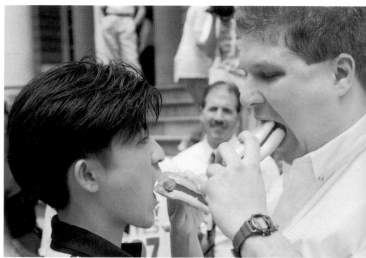

B 1 Write down THREE examples of each of these types of food. Try to think of some UNUSUAL examples, not the most obvious ones. Use a dictionary if necessary.

Appetisers (starters) *avocado paté*	Spices
Fish and shellfish	Dairy products
Poultry	Nuts
Game	Desserts
Herbs	Cakes and pastries

2   Compare your lists and then discuss these questions:

- Which are your favourite foods in each category above?
- Imagine it's your birthday – write a menu, including all your favourite foods.
- What are specialities of your region or country? What are the ingredients required and how are they made?
- How important is food in your life? Do you 'live to eat' or 'eat to live'?
- Why is the title of this unit in French?

A Read the article and decide which word (A–D) best fits each gap.

Feel free to protest

HOBSON'S CHOICE has taken on an added meaning at Berni Restaurants, the chain of more than 230 steak houses owned by Grand Metropolitan.

Nowadays if you don't like what is provided in your meal you don't pay. And that covers the service too.

Slow waitresses, soup-spilling waitresses, surly waitresses, and "please make up your mind" waitresses are out.

Under what Berni calls a customer service guarantee, diners who complain about either the meal or the service have their bill _____ 1 up. One of the intentions is to get round the traditional British habit of not complaining, but not going back either.

A poll conducted by Berni found that 60% of dissatisfied customers said they wouldn't go back to an offending restaurant. To _____ 2 down this reserve, the scheme was initiated by a group of Berni managers and tried out in the north of England, where results were sufficiently encouraging to _____ 3 the scheme to the rest of Britain.

Armed with this knowledge and thinking that it didn't seem too difficult to get a free meal, I descended on the Berni Inn at Wimbledon, where my waitress was Martha, who failed to provide me with any _____ 4 to use the repertoire of "Waiter, there's a fly in my soup" jokes I had rehearsed beforehand. The food proved a match for the service. Simon Smith, the manager, told me he had been pleasantly pleased at a lack of unscrupulous diners trying to take advantage of the scheme. Complaints had generally been _____ 5 .

In fact some people who did complain had to be _____ 6 to leave the bill to him. Many had not even realised the scheme was operating.

"We're finding that those who complained and had their bill torn up are returning and bringing others with them. In the first five weeks we lost £1,000 in unpaid bills, but we're getting a lot of favourable _____ 7 by word of mouth.

"I am sure we'll keep more customers longer this way."

James Allen

1	**A** broken	**B** brought	**C** thrown	**D** torn
2	**A** break	**B** destroy	**C** diminish	**D** reduce
3	**A** change	**B** replace	**C** spread	**D** transfer
4	**A** food	**B** opportunity	**C** possibility	**D** scope
5	**A** correct	**B** exaggerated	**C** excessive	**D** justified
6	**A** forced	**B** ordered	**C** persuaded	**D** requested
7	**A** advertising	**B** propaganda	**C** publicity	**D** publishing

B 👥👥 Discuss these questions:

- Could the Berni scheme operate in restaurants in your country?
- Have you ever complained (or been with someone who complained) in a restaurant? What happened?
- What other situations have you actually been in where you made a complaint?
- What are the qualities of a good restaurant? Describe a good restaurant you have been to and a bad restaurant you remember going to.

C **1** 🔊 Listen to some 'Waiter, waiter!' jokes.

2 👥 Role-play a conversation between a dissatisfied customer and a courteous waiter or waitress.

"Waiter…there are no flies in my soup!"

Running a restaurant

A 👥👥👥👥 **Discuss these questions:**

- What do you think are the pros and cons of running a restaurant? Would you like to run a restaurant? Give your reasons.
- If you were going to open a restaurant or café near where you live, what kind of food would you serve? What kind of atmosphere would you try to create?
- From a restaurateur's point of view, what are the attributes of an ideal customer?
- From a customer's point of view, what are the qualities of a good restaurant?

B Seven paragraphs have been removed from this article. Choose the most suitable paragraph from the list A–G for each gap (1–7) in the article.

The British are coming

"A stone's throw from the Palais des Festivals," says the Michelin Guide. "Pleasant dining room, partly vaulted, recently redecorated: pearl-grey walls, plum furniture and careful lighting. Specialities: foie gras in a potato ribbon; fillet of bass in mussel soup; passion fruit sorbet."

But the bit that matters lies just to the left of that sober piece of text: a single, discreet rosette. It was awarded, last week, to a new Cannes restaurant called Neat, named after its chef, Richard. He has just become the first British restaurateur since the Second World War to win a Michelin star in France.

1 [   ]

"I suppose it would have been sensible to be a little apprehensive," he says. "But to be honest, I didn't even think about it. I'm surrounded by professionals, and provided you're honest, provided you serve up a quality product for a reasonable price, you'll do well. That's always been my philosophy, and it's the same here."

2 [   ]

"In a way, I'm a pure product of France," he says frankly, drawing on a post-lunch cigarette. "I've been working in France or with French people for the past 18 years. It wouldn't be honest or sensible of me to be aggressively British about anything – and I'm hardly about to bite the hand that feeds me."

Nonetheless, his rapid promotion to one-star status in France, an honour for which many French chefs spend years slaving over hot vol-au-vents, has raised eyebrows. The local press has had a field day, and even national television has made the trip down to the chic Mediterranean resort town where Neat, 33, settled with his French wife Sophie in September.

Cannes was, he says, a very deliberate choice for his new venture. It was a challenge he set himself after giving up Pied à Terre, getting married and taking off on a two-year extended honeymoon to India (during which, Neat admits, he did very little except perfect his crawl in various hotel swimming pools and become a "really rather good" amateur chess player).

3 [   ]

"Cannes has a longer season than anywhere else. There are film, TV and music festivals here, conferences and congresses from January to November. And there are 150,000 Brits living within 45 minutes' drive, plus another 50,000 every summer."

4 [   ]

That being no way to run a restaurant, the Frenchman was "practically on his knees, begging us to buy it" seven months later; Neat was born, and at roughly half the price its owners would have had to pay for it half a year earlier. The restaurant, redecorated by Sophie, seats 45 in winter and will take 55 when the terrace is open in summer.

Finding the right staff was no problem, Neat says – though in the end they came from a somewhat unexpected source. The first hire was Mike, an old acquaintance from the Manoir, who was on holiday in Cannes and visiting a girlfriend at the Carlton Hotel nearby.

"He recognised the name and showed up two weeks after we opened," Neat says. "He came in for a coffee and about half an hour later was asking for a job. I told him working here was different to being on holiday, but he was back in a week with his knives. It was a fait accompli."

5

A battalion of Brits behind the saucepans didn't exactly go down a bundle with the local restaurateurs, however, particularly when the sought-after star came Neat's way. The reaction from the local trade was, he concedes, "underwhelming".

But his customers – the congress business, a highly enthusiastic British community, and a small but growing band of Frenchmen – are delighted.

"Sophie tells me the French who come in here are a little bit sceptical at first," Neat says. "But they take the plunge, they see it's a professional operation, they like what they eat – and they come back."

6

There are many in Britain, and a growing number in France, who will dispute the value to a restaurant of a Michelin star. The venerable red guide, which this year celebrates its 100th anniversary, is accused of favouring the traditional over the inventive, and of placing as much emphasis on the fripperies as on the food. More than one chef in both countries has turned down a star.

But Neat, unashamedly, is not one of the doubters. "I've worked in gastronomic restaurants for 13 years now," he says. "I like working in them because you can charge enough to buy the best produce, to get top personnel, and to attract the best clientele – people who really enjoy their food, are knowledgeable about what they're doing."

7

So would he like a second star? "One, two, three, I don't know," he says. "I want to run a good restaurant, but I want a life too. Right now the most important thing is that I can do that right here – and wear shorts and sunglasses 10 months of the year."

John Henley

A   "It's a fact that gastronomy is judged in certain ways. Now I didn't set the goalposts, but I know what they are, and Michelin is the most creditable organisation currently giving ratings to gastronomy. I want to run a restaurant I'm proud of, and Michelin is the measure."

B   "This was a good place for a lot of reasons," he says. "Sophie studied at Nice just along the coast, and the south of France is her adopted home."

C   A month later came Elliot, a friend of Mike's "who does the pastry". Then Warren, Neat's old sous-chef at Pied à Terre, pitched up, and finally Jimmy, who was a good friend of Warren's. It's the best way to recruit people, Neat says: everyone can vouch for everyone else.

D   Neat's three-course lunchtime menu is priced at 220 francs, and the dinner equivalent is 270 francs: good value by Cannes' standards and a downright steal by London's. The dishes, with the exception of his trademark snails with mushrooms and garlic purée, are all new since the chef's Pied à Terre days.

E   Nor, he points out diplomatically, can the quality product he is serving up be described as English in any meaningful sense of the word. Having served under such French gurus as Raymond Blanc at the Manoir aux Quat' Saisons and Joel Robuchon in Paris, and spent 14 months with "the great unwashed" Marco Pierre White to boot, he is definitely more cuisinier than cook.

F   It took the couple and their business partner, Frenchman Bruno Asselin, some time to find the right venue, on the Place Mérimée about 30 yards from the Congress Centre. When they first arrived, the place had just been bought by a former French textiles executive who "rather fancied running a little bistro to keep himself from getting bored in his retirement," Neat says.

G   Words like coals and Newcastle may spring forcefully to mind, but Neat – formerly of the ritzy two-star London eatery Pied à Terre – insists he is not out to prove any kind of nationalist point, even if five out of the six kitchen staff in his new venture are English and it only took him six months to pick up the honour.

C   👥👥 **Ask your partners these questions:**

In an average week . . .
- How often do you eat lunch out? How often do you eat dinner out?
- How many meals do you prepare or help to prepare?
- How many times do you lay the table and do the washing-up?
- How often do you go shopping for food items?
- How often do you eat as a family?
- How do your habits compare with those of a 'typical person' from your country?

5.4 **The passive – 1**　　　　　　　　　　　**GRAMMAR REVIEW**

A 　👥 **Discuss the differences in emphasis (if any) between these sentences:**

1　I'm afraid all the cakes have been eaten.
　　I'm afraid I've eaten all the cakes.
2　Arsenal beat Chelsea in the final.
　　Spurs were beaten in the semi-finals.
　　Manchester United were beaten in the quarter-finals by Southampton.
3　He thinks people are plotting against him.
　　He thinks he's being plotted against.
4　The dough was rolled out and then cut into teddybear shapes.
　　We rolled out the dough and then we cut it into teddybear shapes.
5　There was nothing to do.
　　There was nothing to be done.
6　My wallet has been stolen!
　　That man stole my wallet!
　　Someone has stolen my wallet!
　　I've had my wallet stolen!

B 　👥 **Highlight all the passive verbs and passive participles in *Feel free to protest* on page 55. Discuss why the passive, rather than the active, has been used in each case. If each example is rewritten using an active verb, what difference does this make to the tone, style or emphasis?**

C 　👥 **Rewrite these sentences using the passive: the subject can be omitted where it seems irrelevant or misleading. Your rewritten sentences should be compared with a partner's.**

1　Someone told us that the bill would include service.　*understand*
　　We were given to understand that service would be included.
2　A friend told me that the college has awarded you a scholarship.
3　The crash badly damaged both cars but it didn't cause the injury of anyone.
4　After the lifeguard had rescued the bather, an ambulance took him to hospital.
5　After the surgeon had operated on him, she told him to stay in bed for a week.
6　People all over the world buy McDonald's hamburgers.
7　Everton held Liverpool to a draw.
8　Thousands of demonstrators may crowd into the square tonight.
9　We expected the plane to land at noon, but something has delayed it.　*schedule*
10　The rain brought about the cancellation of the tennis match.　*rain off*
11　They had masses of requests for free samples of the new product.　*flood*
12　Someone has seen an escaped prisoner, whom the police believe to be dangerous.

5.5 **Adjectives and participles**　　**VOCABULARY DEVELOPMENT**

A 　👥 **Discuss the differences in meaning between these pairs of sentences:**

1　She has a talking parrot.　　　　　　　Have you heard her parrot talking?
2　She is an old friend.　　　　　　　　　My friend is quite old.
3　All the people concerned were there.　　All the concerned people were there.
4　It wasn't a proper meeting.　　　　　　The meeting proper began at 9.
5　The members of staff present.　　　　　The present members of staff.
6　Is he the person responsible?　　　　　Is he a responsible person?
7　I have a friend living in London.　　　　She has no living relatives.
8　He is a complete idiot.　　　　　　　　The complete meal cost a mere £5.
9　She has an elder brother.　　　　　　　Her brother is elderly.
10　The film had a very involved plot.　　　The actors involved were unconvincing.

B Study these notes, and fill the gaps in the examples:

Position of adjectives (*tasty*) and participles used as adjectives (*tired or tiring*).

I **Most** adjectives and participles are normally placed **before a noun** or **after a verb**:

*appetising   delicious   delicious-looking   frightened   good-looking   happy   home-made
lonely   refreshing   similar   sleeping   tasty etc.*

He is a very good-looking man.   He is very good-looking.

That was a really ...*tasty*... meal.   Those buns look absolutely .... !

2 A few adjectives are normally only placed **before a noun** (not after a verb):

mere   sheer   complete   utter   total   downright

It took a mere hour to finish.   This is sheer madness.

The journey was a(n) .... disaster.   The meal was a .... success.

3 A few adjectives are normally placed **after a verb** (not before a noun):

*afloat   afraid   alight   alike   aloft   alive   alone   asleep   awake
well   unwell   ill   content*

Are you awake yet?   I don't feel very well.

The fire isn't .... yet.   Don't leave the baby .... all night.

Shh! The baby's .... in its cot.   Her two sisters look ....

4 A few adjectives are normally placed **after a noun**:

galore   manqué   elect   present (= attending)   proper (= itself)

There was food galore at the party.   He is an artist manqué.

The president .... takes office next month.

5 A few adjectives and participles can sometimes be placed after a noun, rather than before it:

*concerned (= affected)   responsible (= who did it)   involved (= included)
imaginable (after a superlative)*

All the people concerned have been notified.

That was the most disgusting meal .... !

6 A few adjectives and participles can come either **before or after a noun**:

affected   available   required   suggested   obtainable

All the people affected have complained.   = All the affected people have complained.

Work expands to take up the time ....   = Work expands to fill the .... time.

7 Most participles used as adjectives (ending in *-ing*, *-ed*, *-en*) and most adjectives ending
in *-able* and *-ible* are placed **after a noun** when extra information is given **afterwards** –
as if in a relative clause:

These are delicious cakes (which have been) made according to my own recipe.

How high are the mountains (which are) visible in the distance?

I love the smell of cakes (which are) .... in the kitchen.

The houses (which were) .... in the storm have been repaired.

A survey .... by Berni revealed some unexpected information.   (see 5.2)

C Insert suitable adjectives from B before or after the nouns in green in these sentences:

1 Do you have all the ingredients?
2 I object to his rudeness.
3 Don't forget to follow the guidelines.
4 The people have all been arrested.
5 Never wake a baby.
6 In the sale there were bargains.
7 I'd love a glass of lemonade.
8 Can I try one of those cakes?
9 She is the nicest person.
10 It seems to me that he is a fool.
11 The meeting began promptly.
12 Some of the people fell asleep.

A **1** Read the report through. Highlight the main points.

Bottled water condemned as 'vast con'

BOTTLED water was one of the "great confidence tricks of modern times" with customers paying 700 times more in the supermarket than for the same quality from the tap, the Water Companies Association said yesterday.

Attacking the bottled water industry for being "vastly over-priced", Pamela Taylor, the chief executive, said there was little to differentiate it from tap water.

Its marketing was based on associations with sport, health and fitness which had no basis in truth, and its packaging and distribution were environmentally damaging, she said.

The difference in price between bottled water and tap water was comparable to the gap in cost between running a Ford Escort and a light aircraft. If household water supplies were charged at the same rate as bottled water, the average household bill would rise to £77,000 a year.

One of the reasons consumers believed bottled water tasted better was because they stored it in the fridge. If tap water was bottled and kept in the fridge it would be impossible to tell the difference, the association said.

Tap water was more tightly controlled than bottled water. The Drinking Water Inspectorate reported last year that 99.7% of all samples passed purity tests. Almost 2% of bottled water failed the same tests, meaning that 10 million litres of bottled water with unacceptable levels of bacteria were sold in British supermarkets each year.

The association also criticised the labelling of bottled water. Table and purified water could be and often were simply bottled tap water. Spring and natural water often had to undergo similar treatment to tap water before it could be bottled.

One of the most telling arguments against bottled water was the harm the trade caused to the environment.

Mike Walker, the association's head of policy, said: "While the bottled water industry is keen to market its product by using natural beauty and unspoilt countryside, bottled water is far more environmentally damaging than tap water. Many of the UK's major brands use plastic bottles. Most of these end their lives in landfill sites."

The transportation of water from places as far away as Israel, Japan, South Korea, and water-short countries such as India and Kenya was condemned as unnecessary and wasteful.

Robert Hayward, the director general of the British Soft Drinks Association, said bottled water was a booming business. "The growth is the result of consumer choice. Consumers buy our products because of their taste, their consistency of quality and their convenience."

Paul Brown

2 Look at the notes below. TWO important points are missing from each set of notes – add these to the notes. Then decide which style of notes might be most helpful for YOU if you were going to write a similar report.

Water Companies Association say bottled water is a con:
marketing: associations with 'sport, health, fitness' – no basis in truth
price: bottled water costs 700 times more than tap water
purity: tap water more closely controlled: 99.7% of tap water
passes tests. 2% of bottled water fails same tests – 10 million
litres with unacceptable levels of bacteria sold each year
labelling: misleading because 'table water' + 'purified water'
often just bottled tap water – 'spring water' + 'natural
water' has to undergo same treatment as tap water
before bottling
distribution: transportation from places overseas + water-short countries
unnecessary + wasteful
British Soft Drinks Association say: 'Consumers buy bottled water because
they prefer its taste, consistent quality and convenience'

Water Companies Association say bottled water a con:

marketing: associations 'sport, health, fitness' - no basis in truth
price: 700 times higher
taste: stored in fridge - tap water in fridge same
labelling misleading: 'table water' + 'purified water' bottled tap water - 'spring water' + 'natural water' same treatment as tap water before bottling
packaging: environmentally damaging - plastic bottles

British Soft Drinks Association say: Consumers prefer taste, consistent quality + convenience of bottled water

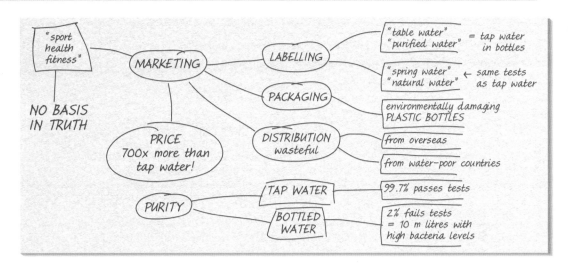

3 👥 List the advantages and disadvantages of each type of notes. If you use a different style altogether, what are the advantages of your style of notes?

B 1 🔊 You'll hear a radio programme about the Fairtrade scheme. MAKE NOTES on the main points that are made.

2 👥 Compare your notes with a partner's. Rewrite your notes before you write an article on this topic:

How can schemes like Fairtrade improve the quality of life for farmers in developing countries? (300–350 words)

5.7 / *should* and *be*

A **1** 👥 **Decide which alternatives fit into the gaps – in most cases more than one alternative can be used.**

1 It's important that he .... told the truth.

  is   be   should be   will be   is going to be

2 I insist that I .... my money back after such a terrible meal.

  given   be given   was given   am being given   should be given

3 This is a big problem – what do you think I .... ?

  shall do   should do   ought to do   can do

4 We were all sitting watching TV when who .... but Billy.

  could arrive   would arrive   should arrive   did arrive

5 I'm sorry that you .... upset about this.

  feel   do feel   will feel   should feel   ought to feel

B **Study these examples before doing C below.**

> **Reactions** When expressing reactions, using *should* is more formal, and sounds rather less direct than a present tense:
>
> I'm very sorry that you should feel upset.
> It's a pity that she should not be on speaking terms with him.
> It's interesting that they should want to visit us.
> It's disgraceful that we should have to pay extra for service.
> It has always worried me that he should feel lonely.
>
> **Suggestions and recommendations** Using *should* or *be* + past participle tends to sound less bossy and more formal than a present tense. Compare these pairs of sentences:
>
> I recommend that he should take up cooking as a career.
> I recommend that he takes up cooking.
> I suggest that she should be asked to make a speech on our behalf.
> I recommend that she is asked.
> I propose that she be given everything she needs.
> I propose that she is given . . .
>
> *Should* can also be used in **conditional** sentences like these:
>
> If you should meet Tim, give him my regards.
> Should the doors be locked, the key may be obtained from the caretaker.   (see 13.4)

C **Complete these sentences, using *should* or *be* + past participle:**

1 It is very important that you .... before you start writing.
2 It is absolutely essential that he .... his work on time.
3 I insist that the washing-up .... before you go out for the evening.
4 It's wrong that the government .... tax on petrol.
5 It's a nuisance that we .... so much homework at the weekend.
6 It's necessary that ....
7 I'm disappointed that ....
8 It's awfully sad that ....
9 It bothers me that ....
10 I propose that Jill .... president of the society.
11 If you .... questions, please do not hesitate to ask.

"One more notch. Room for dessert."

A 1 Before you listen to the recording, look at these diagrams, showing the process of margarine manufacture. As you can see, they are in the wrong order. Using a pencil, number the steps in what looks like the right order. The first and last steps are numbered already.

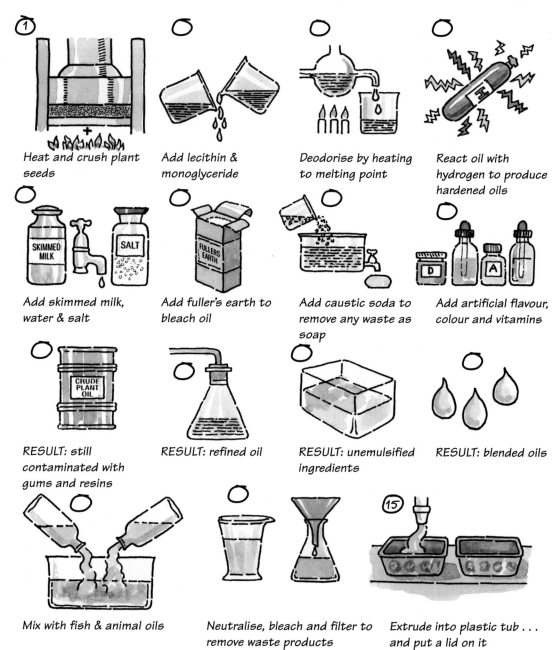

Heat and crush plant seeds

Add lecithin & monoglyceride

Deodorise by heating to melting point

React oil with hydrogen to produce hardened oils

Add skimmed milk, water & salt

Add fuller's earth to bleach oil

Add caustic soda to remove any waste as soap

Add artificial flavour, colour and vitamins

RESULT: still contaminated with gums and resins

RESULT: refined oil

RESULT: unemulsified ingredients

RESULT: blended oils

Mix with fish & animal oils

Neutralise, bleach and filter to remove waste products

Extrude into plastic tub . . . and put a lid on it

2 Listen to the recording and number the diagrams to show the correct sequence of the manufacturing process.

B 1 Students A and B look at Activity 2, C and D look at 15. Each pair has different information about the processes of making wine and brewing beer. Study the information and MAKE NOTES on the main points of the process, or highlight the important information.

2 Student A should join C and B should join D to form new pairs. Tell your new partner what you found out. Discuss what the two processes have in common, and how they are different.

C Write an article explaining either how wine is made or how beer is made.

Make notes first, and write your article WITHOUT quoting verbatim from Activity 2 or 15.

or Make notes on another culinary or non-culinary process, and write a description of the process. You may need to do some research on this.

6

See the world!

6.1 Where would you like to go?

TOPIC VOCABULARY

 A **Discuss these questions:**

- Would you like to visit this place? Why/Why not?
- Which five places in the world would you like to visit one day? Why?
- And which five places have you no desire to visit ever? Why?

B **Fill the gaps in this description of the illustration, using the words on the right:**

Soufrière is a small fishing ~~port~~ on the west ¹ of the ² of St Lucia in the Caribbean. It lies at the centre of a sheltered ³ which forms a natural ⁴ .
The town is dominated by the Pitons: two mountain ⁵ which were once ⁶ , covered in tropical ⁷ . If you travel ⁸ up the river ⁹ you come to a ¹⁰ where there are plantations growing coconuts and tropical fruits, watered by little ¹¹ flowing down from the hills. To the north there are impressive ¹² plunging into the sea and around a ¹³ is a secluded hotel above a little ¹⁴ , from where you can swim out to watch the fish around the coral ¹⁵ .
The ¹⁶ from the hotel is breathtaking.
   Despite its wonderful ¹⁷ , warm ¹⁸ , friendly people and delicious local ¹⁹ , Soufrière isn't a popular tourist destination, perhaps because it lacks the sandy ²⁰ tourists expect in a Caribbean ²¹ .

bay
beaches
cliffs
climate
coast
cove
harbour
headland
inland
island
peaks
plateau
rainforest
reef
resort
seafood
setting
streams
valley
view
volcanoes

C **Choose THREE words or phrases that make sense in each of the gaps:**

1 Not liking crowds, I prefer going on holiday to somewhere that's ....
   abandoned   backward   derelict   deserted   dull   godforsaken   off the beaten track
   out of the way   secluded   spoiled   strange

2 I enjoy visiting places abroad where the people are ....
   churlish   courteous   easygoing   hospitable   morose   sulky   sullen

3 The Vatican in Rome is visited every year by millions of ....
   commuters   holidaymakers   passengers   pilgrims   vagrants   travellers

4 The .... takes up to four hours on the motorway, but it's quicker by train.
   crossing   drive   flight   journey   passage   track   travel   trip   voyage   way

5 I'm going overseas next week and I'll be .... for the rest of the month.
   abroad   absent-minded   away from home   missing   offshore   on the run
   out   out in the country   out of the country

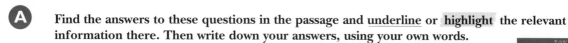 **Note down SIX countries that you have visited – or might visit one day. And SIX MORE countries from which visitors to your country come. Then discuss these questions:**

- What do you call a citizen of each country? What languages do they all speak?
- What are the principal cities called – and how are they pronounced?
- Which nationalities are the most frequent visitors to your country, and what are the attractions of your country to them?

6.2 Learning the language

READING AND SPEAKING

A **Find the answers to these questions in the passage and <u>underline</u> or highlight the relevant information there. Then write down your answers, using your own words.**

1 What did many Turks do when they encountered a non-Turkish speaker?
2 Why was the author confused at the reaction to her *useful phrase*?
3 Why was the hotel porter the first to understand her?
4 Why did Mr Yorum point to himself when they first met?
5 Why did the narrator think he was pointing to himself?
6 Why didn't the writer try to resolve the confusion with Mr Yorum?

I studied my Turkish phrase book, and learned a few of the most useful ones by heart. One was about how I did not understand Turkish well, which I copied into my note-book and carried about with me. Many Turks can't understand that anyone really does not know Turkish; they think that if they say it often enough and loud enough it will register. They did this whenever I said this phrase; it seemed to start them off asking what seemed to be questions, but I only said my piece again, and after a time they gave it up. Sometimes they said "Yorum, yorum, yorum?" as if they were asking something, but I did not know what this word meant, and I thought they were mimicking what they thought I had said.

This was all that happened about it for a few days, then one day when I said my piece to the porter he nodded, and went to the telephone and rang someone up, and presently a man came downstairs and bowed to me as I stood in the hall and said something to me in Turkish. I had better explain here that there was a misunderstanding which was my fault, for I discovered some time afterwards that I had copied the phrase in the book which was just below the one which meant "I do not understand Turkish," and the one I had copied and learnt and had been saying to everyone for days meant "Please to phone at once to Mr Yorum," though this seems a silly phrase to print in a book for the use of people who do not know Mr Yorum at all and never would want to telephone to him. But one day this Mr Yorum turned up at the hotel to stay, and the porter saw then what I wanted him to do, and he rang Mr Yorum in his room and asked him to come down. But I did not know then about my mistake, and when Mr Yorum spoke to me I said again that I did not understand Turkish, and he bowed and pointed to himself. I thought he must be offering to interpret for me, but when I tried English on him he shook his head and said, "Yok, yok," and I could see he knew none. So I looked up the Turkish for "What can I have the pleasure of doing for you?" and said it, but of course I did not understand his answer, and that is the worst of foreign languages, you understand what you say in them yourself, because you have looked it up before saying it, but very seldom what the foreigners say to you, because you have not looked up that at all. So I looked through the book till I found "Who are you, sir?" and he said in reply, "Yorum, Yorum, Yorum." I saw there was some confusion somewhere, but there is always so much confusion in Turkey that I let it go, and ordered drinks for both of us, and we drank them, then he went away, quite pleased that I had telephoned to him to come and have a drink.

from The Towers of Trebizond by Rose Macaulay

B 🏃 **Discuss these questions:**

- Have you had any similar experiences with English or other foreign languages?
- How much of your language does a tourist in your country need to know?
- Which parts of the passage did you find amusing?
- What do you think happened next in the story?

C 🏃 **One of you should look at** Activity 4, **the other at** 16. **These Activities contain the next paragraphs of the story. Find out what happened when Mr Yorum was called down to the hotel lobby yet again. Then tell your partner about it in your own words.**

6.3 **The future**   **GRAMMAR REVIEW**

A 🏃 **Discuss the differences in meaning, if any, between these sentences:**

1 I think I'm going to scream.   I think I'll scream.
2 It's still raining in Scotland.   It's still going to rain in Scotland.
   It will still be raining in Scotland.   It still rains in Scotland.
3 I'll phone him after work.   I'm phoning him after work.
   I'm going to phone him after work.   I'll be phoning him after work.
4 When are we having lunch?   When do we have lunch?
   When are we going to have lunch?   When shall we have lunch?
5 What time shall I get to your house?   What time will I get to your house?
6 I'll work hard tonight.   I'll be working hard tonight.
7 Will you be going shopping today?   Are you going to go shopping today?
   Are you going shopping today?   Will you go shopping today?
   Do you go shopping today?

B **Fill the gaps in these sentences, which all refer to the future, with suitable words. In some cases various answers are possible.**

1 I think I .... sneeze. .... you give me a tissue, please?
2 .... able to make people understand when you .... Turkey?
3 Have you decided how to get there? .... by car or .... a bus?
4 Supposing your car .... on the way there, what .... do?
5 Our flight is due .... at 9.30, but I'm afraid it .... delayed.
6 By the time the plane .... , we .... waiting
   for four hours.
7 No one knows for sure what the future .... us.
8 In the next century, tourism .... more and more
   highly developed.
9 While you .... holiday, I .... in the office.
   I hope you .... a postcard.
10 I've no idea when I .... finished my work.
11 As soon as I .... the results, I .... a ring to
   let you know.
12 It's time we .... what we .... this weekend.
13 I hope nobody .... me at 8 o'clock because
   I .... still .... dinner then.
14 What .... happen at the frontier if I ....
   my passport at home?
15 I'm looking forward .... the book, when you ....
   finished with it.

C **1** 🏃🏃 **Discuss these questions about the future:**

- What are the most interesting things you're going to do during the coming month?
  Which are you looking forward to most?
- Looking ahead ten years or so: how will your life then be different from now?
- How will the world be different ten years from now?

2 🖉 **Write two paragraphs summarising the main points of your discussion.**

One word – different meanings

Homonyms are words which are written the same but have different meanings:

This is a good book.   Can I book two tickets for the concert?
Do you understand this sentence?   His sentence was life imprisonment.
What do you mean?   Don't be so mean!
It's rude to point.   What is the main point?
The point of the knife was blunt.
When do you start work?   This pen doesn't work.
A work of art.

A   👥 **Fill each gap with a word that makes sense in the sentence:**

1 From here to the coast is a two-hour ....
  They avoid the beach in summer because the crowds .... them mad.

2 Turn .... at the next junction.
  Are there any biscuits .... in the tin?

3 Did you enjoy the .... ?
  Can you .... me how to work this gadget?

4 Please do not leave any .... of value in your room.
  Is 'the' the definite or the indefinite .... ?
  I read a fascinating .... in today's paper.

5 Could you wait a .... , please?
  This is the .... time this has happened.

6 I always .... at the sight of blood.
  This photocopy is so .... that I can hardly read it.

7 I didn't expect the bull to .... us.
  There is no .... for this service.

8 Don't you feel .... after eating so many cakes?
  Comedians make their living by being .... in public.

B   👥 **Think of ONE WORD which can be used appropriately in all three sentences, and write it in the box in CAPITAL LETTERS.**

1 If I had a .... for every time he apologised, I'd be a millionaire.
  200 grams is about half a .... in the USA.
  There was no answer so he began to .... on the door.

  1 [　　　　　]

2 Thank you, I really .... what you've done for me.
  The value of a flat will .... over the years.
  You don't .... how much time and effort I've put into this.

  2 [　　　　　]

3 There is plenty of .... evidence linking smoking with cancer.
  It's healthier to sleep on a .... mattress than a soft one.
  Jones and Son are a family .... established in 1977.

  3 [　　　　　]

4 It may rain while we're out, in which .... we can expect to get wet.
  Don't forget to put a label on your ....
  The police are investigating the .... of the missing luggage.

  4 [　　　　　]

5 When the .... was read they discovered they had been left a fortune.
  Where there's a .... there's a way.
  Do come to the party! Please say you .... !

  5 [　　　　　]

6 Put a .... on the pan to keep the flies off.
  Don't worry about the rail fare, we'll .... your expenses.
  In a thunderstorm, don't take .... under a tree.

  6 [　　　　　]

Preparation

Before the next lesson, read the passage in **6.5 B** and do the tasks in **C** and **D**.

6.5 The friendly skies

A **Discuss these questions:**

- Do you enjoy flying or are you afraid of flying? Give your reasons.
- What would you say to a friend who refuses to travel by plane?

B In this passage the writer, Jonathan Raban, is waiting at an airport somewhere in the USA for his flight to Seattle. First read the passage – and enjoy it.

I spend a lot of time anxiously listening to the announcements over the loudspeaker system. In almost all respects, these summonses and bulletins are enunciated with extreme clarity by women speaking in the painfully slow and fulsomely stressed tones of infant teachers in a school for special-need children. It is only when they reach the flight number of the plane concerned or the name of the passenger who must immediately report to the United Airlines information desk that their voices go into misty soft focus. I keep on hearing that I am urgently wanted, but sit tight, fearing paranoia. They don't want me. They can't want me. They want Josephine Rubin, or John A.T. Horobin, or Sean O'Riordain, or Jennifer Raymond, or Jonah the Rabbi, or Rogers and Braybourne.

When I first arrived here, I fed some coins into a newspaper-dispenser and took out a copy of the local broadsheet – the *Post-Dispatch*, the *Courant*, the *Plain Dealer*, the *Tribune*, the *Herald*, or whatever it was. It was an unhappy diversion. It spoke too eloquently of the world one had left behind by coming here – that interesting world of School Board Split, City Cop on Take, Teamsters Boss To Quit, Highways Commission Probe – Official. It made me feel homesick for reality: the only news that interested me now was the depressing stuff on the V.D.U.s. *Cancelled. Delayed.* Did the controllers ever get to write *Crashed, Missing, Hijacked* on these screens?

What puzzles me is that I seem to be entirely alone in my frustration and distress. Almost every flight is going out late, and there must be several thousand people in this airport, switching their departure gates, phoning home, putting another Scotch-and-soda down on their tab in the cocktail lounge. The men's neckties are loosened, their vests unbuttoned. They sit with open briefcases, papers spread in front of them as if this place was a comfortable home-from-home. I watch one man near me. He's got a can of beer, a basket of popcorn, and he's two thirds of the way through a sci-fi thriller by Arthur C. Clarke. The bastard hasn't got a care in the world. His eyes never drift up to the V.D.U.; he never cocks his head anxiously when Teacher starts talking through the overhead speakers. He's on a domestic flight. He's a domestic flier.

An hour and a half later it is still raining, but we're getting somewhere here – at least I thought so 50 minutes ago when I buckled in to seat 38F and began looking out through the lozenge of scratched plastic at the men in earmuffs and storm-gear on the ground below. Since then we haven't budged. We've suffered faint, pastiche imitations of Scott Joplin, Count Basie and Glen Miller on the muzak system. My neighbour in 38E, who is careless of the usual rules of body space, has worked her way slowly through four pages of the *National Enquirer*, moving her lips as she reads. In the seats ahead, there has been a good deal of folding and refolding of copies of *Business Week* and the *Wall Street Journal*. Still no-one seems much disconcerted except me. The inside of the plane is hot and getting hotter. The stewards, flirting routinely among themselves, are proof against any damn-fool questions from me.

The muzak clicks off. A voice clicks on.

"Hi!" – and that seems to be it for a good long time. Then, "I'm, uh, Billy Whitman, and I'm going to be your pilot on this flight here to ... " I think I can hear Mr Whitman consulting his clipboard. " ... uh, Seattle this morning. Well – it was meant to be morning, but it looks to me now to be getting pretty damn close to afternoon ... "

He's putting on the entire cowlicked, gum-shifting country boy performance.

"I guess some of you folks back there may be getting a little antsy 'bout this delay we're having now in getting airborne ... Well, we did run into a bit of a glitch with Control up there, getting our flight-plan sorted ... "

We haven't got a flight-plan? Is Mr Whitman waiting for someone to bring him a *map*?

"But they got that fixed pretty good now, and in, uh, oh, a couple or three minutes, we should be closing the doors, and I'm planning on getting up into the sky round about ten minutes after that. So if you all sit tight now, we'll be getting this show right on the road.

Looks pretty nice up there today … no weather problems that I can see so far … at least, once we get atop this little local overcast … and I'm looking for a real easy trip today. Have a good one, now, and I'll be right back to you just as soon as we go past something worth looking out the window for. Okay?"

Click.

11

After the video and the stewards' dumbshow about what to do in "the unlikely event" of our landing on water (where? the Mississippi?), Captain Whitman takes us on a slow ramble round the perimeter of the airport. We appear to be returning to the main terminal again when the jet takes a sudden deep breath, lets out a bull roar, and charges down the runway, its huge frame shuddering fit to bust. Its wings are actually flapping now, trying to tear themselves out at their roots in the effort to achieve lift-off. It bumps and grinds. The plastic bulkheads are shivering like gongs. Rain streams past the window, in shreds, at 200 miles an hour.

12

This is the bit I hate. We're not going fast enough. We're far too heavy to bring off this trick. We're breaking up. To take this flight was tempting fate one time too many. We're definitely goners this time.

13

But the domestic fliers remain stupidly oblivious to our date with death. They go on reading. They're lost in the stock market prices. They're learning that Elvis Presley never died and has been living as a recluse in Dayton, Ohio. These things engage them. These guys are – bored. The fact, clear enough to me, that they are at this moment rocketing into eternity is an insufficiently diverting one to make them even raise their eyes from their columns of idiot print.

14

Somehow (and this Captain Whitman must know a thing or two) we manage to unpeel ourselves from the obstinate earth, which suddenly begins to tilt upwards in the glass. An industrial outskirt of the city shows as an exposed tangle of plumbing; there's a gridlock of cars on a freeway interchange, their headlamps shining feebly through the drizzle. The airport beneath us is marked out like a schoolbook geometrical puzzle. Then, suddenly, we're into a viewless infernal region of thick smoke, with the plane skidding and wobbling on the bumpy air. It's rattling like an old bus on a dirt road. In 38E we're deep in the miracle of Oprah Winfrey's diet. In 38F we're beginning to suspect that we might conceivably survive.

15

My ears are popping badly. The noise of the engines changes from a racetrack snarl to the even threshing sound of a spin-dryer. On an even keel now, we plough up steadily through the last drifts and rags of storm cloud and the whole cabin fills with sudden brilliant sunshine. We're in the clear and in the blue; aloft, at long last, over America.

16

from *Hunting Mr Heartbreak* by Jonathan Raban

C 👤 → 👤 **Choose the best answer to these questions. Then justify your answers to each other.**

1 The writer hears the announcer calling …
  A children's names   **C** his name
  B other people's names   **D** people with names that sound like his

2 The other people at the airport seem to be …
  A frustrated   **C** anxious
  B distressed   **D** indifferent

3 The word *disconcerted* in ¶4 means …
  A terrified   **C** uncomfortable
  B anxious   **D** squashed

4 The flight attendants are … to answer the writer's questions.
  A willing   **C** unable
  B too busy   **D** happy

5 The pilot's announcement …
  A inspires confidence   **C** doesn't make the writer feel less nervous
  B is not informative   **D** makes the writer panic

6 The person sitting next to the writer is reading …
  A a business newspaper   **C** a news magazine
  B a scandal sheet   **D** a TV guide

7 The writer was the only person on the plane who …
  A thought they would die   **C** was amused by the pilot's announcement
  B read the safety instructions **D** had nothing to read

D **Highlight** the vocabulary in the passage that you want to remember. But that doesn't mean every word you didn't know. For example, you probably didn't know the American slang words in red below, but you can probably guess their meanings from the context:

"… some of you folks back there may be getting a little antsy 'bout this delay we're having now in getting airborne … Well, we did run into a bit of a glitch with Control up there, getting our flight-plan sorted … "

E 👥 **Highlight** THREE parts of the passage that amused you. Point them out to a partner, and compare each other's reactions. Look again at the discussion questions in A – what would be the writer's OWN answers to the questions, do you think?

6.6 **Repetition**   **WRITING SKILLS**

A **1** Read these extracts from a Canadian tourist brochure. **Highlight** the places where the same words or the same grammatical structures are repeated in each extract. (Reasons 5 to 9 are: 5. The Wildlife; 6. The Country Life; 7. The City Life; 8. The History; 9. The Events.)

10 Great Reasons to Visit Saskatchewan

Saskatchewan is a big province that constantly surprises. With its vast and changing landscapes, its colourful events and its rich heritage, it has a lot to offer. Covering it in a few words and photos is no easy task.

In the next 20 pages we present 10 great reasons why you should travel to our province. Why Saskatchewan is special. Why it's a place where you belong.

We have thousands of reasons for you to see Saskatchewan – we're limited to 10 here. We're confident you'll find them reasons enough to visit. And that you'll find more reasons to return.

1 The Prairies

When people think Saskatchewan, they think prairies. They think fields of gold that stretch up against the horizon. They think bold, blue sky. They think vistas that seem flawlessly flat and that from the air resemble a patchwork quilt.

Prairie scenery can be breathtaking. Brilliant mustard and canola waving in the wind. Grain elevators standing like sentinels, signalling the approach of new towns. Sunsets offering their light shows of purple, orange and red.

The prairies are also rolling hills where you'd least expect them. Valleys full of wild flowers, prairie lilies and saskatoons. Plus plains and bush alive with prairie dogs, meadowlarks and white-tailed deer.

This year stop and smell the clover. See the images that have graced a thousand postcards. Visit the prairies.

2 The Parks

Hike a leafy aspen trail. Zip down a monster waterslide. Join a "wolf howl" under clear moonlight. Whatever your interests you can likely satisfy them in Saskatchewan's parks.

With nearly five million acres of Saskatchewan parkland, Mother Nature has plenty of places in which to work her spell on you. At our parks you can sink that championship putt, watch deer and elk by the roadside, relax at a four-season resort, or pitch your tent near a back country gurgling stream.

Waskesiu. Grasslands. Moose Mountain. Cypress Hills. Our parks are destinations, summer and winter. They put you in touch with a simpler, gentler world – a world where the sun shines bright and the deadlines and pressures of ordinary life are far, far away.

3 The Lakes

Get out your swimming trunks, unfurl those sails, dust off your water-skis, take the canoe and tackle box out of storage and book that cabin or resort. Saskatchewan's 100,000 – that's right 100,000! – lakes await you.

4 The Fishing

Picture a lazy day on a crystal clear lake. Morning mist comes off the water. An evergreen shoreline frames your horizon. A bald eagle circles overhead. Then suddenly your line tenses, and everything changes. Your battle with a monster of the deep has begun.

10 The People

If there are 10 great reasons to visit Saskatchewan, then there are a million reasons to come back. Our people. Superhearted. Lively. Famous for their hospitality.

With a mosaic of cultures, Saskatchewan is truly the world in one place. Native Indians and people with British, French and east-European roots. People who celebrate their uniqueness at annual celebrations like Vesna and Folkfest in Sasktatoon, or Mosaic in Regina. Where the food, fun and music of the homelands trail long into the night.

When all is said and done, it's the people you meet who make a vacation unforgettable. We invite you to meet ours. Through them discover the place where you belong.

2 👥 Compare what you've both highlighted and discuss what the effect of the repetition is in each case.

B 1 👥 Make a list of TEN GREAT REASONS why tourists should visit your country, region or city. Then decide what you would write to justify ONE of the attractions.

2 🖊 Write around 100 words describing the attraction you've picked, in the same style as the Canadian brochure.

3 👥 Compare what you've both written. Then write another 100 words about another attraction of your country, region or city.

6.7 / Revision and exam practice   ADVANCED GRAMMAR

Complete the second sentence so that it has a similar meaning to the first sentence using the word given. DO NOT CHANGE THE WORD GIVEN. Use between three and eight words, including the word given.

1 Why on earth didn't you tell me before?

ever   Why ......*ever didn't you*...... tell me before?

2 We went on waiting until midnight for the plane to take off.

still   We .... for the plane to take off.

3 Someone told me my flight was cancelled when I got to the airport.

arriving   .... that my flight had been cancelled.

4 I had never flown before which was why I was very nervous.

having   Never .... I was very nervous.

5 I only want to spend the rest of my life with you.

thing   The .... the rest of my life with you.

6   They go on holiday in the winter and in the summer too.

only

Not .... in the winter but also in the summer.

7   We didn't realise that our hotel was right beside the airport.

did

Little .... our hotel was right beside the airport.

8   I propose that we send him a letter explaining the situation.

be

I propose .... explaining the situation.

9   She always gets the right answers.

never

She .... right answers.

10   We had to write several letters before we got our money back.

manage

Only after writing several letters .... our money back.

When doing this kind of exercise in Part 4 of the Use of English Paper, first identify the structure that is required, then rewrite the sentence. Concentrate on conveying the meaning as well as getting the grammar right. Don't change more than you have to.

6.8   The impact of tourism   LISTENING AND COMPOSITION

A   🔊 **You'll hear an interview about tourism in the Maldives. Answer the questions by filling the boxes with a word or short phrase.**

1   How many inhabited islands are there in the Maldives? [_____ **1**]

2   How many resort islands are there in the Maldives? [_____ **2**]

3   Resort islands are [_____ **3**] to ordinary Maldivians.

4   Most of the tourists who go to the Maldives are from [_____ **4**] .

5   According to the Tourism Master Plan, what are the two major attractions of the Maldives?

[_____ **5a**] and [_____ **5b**] .

6   Most of what the tourists need has to be [_____ **6**] .

7   The regulation of tourism on the Maldives has been [_____ **7**] .

8   It's hard for many staff on a tourist island to [_____ **8**] .

9   One result of *El Niño* is to make the coral less [_____ **9**] .

10   The long-term problem facing the Maldives is [_____ **10**] .

B 🧑🧑🧑🧑 **Discuss these questions:**

- What are your views on the way tourism is managed in the Maldives?
- What harm can tourism cause? What are the benefits of tourism?
- Should poorer countries segregate tourists in hotel zones to 'protect' the local people from them? Or should they discourage tourism altogether?
- What are the problems that face the tourist industry in your country?
- What are the most popular destinations for tourists from your country?
- How are foreign tourists treated in your country? How do they behave there?
- What has been the impact of tourism on your region, or elsewhere in your country?

C ✒ **Write a newspaper article describing the impact of tourism on a place in your country, or in another country you know (300–350 words). Make notes first.**

| 6.9 | *come* and *go* | VERBS AND IDIOMS |

A **Find synonyms for the phrases in red, or explain their meaning. Use a dictionary if necessary.**

1 She was very upset at first, but she came to terms with it eventually.
2 I expected my arrangements to go off without a hitch, but they came to nothing.
3 His early success went to his head and he did no more work the rest of the year.
4 'How is your work coming along?' 'If you come along with me, I'll show you.'
5 It's no good, I've gone off the idea. I can't go through with it.
6 Let's go through this point again, in case it comes up in the exam.
7 Go ahead, you can take my Swiss army knife with you – it may come in useful.
8 She kept teasing the dog, so it wasn't surprising that it went for her.
9 'She's decided to go it alone and start her own business.'
'I only hope it comes to something and doesn't turn out to be a disaster.'
'Don't worry, she's gone into all the financial forecasts very thoroughly.'
10 Her presentation at the conference went down very well.

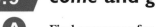

B **Fill the gaps in these sentences with suitable phrases from the list below. You may need to change the form of the verbs.**

1 They .... the brilliant idea of taking in overnight guests.
2 When is her new book .... ?
3 'I see that bus fares have .... again.' 'Well, they never .... , do they?'
4 I've just been reading that fascinating old guidebook. Where did you .... it?
5 She .... him until he gave in and agreed to .... the competition.
6 The day before their holiday, they both .... flu.
7 He stays on the beach, while she .... water-skiing and skin-diving.
8 She took a lot of persuading but eventually she .... to our point of view.
9 I'll wait till the matter .... naturally in the course of the conversation.
10 My suitcase is practically brand new but it .... on the luggage carousel.

come across   come apart   come out   come round
come up   come up with
go down   go down with   go in for
go off   go on at   go up

7

Spending your money

A   **Discuss these questions:**

- Which of the places shown above do you enjoy shopping at? Give your reasons.
- Think of the area you live in. Which is your favourite place locally to get:
  magazines   stationery   books   clothes   CDs   electrical goods
- Do you enjoy going shopping? Give your reasons.

B   In these sentences, THREE of the alternatives are correct and the rest are wrong. Decide which are correct and why the wrong alternatives seem incorrect.

1   Believe it or not, there really are .... of soft drink called *Calpis, Pocari Sweat, Pschitt, Sic* and *Dribly*!
   brands ✓   categories   commodities   makes ✓   species   styles   varieties ✓

2   The .... was thronged with shoppers on the Saturday before Christmas.
   boutique   business   kiosk   mall   shopping centre   precinct

3   They stock a wide range of .... in most department stores.
   articles   goods   materials   merchandise   objects   supplies

4   The goods they have on offer in the market are certainly ....
   a bargain   good value   invaluable   value for money   valued   worthy

5   Complaints about goods should be made to the retailer, not the ....
   author   creator   inventor   manufacturer   supplier   wholesaler

6   Consumer protection laws must be observed by every ....
   end user   patron   purchaser   retailer   trader   vendor

7   An electronic cash register keeps a record of every ....
   bargain   contract   deal   negotiation   purchase   sale   transaction

8   If you want a shop to keep something for you until later, you may have to ....
   give a discount   give a refund   make a down payment   open an account   pay a bribe
   pay cash down   pay a deposit   pay a ransom

9   You can get something repaired free of charge if it's still under ....
   assurance   certificate   guarantee   twelve months old   warranty

10   I enjoy going to that shop because the staff are so ....
   courteous   helpful   humble   knowledgeable   lenient   obsequious   subservient

C **1** 🔊 You'll hear an interview with Amanda Hooper, who is a manager in a department store.

Note down your answers to these questions:

1 What does Amanda enjoy about her job?
2 What are her responsibilities?
3 What are the disadvantages of working in a department store?
4 What are her ambitions?

2 👥 Compare your answers with a partner. Then discuss what YOU would enjoy and not enjoy about doing Amanda's job – and the job of a sales assistant.

D 👥👥 Student A should look at Activity 3, student B at 10, C at 26 (and D at 29) for ideas to share. You'll each have some ideas on how to handle customers.

Decide which of the ideas seem most useful – not only for sales assistants, but also, more generally, when dealing with people in other situations too.

| 7.2 | **Prepositions – 1** | GRAMMAR REVIEW |

Fill each gap in this newspaper article with a suitable preposition.

Money fit to launder

Great inventions rarely work first time. ¹ 1990 the Reserve Bank of Australia, the country's central bank, shipped an order ² commemorative banknotes, ³ the first to be made ⁴ plastic film rather than paper, ⁵ Western Samoa. The Pacific islanders' excitement ⁶ their new two-tala notes soon turned ⁷ anger. Ink rubbed off the surface and smudged the portrait ⁸ Malietoa Tanumafali, the revered head of state, ⁹ whose honour the notes had been issued. ¹⁰ their early days, plastic banknotes shed ink, jammed ¹¹ note-counting machines and often refused to be refolded. But the Reserve Bank, which pioneered the technology, claims to have eradicated the sort of glitches that produced red (and smudged) faces ¹² Western Samoa. Australia issued its own plastic tender ¹³ the first time in 1992. ¹⁴ 1996, the country had taken the last ¹⁵ its paper money ¹⁶ circulation. Now it is persuading other countries to follow its example.

The Australians say plastic cash has two main advantages ¹⁷ the paper variety. First, it is hard to forge. As well as fancy inks and watermarks, it has a transparent window that makes life difficult ¹⁸ counterfeiters. The second advantage is economic. Plastic notes are hard to rip and even survive washing machines. Although each note costs ¹⁹ twice as much as a paper one to make, it lasts up to four times as long. The advantage is even greater ²⁰ humid climates, where paper notes can survive as little as four months.

Armed ²¹ these selling points, the Reserve Bank's printing division is running a healthy export business. It makes plastic notes ²² several countries, including Thailand, Brunei and a forgiving Western Samoa. DuraNote, an American company ²³ a plastic product, claims to be talking to central banks ²⁴ twenty-four countries. "Until recently plastic cash was considered a novelty," says Al McKay ²⁵ DuraNote. "Now the central banks have become more cost-conscious they are taking it very seriously."

Such scrimping ²⁶ costs even extends ²⁷ recycling, it seems. Australia plans to turn worn-out plastic notes ²⁸ wheelbarrows, compost bins and plumbing fittings. There may be money ²⁹ such products, ³⁰ more ways than one.

from *The Economist*

Preparation Before the next lesson, read the article in 7.3 on the next page and do the task in **A1**.

A **1** 🖉 Read this article and MAKE NOTES on which aspects of West Edmonton Mall would appeal to you, and which would not.

2 👥 Compare your notes with a partner, and discuss your reactions to the article.

Canada's palace of kitsch convenience

Dave Hill

1 FIRST IMPRESSIONS of the West Edmonton Mall are numbingly familiar, especially if you enter by the east wing. Outside, the sleet may be whipping across the flatlands of Alberta, but the processed ambience swiftly renders your senses supine in a manner well known to any visitor to Gateshead's Metro Centre or London's Brent Cross.

2 There is antiseptic Muzak and the glare of fluorescent lights. The concourse is decorated with indoor plants and "anchored" – to use the parlance of this most fanatical of service industries – at each end by a major department store.

3 Wander for a day among its glass and plastic halls and discover a complex so vast that its length is three times the height of the Empire State Building. The pursuit of aimless leisure here approaches the surreal. It is not the kind of place you drop in to for a bag of jelly babies and a packet of cigarettes. When you visit West Edmonton Mall and its avalanche of attractions, there is only one thing to do – hand in your coat at the cloakroom and submit.

4 You could go both barmy and bankrupt in this place and it wouldn't hurt a bit. For as well as the consumer seductions of IKEA, Sears, Athletes' World and 800 other shops, a thematic mock-up of New Orleans' Bourbon Street containing several of the Mall's 110 eating establishments, plus a chapel, a nightclub and a bingo hall, West Edmonton Mall offers far more.

5 There is Fantasyland, a full-scale children's funfair complete with dodgems, miniature railway and stomach-churning repertoire of plunges, slides and spins; the World Waterpark, whose main pool features the Blue Thunder wave machine and a labyrinth of spiralling, high-velocity tunnel rides; the Deep Sea Adventure, an artificial oceanscape containing a replica of Christopher Columbus's ship, the Santa Maria, six mini-submarines for sub-aquatic sightseeing, a school of dolphins and an entire community of undersea life;

a competition-standard skating rink, the Ice Palace; an 18-hole miniature golf course; a 19-studio cineplex and, of course, 15 banks and other financial service outlets.

When the Mall's public relations person reaches for comparisons, she does not trouble with the obvious competitors but talks about Disneyland. "We've created a 365-day-a-year summer environment which provides entertainment for people. We have something for everyone. Disney has set the standard, and I like to think we match it."

Mickey Mouse himself would have to admit she has a point. West Edmonton Mall is not so much a shopping city as a fully integrated consumer fantasy that succeeds in being mindless, utterly ridiculous and absolutely out of this world. My girlfriend and I, and our two young children, meandered among the fountains and plastic mouldings in a condition of ever-increasing gormlessness, simultaneously stunned and seduced by the diabolically manufactured mechanism for parting you from your critical faculties and your cash.

Everything is scrupulously designed to prolong your visit and, in the end, everything is welcome. For example, is there a Western parent alive who, in the middle of a frantic day, would not welcome the oasis of a children's facility like Fantasyland?

An hour of such blissful respite, followed by coffee and a sandwich at some glitzy pre-fab café, and we were ready once again to disappear into our consumer daze, blithely coughing up a few more dollars for a tiepin, a woolly hat or baseball pennant, pausing to peer down at the sharks which glide through the depths of the Deep Sea Adventure or to gawp swivel-eyed at the Ice Palace skaters. In its idiotic way, it's all too wonderful for words. I like malls, partly because they usually fulfill their promise to be clean, safe and efficient, but mostly because they emit such a stupefying sensory cocktail of obsession, ostentation and overkill. At West Edmonton Mall – the world's biggest, according to the Guinness Book of Records – these characteristics reach absurd heights.

10 Mall-building is a precise science and this indoor panorama is nothing if not state-of-the-art. It is not that the shopping itself is so very thrilling; as ever with such malls, the stores are plentiful but ultimately banal. Rather, the pleasure is in being part of a quietly lunatic alternative universe where the thin line that divides shopping from entertainment becomes almost totally erased.

11 Entirely the product of private capital, West Edmonton Mall is owned by the Triple Five Corporation, the company of the Ghermazin family (three brothers and their father), who came from Iran to New York as rug traders, moved to Montreal and later made good with the discovery of Albertan oil. West Edmonton Mall has been built with the proceeds, a financial investment well over the $1 billion mark.

12 As well as the World Waterpark, the Ice Palace and Fantasyland, it includes a hotel – the Fantasyland Hotel, naturally – as final confirmation, perhaps, that the Mall is not just a place to pass through, but a modern day pleasure dome.

13 Can you imagine spending your holiday in a glorified shopping precinct? Well, plenty of people do, booking in to any of half-a-dozen themed Fantasyland Hotel quarters with names like "Hollywood", "Polynesian" and "Truck". Others simply take in the Mall as part of bigger package tours. Of the annual 20 million visitors, around nine million are tourists, including a growing proportion of Japanese for whom no North American itinerary is complete without dropping in on Disneyland, Disney World and the Mall.

14 With pilgrims descending on it from all corners of the globe, the Mall enjoys a status approaching that of a sacred monument where worshippers pay homage with their credit cards. As a way to spend your time, West Edmonton Mall is as gratifyingly mind-rotting an experience as you could wish, positive proof that everyone should become a consumer zombie at least once in their lives.

B **1** Highlight the following words in the article and work out their meanings from the context. The paragraph numbers (¶) are given.

¶2 *parlance*	¶3 *avalanche*	¶4 *barmy*	*mock-up*
¶7 *meandered* *critical faculties*	¶8 *oasis*	¶9 *blithely*	*coughing up*
¶10 *state-of-the-art* *banal*	¶11 *proceeds*	¶12 *pleasure dome*	
¶13 *glorified*	¶14 *gratifyingly*		

Match their meanings to the words below.

ability to judge objectively   agreeably   crazy   in a carefree manner   jargon
palace of delights   plethora   profits   refuge   repetitious and dull   replica
seeming more important than in reality   spending   ultra-modern   wandered

2 Now fill the gaps in these sentences with suitable forms of the words in italics above:

1 It was a four-day camel ride before we reached the ....
2 They donated the .... of the jumble sale to charity.
3 They were .... complimentary about my essay, but I thought it was rather .... Maybe their .... are not very sharp!
4 The stream .... across the plain and then flowed into the river.
5 We had to .... £25 when we lost our car park ticket.
6 A shop is a 'retail outlet' in commercial ....
7 They received an .... of replies to the advertisement for 'senior administrator' – but I think they're just looking for a .... office boy.
8 The architect constructed a .... of the new mall to show to her clients.
9 This hi-fi system contains all the latest .... features.
10 He .... strolled into the interview room an hour late – he must be .... !

C Write your answers to these questions:

1 What did the writer and his family buy at the Mall?
2 The builders of the Mall gained their wealth from ....
3 The tourists who visit the Mall are likened to .... visiting a ....
4 How would you describe the tone of the article?
5 To sum up, what is the writer's attitude to the Mall? .... and ....
6 What would appeal to you and not appeal to you about the Mall? Write a summary of your reactions (50–70 words).

7.4 Past and present   GRAMMAR REVIEW

A 👥 **Discuss any differences in meaning between these sentences:**

1 I didn't have time to read the paper   I haven't had time to read the paper
  this morning.   this morning.
2 I had tea when Pam came in.   I was having tea when Pam came in.
3 By the time we had had lunch it was 2.30. By the time we had lunch it was 2.30.
4 Where has Steve gone for his holiday?   Where does Steve go for his holiday?
  Where is Steve going for his holiday?   Where did Steve go for his holiday?
  Where has Steve been going for his holiday?

5 I had hoped you would invite me.   I was hoping you would invite me.
  I did hope you would invite me.   I hoped you would invite me.
6 What are you doing?   What do you do?
  What have you done?   What have you been doing?

B **Fill each of the blanks with a suitable word or phrase.**

1 I _haven't seen_ Ruth for ages. I believe I last _saw her at_ Christmas.
2 Where .... that nice new jumper? The colour really .... you!
3 Come quickly! There .... accident – I think someone .... hurt.
4 Even though .... just .... rain, we .... to go out for a walk, thinking that it
  .... last long – and sure enough the sun soon ....
5 The back door .... just .... painted. If you .... it, you .... paint on
  your hands.
6 It's high time Bill .... to the hairdresser's – he .... his hair cut ....
  Christmas.
7 Here you are at last! We .... waiting for you .... 7.30 – where .... ? Why
  .... you tell us that you .... late? You .... phoned us before we ....
  home, then we .... the beginning of the show.
8 When I .... a child I .... spend all my money on sweets, but now I ....

C 1 👥👥 **Look at these photos and discuss the questions below. MAKE NOTES on your discussion.**

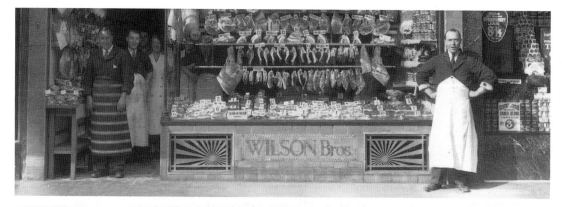

- How have shops and stores changed over the past 10 or 20 years?
- How has your local shopping area changed recently? What new shops have opened up?
  Which shops have closed down or gone out of business? Why?
- How has the awareness (and power) of consumers changed over the years?
- Describe your own shopping habits – past and present.

2 ✏ **Write a couple of paragraphs about your group's discussion, summarising the main ideas.**

A Decide which of these factors are most important when buying the products below:

QUALITY   PRICE   SERVICE   PARKING   CONVENIENCE   FRIENDLY ADVICE
food   clothes   books   electrical goods   CDs   videos or DVDs   souvenirs

B You'll hear a broadcast about Japanese department stores. As you listen for the first time, choose the word or phrase which best completes each sentence:

1 The first Mitsukoshi store opened in ....
   a 1637   **b** 1673   **c** 1736   **d** 1763
2 Mitsukoshi-mae means '..................... Mitsukoshi'.
   a beneath   **c** in front of
   b beside   **d** inside
3 At opening time, the sales staff are all ....
   a standing at the main entrance
   b ready to greet you as you enter their department
   c waiting at their tills
   d handing out brochures
4 The 'Ladies Club' provides ....
   a companionship   **c** free lunches
   b discounts   **d** courses
5 The facilities offered at other Japanese department stores are .... to Mitsukoshi's.
   a identical   **b** inferior   **c** dissimilar   **d** comparable
6 English is spoken by .... of the sales staff.
   a all   **b** most   **c** none   **d** some
7 Japanese department stores are open ....
   a every day of the week   **c** every day except Sunday
   b every day except national holidays   **d** six days a week
8 At one store the sales staff wear badges showing their hobbies so that ....
   a they don't need to wear a uniform   **c** you can discuss hobbies with them
   b customers can relate to them as people **d** they seem more interesting

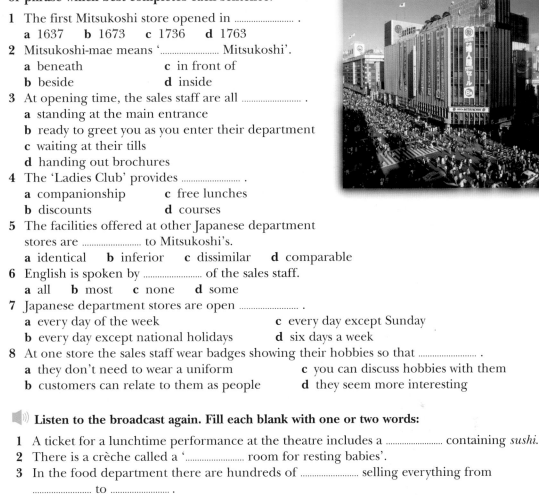

C Listen to the broadcast again. Fill each blank with one or two words:

1 A ticket for a lunchtime performance at the theatre includes a .... containing *sushi*.
2 There is a crèche called a '..................... room for resting babies'.
3 In the food department there are hundreds of .... selling everything from .... to ....
4 On the upper floors you can find many small ....
5 In summer, you can go up to the roof garden where you can sit in a .... and enjoy the .... and the ....
6 Summer in Japan officially begins on .... and ends on ....
7 At the main entrance you can get a .... and brochure in English.
8 As you enter the lift the operator will .... to you and .... you.
9 Department stores in Japan are open from .... to ....
10 Some department stores are owned by .... companies. There you can take the lift down to the .... where your .... is waiting.
11 Japanese department stores compete in terms of .... , how much of a .... it is to go there, and the .... of goods on offer.
12 At Mitsukoshi in London, helping Japanese tourists encourages ....

D Discuss your reactions to the broadcast:

• How do Japanese stores compare with department stores in your country?
• Which of their facilities and services seem most attractive?
• If you were going to open a shop, what would you sell? What facilities and services would you offer to your customers?

7.6 Dear Sir, ...

A Imagine that six months ago you bought a new hi-fi system from a department store. After four weeks the CD player went wrong, and you waited three weeks for the store to replace the hi-fi with a new one. Four weeks later the cassette player went wrong and you had to wait six weeks while the store repaired it. Now something else has gone wrong with it ...

👥 Role-play a conversation between the customer and the department manager.

B ✎ Imagine that you're now living in a different part of the country, so you can't take the hi-fi back to the shop in person and you've been unable to get through on the phone. Write a letter, fax or e-mail to the store (300–350 words).

7.7 Further uses of -ing

A Fill the gaps in the sentences in this revision exercise. (If you have any problems look again at 4.4.)

1 When .... a complaint, I prefer to be friendly and polite, instead of ....
   aggressive or rude.
2 I found out what ingredients the product contained by .... the label. On ....
   that it contained artificial flavouring, I decided against .... it.
3 It's no use .... him, he won't take any notice of you.
4 There's no point in .... the book in translation if it's available in English.
5 It's impossible to sneeze without .... your eyes.
6 In addition to .... this course, she spends a lot of time at home .... things like
   .... novels in English and .... with friends by .... letters.
7 I've heard so much about you, I've really been looking forward .... you.
8 I felt depressed because I'm not used .... alone.

B Study these examples before filling the gaps in the exercise below:

> The possessive (*their*, *everyone's*, *her*, etc.) in these examples seems more formal than a straightforward pronoun or noun (*them*, *everyone*, *Janet*).
>   I very much appreciated their/them coming to see me.
>   We were puzzled about everyone's/everyone feeling ill after the meal.
>   Janet/Her/Janet's arriving on time for a change was quite a surprise.
>
> A possessive is NOT normally used when several words are involved:
> I very much appreciated Janet and Maurice coming to see me.
>
> A possessive can't be used after verbs like *see*, *hear*, *feel*, *notice*, *watch* and *smell*:
>   I didn't hear you calling me. ✓
>   I didn't hear your calling me. ✗
>   Can you smell something burning?

1 Their father doesn't approve of .... home late or .... television either. In fact, he
   insists on .... home before 11 and says that .... books will improve their minds.
2 We were all delighted to hear about Bill .... so well in the interview. His success is due
   to .... such a good impression on the interviewer.
3 They both smoke like chimneys, and I can't get used to .... during meals and
   .... me for a light is particularly irritating.
4 I'll never forget that time we went for a walk with Tony and Jane. Do you remember
   .... into the river and then .... to save him?

C Finish the incomplete sentences so that each means the same as the sentence before it.

1 I don't advise you to travel to London to do your shopping.   It isn't worth ....
2 We were upset that he forgot to inform us.   We were upset about his ....
3 It might be a better idea to save your money, not spend it.   Instead of ....
4 She is a champion athlete and speaks four languages fluently.   Besides ....
5 He has a job in an office and works in a shop at weekends.   As well as ....
6 You won't find out if they're open if you don't phone them.   Without ....
7 He has been in love with her from the moment he first saw her.   Ever since ....
8 It was inconsiderate of you not to consult me beforehand.   Your ....

7.8 Compound nouns   VOCABULARY DEVELOPMENT

A Read these notes. Then look again at the article about West Edmonton Mall in 7.3 and underline the compound nouns in paragraphs 1–6.

There are three types of compound nouns:

1 Noun + noun:
service industry   department store   pleasure dome   credit card   bar code   charity shop

2 Adjective + noun:
central heating   public relations   open air   indoor plants   yellow pages

– These aren't the same as 'normal adjectives', which modify a noun:
efficient heating = the heating is efficient   yellow trousers = the trousers are yellow

3 Longer phrases:
cost of living   rule of thumb   do-it-yourself   value added tax

Most compound nouns consist of two separate words. But some are hyphenated, and some are single words. There are no hard-and-fast rules about this:
dry-cleaning   nightclub   sunglasses   back-seat driver   cover-up

B Form compound nouns from the words in red and blue:

air   burglar   common   driving   estate   agent   alarm   attack   benefit
fancy   generation   greenhouse   hay   breakdown   business   clip   conditioning
heart   hire   income   junk   mail   crossing   dress   effect   fever   food
mother   nervous   package   paper   forecast   gap   licence   mall   meter
parking   pedestrian   pocket   shopping   money   order   purchase   sense
show   unemployment   weather   window   shopping   tax   tongue   tour

C Here are the first words of some common two-word compound nouns. What are the second words? In some cases there may be several possibilities.

inverted *commas*   mineral *water*   general *knowledge/election/public*
one-parent ....   current ....   stainless ....   traveller's ....
compact ....   exclamation ....   swimming ....   skating ....
delivery ....   chain ....   clearance ....   travel ....
wastepaper ....

D Fill the gaps with suitable compound nouns from A, B and C:

1 People in a .... often spend more time .... than actually buying things.
2 I didn't have enough money in my .... to cover a cheque, so I used my ....
3 You can pick up some good bargains at a .... or a ....
4 If you buy something from a .... catalogue, there's a .... to be added on.
5 Those black stripes on the back cover of this book are its ....
6 If you want to buy a house go to an .... , but to book a holiday go to a ....
7 I inadvertently threw my invitation to the .... party into the ....
8 Going on holiday? Don't forget to take your .... and ....

Preparation   Before the next lesson, collect some advertisements from magazines or newspapers. Include at least one that you DISLIKE or disapprove of, as well as ones you do like.

7.9 Advertising: sequencing your ideas

A Paragraphs a–g are in the wrong order. Rearrange them and number them in the correct order.

Benetton 'tasteless' ads in court

1 THE first of a series of lawsuits connected with a world-wide advertising campaign by the clothing giant Benetton opened yesterday, in which the company is accused of causing a sales slump through "tasteless" publicity.

a "Many things come into play, not least a person's business sense. Many of our German branches are doing very well."

b Benetton in turn is suing Mr Hartwich for withholding payments to the fashion chain and yesterday succeeded in postponing the court case until next month, saying it had no inclination to reach an amicable settlement in view of the publicity surrounding Mr Hartwich that had caused sales to drop by up to 60pc. A group of 70 Benetton retailers from four European countries met in Mainz on Sunday to coordinate their rebellion against the Italian company.

c Heinz Hartwich, from Kassel, became the first of a group of retailers in Germany to sue the company for an undisclosed sum in respect of sales losses which they claim are a result of customer boycotts.

d Mr Hartwich alleged that parents had told him that their children would be picked on by friends if they wore Benetton clothes and that shops had received anonymous threats complaining about the advertisements.

e Religious and political circles in Germany have long protested against the advertisements, intended to focus on social issues, which included pictures of the bloodied uniform of a dead Croatian soldier and a baby attached by an umbilical cord.

f Several similar cases of Benetton being sued in France have been settled out of court, but a company lawyer said the "media circus" generated by the complaints in Germany have led the company to fight the issue in court. A spokesman for Benetton said that blaming advertising for poor sales was absurd.

g Some of the more commonly seen ads on hoardings and in magazines included oil-soaked birds and Aids sufferers.

9 Mr Ulfert Engels, a lawyer for Mr Hartwich, said that 150 of Benetton's 650 franchises in Germany have had to close. One third of the remaining 500 have survived only with financial support from the main company.

Robin Gedye

B Explain who or what is referred to by the words highlighted in these quotations from the article:

¶a ... our German branches ...
¶b ... payments to the fashion chain ...   ... saying it had no inclination ...
¶c ... to sue the company ...   ... which they claim ...
¶d ... if they wore ...
¶e ... protested against the advertisements ...
¶f Several similar cases ...

In a composition, the sequence in which points are made change the impact on your reader. Some points need to be arranged in a logical order with related ideas grouped together. Some points can be arranged in different ways to provide different kinds of emphasis.

The first point often 'sets the scene' for the rest of the text, while the final point is usually perceived as the conclusion.

C 👥👥 Look at the advertisement on the right together with the ones you've brought to class. Discuss these questions:

- How effective is each ad?
- Which do you like best and why?
- Which do you disapprove of and why?

While other people are reading their morning paper at Heathrow können Sie die Zeitung in Hamburg lesen.

British Airways news for businessmen is that we have more early flights each day to more European cities than any other airline.

D **1** ✏ Look at the notes below and decide which of the points you would include in an essay on the following topic. Bear in mind that the points must all be relevant, and that you can't make every single point in 300–350 words.

Write an essay outlining the harmful and the beneficial effects of advertising (300–350 words).

- Need created for totally unnecessary products (e.g. kitchen gadgets)
- Plethora of brands of goods, different only in name (e.g. detergents)
- Goods more expensive due to costly advertising budgets
- Young people may be harmed by certain advertisements (e.g. alcoholic drink)
- Ads stimulate envy among the less well-off; may lead to rise in crime rate (e.g. thefts of expensive cars)
- Commercials on TV interrupt programmes – very annoying
- Ads lead to dissatisfaction with one's standard of living – may lead to people trying to live beyond their means
- Ads create desire for more and more material possessions
- Many commercials on TV have insidious tunes that linger in the brain
- Many ads are amusing and informative – often more amusing than the programmes on TV or articles in a magazine
- Ads stimulate competition between companies, thus keeping prices down
- Ads create consumer awareness, giving information about a range of products
- Ads in newspapers and magazines keep their cost down – many couldn't survive without advertisements
- The world would be duller and drabber without amusing and colourful ads

2 Add any important further points you want to make to the notes above.

3 Decide on the best sequence of the points for your essay.

4 ✏ Write your essay, citing examples of particular advertisements that support your arguments.

8

Have I got news for you!

8.1 **The media**   **TOPIC VOCABULARY**

A 👥👥👥👥 **Discuss these questions:**

- What do you think has happened in the photos?
- How do you find out what's in the news?
- Which newspapers do you read regularly? Which do you prefer and why?
- What current affairs programmes do you watch or listen to on the TV or radio?
- If you go to websites for news, which do you prefer and why?
- Which English-language newspapers have you read? What were they like?
- Is there a local English language newspaper in your country? What's it like?
- Do you believe everything you read in the newspapers? Why/Why not?

B 👥👥 **Match the words and phrases in red to their synonyms in blue.**

article	circulation	editorial	issue		critic	the dailies	journalist	lead story
magazines	main story	newsreader			leader	monthlies & weeklies		newscaster
the papers	reporter	reviewer			number	number of copies sold		report

C 👥👥 **Here are some (genuine) newspaper headlines. Explain the double meaning or joke.**

1 POLICE FOUND DRUNK IN SHOP WINDOW

2 Butter battle spreads

3 Hospital guards stab victim

4 Dog rescues cat

5 Mine exploded on building site

6 The teacher from hell

7 Fish talks in Brussels

8 Women who smoke have lighter children

A 👥 **Discuss the differences in meaning (if any) between these sentences:**

1 Could you finish the article? / Were you able to finish the article?
2 Can you carry this box? / Could you carry this box?
3 You can't leave yet. / You needn't leave yet.
4 I don't need to read the paper today. / I needn't read the paper today.
  I don't have to read the paper today. / I shouldn't read the paper today.
  I haven't read the paper today. / I haven't got to read the paper today.
5 There could be an election this year. / There has to be an election this year.
  There should be an election this year. / There will be an election this year.
6 That could be Tony at the door. / That must be Tony at the door.
  That will be Tony at the door. / That can't be Tony at the door.
  That might be Tony at the door. / That should be Tony at the door.

B **Write TWO reports of each sentence; one using a modal verb, and one using a longer phrase, as in the example:**

1 'You must do it now.' — He said that ....
  a   *He said that we had to do it.*
  b   *He said that we were obliged to do it / it was necessary for us to do it.*
2 'Maybe we can help you.' — They said that ....
3 'You can't use a dictionary in the exam.' — He told me that ....
4 'Must you leave so soon?' — She asked me if ....
5 'You mustn't believe everything you read in the newspapers.' — He told us that ....
6 'I daren't dive into the swimming pool.' — She told us that ....
7 'You need to book a table.' — He told us that ....
8 'What time must I arrive there?' — She wondered ....

C 👥 **Rewrite each headline as a full sentence:**

1 **'Non-swimmers on the up' says sports minister**
2 **Ban on smoking in cinemas**
3 **Seat belts to be worn in rear seats**
4 **70 mph speed limit to be lifted**
5 **1000s forced to flee after quake**
6 **RECESSION LOOMS AGAIN**
7 **Left set to win election**
8 **Rail strike stops commuters getting home**

D **1** 👥 Imagine that you're giving advice to a British person who is about to visit your country for the first time. What advice would you give about social customs, rules of behaviour and laws, using these modal verbs:

can / can't   have to / don't have to
need to / don't need to / needn't
must / mustn't   should / shouldn't

2 ✏ Write a paragraph, giving the most important pieces of advice.

A Read this *Guardian* leader. It appeared the morning after the accident in which Diana, Princess of Wales, and Dodi Al Fayed were killed – and before the causes of the accident came to light.

Flying too close to the sun

1 SHE WAS 36. She leaves two young sons. She died at a moment when her personal life had brightened and her public life seemed to be making progress. "Unthinkable," people said when they heard of the news of Princess Diana's death, but few families altogether escape such tragedies. Though treated yesterday as barely more than a sideline, the death of Dodi Al Fayed is a tragedy too. So too is the death of their chauffeur, not even dignified in yesterday's reports with a name. Maybe he too was young; maybe he too leaves young children.

2 Yet the death of Diana was also spectacular, an event which reverberated across the world. She was probably the most famous woman, perhaps the most famous person, of her time. People will remember for years where and when they heard of her death, as they did with the death of John F Kennedy. As with Kennedy and with James Dean, John Lennon and Marilyn Monroe, she was a superstar who died young in violent circumstances, and as with them, it will guarantee her a mythological status.

3 In her time, and with her participation, the process accelerated which has made the British monarchy more and more a mix of fantasy with reality. Its role as the most dignified ingredient in our constitution, once apparently unassailable, is so badly eroded today that it looks beyond repair. The Queen herself commands a continuing respect, but for many people in Britain, the principal use of the Royal Family now is to keep us entertained and titillated and tantalised, to give us something new and spicy to discuss in the pub and the shops. More and more, their story has become a kind of rich psychological drama, more gripping even than any soap opera because its people really exist: a drama in whose cast list Diana had become not just the most alluring but perhaps the most influential player.

4 She came to all this hopelessly unprepared; sweet, shy, gauche, somewhat untutored, plucked from nowhere at 19 to be the bride of the heir to the throne, in the sort of transformation one doesn't expect outside bedtime stories. Even had things gone well, this would have been a brutally tough assignment. As it was, they began to go wrong chillingly soon – as we later learned, within a few months of the marriage. The truth about the marriage, at first shadowy and elusive, seeped gradually into the light: the shade of Camilla; her own uncertain temperament; the post-natal depression; the bulimia; the desperate alienation. Her very misfortunes increased the fascination she held for the Press and the public: not just a romantic figure, but a tragic figure too.

5 As things came apart, she had several options. One – which she briefly chose, but soon abandoned – was to pull out of public life and go into hiding; a second, simply to carry on with the life she wanted and do her best to survive the constant, unrelenting exposure; the third, to turn that exposure to positive use by enlisting it to promote her favourite causes. This last she did to huge beneficial effect.

6 She didn't just meet victims of Aids, she embraced them, in defiance of a tabloid press which taught that they were unclean. Her campaign to ban landmines, from which government agents made public and private attempts to dissuade her, took a cause long and obscurely argued by others without her magnetism, and put it on front pages across the world.

7 In doing this, in exploiting her hybrid role, part royal and part non-royal, she laid herself open to the charge of manipulation. It was hard to escape the impression that while claiming to hate the unsleeping eye of the media, she also craved it: not least because a quiet retreat to obscurity would be bowing her knee to the will of an Establishment which had wronged and damaged her and now wanted her out of the way. The result was to put her even more on the nation's centre stage. Increasingly, the story of the Royal Family's troubles came to resemble a script where the scriptwriters had excelled themselves in piling one twist on another. No scriptwriter, in this sense, could have contrived a more symbolic dénouement than that which occurred in the midnight streets of Paris this weekend.

8 And now the princess takes her place in the long and melancholy record of queens and princesses who led sad lives and met still sadder deaths. She will enter into legend, where it may come to be said of her that she met the fate which so often awaits those who fly too near to the sun.

B **Highlight** the following words and phrases in the article. Match their meanings in this context to the definitions below.

¶1 sideline   dignified
¶2 reverberated   mythological status
¶3 accelerated   unassailable   eroded   titillated and tantalised   spicy   alluring
¶4 gauche   chillingly   elusive   alienation
¶5 unrelenting   causes
¶7 hybrid   craved   Establishment   dénouement

attractive   awkward   charities   continuous   couldn't live without   damaged   echoed
ending   excited and fascinated   exciting   feeling of isolation   frighteningly   invulnerable
legendary position   mixed   mysterious   ruling classes   shown respect   went faster
unimportant event

C 👥👥 **Discuss these questions:**

• Do you remember where you were when you heard about Princess Diana's death? How did the news affect you?
• What points are made in the article which praise Princess Diana?
• What points are more critical of her and of the Royal Family?
• How would you feel if photographers took photos of YOU everywhere?
• Who is most to blame for invading the privacy of famous people: the photographers or the people who buy newspapers and magazines?
• Does the press have too much power? What should be done to control the press?

8.4 '...that is part of the job' LISTENING

A 🔊 **Jayne Evans is a news journalist. Complete the sentences with a word or short phrase.**

1 When you're a news journalist, you're never really [1] .

2 A news anchor reads from an autocue but must be ready to [2a]
those words if instructed, and remain [2b] .

3 Shocking stories are very [3] but she must report them calmly.

4 It's almost impossible to remain detached when reporting disasters, but that is
[4] .

5 In her career she has to enjoy the [5] .

6 The funniest situation she has been in was when [6] .

7 Being a news journalist is almost like being another [7] service.

8 Although your adrenalin is pumping, your report must be [8] .

B **Discuss your reactions to the interview:**

- What kind of personality and skills do you need to be a news journalist?
- What would it be like to have Jayne's job? Do you envy her? Why (not)?
- What difference does it make to see a TV on-the-spot report, rather than hear a news anchor person give the same information?
- How can reporters manage to give unbiased versions of events?

8.5 ⟍ **Cream and punishment**

READING

A Six paragraphs/sentences have been removed from this article. Choose the most suitable paragraph/sentence from the list A–F for each gap (1–6) in the article.

Cream and punishment

"WATCH this bit carefully," says Noël Godin, fast-forwarding the video to the right place. "Bill Gates is walking towards the government building, slowly, slowly, his security guards all around him. Meanwhile, 30 pie-throwers, who have been standing in groups of three, suddenly come together, and, in a whirlwind of cakes, they strike their target. Gloup. Gloup. Gloup."

With a contented chuckle, Godin leans back in the black-leather sofa in his Brussels flat. On the screen, his victim is wiping cream pie from his face. "See, he is trying to suppress a small smile," says Godin, delightedly. Suppressing it very successfully, it appears. Gates looks completely stunned.

1 ☐

The first few seconds after an attack reveal the true character of the target, believes Godin. Jean Luc Godard, the film director, showed 'real stature'. "He smiled, pulled off his bespattered jacket, lit a cigar and said: 'It tastes rather good.'"

Godin, who also acts under the pseudonym *Georges le Gloupier*, shakes his head sorrowfully. "After nearly 30 years of attacks, Godard is the only one who turned the situation to his advantage. I was very pleased with his reaction and I will never attack him again." Sylvie says that he is exhausted after all the excitement surrounding the Bill Gates coup.

2 ☐

Godin prides himself on the rigorous selection of his targets, mostly those who have an inflated sense of their own importance and little sense of humour. But he also targets those who, in his opinion, abuse their power or simply get in the way of the total freedom he thinks should be every person's right. Any politician is fair game, although he is wary about attacking them individually as he does not want to give them 'free publicity'.

3 ☐

His list of potential targets in England is growing. "Mr Virgin [Richard Branson] would be a good idea and Rupert Murdoch is also on the list." When she comes here, perhaps later this year, priority number one will be Lady Thatcher. "We will not leave her in peace just because she no longer has power. She is a symbolic target and we will go on a safari mission after her." After that, he is not sure.

4

So, during the Gates attack, he stood in a side street, waiting to intervene with back-up cream pies if needed. Sylvie, who has long feared that he will get himself shot by an over-alert bodyguard, is pleased, but Godin says that he will still deliver the pie to some of his victims, just to keep his hand in.

5

He works on a very low budget, with cream pies donated by local pâtissiers and part-time gloupiers drawn from friends, would-be actors and students.
 "I am very careful about who I target. For example, I have been offered lots of money to do Sharon Stone and Catherine Deneuve. But I like them both. I'm not a cream-cake mercenary. I will accept sponsorship, but only for targets I think are worthy."

6

Ideally, he would like more people to follow his example. "Unlike Bill Gates, I don't feel I have a monopoly on my trade. Quite the reverse. If everyone attacked big bosses and pompous people, the message might start getting through. Custard pies are a sort of esperanto: a universal language."

Helena de Bertodano

A Bill Gates, as "a symbol of the new merchant arrogance", has been Number One on his hit list for some time. Now Bill Clinton and the Pope have replaced Gates as top targets, with Margaret Thatcher and Tony Blair running close behind.

B Godin, 52, loves watching re-runs of his attacks and if Sylvie, his partner, were not here to restrain him, he would probably have rewound the tape and started again. Last month's attack on Bill Gates was his most high-profile yet and has earned him a new fan club in the United States, with an Internet site and lengthy articles about him appearing in papers such as The Wall Street Journal.

C I ask him if it has ever occurred to him that he might be a little mad. "Of course. Like Falstaff. The world needs a bit of madness."

D Inevitably, he has become a target of his own joke. Once, on a talk show, the presenter planted a cream pie in his face. How did he react? "I went and sat on the knee of the most important guest and wiped myself all over him." Does he ever get angry when he is flanned? "I laugh every time. If not I would be a perfect imbecile."

E These days Godin himself reluctantly stands back from the front line of attack. He is so well-known in Belgium that his presence would be a giveaway. "When I go to the theatre, even in a private capacity, there is instant panic around me."

F Usually he only carries out one or two attacks a year. Each *entartement*, or flanning, is meticulously planned and he agrees that it is a form of terrorism. "It is a burlesque terrorism. We do not wound our victims, they are only wounded in their *amour propre*." Sylvie points out that they were very careful not to ram Bill Gates' glasses too hard against his nose.

B 👥👥 Discuss these questions:
- Do you approve or disapprove of Noël Godin's philosophy and tactics? Why?
- Which famous people would you like to attack with a cream pie? Why?

C ✎ Summarise Noël Godin's attitude to famous people (50–70 words).

1 👥 Before writing, first make notes and discuss them with a partner.

2 When you've written your summary, compare it with a partner's.

8.6 Prefixes

All the prefixes in this section are 'ACTIVE' prefixes – they can be used to form new words or phrases.

A Study the examples and then add the words below to the appropriate lists:

anti-	(= opposed to)	anti-nuclear anti-government anti-war
pro-	(= supporting)	pro-environment pro-nationalist pro-strike
pre-	(= before)	pre-recorded pre-Christmas pre-prepared
super-	(= larger/greater than usual)	superglue super-rich superpower
half-	half-finished half-empty half-full half-frozen	

American   asleep   brother   cooked   democracy   expect   federal   feminist
intelligent   monarchy   packed   star   store   test   time   truth   union   way

B Study the examples and then add the words below to the appropriate lists:

re	(= again)	re-elect rewritten recycled
un	(= reverse action)	unbutton undress untie
over	(= too much)	over-react overcooked overindulge
under	(= too little)	underfunded underdeveloped
out	(= more than)	outlive outrun outsell

appear   block   build   capture   estimate   fasten   fillable   grow
load   number   print   simplify   united   usable   value   vote   work

C Study the examples and then add the words below to the appropriate lists:

self-	(= by or for itself/oneself)	self-adjusting self-catering self-contained
co-	(= together)	co-author co-educational
counter-	(= against)	counter-attack counter-productive counter-intuitive
ex-	(= former)	ex-colleague ex-boyfriend ex-boss
semi-	(= half)	semi-professional semi-final semi-precious
sub-	(= below)	sub-zero sub-committee

automatic   circular   defeating   director   educated   employed   exist
explanatory   governing   heading   measure   official   owner   policeman
preservation   president   productive   standard   sufficient   title

The examples in A, B and C show which prefixes generally take hyphens. When pronunciation might be difficult, a hyphen is generally used: *re-election* (not *reelection*) and *super-rich* (not *superrich*). If in doubt, use a hyphen.

D Fill each gap using a prefix with a suitable form of the words in red:

1 It's an .... to say that a change of leader will solve all our problems.   simple
2 The minister was accused of .... the numbers of unemployed.   estimate
3 The .... members were .... by the moderate union members.   strike   vote
4 It may be .... to force them into making a decision, and if you upset   produce
   them they're quite likely to ....   react
5 Foreign-language films may be dubbed or shown with ....   title
6 Magazines devoting page after page to reports on the lives of the ....   rich
   and .... usually .... more serious magazines.   star   sell
7 You needn't refer to the manual: the use of the camera is ....   explain
8 He .... his .... to turn up at the wedding ceremony.   expect   wife
9 The .... began after the troops received a .... signal.   attack   arrange
10 He went out into the snow and .... later looking ....   appear   frozen

8.7 *There ...* — ADVANCED GRAMMAR — 8

A **1** Rephrase each sentence, using *there ...* :

1 Someone is waiting to see you. *There's someone waiting to see you.*
2 Most political problems have no easy answers.
3 It's pointless trying to explain the problem to them.
4 Some papers give more coverage to sport than others.
5 Luckily for us a telephone box was nearby.
6 It's unnecessary to shout, I can hear you perfectly well.
7 Mitsukoshi has 14 branches in Japan and 14 associate stores.
8 Come quickly! An accident has happened! Someone may have been hurt.
9 He stood in the doorway with a sheepish grin on his face.
10 I was waiting in the lecture hall with fourteen other students.

Verbs that describe actions (rather than states) can't be used with *there*:

There fell an apple off the tree. ✗

2 Discuss the difference in emphasis when *there* is used in each sentence.

B Fill the gaps in these examples with suitable words:

1 We expect there .... difficulties ahead.
2 There .... misunderstanding about this: you have to arrive at 7.15 sharp.
3 There .... a time when everyone has to face up to their responsibilities.
4 There .... nonsense talked about politics by people who ought to know better.
5 There .... more question I'd like to ask.
6 There's no .... that some newspapers distort the truth.
7 We were surprised/amazed/shocked at there .... so many people present.
8 There .... to be something wrong with my back, doctor.

Yesterday there came my friend to see me. ✗

There arrived the train on time. ✗

C Explain the meaning of each headline in a full sentence, using *there*:

1 'Fewer than 5,000 attend peace demo' The police say ...
2 More sunshine next week The forecasters say ...
3 'NO DOUBT ABOUT A VICTORY' The England soccer manager says ...
4 'Too many cars cause pollution and accidents' Environmentalists say ...
5 General election possible this year According to the newspaper ...
6 Peace moves in teachers' dispute There ...
7 Road accidents down this year There ...
8 None killed in ferry sinking There ...

D Student A should look at Activity 8, student B at 17 and C at 27. There's a short news item for you to read and then retell to your partners in your own words, using *There ...*

8.8 Hitting the headlines — LISTENING AND SPEAKING

A 🔊 You'll hear a radio programme. Indicate where the events in 1–8 happened by writing the appropriate letter in each box.

In each box write:

	I	if it happened in Italy
or	**J**	if it happened on the way to Japan
or	**USA**	if it happened in the USA

1 One can of beer every evening.
2 Police knew the licence number of the car.
3 Roller-skating champion.
4 Accurate throwing caused deaths.
5 Shortage of fresh water.
6 Video camera stolen, but not videotape.
7 Waving to relatives was dangerous.
8 Workmates were very kind to their colleague.

1	
2	
3	
4	
5	
6	
7	
8	

B Which places in the world are in the news this week? What headline news has come from each of the continents during the past month?

C **1** Before the next lesson, listen to the news on the radio or TV (or read the news on the Internet) and make notes on the main points of TWO interesting stories.

2 Then, back in class, tell your partners about your stories.

8.9 **Freedom**

SPEAKING

A Read this poem and then discuss the questions below.

> ### EPITAPH ON A TYRANT
>
> Perfection, of a kind, was what he was after,
> And the poetry he invented was easy to understand;
> He knew human folly like the back of his hand,
> And was greatly interested in armies and fleets;
> When he laughed, respectable senators burst with laughter,
> And when he cried the little children died in the streets.
>
> W.H. Auden (1938)

- Which tyrants and dictators spring to mind when you read the poem?
- Why is it that tyrants and dictators succeed in politics – and on a smaller scale in business and family life too?
- What can the individual (i.e. you and I) do to stop them from succeeding?
- How important is it for a country to have a strong, charismatic leader?

B Which of these quotations do you agree with, and which do you disagree with? Which do you agree with up to a point? Give your reasons.

'All men are created equal.' – Thomas Jefferson (1743–1826)

'The ballot is stronger than the bullet.' – Abraham Lincoln (1809–1865)

'No one can be perfectly free till all are free; no one can be perfectly happy till all are happy.' – Herbert Spencer (1820–1903)

'Nationalism is an infantile disease. It is the measles of mankind.' – Albert Einstein (1879–1955)

'Unhappy the land that is in need of heroes.' – Bertolt Brecht (1898–1956)

'Politics is too serious a matter to be left to the politicians.' – General de Gaulle (1890–1970)

'Political power grows out of the barrel of a gun.' – Mao Zedong (1893–1976)

'Ask not what your country can do for you; ask what you can do for your country.' – John F. Kennedy (1917–1963)

'All animals are equal, but some animals are more equal than others.' – *Animal Farm* by George Orwell (1903–1950)

'There is no such thing as a free lunch.' – anon

C Take turns to talk for about two minutes WITHOUT INTERRUPTION on ONE of the topics below. Then the others should react to your talk by answering these questions:

- Is there anything you'd like to add?
- Is there anything you don't agree with?

> Should individuals be free to decide whether or not to do the following things – or should there be laws to control them?
>
> | | |
> |---|---|
> | drink alcohol at any age | drive at any speed |
> | take drugs | have an abortion |
> | do military service | immigrate into your country |
> | wear seat belts in cars | own a gun |

In Part 3 of the Speaking Paper you'll have to speak for two minutes about a topic you are given. You don't have time to prepare a talk, so this is quite hard to do. You have to express your opinions and develop the topic. This is something you can practise on your own at home, preferably using a cassette recorder with a microphone.

After both candidates have spoken and answered follow-up questions, the interlocutor leads a general discussion on a related topic.

8.10 Long and short sentences WRITING SKILLS

 A Read this magazine article and then discuss the questions below:

These are bad times for talking. According to a recent study, dinnertime conversation is disappearing, with people now preferring to eat meals in front of the television. "Social conversation will soon be a thing of the past," said one researcher. It already is in Australia, where one couple haven't spoken to each other for 43 years. Doris and Ivan Weeds stopped communicating in 1954, shortly after their marriage. "We talked incessantly when we were courting," recalled Mrs Weeds, "and I guess we just said everything we had to." They've since lived in near total silence, chattering away happily to friends, but saying nothing whatsoever to each other. Early in the Seventies Mr Weeds did break his silence to ask his wife if she wanted to go to Thailand, and she broke hers to say no, but otherwise all has been mutual muteness, a fact which, insists Mrs Weeds, in no way affects their love for each other. "There are many ways of saying, 'I love you' without actually saying it," she explained, "like blowing kisses, and tap dancing together."

Paul Sussman

1 Which is the shortest sentence? What is the effect of this?
2 Which is the longest sentence? How many different ideas and clauses are there in that sentence? What is the effect of this?
3 How much is direct speech used? (How would the effect be different if reported speech had been used instead?)

 B Re-read the first TWO paragraphs of *Flying too close to the sun* on page 86 and *Cream and punishment* on page 88.
Then discuss the same questions.

C **1** ✏ Rewrite these notes, using a suitable mixture of long and short sentences, and direct or reported speech.

Possibly worst day in history of crime - Miami thief Natron Fubble, 35 - 'World's Most Inept Robber'

Early morning raid on delicatessen - shop owner hit Mr Fubble with giant salami - broke his nose

Attempted bank robbery - met mother in same bank - sent to do shopping for her

Climax: late in afternoon - another failed hold-up - pursued by irate customers - hid in boot of empty car - car was police surveillance vehicle - owners returned from cup of coffee - drove 5 days across America tailing lorry

Whimpers eventually heard near Seattle - removed at gunpoint, arrested

Sentenced to two years - despite claim: 'On top-secret undercover mission for FBI'

2 👥 Read each other's stories. What are the best features of each?

3 ✏ Write a final version, combining the best features of the versions you've read.

Shorter sentences tend to be easier to understand (and easier to write) than long ones, but lots and lots of very short sentences may look silly. 'A good balance' of long and short sentences is preferable.

Put yourself in your reader's position as you write and bear in mind these questions:

'Would I like to be reading this?'   'Have I made my meaning clear?'

8.11 **Points of view**

SPEAKING AND COMPOSITION

A **1** 👥 The class is divided into an even number of pairs (or groups of three). Half the pairs should work out together how they would tell the story of what happened in the photos from the point of view of the person on the LEFT of each photo – the other half from the point of view of the person on the RIGHT of each photo.

2 👥 → 👥 Then each 'left-hand' pair joins a 'right-hand' pair to tell their stories.

B **1** Find an interesting news story in a newspaper – it can be in your own language, not in English – preferably one involving more than one person. Alternatively, you may prefer to use a photograph instead.

2 Make notes on the events that occurred. Don't attempt to translate the article into English but use your own words.

3 ✎ Write a report to the police on what happened, from the point of view of one of the protagonists (300–350 words). Use section headings in your report.

8.12 *bring* and *get*　　　　　　　　　　**VERBS AND IDIOMS**

A Explain the phrases in red, or find synonyms. Use a dictionary if necessary.

1　Talking to her really brought it home to me how important it is to bring children up in the right way. They shouldn't be allowed to get away with bad behaviour.
2　Whatever brought this problem about, we must get round it somehow.
3　They hope to get over their difficulties by bringing in a management consultant.
4　Her attitude brings out the worst in me, I'm afraid. I just can't get on with her. The whole situation's really getting me down.
5　He told an anecdote which brought the house down. But I didn't get the joke.
6　He gets terribly upset when he thinks people are getting at him, but he usually gets over it fairly quickly.
7　I've been cheated and I want to get my own back. How can I get even with them?
8　Time's getting on, I think we'd better get the meeting over with.
9　It was hard to get it across to them that they had to work harder.
10　What did he mean? I really didn't understand what he was getting at.
11　He's terribly gauche and shy with strangers, he needs someone to bring him out.
12　'I had a terrible night: I didn't manage to get off to sleep till 3 a.m. I was so worried about getting behind with my work.'
　　'You should have got up and got on with some reading. You could have got through quite a lot during that time.'

B Fill the gaps with suitable phrases from the list below. You may need to change the form of the verbs.

1　She's a very gregarious person and seems to .... everyone.
2　I promised to go food shopping for them and now I can't .... it.
3　Was it because they pleaded guilty that they .... a fine, instead of a jail sentence? Or was it because the judge had been .... ?
4　There's no point in having good ideas if you don't .... them .... in writing.
5　The UN intervention .... a peaceful settlement of the conflict.
6　If you want to .... in politics you have to have the right connections and .... the people who matter.
7　I'm sorry to .... the subject of politics, I know it's a sore point with you.
8　I know how to handle him, so leave it to me – I'll be able to .... him.
9　I haven't done the work yet and I don't know when I'll .... it.
10　I have to be at work early tomorrow, can you .... me .... at 5.30?
11　I'm sorry to .... this .... – I know it's embarrassing.
12　What have the children been .... while I've been away?

bring about　　bring up
get at　　get down　　get in with
get off with　　get on　　get on to
get on with　　get out of　　get round
get round to　　get up　　get up to

9

A learning curve

9.1 Happy days?   LISTENING AND TOPIC VOCABULARY

A 🔊 **You'll hear three people remembering their schooldays. Fill the gaps in these notes:**

1 **Ruth**, at her comprehensive school in Wales, hated .... lessons because the teacher, Mr James, seemed to .... She didn't like .... because at 14 she didn't appreciate the .... of science.

2 **Sarah**'s favourite subject at her school in England was .... The teacher not only had a passion for her .... but also ....

3 **Christine** describes four phases in the way the girls viewed the boys at her school in Scotland:
   a From the ages of 5 to 10 she thought the boys were ....
   b From 10½ to 14 the girls thought the boys were ....
   c At 14 or 15 they admired the older boys but their contemporaries were ....
   d In the sixth form the boys and girls formed lovely ....

4 **Christine** remembers Miss Rae, who was a .... Pupils who made spelling mistakes were .... Anne Black was punished because she was .... and she spelt words in the way she .... them. Since that time Christine has always .... of teachers intimidating pupils.

B 👥👥 **Compare your reactions to the interviews:**
   • Did you have any similar experiences at school?
   • What is the point of going to school? What should the aims of education be?
   • Is it better to specialise or to have a broad education?
   • What should be the balance between a theoretical, academic approach and a more practical, vocational education?

C 👥 **Discuss which of these words and phrases have similar meanings, or are used in similar situations. In some cases there are various ways of linking them. <u>Underline</u> one word in each list which seems to be the odd one out and is NOT connected with education or training.**

1 award   grant   loan   prize   <u>reward</u>   scholarship
award → grant → scholarship   grant → loan   prize → award
reward isn't connected with education, unless discussing its rewards or pleasures

2 certificate   degree   diploma   doctorate   licence   recommendation
reference   testimonial

3 article   assignment   composition   dissertation   essay   paper   report   thesis

4 comprehensive school   grammar school   gymnasium   junior school   kindergarten
law school   medical school   nursery school   primary school   secondary school

5 BA   bachelor   BSc   doctorate   first degree   MA   master's   MSc   PhD

6 credits   grades   marks   numbers   scores

7 continuous assessment   evaluation   examination   questionnaire   study   test

8 class   conference   lecture   seminar   study group

9 apprentice   contestant   freshman   graduate
participant   post-graduate   pupil   schoolchild
student   trainee   undergraduate

10 academic year   financial year   half-term   holiday
semester   term   vacation

11 correspondence course   degree course   distance learning course
evening course   part-time course   race course   sandwich course

12 associate professor   business associate   coach   don   instructor
lecturer   professor   teacher   trainer   tutor

D Look at the photos and discuss these questions:

- What are the pros and cons of the kinds of schools shown?
- What do you remember most fondly about being in primary school?
- Describe your favourite primary school teacher.
- What did/do you enjoy most at secondary school? What did you dislike most?
- Which were/are your favourite subjects? Why?
- Describe a typical school day for a secondary school pupil in your country.
- How much do you think on-line learning is replacing classrooms?

9.2 Writing an application   COMPOSITION

A Imagine that you are attending an interview for a job or for a place on a higher education course. Describe your own education to your partner, concentrating on your achievements and the qualifications you have attained. Take it in turns to be the interviewer.

B **1** Imagine that you are keen to apply for the scholarship in this advertisement. Note down some reasons why YOU would benefit from learning Japanese.

2 Compare your notes with a partner.

(If you *are* Japanese, write an application for a similar scholarship, offered by the same organisation, to learn another language, such as Spanish or German, but not English.)

SAKURA SCHOLARSHIP SCHEME

Learn Japanese in Japan

Sakura Scholarships offer students the opportunity of taking part in a three-month Japanese language course in the historic city of Kyoto. The Scholarship covers free accommodation, meals and tuition. Return air fares between their country of residence and Osaka are paid, and $1000 pocket money is also provided.

To apply for one of these Scholarships, you should write 300–350 words describing your own education so far, and giving reasons why you think you would benefit from participation in the Sakura Scholarship Scheme.

The closing date for applications is February 1. Applicants who have been selected for the short list will be notified by March 31. The final selection will be made on the basis of interviews held during May.

Applications are open to all students, regardless of age, sex or nationality, and are also welcome from people who are not currently full-time students.

Please send your application to Ms Kyoko Matsumoto, Sakura Scholarship Scheme, Sakura Trading Co, 200 East Avenue, London E9 7PS

3 Write an appropriately dazzling application for the scholarship (300–350 words).

A **1** Read this article, then look at the questions below and decide on your answers.

My lessons in the classroom

"You must be mad!" was the general comment of family, friends and colleagues. "Giving up a teaching post now, when there isn't much chance of finding another one, ever!   1

"And what about all that lovely money you're earning, and all those long holidays!"   2

But I had already come to my lonely decision, after months of concealed suffering. I knew I could no longer continue in the teaching profession. To wake in the morning with a fear of the day ahead, to force a hasty breakfast down an unwilling throat, and then set off for work with pounding heart and frozen face had become habitual, and I had turned to tranquillizers to help me along.   3

It had not always been as bad as this. Ten years ago I managed well enough, and the holidays for rest and recuperation used to come round just in time.   4

But I, in common with most other teachers, am enormously self-critical, and I knew now that I was no longer "managing". My classes were noisy, the children were not learning very much, my attempts to cope with changing teaching methods were patchy, I had run out of enjoyment and enthusiasm. It was time to stop.   5

But was it all my own failure? In fairness to myself, I don't think it was. I had plenty of ideas, I loved my subject, and, by and large, I liked children.   6

I had been idealistic. But the reality I faced was bored children, over-stimulated by video-watching the night before and tired out by a late bedtime. They were children who were given the wrong food at the wrong time, who came breakfast-less to school and then stuffed themselves with gum, crisps and sweets bought on the way; who were "high" with hunger in the lesson before lunchtime and giggled restlessly as the smell of chips from the school kitchen came wafting to all floors.   7

There were children who absorbed all the smutty side of sex before they were 10, and were constantly teasing and titillating each other; bright, hard-working little girls who changed, under the pressures of peer group and advertising, into assertive, screeching empty-heads, with make-up in their pencil cases and a magazine concealed on their desks.   8

Then there were the ones from difficult homes, such as Simon, whose parents had split up after many years together and who was not wanted by either – his tired eyes flickered all round when I tried to remonstrate with him privately, and his pale face never stopped twitching. But he could bring chaos to my lessons with his sniggerings and mutterings.   9

The rudeness I had to put up with, and the bad language, appalled me. I had no redress, as the only form of punishment available was a detention, which meant keeping myself in too.   10

Sometimes parents could be contacted, and their help sought, but frequently they were as bewildered and incapacitated as we ourselves.   11

A frequent image came before me, as I lay in bed after an early wakening – the maths room, after a "wet break", chairs turned over, books and orange peel on the floor.   12

The tenth year are due for their English lesson, so I come in and attempt to assert myself and restore order. Jeremy is telling jokes. Donna is cackling. Andrew is standing on a desk and yelling out of the window.   13

At one time my very presence in the doorway would have been enough to ensure a partial silence. Now they give a vague "Hello, Miss", and carry on.   14

I distribute the work sheets, expensively photocopied, and we try to start, but two slow girls are making noises: "Miss, I can't understand this!" And James is quietly reading his football magazine, Jeremy continues to tell jokes, more quietly now, and Michele bares her gum-filled teeth and urges Paul to shut his face.   15

I have been trying to create the basic conditions in which teaching becomes possible, but I have failed, and no longer have the stomach for the job. And that is why I'm giving up.   16

Anne Bonsall

2 Highlight the relevant information in the passage. Make notes on your answers to these questions

1 Why were the writer's friends and family taken by surprise?
2 Why was the writer's heart pounding as she set off for work?
3 How well had she managed to adapt to new methods during her ten years' teaching?
4 Why did the hard-working little girls change?

5   Why was the writer unwilling to punish pupils who misbehaved?
6   Who are referred to as *we ourselves* in ¶11?
7   How do the tenth year English class react to the writer's entry into the room?
8   What is meant by *the stomach for the job* in the last line?

3 👤 → 👤 **Write down your answers to the questions. Compare your answers.**

B   Find words or phrases in the passage that mean the same as these:

beating loudly   incomplete   hungry   tell off   laughing disrespectfully
way of putting things right   unable to take action   exercise control   laughing shrilly

C   ✏ Why doesn't the writer blame her lack of success as a teacher on her own shortcomings? **Summarise the reasons in 50–70 words.**

MAKE NOTES on the reasons. Compare your notes with another pair, and make sure you have only noted down the relevant information. Then write your summary.

In Part 5 of the Use of English Paper, when writing a summary, remember that you should try to use your own words and not quote directly from the passage. Make sure that you only select the required information – you'll lose marks if you write more than 70 words.

9.4   **'It's just the most wonderful thing'**   **LISTENING**

A   🔊 You'll hear interviews with Sarah Wilson, a teacher at St Mary's School in Cambridge, and Claudine Kouzel, a sixth-former. Tick the boxes in Question 1 and write a word or short phrase in the boxes for Questions 2 to 8.

1   Sarah explains why she enjoys being a teacher.
    Tick the things she mentions:

the long holidays	☐	helping students to manage their work	☐
a good lesson	☐	working with people	☐
helping students to pass exams	☐	making a contribution to students' lives	☐
the funny things that happen	☐	finding quick solutions to students' problems	☐
communicating her love of English literature	☐		

2   She says she needs the holidays to ⬚⬚⬚ **2** who she is.

3   She doesn't like having to balance the needs of the ⬚⬚⬚ **3a**

    with the needs of the ⬚⬚⬚ **3b** .

4   She recommends teaching as a profession to someone who not only loves their

    ⬚⬚⬚ **4a** but also likes ⬚⬚⬚ **4b** .

5   Claudine is hoping to study ⬚⬚⬚ **5a** at university, but she

    doesn't know if she'll do a ⬚⬚⬚ **5b** before starting university.

6   Claudine enjoys school because she has her ⬚⬚⬚ **6a** around,

    and she has the ⬚⬚⬚ **6b** of her teachers.

7   It's hard for her to balance ⬚⬚⬚ **7a** activities with her heavy

    ⬚⬚⬚ **7b** .

8   She prefers a single-sex school because there are fewer ⬚⬚⬚ **8a** ,

    which helps her to ⬚⬚⬚ **8b** on her work.

B   👥👥 **Discuss these ideas:**

• Would you like to be a teacher? Why (not)?
• What are the differences between St Mary's School and Anne Bonsall's school in **9.3**?
• Is it usual for students to do a 'gap year' in your country? Why (not)?
• What are the qualities of a 'good student' or a 'good pupil'?

9.5 Question tags and negative questions GRAMMAR REVIEW

A 👥 **Discuss the differences in meaning or emphasis (if any) between the sentences.**

1 He didn't use to play squash, did he?   Didn't he use to play squash?
   He used to play squash, didn't he?   Did he use to play squash?
   He used to play squash, did he?

2 Isn't this a great party!   This is a great party, isn't it?
   This is a great party!   What a great party!

3 So you enjoyed my talk, did you?   So didn't you enjoy my talk?
   So you didn't enjoy my talk?   So did you enjoy my talk?

4 Isn't it strange that everyone thinks they are experts on education?
   It's strange that everyone thinks they are experts on education.

5 Didn't she do well in her exam!   Didn't she do well in her exam?
   She did very well in her exam.   Did she do well in her exam?
   How did she do in her exam?

B **Add question tags to these sentences. Then rewrite the first four sentences as negative questions.**

Apart from rhetorical questions, question tags and negative questions are rare in writing, except in personal letters.

1 We'd better stop work soon, ... ?
2 I'm right about this, ... ?
3 You'd rather stay in bed than get up early, ... ?
4 Anyone can apply for the scholarship, ... ?
5 If we don't get a move on, there won't be much time left, ... ?
6 Let's have a rest, ... ?
7 Nobody anticipated what would happen, ... ?
8 Do try to relax, ... ?
9 He never used to study so hard, ... ?
10 They ought to work much harder, ... ?

C 🔊 **Listen to the recording and decide whether the speakers sound SURE or UNSURE about the information they're giving. You'll hear these examples first:**

This is a great par_{ty}, isn't _{it!} ↘   = I'm sure – but I want you to agree

He used to play _{squash,} didn't ^{he?} ↗   = I'm unsure – but I think you know

sure or unsure?   sure or unsure?

1	
2	
3	
4	
5	

6	
7	
8	
9	
10	

D **1** **Rewrite each sentence so that its meaning remains unchanged, using a question tag at the end, as in the example. The passive is required in each one.**

1 Experts are finding new ways of using computers all the time.   New uses ....
   New uses for computers are being found all the time, aren't they?

2 One day robots and computers will do all our work for us.   All our work ....

3 I don't think that computers could be installed in every classroom.   Computers ....

4 No one has yet invented a robot teacher.   No robot teachers ....

5 The government should pay teachers on results.   Teachers ....

6 Students' parents often support them.   Students ....

7 The government might raise the school-leaving age to 19.   The school-leaving ....

8 Schools would have to employ more teachers in that case.   More ....

2 **Rewrite each of your passive sentences as negative questions.**

Aren't new uses for computers being found all the time?

A **1** Look at the examples. What is the equivalent verb for each of the abstract nouns?

-ation	*evaluation evaluate* *recuperation recuperate* *cooperation* *administration*
-ion	*detention detain* *destruction* *satisfaction* *suspicion*
-ment	*accomplishment* *astonishment* *enjoyment* *punishment*

2 Form abstract nouns from these verbs, adding them to the appropriate list above.

apply   achieve   acknowledge   amuse   concentrate
contribute   describe   embarrass   encourage   explain
invent   isolate   justify   manage   negotiate   object
oppose   pronounce   receive   recommend   represent   vary

B **1** Look at the examples. What is the equivalent adjective or noun for each of the abstract nouns?

-ty	*anxiety anxious* *reality real* *humility* *seniority*
-ance	*brilliance brilliant* *insignificance* *intolerance*
-ence	*absence* *presence* *intelligence* *reference*
-ism	*realism* *absenteeism* *nationalism* *optimism*
-ness	*clumsiness* *fairness* *happiness* *rudeness*
-ship	*apprenticeship* *relationship* *scholarship* *sponsorship*

2 Form abstract nouns from these adjectives and nouns, adding them to the appropriate list above.

authentic   available   careless   companion   creative   diffident   equal
extravagant   familiar   favourite   friend   generous   half-hearted
honest   incompetent   inconvenient   independent   insolent   leader
loyal   mischievous   narrow-minded   productive   professional
relevant   reliable   self-confident   selfish   stable   symbolic

C → Add two more nouns to each group in A and B, then compare your ideas with another pair.

D What adjective is each of these nouns associated with, or derived from?

-dom	*wisdom wise* *boredom* *freedom*
-th	*breadth* *filth* *health* *length* *stealth* *strength* *warmth* *wealth* *width*
-cy	*democracy* *bureaucracy* *delicacy* *efficiency* *fluency* *frequency* *inadequacy* *inefficiency* *redundancy* *urgency*
and ...	*delight delighted* *enthusiasm* *hysteria* *hunger* *pride* *sarcasm* *success*

E Fill the gaps in these sentences with suitable nouns from A, B and D:

1 They apologized for the .... we had been caused.
2 We were sceptical about the .... of the statistics he had quoted.
3 She was full of .... for her job and her talk included a fascinating .... of a typical day's work.
4 Contending with .... in government offices leads to .... and delays.
5 Teachers should not show .... to individual pupils – their motto should be .... to each child and they should encourage .... among their pupils.
6 I didn't quite see the .... of the answer he gave and I asked him to give us some .... for it. His .... was totally convincing.
7 I have all the right .... for the job but I don't know what the salary will be, because the advertisement says that it's 'subject to .... '.
8 They want me to supply them with three character .... , as they are particularly interested in my qualities of ....
9 Two things I disapprove of are .... and ....
10 Two qualities I appreciate in a person are .... and ....

A Read this article and then answer the multiple-choice questions opposite:

Managing your study time

1   I was in a student coffee bar during my first week at university soaking in the atmosphere when a lad from Oldham, of conspicuously cool and languid manner, announced calmly that he intended to get a first in classics. He would work 25 hours a week, study five hours a day on weekdays and leave the weekends free. That would be sufficient.

2   I was vaguely committed to endless hours of work. I imagined that at some point I would spend weeks of intensive study. The vice-chancellor had told us in his address to freshers to look at the person on either side and note that in all probability one of us would not be around the following year. The message struck home: I would turn myself into a paragon of academic virtue. I could see that the classicist in the coffee bar had got it all wrong, or was bluffing.

3   Three years later he sailed to his first whilst other friends struggled to very modest achievements. As I discovered when sharing his lodgings, he worked more or less to the plan he had outlined. He slept late in the mornings, only stirring himself if there was a lecture to attend. He played cards with the rest of us after lunch. Then he moved to his desk and stayed there till around seven. The evenings he spent more wildly than most – hence the late mornings. Nevertheless, when I came to look back I realised he had studied more than anyone else I knew. Through sticking assiduously to a modest but well-defined, realistic plan, he had achieved a great deal. He had enjoyed work much more, too. He argued that it was not possible to work productively at intensive intellectual tasks for more than a few hours at a time. I aimed to do much more. But I was easily distracted. By the time it was apparent that stretches of a day had slipped away, I felt so guilty that I blotted studies out of my mind, comforting myself with the thought of all the days which lay ahead.

4   I was too inexperienced at looking after my own affairs to realise I was already failing one of the major tests of studenthood, the organisation of time. I thought that success in studying was to do with how brilliantly clever and original you were; I had yet to discover that one of the central challenges of adult life is time management.

5   At school the work timetable was defined for us and teachers made sure we fitted all that was required into the school year. At university I was at sea. Time came in great undifferentiated swathes. What to do with it all? With 168 hours in a week — or 105, allowing nine a day for sleeping and eating — how many was it reasonable to spend on study? Individuals vary and different subjects make different demands. Nevertheless with a target you can plan your studies, not just stumble ahead in hope. The sketchiest of weekly timetables, setting aside 40 hours to cover all study, is an invaluable aid in defining time. Then you can divide it into segments and use it strategically, rather than let it dribble away.

6   Defining what to do is harder. Take the booklists. How many books are students expected to read? How long should a book take? It took me so long to read just a few pages that I felt defeated when I looked ahead. Should I take notes? How many? What would I need them for?

7   I would sit in the library for a whole day, dipping into one book after another, often with glazed over eyes. What was my purpose? How would I know when I had achieved it? By comparison I went to lectures gratefully – at least I knew when they started and finished. Although my lecture notes weren't up to much, I could tell myself I had accomplished something, which would bring down my anxiety level.

8   Much later I discovered I could learn a great deal from a close reading of selected sections; that taking notes could sometimes be very satisfying and at other times was not necessary. The trick was to take control; to decide what I wanted to find out – something specific – and then work at it until I had taken in enough to think about for the time being.

9   Dividing big jobs into smaller sub-tasks helps to bring work under control, allows you to set targets and check your progress. There is so much pressure to be ambitious – to go for the long dissertation, to read the huge tomes. Yet achievement arises out of quite modest activities undertaken on a small scale. The trouble with the big tasks is that you keep putting them off. Their scope and shape is unclear and we all flee from uncertainty. The more you can define your work as small, discrete, concrete tasks, the more control you have over it.

10   Organising tasks into the time available can itself be divided into strategy and application. It is useful to think of yourself as "investing" time. Some tasks require intense concentration and need to be done at a prime time of day, when you are at your best and have time to spare. Others can be fitted in when you are tired, or as "warm-up" activities at the start of a session. Some, such as essay writing, may best be spread over several days. Some need to be done straight away.

11   There are few reliable guidelines. Essentially you have to keep circling round a self-monitoring loop: plan an approach to a task, try it out, reflect afterwards on your success in achieving what you intended and then revise your strategy.

12   Once you start to think strategically, you begin to take control of your studies rather than letting them swamp you.

Andrew Northedge

Choose the word or phrase which best completes each sentence:

1 The vice-chancellor's speech .... the writer.
   a amused   **b** failed to convince   **c** frightened   **d** terrified

2 The lad from Oldham's time at university was .... than the writer's.
   a less successful   **b** more fun   **c** more intellectual   **d** more strenuous

3 While he was in the university library the writer ....
   a couldn't concentrate   **c** read books from cover to cover
   b dozed off   **d** worked hard

4 Towards the end of his time at university the writer ....
   a gave up hope   **c** worked harder
   b organised himself better   **d** wrote a long dissertation

5 The writer recommends ....
   a studying for a short time every day   **c** finishing one task before starting another
   b studying only when you are alert   **d** deciding when each kind of task is best done

6 *Circling round a self-monitoring loop* (¶11) means ....
   a approaching studies in a circuitous way   **c** continuing to study for a long time
   b planning your study methods   **d** evaluating the success of your study methods

B Highlight these words and phrases in the passage, and use a dictionary to look up the meanings of any you are unsure of. Make sure you look at the examples given as well as the definitions. Then look again at the words in context.

   bluffing (¶2)   assiduously (¶3)   blotted out (¶3)   at sea (¶5)   segments (¶5)   strategically (¶5)
   dribble away (¶5)   dipping into (¶7)   glazed over (¶7)   prime (¶10)   swamp (¶12)

C 👥 → 👥 Highlight FOUR phrases in the passage which you consider to be key phrases. Then compare your ideas with another pair and discuss these questions:

- Which of the advice given in the passage do you agree with?
- Which do you already follow? Which ought you to follow?
- How does a British university, as described in the passage, differ from a university in your country?

9.8 Reporting – 2   **ADVANCED GRAMMAR**

A 👥 Each of the statements on the left is reported in two different ways. What is the difference in emphasis between the two reports on the right?

1 "I'll be arriving tomorrow."   He told me that he would be arriving tomorrow.
                               He told me that he would be arriving the next day.

2 "You should spend more   She advised me to spend more time reading.
   time reading."   She urged me to spend more time reading.

3 "I don't think your plan   He dismissed my plan as unrealistic.
   will work."   He had doubts about the effectiveness of my plan.

4 "I'll phone them soon."   He promised to make the call soon.
                               He said that he was going to make the call soon.

5 "You're absolutely right."   She agreed.
                               She assured me that I was right.

B 1 🔊 You'll hear the same words spoken in five different ways, each conveying a different attitude or mood. Select ONE adjective to describe each attitude:

1	
2	
3	
4	
5	

amazed   *angry*   *depressed*

diffident   *disappointed*   *impressed*

half-hearted   *heart-broken*

hysterical   *sarcastic*   *shocked*

2 Write four sentences SUMMARISING what Speakers 2 to 5 said, imagining that you were the person addressed. For example:

   1 The first speaker complained that my work hadn't improved and compared it unfavourably with everyone else's.

C 👤→👤 **Use these verbs to report what the people said in as few words as possible. Then compare your sentences with a partner's.**

assure   claim   congratulate   disagree   deny✓   insist   promise   remind   regret   reproach   suggest   warn

1   "No, it wasn't me. I didn't borrow your bike."   *She denied borrowing my bike.*
2   "I'll let you know as soon as they get here. OK?"
3   "Don't forget: you've got to hand in your work this evening."
4   "It's a shame you couldn't make it to the party last night."
5   "Well done! I always thought you'd pass."
6   "Don't worry, as long as you keep your head, you'll manage all right."
7   "You really must come and visit us next weekend!"
8   "I don't really think that what you said makes sense."
9   "If you park on this double yellow line, you'll get a ticket."
10   "You shouldn't have behaved like that. You should be ashamed of yourself."
11   "If I had more time, I'd help you with your work."
12   "Might it be a good idea if we all organised our time more efficiently?"

9.9 Progressive v. traditional methods

LISTENING AND
COMPOSITION

A 1 👥 **Read this description of Summerhill School, then discuss these questions:**

• What might you like and dislike about attending Summerhill?
• What do you think the drawbacks of Neill's approach might be?

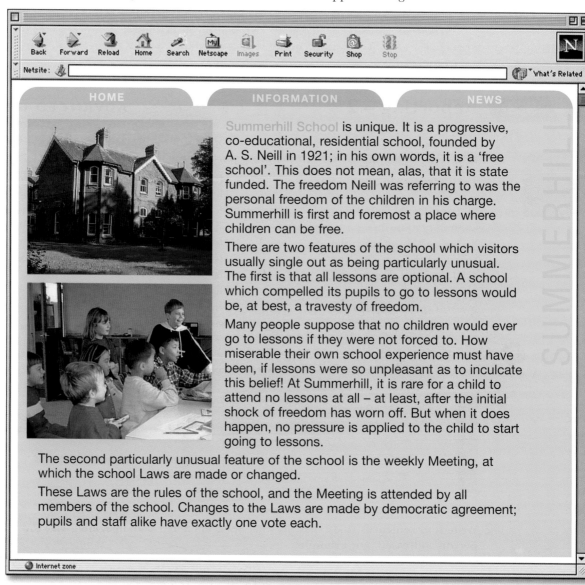

HOME   INFORMATION   NEWS

Summerhill School is unique. It is a progressive, co-educational, residential school, founded by A. S. Neill in 1921; in his own words, it is a 'free school'. This does not mean, alas, that it is state funded. The freedom Neill was referring to was the personal freedom of the children in his charge. Summerhill is first and foremost a place where children can be free.

There are two features of the school which visitors usually single out as being particularly unusual. The first is that all lessons are optional. A school which compelled its pupils to go to lessons would be, at best, a travesty of freedom.

Many people suppose that no children would ever go to lessons if they were not forced to. How miserable their own school experience must have been, if lessons were so unpleasant as to inculcate this belief! At Summerhill, it is rare for a child to attend no lessons at all – at least, after the initial shock of freedom has worn off. But when it does happen, no pressure is applied to the child to start going to lessons.

The second particularly unusual feature of the school is the weekly Meeting, at which the school Laws are made or changed.

These Laws are the rules of the school, and the Meeting is attended by all members of the school. Changes to the Laws are made by democratic agreement; pupils and staff alike have exactly one vote each.

2  Beth Titchener is a pupil at Summerhill, Michael Newman is a teacher there. Listen to the interviews and choose the best answer for each of the questions.

Beth Titchener

1 Beth enjoys being a pupil at Summerhill because she can
  a skip lessons **b** make her own decisions **c** speak at the Meetings `[ 1 ]`
2 She left her previous school because it
  a was boring **b** didn't give her enough freedom **c** made her unhappy `[ 2 ]`
3 She attended all the Japanese lessons because
  a she wanted to understand her Japanese friends **b** the lessons were interesting
  c she thought Japanese lessons would be fun `[ 3 ]`
4 Because pupils at Summerhill come from many different countries
  a British pupils are outnumbered **b** not everyone can speak English well
  c everyone is valued as an individual `[ 4 ]`

Michael Newman

5 Michael enjoys teaching at Summerhill because
  a it's easy to control the classes **b** the teachers and kids are friends
  c everyone gets on really well with each other `[ 5 ]`
6 To an outside observer his English lessons would
  a seem chaotic **b** appear disorganised **c** not seem unusual `[ 6 ]`
7 Michael's previous job was teaching English
  a to Italians **b** in an English grammar school **c** in a community school `[ 7 ]`
8 At the Meetings, Summerhill pupils learn how to
  a speak in public **b** value the opinions of younger pupils
  c make decisions about moral issues `[ 8 ]`

3 Discuss these questions:

- What are your views on Summerhill and similar schools?
- Would you send your children to such a school? Give your reasons.
- What features of Summerhill ought to be a part of mainstream schools?
- What are your views on progressive v. traditional teaching methods?
- What are your views on comprehensive v. selective schools?

B In this section we'll concentrate on making and using notes when writing a composition with the clock running. Keep a record of how long each of the following steps takes you:

1 MAKE NOTES for an essay on this topic:

Give your views on progressive versus traditional methods of education (300–350 words).

2 EDIT your notes: eliminate the irrelevant points and the less important points. Decide on the best sequence of points.

3 Write your essay, timing yourself to see how long the whole process takes.

In the exam you'll have two hours to write two compositions, but this includes the time you need to decide which topics to choose, and time to check your work through for mistakes afterwards. Ideally, though, planning (including writing your notes) and actually writing each composition should take no longer than 50 minutes. It's not wise to allow a full hour for both.

"I had all the right answers, but I had them in the wrong order."

10 Mother nature

A 1 🏃🏃🏃🏃 **Discuss these questions:**

- What are your reactions to the two pictures? What are the implied attitudes to animals, nature and the countryside?
- Do you have any pets at home – or do any of your relatives have them?
- To what extent would you describe yourself as an animal-lover or a nature-lover?
- In what ways do you try to be 'environmentally friendly'?

2 Note down TEN vocabulary items connected with the topic of this unit.

B 1 👥 **Choose one word that best completes each of the sentences:**

1 Many species of animals and plants today are ....
  dangerous   endangered   precarious   risked   risky

2 Modern farm animals and crops are the result of centuries of selective ....
  breeding   cultivation   education   mating   reproduction

3 It took a long time for the theory of evolution to be ....
  absorbed   accepted   acknowledged   tolerated

4 My friend is a keen amateur ....
  natural historian   naturist   naturalist   nationalist

5 He gets very .... about experiments being carried out on live animals.
  worked down   worked out   worked over   worked up

6 One of the effects of acid rain is that it causes plants to ....
  contract   flourish   shrink   thrive   wither

7 Waste paper can be .... instead of being burnt.
  decomposed   incinerated   recycled   revamped

8 There are over 850,000 named .... of insects on this planet.
  colonies   families   species   styles   varieties

9 Rabbits and mice are ....
  amphibians   carnivores   marsupials   rodents

10 Crocodiles and alligators are ....
  crustaceans   herbivores   mammals   reptiles

11 The lioness lay in wait for her ....
  game   lunch   prey   target   victim

12 Cattle and chickens are .... animals.
  domestic   domesticated   house-trained   obedient   tame   wild

13 Rats, mice and cockroaches are usually considered to be ....

    pets   cuddly   mischievous   vermin   weeds

14 Your cat has scratched me with its ....

    claws   fangs   hoofs   nails   paws   pincers   whiskers

15 We all admired the parrot's beautiful ....

    coat   bark   fleece   fur   hide   plumage

16 Many insects, such as wasps and ants, use their .... to touch objects.

    aerials   antlers   feelers   horns   whiskers

17 We saw a huge .... of birds through our binoculars.

    crowd   flock   herd   pack   shoal   swarm

18 Squirrels and rabbits are .... little creatures.

    amiable   courteous   delicious   elegant   endearing   extravagant   fierce   tasty

2 Look again at the words that you DIDN'T use in the gaps. Why is each wrong in the context? Highlight any of them that you want to remember.

10.2 'Our cousins in the ocean'   LISTENING

A 👥 You'll hear an interview with Ray Gamble, an expert on whales. Before you hear it, discuss with your partner what you already know about whales.

B 1 🔊 In the first part of the interview you'll hear about different people's attitudes to 'saving the whales'. Answer these multiple-choice questions.

1 The Inuit peoples (Eskimos) of the Arctic ...
    a hunt whales together for enjoyment
    b would die out if they didn't hunt whales
    c depend on whale meat and products for their survival
    d don't actually like the taste of whale meat

2 When Ray watched Eskimos hunting whales he found the experience ...
    a sickening   **b** fascinating   **c** shocking   **d** unsettling

3 To Western people today the whale represents the idea of
    a beauty   **b** freedom   **c** pleasure   **d** food

4 For Western people, the whale is no longer thought of as a source of ...
    a meat   **b** oil   **c** raw materials   **d** wonder

5 Nowadays Western people view commercial whale hunters as ...
    a brutal   **b** primitive   **c** distasteful   **d** profitable

2 🔊 In the second part of the interview, Ray talks about why he thinks whales are exciting animals. Put a tick beside the reasons he gives.

he feels an inexplicable affinity with them ☐	their brains are large ☐
they have feelings like human beings ☐	all whales are enormous ☐
they can move in spectacular ways ☐	they can perform tricks ☐
they can communicate with each other ☐	they may be on the verge of extinction ☐
some whales are impressively large ☐	they are perfectly suited to living in the sea ☐

C 👥👥 Discuss your reactions to the recording.

- What other species do you know about which are endangered?
- Why is it important that endangered animals and plants don't become extinct?
- How can endangered species be protected?

10.3 The Third Chimpanzee

A **1** Read this text and then answer the questions opposite:

It is obvious that humans are unlike all animals. It is also obvious that we are a species of big mammal, down to the minutest details of our anatomy and our molecules. That contradiction is the most fascinating feature of the human species. It is familiar, but we still have difficulty grasping how it came to be and what it means.

On the one hand, between ourselves and all other species lies a seemingly unbridgeable gulf that we acknowledge by defining a category called 'animals'. It implies that we consider centipedes, chimpanzees and clams to share decisive features with each other but not with us, and to lack features restricted to us. Among these characteristics unique to us are the abilities to talk, write, and build complex machines. We depend completely on tools, not just on our bare hands, to make a living. Most of us wear clothes and enjoy art, and many of us believe in a religion. We are distributed over the whole Earth, command much of its energy and production, and are beginning to expand into the ocean depths and into space. We are also unique in darker attributes, including genocide, delight in torture, addictions to toxic drugs, and extermination of other species by the thousands. While a few animal species have one or two of these attributes in rudimentary form (like tool use), we still far eclipse animals even in those respects.

Thus, for practical and legal purposes, humans are not animals. When Darwin intimated in 1859 that we had evolved from apes, it is no wonder that most people initially regarded his theory as absurd and continued to insist that we had been separately created by God. Many people, including a quarter of all American college graduates, still hold to that belief today.

On the other hand, we obviously are animals, with the usual animal body parts, molecules and genes. It is even clear what particular type of animal we are. Externally, we are so similar to chimpanzees that eighteenth-century anatomists who believed in divine creation could already recognize our affinities. Just imagine taking some normal people, stripping off their clothes, taking away all their other possessions, depriving them of the power of speech, and reducing them to grunting, without changing their anatomy at all. Put them in a cage in the zoo next to the chimp cages, and let the rest of us clothed and talking people visit the zoo. Those speechless caged people would be seen for what we all really are: a chimp that has little hair and walks upright. A zoologist from outer space would immediately classify us as just a third species of chimpanzee, along with the pygmy chimp of Zaire and the common chimp of the rest of tropical Africa.

Molecular genetic studies over the last half-a-dozen years have shown that we continue to share over ninety-eight per cent of our genes with the other two chimps. The overall genetic distance between us and chimps is even smaller than the distance between such closely related bird species as red-eyed and white-eyed vireos, or willow warblers and chiffchaffs. So we still carry most of our old biological baggage with us. Since Darwin's time, fossilized bones of hundreds of creatures variously intermediate between apes and modern humans have been discovered, making it impossible for a reasonable person to deny the overwhelming evidence. What once seemed absurd – our evolution from apes – actually happened.

Yet the discoveries of many missing links have only made the problem more fascinating, without fully solving it. The few bits of new baggage we acquired – the two per cent of our genes that differ from those of chimps – must have been responsible for all of our seemingly unique properties. We underwent some small changes with big consequences rather quickly and recently in our evolutionary history. In fact, as recently as a hundred thousand years ago that zoologist from outer space would have viewed us as just one more species of big mammal. Granted, we had a couple of curious behavioural habits, notably our control of fire and our dependence on tools, but those habits would have seemed no more curious to the extraterrestrial visitor than would the habits of beavers and bowerbirds. Somehow, within a few tens of thousands of years – a time that is almost infinitely long when measured against one person's memory but is only a tiny fraction of our species' separate history – we had begun to demonstrate the qualities that make us unique and fragile.

What were those few key ingredients that made us human? Since our unique properties appeared so recently and involved so few changes, those properties or at least their precursors must already be present in animals. What are those animal precursors of art and language, of genocide and drug abuse?

Our unique qualities have been responsible for our present biological success as a species. No other large animal is native to all the continents, or breeds in all habitats from deserts and the Arctic to tropical rainforests. No large wild animal rivals us in numbers. But among our unique qualities are two that now jeopardize our existence: our propensities to kill each other and to destroy our environment. Of course, both propensities occur in other species: lions and many other animals kill their own kind, while elephants and others damage their environment. However, these propensities are much more threatening in us than in other animals because of our technological power and exploding numbers.

from *The Rise and Fall of the Third Chimpanzee* – Jared Diamond

Write your answers to these questions:

1 What are the other two species of chimpanzee?
2 How is the human use of tools different from the way other animals use them?
3 Which other creatures can be found in every continent?
4 Which other creatures kill members of the same species?
5 Which other creatures do harm to their environment?

6 Summarise the reasons why a zoologist from outer space would classify humans as a third species of chimpanzee (50–70 words).

2 **Compare your answers.**

B **Find words in the passage with similar meanings to these words and phrases and** highlight **them in context:**

¶1   very smallest
¶2   difference   more evil   characteristics   primitive   outdo
¶3   suggested   at first
¶4   resemblances   making incoherent sounds
¶5 & 6 influences
¶7   properties which existed before
¶8   tendencies

In the exam you can't use a dictionary – and there's no time to ponder over words you don't understand. So, when there are unfamiliar words in a text, you have to guess what they mean – and hope for the best. But only bother do do this if the words are relevant to a particular question.

10.4 **Conditionals – 1**   **GRAMMAR REVIEW**

A  **Discuss any differences in meaning or emphasis between these sentences:**

1 I feel upset when I think about the destruction of the rainforests.
   I'd feel upset when I thought about people destroying the rainforests.
   I'd feel upset if I thought about the rainforests being destroyed.
   I feel upset if I think about the destruction of tropical rainforests.
   I felt upset when I thought about jungles being destroyed.

2 If you don't leave now, you'll be late.
   If you leave now, you won't be late.
   If you left now, you wouldn't be late.
   If you didn't leave now, you'd be late.
   Unless you leave now, you'll be late.

3 If you're interested I'll tell you about my dream.
   If you were interested I'd tell you about my dream.

4 When I have time, I'll feed the cat.
   If I have time, I'll feed the goldfish.
   If I had time, I'd feed the ducks.
   If I had time, I'd have fed the birds.
   When I had time, I'd feed the rabbits.
   If I'd had time, I'd have fed the dog.

B **Rewrite each sentence, beginning each new sentence with** *If . . .* **, keeping the meaning as close as possible to the original sentence.**

1 Don't go too close to that dog in case it bites you.   If . . .
2 I couldn't give you a hand because I didn't realise that you needed help.   If . . .
3 The amount of carbon dioxide in the atmosphere must be reduced,
    otherwise the ozone layer will be permanently damaged.   If . . .
4 Forests once covered most of Europe, before they were cut down.   If . . .
5 Pollution is caused by ignorance about its effects on the environment.   If . . .
6 Animals can't speak in their own defence, so we must speak up for them.   If . . .
7 Everyone should drive more slowly so that there is less pollution.   If . . .
8 Without acid rain these lakes would still have fish in them.   If . . .

C Complete each sentence with your own ideas, as in the example.

1 Would you feel sick if *you had to eat raw fish?*
2 If he hadn't been so generous, ...
3 If you aren't careful, ...
4 If she doesn't phone me by Friday, ...
5 If everyone cared more about the environment, ...
6 If any species becomes extinct, ...
7 If human beings became extinct, ...
8 Unless the governments of the world cooperate, ...

D **1** 👥👥 **Discuss these questions:**

- What might happen if global warming continues?
- What might happen if everyone voted for the Green Party?
- What might happen if everyone stopped eating meat and fish?
- What might have happened if recycling hadn't become popular?

2 ✒ **Write a paragraph summarising your discussion. Compare your summary with another group.**

10.5 Showing your attitude

WRITING SKILLS

A The writer of this passage, a zoologist and zoo owner, wants to convince the reader of his views on zoos and safari parks.

Look at the highlighted examples, then decide which alternatives below fit best in gaps 1–8.

I must agree with you (if you are anti-zoo), that not all zoos are perfect. Of the 500 or so zoological collections in the world, a few are excellent, some are inferior and the rest are
¹ . Given the premises that zoos can and should be of value scientifically, educationally and from a conservation point of view (thus serving both us and other animal life), then I ²
that one should strive to make them better. I have had, ironically enough, a great many ³
opponents of zoos tell me that they would like all zoos closed down, yet the same people accept with equanimity the proliferation of safari parks, where, by and large, animals are ⁴ worse off than in the average zoo. An animal can be ⁵ unhappy, ⁶ ill-treated, in a vast area as in a small one, but the rolling vistas, the ⁷ trees, ⁸ criticism, for this is the only thing that these critics think the animals want.

1 appalling · bad   3 rabid · strong   5 equally · just as   7 ancient · old
2 believe · feel very strongly   4 far · much   6 as · just as   8 obliterate · prevent

B Highlight the words and phrases in the rest of the passage which show the writer's feelings, attitude and passionately held opinions.

It is odd how comforted people feel by seeing an animal in a large field. Safari parks were invented purely to make money. No thought of science or conservation sullied their primary conception. Like a rather unpleasant fungus, they have spread now throughout the world. In the main, their treatment of animals is disgraceful and the casualties (generally carefully concealed) appalling. I will not mention the motives, or the qualifications of the men who created them, for they are sufficiently obvious, but I would like to stress that I know it to be totally impossible to run these vast concerns with a knowledgeable and experienced staff, since that number of knowledgeable and experienced staff does not exist. I know, because I am always on the look-out for such rare beasts myself.

I am not against the conception of safari parks. I am against the way that they are at present run. In their present form, they represent a bigger hazard and a bigger drain on wild stocks of animals than any zoo ever has done. Safari parks, properly controlled and scientifically run, could be of immense conservation value for such things as antelope, deer and the larger carnivores. But they have a long way to go before they can be considered anything other than animal abattoirs in a sylvan setting.

I feel, therefore, that one should strive to make zoos and safari parks better, not simply clamour for their dissolution. If Florence Nightingale's sole contribution, when she discovered the appalling conditions in the hospitals of the last century, had been to advocate that they should all be closed down, few people in later years would have praised her for her acumen and far-sightedness.

My plan, then, is that all of us, zoo opponents and zoo lovers alike, should endeavour to make them perfect; should make sure that they are a help to animal species and not an additional burden on creatures already too hard pressed by our unbeatable competition. This can be done by being much more critical of zoos and other animal collections, thus making them more critical of themselves, so that even the few good ones will strive to be better.

from *The Stationary Ark* by Gerald Durrell

C **1** Here are more examples of words and phrases which show a writer's attitude. **Highlight** the ones that you would like to remember.

1 It is … that animals are kept in captivity.
appalling   disgraceful   dreadful   frightful   shocking   terrible   absurd
incomprehensible   odd   ridiculous   strange   ironic

2 Some zoos are … but most of them are … .
admirable   excellent   fine   praiseworthy   appalling   atrocious   disgraceful   dreadful
frightful   shocking

3 … something must be done as soon as possible.
Clearly   Obviously   Quite frankly   There is no doubt that   Undoubtedly
You must agree that   Without a shadow of doubt   As far as I'm concerned
I feel very strongly that   My view is that   I would like to stress that   It seems to me that
Personally I believe that   It is generally agreed that

4 … , there is a straightforward solution to this problem.
Ironically enough   Strangely enough   Oddly enough   Actually   In fact   In spite of this
Mind you   Nevertheless   Still

5 I … good zoos but I … bad ones.
am all in favour of   advocate   applaud   approve of   favour   support   am against
condemn   strongly disapprove of   object to   reject the idea of

2 Fill these gaps with words or phrases you highlighted in C1 above:

1 It is .... that most safari parks are simply money-making enterprises.
2 .... there are some zoos which are run to make a profit, but not all.
3 .... , some zoos are absolutely ....
4 I .... zoos as such – .... I enjoy a day at the zoo.
5 .... hunting animals is a(n) .... leisure activity.
6 .... there is nothing wrong with people having pets, ... keeping a large dog in a city apartment is ....

D Write a couple of paragraphs, giving your own views on ONE of these topics you feel strongly about:

Using animals in laboratories for testing cosmetics   Killing animals for 'sport'
Keeping large, fierce dogs as 'pets'   The destruction of the rainforests
Training animals to perform in circuses   Eating meat

10.6 Uses of the past   ADVANCED GRAMMAR

A 👥 Discuss the differences in meaning (if any) between these sentences:

1 I wish that dog would stop barking.   I wish that dog had stopped barking.
I wish that dog didn't bark.   I want that dog to stop barking.
2 It's time for you to do the washing-up.   It's time you did the washing-up.
3 If only it were Friday!   If it were only Friday …
Only if it was Friday …   If it's only Friday …
4 Would you rather I didn't help you?   Would you rather not help me?
Would you prefer it if I didn't help you?   Would you prefer me not to help you?
5 I was going to phone her tonight.   I intended to phone her tonight.
I am to phone her tonight.   I was to have phoned her tonight.
6 I wish I knew the answer.   I wish to know the answer.

B **Fill each gap with suitable words or phrases:**

1 I do wish you .... me when I'm trying to study.
2 It's high time something .... industry from polluting the environment.
3 You're very late! I'd prefer .... a little earlier next time.
4 If only people .... the dangers of global warming 20 years ago!
5 I wish .... ride a horse.
6 I wish there .... to save the whales.
7 We .... and see you on Sunday but there wasn't enough time.
8 What a noise you're making! I'd rather .... a bit more quietly.
9 Well, it's 9.30, do you think it's .... yet?
10 Isn't it time the cat ....? It looks very hungry.

10.7 **Biological diversity**   R E A D I N G

A **Read this passage and then answer the questions on the next page.**

So much to save

[1] THE idea of preserving biological diversity gives most people a warm feeling inside. But what, exactly, is diversity? And which kind is most worth preserving? It may be anathema to save-the-lot environmentalists who hate setting such priorities, but academics are starting to cook up answers.

[2] Andrew Solow, a mathematician at the Woods Hole Oceanographic Institution, and his colleagues argue that in the eyes of conservation, all species should not be equal. Even more controversially, they suggest that preserving the rarest is not always the best approach. Their measure of diversity is the amount of evolutionary distance between species. They reckon that if choices must be made, then the number of times that cousins are removed from one another should be one of the criteria.

[3] This makes sense from both a practical and an aesthetic point of view. Close relatives have many genes in common. If those genes might be medically or agriculturally valuable, saving one is nearly as good as saving both. And different forms are more interesting to admire and study than lots of things that look the same.

[4] Dr Solow's group illustrates its thesis with an example. Six species of crane are at some risk of extinction. Breeding in captivity might save them. But suppose there were only enough money to protect three. Which ones should be picked?

[5] The genetic distances between 14 species of cranes, including the six at risk, have already been established using a technique known as DNA hybridisation. The group estimated how likely it was that each of these 14 species would become extinct in the next 50 years. Unendangered species were assigned a 10% chance of meeting the Darwinian reaper-man; the most vulnerable, a 90% chance. Captive breeding was assumed to reduce an otherwise-endangered species' risk to the 10% level of the safest. Dr Solow's computer permed all possible combinations of three from six and came to the conclusion that protecting the Siberian, white-naped and black-necked cranes gave the smallest likely loss of biological diversity over the next five decades. The other three had close relatives in little need of protection. Even if they became extinct, most of their genes would be saved.

Building on the work of this group, Martin Weitzman, of Harvard University, argues that conservation policy needs to take account not only of some firm measure of the genetic relationships of species to each other and their likelihood of survival, but also the costs of preserving them. Where species are equally important in genetic terms, and – an important and improbable precondition – where the protection of one species can be assured at the expense of another, he argues for making safe species safer, rather than endangered species less endangered.

In practice, it is difficult to choose between species. Most of those at risk – especially plants, the group most likely to yield useful medicines – are under threat because their habitats are in trouble, not because they are being shot, or plucked, to extinction. Nor can conservationists choose among the millions of species that theory predicts must exist, but that have not yet been classified by the biologists assigned to that tedious task.

This is not necessarily cause for despair. At the moment, the usual way to save the genes in these creatures is to find the bits of the world with the largest number of species and try to protect them from the bulldozers. What economists require from biologists are more sophisticated ways to estimate the diversity of groups of organisms that happen to live together, as well as those which are related to each other. With clearer goals established, economic theory can then tell environmentalists where to go.

from The Economist

Answer these multiple-choice questions about the article:

1 Dr Solow believes that ....
   a all species should be saved   **c** very rare species can't be saved
   b all very rare species should be saved   **d** only some species are worth saving
2 Dr Solow's work depended on ....
   a previous biological research   **c** the premise that not all species are the same
   b the cost of preserving cranes   **d** the premise that all cranes should be protected
3 Endangered species of cranes can be saved by ....
   a keeping them in zoos or wildlife parks   **c** stopping hunters from killing them
   b protecting their habitats   **d** encouraging them to mate with their cousins
4 Three of the six species of endangered cranes ....
   a were so rare they couldn't be saved   **c** were less interesting to admire than others
   b could be allowed to become extinct   **d** shouldn't be protected
5 Dr Weitzman's ideas ....
   a disregard Dr Solow's   **c** take Dr Solow's ideas one step further
   b contradict Dr Solow's   **d** confirm Dr Solow's
6 Dr Weitzman believes that if two species are equally important genetically we should
   protect ....
   a the rarer one   **c** them both
   b the less endangered one   **d** the one that is more attractive
7 Most species are endangered because ....
   a they are hunted or picked   **c** we don't care enough about them
   b biologists haven't classified them   **d** the places they live in are being destroyed
8 According to the writer what has to be done first is for ....
   a biologists to instruct economists   **c** economists to instruct biologists
   b developers to stop destroying habitats **d** biologists to classify undiscovered species

---

When answering multiple-choice questions, it's sometimes easier to eliminate (and cross out) the wrong answers first, and *then* decide what
the right answers might be. Be careful though: sometimes it's the least likely looking answer that is actually right – especially if the writer holds
unconventional views, or if you're reading about an unfamiliar topic!

B   **Find words in the passage with similar meanings to these words and phrases and highlight
them:**

    ¶1 an unacceptable idea   formulate   ¶2 assert   ¶4 theory   ¶5 death   calculate
    ¶7 produce

10.8 *put* and *set*   **VERBS AND IDIOMS**

A   **Which of the following would be preceded by *put* and which by *set*?**

    pressure on someone   a trap for someone   your teeth on edge   two and two together
    someone at their ease   a question to someone   a stop to something   a good example
    someone in the picture   fire to something   your watch   pen to paper   the scene

B   **Find synonyms for the phrases in red, or explain their meaning. Use a dictionary if necessary.**

1 I think I put my foot in it when I asked him what the matter was.
2 Having the car fixed set me back £250! That's put paid to my holiday plans.
3 Keep your options open: don't put all your eggs in one basket.
4 If you take a flash photo while he's playing the violin you may put him off.
5 Her bad performance in her flute exam can be put down to nerves. Let's
  hope it doesn't put her off playing altogether.
6 You've let her get away with being late too often: it's time you put your
  foot down.
7 The bad weather has set the building programme back by several weeks.
8 When they set up the scheme they set out to make it as innovative as possible.
9 You're always putting me down! Put yourself in my shoes and imagine what
  it feels like. Don't you realise that it puts both of us in a bad light?
10 I wouldn't put it past him to have made the whole story up. I'm sure he was
  putting me on!

C Fill the gaps in these sentences with suitable phrases from the list below.
You may need to change the form of the verbs.

1 It wasn't his idea – someone else must have .... him .... it.
2 They were going out together for five years before they .... home together.
3 He has tremendous ideas but he's not very good at .... them ....
4 I don't want to .... you .... but I've got nowhere to stay.
Can you .... me .... for the night?
5 If you don't like the situation, you'll just have to .... it, I'm afraid.
6 I .... my order last month and I still haven't received the goods.
7 Holidays are expensive: you can save up by .... a little money each month.
8 In her book she .... to examine the wide variety of species in the world.
9 5,000 words! You must have .... a lot of hours on this work.
10 They won't turn on the central heating until the really cold weather ....

put across/over   put aside/put away/set aside   put in   put in   put out
put up   put up to   put up with   set in   set out   set up

10.9 Different styles

VOCABULARY DEVELOPMENT AND
WRITING SKILLS

A **1** How would you describe the style of each of these sentences: FORMAL, COLLOQUIAL, or NEUTRAL (i.e. neither stiffly formal nor very colloquial)?

1 a Different forms are more interesting to admire and study than lots of things that look the same.
  b It's a lot more interesting to admire and study different forms than lots of things that look the same.
  c Different forms are more interesting to admire and study than a large number of similar looking species.

2 a I do like little kittens and puppies – they're ever so sweet, aren't they?
  b I consider young kittens and puppies to be the most endearing creatures.
  c Small kittens and puppies are delightful, I think.

2 Highlight some examples of NEUTRAL style in the first half of *So much to save* on page 112.

B Rewrite these colloquial sentences in a more neutral (i.e. more formal but not stiffly formal) style:

1 It's a lot better to use renewable energy – not fossil fuels like coal, gas and oil.
  Renewable energy resources are preferable to fossil fuels, such as coal, gas and oil.
2 How's your dad? Is he OK again yet?
3 Well, she hit the roof when they broke it to her that she'd got the sack.
4 To grow organic fruit and vegetables they don't use artificial fertilisers, you know.
5 We were ever so scared when this huge great dog came bounding up to us.
6 For pity's sake, mind what you're doing with that knife!
7 There's no point in testing cosmetics on animals – and it's cruel too.
8 Why on earth didn't you turn the light off when you left the room?
9 Hey, it looks as if it's going to rain pretty soon.
10 Don't throw litter in the street – put it in a bin or something, for goodness sake.

> When writing a composition in the exam it's best to aim for a fairly neutral style, rather than a style that is over-colloquial or stiffly formal. However, a personal letter should be written in a friendly, colloquial style.

C Rewrite these formal sentences in a more neutral, less formal style:

1 It is unwise to bathe here due to possible contamination of the water.
  It's not advisable to go swimming here because the water may be polluted.
2 Meteorologists maintain that the rate of increase in the global warming process is accelerating.
3 It is conceivable that a slight rise in temperature would have a dramatic effect on the ice in polar regions.
4 Discarding cans and bottles leads to excessive consumption of energy and materials. It is preferable to recycle them.
5 The serving of luncheon commences at noon.
6 Passengers are requested to exercise caution when alighting from the train.
7 We regret that the playing of musical instruments is not permitted on the premises.
8 Whilst all vegetarians eschew meat, vegans consume neither fish nor dairy products.

> Contractions (*isn't*, *it's*, etc.) are often used in a neutral style. In the exam you wouldn't be penalised for using them, but it may be safer to stick to full forms. In academic essays or job applications contractions should not be used, though.

A   First, read this through, just to get the gist before you look at the alternatives in B below:

I t is not ___¹ to ___² an unknown animal. Spend a day in the tropical forests of South America, turning over logs, looking beneath bark, sifting through the moist litter of leaves, followed by an evening ___³ a mercury lamp on a white screen, and one way and another you will ___⁴ hundreds of different kinds of small creatures. Moths, caterpillars, spiders, long-nosed bugs, luminous beetles, harmless butterflies ___⁵ as wasps, wasps shaped like ants, sticks that walk, leaves that open wings and fly – the variety will be ___⁶ and one of these ___⁷ will almost certainly be undescribed by science. The difficulty will be to find ___⁸ who know enough about the groups ___⁹ to be able to single out the new one.

   No one can say ___¹⁰ how many species of animals there are in these greenhouse-humid dimly lit jungles. They contain the ___¹¹ and the most varied assemblage of animal and plant life to be found anywhere on earth. Not only are there many categories of creatures – monkeys, rodents, spiders, hummingbirds, butterflies, but most of those types ___¹² in many different ___¹³ . There are over forty different species of parrot, over seventy different monkeys, three hundred hummingbirds and tens of thousands of butterflies. If you are not ___¹⁴ , you can even be ___¹⁵ by a hundred different kinds of mosquito.

from Life on Earth by David Attenborough

B **1**   Decide which words are most suitable to fit in each of the numbered gaps above – some are grammatically or stylistically unsuitable.

In Part I of the Use of English Paper there are no alternatives to help you. Bear in mind the context, the sense of the passage, and its style. In the exam some of the gaps require grammatical words: prepositions, articles, conjunctions, etc.

  1 difficult ✓   hard ✓   problematic ✗   strenuous ✗   tricky ✗
  2 come across   discover   find   identify   meet
  3 lighting   pointing   reflecting   shining
  4 collect   discover   gather   glimpse   identify   pick up
  5 disguised   dressed   masquerading   posing
  6 ample   big   enormous   huge   immense
  7 animals   creatures   insects   things   types
  8 experts   friends   guys   people   specialists
  9 characteristics   concerned   themselves   there
 10 almost   exactly   just   nearly   precisely   quite   sincerely
 11 best   biggest   deepest   richest   strangest   thickest   wildest
 12 are   become   exist   happen   remain   survive
 13 forms   manners   types   ways   zones
 14 asleep   awake   careful   cunning   fortunate   unlucky
 15 attacked   bitten   poisoned   stung   threatened

2 Where you ticked more than one answer, which is the one you feel is the best?

A Look at the statistics, quotations and photos below and opposite and discuss your reactions.

According to the experts:

- Between 2000 and 2010 10% of the estimated 30 million species of plants and animals will be lost forever. By 2030 another 20% are likely to be lost. The extinction of one plant species can cause the loss of 30 dependent organisms.
- Half the world's rainforests have already been destroyed. Of the remaining half, two thirds will disappear by 2030.
- Between 2000 and 2010 the average temperature will rise by 1°C. By 2100 it will rise by 3° to 5°C. This will have unpredictable effects on local weather patterns. By 2100 the sea level is likely to rise between 10cm and 2m.
- There are 750 million motor vehicles in the world. By 2030 there will be 1,100 million.
- The total world population is over 6,000 million. By 2030 there may be 8,000 to 10,000 million mouths to feed and by 2100 11,000 to 14,000.
- Glaciers melting in Greenland are sending more and more icebergs into the North Atlantic and cooling the ocean. This may divert the Gulf Stream and bring much colder weather to Western Europe.

Greenpeace

'This is what you should do: love the Earth and sun and the animals, despise riches, give alms to everyone that asks, stand up for the stupid and crazy, devote your income and labour to others, hate tyrants, argue not concerning God, have patience and indulgence towards the people, take off your hat to nothing known or unknown or to any man or number of men . . . re-examine all you have been told at school or church or in any book, dismiss what insults your own soul, and your very flesh shall be a great poem.'

Walt Whitman

If the Earth
were a few feet in diameter,
floating a few feet above a field somewhere,
people would come from everywhere to marvel
at it. People would walk around it marvelling at its
big pools of water, its little pools and the water flowing
between. People would marvel at the bumps on it and the
holes in it. They would marvel at the very thin layer of gas
surrounding it and the water suspended in the gas. The people
would marvel at all the creatures walking around the surface of
the ball and at the creatures in the water. The people would
declare it as sacred because it was the only one, and they would
protect it so that it would not be hurt. The ball would be the
greatest wonder known, and people would come to pray to
it, to be healed, to gain knowledge, to know beauty and to
wonder how it could be. People would love it and defend
it with their lives because they would somehow
know that their lives could be nothing
without it. If the Earth were
a few feet in diameter.

Joe Miller

B 🖋 Write an article for a magazine explaining your views for and/or against ONE of the following points of view (300–350 words).

> The future of the planet looks bleak, but there's nothing I can do about it.

> What happens in poor countries on the other side of the world doesn't concern me.

> There's no point in worrying about things that will only affect our grandchildren.

> The world will be a better place for our children and grandchildren.

11 Another world

11.1 Enjoying reading   LISTENING AND TOPIC VOCABULARY

A 🔊 **You'll hear Christine, Jonathan, Karen and William talking about reading. Indicate which of the speakers expresses each of these opinions by writing C, J, K or W in each box. If more than one person expresses the same opinion, write more than one letter in the box.**

1   I forget the real world when I'm reading a book.   **1**

2   I can experience the world through another person's eyes.   **2**

3   I learn about history from the books I read.   **3**

4   I like the feel of a book in my hands.   **4**

5   I love stories where you want to know what will happen in the end.   **5**

6   I love to re-read passages I have enjoyed.   **6**

7   I prefer books to films.   **7**

8   I prefer books to TV.   **8**

9   Reading a book can remind you of other places.   **9**

10 Reading a book can take you to another world.   **10**

B 👥 **Discuss these questions:**

- Which of the people interviewed do you identify with most?
- What enjoyment do you get from reading for pleasure?
- What kinds of books and magazines would you like to read if you had more time?
- Name one fiction or non-fiction book you've enjoyed. What did you enjoy about it?
- 60% of people read a book at least once a month (but 40% don't)! How many books do you read in a year? How many are in your own language, and how many in English?

C **In these sentences THREE of the alternatives are correct and the rest are wrong. Tick the correct words.**

1   As I prefer fiction to non-fiction I often read ....
   best-sellers   biographies   memoirs   thrillers   whodunits

2   Before buying a book it's a good idea to read the ....
   bibliography   blurb   contents   dustjacket   sleeve

3   The opening page of a book often has a(n) ....
   appendix   dedication   foreword   index   preface

4   I've just read the reviews of a newly-published .... of poetry.
   album   anthology   book   collection   gathering

5   The plot of a popular romantic novel is not usually very ....
   complex   intricate   involved   mixed   multiple

6   It was a very long book and it took me ages to .... through it.
   flip   get   struggle   thumb   wade

7   The contents page of a book usually gives the titles of all the .... in it.
   chapters   excerpts   extracts   passages   sections   units

8   The language she uses can be interpreted literally or ....
   descriptively   figuratively   illustratively   metaphorically   symbolically

9   Although the book has a serious .... , it is very accessible and witty.
   author   message   plot   purpose   satire   side

10 His books not only have exciting plots but are also very ....
   gripping   readable   thought-provoking   thrilling   well-written

D These abbreviations are found in non-fiction books and footnotes, as well as in reports and articles. Rewrite each one as a complete word or phrase.

e.g. *for example*   etc. *and so on/and so forth /et cetera*
i.e.   cf.   ff.   pp.   ibid.   viz.   N.B.   sic   ©   ¶

11.2 **'My last novel is the best work I can do'**   LISTENING

A 👥 You'll hear an interview with the novelist William Boyd. First, discuss how he might answer these questions:

- Do you have regular working hours?
- How do you invent your characters?
- What do you really enjoy about what you do?
- Do you write on a computer?
- Which of your novels is your favourite?

B 🔊 Listen to the interview and fill each box with a word or short phrase:

1 William Boyd's first writing job was as a ⬚ **1** critic.

2 At the moment his working hours are ⬚ **2** .

3 His characters are not based on ⬚ **3** .

4 In order to write from a woman's perspective he forgets ⬚ **4a** and focuses on ⬚ **4b** .

5 Tick the reasons he gives for enjoying what he does:
being autonomous ☐   being famous ☐   feeling free ☐
making money ☐   being self-sufficient ☐   solitude ☐

6 Writers who moan about how hard it is to write should ⬚ **6** .

7 He finds that he can write anywhere because, when he was younger, he worked in ⬚ **7** .

8 He writes the ⬚ **8** of his novels in longhand.

9 He thinks that it's a mistake to ⬚ **9a** what your 'ideal reader' wants to read. A writer should be ⬚ **9a** to him/herself.

10 Which of his novels is his favourite? ⬚ **10** .

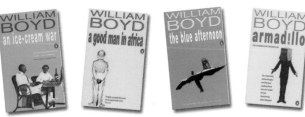

C 👥👥 Discuss these questions:

- What do you think you might enjoy / not enjoy about William Boyd's novels?
- Who is the most famous living writer in your country? What do you know about him/her?
- What is the most famous classic book written in your language? Describe it.
- Who are your favourite British and American writers? What do you like about their works?

11.3 **Setting the scene...**   **READING AND SPEAKING**

 Here are the opening paragraphs of three bestselling British novels. Read each extract carefully, then discuss the questions below:

A Read the beginning of *Brazzaville Beach* (1990) by William Boyd and answer the questions below:

I live on Brazzaville Beach. Brazzaville Beach on the edge of Africa. This is where I have washed up, you might say, deposited myself like a spar of driftwood, lodged and fixed in the warm sand for a while, just above the high tide mark.

The beach never had a name until last April. Then they christened it in honour of the famous *Conferençia dos Quadros* that was held a few years ago in Congo Brazzaville in 1964. No one can explain why but, one day, over the laterite road that leads down to the shore, some workmen erected this sign: 'Brazzaville Beach', and written below that, *Conferençia dos Quadros, Brazzaville, 1964.*

It is an indication, some people say, that the government is becoming more moderate, trying to heal the wounds of our own civil war by acknowledging a historic moment in another country's liberation struggle. Who can say? Who ever knows the answers to these questions? But I like the name, and so does everyone else who lives around here. Within a week we were all using it unselfconsciously. Where do you live? On Brazzaville Beach. It seemed entirely natural.

I live on the beach in a refurbished beach house. I have a large cool sitting-room with a front wall of sliding meshed doors that give on directly to a wide sun-deck. There is also a bedroom, a generous bathroom with bath and shower, and a tiny dim kitchen, built on to the back. Behind the house is my garden: sandy, patchy grass, some prosaic shrubs, a vegetable plot and a hibiscus hedge, thick with brilliant flowers.

2 How many other characters are mentioned? What is the effect of this?
3 What do we find out about the place and time that are described?
4 How many times is the word *beach* used? What is the effect of this?
5 How is each paragraph different in content and style?

B Read the beginning of *A Dark-Adapted Eye* (1986) by Barbara Vine and answer the questions below:

1

On the morning Vera died I woke up very early. The birds had started, more of them and singing more loudly in our leafy suburb than in the country. They never sang like that outside Vera's windows in the Vale of Dedham. I lay there listening to something repeating itself monotonously. A thrush, it must have been, doing what Browning said it did and singing each song twice over. It was a Thursday in August, a hundred years ago. Not much more than a third of that, of course. It only feels so long.

In these circumstances alone one knows when someone is going to die. All other deaths can be predicted, conjectured, even anticipated with some certainty, but not to the hour, the minute, with no room for hope. Vera would die at eight o'clock and that was that. I began to feel sick. I lay there exaggeratedly still, listening for some sound from the next room. If I was awake my father would be. About my mother I was less sure. She had never made a secret of her dislike of both his sisters. It was one of the things which had made a rift between them, though there they were together in the next room, in the same bed still. People did not break a marriage, leave each other, so lightly in those days.

I thought of getting up but first I wanted to make sure where my father was. There was something terrible in the idea of encountering him in the passage, both of us dressing-gowned, thick-eyed with sleeplessness, each seeking the bathroom and each politely giving way to the other.

1 What do we find out about Vera? Why is she going to die?
2 How many times is the word *die* or *death* used? What is the effect of this?
3 What do we find out about the narrator?
4 What do we find out about the place and time that are described?

C Read the beginning of *Nice Work* (1988) by David Lodge and answer the questions below:

Monday January 13th, 1986. Victor Wilcox lies awake, in the dark bedroom, waiting for his quartz alarm clock to bleep. It is set to do this at 6.45. How long he has to wait he doesn't know. He could easily find out by groping for the clock, lifting it to his line of vision, and pressing the button that illuminates the digital display. But he would rather not know. Supposing it is only six o'clock? Or even five? It could be five. Whatever it is, he won't be able to get to sleep again. This has become a regular occurrence lately: lying awake in the dark, waiting for the alarm to bleep, worrying.

Worries streak towards him like enemy spaceships in one of Gary's video games. He flinches, dodges, zaps them with instant solutions, but the assault is endless: the Avco account, the Rawlinson account, the price of pig-iron, the value of the pound, the competition from Foundrax, the incompetence of his Marketing Director, the persistent breakdowns of the core blowers, the vandalising of the toilets in the fettling shop, the pressure from his divisional boss, last month's accounts, the quarterly forecast, the annual review ...

In an effort to escape this bombardment, perhaps even to doze awhile, he twists onto his side, burrows into the warm plump body of his wife, and throws an arm round her waist. Startled, but still asleep, drugged with Valium, Marjorie swivels to face him. Their noses and foreheads bump against each other; there is a sudden flurry of limbs, an absurd pantomime struggle. Marjorie puts up her fists like a boxer, groans and pushes him away. An object slides off the bed on her side and falls to the floor with a thump. Vic knows what it is: a book which one of Marjorie's friends at the Weight Watchers' club has lent her, and which she has been reading in bed, without much show of conviction, and falling asleep over, for the past week or two.

1 What do we find out about Victor Wilcox?
2 What do we find out about Marjorie?
3 What do we find out about the place and time that are described?
4 How many of Victor's worries are listed in the second paragraph? What is the effect of this?
5 How is each paragraph different in content and style?

D Discuss these questions:

• What do you think is going to happen in each of the stories?
• Which of the three novels would you like to read more of, and why?
• Which seems to have the most readable or attractive style?

11.4 ## Describing a book SPEAKING AND COMPOSITION

A Discuss these questions about reading in general:

• How much reading do you do? How much time do you spend each week reading books, and how much time reading newspapers or magazines? How much do you read in English, rather than in your own language?
• What kinds of books do you enjoy reading? Do you choose different sorts of books for different occasions (journeys, holidays, reading in bed, etc.)?
• If you could choose between reading a book or seeing the same story as a film, on video or on TV, which would you prefer? Why?
• Who are your favourite authors? Describe the kinds of books they write.
• Describe one book you have particularly enjoyed reading recently. What did you like about it? What were its faults?
• Are there any books you'd like to re-read one day (or is there one that you have re-read)? What are the qualities of such a book?
• Is there any particular book you'd recommend to your partners? What do you think they'd enjoy about it?

"They're books, dad needs them for reading."

In the exam, if one of your compositions is too short you'll lose marks.

If one of your compositions is too long, not only will it probably contain more mistakes but writing all those extra words will take up more of your time.

 B 🖋 **Write a composition on ONE of these topics (300–350 words):**

Either: Write a review for a student magazine of a book you have particularly enjoyed reading, making it sound as appealing as possible to potential readers.

or: Write an essay explaining what you find particularly striking or moving about the prescribed book you are reading.

Make notes before you start writing. Try to cover the following aspects of the book:

Theme   Plot   Characters   Style   Message   Relevance to your life

Do you know how many lines of your handwriting are equivalent to 100 words? And how many lines are equivalent to 350 words?

To check how long a composition is: count the words in 10 lines, divide by 10 (to get the average number of words per line) and then multiply the answer by the total number of lines.

11.5 Conjunctions and connectors – 1 GRAMMAR REVIEW

 A **1** Study these examples and highlight the conjunctions and connectors you want to remember:

> **Explaining results and reasons**
> because   and so   since   as   the reason why   consequently   therefore
> as a result of this
>
> **Contrasts, unexpected results**
> but   although   nevertheless   all the same   however   though   even though
> and yet   still   on the other hand
>
> **Mentioning exceptions**
> but not   apart from   except   with the exception of
>
> **Reservations, qualifications**
> anyway   at least   at any rate   in any case
>
> **Making further points**
> and also   moreover   what is more   yet   besides   furthermore
> not only ... but also
>
> **Emphasising**
> especially   in particular   above all   particularly   chiefly   primarily
>
> **Clarifying**
> i.e.   in other words   that is to say   which means that
>
> **Giving examples**
> e.g.   for example   such as   for instance   like
>
> **Not mentioning further examples**
> etc.   and so forth   and so on   as well as other similar things/books

2 **Rewrite these sentences using conjunctions and connectors you highlighted above:**

1 She likes reading but she doesn't have much time for it.
She doesn't have much time for reading even though she enjoys it a lot.

2 Many blockbusters, e.g. James Mitchener's *Alaska*, are over 1,000 pages long.

3 He enjoys reading biographies – especially ones about politicians.

4 Science fiction is an acquired taste – anyway that's what sci-fi fans say.

5 She prefers reading non-fiction books, i.e. biographies, history books, etc.

6 The book contained a lot of explicit sex and violence and so it was a best-seller.

7 He reads thrillers but he doesn't read much else.

8 Reading is an inexpensive hobby and it is enjoyable.

B Fill each gap with a suitable conjunction or connector – without using *and* or *but*.

1 All of E.M. Forster's novels, ... *A Passage to India*, are set in Europe.
2 Jane Austen's novels were popular in her day, ... they are still widely read.
3 Katherine Mansfield's short stories are brilliant examples of the genre; .... I'd recommend the ones she wrote later in her life.
4 I've never appreciated D. H. Lawrence's work .... he's supposed to be a great English writer – .... I think he's rather overrated.
5 Charles Dickens' novels, ... *Oliver Twist*, were published monthly as serials; .... each new instalment was eagerly awaited by readers.
6 Mary Ann Evans was an independent, free-thinking woman; .... all her novels were written under a male pseudonym: George Eliot.
7 Kingsley Amis' *Lucky Jim* is his best work – .... that's what I think.
8 Anne, Charlotte and Emily Brontë all wrote novels which are well worth reading – .... Emily's *Wuthering Heights* and Charlotte's *Jane Eyre*.

11.6 Collocations: idioms   VOCABULARY DEVELOPMENT

A In some fixed, idiomatic phrases, words go together like *salt and pepper, fish and chips, sweet and sour*, or *Marks and Spencer*. Fill the gaps in these sentences with suitable expressions from the list below:

1 Can we discuss the .... of your proposals later on?
2 Can you show me the .... to support your argument?
3 They get on quite well together, even though they have their little ....
4 You gain some things and you lose others: it's a case of ....
5 The police are responsible for maintaining ....
6 It was .... whether the rescuers would get there in time.
7 They've shared a lot of experiences: they've been through .... together.
8 You can't claim on insurance for .... , only for damage.
9 I need another £100 .... the amount I've already saved up.
10 Nuclear physicists who are also bestselling writers are ....
11 He makes a little money out of writing but teaching is his ....
12 After all their adventures, they reached home ....

bread and butter   facts and figures   few and far between   law and order   over and above
pros and cons   safe and sound   swings and roundabouts   thick and thin   touch and go
ups and downs   wear and tear

B Look at these examples and then match the words in the lists below together:

a swarm of bees   a bag of flour   a box of matches   a tank of petrol
a pair of scissors   a pair of binoculars   a pair of sunglasses   a pair of tights

a/an	basket	bucket	bunch	carafe	**of**	beans	bother	bread	cake
	cup	flight	flock	gust	herd		cards	cattle	equipment	flowers
	item	jug	loaf	pack	pair		fruit	helpers	hills	honey
	piece	pot	puff	range	sack		luggage	milk	potatoes	sheep
	school	slice	spoonful	spot			smoke	socks	stairs	sugar	tea
	team	tin or can	tube			tights	toothpaste	tweezers	water
						wind	wine or water	whales	

C Fill these gaps with suitable expressions from B:

1 In the distance we could see .... and beyond that a snow-capped mountain.
2 If you give your hostess .... , she'll be very pleased.
3 How many .... are you allowed to check in for this flight?
4 If you've got .... , we can play poker.
5 There was a sudden .... and her umbrella blew inside out.
6 We want .... to help us to redecorate our flat.
7 I'm having .... with my work, could you help me?
8 Don't be so silly! There's no need to be scared of ....
9 I went down .... and came to a locked door.
10 I've got a splinter in my finger, have you got .... I can borrow?

D Match the two halves of these idiomatic expressions:

muscular:	He's as strong as …	toast
short-sighted:	She's as blind as …	a horse/an ox
not rough:	The sea was as calm as …	a fiddle
without obligations:	She's as free as …	the hills
unemotional:	He's as cool as …	a sheet
tough:	She's as hard as …	a mouse
self-effacing:	He's as quiet as …	nails
healthy:	She's as fit as …	a picture
pale:	He looked as white as …	a cucumber
ancient, traditional:	That story is as old as …	the air
attractive:	She looked as pretty as …	a millpond
well-behaved:	The children were as good as …	a feather
not heavy:	She's as light as …	gold
cosy:	We were as warm as …	a bat

11.7 A good beginning

WRITING SKILLS

A Read this article about first lines and first novels and then compare your reactions to it.

Sifting the nodders from the shakers

"I WAS gazing out beyond Beachy Head contemplating the ruins of my life." This, in the jargon of book publishing, is a shaker, a complete no-no as an opening line. Unless the author performs some miracle in the next couple of paragraphs, the publishing company's reader will flick to the next chapter and, if there's more of the same, cast the manuscript aside.

A similar fate awaits books that begin: "The day after my husband died"; "Picking up the pieces was never going to be easy" or, what one publisher describes as the Enid Blyton* opener: "Peter and Bob decided to go to the market in Leeds that day". These are all shakers (as in head-shakers) of the first order.

On the other hand, the first line of Tolstoy's *Anna Karenina* – "All happy families resemble one another, but each unhappy family is unhappy in its own way" – is what another publisher describes as a nodder, in the sense that it makes you think Yes, there's something I recognise in that. For the unpublished author, the first line or paragraph is all-important.

Mass literacy and the premise that "everyone has a book in them" causes thousands of unsolicited manuscripts to thud on to the doormats of publishers and literary agents every week. Nearly all are rejected. One agency calculated that all but 0.001 percent are sent back.

Stephen Burgen

* Enid Blyton wrote in a very easy style. She wrote lots and lots of story books for boys and girls.

B → Look at the first lines of the passages in 11.3 on pages 120–1 and 11.9 on page 126 – and the passages in units 12 and 13. Choose five that are 'nodders', in your view – and any that you think are 'shakers'. Compare your findings with another pair.

C **1** Look at these first lines of some students' compositions on the topic 'The effect of tourism on a place in my country' (which you tackled in unit 6). Which of them make you want to read on?

a The first time I went to Venice it was rainy and quite chilly. I remember it was December and so there were not many tourists around. That's the very time you have to go there - in the middle of winter when it's freezing and foggy.

b Switzerland has been traditionally a very famous country for tourism. But having a huge number of tourists every year causes a lot of problems for a small country like mine.

c Gordes is a magically beautiful village in the south of France. Its medieval houses are perched on a cliff, looked down upon by a church. The view it offers over Provence is breathtaking: an endless landscape of lavender fields, vineyards and poplars, vanishing into the distance in a dim April haze.

d Venice has always been a tourist resort and probably tourism will be its main source of income for ever. Venice itself was conceived as a tourist destination and therefore it is impossible to imagine it otherwise.

e Tourism in the Canary Islands has had a great impact on the way of life of the local people and on the scenery of the islands. Before tourism became one of the main sources of income for the islands, most of the people lived from agriculture and fishing.

f The sun is burning. For three days now it has been extremely hot. The asphalt on the street seems to be melting away, trapping the cars that try to force their way to the beach.

2 How could you improve each one, particularly the very first sentence of each?

D **1** Look at the first lines of your own recent compositions. Which do you think are 'nodders' and which are 'shakers'? Write improved opening lines for the ones you're not satisfied with.

2 Show your improved versions, together with the original first lines, to a partner and ask for comments.

11.8 *It . . .* constructions ADVANCED GRAMMAR

A Discuss the differences in emphasis between these sentences:

1 Did Jane Austen write *Emma*?
Was it Jane Austen who wrote *Emma*?
Was Jane Austen the author of *Emma*?
Was the author who wrote *Emma* Jane Austen?

Was *Emma* written by Jane Austen?
Was it *Emma* that Jane Austen wrote?
Was Jane Austen the author who wrote *Emma*?

2 What I enjoy reading is thrillers.
Thrillers are what I enjoy reading.

I enjoy reading thrillers.
It's thrillers that I enjoy reading.

3 It was me who borrowed your book.

I borrowed your book.

B Fill these gaps with suitable words or phrases:

1 It was .... that he managed to .... of the mountain so quickly.
2 Was it Hemingway or Steinbeck who .... *A Farewell to Arms*?
3 It's .... that you .... me about the danger.
4 It's not because he .... , it's because he .... that he can't make friends.
5 It wasn't .... before we .... what a big mistake ....
6 Why .... that my friends are so unpunctual and .... on time?
7 If you call the office I expect it .... John .... the phone.
8 It used .... my sister .... the great reader in our family, but now it .... the most books.

Verbs and adverbs of manner can't be used with *It's ... that ...*:

It's fall over that he did. ✗   It was fast that he ran. ✗   It was well that she did in the test. ✗

C Rewrite these sentences, using an *It . . .* construction to emphasise the words in red:

1 She finished reading the book only yesterday.   It ....
2 Do you enjoy the humour of her stories?   Is it ....
3 Did you read *Emma* or *Persuasion* recently?   Was it ....
4 I went to bed early because I was feeling worn out. It was because ....
5 A strange noise woke me up in the early hours.   It ....
6 I heard the noise at half past four in the morning. It ....
7 I realised what had happened when I looked out of the window. It ....
8 Then I found I couldn't get back to sleep.   It ....
9 I finally did get to sleep at about eight o'clock. It ....
10 I didn't wake up until lunchtime.   It wasn't ....

11.9 Three American novels

A These are the opening paragraphs of three well-known American novels. Read them through before you answer the questions below.

1 In the late summer of that year we lived in a house in a village that looked across the river and the plain to the mountains. In the bed of the river there were pebbles and boulders, dry and white in the sun, and the water was clear and swiftly moving and blue in the channels. Troops went by the house and down the road and the dust they raised powdered the leaves of the trees. The trunks of the trees too were dusty and the leaves fell early that year and we saw the troops marching along the road and the dust rising and leaves, stirred by the breeze, falling and the soldiers marching and afterwards the road bare and white except for the leaves.

The plain was rich with crops; there were many orchards of f̶ ̶ ̶ ̶ beyond the ̶ ̶ ̶ ̶ the m̶ ̶ ̶ ̶ ̶

2 To the red country and part of the grey country of Oklahoma the last rains came gently, and they did not cut the scarred earth. The ploughs crossed and recrossed the rivulet marks. The last rains lifted the corn quickly and scattered weed colonies and grass along the sides of the roads so that the grey country and the dark red country began to disappear under a green cover. In the last part of May the sky grew pale and the clouds that had hung in high puffs for so long in the spring were dissipated. The sun flared down on the growing corn day after day until a line of brown spread along the edge of each green bayonet. The clouds appeared, and went away, and in a while they did not try any more. The weeds grew darker green to protect themselves, and they did not spread any more. The surface of the earth crusted, a thin hard crust, and as the sky became pale, so the earth became pale, pink in the red country and white in the grey country.

In the water-cut gullie̶ ̶ ̶

3 We drove past Tiny Polski's mansion house to the main road, and then the five miles into Northampton, Father talking the whole way about savages and the awfulness of America, how it got turned into a dope-taking, door-locking, ulcerated danger-zone of rabid scavengers and criminal millionaires and moral sneaks. And look at the schools. And look at the politicians. And there wasn't a Harvard graduate who could change a flat tyre or do ten push-ups. And there were people in New York City who lived on pet food, who would kill you for a little loose change. Was that normal? If not, why did anyone put up with it?

'I don't know,' he said, replying to himself. 'I'm just thinking out loud.' Before leaving Hatfield, he had parked the pick-up truck on a rise in the road, and pointed south.

'Here come the savages,' he said, and up they came, tracking across the fields from a sickle of trees through the gummy drizzling heat-outlines of Polski's barns. They were dark and their clothes were rags and some had rags on their heads and others wide-brimmed hats. They were men and boys, a few no older than me, all of them carrying long knives.

Father's finger scared me more than th̶ ̶ ̶ ̶

B 👥 **Refer back to the three extracts and discuss these questions:**

1 Which book on the right do you think each extract comes from?
2 Which extract conveys an impression of time passing?
3 Which conveys an impression of movement?
4 Which conveys an impression of a degenerating, violent world?
5 How are these impressions conveyed? What stylistic devices are used to create the impressions?
6 Which uses the fewest modifying adjectives?
7 Which uses the simplest grammatical structures?
8 Which uses the style of spoken conversational English?
9 Which uses repetition to achieve its effect?
10 What do you think might be the THEME of the book each extract comes from? What might come next in the story?

A 👥 **Read about the Rocket eBook and then discuss the questions below:**

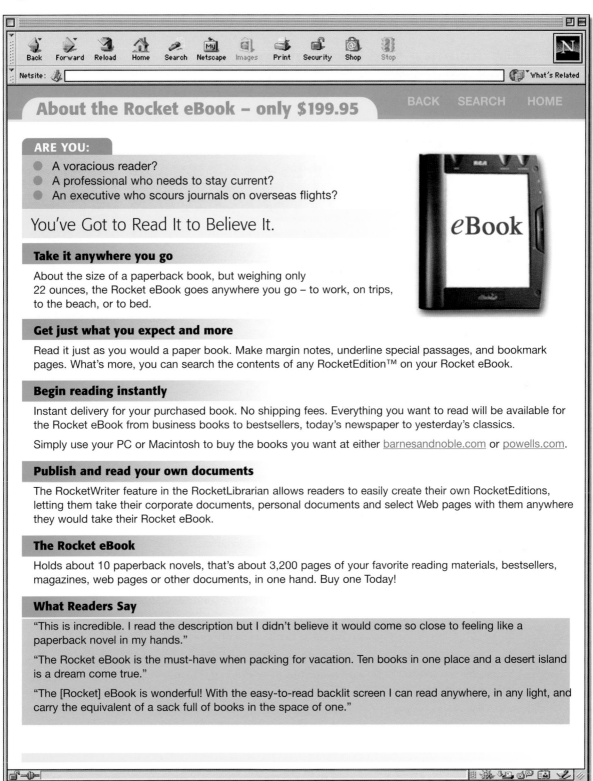

Netsite:

About the Rocket eBook – only $199.95 BACK SEARCH HOME

ARE YOU:
- A voracious reader?
- A professional who needs to stay current?
- An executive who scours journals on overseas flights?

You've Got to Read It to Believe It.

Take it anywhere you go

About the size of a paperback book, but weighing only 22 ounces, the Rocket eBook goes anywhere you go – to work, on trips, to the beach, or to bed.

Get just what you expect and more

Read it just as you would a paper book. Make margin notes, underline special passages, and bookmark pages. What's more, you can search the contents of any RocketEdition™ on your Rocket eBook.

Begin reading instantly

Instant delivery for your purchased book. No shipping fees. Everything you want to read will be available for the Rocket eBook from business books to bestsellers, today's newspaper to yesterday's classics.

Simply use your PC or Macintosh to buy the books you want at either barnesandnoble.com or powells.com.

Publish and read your own documents

The RocketWriter feature in the RocketLibrarian allows readers to easily create their own RocketEditions, letting them take their corporate documents, personal documents and select Web pages with them anywhere they would take their Rocket eBook.

The Rocket eBook

Holds about 10 paperback novels, that's about 3,200 pages of your favorite reading materials, bestsellers, magazines, web pages or other documents, in one hand. Buy one Today!

What Readers Say

"This is incredible. I read the description but I didn't believe it would come so close to feeling like a paperback novel in my hands."

"The Rocket eBook is the must-have when packing for vacation. Ten books in one place and a desert island is a dream come true."

"The [Rocket] eBook is wonderful! With the easy-to-read backlit screen I can read anywhere, in any light, and carry the equivalent of a sack full of books in the space of one."

- What are the main attractions of the eBook? If you had one, how much would you use it?
- What do you think are the main drawbacks of the eBook?

B 🖉 **Imagine that you have been using an eBook for a month. Write an article about your experience.**

If you're doing a set book, it's worth searching the Internet for any study aids on the book you're reading. Your first port of call should be www.sparknotes.com, which provides free notes on a large number of books.

12 The cutting edge

12.1 Science and technology

TOPIC VOCABULARY

A 👥 **Discuss these questions:**

• What do you think each photograph shows?
• What other 20th century inventions or scientific breakthroughs have changed our lives as much as, or even more than, the inventions shown in the photos?

 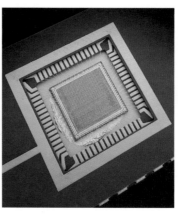 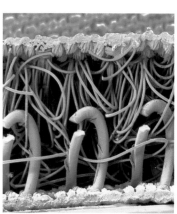

B 👥 **Choose ONE answer to complete each sentence.**

1 Technology deals with the .... of science.
apparatus   application   empiricism   practicability

2 .... is one of the physical sciences.
anatomy   botany   meteorology   sociology

3 .... is one of the life sciences.
archaeology   astronomy   astrology   zoology

4 .... is one of the social sciences.
anthropology   geology   chemistry   physics

5 IT (Information Technology) is the study of ....
computers   libraries   laboratories   keyboards

6 If the warning light should come on, turn the red .... to off.
button   dial   knob   lever

7 Albert Einstein was the most brilliant mathematician of his ....
class   country   generation   year

8 A scientific hypothesis is tested in a series of .... experiments.
controlled   limited   supervised   theoretical

9 The success of her research can be attributed to 10% .... and 90% hard work.
common sense   greed   effort   inspiration

10 His ideas are invariably criticised as .... by fellow scientists.
imaginative   impractical   ingenious   theoretical

11 A food processor has become an indispensable piece of .... in the home.
contraption   device   equipment   gadget

12 The designer has applied for a .... for her new invention.
copyright   patent   royalty   trade mark

13 It must have taken a genius to .... this complicated apparatus.
think of   think out   think through   think up

14 This appliance has to be plugged into a(n) .... to make it work.
cable   inlet   plug   socket

15 Many solutions to technical problems are discovered by ....
experience   hit and miss   rule of thumb   trial and error

A 🔊 **You'll hear part of a broadcast about the Freedom Ship. Write a word, number or short phrase to answer these questions about the project.**

1 How many homes will there be on board? `_____` 1

2 How much is the cheapest home? `_____` 2

3 How much is the most expensive home? `_____` 3

4 How will people get to and from the port? `_____` 4

5 What proportion of the time will the ship be stationary? `_____` 5

6 How long will the ship be? `_____` 6

7 How wide will the ship be? `_____` 7

8 How long will it take to travel around the world? `_____` 8

9 What is the largest plane that will be able to land? `_____` 9

10 Why will there be a lot of open-air space and parks? `_____` 10

11 What educational facilities will there be? `_____` 11

12 How much tax will residents have to pay? `_____` 12

13 How will residents be encouraged to run businesses? `_____` 13

14 What will be done with non-recyclable waste? `_____` 14

15 What kind of fuel will the ship use? `_____` 15

16 How will the ship be affected by rough seas? `_____` 16

B **1** 👥👥 **Discuss these questions:**

- What would be the advantages and disadvantages of living on the Freedom Ship?
- Would you like to study in the Freedom Ship's university? Why (not)?
- Do you think this scheme will ever be realised? Give your reasons.

2 👥👥 **Design your own ideal city of the future. What facilities would it have? How would it be constructed? How large would it be?**

3 **Give a short presentation of your ideas to another group or to the whole class.**

1 **Read this article and** highlight **the parts that amuse you, or which strike a chord with you.**

DESIGN FLAWS

I have a teenaged son who is a runner. He has, at a conservative estimate, 6,100 pairs of running shoes, and every one of them represents a greater investment of cumulative design effort than, say, Milton Keynes.

These shoes are amazing. I was just reading a review in one of his running magazines of the latest in 'sport utility sneakers', as they are called here, and it was full of passages like this: 'A dual-density EVA midsole with air units fore and aft provides stability while a gel heel-insert absorbs shock, but the shoe makes a narrow footprint, a characteristic that typically suits only the biomechanically efficient runner.' Alan Shepard went into space with less science at his disposal than that.

So here is my question. If my son can have his choice of a seemingly limitless range of scrupulously engineered, biomechanically efficient footwear, why does my computer keyboard suck? This is a serious enquiry.

My computer keyboard has 102 keys – almost double what my old manual typewriter had – which on the face of it seems awfully generous. Among other typographical luxuries, I can choose between three styles of bracket and two kinds of colon. I can dress my text with carets (^) and tildes (~). I can have slashes that fall to the left or to the right, and goodness knows what else.

I have so many keys, in fact, that over on the right-hand side of the keyboard there are whole communities of buttons of whose function I haven't the tiniest inkling. Occasionally I hit one by accident and subsequently discover that several paragraphs of my w9rk n+w look l*ke th?s, or that I have written the last page and a half in an interesting but unfortunately non-alphabetic font called Wingdings, but otherwise I haven't the faintest idea what those buttons are there for.

Never mind that many of these keys duplicate the functions of other keys, while others apparently do nothing at all (my favourite in this respect is one marked 'Pause', which when pressed does absolutely nothing, raising the interesting metaphysical question of whether it is therefore doing its job), or that several keys are arrayed in slightly imbecilic places. The delete key, for instance, is right beside the overprint key, so that often I discover, with a trill of gay laughter, that my most recent thoughts have been devouring, Pacman-like, everything I had previously written. Quite often, I somehow hit a combination of keys that summons a box which says, in effect, 'This Is a Pointless Box. Do You Want It?' which is followed by another that says, 'Are You Sure You Don't Want the Pointless Box?' Never mind all that. I have known for a long time that the computer is not my friend.

But here is what gets me. Out of all the 102 keys at my disposal, there is no key for the fraction ½. Typewriter keyboards always used to have a key for ½. Now, however, if I wish to write ½, I have to bring down the font menu and call up a directory called 'WP Characters', then hunt through a number of sub-directories until I remember or more often blunder on the particular one, 'Typographic Symbols', in which hides the furtive ½ sign. This is irksome and pointless and it doesn't seem right to me.

But then most things in the world don't seem right to me. On the dashboard of our family car is a shallow indentation about the size of a paperback book. If you are looking for somewhere to put your sunglasses or spare change, it is the obvious place, and it works extremely well, I must say, so long as the car is not actually moving. As soon as you put the car in motion, however, and particularly when you touch the brakes, turn a corner, or go up a gentle slope, everything slides off. There is, you see, no lip round this dashboard tray. It is just a flat space, with a dimpled bottom. It can hold nothing that has not been nailed to it.

So I ask you: what, then, is it for? Somebody had to design it. It didn't just appear spontaneously. Some person – perhaps, for all I know, a whole committee of people in the Dashboard Stowage Division – had to invest time and thought in incorporating into the design of this vehicle a storage tray that will actually hold nothing. That is really quite an achievement.

But it is nothing, of course, compared with the manifold design achievements of those responsible for the modern video recorder. Now I am not going to go on about how impossible it is to programme the typical video recorder because you know that already. Nor will I observe how irritating it is that you must cross the room and get down on your belly to confirm that it is actually recording. But I will just make one small passing observation. I recently bought a video recorder and one of the selling points – one of the things the manufacturer boasted about – was that it was capable of recording programmes up to twelve months in advance. Now think about this for a moment and tell me any circumstance – and I mean any circumstance at all – in which you can envision wanting to set a video machine to record a programme one year from now.

I don't want to sound like some old guy who is always moaning. I freely acknowledge that there are many excellent, well-engineered products that didn't exist when I was a boy – the pocket calculator and kettles that switch off automatically are two that fill me yet with gratitude and wonder – but it does seem to me that an awful lot of things out there have been designed by people who cannot possibly have stopped to think how they will be used.

Just think for a moment of all the everyday items you have to puzzle over – fax machines, photocopiers, central heating thermostats, airline tickets, television remote control units, hotel showers and alarm clocks, microwave ovens, almost any electrical product owned by someone other than you – because they are ill thought out.

And why are they so ill thought out? Because all the best designers are making running shoes. Either that, or they are just idiots. In either case, it really isn't fair.

Bill Bryson

2 Find words in the text which mean the same as the following:

¶3 *infinite*   ¶4 *decorate*   ¶5 *typeface*   ¶6 *idiotic*   ¶7 *discover by accident*   ¶8 *hollow area*
¶9 *without human intervention*   *numerous*   ¶10 *imagine*   ¶11 *complaining*

B Choose the word or phrase which best completes each sentence:

1 The writer finds his computer keyboard ...
  a inefficient   **c** frustrating
  b confusing   **d** infuriating
2 *with a trill of gay laughter* (¶6) is an example of ...
  a heavy irony   **c** his cheerfulness in the face of adversity
  b gentle irony   **d** a paradox
3 What irritates the writer most about his computer is ...
  a the pointless boxes that appear   **c** the lack of a ½ key
  b how easy it is to delete accidentally   **d** the keys he never uses
4 The indentation on his car's dashboard works fine ...
  a when the car is driven slowly   **c** except when it is used for loose change
  b when the car is stationary   **d** except when the car is parked on a slope
5 The facility of being able to set a video recorder to record 12 months from now is ...
  a a useful feature   **c** pointless
  b a good marketing feature   **d** likely to make programming it harder
6 The problem with many products is that the designers ...
  a have concentrated on appearance   **c** are inadequately trained
  b haven't considered the users   **d** know how to use their own products

C Write a SUMMARY of what the writer LIKES about modern design and technology (50–70 words).

D Discuss these questions:
- What did you find funny about the article? Tell each other which parts struck a chord with you.
- Look again at paragraph 10. Is the writer just *an old guy who is always moaning*?
- Look again at paragraph 12. Which of the products have you had to puzzle over? Do you share the writer's feelings about them?

12.4 Verbs + prepositions

A Read each set of notes and then do the exercises below. Choose from among these prepositions:

about   against   at   by   for   from   in   on   out   of   to   with

1 Some verbs normally **HAVE TO BE** followed by a preposition:

Who does that white coat belong to?
You must be confusing me with someone else.
Where do you come from?

Fill in the missing prepositions in this list:

combine something	*engage*	*part* ....
compare something	*invest*	*reason* ....
contrast something	*lean*	*rely* ....
depend	*mistake it/them*	*separate something* ....

2 Some verbs **CAN** be used with a prepositional phrase (but they needn't be):

I think he applied last week.
Yes, but what did he apply for? Who did he apply to? When did he apply?
He applied to his father's company for a job.

Add the missing prepositions. The verbs in blue can be used with more than one preposition.

agree	*insist*	*smell* ....
apologise	*interfere*	*struggle* ....
approve	*intrude*	*succeed* ....
bargain	*negotiate*	*suffer* ....
care	*object*	*talk* ....
decide	*quarrel*	*vote* ....
experiment	*resign*	*watch* ....
hope	*retire*	*worry* ....

3 Some verbs normally followed by an object can **ALSO** be used with prepositional phrases:

She accused someone. Yes but what did she accuse them of?
He borrowed something. Yes, but who did he borrow it from?

Add the missing prepositions. The verbs in blue can be used with more than one preposition.

admire him	*deliver it*	*thank her* ....
blame her	*punish him*	*threaten them* ....
congratulate him	*rescue them*	*use it* ....
consult her	*respect her*	*warn him* ....
convince them	*take it*	

B Fill each gap with a suitable preposition.

Penguin power pushes
propellers aside

A ship that flaps its way [__1__] the water like a penguin is to be built [__2__] the United States after engineers realised that the bird is much better at moving [__3__] the water than a propeller-driven boat.

Boat builders have been using propellers [__4__] over 150 years but researchers have been uncomfortable at the knowledge that the aquatic world, [__5__] 150 million years [__6__] evolutionary experience, has ignored propellers as a means of moving [__7__] water.

After studying the fins [__8__] various fish, the researchers, [__9__] the Massachusetts Institute of Technology, realised that penguins slide [__10__] water at least 15 per cent more efficiently than boats.

From videos of swimming penguins, the researchers watched the birds' pectoral fins waft towards and away from each other. The sideways forces cancelled each other out and the resulting thrust was almost entirely forwards. Last month the engineers, led [____]¹¹ Prof Michael Triantafyllou, demonstrated a 12ft computer-controlled boat [____]¹² two "oscillating foils" based [____]¹³ the same principles.

The foils [____]¹⁴ the prototype boat look just like two ordinary rudders, but they work [____]¹⁵ an entirely different way. Two large motors swivel the foils towards and away from each other [____]¹⁶ a rudder-like movement. Two smaller motors also make the foils twist slightly.

[____]¹⁷ ensuring that the foils work together to make an opening and closing motion, their sideways forces cancel each other out just as with a penguin.

The prototype boat's maiden voyage [____]¹⁸ Charles River, Boston, was a success. Triantafyllou has now agreed [____]¹⁹ a shipyard to build a 40ft wide, 150ft long version [____]²⁰ the penguin-inspired ship. [____]²¹ larger fins mounted underneath the stern the efficiency could be even better, he says. And the fish-like wake is difficult to detect, which could be an advantage [____]²² military vessels.

The group's first attempt [____]²³ fish-like propulsion led to Robotuna, a robot that swims like a tuna. The scientists say the penguin is a better bet [____]²⁴ human transport because it holds its body still as it swims.

Aisling Irwin

12.5 The passive – 2   ADVANCED GRAMMAR

(A) 1 Study the following reasons and then decide which of them apply to sentences 1–10 below:

> **Why the passive is used**
>
> The passive may be used for a variety of reasons, including the following:
> a to dissociate speakers or writers from an unpopular decision or announcement
> b to give an impression of objectivity – especially in scientific or technical texts and in news reports
> c to give the effect of formality
> d to arouse sympathy for the victim
> e to describe actions where the people responsible are unknown, unimportant or irrelevant – or obvious
> f to avoid blaming anyone directly for what has happened
> g for variety – to make a change from using the active
> h when using the passive makes the sentence easier to read and the meaning easier to understand than a clumsy or inelegant active sentence – i.e. the passive is more concise
> i to emphasise the people responsible (using by …)

1 Dictionaries may not be used in the examination. ....
2 He was criticised by his father, but praised by his mother. ....
3 He's been misunderstood and made to feel inadequate all his life. ....
4 It has been decided to restrict parking by students in the college grounds. ....
5 Several people have been injured in accidents at this junction. ....
6 The solution was heated to boiling point and then allowed to cool to 20°. ....
7 Although we arrived early, we were kept waiting for an hour. ....
8 We arrived late because our flight was delayed. ....
9 The documents are being photocopied at the moment. ....
10 Some money has been taken from my room. ....

2 Now rewrite each sentence in the active voice. How does the emphasis of each sentence change when it's rewritten?

(B) Rewrite each of these sentences using the passive, starting with the words on the right:

1 Everyone looks down on her and she's fed up with it.   She's fed up with ....
2 The children's grandparents looked after them.   The children ....
3 My assistant is dealing with this matter.   This matter ....
4 Customers must pay for any breakages.   All breakages ....
5 You can't rely on Tony to finish the work on time.   Tony can't ....

6 I'll get someone to see to the repairs right away.   The repairs ....

7 Someone had broken into her apartment during the night.   Her apartment ....

8 People often look on scientists as experts.   Scientists ....

9 Someone pointed out to me that I was wearing odd socks.   It ....

10 People might refer to him as 'technophobic'.   He ....

11 Without permission for a new runway they can't expand
the airport.   Until permission ....

12 Electronics might intimidate some people, but not me.   Some ....

13 I can't figure out how to dispose of all these old magazines.   How can all ....

14 You'll have to get rid of all those old magazines.   Those old magazines ....

15 They have accounted for all the survivors of the accident.   All the ....

12.6 *give* and *take*

VERBS AND IDIOMS

A Which of the following would you GIVE and which would you TAKE?

> a liking to someone or something   a photograph   a pride in something   advice to someone
> an answer   an explanation   an interest in something   encouragement   evidence
> issue with someone   part in something   permission   pity on someone   someone a kiss
> someone a lift   someone a ring   someone a shock   someone some help
> your time over something

B Find synonyms for the phrases in red, or explain their meaning. Use a dictionary if necessary.

1 Don't take it for granted that everything's going to be easy: you should be prepared to take the rough with the smooth when you take up a new job.

2 When we criticised him I half expected him to take offence, but he took it in good part, and in the ensuing discussion he gave as good as he got.

3 She was quite taken aback when I took her up on her offer.

4 They were quite taken with each other on their first meeting.

5 He nearly took us in, but he gave himself away when he started giggling.

6 He took exception to the fact that she was starting to take him for granted.

7 I know you're annoyed but don't take it out on me – take it up with the people who were responsible.

8 Cheer up! Why don't you take him out for a meal, it may take you out of yourself.

9 She can take off her father's voice and mannerisms brilliantly – especially the way he takes off his glasses when his patience is about to give out.

10 There was so much information that I couldn't take it all in.

C Fill the gaps in these sentences with suitable phrases from the list below. You may need to change the form of the verbs.

1 The sight was so beautiful it .... her breath ....

2 I remember .... the message but I've forgotten where I put it.

3 About 75% of the land area of Britain is .... agriculture.

4 You really should .... insurance before you travel.

5 You've .... more work than you can manage and it seems to be .... it .... of you. Why don't you .... a few days .... ?

6 I used to go jogging but now I .... it .... Perhaps I'll .... swimming instead.

7 I'm feeling a bit tired of driving, would you mind .... for a while?

8 I apologise. I .... all those things I said about your new hairstyle.

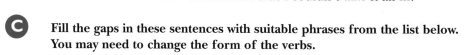

> give over to   give up   take away   take back   take down
> take off   take on   take out   take out   take over   take up

A 👥 **Read these notes and then look at the pairs of nouns below:**

- How are the nouns different? What do they have in common – if anything?
- What abstract noun or verb is associated with each noun – or does a phrase have to be used instead?

> These suffixes can be used to form nouns from verbs, or from abstract nouns:
>
> **-er** *employer   gangster   examiner   adviser   reviewer   office cleaner*
> *computer   vacuum cleaner   timer   tranquilliser*
> **-ee** *employee   trainee   addressee   absentee*
> **-or** *inventor   supervisor   operator   juror   perpetrator   impersonator*
> **-ist** *scientist   technologist   terrorist   environmentalist*

astrologer • astronomer   *Astronomers look through telescopes but astrologers work out horoscopes.*
Both an astronomer and an astrologer study the stars.
The nouns are astrology and astronomy.

administrator • dictator	attacker • hijacker	bartender • moneylender
chauvinist • feminist	councillor • counsellor	demonstrator • spectator
employer • employee	fortune-teller • storyteller	landowner • loner
miner • minor	pawnbroker • stockbroker	payer • payee
persecutor • prosecutor	predecessor • successor	psychologist • psychiatrist
researcher • searcher	shareholder • householder	troubleshooter • troublemaker

B **Read these notes and then form verbs from the adjectives and nouns below, using *-ise/-ize* or *-en*:**

> These suffixes can be used to form verbs from adjectives and nouns:
>
> **-en** *dampen   ripen   harden*
> **-ise/-ize** *modernise   advertise   popularise*
>
> British English spelling: *-ise* or *-ize* (as you prefer)
> American English spelling: *-ize*

context *contextualise* deaf emphasis familiar general glamour loose moist
national sharp straight strong subsidy summary sweet sympathy synthetic
thick tight victim visual wide

C **1** Highlight the words you'd like to remember – and any spellings you find troublesome. Use a dictionary, paying particular attention to the examples.

2 👥 Write a short exercise with gaps and give the sentences to another pair to do.
e.g. *A person who is sent for to deal with problems is a* .... (troubleshooter)

Thinking about the reader READING AND WRITING SKILLS

A **1** **Read the text through before looking at the questions below.**

Over the years I have fumbled my way through life, walking into doors, failing to figure out water faucets, incompetent at working the simple things of everyday life. "Just me," I would mumble. "Just mechanical ineptitude." But as I studied psychology and watched the behavior of other people, I began to realize that I was not alone. My difficulties were mirrored by the problems of others. And we all seemed to blame ourselves. Could the whole world be mechanically incompetent?

The truth emerged slowly. My research activities led me to the study of human error and industrial accidents. Humans, I discovered, do not always behave clumsily. Humans do not always err. But they do when the things they use are badly conceived and designed. Nonetheless, we still see human error blamed for all that befalls society. Does a commercial airliner crash? "Pilot error," say the reports. Does a Soviet nuclear power plant have a serious problem? "Human error," says the newspaper. Do two ships at sea collide? "Human error" is the official cause. But careful analysis of these kinds of incidents usually gives the lie to such a story. At the famous American nuclear power plant disaster at Three Mile Island, the blame was placed on plant operators who misdiagnosed the problems. But was it human error? Consider the phrase "operators who misdiagnosed the problems." The phrase reveals that first there were problems – in fact, a series of mechanical failures. Then why wasn't equipment failure the real cause? What about the misdiagnoses? Why didn't the operators correctly determine the cause? Well, how about the fact that the proper instruments were not available, that the plant operators acted in ways that in the past had always been reasonable and proper? How about the pressure relief valve that failed to close, even though the operator pushed the proper button and even though a light came on stating it was closed? Why was the operator blamed for not checking two more instruments (one on the rear of the control panel) and determining that the light was faulty? (Actually, the operator did check one of them.) Human error? To me it sounds like equipment failure coupled with serious design error.

And, yes, what about my inability to use the simple things of everyday life? I can use complicated things. I am quite expert at computers, and electronics, and complex laboratory equipment. Why do I have trouble with doors, light switches, and water faucets? How come I can work a multimillion-dollar computer installation, but not my home VCR? While we all blame ourselves, the real culprit – faulty design – goes undetected. And millions of people feel themselves to be mechanically inept. It is time for a change. ■

from the Preface to *The Psychology of Everyday Things* by Donald A. Norman

2 **Go through the text and answer these questions:**

1 Highlight THREE sentences that seem to sum up the writer's message.
2 Look at the cases where he uses *I, me* or *my* and underline them – what is the effect of this?
3 How many times does the writer use *we* or *ourselves*?
4 How many times does he use *you* or *your*, addressing the reader directly?
5 How many times does he use imperatives, addressing the reader directly?
6 How many questions does the writer ask? What is the effect of this?
   Put a ring round all the question marks: (?) (?)
7 How many answers does he give?
   How many questions are unanswered?
8 How well does the writer succeed in involving the reader?
9 What kind of reader does the writer seem to have in mind?
   To what extent are YOU that kind of reader?
10 How does the kind of reader he has in mind affect:
    a the content of the text
    b the style of the text

B **1** **Think of another subject you feel strongly about and which you have some personal knowledge of: e.g., traffic problems in your city, bureaucracy, energy conservation, etc. Make notes on your experiences and your views.**

2 Write a paragraph in a similar style to the text. Use the first person and answered or unanswered questions.

A **1** 👥👥👥 Discuss these questions:
- Which of the things look easier to use? Why is this?
- Can you programme a video recorder to record a TV programme? Have you ever set one wrong? Was it your fault or the designer's?

2 👥👥 Now one of you should look at Activity **6**, one at **19** and one at **28**. You'll have some more questions to ask each other about the design of everyday equipment (based on the ideas of Donald A. Norman).

B **1** Spend some time researching and thinking about the ideas you discussed earlier, looking at the way you and other people interact with doors, watches, switches, numbers, etc.

2 👥👥👥👥 Find out about each other's ideas and experiences. Discuss how you will organise and sequence your ideas for an article with this headline:

User-friendly? I don't think so!

(300–350 words)

3 🖊 Write your article, giving examples from what you discussed in A2 and discovered in your research. Make notes before you start.

COMPUTER SCIENCE

"A virus ate my homework."

13

Just good friends?

13.1 **Friends . . . and enemies** LISTENING & TOPIC VOCABULARY

Edward Hopper: Nighthawks, *1942 (detail)*

A   **Discuss these questions about the picture:**

- Where are the people? Who are they? How do they feel?
- What has happened earlier, what's happening now and what's going to happen?
- What have they said to each other earlier? What are they saying now? What are they going to say? What is their relationship?
- How does the picture make **YOU** feel? Would you like to be one of the people? Why (not)?

B   **One of you should look at Activity 7, the other at 20. You'll each have another picture to look at and describe. Ask each other questions to find out how the picture illustrates the relationships between the people.**

C   **You'll hear Ruth, William and Sarah talking about friendship. Indicate which of the speakers expresses each of the opinions listed by writing the appropriate letter in each box.**

Write R for Ruth, or W for William, or S for Sarah. Write more than one letter in the box if a view is expressed by more than one person.

1 A good friend can support you when you're feeling sad.	1
2 A good friend can tell you if you're behaving stupidly.	2
3 I don't like the partners my best friend chooses.	3
4 I have known by best friend since we were children.	4
5 I still spend a lot of time with my best friend.	5
6 It's hard for an adult to make new friends.	6
7 It's hard to break into an established circle of friends.	7
8 My best friend likes to do different things from me now.	8

D   **Discuss these questions:**

- Which of the experiences you heard about in **C** struck a chord with you?
- Describe the person who was your own best friend as a child – how has your relationship changed since you first got to know each other?
- What do you appreciate about the friends you have now? Explain why you get on well.
- Is it better to have just one or two close friends, or friends you don't know so well?

E 1 👥 Discuss the relative importance of the following qualities in a friendship or a relationship. Note down THREE important qualities that are missing from the list.

cheerfulness   commitment   compassion   compatibility   consideration   enthusiasm
generosity   good looks   intelligence   kindness   loyalty   optimism   passion   patience
politeness   punctuality   realism   reliability   responsibility   sincerity   thoughtfulness

2 And how important are the following factors in a friendship or a relationship?

age   family background   mutual interests   a sense of humour   social class
shared attitudes to religion, politics, etc.   similar personalities

3 Which FIVE features from the two lists in E1 and 2 are the most important and why? Which are the five LEAST important features?

F 1 🔊 You'll hear the same words spoken in different ways. Decide which word from the list on the right best describes each speaker's mood or tone.

1	
2	
3	
4	
5	

annoyed   jaded

anxious   patient

businesslike   sarcastic

despondent   timid

eager   impatient

2 👥 Discuss how each speaker's TONE OF VOICE conveyed their mood. Consider their speed of delivery, the amount of hesitation, the pitch of their voice, the way they emphasised words, the way they sighed or laughed or made other noises, etc.

Well, good evening. Thank you both for getting here on time and for waiting so patiently. Everyone else seems to be rather late, or maybe they haven't been able to make it. Anyway, we'll make a start I think, and if any of the others do come we can always fill them in on what's happened so far...

3 👥 Take it in turns to read the speech aloud in different ways. Can your partner guess what mood you're trying to convey?

13.2   As the saying goes...   GRAMMAR REVIEW

A These sayings and proverbs all have something to do with relationships. Rewrite each one starting with the words on the right, keeping the meaning as similar as possible to the original sentence. (This exercise revises some of the points covered in the Grammar review sections earlier in the book.)

1 A friend in need is a friend indeed.   Someone who *helps you if you're in trouble* is a
                                                true friend.
2 It takes two to make a quarrel.   When there .... , both parties ....
3 Actions speak louder than words.   What really .... do, not .... say.
4 It takes all sorts to make a world.   The world is .... people.
5 Live and let live.   Be .... and .... what they want to do.
6 It's easy to be wise after the event.   You couldn't .... happen.
7 Blood is thicker than water.   Family .... other relationships.
8 Like father like son.   A son tends .... father.
9 Many a true word is spoken in jest.   A remark ....
10 Out of sight, out of mind.   Absent friends ....
11 Absence makes the heart grow fonder.   When people ....
12 One good turn deserves another.   After someone ....
13 Where there's a will there's a way.   If you ....
14 Love is like the measles, we all have   Everyone .... , but they .
    to go through it.   .... eventually.

B 👥 Discuss which of the sayings you agree with, comparing them with your own experiences.

Proverbs should be used sparingly in conversation, and they can sound very odd when used inappropriately. We can soften their effect by adding...
– *as they say* or ... – *as the saying goes:*
"*Well, it's easy to be wise after the event – as the saying goes.*"

13.3 Family life

A Read the three extracts and discuss the questions that follow.

CHAPTER ONE

THIS is the story of a five-year sojourn that I and my family made on the Greek island of Corfu. It was originally intended to be a mildly nostalgic account of the natural history of the island, but I made a grave mistake by introducing my family into the book in the first few pages. Having got themselves on paper, they then proceeded to establish themselves and invite various friends to share the chapters. It was only with the greatest difficulty, and by exercising considerable cunning, that I managed to retain a few pages here and there which I could devote exclusively to animals.

I have attempted to draw an accurate and unexaggerated picture of my family in the following pages; they appear as I saw them. To explain some of their more curious ways, however, I feel that I should state that at the time we were in Corfu the family were all quite young: Larry, the eldest, was twenty-three; Leslie was nineteen; Margo eighteen; while I was the youngest, being of the tender and impressionable age of ten. We have never been very certain of my mother's age, for the simple reason that she can never remember her date of birth; all I can say is that she was old enough to have four children. My mother also insists that I explain that she is a widow for, as she so penetratingly observed, you never know what people might think

I did not kill my father, but I sometimes felt I had helped him on his way. And but for the fact that it coincided with a landmark in my own physical growth, his death seemed insignificant compared with what followed. My sisters and I talked about him the week after he died, and Sue certainly cried when the ambulance men tucked him up in a bright-red blanket and carried him away. He was a frail, irascible, obsessive man with yellowish hands and face. I am only including the little story of his death to explain how my sisters and I came to have such a large quantity of cement at our disposal.

In the early summer of my fourteenth year a lorry pulled up outside our house. I was sitting on the front step rereading a comic. The driver and another man came towards me. They were covered in a fine, pale dust which gave their faces a ghostly look. They were both whistling shrilly completely different tunes. I stood up and held the comic out of sight. I wished I had been reading the racing page of my father's paper, or the football results.

'Cement?' one of them said. I hooked my thumbs into my pockets, moved my weight to one foot and narrowed my eyes a little. I wanted to say something terse and appropriate, but I was not sure I had heard them right

I was born poor in rich America, yet my secret instincts were better than money and were for me a source of power. I had advantages that no one could take away from me – a clear memory and brilliant dreams and a knack for knowing when I was happy.

I was at my happiest leading two lives, and it was a satisfaction to me that the second one – of the dreamer or the sneak – I kept hidden. That was how I spent my first fifteen years. Fifteen was young then and I knew this: The poor don't belong. But one summer out of loneliness or impatience my second self did more than wake and watch, and more than remember. He began to see like a historian, and he acted. I have to save my life, I used to think.

Early that summer I was walking down a lovely crumbling little street lined with elms, called Brookview Road. The city of Boston, with its two tall buildings

👥 **Discuss these questions and note down your answers:**

1 Which extract comes from which of these books:

2 Which of the extracts makes you want to read on? Give your reasons.
3 What do the extracts have in common?
4 What are the main differences between the three extracts?
5 What kind of young person does each narrator seem to be?
6 In the first extract, how did the narrator's family *invite various friends to share the chapters*? And what does he mean by *'their more curious ways'*?
7 In the second extract, why do you think the narrator was *'rereading a comic'*? Why did he *'wish he had been reading the racing page of his father's paper'*?
8 In the third extract, what is meant by *'The poor don't belong'*?
9 What do we learn of the relationship between the narrator and his family in each extract?

B 👥→👥 **Compare your answers to the questions. Then discuss which of the qualities in 13.1 E1 are most important in FAMILY relationships between parents and children, and between sisters and brothers.**

C **Highlight any words in the extracts in A which you didn't understand (or had to guess). Use a dictionary to check their meanings.**

13.4 **Conditionals – 2**   **ADVANCED GRAMMAR**

A 1 👥 **Discuss any differences in style or meaning between the sentences in each group:**

1 If it weren't for the children they would have split up by now.
   If it wasn't for the children they would have split up by now.
   Were it not for the children they would have split up by now.
   If they didn't have children they would have split up by now.

2 If you should see Terry could you give him my regards?
   When you see Terry could you give him my regards?
   If you happen to see Terry could you give him my regards?
   If you see Terry could you give him my regards?
   Should you see Terry could you give him my regards?

3 If you wouldn't mind waiting I'll let them know you're here.
   If you don't mind waiting I'll let them know you're here.
   If you wait I'll let them know you're here.

4 Had it not been for your help I couldn't have done it.
   Without your help I couldn't have done it.
   If it hadn't been for your help I couldn't have done it.
   If you hadn't been so helpful I couldn't have done it.
   I'm glad you helped me otherwise I couldn't have done it.

2 **There are NO COMMAS in any of the above sentences. Which of them would be easier to understand if they were to have commas?**

B **Finish the incomplete sentences in such a way that each one means the same as the complete sentence before it:**

1 Please do take a seat and I'll bring you some coffee.   If you ....
2 Their relationship was doomed because of their incompatibility.   Had ....
3 I might miss my connection, if so I'll try to call you to let you know.   Should ....
4 They didn't get married because their parents were against it.   But ....
5 You probably won't have time – but I'd like you to come and see us.   If ....
6 There was such a lot of traffic: that's why we're late.   Had ....
7 She could tell him she's leaving, but it would upset him.   If ....
8 They have a wonderful relationship, and have decided to get married.   Were ....
9 She's very patient and loyal, that's why she hasn't left him.   If it ....
10 If you don't work hard at a relationship it's not likely to last.   Without ....

C 1 👥 ✎ **Write FIVE sentences about your own friends and relatives, and your relationships with them using the following structures:**

   Had...   If it weren't for...   Were...   Should...   Without...

2 👥→👥 **Compare your sentences.**

13.5 ...till death us do part?

A **1** Read this extract through carefully, preferably before the lesson.

Whenever Henry Wilt took the dog for a walk, or, to be more accurate, when the dog took him, or to be exact, when Mrs Wilt told them both to go and take themselves out of the house so that she could do her yoga exercises, he always took the same route. In fact the dog followed the route and Wilt followed the dog. They went down past the Post Office, across the playground, under the railway bridge and out on to the footpath by the river. A mile along the river and then under the railway line again and back through streets where the houses were bigger than Wilt's semi and where there were large trees and gardens and the cars were all Rovers and Mercedes. It was here that Clem, a pedigree Labrador, evidently feeling more at home, did his business while Wilt stood looking around rather uneasily, conscious that this was not his sort of neighbourhood and wishing it was. It was about the only time during their walk that he was at all aware of his surroundings. For the rest of the way Wilt's walk was an interior one and followed an itinerary completely at variance with his own appearance and that of his route. It was in fact a journey of wishful thinking, a pilgrimage along trails of remote possibility involving the irrevocable disappearance of Mrs Wilt, the sudden acquisition of wealth, power, what he would do if he was appointed Minister of Education or, better still, Prime Minister. It was partly concocted of a series of desperate expedients and partly in an unspoken dialogue so that anyone noticing Wilt (and most people didn't) might have seen his lips move occasionally and his mouth curl into what he fondly imagined was a sardonic smile as he dealt with questions or parried arguments with devastating repartee. It was on one of these walks taken in the rain after a particularly trying day at the Tech that Wilt first conceived the notion that he would only be able to fulfil his latent promise and call his life his own if some not entirely fortuitous disaster overtook his wife.

Like everything else in Henry Wilt's life it was not a sudden decision. He was not a decisive man.

6

from Wilt by Tom Sharpe

2 Note down your answers to these questions:

1 Who decided what time Clem should go for a walk?
2 Who decided on the route for the walk?
3 What do you think a *semi* (line 6) is?
4 Why did Clem feel more at home where the houses were larger?
5 Why did Wilt feel uneasy there?
6 What did Wilt do during the rest of the walk?
7 What were the three directions in which his thoughts took him?
8 How do you think Wilt fared in arguments in real life?
9 What do you think Wilt does at *the Tech*?
10 What might *some not entirely fortuitous disaster* be?
11 Why aren't we told Mrs Wilt's first name?
12 Why is Henry Wilt referred to as *Wilt* (rather than Mr Wilt or Henry)?

B **1** Now read this extract and compare it with the extract above. Find out what the two extracts have in common. How are they different?

Henry Farr did not, precisely, decide to murder his wife. It was simply that he could think of no other way of prolonging her absence from him indefinitely.

He had quite often, in the past, when she was being more than usually irritating, had fantasies about her death. She hurtled over cliffs in flaming cars or was brutally murdered on her way to the dry cleaners. But Henry was never actually responsible for the event. He was at the graveside looking mournful and interesting. Or he was coping with his daughter as she roamed the now deserted house, trying not to look as if he was glad to have the extra space. But he was never actually the instigator.

Once he had got the idea of killing her (and at first this fantasy did not seem very different from the reveries in which he wept by her open grave, comforted by young, fashionably dressed women) it took some time to appreciate that this scenario was of quite a different type from the others. It was a dream that could, if he so wished, become reality.

One Friday afternoon in September, he thought about strangling her. The Wimbledon Strangler. He liked that idea. He could see Edgar Lustgarten narrowing his eyes threateningly at the camera, as he paced out the length of Maple Drive. 'But Henry Farr,' Lustgarten was saying, 'with the folly of the criminal, the supreme arrogance of the murderer, had forgotten one vital thing. The shred of fibre that was to send Henry Farr to the gallows was – '

What was he thinking of? They didn't hang people any more. They wrote long, bestselling paperback books about them.

from The Wimbledon Poisoner by Nigel Williams

2 👥 Discuss these questions:

- Which parts of the two passages amused you? Can you explain why? (If neither passage amused you at all, what did you find annoying about them?)
- Both books were written by men – but what kind of readers were they written for? Would they appeal more to men or women, or to both?
- Look at the first sentences: Are they both 'nodders' (see 11.7)?
- What do you think is going to happen in each story? Will either of the Henries actually succeed in murdering his wife, or not?

13.6 Underlying meanings   VOCABULARY DEVELOPMENT

A 👥 Some words have particular associations with other words and ideas. Highlight these examples in the extract from Wilt in 13.5A. Decide what CONCEPT or UNDERLYING MEANING the writer expects the reader to associate each phrase with.

yoga exercises	*parried*
a semi (= semi-detached house)	*a pilgrimage*
Rovers and Mercedes	*the Tech* (= technical college)
an itinerary	*fulfil his latent promise*

B Read these notes and then decide which of the words in each pair below seem to have more pejorative associations:

Some words have pejorative or uncomplimentary associations:
    That's a stupid mistake!   She's a very fussy person.

Some words have less pejorative or more positive associations:
    That's a silly mistake!   She's a very discerning person.

Associations very much depend on the context in which words are used.

cautious · prudent	cooperative · obedient	difficult · challenging
dreamer · idealist	frank · sincere	gullible · trusting
humble · modest	laid back · lazy	light-hearted · frivolous
moody · depressed	naive · innocent	optimistic · impractical
oversight · mistake	realistic · pessimistic	solemn · serious
stubborn · resolute	studious · hard-working	tease · mock

C 1 Choose FIVE of the following ideas and write down five nouns or adjectives that you associate with each of them. Pick words that reflect your feelings – as in the examples:

For example, *clever* and *bright* are generally complimentary, but to call someone *a clever dick* or a *bright spark* is disparaging. It's also possible to use complimentary words in a sarcastic or ironic way: *That was <u>very</u> clever of you!*

Being at home	*security predictable reassurance mother warmth*	
Away from home	*freedom danger excitement interesting cold*	
Being with a friend	Meeting a stranger	Being alone
Parents	Marriage	Children
Taking an exam	Learning English	Music
Earning a living	Holidays	School
Shopping	Reading	Television

2 👥 Compare your ideas. Which of the words you wrote down seem to have negative and which have positive associations?

"Leave those… Kevin will do the washing up."

A   Read the passage and then discuss the questions below with a partner.

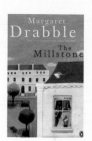

M y career has always been marked by a strange mixture of confidence and cowardice: almost, one might say, made by it. Take, for instance, the first time I tried spending a night with a man in a hotel. I was nineteen at the time, an age appropriate for such adventures, and needless to say I was not married. I am still not married, a fact of some significance, but more of that later. The name of the boy, if I remember rightly, was Hamish. I do remember rightly. I really must try not to be deprecating. Confidence, not cowardice, is the part of myself which I admire, after all.

Hamish and I had just come down from Cambridge at the end of the Christmas term: we had conceived our plan well in advance, and had each informed our parents that term ended a day later than it actually did, knowing quite well that they would not be interested enough to check, nor sufficiently au fait to ascertain the value of their information if they did. So we arrived in London together in the late afternoon, and took a taxi from the station to our destined hotel. We had worked everything out, and had even booked our room, which would probably not have been necessary, as the hotel we had selected was one of those large central cheap-smart ones, specially designed for adventures such as ours. I was wearing a gold curtain ring on the relevant finger. We had decided to stick to Hamish's own name, which, being Andrews, was unmemorable enough, and less confusing than having to think up a pseudonym. We were well educated, the two of us, in the pitfalls of such occasions, having both of us read at one time in our lives a good deal of cheap fiction, and indeed we both carried ourselves with considerable aplomb. We arrived, unloaded our suitably-labelled suitcases, and called at the desk for our key. It was here that I made my mistake. For some reason I was requested to sign the register. I now know that it is by no means customary for wives to sign hotel registers

from The Millstone *by Margaret Drabble*

1 What kind of person does Rosamund, the narrator, seem to be?
2 Find an example of the narrator poking fun at herself.
3 How would you describe the tone or style of the passage?
4 What do you think is going to happen in the rest of the novel? What clues are given in the passage? Why is it called *The Millstone* do you think?

B 1 👥 **The author wrote the story in the first person. Why do you think she did this? What would be the effects of changing *my* to *her*, *I* to *she*, *we* to *they* and *our* to *their*?**

2 Look again at 13.5. If the extracts from *Wilt* and *The Wimbledon Poisoner* were in the first person, what effect would this have on them?

If the extracts in 13.3 were in the third person, what effect would this have?

C 1 ✎ Think of an embarrassing, amusing or memorable experience you've had (or can imagine having). Write TWO versions of the opening paragraph of a story about the experience: one in the first person (using *I/me/my*), the other in the third person as if you're writing about a 'character' (about 50 words each).

2 👥 Compare your paragraphs. Discuss which version was easier to write and which is most convincing.

If you're writing an article or a letter in the exam, narrative can help to engage the reader.

A fictional or semi-fictional story can be easier to handle than one which sticks strictly to the truth, because you can make the events fit the time and space available – and it may be easier to restrict the vocabulary to words you know.

A 🔲 A proposal is like a report, except that the focus is on the future. Proposals include recommendations for discussion or for action. Proposals include section headings. Read this information and then MAKE NOTES on your ideas for the facilities the proposed students' centre should provide.

Lion Yard to become International Student Centre?

The owners of Lion Yard, which has been empty for over a year, have offered the building to the city on condition that it is converted into an international student centre.

Lion Yard was built in 1800 as a leather warehouse and is a historic building. Any conversion of the building would have to retain its exterior and remain faithful to the historical nature of the interior.

The Mayor is asking students to submit economically viable proposals on what facilities the new Centre should provide, to make the best use of the building whilst retaining its historic character.

International Student Centre?

Students find it hard to make friends

A recent survey among students revealed that many feel that they have a narrow circle of friends and that their social life would be much better if they could widen this circle. Many students say that their only friends are their class-mates. They find it hard to make contact with students from other faculties and other year groups and institutions.

A new Student Centre, which would enable students from different colleges and institutions to meet socially, could help to bridge that gap.

B ✏️ Write your proposal (300–350 words). Use section headings.

"Trust me, he'll come running home when he hears the can opener"

14

All in a day's work

14.1 / Work and business

VOCABULARY AND LISTENING

A **1** 🔊 You'll hear a doctor, a butler/house-manager, and a photographer describing their jobs. MAKE NOTES on which aspects of their work each one enjoys most and which aspects they don't enjoy.

2 👥 Discuss these questions:
- What are the pros and cons of each person's job?
- Which of the jobs would you prefer to have? Give your reasons.
- What would be the ideal job for you – and why?

B Choose the best word or phrase to fill each gap in each text. Look at the example first:

In Part I of the Reading Paper you'll have to do three vocabulary exercises similar to these. Some of the questions in the exam will be harder than these.

A large company is owned by its _____ ⁰, who may be individual _____ ¹ or major financial _____ ², but it is controlled by a board of _____ ³. Many _____ ⁴ corporations are divided into different divisions. For example Vivendi, a French-based corporation, has _____ ⁵ all over the world, including Universal Studios and Connex, who run trains. But the _____ ⁶ of the company is in France.

0	**A** staff	**B** shareholders ✓	**C** managers	**D** customers
1	**A** unions	**B** clients	**C** banks	**D** investors
2	**A** societies	**B** institutes	**C** institutions	**D** guilds
3	**A** bosses	**B** managers	**C** presidents	**D** directors
4	**A** multi-national	**B** nationalised	**C** local	**D** cosmopolitan
5	**A** branches	**B** departments	**C** subsidiaries	**D** offices
6	**A** directors	**B** headquarters	**C** bosses	**D** factories

When designer Jane Rodgers was _____ ⁷ up by the boss of an internet start-up company serving the film industry, she thought she knew what she was in for. "I researched the guy and his _____ ⁸ businesses, bought a new suit and lied to my boss about having to leave early for a doctor's appointment on Tuesday evening." Rodgers met her _____ ⁹ new employer not in his office but in a bar in Hoxton, an up-and-coming area of East London. "Imagine my surprise when, after five minutes of chitchat, first date questions really, he leaned towards me, stared earnestly into my eyes and told me: 'Jane, I think you're the one.' I felt like it was me as a person that was being _____ ¹⁰." He had neither seen her CV nor told her what the job _____ ¹¹, but he was determined to _____ ¹² her. She declined the offer.

7	**A** e-mailed	**B** called	**C** telephoned	**D** contacted
8	**A** previous	**B** further	**C** past	**D** prior
9	**A** future	**B** probable	**C** prospective	**D** likely
10	**A** seen	**B** scrutinised	**C** addressed	**D** interviewed
11	**A** earned	**B** consisted	**C** included	**D** involved
12	**A** rent	**B** interview	**C** fire	**D** hire

The selection and _____ [13] staff is the responsibility of the human _____ [14] department. They carry out interviews after looking at the suitability of all the applicants, looking at their _____ [15] and making a short list of candidates to interview. This department is also responsible for the _____ [16] and welfare of staff. If the company is in financial _____ [17] and has to cut back on its staff and make people _____ [18], they are also responsible for dealing with this.

13 **A** finding	**B** recruitment	**C** advertising	**D** choice
14 **A** personnel	**B** awareness	**C** personal	**D** resources
15 **A** photographs	**B** portfolios	**C** CVs	**D** referees
16 **A** instruction	**B** training	**C** education	**D** induction
17 **A** difficulties	**B** hardships	**C** dilemmas	**D** embarrassments
18 **A** idle	**B** jobless	**C** redundant	**D** unemployed

14.2 Collocations: verb phrases VOCABULARY DEVELOPMENT

A **1** Which of the following things *break*? And which can *change*?

waves   traffic lights   a boy's voice   a storm   the weather   your mood   day

2 Which of the following things can you *break*? And which can you *change*? (Some can be used with either verb, with different meanings.)

a promise   a world record   an appointment   a tablecloth   crockery   direction
gear   money   someone's heart   the bed or the sheets   a habit   the ice   the law
the news to someone   the silence   the subject   trains   your arm   your clothes
your leg   your mind   your shoes

And in what circumstances might you break or change each of them?

B Which of the following things can you *follow*? And which can you *lose*? (Some can be used with either verb, with different meanings.)

an argument   a line of argument   a route or directions   a story   trade or profession
advice or instructions   someone's example or their lead   an idea   control over something
face   heart   a football team   a football match   interest in something
the fashion or a trend   the thread of a story   track of something   weight   your job
your nerve   your temper   your voice if you have a cold   your way or bearings

And in what circumstances might you follow or lose each of them?

C Fill the gaps in these sentences with suitable words from the list below, changing the form of the verb as necessary.

1 Can I _____ you a favour? I'd like you to _____ me a hand with _____ this heavy package.
2 If you want to _____ a bank account, they may ask you to _____ references.
3 I'd like to _____ the order which I _____ last week – I've _____ my mind about wanting it.
4 Always _____ careful attention to what the interviewer says. You should answer clearly but there's no need to _____ your voice above the normal level. Don't reply too quickly: give yourself time to _____ your thoughts.
5 When he _____ me the chocolates, I couldn't _____ the temptation to _____ them even though I was trying to _____ weight.
6 Although she _____ a very busy life, _____ her own business, she tries to _____ a balance between the demands of her work and her private life.
7 She tried to _____ light on the situation by _____ our attention to the fact that we would have to _____ the costs of the scheme.
8 No one _____ any objection when we _____ the decision to _____ the next meeting on Sunday.

accept   ask   bear   cancel   change   collect   draw   hold   lead   lend   lift   lose
offer   open   pay   place   raise   raise   reach   resist   run   strike   supply   throw

This section deals with only a small portion of a vast topic. The only way to learn collocations of this kind is by reading and listening carefully – and by referring to a dictionary to check up when necessary.

Which of these students' endings to a job application letter are most effective? Which encourage the reader to look favourably on the application?

1

> In order to improve my English skills I would like to work for about two years in England and I think the position as a junior commercial banker would fit with my imagination. I am ready for further discussions. Give me a ring or write to me.

3

> I have a good knowledge of English and German, and I am learning Spanish.
>   I enclose my curriculum vitae and will be available for interview any day after September 1. My present position is subject to one month's notice.
>   I look forward to your reply.

2

> Besides my mother tongue, German, I can also speak English and Japanese fairly well.
>   If you feel that my qualifications meet with your requirements, I shall be pleased to come for an interview.
>   Please find enclosed a curriculum vitae, educational reports and certificates of training.

4

> I can type and take shorthand, I enjoy contact with people and I am a willing and responsible person.
>   I am very interested in the job you are offering and reckon myself to be the right person for it.
>   I look forward to hearing from you,

 Look at the final paragraphs of the passages in 9.3, 9.7, 10.7, 12.3, 12.4B, 12.8 and 14.5, taking account of the very last sentence in particular. Discuss these questions:

- Which one has the least effective ending? Which one has the most effective ending? Why?
- Do short sentences seem more effective than long, complex ones? Why (not)?
- Why is a good ending important?

 Now look at the final paragraphs of your own recent compositions:

- Which of them are you most pleased with? Why?
- Which of them could be improved? Rewrite the last sentences of these.

 Study the notes and examples and fill the gaps in the sentences below. Highlight any phrasal verbs that you're unfamiliar with and look them up.

> **1** Some phrasal verbs are **intransitive** (they don't take an object):
>
> When we challenged him to justify his point of view he backed down.
> He wasn't being serious, but I didn't catch on until he started smiling.
>
> **But not:** I didn't catch immediately on. ✗
>
> | | | | | | |
> |---|---|---|---|---|---|
> | check up | climb down | cool off | close in | die out | fall apart |
> | fall behind | pass away | pay up | ring off | settle down | settle up |
> | shop around | speak up | stand out | stay on | stop over | wear off |

a If you want to save money you should .... before making a purchase.
b After a few moments' silence, one of them .... and asked a question.
c The effects of the wine .... by the next morning.

> **2** With most **transitive** phrasal verbs (i.e. verbs that take an object), the object can come in various positions, but not if the object is a pronoun:
>
> They've brought the meeting forward.   They've called the meeting off.
> They've brought forward the meeting.   They've called off the meeting.
> They've brought it forward. They've called it off.
> The meeting's been brought forward.   The meeting's been called off.
> **But not:** They've brought forward it. ✗   They've called off it. ✗

carry out	cut back	dream up	drive out	explain away	follow up
hand in	leave behind	pay back	rip off	send up	sort out	think up
tone down	trade in	try out	use up	win over	write out

a Thanks for lending me the money, I promise I'll .... on Friday.
b Everyone was .... by the force of her arguments.
c The little boy was very upset because his mother ....

3 With some transitive phrasal verbs the **object** must come immediately **after** the verb:
   They tried to catch me out by asking me a trick question.
   They tried to catch the interviewees out by asking them trick questions.
   But not: They tried to catch out me. ✗

   | call back | count in | cut off | give up | invite out | order about | see out | show around |
   | start off | tear up |

a When they left I went downstairs with them and ....
b Pam is a new student, could one of you .... , please?
c I wanted to .... on Friday night, but she said she was washing her hair.

4 Some phrasal verbs can be followed by a preposition:
   I was trying to catch up <u>on</u> the work I'd missed.
      (**but**   I've missed a lot of work and I'm trying to catch up.)
   He disliked having to clean up <u>after</u> his guests.
      (**but**   He disliked having to clean up.   He disliked having to clean everything up.)

   | tidy up <u>after</u> | check up <u>on</u> | crack down <u>on</u> | creep up <u>on</u> |
   | miss out <u>on</u> | play along <u>with</u> | wait up <u>for</u> |

a I wasn't invited to the party and I was afraid I might be .... the fun.
b I'm just interested in how you're getting on – I'm not ....

5 Some phrasal verbs **MUST** be used with a preposition:
   You shouldn't talk down <u>to</u> children.
   He finds it hard to live up <u>to</u> his mother's expectations.

   | come up <u>against</u> | face up <u>to</u> | grow out <u>of</u> | lead up <u>to</u> | stick up <u>for</u> |

a When they set up their new business they .... a lot of problems.
b She was being unusually polite to me and I wondered what it was all ....

The object of a **verb + preposition** (see 12.4) **MUST** come after the preposition:
We were counting on him to help us.   We were counting on Bill to help us.
   But not: We were counting him on. ✗   We were counting Bill on. ✗
I talked her out of giving up.   I talked Jo out of giving up.   She was talked out of giving up.
   But not: I talked her giving up out of. ✗   She was talked giving up out of. ✗

B Fill each of the blanks with a suitable phrasal verb from 1 to 5 above.

1 If you've got a parking ticket you can't just .... – you'll have to ....
2 It was clearly my fault but I was able to .... an excuse to ....
3 He was threatening to .... his notice, but I managed to .... and persuade him to ....
4 I'm relying on you to .... if there's any trouble.
5 Let's hope you aren't .... by this question!
6 If you already have a car, you can .... when you buy a new one.
7 I'm going to be back very late tonight – don't ....
8 He eventually .... after we'd presented all the arguments.
9 Customs officers have been .... people who are over the duty free limit.
10 She used to be a very sulky little girl, but she .... eventually.

14.5 Learning to be happy

A Read the first paragraph of this article: what are YOUR answers to the questions?

Learning to be happy

WHY DO some people exude humour and good cheer while others seem to treat every day like a funeral? What makes the elderly more contented with their lot than the young? And why isn't winning the National Lottery necessarily a good thing?

As another grey Monday morning dawns, these are some of the questions that make Michael Argyle, Emeritus Professor of Psychology at Oxford Brookes University, go into work with a spring in his step.

While his colleagues work themselves into a frenzy measuring the effects of Prozac on depressed lab rats, Professor Argyle, who is a youthful 71, is turning his mind to a far more rewarding area of study: happiness.

B Read the rest of the article and then answer the questions that follow:

1 Who has it and who doesn't? And how do those of us with less of it get more? It is a riddle that has exercised philosophers ever since Aristotle first identified happiness as the end of all human activity. Wealth and health are thought to be a means to it, but the thing itself always seems to be just beyond our grasp.

2 After a decade studying happiness or "subjective well-being", to give it its proper psychological term, Argyle concludes that the best guarantee of long-term happiness is something called "serious leisure" – a hobby or activity that involves your whole being.

3 It could be bridge or it could be bungee jumping. Or it could be an activity as innocuous as reading or housework.

4 It could even be Scottish country dancing – a passion the professor admits to indulging twice a week.

5 "It's extremely invigorating and a great source of euphoria," says Argyle. "It's also a highly social activity, which is a very important component of happiness. The music is cheerful. The point is it doesn't really matter what you do as long as you find the activity challenging and absorbing."

6 Other experts, like Mihaly Csikszentmihaly, Professor of Psychology at the University of Chicago, concur. He has a similar theory called "flow". This is what a chess player senses at the most intense point in a game or skiers feel when they hit a particular groove on a black run, a feeling they describe as being "at one with the slope".

7 "Flow is produced by the balance between the demands of what you are doing and the skill which you have to do it," explains Argyle. "It's a state of loss of self-awareness, brought about by facing challenges with necessary skills."

8 Because most people are by nature lazy and undisciplined, the majority find it easier to achieve flow when they are forced to rise to challenges imposed on them from outside, hence the importance of work as a source of happiness.

But work can also be a huge source of stress and there seems to be less time than ever for the simple pleasures of life.

This is where Professor Argyle's theories come in. Flow, he argues, is all very well for the adrenalin-driven commodities traders of this world, but those of us who don't have a high-powered job in the City – or any job for that matter – may have to look elsewhere for contentment.

"There really is a problem here," he writes in his latest book, *The Social Psychology of Leisure*, "in that free time has greatly increased but those who have the greatest increase have not been able to convert it into satisfying forms of leisure."

The best example is TV. Recent studies have shown that Britain is in danger of becoming a nation of couch potatoes and Argyle agrees that because of its essential passivity TV is one of the activities least likely to produce flow. "The bad thing about TV is it means you are not doing something else, like talking to your friends."

On the other hand, Argyle points out that TV is often the focus for family gatherings and that soap operas can provide a sort of "fantasy social life".

So what sort of "serious leisure" activities should we be considering if we want a slice of Nirvana?

One answer is to ask the subject to write down what they do at each hour of the day, and how it makes them feel. This technique, known as "pleasant activities therapy", was invented by Peter Lewinsohn. The data is fed into a computer which comes up with the activities that tend to produce the greatest happiness for the greatest number.

Professor Argyle's own study of leisure groups put dancing at the top of the contentment charts, which you may or may not see as a happy coincidence given the professor's own passion for hopping about in a kilt ("it's a bit of an in-joke in the department, actually," says Argyle, grinning).

Next comes church, not so much for its religious aspects, although these are important (belief in the afterlife and all that), as mingling with other worshippers.

"Church is a great source of comfort and companionship, particularly for the elderly and isolated," says Argyle, who happens to be a devout Anglican and an active member of the university congregation.

Next is any other activity that involves contact with people – such as volunteer work, or simply sitting around and relaxing with family and friends – followed by reading, making or fixing things and team sports. Cooking, housework and shopping are all ranked above watching TV.

But isn't all this ranking of different leisure activities beside the point? After all, there are plenty of compulsive-depressive types (bond dealers come to mind) who work all hours, go skiing every weekend and still end up committing suicide at 35.

For a moment Argyle looks as if he might frown.

"Just as there are happy people, there are unhappy people," he says, answering one of the questions posed at the outset of this article. The difference is that unhappy people look at themselves when things go wrong, but happy people only look at themselves when things go right. "The Americans call it the Pollyanna effect – always looking on the bright side."

Argyle can even demonstrate this phenomenon using something he calls the Oxford Happiness Inventory. This was compiled by inverting items from something called the Beck Depression Inventory. There are 29 multiple-choice questions like: "Do you laugh never/sometimes/a lot/all the time?" and: "Are you optimistic about the state of the world?"

Whatever personality type you are, however, he argues that a happy marriage can more than make up for it. Indeed, Argyle, who has been married 46 years and has four children and eight grandchildren, argues that a loving relationship is by far the greatest single source of contentment (conversely, an unhappy marriage is one of the greatest sources of distress).

So what about the answers to some of those questions posed at the outset: why are the old more content than the young and why isn't winning the National Lottery necessarily a good thing?

The answer to the first is the flipside of flow: what Professor Argyle calls "a cognitive appraisal of the goal-achievement gap".

"When you're young the gap between your goals and your ability to achieve them tends to be wider hence anxiety. But when you're older you've achieved more and don't aspire to as much."

Okay, but surely winning the Lottery can't make you any more anxious?

"Actually, lots of people's lives seem to be wrecked by it," says Argyle, deadly serious. "They give up their work, so they lose their job aspirations. Then they move house and their new neighbours ignore them. Finally, they row with their family."

Argyle is getting gloomier by the minute.

"Look," he says. "If wealth were the source of happiness you would expect that as societies got richer the sum of happiness would increase. In fact that's not the case at all. Unfortunately, the only thing that seems to matter to some people is being better off than the next person."

Mark Honigsbaum

Choose the best alternative to fill each gap.

1 According to Prof Argyle 'serious leisure' is something you ....
are passionate about   spend all your spare time doing   take up when you're older

2 In principle, Prof Csikszentmihaly and Prof Argyle ....
see eye to eye   see things differently   have nothing in common

3 Prof Csikszentmihaly believes that work brings happiness to ....
few people   most people   some people

4 Prof Argyle says many people can't find happiness at work because they don't have ....
enough free time   demanding jobs   enough time to enjoy their work

5 People can be helped to find happiness by ....
being told jokes   reflecting on how they spend their time   observing others having fun

6 Prof Argyle believes that ....
everyone can be happy   happiness can be learnt   not everyone can be happy

7 Older people tend to be happier than younger people because they ....
are less worried about being successful   have learnt that it's no use worrying about failure

8 Lottery winners often ....
spend all their money very quickly   become very unhappy   give their money away

C Find each of the phrases below in the article and highlight them. Then decide which of the meanings on the right is correct in the context:

¶1	exercised	*kept fit · kept busy*
¶1	end	*finish · goal*
¶2	concludes	*judges · finishes*
¶3	innocuous	*dull · innocent*
¶5	euphoria	*exhilaration · excitement*
¶10	adrenalin-driven	*motivated by excitement · motivated by fear*
¶12	couch potatoes	*people who watch too much TV · people who eat too much*
¶17	mingling	*combining · socialising*
¶18	devout	*believing · benevolent*
¶23	inverting	*reversing · devising*
¶26	flipside	*opposite · less good side*

D Discuss your reactions to the article. Which of Prof Argyle's views do you agree with most strongly – and which points do you disagree with?

14.6 ## Beat the clock

READING

A Five paragraphs have been removed from this article. Choose the most suitable paragraph from the list A–E for each gap (1–5) in the article.

Beat the clock

When designer Jane Rodgers was called up by the boss of an internet start-up company serving the film industry, she thought she knew what she was in for. "I researched the guy and his previous businesses, bought a new suit and lied to my boss about having to leave early for a doctor's appointment on Tuesday evening." Rodgers met her prospective new employer not in his office but in a bar in Hoxton, an up-and-coming area of East London. "Imagine my surprise when, after five minutes of chitchat, first date questions really, he leaned towards me, stared earnestly into my eyes and told me: 'Jane, I think you're the one.' I felt like it was me as a person that was being scrutinised." He had neither seen her CV nor told her what the job involved, but he was determined to hire her. She declined the offer.

1

"Personality is becoming increasingly important" observes Andrew Swift of recruitment consultants Price Jamieson. "There's a chronic staff skills shortage in areas such as new media, so companies are looking at who will fit in with their culture, rather than who has experience. Technology is changing so fast anyway that there's no point recruiting people who have today's skills. What we need are people with creative, dynamic personalities who are not afraid to push forward into the unknown. "Traditional interview rules are all well and good, but when people need staff in a hurry, they learn the benefits of intuition."

2

London-based psychologist Ros Taylor has just interviewed the chief executives of 80 blue-chip companies about the human side of running a successful business. "Really, to make a good impression, you don't even get time to open your mouth," she says, pointing out that often employers will be observing a candidate from the moment they park their car outside the office. "An interviewer's response to you will generally be pre-verbal – how you walk through the door, what your posture is like, whether you smile, whether you have a captivating aura, whether you have a firm, confident handshake. You've got about half a minute to make an impact and after that all you are doing is building on a good or bad first impression." Thirty seconds is hardly enough time to think consciously, Taylor adds: "It's a very emotional response."

3

Ben Williams, an occupational psychologist involved in interview training, doesn't agree that a candidate has the luxury of 30 seconds. "I'd argue that it's more like a third of a second, which is basic human reaction time. In that time, like animals, we make a judgement based on whether there is a perceived threat, in which case our instinct is to run, or a favourable response, when we feel it's safe to approach. Everything that happens after only backs that up."

4

Psychologists call this tendency to fixate on character traits and overlook context the Fundamental Attribution Error – that the way a person will behave in an interview situation reflects the way that person will always behave. In other words, we don't need to know someone in order to believe that we do know them.

5

Perhaps the job interview itself has become an outmoded concept. There's a joke doing the rounds of personnel departments at the moment. A human resources officer gets a call from Satan: would she like to work in Hell? She pops down for a meeting and likes what she sees – wild partying and champagne flowing. "OK, when do I start?" On Monday morning when she reports for work, Hell is a very different place. There's no party, everyone is depressed. "What's happened to this place?" she asks. Satan laughs. "Oh that – that was just the job interview. You're an employee now."

Anita Chaudhury

A

Experts like Williams are often called in by employers to bring a more objective approach to recruitment; intuition is not a skill he seeks to encourage in his clients. "Things like psychometric testing are designed to limit the effect of first impressions. We also train interviewers to be a case of the 'halo effect' – when you instantly like someone and everything they subsequently reveal becomes a self-fulfilling prophecy because you only want to believe the good stuff."

B

The New Yorker recently looked into this issue. Malcolm Gladwell observed that job interviews are increasingly becoming encounters in which charisma and gut reaction are vital. "Hiring someone is essentially a romantic process. We are looking for someone with whom we have a certain chemistry, we want the unlimited promise of a love affair." The structured interview, by contrast, seems to offer only the dry logic and practicality of an arranged marriage.

C

In fact, Rodgers' experience is not as unusual as it sounds. As the skills shortage in the new economy spirals out of control, your CV is likely to be the last thing on a prospective employer's mind. Last weekend, a study presented to the American Psychological Society in Miami revealed that most interviewers decide within a minute whether someone is suitable for the job. But this is by no means an American trend. Stressed-out British executives, faced with the longest working hours in Europe, are waking up to the wisdom of employing people who may not be qualified for the job but at least will be fun to work with when the team has to pull off an all-nighter.

D

Addie Churchill, who runs a PR company with clients including Carlton TV and Disney, admits she always goes on gut feeling. "It sounds like a dangerous thing to rely on but I have learned the hard way that if you get a strong vibe about someone, 99% of the time it's accurate. I recently hired an account executive within moments of him walking through the door. I knew he was the right person because we just clicked, but I also knew he didn't have the right experience, that it would take three months to knock him into shape. It was the right decision. It happens the other way round, of course – you instantly know someone is wrong for the job but have to go through the interview process anyway. Using gut feeling isn't risky, but you need to know how to use it."

E

So is the job interview dead? Not quite. But research from the University of Toledo in America reveals that only the first 15 seconds really matter. Researchers interviewed 98 volunteers of various ages and backgrounds for 20 minutes; each interviewer then filled out a six-page evaluation of the candidate. Originally the study was to establish whether applicants who had been coached in body language would get better ratings than those who hadn't (they didn't) – but then another student decided to use the interview videos to test out the idea that "the handshake is everything". She took 15 seconds of footage, showing applicants as they knocked on the door, came in, shook the hand of the interviewer and sat down. Then she got a series of strangers to rate the applicants based on that clip, using the same criteria as were used in the longer interviews. Even with such a short tape, their ratings were very similar.

B **1** Highlight the most important point made in each paragraph of the article.

2 Then join a partner and compare what you've both highlighted. What kind of training would you give to people who are going to attend interviews?

ALL IN A DAY'S WORK

A You'll hear part of a seminar for job-seekers. Listen to the recording and tick only the advice and information that the speakers actually give.

This is similar to Part 4 of the Listening Paper – except that in the exam there are only 6 opinions to choose between.

In each box write:

	Anne	for a view expressed only by Anne
or	**Kerry**	for a view expressed only by Kerry
or	**Both**	for a view expressed both by Anne and Kerry
or	**Neither**	for a view expressed by neither of them

■ THE APPLICATION FORM

1	Photocopy it and practise filling in the copy first.	1
2	Write your final version neatly and clearly.	2
3	Use a separate sheet for any extra information you want to give.	3
4	Personnel officers read application forms very carefully.	4
5	Use words that show you want to be successful.	5
6	Mention any unusual hobbies or jobs.	6

■ THE INTERVIEW

7	Be confident.	7
8	Avoid answering questions about your leisure interests.	8
9	Do some research into the company's competitors.	9
10	Ask the interviewer to explain what his or her company does.	10
11	Expect to be surprised.	11
12	You may have to have lunch with the interviewer.	12
13	The interviewer may insult you.	13
14	Remain calm whatever happens.	14
15	Arrange to participate in some mock interviews beforehand.	15
16	Tell the interviewer that you are sensitive and clever.	16

■ 'CREATIVE JOB SEARCHING'

17	This technique is better than applying in the conventional way.	17
18	Get in touch with employees in companies in your chosen field.	18
19	You will get a job if you are persistent enough.	19
20	If you're personally known to a company you stand a better chance.	20

B 🧍🧍🧍🧍 Discuss these questions:

- Which of the advice do you disagree with? What other advice would you give to job-seekers?
- If you were looking for an employee, what qualities would you be looking for?
- What do you find most difficult about EXAM interviews? What aspects of your performance would you most like to improve?

C ✎ Write a letter of application. Find an advertisement for a job you find attractive, or which is suitable for someone with your talents, experience and qualifications.

Describe yourself and explain why you are the ideal person for the job (300–350 words).

"Thanks, and I assure you you've picked the right man for the job, Dad."

A

Read this text and think of the word that fits best in each space. Use only one word.

This exercise is similar to Part 1 of the Use of English Paper. In the exam, you should write your answers in CAPITAL LETTERS on the Answer Sheet.

Grounds for optimism

Brazil's coffee growers had a problem in the 1930s – record harvests had caused the coffee price to plummet. Growers were _____ ¹ to burn or dump millions of tons of coffee beans into the sea.

The Brazilian Coffee Institute _____ ² Nestlé, the Swiss food company, to see if it could come up with new _____ ³ based on coffee. Nestlé had already made a _____ ⁴ for itself by producing powdered milk and chocolate, and preserving other perishable foodstuffs.

Nestlé's scientists, after several years of _____ ⁵ , found that they were able to retain the aroma and taste of coffee in a soluble form by adding hydrocarbons. The result went on _____ ⁶ in 1938 as Nescafé.

UK production began the following year at Nestlé's factory in west London. But the war intervened, slowing _____ ⁷ of Nescafé and other Nestlé products. The group's _____ ⁸ crashed from $20m in 1938 to $6m in 1939, and it moved part of its operations from isolated Switzerland to the USA.

But help was at _____ ⁹ . US troops pouring across Europe and Asia found Nescafé in their ration packs. Liberated populations, many of whom had been drinking ersatz coffee made from acorns and had little _____ ¹⁰ of real coffee imports for some time to come, quickly _____ ¹¹ a taste for the instant coffee carried by their liberators.

In one year the whole _____ ¹² of the Nescafé's US plant went to the armed forces.

Continued research at Nestlé led to a new _____ ¹³ producing a soluble residue which was 100% coffee. This was _____ ¹⁴ under the Nescafé name in 1952, just in time to _____ ¹⁵ from the boom in coffee drinking as young people flocked to coffee bars to listen to the new rock and roll music.

B

Read the second part of the article. Use the word given in CAPITALS at the end of some of the lines to form a word that fits in the space in the same line.

This exercise is similar to Part 2 of the Use of English Paper, but in the exam there are only 10 spaces to fill. In the exam, you should write your answers in CAPITAL LETTERS on the Answer Sheet.

Further research by Nestlé's _____ ¹⁶ to capture more fully the taste of home-made coffee resulted in the _____ ¹⁷ of the freeze-drying process in 1966 and the launch of Nescafé Gold Blend.

In simple terms, Nescafé is made by selecting the right mix of beans, extracting liquid coffee in much the same way as the conventional coffee machine, and then freeze-drying the results. The _____ ¹⁸ skills lie in the roasting, extracting and dehydrating processes employed.

There are two basic coffee plants: arabica, a highly _____ ¹⁹ variety grown in central and south America and the east coast of Africa at altitudes between 600 and 2,000 metres, and robusta, a more pungent, stronger-tasting coffee grown below 600 metres in parts of Africa and Asia. Arabica accounts for two-thirds of world coffee _____ ²⁰ , robusta for the rest.

Nestlé estimates that on average 3,000 cups of Nescafé are drunk every second, with an overall _____ ²¹ of no fewer than 100bn cups per year. More than 40m cups of Nescafé are drunk every day in Britain.

In 1974 the Nestlé board, concerned about the company's _____ ²² upon _____ ²³ commodity prices and sources of supply in politically and economically unstable regions, decided to _____ ²⁴ outside its core food business. The company bought a large stake in the French cosmetics group L'Oréal.

In the next three years the price of coffee quadrupled and the price of cocoa tripled. Nevertheless, Nescafé continued to be a big _____ ²⁵ , and a greater variety of coffee drinks was brought out under its brand name. These included Blend 37, with a more _____ ²⁶ coffee taste, an after-dinner coffee using just arabica beans, _____ ²⁷ Nescafé and an instant cappuccino.

In the 1960s Nescafé started to replace its tins with glass jars. More _____ ²⁸ was its 1980s–90s Gold Blend TV campaign, a mini soap opera about the developing _____ ²⁹ between a young couple. It grabbed the nation's attention, perhaps more for its story line than the _____ ³⁰ .

SCIENCE
INVENT

TECHNOLOGY

AROMA

PRODUCE

CONSUME

DEPEND
CERTAIN
DIVERSE

SELL

CONTINENT
CAFFEINE

STRIKE
RELATION
PRODUCE

15
Is it art or entertainment?

15.1 | The tingle factor

A Read this article and then answer the questions that follow:

The tingle factor

Music makes us emotional – but how?
Psychiatrist Raj Persaud finds out

We've all felt something like it – a lump in the throat at a romantic song, a tingle up the spine from a Beethoven quartet or a rush of energy at a club. Music, perhaps more than any other art form, has a direct line to the emotions. The question is, how? Serge Dorny, artistic director of the London Philharmonic Orchestra, has taken a psychological approach in programming the orchestra's forthcoming festival, Regeneration, using music to interpret the anticipated emotional upheaval of the new century. He has juxtaposed Bernd-Alois Zimmerman's dark piece Photoptosis, for instance, which explores anxiety and desperation (the composer eventually killed himself) with Scriabin's heady, excitable Poem of Ecstasy and Beethoven's life-affirming, optimistic violin concerto.

There can be little doubt that music has a profound impact on mood. A recent startling study from America found a strong association between suicide rates and the amount of air time devoted to country and western music on local radio. Were the mournful themes of country music causing listeners to feel low, or did they choose the music because it reflected their negative mood?

One popular theory is that music provokes our emotions because of the context in which we normally hear it – so a funeral march, for instance, produces sadness because we hear it at depressing times. But researchers into the psychology of music can predict what sequences of notes reliably provoke the same emotional reactions in different people. For example, it has been found that sadness and even tears tend to be produced by repetitive phrases which lead to predictable sequences, but which then vary leading to anticipated resolutions. Shivers and goose pimples tend to be a result of unexpected harmonies. It seems that expectancy and violation of expectancy play a major part in emotional reactions to music, and rhythm seems key.

Conventionally, fast tunes have energetic connotations, and slow tunes more leisurely ones. Since when events occur rapidly more energy is consumed than when they take place slowly, it seems that there is something intrinsically energetic and positive about fast music. Slow music therefore could be associated with low energy, and perhaps sadness. This could explain the consensus about the emotional content of pieces of music, even when these pieces are unknown to different listeners. As musicologist and psychiatrist Dr Anthony Storr puts it: "No one calls Rossini's overture to The Barber of Seville tragic; no one thinks of Beethoven's Fifth Symphony as merely pretty."

Music also intensifies emotions already present – think of a chanting football crowd, or the rabble-rousing sounds of a military band. Storr points out that because music brings about similar emotional responses in different people at the same time, it is relied on to create a sense of unity – which also highlights the political use of music to unite and so perhaps control a crowd.

Storr argues that this power derives from the way music structures time, imposing order and ensuring that the emotions aroused by a particular event peak at the same moment. In fact the rhythmical nature of music may hold the secret to its emotional impact, since rhythm is so rooted in our bodies in the form of breathing, heart beat, walking, even sex.

It is possible, too, that our choice of music could reveal the emotional states we prefer, and so provide clues to personality. Dr William McCown and colleagues at the department of psychology at Northeast Louisiana University, noting the spread of bass-enhancing technology in personal audio equipment, found that the preference for exaggerated bass in music was associated with impulsiveness and a preference for unusual experiences.

They argue that since, in what they term "primitive" cultures, the bass is associated with warfare and uninhibited actions, exaggerated bass may actually encourage wild behaviour – which could explain why such music is frequently heard in clubs. Something to think about, perhaps, next time you strut your stuff at Home or Fabric.

1 Music is more likely to evoke .... than other art forms.
   A uncomfortable feelings   **C** an emotional response
   B strong memories   **D** a violent reaction

2 People who listen to country and western music on the radio ....
   A enjoy feeling sad   **C** choose it because they feel sad
   B are driven to feel suicidal   **D** are more likely to kill themselves than others

3 An emotional response to music is triggered when ....
   A you are feeling tired   **C** you are feeling vulnerable
   B what you expect doesn't happen   **D** you are shocked by it

4 It is .... certain pieces of music evoke the same response in everyone.
   A untrue that   **C** agreed that
   B doubtful whether   **D** quite certain that

5 Some music can lead groups of people to ....
   A disagree with each other intensely   **C** start marching
   B feel the same way as each other   **D** join together and start singing

6 People who like deep notes tend to be more ....
   A active   **C** likely to make quick decisions
   B emotional   **D** indecisive

B   **Discuss these questions:**

- What kinds of music send a tingle up your spine? Can you think of specific examples of favourite songs or pieces of music?
- What kinds of music leave you cold? What kinds of music do you dislike – and why?
- Do you choose music to suit your mood? Do you like a heavy bass rhythm?

15.2   'You're being paid to be a child!'   LISTENING

In Part 3 of the Listening Paper you'll have to answer multiple-choice questions like these. In the exam, there are only five questions to answer.

Simon Russell Beale has performed at the Royal National Theatre and with the Royal Shakespeare Company, most recently in the part of Iago in Shakespeare's *Othello*. Listen to the interview and choose the alternative which fits best according to what he says.

1 On the world tour, the audiences' response to *Othello* was ...
   A friendly   **B** unpredictable   **C** slow   **D** enthusiastic   `1`

2 Shakespeare's plays are different from modern plays because the actor and audience are subconsciously aware of a continuous ...
   A relevance to today   **B** stream of imagery   **C** beat   **D** series of emotions   `2`

3 Performing Shakespeare in modern dress can be effective as long as ...
   A guns aren't used instead of swords   **B** it doesn't distract from the language
   C there are no anachronisms   **D** the actors really make the play believable   `3`

4 The actors Simon has worked with are very ...
   A creative   **B** cheerful   **C** funny   **D** intelligent   `4`

5 Simon finds acting in front of a camera difficult because he ...
   A doesn't have the right kind of energy   **B** is mainly a stage actor
   C finds it hard to suddenly begin performing   **D** doesn't enjoy filming   `5`

6 The pace of a screen performance is controlled by the director and the ...
   A scriptwriter   **B** actors   **C** editor   **D** camera operator   `6`

7 For Simon, one of the pleasures of his job is that he enjoys ...
   A playing   **B** showing off   **C** standing on stage   **D** being famous   `7`

8 What advice would Simon give a would-be actor?
   A Be careful!   **B** Don't do it!   **C** Have a go!   **D** Wait until you're older!   `8`

15.3 Prepositions – 2

 A Fill the gaps in these sentences with a suitable preposition from the list. Some are used more than once.

after   at   before   below   beside   besides   by   during   for   from   in   into
in front of   next to   on   on top of   opposite   over   to   under   with

1 There's a free seat .... me here – sit .... me and keep me company.
2 The temperature .... the South Pole .... winter is usually .... 50 degrees .... zero.
3 The *Mona Lisa*, which is .... the Louvre .... Paris, was painted well .... 400 years ago.
4 Would you prefer to go .... car, ... the bus or .... foot?
5 The Odeon is directly .... the bus station, a few metres .... the square. If you're approaching it .... the west, turn .... the left when you see the university .... your right.
6 'Try to arrive .... time .... future,' he said to me .... a whisper.
7 I couldn't see very well because someone .... a big hat was sitting .... me .... the cinema. And I couldn't hear the soundtrack because some people were talking .... loud voices .... the film.
8 .... painting lovely pictures she's very good .... sculpture.
9 G comes .... F .... the alphabet, and .... H.
10 She was working .... the painting .... five weeks .... the spring.
11 Instead of keeping his money .... the bank he hides it .... the carpet. He keeps his small change .... a biscuit tin .... the wardrobe.
12 When they walked .... the room hand .... hand, they saw her sitting .... an armchair .... the window .... a big smile .... her face.

B Fill each of the gaps in this text with a suitable preposition or prepositional phrase:

The artist's daughter Betty is painted ¹ photographic detail. She sits very near the surface ³ the picture, as ⁴ a close-up camera shot. The painting could not really be called a portrait ⁵ Betty, however, as it teaches us very little ⁶ her. Richter has chosen to paint his daughter as she turns away; her face is invisible. Instead he has concentrated ⁷ the red, white and pink patterns ⁸ her jacket and dress, and her hair gathered ⁹ the back ¹⁰ her head. Richter has undermined accepted notions ¹¹ painting and representation, giving us a painting that literally turns its back ¹² convention. Continually discovering new ways ¹³ expression, Richter's work is extremely diverse. The wall ¹⁴ the background ¹⁵ this painting resembles some of the very abstract works that Richter creates. These monochrome, thickly painted canvases evoke sadness and despair and were executed ¹⁶ response ¹⁷ the Vietnam war.

Gerhard Richter: Betty, 1988 (oil on canvas – 102 × 72 cm)

from *The Art Book* (Phaidon Press)

 C Discuss your reactions to the painting reproduced above and the description you've read.

A Replace the conjunctions in these sentences with the words given in red:

1 I don't know much about art but I know what I like.   Despite ....
2 Not only does he paint in oils, but he also paints watercolours.   Besides ....
3 You won't get seats for the show unless you go to the box office today. Without ....
4 The performance was cancelled because the tenor and soprano
  were both ill.   Due to ....
5 I like all kinds of music but I don't like jazz.   Except for ....
6 He was missing his wife and he was missing his children too.   As well as ....
7 You didn't enjoy the film, and neither did I.   Like ....
8 The pianist gave a wonderful performance, so I enjoyed the concert. But for ....

B Read these notes. Then fill the gaps in the sentences below – and then write a CONTINUATION for each sentence using some of the phrases in red.

These phrases are used when making generalisations:

as a rule   broadly speaking   everyone would agree that   generally speaking   in many cases
in most cases   in some cases   it is often said that   it is recognised that
it is sometimes said that   many people believe   on the whole

These phrases are used when explaining exceptions:

apart from   but all the same   but every so often   but now and then
but in other cases   but in this one case   but there are exceptions to every rule
except for   however   on the other hand   to some extent   to a certain extent

1 *Some people say that* modern art is overrated, but ....
2 .... artists lead a good life: their hobby is their profession, but ....
3 .... Hollywood movies are ephemeral, ... you see one you can't forget.
4 .... watching television is rather a waste of time, ...
5 .... politicians are honourable, dedicated people, ...
6 .... reading is a wonderful source of pleasure; ....
7 .... people work because they have to, not because they want to, ...
8 .... I enjoy all kinds of music, ...

C **1** Look at this picture: why is it called *The Fall of Icarus*? Talk about the various things that are going on in the picture and make notes on the main points.

Pieter Brueghel (1527–1569) *The Fall of Icarus* (oil on canvas – 73.5 × 112 cm)

2 👥 **Look at the poem in** Activity 1 **and then discuss these questions:**

- What did you find out about the picture that you hadn't noticed already?
- Did the poem make you think differently about the picture? In what ways?
- What are the main points made in the poem?

3 🖋 **Write a description of the painting, explaining what it shows and what you think about it (about 150 words). Try to use some of the conjunctions and connectors in red on page 159.**

15.5 ▷ Use of English Part 5: *Guernica*　　　EXAM PRACTICE

Pablo Picasso's *Guernica* was painted after the bombing of a Basque town in 1937 during the Spanish Civil War. The painting itself is nearly eight metres across, but the reproduction below gives an idea of what it looks like.

Pablo Picasso (1891–1973) – *Guernica* (oil on canvas – 350 × 777 cm)

A **1** 👥 **Before you read this text, discuss your reactions to the picture.**

2 👥 **Read the text and answer each of the questions that follow in a word or short phrase:**

In Part 5 of the Use of English Paper you'll have to read two texts, answer questions and write a 50–70 word summary. In this section there is only one text to read.

Guernica was the last great history-painting. It was also the last modern painting of major importance that took its subject from politics with the intention of changing the way large numbers of people thought and felt about power. Since 1937, there have been a few admirable works of art that contained political references – some of Joseph Beuys's work or Robert Motherwell's *Elegies to the Spanish Republic*. But the idea that an artist, by making a painting or sculpture, could insert images into the stream of public speech and thus change political discourse has gone, probably for good, along with the nineteenth-century ideal of the artist as public man. Mass media took away the political speech of art. When Picasso painted *Guernica*, regular TV broadcasting had been in existence for only a year in England and nobody in France, except a few electronics experts, had seen a television set. There were perhaps fifteen thousand such sets in New York City. Television was too crude, too novel, to be altogether credible. The day when most people in the capitalist world would base their understanding of politics on what the TV screen gave them was still almost a generation away. But by the end of World War II, the role of the 'war artist' had been rendered negligible by

1

5

10

looked like bad, late German Expressionism, or the incontrovertible photographs from Belsen, Majdanek, and Auschwitz? It seems obvious, looking back, that the artists of Weimar Germany and Leninist Russia lived in a much more attenuated landscape of media than ours, and their reward was that they could still believe, in good faith and without bombast, that art could morally influence the world. Today, the idea has largely been dismissed, as it must be in a mass media society where art's principal social role is to be investment capital, or, in the simplest way, bullion. We still have political art, but we have no *effective* political art. An artist must be famous to be heard, but as he acquires fame, so his work accumulates 'value' and becomes, ipso facto, harmless. As far as today's politics is concerned, most art aspires to the condition of Muzak. It provides the background hum for power. If the Third Reich had lasted until now, the young bloods of the Inner Party would not be interested in old fogeys like Albert Speer or Arno Breker, Hitler's monumental sculptor; they would be queuing up to have their portraits silkscreened by Andy Warhol. It is hard to think of any work of art of which one can say, *This* saved the life of one Jew, one Vietnamese, one Cambodian. Specific books perhaps; but as far as one can tell, no paintings or sculptures. The difference between us and the artists of the 1920s is that they thought such a work of art could be made. Perhaps it was a certain naïveté that made them think so. But it is certainly our loss that we cannot.

15

20

25

30

from *The Shock of the New* by Robert Hughes

In Part 5 of the Use of English Paper there aren't as many questions as this. These are to give you extra practice!

1 What does the writer mean by *insert images into the stream of public speech* in line 6?
2 How do people in the West nowadays form their political opinions, according to the writer?
3 Why does the writer say so much about television in lines 9 to 14?
4 Why is the word *effective* in italics in line 21?
5 Why is the word *value* in inverted commas in line 22?
6 According to the writer, what is the function of art today?
7 How does the writer feel about the ineffectiveness of political art today?

B 👥 **Discuss these questions:**

- To what extent do you agree with the writer's views?
- What do you think is the purpose of a work of art?
- What influence can a painting, or any other work of art, have on your own feelings and attitudes?
- Does a critic like Robert Hughes perform a useful function in explaining and interpreting works of art as well as evaluating them?
- Does the same hold good for a music critic, a film critic, a TV critic, a restaurant critic or a sports writer?

C 👥 **Discuss these exam tips with a partner. Which of them might work for you? Are there any other tips you can add?**

1 Part 5 of the Use of English Paper is worth 22 marks (30% of the marks for the whole paper). Aim to spend about 20–25 minutes on it – but don't spend too long on it at the expense of the other questions.

2 The 4 questions on language awareness (style, emphasis or vocabulary) are worth 2 marks each. These can be answered briefly – in a word or short phrase. Don't bother to write full sentences for these answers. Use a highlighter or a pencil to help you to focus on the quoted phrases in context in the text.

3 The summary task is worth 14 marks (4 for content and 10 for summary writing skills). You have to extract information from both texts for this – and you must write fewer than 70 words. Check for any irrelevancies in your notes before you start writing.

4 Make notes before you put pen to paper – space is limited and there may not be enough room for extensive corrections later.

5 In the summary, try to rephrase some of the information in your own words, but don't waste too much time trying to think of a synonym for every word – just avoid direct quotation as far as possible!

Two reviews

A Read these reviews and then answer the questions below:

Jakob the Liar by CLARK COLLIS

There was once a time when a comedy about the holocaust would have been considered an audaciously brave and/or audaciously stupid move. Unfortunately for *Jakob the Liar*, the conclusion of that particular period in cinema history occurred last year, with the release of Roberto Benigni's *Life is Beautiful*.

As a result, what would otherwise have been, if nothing else, at least controversial, simply comes across as a vehicle for Robin Williams at his most unpleasantly sentimental.

The artist formerly known as Mork plays the economically truthful Jakob, a mild-mannered Jewish baker-cum-boxing manager who we discover failing to make ends meet in a Polish ghetto towards the end of World War II.

After accidentally learning that Germany is losing the battle for the Eastern front, Williams spreads the good news – and before you can say, 'Goooooooooood morning, Warsaw!' the entire community is under the misapprehension that he has somehow saved a radio from Nazi confiscation.

Which presents something of a dilemma for our supposedly unheroic hero. Should he tell the truth and destroy his increasingly suicidal friends' last hopes?

Or should he risk execution by pretending that he does have a radio, enabling him to do a lot of funny voices behind a screen for the entertainment of the cute little concentration camp-escaping child that he stumbled across way back in Act One?

Anyone who bets on the first option has clearly never seen a Robin Williams movie – although they would certainly be well advised not to make this their first.

Since it was based on a book by camp survivor Jurek Becker, no one could argue that director Kassovitz's intentions are less than noble. But as entertainment, the end product is as turgid a film about mass genocide as we are ever likely to see.

Moreover, while the support from fellow players Alan Arkin, Liev Schreiber and Nina Siemaszko, as Williams' fellow persecutees, is competent enough, the entire enterprise has been smothered with such a sickly layer of glutinous Hollywood sentimentality – replete with a predictably semi-happy ending – that diabetics should probably consult their doctor before even seeing the trailer.

1 *Jakob the Liar* is ....
   a a controversial film   **c** not controversial
   b a moving film   **d** better than *Life is Beautiful*
2 The writer finds Williams' performance ....
   a distasteful   **c** better than in his previous films
   b charming   **d** dull
3 What does Jakob do when his fellow-inmates think he has a radio?
   a He has a lot of fun   **c** He tells them that Germany is losing the war
   b He keeps up the pretence   **d** He tells the truth
4 Which of these phrases is **NOT** used humorously or sarcastically?
   a the cute little concentration camp-escaping child that he stumbled across
   b they would certainly be well advised not to make this their first
   c no one could argue that director Kassovitz's intentions are less than noble
   d diabetics should probably consult their doctor before even seeing the trailer

What Dreams May Come by KIM NEWMAN

One advantage of recent advances in special effects technology is that films can take you to places you've never seen before, and couldn't even imagine. *What Dreams May Come* takes you somewhere you may not want to experience quite yet. Chris Nielsen (Robin Williams), a doctor whose happy marriage has already been blighted by the deaths of his kids, is killed in an accident and wakes up in a private universe which takes the shape of his wife's semi-Impressionist paintings. Death isn't so bad, especially with guide Albert (Cuba Gooding Jr.) around to give tips and reunite him with his put-down dog and lost little girl. However, Chris' wife Annie (Annabella Sciorra) can't take another bereavement and commits suicide. Since this condemns her to the Hell section of this afterworld, Chris strives – guided by Max Von Sydow – to haul her out of the slough of despair and bring her to the happy lands, even though everyone says this is futile.

Adapted from a cranky mystic novel by Richard Matheson and directed with visual genius by Vincent Ward, this is one of those failures that has so many near-great things that it almost gets by on guts. Few films have the nerve or the imagination to create a world beyond, and the settings are consistently incredible, whether in the idyllic heaven or the paved-with-agonised-faces hell.

The problem is that, despite mostly strong performances, there's something not right about the central perfect relationship so you get distracted arguing with all the religious guff. It feels like what you'd get if you took the legend of Orpheus and previewed it in Pasadena, then rewrote the classical tragedy as a feelgood Hollywood hug-fest. After the underrated excellence of *Map Of The Human Heart*, Vincent Ward is entitled to a misstep and we probably ought to be grateful that this one is as interesting as it is.

5 When Dr Nielsen dies and wakes up in the afterworld ....
   a he is all alone
   b he is very unhappy
   c he meets his dog again
   d his wife is by his side

6 What does the writer mean by *incredible* in the second paragraph?
   a absurd
   b very strange
   c not believable
   d wonderful

7 Why does Annie kill herself?
   a She wants to join Chris in heaven
   b She is all alone in the world
   c Too many of her nearest and dearest have died
   d She doesn't realise she'll go to Hell

8 The writer thinks that *What Dreams May Come* is ....
   a a brave attempt
   b not worth seeing
   c well worth seeing
   d nearly as good as the director's previous film

B 1 **Discuss these questions:**
   • Which of the films would you LEAST like to see? Why?
   • What was the WORST film you've ever seen? Tell your partners about it.
   • How seriously do you take reviews? How much do they influence your decision whether to see a movie, buy a CD, eat at a restaurant or go to a show?

2 **Before one of you looks at Activity 5, and the other at 18, read this introduction:**

Movie clichés

Apparently there are only half a dozen basic movie plots. However, the list of movie clichés is endless. Many of them are necessary short cuts (movie people never ask for change in a shop or from a taxi driver, for instance), but the rest are gratuitous. Still, they can alleviate the tedium of watching a bad film.

15.7 **Writing Part 2**

A  Discuss this exam advice for Paper 2 with a partner. Which pieces of advice are the most useful? Which might not work for you? Can you add any more advice to the list?

---

1 Follow the instructions exactly. If the instructions say 'Write a letter to a friend', for example, your work must look like a personal letter and NOT like a business letter! This may sound obvious but it's easy to overlook important instructions when you're in a hurry.

2 Make sure you understand the instructions for each question. If you don't fully understand a particular question, it's best not to answer it. Answers that 'wantonly misinterpret the question' are penalised.

3 If you choose a question which asks you to tell a story, such as an article about a memorable journey, you don't have to tell the truth. In fact, it may be more interesting and easier to use your imagination and make up a story.

4 Decide which of the questions are the easiest for you to answer – maybe cross out the ones you don't want to do and then choose between the ones that remain.

5 Make notes for both questions. If at this stage you find you haven't got enough ideas on one of them, there may be time to choose another one.

6 Check if any particular grammatical structures seem to be needed for the subject: conditionals, modal verbs, past/present perfect, etc.

7 Examiners prefer compositions that are easy to read (and neatly written). If in doubt, use a straightforward neutral style – generally this is preferable to a very informal or very formal style.

8 Allow enough time at the end for editing your work and proof-reading it, i.e. checking it through for spelling mistakes, grammatical errors and slips of the pen.

B 1  Re-read the two movie reviews in 15.6. Choose the ONE which you prefer and make notes on these aspects of the movie that are mentioned by the writer:

	information	favourable view	critical view
the plot			
the script			
the actors			
the look			
the director			
the music			
comparisons			
conclusion			

- Which aspects were NOT mentioned in the review? Why weren't they mentioned?
- What is the main impression the review gives? Does it make you want to see the film or not?

2  Pick a film you've both seen and discuss all the aspects noted above. Which of the points you discuss would be worth mentioning in a 300–350 word review – and which would be best omitted?

C ✐ Write a review of a film you have seen recently (300–350 words).

"Are you sure this is a film noir"

Part 1 of the Reading Comprehension Paper consists of 18 multiple-choice questions on missing words from three texts. The questions focus on different aspects of vocabulary and grammar. Look at the annotated questions (1–6) and then answer questions 7–12 unaided.

The Beach   by ANGIE ERRIGO

Getting away from it all on an _____¹ tropical beach is not the idyll of your lottery winning dreams in this unnerving drama of a hidden Eden where obsessive travellers disassociate from the world.

Leonardo DiCaprio is backpacker Richard, who thinks he's worldly-wise, but is so "the young American abroad" when he seeks adventure and danger in Thailand. A strange _____² with crazed Daffy (Robert Carlyle), who rants of a perfect, secret beach, seems the travel tip for him. And he recruits a French girl he fancies rotten (Virginie Ledoyen) and her amiable boyfriend (Guillaume Canet) to _____³ him on a mysterious, funny, scary journey to the spectacularly beautiful (take a bow, cinematographer Darius Khondji) haven.

There Sal (Tilda Swinton) holds sway over a community of drop-outs who are kind of a _____⁴ between the *Swiss Family Robinson* and an apocalyptic water sport cult. Like Garland's novel, the film will be compared with *Lord Of The Flies* as the absence of societal constraints and concerns creates a moral vacuum for wild things to rumpus mightily. *The Beach* is more a _____⁵ of the modern world, though, with a more experienced gang and their alternative attempts to connect with _____⁶ riven by their secrets, desires, jealousies and competitiveness. They import their own serpents into this paradise.

Choose the best word or phrase to fill each gap in the text:

In the exam it's a good idea to put a pencil mark beside the questions you can't answer and come back to them later. It's usually best to eliminate the answers you know to be wrong first,

1 **A** abandoned *not appropriate* **B** unspoilt ✓ **C** tropical *not grammatical* **D** Asian *OK but not the best*

2 **A** meeting *OK but not the best* **B** rendezvous *not quite right* **C** date *not appropriate* **D** encounter ✓

3 **A** encounter *doesn't make sense* **B** join ✓ **C** travel *not grammatical* **D** escort *not appropriate*

4 **A** mixture *OK but not the best* **B** blend *not appropriate* **C** cross ✓ **D** association *different meaning*

5 **A** microcosm ✓ **B** symbolic *not grammatical* **C** comparison *doesn't make sense* **D** reflection *OK but not the best*

6 **A** themselves *doesn't make sense* **B** a team *silly* **C** each *not grammatical* **D** one another ✓

Richard is more than a little disturbed, as we learn from a voiceover that _____⁷ on intrusive but underlines his alienation. His fixation with Vietnam movies could be spelled out more clearly to _____⁸ his solitary stint in the jungle turning into a pathological commando game, Heart Of Darkness for the Sega generation.

DiCaprio's _____⁹ as the smartarsed thrill-seeker and the more wry narrator with _____¹⁰, but he works very hard for his reputed $20 million fee when required to turn into a bug-eating nutter. _____¹¹ the dodginess of this interlude, however, Boyle's direction holds a true line between allure and horror, and John Hodge's _____¹² is intriguing and forceful. It's much better than rumoured: entertaining, engrossing, and ripe for discussion – somewhere civilised – afterwards.

then if you're still unsure you may have to guess. It's better to make a wild guess than not to answer at all.

7 **A** frontiers **B** borders **C** approaches **D** comes close
8 **A** explain **B** justify **C** interpret **D** describe
9 **A** role **B** part **C** voice **D** perfect
10 **A** foresight **B** hindsight **C** retrospect **D** knowledge
11 **A** Although **B** In spite **C** Despite **D** Because of
12 **A** script **B** book **C** story **D** plot

Use of English Part 4

Part 4 in the Use of English Paper also tests both vocabulary and grammar. Look at the annotated answers to the first questions and then do the rest unaided. Complete the second sentence so that it has a similar meaning to the first sentence, using the word given. Do not change the word given. You must use between three and eight words, including the word given.

1 Because of the rain the only thing we could do was go to the art gallery.
   alternative
   As it .... go to the art gallery.

was raining there was no alternative but	X 'to' omitted
was wet we decided to	? 'alternative' omitted
was raining there were no alternatives so we had to	X word changed + too many words
was raining we had no alternative but to	✓ correct
was raining our only alternative was to	✓ correct

2 I remember very few things about the film.
   scarcely
   I .... the film.

(can) scarcely remember a thing about	X brackets not advisable
can scarcely remember	X meaning changed
can scarcely remember anything about	✓
scarcely remember anything about	✓
can scarcely remember a thing about	✓

3 A silent movie can't be compared to a modern film.
   comparison
   There .... a modern film.

can be no comparison between a silent movie and	X too many words
isn't a comparison to be made between a silent movie and	X meaning changed + too many words
is difficulty in comparing a silent movie with	X word altered
is no comparison between a silent movie and	✓
's no comparison between a silent movie and	✓ contractions are OK

When doing a transformation exercise like this, make absolutely sure that you've included all the information given in the original sentence, and that you haven't inadvertently changed the meaning or emphasis of the sentence. And make sure the grammar in your rewritten sentence and the spelling are OK.

4 Not many people are expected to attend the show.
   poorly
   The show .... attended.

5 You can't possibly expect me to pay for the tickets.
   question
   There .... the tickets.

6 After making *Titanic*, Leonardo DiCaprio appeared in *The Beach*.
   previous
   Leonardo DiCaprio .... *Titanic*.

7 It was stupid of her to turn down the offer of free tickets for the opera.
   fool
   She .... of free opera tickets.

8 I never thought of taking up painting as a hobby.
   occurred
   It .... painting as a hobby.

Find synonyms for the phrases in red, or explain their meanings. Refer to a dictionary if necessary.

1 I know it's a very old car but I think it's still good for a few more years.
2 'What do you enjoy most about your work?' 'That's a good question!'
3 I asked him to apologise and he did so, but with bad grace.
4 I made ten photocopies and then one more for good measure.
5 Don't do someone a good turn in the hope of getting something in return.
6 Have you finished in the shower, or are you planning to stay in there for good?
7 I'm not myself today – I had rather a bad night.
8 Is it bad manners to read while you're eating a meal?
9 After that things went from bad to worse.
10 I didn't get the job, but it's all to the good because it wasn't really right for me.
11 He can't be trusted: he's good for nothing and a thoroughly bad lot.
12 'Work hard and play hard' is an old saying that still holds good today.

B **Fill the gaps in these sentences with suitable phrases from the list on the right. The verbs may need to be changed to fit the context.**

1 You can .... as an entertainer, if you're successful.
2 Make sure you arrive .... for the interview – that usually ....
3 She promised to phone me first thing today and she was ....
4 I've had the machine overhauled and serviced – now it's ....
5 I can't run because I've got ....
6 The company is .... : more staff are being made redundant.
7 The service here is terrible – I .... to complain to the manager.
8 I know the managing director personally, so I'll .... for you.
9 I took the machine to pieces but couldn't fix it – in the end I ....
10 Things may go wrong if we continue, I think we should stop now ....
11 We made the offer .... and didn't expect these problems would arise.
12 Lunchtime already! It's .... I brought some sandwiches.

a bad leg/ankle/ knee
give up as a bad job
in a bad way
a good job
as good as new
as good as her word
make good money
have a good mind
in good faith
in good time
make a good impression
put in a good word
while the going's good

"OK, 'Leo', break's over."

16

Look after yourself!

16.1 **A healthy life?**   **READING AND VOCABULARY**

A   Read this article and then answer the questions that follow:

Programme
for Natural Healing

Everyone worries about their health. For some it's about losing a bit of weight, others that they'll inherit diseases which afflicted their parents. But what if someone told you in just two short months you could be feeling on top of the world? That's exactly what Andrew Weil has to say in his latest book, *8 Weeks to Optimum Health*. Weil – a doctor and bestselling author of *Spontaneous Healing* – believes we can all optimise the functioning of the body's natural healing system, not just on a day-to-day basis but also in responding to everyday illnesses and more serious medical conditions. He has drawn up a programme which makes simple changes to our lifestyle in terms of diet, exercise, supplements and mental and spiritual development, in turn prompting "long-lasting and dramatically beneficial effects for our health". Of course, everyone is different so Weil also provides specific guidance for men and women, pregnant women, people under 20, over 50 and over 70, those who are overweight, people at risk from cardiovascular disease and cancer and those who have young children. There are even sections devoted to the health of those who live in big cities and who travel frequently.

So how does it work? Weil says it has much to do with the body's own healing system. "Health is wholeness and balance, an inner resilience that allows you to meet the demands of living without being overwhelmed. If you have that kind of resilience, you can experience the inevitable interactions with germs and not get infections, you can be in contact with allergens and not suffer allergies and you can sustain exposure to carcinogens and not get cancer."

Week one begins with a general cupboard clearance – out must go all unhealthy foods like oils and artificial sweeteners – and an introduction to vitamin C, walking and eating more broccoli – a nutrient and fibre-rich vegetable. Breath observation – pay attention to your breathing patterns – also starts now.

As the weeks progress, so Weil steps up the demands. Week two calls for an increase in your consumption of whole grains and an end to drinking chlorinated water. He also suggests attempting a one-day "news-fast". With each week comes the adoption of new supplements and fresh dietary habits. Exercise is increased and more mental and spiritual tasks are set. Alongside each chapter he includes true stories of those 'healed' by the plan, plus various healthy recipes. But he warns: "Perfect health is not possible – beware of persons and products that promise it. Health is not static: it is normal to lose it periodically in order to come back to it in a better way."

Weil says the eight-week programme gives users the information needed to keep their healing system in working order. "It shows you how to build a lifestyle that will protect you from premature disability and death and it teaches practices and skills that will enable you to prepare body, mind and spirit for any eventual health crisis you may face. Start it now and reap the benefits for the rest of your life."

1 People are concerned about...
   A receiving conflicting advice from medical experts   **C** their parents falling ill
   B suffering from the same illnesses as their parents   **D** gaining too much weight
2 Dr Weil believes that everyone should...
   A be sceptical about his methods   **C** follow the same programme
   B use different methods   **D** eat less and exercise more

3 Dr Weil believes that everyone...
   A can develop immunity to germs
   B can cope with potential sources of illness
   C should avoid contact with germs
   D is at risk from infection
4 Following Dr Weil's methods over the weeks...
   A you have to put more and more effort into it
   B you must expect to be ill occasionally
   C you shouldn't watch the news on TV
   D you will never suffer from illness
5 Dr Weil's programme will be effective if you...
   A don't expect results for at least two months
   B have faith in it
   C begin at once
   D follow every step rigorously

In the exam read each text in Paper 1 twice: once quickly to get the gist and again more carefully to find the answers. In Parts 2–4, each correct answer gains **TWO** marks. Some alternatives in multiple-choice questions are designed to be tricky and distract you from the right answer – so don't jump to conclusions.

Use a highlighter or pencil to mark any questions that you're still unsure about. It may be best to come back to them later on, rather than read the text again straight away.

B 🚶🚶🚶🚶 **Discuss these questions:**

- What do you think about Dr Weil's programme? Would it work for you?
- How do YOU stay healthy and fit? What kind of exercise do you take?
- How careful are you about your diet?
- Do you worry about your health? What special precautions do you take against falling ill?

C Choose the THREE best answers to fill the gap in each sentence.

1 He will have to go on a diet because he is getting ....
   dense   flabby   buxom   robust   plump   stout

2 If he still feels ill after taking this treatment, he should see ....
   a consultant   a midwife   a specialist   his GP   a quack

3 She needs to put on some weight after her illness because she is too ....
   fragile   lean   light   skinny   slim   thin   slender

4 Many illnesses today are related to ....
   grief   stress   tension   worry   sadness   suffering

5 What treatment should be given to someone who has .... ?
   fainted   lost consciousness   passed away   passed out   passed through

6 I'm a bit worried about the .... I've been having in my back.
   agony   twinges   ache   pain   suffering   wound

7 Illness can be stopped before it happens by means of ....
   after care   vaccines   preventive medicine   therapy   healthy living

8 The nurse made her take .... to help her sleep better.
   a lotion   a sedative   a pain-killer   an ointment   a tranquilliser

9 Take two of these .... three times a day after meals.
   drugs   capsules   sweets   tablets   pills   placebos

10 Everyone hoped that he would .... after the operation.
   pull out   pull through   get better   pull over   get well   get up

11 You really must see a doctor about that ....
   pimple   rash   blister   scratch   swelling   inflammation

12 Keep away from other people if you have a disease that is ....
   catching   contagious   antiseptic   catchy   infectious

13 Once a year it's a good idea to go to the doctor for ....
   an examination   a check-up   an operation   a post-mortem   a medical

14 She had to go to hospital when she ....
   had a break   broke up   pulled a muscle   sprained her ankle   fractured her wrist

15 Medical experts take the claims of .... medicine more seriously nowadays.
   alternative   complementary   conventional   fringe   mainstream   orthodox

D In these sentences only ONE of the four alternatives given is correct. Choose the correct alternative.

1 An illness that is caused by the mind is known as a .... illness.
pschyosamatic   pschyosomatic   psychosamatic   psychosomatic

2 Before the operation the patient was given a general ....
anaesthetic   anesthaetic   anasthetic   anisthetic

3 The doctors examined the patient and came to the conclusion that he was ....
a loony   off his rocker   silly   unbalanced

4 Malaria is .... by the female anopheles mosquito.
broadcast   sent   transmitted   transported

5 Realising that she was probably pregnant she consulted a ....
chiropodist   gynaecologist   osteopath   pediatrician

6 We realised he must be ill when he ....
threw down   threw out   threw in   threw up

7 Hayfever is a very common type of ....
allergy   antagonism   symptom   therapy

8 Smallpox, once responsible for millions of deaths, has been completely ....
abolished   erased   eradicated   exterminated

9 The consultant operated on the patient when he complained of pains in his ....
insides   paunch   tummy   stomach

10 He has a morbid fear of going outside his home, known to doctors as ....
agoraphobia   arachnophobia   claustrophobia   xenophobia

E 🔊 You'll hear ten 'Doctor, doctor' jokes – which do you think is the funniest?

16.2 Speaking

EXAM PRACTICE

In the Speaking Paper candidates are assessed on their:

grammatical resource (accuracy and range of grammar) · lexical resource (vocabulary) · discourse management · pronunciation of sentences · interactive communication · vocabulary resource

Part 1: The interlocutor talks with each candidate about general topics (3 minutes).

Part 2: The candidates look at visual prompts and the interlocutor leads them into a discussion (4 minutes).

Part 3: Each candidate is given a written question. They have to talk uninterrupted for 2 minutes each, then a discussion follows (12 minutes).

A 👥 **Conversation with interlocutor**   One of you should look at Activity 11, the other at 21. You'll have some general questions to answer.

B 👥 **Conversation about pictures**   One of you should look at Activity 12, the other at 22. You'll each have a picture to describe and discuss.

C 👥 **Long turns and discussion**   One of you should look at Activity 13, the other at 23. You'll each have a topic to talk about for two minutes and then discuss together.

In the exam, don't be the passive partner – take the initiative just as you would in a normal conversation. If you're reticent, it may be quite difficult for the assessor to assess how well you speak English. Remember that it's how well you communicate that's being assessed, not whether your answers are correct, intelligent or sensible – or even wholly true!

A cheerful, confident manner is also very helpful. The assessor will try to put you at your ease, but the best way to feel confident is to have plenty of practice before the exam. Team up with another student and try the Speaking tests in *Cambridge Proficiency Practice* 1. You can practise giving a two-minute talk on your own, preferably recording your voice onto cassette or minidisc.

A 👥 **Discuss any differences in meaning or style between these sentences:**

1 The doctor I spoke to yesterday told me not to worry.
  The doctor, whom I spoke to yesterday, told me not to worry.
  The doctor, who I spoke to yesterday, told me not to worry.
  The doctor to whom I spoke yesterday told me not to worry.
2 He told us about the treatment, which made him feel better.
  He told us about the treatment that made him feel better.
3 They operated on the first patient who was seriously ill.
  They operated on the first patient, who was seriously ill.

B **Fill the gaps with *who, whose, which* or *that*. Add COMMAS where necessary.**

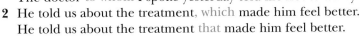

The Californians have come up with a device for people   ¹have their own small swimming
pool   ² should transform their lives as much as those indoor exercise bikes   ³
were so popular in the 1970s did. Swimming   ⁴ is recognised to be one of the best
ways of keeping fit is impractical in pools   ⁵ are too small for serious swimming. But
the *Hydroflex* is a new device   ⁶ can keep swimmers in the same spot and still allow
them to do all the strokes. It consists of a plastic bar   ⁷ is attached to the side of the
pool by two lines and to the swimmer by a waist belt. The swimmer   ⁸ legs are
protected from the lines by the bar remains stationary while swimming. It sounds like an activity
          ⁹ is only suitable for people   ¹⁰ desire to keep in shape helps them to ignore
the taunts of neighbours   ¹¹happen to spot them in the pool.

C **Complete each sentence with suitable words. Add COMMAS wherever they are needed.**

1 He's the only person I know .... ten kilometres a day before breakfast.
2 I swam twenty lengths .... me a long time.
3 He has two sisters both .... doctors. The younger of the two .... Jane qualified
  last year. He also has two brothers neither .... know anything about medicine.
4 One of the children must have swallowed the pills .... left in the bathroom.
5 All .... people say about hospitals is true.
6 She loves talking about her operation .... us all feel ill.
7 The matron is the .... is in overall charge of the nursing staff.
8 Taking a degree in medicine .... longer than most other university courses is the only
  method .... one can become a doctor.

16.4 **Listening Part 1** EXAM PRACTICE

In Part 1 of the Listening Paper you hear four extracts, each with two multiple-choice questions. Make sure you read the questions before you listen
to the recording. (You'll hear each clip twice.)

🔊 **Extract One**
You hear a doctor talking to her patient.

1 When was the patient injured?
  A Tuesday **B** Wednesday **C** Thursday   `1`
2 The doctor is
  A helpful **B** sympathetic **C** unsympathetic   `2`

Extract Two

You hear part of a radio programme about homeopathy.

3 Samuel Hahnemann's purpose of 'proving' substances was to ...
  A cure his patients **B** discover the effects of different substances
  C test his technique of dosage   `3`

4 The efficacy of homeopathy depends on ...
   A the similarities between symptoms and the effects of various substances
   B patients getting worse before they get better
   C giving patients very small doses of poison

`[ 4 ]`

Extract Three

You hear a doctor talking about his relationship with patients.

5 A patient is more likely to believe that practitioners can cure them if they have ...
   A a good bedside manner   **B** smart consulting rooms
   C letters from cured patients

`[ 5 ]`

6 The doctor's own patients recovered, he suggests, because ...
   A their own bodies cured them   **B** they trusted him
   C they were not really ill

`[ 6 ]`

Extract Four

You hear two friends talking about dreams.

7 According to the man, dreaming is like
   A being another person   **B** visiting other countries
   C running from place to place

`[ 7 ]`

8 Compared to our waking lives, dream experiences are more
   A interesting   **B** vivid   **C** intense

`[ 8 ]`

16.5 Use of English Part 2   EXAM PRACTICE

In Part 2 of the Use of English Paper you have to form a word that fits in the space. Make absolutely sure the word is grammatically correct in the context. Each question of the ten questions is worth one mark. Here, to give you extra practice, there are 15 questions.

Use the word given in capitals at the end of some lines to form a word that fits in the space in the same line. Write your answers in CAPITAL LETTERS.

More than half the world's population consider _____ [1] shy, delegates   **THEM**
to the first international _____ [2] on shyness, being held in   **CONFER**
Cardiff, will be told today. One in 10 cases is severe. Effects include
mutism, speech problems, _____ [3], blushing, shaking and   **LONELY**
trembling, lack of eye contact, _____ [4] in forming relationships and   **DIFFICULT**
social phobia – the most extreme form of shyness, defined by the
American Psychiatric Association as a pronounced and _____ [5] fear   **PERSIST**
of social or performance situations in which _____ [6] may occur. Shy   **EMBARRASS**
people tend to blame themselves for social _____ [7] and attribute   **FAIL**
success to _____ [8] factors. They expect their behaviour to be   **OUT**
_____ [9], remember only negative information about themselves   **ADEQUATE**
and accept without challenge adverse comments from others.

The causes are complex and not fully understood. The latest theory is
that it can be traced to genes as well as to social _____ [10].   **CONDITION**
One estimate, based on research with twins, is that around 15 per cent
of the population are born with a _____ [11] to shyness. Some   **DISPOSE**
_____ [12] believe there are two types: an early developing, fearful   **PSYCHOLOGY**
shyness and a later developing, _____ [13] shyness. The fearful   **CONSCIOUS**
version emerges often in the first year of life and is _____ [14] to be   **THINK**
_____ [15] inherited.   **PART**

Sigmund Freud (1856–1939)

In Part 2 of the Listening Paper you have to complete nine sentences with specific information or an opinion. You'll hear just one person speaking, or one person being interviewed.

A **In the recording Professor Carl Abrahams is talking about Sigmund Freud. Complete the sentences with a word or short phrase:**

1 According to Professor Abrahams, some patients

[1   ] after psychoanalysis.

2 Freud's own account of the wolf man case was [2   ].

3 Although Freud was not a good doctor, he was a good [3   ].

4 An innocent [4   ] is commonly believed to betray

concealed secret desires.

5 When they first came out, Freud's books got [5   ].

6 Freud asserted that sexuality and [6   ] were directly related.

7 Freud's technique of 'free association' was [7   ].

8 The popularity of Freud has [8   ] research into mental

disorders.

9 People who consult psychoanalysts are being [9   ] by them.

In the exam you'll hear each recording twice. You'll have about 45 seconds to read the questions through beforehand and about 15 seconds between each playing to check your answers. Answer the easier questions during the first listening and make a pencil mark beside the ones you can't get and listen carefully for them during the second listening. Don't leave any blanks – make a guess if you really don't know an answer.

Beware of distractingly plausible answers and don't rely on what you already know. Concentrate on what the speakers actually say, not what you'd say if you were talking about the same topic.

B **Discuss these questions:**
- How would you describe Professor Abrahams' attitude during the interview? Write down three descriptive adjectives to characterise your impression of him.
- To what extent were you convinced by what he said?
- How can a psychiatrist (or psychoanalyst or psychotherapist) help someone with their problems?
- What is the difference between a psychologist and a psychiatrist?

16.7 **Synonyms and homonyms** VOCABULARY DEVELOPMENT

Synonyms are useful in Part 5 of the Use of English Paper, where you are expected to use your own words as far as possible and to avoid quoting directly from the text. In your compositions you can avoid repetition or an over-simple style by choosing suitable synonyms.

When you're writing, and you can't think of a suitable synonym on the spur of the moment, leave a gap (like this:), or p il in the word you want to replace, and come back later to fill it in.

A 🔊 **You'll hear the same words spoken in eight different ways – pay attention to the underlying meaning conveyed by each speaker's tone of voice:**

> *Ah, there you are. I was wondering where you'd got to. Luckily I had some work to get on with so I wasn't bored. Anyway, even if the film has started by the time we get there, I don't think it'll matter, do you?*

1 Decide which word from the list on the right best describes each speaker's tone:

1		5	
2		6	
3		7	
4		8	

amused   bored
cross   friendly
furious   kind
sad   unemotional

2 🔊 **Listen to the recording again and note down at least one other adjective (or phrase) to describe the tone of each speaker. Compare ideas with your partners.**

B **Look at these words and match them with their synonyms below.**

amazed   annoyed   clever   confused   cured   depressed   determined   different
disappointed   dull   encouraged   exciting   frightened   glad   respected   revolting
shocked   upset   worried   worrying

admired   anxious   astonished   better   bewildered   delighted   despondent   disgusting
disillusioned   distressed   disturbing   diverse   dreary   heartened   horrified   indignant
persistent   scared   talented   thrilling

C **Replace each word in red with a synonym which might impress the examiners – or which can help you to avoid repetition. (You may have to rewrite the whole sentence.)**

1 Surfing can be dangerous, but hang-gliding is much more dangerous.
2 There are many good ways of keeping fit – jogging is very good.
3 I was happy to meet my old friends again. It was good to talk about old times.
4 I'm sorry that you were unwell yesterday. You look all right today.
5 It was kind of you to offer to help, but the work wasn't difficult.
6 We went for a nice walk at the weekend, ending up at a nice restaurant.
7 The original novel was interesting, but the film they made of it was boring.
8 The meal we had last night was good, but the wine wasn't good.

D **Replace the verbs in red with suitable phrasal verbs. (This exercise revises some of the phrasal verbs you have come across in previous units.)**

1 Freud had the theory that pleasure and sexuality were directly linked.
2 I couldn't make them understand that I was tired and this really depressed me.
3 I withdraw that remark I made about you.
4 If you have a pain in your back you'll just have to endure it.
5 I find that stress at work often causes a headache.
6 I hope you aren't delayed in the rush-hour traffic.
7 She invented the whole story and she deceived us all!
8 His suitcase disintegrated on the luggage carousel.
9 Having heard all the arguments I've decided to support your idea.
10 Would it inconvenience you if I stayed for dinner?

A 👥 **Discuss the notes below and add your own views to them. Decide which of the points you'll include and which you'll leave out in an essay on this topic:**

We are constantly bombarded with advice from experts on ways of staying healthy and surviving to a ripe old age. Which aspects of their advice do you think it is practicable to follow? Read this leaflet and then write an essay giving your views on this topic. (300–350 words)

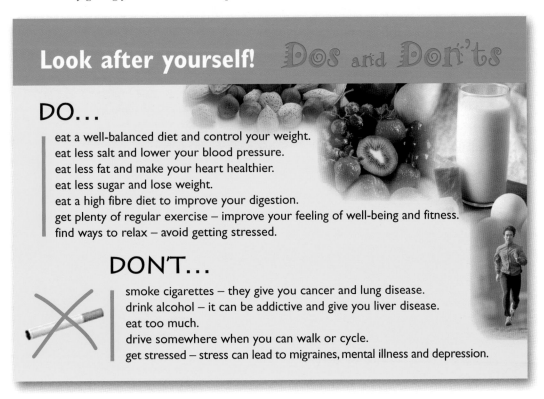

Look after yourself! Dos and Don'ts

DO...

eat a well-balanced diet and control your weight.
eat less salt and lower your blood pressure.
eat less fat and make your heart healthier.
eat less sugar and lose weight.
eat a high fibre diet to improve your digestion.
get plenty of regular exercise – improve your feeling of well-being and fitness.
find ways to relax – avoid getting stressed.

DON'T...

smoke cigarettes – they give you cancer and lung disease.
drink alcohol – it can be addictive and give you liver disease.
eat too much.
drive somewhere when you can walk or cycle.
get stressed – stress can lead to migraines, mental illness and depression.

B **1** ✏ **Make your own notes and then write the essay. Try to do everything in ONE HOUR: making notes, writing the composition and checking your work.**

2 👥 **Show your completed essay to your partner and ask for comments.**

What are the examiners looking for in the Writing Paper?
1 How well you have fulfilled the task set. (The five questions in Part 2 provide five different tasks: each demands different responses and techniques.)
2 The relevance and organisation of your composition as a whole, as well as the quality of the individual paragraphs.
3 The quality of the language you use: the range and appropriateness of vocabulary and sentence structure; the correctness of grammar, punctuation and spelling.
4 Your ability to display a breadth of experience or background knowledge, and your use of illustration and allusion.
5 A 'balance between accuracy and imagination' in each composition: the examiners try to give equitable treatment to compositions which are 'pedestrian but accurate' and those which are less accurate but 'lively and imaginative'.

In Part 3 of the Reading Paper you have to decide which paragraph fits in the spaces in the text. To add to the difficulty, there's one extra paragraph which doesn't fit anywhere. In the exam there are seven paragraphs missing, but here only six are missing.

Six paragraphs/sentences have been removed from this article. Choose the most suitable paragraph/sentence from the list A–G for each gap (1–6) in the article. There is one extra paragraph you don't need to use.

Jane Clarke

Taking the waters

While we can survive for some time without food, we can only live for a few days without water. A persistently dehydrated body can lead to lethargy, poor skin, high cholesterol levels, urinary-tract infections such as cystitis and bowel problems such as constipation.

| 1 |

Even high blood fat (cholesterol and triglycerides) levels can be aggravated by lack of water; without it, fibre (found in whole grains, pulses, oats, fruits and vegetables) cannot swell and stimulate the body to produce High Density Lipoprotein, aka 'good cholesterol'. HDL picks up Low Density Lipoprotein – 'bad cholesterol' – and takes it to the gut, where it is excreted.

| 2 |

Most adults should drink two or three litres (about four or five pints) of water every day. Those who exercise, and pregnant women, need even more. Exercise causes the body to lose fluid, which can lead to over-heating, dizziness and tiredness. During pregnancy, the fluid requirement increases to nourish the foetus, while breast-feeding mums need extra fluid to produce milk. Children can lose a lot of water through their skin, because they're generally more active. Urine is one of the best guides to the adequacy of fluid intake.

| 3 |

When you boost your water intake, you will find yourself using the loo more frequently, but your body will soon adapt. If you have other symptoms – a need to pass urine excessively, blood in urine, pain or extreme itchiness or discomfort – it may mean that you have a urine infection, which will need medical attention.

| 4 |

With digestive disorders such as a hiatus hernia or oesophagitis (inflammation of the oesophagus), having too much liquid can cause the stomach contents to leak up into the oesophagus, irritate the oesophagus walls and bring on heartburn. To avoid this, take only small sips with your meal to refresh your palate, but make up your fluid requirement between meals.

| 5 |

Some people find bottled water unnecessary and uneconomical. A litre of tap water costs 0.06 pence, approximately – that's up to a thousand times cheaper than bottled water. There is also the cost to the environment (plastics for packaging and energy for transport). If the taste puts you off tap water, your water supplier will be able to test for contamination (which can occur in old pipes, for example) or bacterial overgrowth. Water companies now have a legal duty to meet safety standards and are 'committed to improvements in the palatability of water, particularly taste and clarity', according to Water UK.

| 6 |

Also, it doesn't have to be served cold – there are many fruit and herbal teas and tisanes on the market; you could even make your own using fresh mint, or root ginger with lemon and honey. Remember that water that contains caffeine – from coffee, tea, colas or hot chocolate – does not count towards your daily two- to three-litre intake because caffeine is dehydrating. Enjoy two or three cups (the daily recommendation), but then take care to keep up necessary levels of pure water – your best liquid asset.

A A water filter can remove some of the undesirable tastes, but make sure it is regularly serviced, otherwise you will be contaminating your water by passing it through an unclean filter. Bottled water is handy to carry around with you, to give to your child to take to school or to have sitting on your desk – all good ways of reminding you to drink a glass an hour. You can make water more interesting by adding shavings of fresh ginger, slices or squeezes of fresh lemon or lime, a few drops of orange-blossom water or a dash of elderflower or lime cordial.

B An adult's body is made up of about 65 per cent water, and this has to be topped up to keep it healthy, flexible and young-looking. We need water to keep the body flushing waste products, maintain healthy skin, hair and organs, produce digestive enzymes, regulate our temperature (cooling by evaporation through the skin) and aid uptake of essential nutrients such as vitamins, minerals and natural sugars.

C For people who have a poor appetite, or who need to put on weight or maximise their calorie intake, it is important not to drink large amounts of water at meal times. Water itself does not disturb digestion, but if you fill yourself up with fluid, you'll have less room for food.

D I recently discovered when advising a high-altitude level climber (Mount Everest, K2, etc.) that checking the colour of urine can be a life-saving exercise. Urine should be pale in colour, and you should go to the loo regularly throughout the day. If urine is dark, you are not drinking enough water – which can quickly lead to death if you're 24,000ft above sea level. If you think two litres of water is a lot, imagine having to drink eight to 10 – the average daily fluid requirement for high-altitude climbers!

E We lose water mainly through our kidneys and skin (the skin's inner layer, dermis, is made up of 70 per cent water and acts as a natural reservoir). We also lose a lot of water when we suffer sickness, diarrhoea or any infection that causes fever. Now that the majority of us live in centrally heated houses and work in offices with heating and air conditioning, we lose more water through our skin than people did in the past. Our diets now also contain higher levels of salt, additives and sugars, all of which place extra strain on the body's water reserves.

F Many people wonder why doctors and medical people make so much fuss about water, but the reason is clear: water is good for you. And the more you drink the better it is for your health. Most people drink far less than they should and they are not aware of this.

G Whether you get your water from a tap or a bottle is up to you. Mineral and spring water are ground waters, which means they landed as rain, seeped through rocks and collected in underground pools. When this water reaches the surface, it can be bottled and labelled as spring water. 'Natural mineral water' is more rigidly defined and is better regulated; it has to come from a source which is naturally protected, of a constant composition and free from pollution. A small amount of water can be found to be naturally sparkling, but most sparkling water has had carbon dioxide pumped into it. This poses no threat to health.

16.10 Use of English Part 3

EXAM PRACTICE

In Part 3 of the Use of English Paper there are six sets of three sentences, each with a missing word. You have to think of a word that fits in all three sentences. If you can only think of a word that fits in two of them, it might be worth guessing that this is the missing one in the third.

Make sure the word you choose is grammatically correct – does it need an 's' or 'ed' on the end?

Think of ONE WORD which can be used appropriately in all three sentences.

1 I suppose you think my opinions don't .... – well, they do!
He was found guilty on one .... of murder and two of assault.
I hope it won't .... against me if I don't come to your party.

2 When his health deteriorated the surgeon decided to ....
You can find instructions on how to .... the machine in the manual.
Parking restrictions only .... from 8 am to 6 pm.

3 The .... of the organisation was born two hundred years ago.
The crew abandoned ship when it began to .... on the rocks.
Their plans are going to .... if they don't keep to their budget.

4 Her constant criticism .... my enthusiasm.
Pollution is exacerbated by the fumes from car and lorry ....
Going up a mountain .... even experienced climbers.

5 She hates working for other people, and prefers to run her own ....
Young people .... less and less respect for their elders these days.
Recent reports .... a sharp rise in the numbers of overweight people. | **5**

6 The headings are usually printed in bold ....
She doesn't want to see him again because he isn't her ....
I wish I had learned to .... when I was younger, it's so difficult now. | **6**

16.11 Use of English Part 5: Floating

EXAM PRACTICE

In Part 5 of the Use of English Paper you have to read two texts and answer four language awareness questions (each worth two marks). You then have to write a 50–70 word summary of some information contained in the two texts (worth 14 marks).

There are more than four questions here, to give you extra practice.

 A **Read the text and answer the questions below:**

Fee floating

STRESSED executives used to unwind with a few cigarettes and a pint of lager. No longer. Fear of the two big Cs – cancer and corpulence – has encouraged them to take to more exotic therapies. The big hit of the moment is floating about in tanks of salt water. Today only slobs smoke and slurp; sensible people float and free-associate.

The idea behind floating is simple: deprive the body of physical sensations and you free the mind for meditation. The fad started 20 years ago in California. While he was investigating the side-effects of sensory-deprivation, a neuro-physiologist called John Lilley had the bright idea of immersing his assistants in tanks of salt water. They emerged euphoric, jabbering about inner peace and mystical visions.

The first British tank was set up six years ago in a seedy bit of south London. There are now more than 40 of them open to the public and almost as many private ones – a tank can be yours for just £2,000 ($3,400). They have even found their way into night clubs. Seasoned floaters report a recent surge in interest. "Neighbours", a television soap-opera, has featured it; Jason Donovan, a pop star, has discovered it; even the medical profession has put in a good word for it.

Floating is certainly a weird sensation. The tank is a light-proof and sound-proof closed shell about the size of a small sauna. You lie (alone) in the darkness, with your head resting on a floating pillow and your body suspended in ten inches of warm water, salted about as heavily as the Dead Sea. For the first few minutes you listen to a tape of warbling flutes and twittering birds. Then everything falls silent.

At first, you concentrate on the physical sensation of floating. Next you start to worry about unpaid bills and unfinished jobs. Finally, you drift off into a meditative limbo – the middle-zone, the cognoscenti call it. Snatches of music and exotic images – some of them startlingly vivid – drift in and out of your mind. Floaters usually lose track of time, unaware of whether they have been in the tank for five minutes or five hours. Not so the proprietors: after your allotted hour, a tape of bellowing whales and crashing waves summons you out of your reverie. Even in the new age, time is money.

Floating leaves you feeling spaced-out without the physical side-effects of chemicals or the mental tedium of meditation. But beware the lure of salt water. The contrast between the womb-like security of the tank and the bustle of the street sends the pulse racing and the senses reeling – and undoes the benefits of an hour in less than ten minutes. Frequent floaters go to ever greater lengths to attain nirvana: some float for up to eight hours a day. And none of this comes cheap: an hour in the tank will set you back £20.

from *The Economist*

For questions 1–7 write a word or short phrase. You do not need to write complete sentences.

1 Why did the writer use the word *jabbering* in line 15?
2 What impresssion does the writer give by using the word *seedy* in line 18?
3 Why did the writer use the expression *warbling flutes* in lines 33–4?
4 Why is the word *alone* in brackets in line 29?
5 What are said to be the disadvantages of taking drugs and meditation?
6 Why might floaters feel worse after a session in the tank?
7 Explain in your own words how floaters are informed that their time is up.

8 In 50–70 words, summarise the history of floating.

B **Compare your answers.**

The summary writing task tests information selection, linking and sentence construction. Four of the 14 marks are awarded for including the relevant points, the rest are for summary writing skills.

16.12 *mind, brain* **and** *word*   IDIOMS

A **Find synonymous words or phrases to replace the phrases in red, using a dictionary if necessary.**

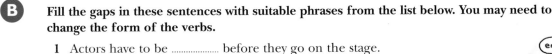

1 Don't expect him to spare your feelings: he always speaks his mind.
2 Being insured costs a lot of money but it gives you peace of mind.
3 I was so annoyed that I couldn't resist giving him a piece of my mind.
4 She gave me her word that she would pay me back the next day.
5 She's so indecisive: she can never make up her mind what to do.
6 We were in two minds whether to phone you or not.
7 He's so garrulous that you can't get a word in edgeways.
8 It'll all end in tears, mark my words!
9 I can still see the whole scene in my mind's eye.
10 I'm sorry I didn't post the letter, it slipped my mind, I'm afraid.
11 Their new car is the last word in luxury.
12 'No, you can't stay out all night.' 'Is that your last word?' 'Yes.'

B **Fill the gaps in these sentences with suitable phrases from the list below. You may need to change the form of the verbs.**

1 Actors have to be .... before they go on the stage.
2 You're an expert on this subject, would you mind if I .... ?
3 He's usually so trustworthy, he's the last person I'd expect to ....
4 I couldn't think what to do, then suddenly I had a ....
5 Sit down, listen to some music and try to .... your problems.
6 I'm so angry about the way I was treated that I .... write a letter of complaint.
7 Idioms like these can't be translated .... into another language.
8 Who are you going to believe? We both denied responsibility so ....
9 You look preoccupied, as if you ....
10 Many English jokes depend on a ....
11 If you .... about coming with us, just give me a call.
12 I was .... but I couldn't solve the problem.

brainwave	change your mind	go back on her/his word	have a good mind to
have something on your mind	take your mind off	word for word	word perfect
it's his/her word against mine	pick your brains	play on words	rack my brains

"He pretends to throw the stick, I pretend to chase it.
Is this normal?"

17

The past is always with us

EXAM PRACTICE

A **Look at the pictures and discuss these questions:**

- What is each person famous for? What were his achievements?
- Why do we hear about so few women in history? Who are the most famous women in your country's history? What are they famous for?
- How interested are you in history? Give your reasons.

B Fill each gap with ONE suitable word.

In Part 1 of the Use of English Paper you should read the whole text through before filling any of the blanks. If you can't think what to put in some of the gaps, leave them blank and allow yourself enough time to come back to them later. If you're unsure of an answer, write it in pencil and come back to it later. Remember to write your answers in CAPITAL LETTERS on the Answer Sheet.

Make sure the words you choose not only make sense in the context but are grammatically correct – and that you spell them correctly. If you aren't sure, try to decide what kind of word is missing: noun, adjective, adverb, verb, etc.

JEANS

'G ÈNES' is the French name for Genoa, and by extension for a traditional ¹ of trousers worn by Genoese sailors. Serge de Nîmes was the ² of a tough blue sailcloth, now corrupted to 'denim', traditionally ³ in the French town. Levi Strauss (1829–1902) was a ⁴ of Bavaria who ⁵ to New York at the age of fourteen and who ⁶ his brothers in their ⁷ of supplying the prospectors and frontiersmen of the Californian Gold Rush. Some time in the 1860s Levi's company had the ⁸ of matching the denim cloth with the Genoese trousers, and of ⁹ the pockets and seams with brass horse-harness rivets.

Thus was produced the most durable and universal item in the ¹⁰ of fashion design – a German immigrant using French materials and Italian style to invent an archetypal American ¹¹.

'Blue jeans' remained workaday clothing in North America for almost a ¹², before taking Europe (and the ¹³ of the world) by ¹⁴ in the 1960s, a prime ¹⁵ of 'Americanization'.

from Europe A History by Norman Davies

C Read this text and then answer the multiple choice questions that follow:

You'll have to answer multiple choice questions like these in the Reading Paper Parts 2 and 4 (and also in the Listening Paper Parts 1 and 3). If you don't know which answer is right, first eliminate the ones you think are wrong. Then choose between the ones that might be right. If in doubt, guess! Don't leave a blank.

MURANO

1 MURANO is an island in the Venetian lagoon. It is the site of a Romanesque church, Santa Maria e Donate, dating from 999, and the glassworks of the former Venetian Republic.

2 Glass-making has been practised in Europe since ancient times, but Greek and Roman glass was coarse in texture and opaque in colour. It was only at Murano, near the turn of the thirteenth century, that the glass-masters created a product that was both tough and transparent. For several decades the formula remained secret: but then it leaked to Nuremberg, whence it spread to all corners of the continent.

3 Transparent glass made possible the science of optics, and was crucial in the development of precision instruments. The principles of the lens and the refraction of light were known by the time, c.1260, that Roger Bacon was credited with designing the first pair of spectacles. (There is a portrait of the Emperor Henry VII (d. 1313) wearing spectacles in one of the stained glass windows of Strasburg cathedral.) Glass windows gradually came into fashion between the fourteenth and sixteenth centuries, first in churches and palaces and later in more humble dwellings. Glass flasks, retorts, and tubes facilitated the experiments of alchemy, later of chemistry. Glass cloches and greenhouses transformed market-gardening. The microscope (1590), telescope (1608), barometer (1644), and thermometer (1593), all glass-based, revolutionized our views of the world. The silvered mirror, first manufactured at Murano, revolutionized the way we see ourselves.

4 The social consequences of glass were far-reaching. The use of spectacles extended the reading span of monks and scholars, and accelerated the spread of learning. Windows increased the hours and efficiency of indoor work, especially in northern Europe. Workplaces could be better lit and better heated. Greenhouses vastly improved the cultivation of flowers, fruit, and vegetables, bringing a healthier and more abundant diet, previously known only in the Mediterranean. Storm-proof lanterns, enclosed coaches, and watch-glasses all appeared, whilst precision instruments encouraged a wide range of scientific disciplines, from astronomy to medicine.

5 The mirror had important psychological consequences. People who could see a sharp image of their own faces developed a new consciousness. They became more aware of their appearances, and hence of clothes, hairstyles, and cosmetics. They were also led to ponder the link between external features and the inner life, in short, to study personality and individuality. They developed interests in portraiture, biography, and fashion. The very unmedieval habits of introspection were strongly reflected in Rembrandt's paintings, for example, and ultimately in the novel.
The *Galerie des Glaces* (Hall of Mirrors) at the palace of Versailles was opened on 15 November 1684. It was a wonder of the age. Spanning the full façade of the central pavilion and overlooking the park, its colossal mirrors reflected the light of seventeen huge windows and seventeen colossal chandeliers. It was the secular counterpart to the medieval stained glass of Chartres.

6 The ancients had seen through glass darkly. The moderns saw through it clearly, in a shocking, shining cascade of light that reached into their innermost lives.

from *Europe A History* by Norman Davies

1 The method of making glass one could see through ...
   A was already practised in Ancient Greece
   B developed slowly between 999 and 1200
   C was perfected in Nuremberg
   D was, for many years, only known to Murano glassmakers

2 The new type of glass was first used in ...
   A windows for religious buildings
   B bottles and containers
   C windows in normal houses
   D reading glasses

3 Glass improved everyday life in the north of Europe because ...
   A spectacles helped people to read
   B flowers could be grown in cold weather
   C it was easier to see indoors
   D the study of medicine developed

4 Before people used mirrors they ...
   A didn't care how they looked
   B didn't examine their own behaviour
   C had no idea how they looked
   D behaved inconsiderately

5 Without the new type of glass there would have been no ...
   A cathedrals   B paintings   C bottles   D scientific instruments

D **Discuss these questions:**
- Name three significant events in your country's history. When did they happen and why are they memorable?
- What was the most significant world event of the last ten years?

A Read and listen to these poems before you look at the questions in B below.

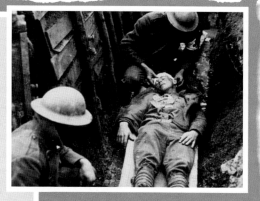

THE SOLDIER

If I should die, think only this of me;
    That there is some corner of a foreign field
That is for ever England. There shall be
    In that rich earth a richer dust concealed;
A dust whom England bore, shaped, made aware,
    Gave, once, her flowers to love, her ways to roam,
A body of England's breathing English air,
    Washed by the rivers, blest by suns of home.

And think, this heart, all evil shed away,
    A pulse in the eternal mind, no less
        Gives somewhere back the thoughts by England given;
            Her sights and sounds; dreams happy as her day;
        And laughter, learnt of friends; and gentleness,
            In hearts at peace, under an English heaven.

Rupert Brooke

THE GENERAL

'Good-morning; good-morning!' the General said
When we met him last week on our way to the Line.
Now the soldiers he smiled at are most of 'em dead,
And we're cursing his staff for incompetent swine.
'He's a cheery old card,' grunted Harry to Jack
As they slogged up to Arras with rifle and pack.

But he did for them both with his plan of attack.

Siegfried Sassoon

FUTILITY

Move him into the sun –
Gently its touch awoke him once,
At home, whispering of fields unsown.
Always it woke him, even in France,
Until this morning and this snow.
If anything might rouse him now
The kind old sun will know.

Think how it wakes the seeds, –
Woke, once, the clays of a cold star.
Are limbs, so dear-achieved, are sides,
Full-nerved – still warm – too hard to stir?
Was it for this the clay grew tall?
– O what made fatuous sunbeams toil
To break earth's sleep at all?

Wilfred Owen

B Discuss which of the alternatives best reflects the meaning and mood of each poem.

1 In Rupert Brooke's *The Soldier*, the poet is praising...
  A England's brave soldiers   **C** England's scenery and people
  B England's free and democratic society **D** England's heritage and history
2 The England described in the poem is England...
  A during peacetime   **C** in spring or summer
  B during the poet's youth   **D** during the previous century
3 If he dies the poet is sure that...
  A he will be remembered   **C** his Englishness is immortal
  B England will remain unchanged **D** his friends and relations will remember him
4 If the idea of 'England' were replaced by 'Germany' or another country, the poem would...
  A no longer make sense   **C** still mean the same
  B have a different significance   **D** be more moving
5 The tone of *The Soldier* is...
  A sentimental   **B** optimistic   **C** pessimistic   **D** detached

6 In Wilfred Owen's *Futility*, the soldier described...
  A has only just died   **C** has been dead for a long time
  B is sure to die soon   **D** is likely to survive
7 According to the poem it is pointless that...
  A any man should die in war   **C** a dead man should be moved into the sun
  B a man should grow up to die in this way **D** a dead body should be buried
8 The tone of *Futility* is...
  A resigned   **B** sardonic   **C** lyrical   **D** emotional

You won't have to answer questions about poems in the exam! But there will be language awareness questions, focusing on style, emphasis or implications.

9 In Siegfried Sassoon's *The General*, the smiling general is...
   A insincere   **B** incompetent   **C** happy   **D** brave

10 'Harry and Jack' are...
   A two typical private soldiers   **C** two now-dead friends of the poet
   B two young officers   **D** two living friends of the poet

11 The soldiers who marched past the general last week...
   A disliked him   **B** respected him   **C** liked him   **D** didn't notice him

12 The tone of *The General* is...
   A serious   **B** humorous   **C** sarcastic   **D** emotional

C One of you should look at Activity **9**, one at **25** and the other(s) at **30**. You'll each have some information about each poet's life to share with your partners. Then discuss these questions:

- How does knowing more about each poet's life influence your response to the poems?
- Which of the poems made the greatest impact on you? Why?
- Which poems or works of literature came out of wars that your country has been involved in?
- Why is it that some people find films and books about war fascinating?

17.3 Modifying adjectives and participles

VOCABULARY DEVELOPMENT

A 1 Which of these sentences look right – and which are wrong?

They were extremely pleased with my work.
It was very delightful to have met you.
It is extremely important to read the question carefully.
It is very essential to make notes before you start writing.
It is extremely vital to check your answers for slips of the pen.

2 Tick the words that are 'GRADABLE' (i.e. they can be intensified by words like *very* or *extremely*) and put a cross by the ones that are 'non-gradable' or 'ABSOLUTE' (not usually intensified by *very*).

livid ☒ indignant ☑   good ☑ perfect ☒
absurd ☐ preposterous ☐ improbable ☐
intelligent ☐ sensible ☐ brilliant ☐
amazed ☐ surprised ☐ astounded ☐
terrifying ☐ frightening ☐
fatal ☐ hazardous ☐ deadly ☐ harmful ☐
happy ☐ euphoric ☐
genuine ☐ believable ☐

identical ☐ similar ☐
interesting ☐ fascinating ☐
priceless ☐ valuable ☐
worthless ☐ futile ☐ inexpensive ☐
delightful ☐ pleasant ☐
essential ☐ important ☐

B Fill each gap with a suitable modifier from the list, but don't repeat the same one in the same sentence.

absolutely   badly   considerably   deeply   exceptionally   extraordinarily   fully   highly
perfectly   quite   really   remarkably   thoroughly   totally   unexpectedly   utterly

1 He was .... determined to succeed, and he was .... disappointed when he didn't. We were .... amused, but pretended to be .... sympathetic.

2 The amount of work that is required is .... greater than we expected, and we'll have to make a(n) .... great effort to finish it on time.

3 We were .... delighted to hear he was marrying such a(n) .... nice woman.

4 He was feeling .... depressed after his illness, but he made a .... quick recovery, and was .... cheerful after that.

5 We felt we had been .... let down when they told us our application had been rejected. We were .... embarrassed because we'd told all our friends.

6 I'm sure her business will be .... successful, as she is a .... capable person, even though it's .... true that most new businesses don't succeed.

7 It was a(n) .... wonderful film and I thought the performances were .... moving. It was .... different from any other film I've ever seen.

8 The role of women in history is not .... recognised by many historians, who tend to be .... traditional in their attitudes.

C   For each sentence, write a new sentence as similar in meaning as possible to the original sentence, using the word given but without altering the word in any way. Use three to eight words.

impossible

1   Some people simply can't remember historical dates at all.
Some people find that .... remember historical dates.

delighted

2   We should be very happy indeed to accept your invitation.
We should .... accept your invitation.

forgotten

3   It happened so long ago that no one remembers it at all now.
It happened so long ago that ....

futile

4   There's no point at all in asking him to be tactful.
It is .... to be tactful.

livid

5   She was very angry indeed when she found out about our plans.
She .... find out about our plans.

improbable

6   There is no likelihood at all of his succeeding.
It is .... succeed.

essential

7   You must *not* forget to check your work through for mistakes.
It is .... to check your work through for mistakes.

fascinating

8   We really were extremely interested in the lecture.
We ....

17.4   **The end of the war**   **READING**

A   Read this extract, which describes the last months of the First World War, as seen from one young man's point of view. Then answer the questions on the next page.

Nancy's brother, Tony, had also gone to France now, and her mother made herself ill by worrying about him. Early in July he should be due for leave. I was on leave myself at the end of one of the four-months' cadet courses, staying with the rest of Nancy's family at Maesyneuardd, a big Tudor house near Harlech. This was the most haunted house that I have ever been in, though the ghosts, with one exception, were not visible, except occasionally in the mirrors. They would open and shut doors, rap on the oak panels, knock the shades off lamps, and drink the wine from the glasses at our elbows when we were not looking. The house belonged to an officer in the Second Battalion, whose ancestors had most of them died of drink. The visible ghost was a little yellow dog that would appear on the lawn in the early morning to announce deaths. Nancy saw it through the window that time.

The first Spanish influenza epidemic began, and Nancy's mother caught it, but did not want to miss Tony's leave and going to the London theatres with him. So when the doctor came, she took quantities of aspirin, reduced her temperature, and pretended to be all right. But she knew that the ghosts in the mirrors knew the truth. She died in London on July 13th, a few days later. Her chief solace, as she lay dying, was that Tony had got his leave prolonged on her account. I was alarmed at the effect that the shock of her death might have on Nancy's baby. Then I heard that Siegfried [Sassoon] had been shot through the head that same day while making a daylight patrol through long grass in No Man's Land; but not killed. And he wrote me a verse-letter from a London hospital beginning: *I'd timed my death in action to the minute...*

It is the most terrible of his war-poems.

Tony was killed in September. I went on mechanically at my cadet-battalion work. The new candidates for commissions were mostly Manchester cotton clerks and Liverpool shipping clerks – men with a good fighting record, quiet and well behaved. To forget about the war, I was writing *Country Sentiment,* a book of romantic poems and ballads.

In November came the Armistice. I heard at the same time of the deaths of Frank Jones-Bateman, who had gone back again just before the end, and Wilfred Owen, who often used to send me poems from France. Armistice-night hysteria did not touch our camp much, though some of the Canadians stationed there went down to Rhyl to celebrate in true overseas style. The news sent me out walking alone along the dyke above the marshes of Rhuddlan (an ancient battlefield), cursing and sobbing and thinking of the dead.

Siegfried's famous poem celebrating the Armistice began:

> *Everyone suddenly burst out singing,*
> *And I was filled with such delight*
> *As prisoned birds must find in freedom...*

But 'everyone' did not include me.

from Goodbye to All That by Robert Graves

1 According to the writer, the invisible ghosts...
   A really did not exist   **C** really did exist
   B were visible only to Nancy   **D** were the ghosts of soldiers who had died
                                                      at the Front
2 The doctor who came to see Nancy's mother...
   A knew she was dying   **C** did not realise she was very ill
   B did not examine her thoroughly   **D** gave her tablets to bring down her temperature
3 The writer mentions the deaths of...
   A five people he knew well   **C** four people he knew well
   B three people he knew well   **D** two people he knew well
4 The writer, at the time, was...
   A fighting at the Front   **C** training soldiers who wanted to be officers
   B training new recruits   **D** training would-be officers, fresh from school
5 When the Armistice was announced the writer...
   A was overjoyed   **C** had mixed feelings
   B became hysterical   **D** was overwhelmed with grief
6 The tone of the writing in the extract seems...
   A emotional   **B** cynical   **C** detached   **D** careless

B   **Discuss your reactions to the text with a partner.**

When tackling a reading text in the exam, you may prefer to read it quickly through to get the gist before looking at the questions – or look at the questions first and then read the text through.

Some of the alternatives given in the questions may be tricky or deceptively plausible, which may distract you from the best alternative – so don't jump to conclusions. Be ready to eliminate the wrong answers and find the right one by a process of elimination.

Read carefully through the text to find the answers, highlight any relevant parts so that you can find them again quickly later. In the exam each correct answer gains two marks.

17.5 Adjectives + prepositions   GRAMMAR REVIEW

A   **Discuss the differences in meaning between the adjectives in these sentences. Who or what might *it* or *them* refer to at the end of each sentence?**

1 Drink up: it's good for you.   She is very good at it.
  He was very good about it.   She was very good to them.
2 She was angry with them.   He was angry about it.
3 I knew I was right about them.   The choice was right for them.
4 We were pleased with them.   We were pleased for them.
  He sounded pleased about it.
5 She was sorry for them.   He was sorry about it.

B   **Decide whether *of* or *to* is used after each of these adjectives:**

accustomed   ahead   allergic   ashamed   aware   capable   comparable   conscious
courteous   critical   cruel   devoid   devoted   envious   equivalent   guilty   hurtful
identical   impolite   indifferent   inferior   intolerant   irrelevant   kind   loyal
preferable   proud   scared   sensitive   short   similar   superior   susceptible
unfaithful   unworthy   wary   weary

C   **Which of the prepositions is used after each of these adjectives?**

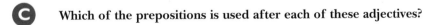

absent   annoyed   apprehensive   bewildered   comparable   compatible   consistent
conversant   curious   *about*   *for*   *from*   *on*   *with*   dependent   dubious
familiar   famous   far   free   fussy   guilty   indignant   intent   keen   level
patient   responsible   sceptical   vague

D **Fill each gap with one word only, chosen from the previous two exercises:**

1 We felt .... about the reception we might get, even though we knew that we'd be forgiven when we explained how .... we were for being late.

2 He is .... to his children and feels .... of them, but he does get .... with them if they are ever .... to people. Usually he feels .... about this afterwards, even though he knows it is .... for them.

3 I know I'm being .... of your staff but I'm not .... to being treated in this way. Who is the person who is .... for this?

4 She pretended to be .... to our sarcastic remarks, but in fact she's quite .... to being made fun of. Personally I'm .... about the effectiveness of sarcasm and I'm .... of the fact that it can be very .... to people.

5 Although he's usually .... on getting his own way, he didn't seem to be .... of convincing anyone at the meeting – on this occasion I felt quite .... for him, but I was .... of telling him so.

17.6 Listening Part 3: Emigration   EXAM PRACTICE

Part 3 of the Listening Paper is an interview or discussion. There are five multiple-choice questions which focus on only some of the information or opinions given. Read the questions carefully before you hear the recording, so that you know what to listen out for. (In the exam there are only five questions to answer.)

A 🔊 **You'll hear part of a lecture about emigration. Choose the alternative which fits best according to what you hear.**

1 The total number of emigrants from Great Britain in the 19th century was . . .
A about 2 million   C around 11 million
B under 6 million   D over 13 million   `1`

2 Soon after their arrival in the United States, most immigrants were . . .
A homesick   C pleasantly surprised
B hungry   D disillusioned   `2`

3 Most Irish emigrants left their country because they didn't have enough . . .
A money   C food
B religious freedom   D independence   `3`

4 Most Indians did not go to other countries intending to . . .
A work   C make their fortunes
B become labourers   D settle   `4`

5 The total number of US immigrants between 1830 and 1930 was . . .
A 30 million   C 53 million
B 35 million   D 105 million   `5`

6 One can deduce the origins of American citizens of European origin by . . .
A noticing their foreign accents   C looking at the colour of their skin
B looking through a telephone directory   D asking what kind of food they like   `6`

7 According to the speaker, more recent immigrants in the 20th century . . .
A were less likely to integrate   C don't mix with former immigrants
B send money home to their families   D are less successful   `7`

8 The speaker implies that immigration has contributed to . . .
A prejudice against immigrants   C a rich mixture of different cultures
B the loss of immigrants' cultural heritage   D the language of the host country   `8`

B 👥 **Discuss these questions:**

• Which countries have people from your country emigrated to in the past?
• Do you have any relatives who have emigrated? Do you keep in touch?
• Would you consider emigrating to another country? Give your reasons.
• Which countries have immigrants to your country come from? Why did they come?

Part 4 of the Listening Paper is a discussion. The three-way matching questions require you to decide which of the speakers expressed a particular opinion – or whether they both did. Read the questions carefully before you hear the recording, so that you know what to listen out for.

This is the last Listening exercise. Before the exam, practise doing some Listening tests from Cambridge Certificate of Proficiency in English 1 – under exam conditions if possible.

🔊 **You will hear part of a radio discussion. Indicate which of the speakers expresses each of the opinions listed by writing the appropriate letter in each box.**

In each box write:

	A	for a view expressed only by Alan
or	**J**	for a view expressed only by Jane
or	**B**	for a view expressed both by Alan and Jane

1 The First World War was inevitable. `[ ] 1`

2 Britain was neutral until Belgium was invaded. `[ ] 2`

3 In 1914 the German plan to encircle the French forces misfired. `[ ] 3`

4 The Western Front hardly shifted from 1915 to 1918. `[ ] 4`

5 Things that happened in the First World War made the Second World War inevitable. `[ ] 5`

6 The Russian Revolution began with the support of Germany. `[ ] 6`

17.8 | Writing Parts 1 and 2

EXAM PRACTICE

In Part 1 of the Writing Paper you have to answer a compulsory question based on a short text and, perhaps, a diagram or picture. Make sure your answer sticks to the instructions closely and that you have a clear idea of who your supposed reader is. You may have to write an article, an essay, a letter or a proposal.

A ✎ **Prepare and write this composition task, allowing yourself sixty minutes only. This hour includes: time to think, time to make notes, time to write the letter – and, afterwards, to check your work through for mistakes. Do this without using any reference books (300–350 words).**

This extract is part of a newspaper article about teaching history. Readers were asked to send in their own opinions. You decide to write a letter responding to the points raised and expressing your own views.

Looking to the future?

Moves are afoot to reform the syllabus in secondary schools. The Education Minister has said that history has no place in a forward-looking society. Its place in the curriculum will be taken by extra lessons in information technology, maths and science.

"History had a place when this country could look back proudly on its past. Now we are looking to the future and history has had its day."

There is as yet no word from the Minister on the fate of the country's history teachers, most of whom are not qualified to teach more "forward-looking" subjects.

In Part 2 of the Writing Paper you have a choice of questions, including questions on each of the set texts (not included here). You may have to write an article, a proposal, a report, a review or a letter.

 B **Write 300–350 words on one of these topics:**

1 Write a report of a historical event in the style of a modern newspaper article.
2 Describe the life and achievements of a famous historical figure from your country.
3 Write a first-person narrative about a historical event, as if you were one of the people present at the time, ending with the words: ". . . only then did I realise that I had been involved in a significant moment in history."

Checking your work: Look carefully for any mistakes or slips of the pen you may have made, like the ones illustrated here:

Its important to emphasise that . . .   *Rarely it is possible to . . .*
Perhaps it should pointed out that . . .   *I decided to do a long journey . . .*
Historie can be a facsinating subject.   *We enjoied the peformance.*

By now you're probably familiar with the kind of 'silly mistakes' that you make yourself when you're under pressure. As long as these are spotted and corrected before your work is handed in, there's nothing to worry about – but make sure you do allow yourself enough time for this!

Look back at two or three of your most recent compositions and highlight any 'silly mistakes' you made. Make sure you check your work for mistakes like these in the exam.

17.9 Speaking   EXAM PRACTICE

In Part 1 of the Speaking Paper you give information about yourself and are asked to give some opinions. In Part 2 (two-way conversation) you are given visual and spoken prompts, which generate a discussion. In Part 3 (long turns and discussion) you have to talk for two minutes, working from a prompt card. Then a discussion ensues, exploring the topics of the long turns further.

 A 👥 Conversation about pictures. **Look at the pictures and discuss these questions together:**

* What's happening in the pictures? What kind of people do you think they are?
* What would it have been like to be a member of each family, do you think?
* What other aspects of family life in the first half of the 20th century would you like to see photos of? Why?

B **1** 👥 Long turns and discussion.

Student A
Talk for two minutes about this topic:
What changes have happened in the home since the first photo was taken?
➤ food and cooking
➤ family life
➤ hobbies and leisure activities

Student B
Talk for two minutes about this topic:
What changes have happened in travel and transport since the second photo was taken?
➤ cycling
➤ motoring
➤ travel abroad

2 👥 **Now discuss these questions:**

- How has life improved since those days?
- Is it worth studying history and finding out how people used to live?
- What is your favourite period of history? Why?

To help you feel more confident about the procedure for the exam, spend some time doing practice Speaking tests from one of the Cambridge Proficiency Examination Practice Books with a partner.

Try to give a good impression of your spoken English. Don't just wait to be asked questions – behave and speak as you would in a real conversation. Each part of the Speaking test is all based on the same general topic, but you won't lose marks if you go off at a tangent.

18 Modern life

18.1 Reading Part 2

In Part 2 of the Reading Paper you read four texts on the same theme: these may be articles from newspapers or magazines, advertisements, fiction or non-fiction. You should expect all kinds of questions, focusing on content, detail, attitude, opinion – as well as questions about the style of the text. There are eight questions, each worth two marks.

 A Read these four texts and choose the answer which you think fits best according to the text.

GIRL PAYS THE PRICE FOR LETTER TO PUTIN

A grammar school student in a tiny village deep in the Russian countryside who made the mistake of sending a letter to the president, Vladimir Putin, found herself stripped of the graduation honours she deserved and enrolled in a dairy academy instead of heading for medical school.

The letter was not political, and its author, Anya Provorova, certainly meant no disrespect. She and five graduating classmates of the little school in Vorobyovo, about 250 miles north of Moscow, had only fallen back upon centuries of Russian tradition and sent the Kremlin a request for help.

It wasn't that crucial – all they wanted was a video camera so they could record their graduation – but it seemed worth a try. It couldn't hurt to ask, could it?

It could, and it did.

The problem was this: in her salutation to "The Esteemed Vladimir Vladimirovich Putin", Ms Provorova neglected to finish the phrase with an exclamation point. Moreover, she used the Russian word for "you" in referring to the president, without giving it a capital letter.

As a result, her grades were lowered and she is heading to the local dairy institute.

"I don't think it's fair, especially because the medal commission had already confirmed my marks," she said. "I don't think these mistakes should be enough of a reason to lower my score."

She learned of her reprimand on June 15, at her graduation, after the school commission had condemned the letter to Mr Putin, and chastised the students for their immaturity.

There the story might have ended had not the regional correspondent for the national newspaper, Izvestia, learned of what had happened.

After the story appeared on Tuesday, school officials in the northern district denied that the withdrawal of the medals had anything to do with the letter.

Will Englund

1 Why did Anya fail to graduate?
  A She didn't sign the letter correctly.
  B Because of her poor spelling.
  C Writing to the president was against the rules.
  D She made two small punctuation errors.

2 What did Anya hope to do after leaving school?
  A Meet the president in person.
  B Win a medal for being a good student.
  C Become a graduate.
  D Study to be a doctor.

Boy falls victim to town with no scents

WHEN Gary Falkenham ran a few smears of Dippity-Do gel through his hair it was simply with the intention of enhancing his appearance. Not unnaturally, the 17-year-old also applied a dab of deodorant under each armpit.

Almost anywhere else these events might have passed without attracting undue attention, but Mr Falkenham lives in Halifax, Nova Scotia. Halifax has what its city council calls a "no-scent encouragement programme".

The schoolboy was expelled for two days after a teacher complained about the aroma he brought with him to the classroom. She said that it made her feel ill.

The elected representatives of the city – noted for the pungent fragrance of newly landed fish – believe that commercially produced scents contain untested carcinogenic chemicals and have banned them in public places.

The perfumes industry says their policy stinks.

Betty Bridges, a nurse from Virginia who travelled to the Canadian city to bolster the war on cologne, said: "The end result is that you have products that are being used by virtually the entire population but nobody knows what they'll do."

Ms Bridges, who often wears a breathing mask, has suffered for the past five years from multiple chemical sensitivity. She says that substances from perfumes have been found in breast milk and are linked to neurological disorders.

Conversely, Charles Low, the president of the Canadian Cosmetic, Toiletry and Fragrance Association, said: "The question we're here to answer fundamentally is: 'are fragrances and scented products safe for human use?' Our answer is yes."

As for Mr Falkenham, he was arrested by the Royal Canadian Mounted Police – who always get their man, whether or not he is wearing Dippity-Do – and released without charge.

Michael Ellison

3 Which of the following supports the 'no-scent encouragement programme' most strongly?
   A Gary Falkenham   **C** Gary's teacher
   B Charles Low   **D** Betty Bridges

4 What smell predominates in Halifax?
   A deodorant   **C** fish
   B chemicals   **D** fragrances

Year in jail for airliner mobile phone man

A man who repeatedly refused to turn off his mobile phone during an international flight was jailed for 12 months yesterday.

Airlines, police and the pilots' association welcomed the prison term imposed on Neil Whitehouse, 28, an oil worker, by a judge at Manchester crown court.

He was convicted of "recklessly and negligently" acting in a manner likely to endanger the British Airways Boeing 737 flight from Madrid to Manchester in September last year.

Judge Anthony Ensor told him: "Clearly you have no regard to the alarm and concern of passengers by your stubborn and arrogant behaviour. Any sentence must not only punish you but act as a warning to others."

He called on the Civil Aviation Authority to conclude investigations into legislation specifically banning mobile phones on planes.

"Proliferation of ownership of mobile phones and an increasing number of reports from pilots of electro-magnetic interference makes this a priority," he said.

At his trial last month the jury heard how Whitehouse, of Mansfield, Nottinghamshire, refused to switch off the phone despite requests from the captain and cabin crew.

Jamie Wilson

5 Who is looking into the possibility of introducing a law prohibiting mobile phones on planes?
   A The police   **C** The pilots' association
   B The Civil Aviation Authority   **D** The airlines

6 Why did the judge impose such a heavy sentence?
   A Because Whitehouse was arrogant.
   B Because the plane nearly crashed.
   C Because the plane made an emergency landing.
   D To discourage others from copying Whitehouse.

When high life was just a carousel

IT SOUNDED like the kind of glamorous job most people dream of. It required Geoffrey Senior to dress in smart suits, stay in expensive hotels and travel like a model executive back and forth to Heathrow airport.

In 12 months Mr Senior, aged 21, saw £300,000 pass through his hands, but the high life ended yesterday in a three-year prison sentence. The young, penniless, homeless man's luck ran out when a policeman stopped him pushing a trolley loaded with luggage away from a domestic flight terminal's carousel.

Mr Senior's version of the Generation Game – selecting his favourite items from a moving belt but without having to memorise them first – was the sort of profitable low-risk enterprise which has earned Heathrow the nickname Thiefrow and left senior police officers agog at criminal takings estimated at between £4 million and £10 million a week.

At the peak of summer nearly 200,000 people pass through the airport every day, making the remotest parts of the Piccadilly Line an El Dorado for the criminals working the terminals.

"Those like you who haunt Heathrow stealing people's baggage are an absolute menace to society," said Judge George Bathurst Norman in sentencing Mr Senior, who pleaded guilty to eight charges of theft.

Michael Orsulik, prosecuting, told the court that Mr Senior used to go smartly dressed to Terminal One and watch the domestic flight baggage carousel from an upstairs balcony. "If there was baggage going round on it and not many people about he would go down and help himself to items of luggage which took his fancy. He would then take them somewhere quiet, search through and help himself to things worth selling."

In one suitcase Mr Senior found £7,000 in cash. The money was spent on food, clothes and living it up.

David Sharrock

7 Who did Geoffrey Senior steal luggage from?
   A His fellow-passengers.
   B Passengers arriving from abroad.
   C Passengers who were delayed at passport control.
   D Passengers from British cities.

8 What did he do with most of the things in the luggage?
   A He took them home and kept them.
   B He stored them in a locker.
   C He sold them.
   D He left them behind.

B **Discuss these questions:**

   • What do you find most difficult about answering questions like these?
   • Is there any advice you can offer each other?
   • What tips from previous units do you try to follow when doing this kind of test?
   • Do you prefer to read all the texts quickly through first, before looking at the questions?

18.2 Use of English Part 3

EXAM PRACTICE

In Part 3 of the Use of English Paper you have to find a word that fits in all three sentences. The words are likely to be different parts of speech and may well have quite different meanings.

A Think of ONE WORD which can be used appropriately in all three sentences. Write your answers in CAPITAL LETTERS.

1 The bodywork is a bit rusty but the engine is ....
   E-commerce shares are not considered to be a .... investment.
   There was a strange .... followed by complete silence.

   [1]

2 There will be a .... drop in temperature when night falls.
   It will be very cold tomorrow in .... contrast to today.
   He has a .... eye for a bargain.

   [2]

3 The authorities put up .... all over town about the meeting.
   The barmaid never .... him when he tries to catch her eye.
   The film got very good .... but I found it disappointing.

   [3]

4 Everyone had lots of fun at the village ....
  We had a .... amount of sunshine last month.
  I usually make notes for an essay before I write a .... copy. | 4

5 She hopes to .... a good job when she finishes her studies.
  In the 19th century, most people lived off the ....
  Why don't we send him ahead to see how the .... lies. | 5

6 I don't know how you can .... it with your conscience, spending
  so much money on new shoes.
  I've just put up this picture, can you tell me if it's .... ?
  I'm so hungry, I haven't had a .... meal for ages. | 6

B 👥👥 **Discuss these questions:**
  • What do you find most difficult about this kind of task?
  • Is there any advice you can offer each other?

18.3 Use of English Part 4 EXAM PRACTICE

In Part 4 of the Use of English Paper, each correct sentence is worth two marks. A partially correct sentence gets one mark.

A **Complete the second sentence so that it has a similar meaning to the first sentence using the word given. DO NOT CHANGE THE WORD GIVEN. You must use between two and eight words, including the word given.**

depends

fear

gradual

had

takes

doubt

rely

what

1 Without the cooperation of the public, the police cannot prevent crime.
  The work .... the cooperation of the public.

2 She was afraid to scream because she didn't want to awaken the neighbours.
  She .... up the neighbours.

3 The number of murders has been going up little by little each year.
  There has been .... number of murders every year.

4 Their flat has been broken into twice this year.
  They .... twice this year.

5 She has a one-hour journey to work every day.
  Her .... every day.

6 If the traffic is bad, we can't predict exactly when we'll get there.
  If the traffic is bad, there .... time we'll arrive.

7 He may not be a very dependable person.
  You may .... him.

8 I hate the stresses and pressures of modern life.
  The stresses and pressures .... hate.

B 👥👥 **Discuss these questions:**
  • What do you find most difficult about this kind of task?
  • Is there any advice you can offer each other?

The text in Part 3 of the Reading Paper may be an article from a newspaper or magazine, or from a fiction or non-fiction book. There are seven paragraphs or sentences to fit into the spaces, giving a total of 14 marks.

Look for little clues: linking words, names and pronouns, times and places, words like *this, that, these*. Also consider the overall meaning of the text and the way that the main ideas follow on from each other.

 A   Seven paragraphs have been removed from this article. Choose the most suitable paragraph from the list A–H for each gap (1–7) in the article. There is one extra paragraph which you don't need to use.

WHY NO ONE WALKS

I'll tell you this, but you have to promise that it will get no further. Not long after we moved here we had the people next door round for dinner and – I swear this is true – they drove.

> 1

A researcher at the University of California at Berkeley recently made a study of the nation's walking habits and concluded that 85 per cent of people in the United States are 'essentially' sedentary and 35 per cent are 'totally' sedentary. The average American walks less than 75 miles a year – about 1.4 miles a week, barely 350 yards a day. I'm no stranger to sloth myself, but that's appallingly little. I rack up more mileage than that just looking for the channel changer.

> 2

I walk to town nearly every day when I am at home. I go to the post office or library or the local bookshop, and sometimes, if I am feeling particularly debonair, I stop at Rosey Jekes Cafe for a cappuccino. Every few weeks or so I call in at the barbershop and let one of the guys there do something rash and lively with my hair. All this is a big part of my life and I wouldn't dream of doing it other than on foot. People have got used to this curious and eccentric behaviour now, but several times in the early days passing neighbours would slow by the kerb and ask if I wanted a lift.

> 3

'Honestly, I enjoy walking.'

> 4

People have become so habituated to using the car for everything that it would never occur to them to unfurl their legs and see what they can do. Sometimes it's almost ludicrous. The other day I was in a little nearby town called Etna waiting to bring home one of my children from a piano lesson when a car stopped outside the local post office and a man about my age popped out and dashed inside (and left the motor running – something else that exercises me inordinately). He was inside for about three or four minutes, then came out, got in the car and drove exactly 16 feet (I had nothing better to do so I paced it off) to the general store next door, and popped in again, engine still running.

> 5

She looked at me as if I were tragically simple-minded and said, 'But I have a programme for the treadmill. It records my distance and speed, and I can adjust it for degree of difficulty.' It had not occurred to me how thoughtlessly deficient nature is in this regard.

According to a concerned and faintly horrified recent editorial in the Boston Globe, the United States spends less than 1 per cent of its $25 billion-a-year roads budget on facilities for pedestrians. Actually, I'm surprised it's that much. Go to almost any suburb developed in the last thirty years – and there are thousands to choose from – and you will not find a pavement anywhere. Often you won't find a single pedestrian-crossing. I am not exaggerating.

> 6

Although the bookshop was no more than 50 or 60 feet away, I discovered that there was no way to get there on foot. There was a traffic crossing for cars, but no provision for pedestrians and no way to cross without dodging through three lanes of swiftly turning traffic. I had to get in the car and drive across.

At the time it seemed ridiculous and exasperating, but afterwards I realized that I was probably the only person ever even to have entertained the notion of negotiating that intersection on foot.

> 7

In 1994 Laconia dug up its pretty brick paving, took away the benches and tubs of geraniums and decorative trees, and put the street back to the way it had been in the first place. Now people can park right in front of the shops again and downtown Laconia thrives anew. And if that isn't sad, I don't know what is.

BILL BRYSON

A 'Well, if you're absolutely sure,' they would say and depart reluctantly, even guiltily, as if they felt they were leaving the scene of an accident.

B And the thing is this man looked really fit. I'm sure he jogs extravagant distances and plays squash and does all kinds of exuberantly healthful things, but I am just as sure that he drives to each of these undertakings. It's crazy. An acquaintance of ours was complaining the other day about the difficulty of finding a place to park outside the local gymnasium. She goes there several times a week to walk on a treadmill. The gymnasium is, at most, a six-minute walk from her front door. I asked her why she didn't walk to the gym and do six minutes less on the treadmill.

C The fact is, Americans not only don't walk anywhere, they won't walk anywhere, and woe to anyone who tries to make them, as a town here in New Hampshire called Laconia discovered to its cost. A few years ago Laconia spent $5 million pedestrianizing its town centre, to make it a pleasant shopping environment. Aesthetically it was a triumph – urban planners came from all over to coo and take photos – but commercially it was a disaster. Forced to walk one whole block from a car park, shoppers abandoned downtown Laconia for suburban malls.

D But they always looked so upset when I said this, that I gave in and accepted the lift. I didn't have the heart to make them feel they were leaving me to my fate.

E I had this brought home to me last summer when we were driving across Maine and stopped for coffee in one of those endless zones of shopping malls, motels, petrol stations and fast-food places that sprout everywhere in America these days. I noticed there was a bookshop across the street, so I decided to skip coffee and pop over. I needed a particular book and anyway I figured this would give my wife a chance to spend some important private quality time with four restive, overheated children.

F I was astounded (I recall asking them jokingly if they used a light aircraft to get to the supermarket, which simply drew blank looks and the mental scratching of my name from all future invitation lists), but I have since come to realize that there was nothing especially odd in their driving less than a couple of hundred feet to visit us. Nobody walks anywhere in America nowadays.

G 'But I'm going your way,' they would insist when I politely declined. 'Really, it's no bother.'

H One of the things we wanted when we moved to America was to live in a town within walking distance of shops. Hanover, where we settled, is a small, typical New England college town, pleasant, sedate and compact. It has a broad green, an old-fashioned Main Street, nice college buildings with big lawns, and leafy residential streets. It is, in short, an agreeable, easy place to stroll. Nearly everyone in town is within a level five-minute walk of the shops, and yet as far as I can tell virtually no one does.

 B 👥 **Discuss these questions:**
- What do you find most difficult about this kind of task?
- Is there any advice you can offer each other?

"My dog takes his walks pretty seriously"

18.5 **Use of English Part 5**   EXAM PRACTICE

A Read the two extracts from *Cities Fit To Live In* by Barrie Sherman, and answer the questions. For questions 1–4, answer with a word or short phrase. For question 5, write a summary according to the instructions given.

LONELINESS

Greta Garbo was always crying that she 'wanted to be alone'. In An Enemy of the People Ibsen says that 'the strongest man in the world is the man who stands alone'. Ibsen may be correct, since most people want and need company. Loneliness is a terrible thing, and all the worse in a city with so many people around.

Working men sitting each to his own table, each staring down at his pint of beer. Silence, no eye contact, no movement, no communication, except to order another drink. This is one kind of urban loneliness. An elderly woman, living alone, with her children in another city, barely mobile and visited only by meals on wheels and a once-a-week home help who is too busy to gossip. Her friend is her TV   8 set. This too is modern urban loneliness.

But there is so much more. Young mothers trapped in high-rise flats which could have been designed to promote loneliness. Drug addicts locked into worlds of their own. Unemployed people, children unable to make friends, self-conscious adolescents, visitors, desperately shy people, disabled people, people with speech impediments, people who cannot understand the language, people with psychiatric disorders, and separated and divorced people – they may all need companionship at one time or another, perhaps all the time. 'All the lonely people, where do they all come from?' sang the Beatles. From the cities, where else?

Loneliness is corrosive. A lonely person becomes a withdrawn person and finds it hard to make contact   16 with others. Loneliness feeds upon itself. It is a complex problem. The lonely are not joiners, mixers or clubbable people. So while it is easy to develop clubs, groups, teams, games, parties, card schools and socials, or to promote acquaintanceships, friendships, even love affairs, the truly lonely are never involved.

In some cities the culture mitigates loneliness. Barcelona and Bombay have an extended family system. Liverpool and Dublin have well developed community systems. In Amsterdam, there are public places where people are encouraged to meet and spend time. Other cities make resources available to help old people and disabled people meet other people.

Loneliness is, by and large, preventable and curable. Healthy cities ensure that this is not only recognised but that something positive is done about it.

1 What is implied by the phrase 'Her friend is her TV set' in line 8?

....

2 What is meant by the word 'corrosive' in line 16?

....

EXCITEMENT

Cities are exciting places, or at least they should be. People need excitement. They need to have their adrenalin flowing, and their imaginations stimulated. Excitement provides life's high points which become the memories and conversation pieces of later life. However, excitement can come in many guises, and some are not as good for health as others. For example, danger and 'sin' both breed excitement, but danger is associated with physical assault, and the excitement associated with it is not to be recommended. But taken overall, excitement stimulates, making the body and the psyche tingle with pleasure or anticipation.

Elderly people may find a trip to the shops exciting; for a disabled person any trip from their house may be equally exciting. People from the countryside or small towns tend to find the city exciting. Not only would a city-dwelling young person disagree, but he or she might well describe a night club or an adventure playground as exciting, things which an older person might look upon as a form of torture. Healthy cities provide exciting things to do for all their citizens irrespective of age or physical abilities.

Excitement is also about expectations. Some cities have reputations for excitement. Amsterdam, New York, Paris, Barcelona are all known as exciting cities. Excitement is also about people, especially people in large numbers. If people expect things to happen, more often than not they will, even if the excitement is hardly in evidence to other people. In terms of stimulating the senses or health, it does not matter; it is as valuable as the real thing. This is especially true of the suburbs attached to exciting cities. While these may be as placid and dull as most suburbs, the excitement of the city rubs off on them, sometimes undeservedly.

3 What point is the writer making in the second paragraph?

....

4 What is the meaning of 'rubs off' in the last line?

....

5 In 50–70 words, summarise the advantages and disadvantages of living in a city mentioned by the writer. Use your own words as far as possible.

B **Discuss these questions:**

- What do you find most difficult about this kind of task?
- Is there any advice you can offer each other?

18.6 Writing Parts 1 and 2   EXAM PRACTICE

You have two hours for two compositions in the Writing Paper. Allow yourself enough time to make notes before you start writing – and enough time to check your work through before you hand it in. Don't forget to put the number of the question in the box at the top of the answer paper.

Marking Each piece of work is assigned to a "band" ranging from Band 0 ('Negligible or no attempt at the task set') via Band 3 ('Satisfactory realisation of the task set') up to Band 5 ('Outstanding realisation of the task set'). The examiners' first priority is to assess your efforts at communication and give you credit for that, including the clarity and organisation of your composition. Good spelling, punctuation, paragraphing and easily legible handwriting are important. If you fail to answer the question, there are penalties for reproducing "blatantly irrelevant material learned by heart" or for "grossly or wantonly misinterpreting the question".

Length You must write 300–350 words. You don't get credit for extra length, which anyway will probably increase the total number of inaccuracies in your work.

Question 1 In this directed writing task, structured information is provided. You have to respond to a clearly-defined task and the appropriateness of your response and style and register are particularly important.

Question 5 In Question 5 you have to show that you have read and (hopefully) enjoyed a set text and can demonstrate this in an appropriately illustrated description and discussion. Credit is given for breadth, development and relevance of argument, and for the abundance and appropriateness of illustration and quotation.

In the exam there is a specific question on each set book – not generic questions as here.

A **Part 1**

You must answer this question. Write your answer in 300–350 words in an appropriate style.

1 You have been sent the following newspaper cutting. Prepare a suitable handout for visitors and tourists, to be given when they arrive at airports and frontiers in your country.

 Reports in the foreign press

THERE have been a growing number of reports in newspapers abroad that there is a "crime wave" in this country and that tourists are being targeted by muggers, pickpockets and other criminals. The Minister of Tourism fears that foreign visitors may assume they are likely to be robbed once they set foot in the country, and consequently choose different holiday destinations.

The Minister of Tourism stated yesterday, "We want to give all arriving visitors a handout, warning them of the dangers. But we mustn't alarm them unduly. The handout should offer advice on how to minimise the risks by taking the right precautions."

She announced a competition, open to everyone, for a suitable handout which will reassure tourists. The originator of the best handout is to receive a generous cash prize.

Part 2

Write an answer to ONE of these questions. Write your answer in 300–350 words in an appropriate style.

2 A travel guide has asked you to write a review of your city, suburb, town or village which will give visitors a good idea of what to do and where to go.

Write your REVIEW.

3 'The punishment should fit the crime.' This has been the theme of a series of articles in your local newspaper. Write a letter to the newspaper, giving your views.

Write your LETTER.

4 A monthly magazine has invited readers to contribute to a special issue on Freedom. Write a story for the magazine beginning or ending with the words: 'Free at last!'

Write your ARTICLE.

5 Basing your answer on your reading of the prescribed book you have studied, answer ONE of the following.

   a Describe and give examples of the way in which the writer builds up a sense of excitement and tension as the plot unfolds. Write a letter recommending your book to next year's Proficiency class in your college.

   Write your LETTER.

   b What makes the book you have read stand out as a 'work of literature' above the common run of popular fiction? Write an article about the book you have read.

   Write your ARTICLE.

   c 'Any good work of fiction has just the same ingredients as a detective story.' Write an essay explaining to what extent this view is applicable to the text you have read.

   Write your ESSAY.

B   **Discuss these questions:**

   • What do you find most difficult about the Writing Paper?
   • Is there any advice you can offer each other?

18.7   One last word . . .

I do hope you've enjoyed using 'New Progress to Proficiency' and I'd like to wish you the best of luck in your exam!
   Best wishes,

Leo Jones

Communication Activities

1 Read this poem and then discuss the questions on page 160.

MUSÉE DES BEAUX ARTS

About suffering they were never wrong,
The Old Masters: how well they understood
Its human position; how it takes place
While someone else is eating or opening a window or just walking dully along;
How, when the aged are reverently, passionately waiting
For the miraculous birth, there always must be
Children who did not specially want it to happen, skating
On a pond at the edge of the wood:
They never forgot
That even the dreadful martyrdom must run its course
Anyhow in a corner, some untidy spot
Where the dogs go on with their doggy life and the torturer's horse
Scratches its innocent behind on a tree.

In Brueghel's Icarus, for instance: how everything turns away
Quite leisurely from the disaster; the ploughman may
Have heard the splash, the forsaken cry,
But for him it was not an important failure; the sun shone
As it had to on the white legs disappearing into the green
Water; and the expensive delicate ship that must have seen
Something amazing, a boy falling out of the sky,
Had somewhere to get to and sailed calmly on.

W.H. Auden

2 How red wine is made

Ingredients: grape juice, grape skins and stems

- After the grapes have been picked they are taken to the winery where they are put into a machine which crushes them and removes the stems, but not the skins and pips*. This end product is called *must*. It takes 3kg of grapes to make one bottle of wine.
- The must is emptied into tanks or vats. The grape skins have their own natural yeasts which ferment with the sugar in the grape juice to produce alcohol and carbon dioxide. During fermentation, the skins and pips form a thick layer on the surface.
- Fermentation stops after a week or so. The new wine is drained off and the residue of skins and pips is pressed to extract another 20%.
- Wine for everyday drinking is stored in glass-lined cement or stainless steel tanks: the secondary fermentation takes place, making the wine softer and rounder before it is ready to be bottled. Some quality wines may be aged in oak casks, which imparts a special flavour to the wine.
- Before bottling, the wine is *racked* – egg white or another substance is added to carry the sediment to the bottom of the cask.
- The wine is bottled, capped and labelled by machine. Quality wines can be further aged in their bottles, but everyday wine is ready for drinking right away.

* To make white wine, the juice is immediately separated from the skins and pips. To make rosé wine, it is separated after a day or less.

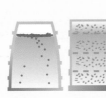

199

3 In your own words, tell your partners about the ideas in this paragraph:

Handling customers well

The benefits of handling customers well are two-fold. Firstly, your job becomes more rewarding, as you are developing your techniques while using them and thus feel your job is really worthwhile. Secondly, your customers go away happy, which underlines your pride in becoming more competent. Satisfied customers don't just come back to your firm again, they tend to look for you personally and they also tell their friends to seek you out.

from *So you think you can cope with customers?* – A Video Arts Guide

4 This is the next paragraph of the story in 6.2. In your own words, tell your partner what happened. Then find out from your partner what happened in the end.

The hotel people began to be more pleased with me too, so I thought Mr Yorum must be quite an important man. Several more times on other days I told them I didn't understand Turkish, and each time they rang Mr Yorum and he came, and sometimes I paid for the drinks and sometimes he did. He and the hotel staff must have thought I had taken a great fancy to him or else that I was working up to some deal I wanted to do with him. The fourth time he came I had a bright idea that I would give him one of the missionary manuals that aunt Dot had left behind in her rucksack, because I thought each manual which I got rid of would lighten the rucksack.

5 Don't read the complete sentences aloud – rely on your memory and try to use your own words.

Movie clichés

1 At least one of every pair of identical twins is born evil.
2 It does not matter if your gang is heavily outnumbered in a fight involving martial arts, your enemies will still wait patiently to attack you one by one.
3 When you turn out the light to go to bed, everything in your bedroom will still be clearly visible, and become a slightly bluish colour.
4 If you are a young, pretty woman, it is possible to become a world expert on nuclear fission at the age of 22.
5 During all police investigations, it will be necessary to visit a strip club at least once.
6 You're very likely to survive any battle in any war unless you make the mistake of showing someone a picture of your sweetheart back home.
7 The Eiffel Tower can be seen from the window of any building in Paris.

6 Study these ideas and then ask your partners the questions:

Doors Most doors have to be pushed or pulled:
- Is there an easily visible handle on the side you have to pull and NO handle on the side you have to push? Is it necessary to have PUSH or PULL written on every door?
- Some doors open both ways, but how can you tell?
- Have you ever pushed instead of pulled? Was it your fault or the designer's?
- If revolving doors aren't already moving, how do you know which way to push? Do they always go round clockwise or do they go anti-clockwise?
- How do people know whether a door is automatic and doesn't need pushing? If it's 'obvious', why is this so? Have you ever pushed an automatic door?

Clocks and watches Think of the digital watches or clock radios you have used:
- How many different functions do they have?
- Can you make them do everything they're supposed to do? Or do you have to read the instructions?
- Have you ever set the alarm wrong? Was it your fault or the designer's?

7 Describe this picture to your partner. Find out about your partner's picture by asking the same questions as you discussed in 13.1 B.

Edward Hopper: *Room in New York,* 1932 (detail)

8 Retell this news story in your own words, beginning: *There was …*

Whatever you might say about women drivers, at least they are more responsible than men. Responsibility takes on a whole new meaning, however, when it comes to Ms Chrysanthemum Choo, arguably the world's safest ever motorist. Ms Choo, 30, of Miami had returned to her car after a shopping expedition, started the engine and patiently waited for an opportunity to pull out on to the main road. Eight hours later she was still patiently waiting. 'I like to be careful,' she explained. 'There were many cars around and I didn't want to do anything rash.' Things quietened down considerably during the night, but unfortunately by that point Ms Choo had fallen asleep, waking up just in time for the morning rush hour. It was another four hours before the desperate driver eventually saw her chance. Overcome with relief she slammed her foot on the accelerator and sped on to the road – straight into the side of a passing police car. 'I obviously wasn't careful enough,' she admitted.

9 **Rupert Brooke (1887–1915)** became an army officer at the outbreak of the war in 1914. He died of blood poisoning from a mosquito bite on his way to the Turkish front by ship, and never saw active service. He was buried on the Greek island of Skyros. His best-known poems are patriotic and romantic, contrasting with the bitterness of Owen and Sassoon.

10 In your own words, tell your partners about the ideas in this paragraph:

Your behaviour creates an impression

People gain a general impression of you from a combination of your facial expression and head movements, your gestures with your hands and arms, and the rest of your body including your legs. They will tend to see you as defensive if you avoid looking at them, clench your hands or cross your arms, keep rubbing an eye, ear or your nose, lean away from them, cross your legs or swivel your feet towards the door. They will tend to see you as anxious if you blink frequently, lick your lips, keep clearing your throat, put your hand over your mouth while you are speaking, tug at your ear, fidget in your chair or move your feet up and down.

from *So you think you can cope with customers?* – A Video Arts Guide

11 Ask your partner these general questions:

- Where are you from?
- Do you live locally?
- Are you studying or do you work?
- How close to your school/work do you live?
- What do you like about the area you live in?
- Could you tell us something about your work/study?
- What about your early school days? What were they like?
- Could you tell us something about your plans for the future?
- Which countries in the world would you most like to visit?
- What are employment opportunities like in this area?
- How easy do you think it will be to maintain the level of English you have achieved?

12 Look at this picture and then discuss these questions:

- What's happening in this picture?
- How do you think the people are feeling?
- Why are they taking part in this class?
- Would you like to be taking part? Why/Why not?
- How important is keeping fit to you?
- What do you do to keep yourself fit?
- How do you try to stay healthy?

13 Speak for two minutes on this topic:

What are your views on living a healthy life?

- ➤ exercise and keeping fit
- ➤ eating the right foods
- ➤ avoiding unhealthy things like alcohol and tobacco

14

cli·ché /ˈkliːʃeɪ; US kliːˈʃeɪ/ n (**a**) [C] phrase or idea which is used so often that it has become stale or meaningless: *a cliché-ridden style.* (**b**) [U] use of such phrases: *Cliché is a feature of bad journalism.*

irony /ˈaɪərənɪ/ n **1** [U] expression of one's meaning by saying the direct opposite of one's thoughts in order to be emphatic, amusing, sarcastic, etc: *'That's really lovely, that is!' he said with heavy irony.* **2** [U, C] situation, event, etc that is desirable in itself but so unexpected or ill-timed that it appears to be deliberately perverse: *the irony of fate* ○ *He inherited a fortune but died a month later; one of life's little ironies.*

accent /ˈæksent, -sənt/ n **1** [C] an emphasis given to a syllable or word by means of stress or pitch¹(2): *In the word 'today' the accent is on the second syllable.* **2** [C] a mark or symbol, usu above a letter, used in writing and printing to indicate emphasis or the quality of a vowel sound: *'Café' has an accent on the 'e'.* **3** [C, U] a national, local or individual way of pronouncing words: *speak English with a foreign accent* ○ *a voice without (a trace of) accent.* Compare DIALECT. **4** [C usu *sing*, U] a special emphasis given to sth: *In all our products the accent is on quality.*

sar·casm /ˈsɑːkæzəm/ n [U] (use of) bitter, esp ironic, remarks intended to wound sb's feelings: *her constant sarcasm about his poor work.*

▷ sar·castic /sɑːˈkæstɪk/ (also *infml* **sarky**) *adj* of or using sarcasm: *a sarcastic person, tone, remark.* **sar·cast·ic·ally** /-klɪ/ *adv.*

slo·gan /ˈsləʊgən/ n word or phrase that is easy to remember, used as a motto eg by a political party, or in advertising: *political slogans* ○ *'Power to the people' is their slogan.*

pro·verb /ˈprɒvɜːb/ n short well-known saying that states a general truth or gives advice, eg 'It takes two to make a quarrel' or 'Don't put all your eggs in one basket': *the Book of Proverbs,* ie one of the books of the Old Testament containing the proverbs of Solomon.

dialect /ˈdaɪəlekt/ n [C, U] the form of a language used in part of a country or by a class of people with grammar, words and pronunciation that may be different from other forms of the same language: *the Yorkshire dialect* ○ *a play written in dialect* ○ *dialect words/pronunciations.* Compare ACCENT 3.

▶ **dialectal** /ˌdaɪəˈlektl/ *adj*: *dialectal differences between two areas.*

from *Oxford Advanced Learners Dictionary of English*

15

How beer is brewed

Ingredients: water, malted barley, hops and yeast

1 Barley is germinated under controlled conditions, which brings out its sweetness, and then baked: the longer it is baked the darker and more caramelised it becomes.
   This *malt* is then milled and sent to the brewery.
2 At the brewery the malt is mixed with water and boiled.
3 The liquid, called the *wort,* is strained off and piped into a *kettle* where hops are added and it is boiled again. (Hops add flavour and bitterness to the product.)
4 The liquid is strained and cooled and then piped to a fermenting vessel, where a special yeast is added. Fermentation takes place, turning the natural sugar in the malt into alcohol and carbon dioxide. This takes about five days.
5 The beer is filtered and piped into cold sealed tanks where secondary fermentation takes place, improving the flavour of the beer and giving it 'character'.
6 The beer is strained off and then bottled, or piped into metal casks ready to be delivered.

16

Your partner has the previous paragraph to this one – find out what happened. Then, in your own words, tell your partner what happened in the end.

So I went and got this manual, which was called "Why I belong to the Church of England", and was slightly translated into Turkish, and I gave it to Mr Yorum, who thanked me and looked at it with surprise, and it must have dawned on him that I was a missionary and was trying to convert him and that this was why I kept sending for him.

After that he must have told the hotel staff not to ring him for me again, for when I said please to telephone him at once they shrugged and threw out their hands and looked at me despisingly. Soon after this I looked at my phrasebook and saw what I had been saying all the time.

17

Retell this news story in your own words, beginning: *There was …*

Nothing is more annoying than parking your car in a car park and then returning to discover you can't remember where you've left it. Imagine how elderly French couple René and Lucille Schubelle felt, therefore, when they returned from a shopping expedition to discover that not just their car but the entire car park had disappeared. Mr and Mrs Schubelle, both 84, of Calais had left their Renault Clio in 'one of those new-fangled municipal parking garages' on the seafront. When they came back two hours later, however, laden down with shopping, they were surprised to discover that the entire car park had vanished into thin air. Thinking perhaps it was 'something to do with terrorists', they contacted the police, who, after a brief investigation, discovered that what the Schubelles had taken to be a multistorey car park was in fact the car deck of a cross-Channel ferry. 'When we told them their car had gone to England they got very confused,' said one official. 'They seemed to think it was a punishment for having a dirty windscreen.'

18

Don't read the complete sentences aloud – rely on your memory and try to use your own words.

Movie clichés

8 A man will show no pain while taking the most ferocious beating but will wince when a woman tries to clean his wounds.
9 Even when driving down a perfectly straight road, it is necessary to turn the steering wheel vigorously from left to right every few moments.
10 A detective can only solve a case once he has been suspended from duty.
11 If you decide to start dancing in the street, everyone you meet will know all the steps.
12 When they are alone, all foreign military officers prefer to speak to each other in English.
13 Whenever it rains, the sun is shining in the background.
14 When someone is upset, as soon as they get home, they lean against the front door.

19 Study these ideas and then ask your partners the questions:

Showers Think of the showers you have used:
- How do you know how to turn it on? How do you know how to make it hotter? How do you know how to increase the flow?
- Do they all follow these conventions?

increase/more reduce/less

- Have you ever been scalded in a shower? Was it your fault or the designer's?

Numbers Make a list of all the numbers you have to remember, or need to look up quite often: e.g. postcodes, other people's birthdays, passport number, credit card, PINs, phone numbers, etc.
- How many numbers are there? How many can you remember without looking them up?
- Have you ever got any of these numbers wrong? What happened?
- Do you have any special techniques for remembering hard-to-recall numbers?

20 Find out about your partner's picture by asking the same questions as you discussed in 13.1 B. Describe this picture to your partner:

Edward Hopper: *Conference at Night.*

21 **Ask your partner these general questions:**

- Where are you from?
- Are you studying or do you work?
- Do you live with friends or family?
- Could you tell us something about your work/study?
- Could you tell us something about the house or apartment you live in?
- What about your early school days? What were they like?
- Let's think about not working or studying. What do you do to relax?
- Could you tell us something about why you are learning English?
- Apart from languages, what other skills will it be important to learn in the future?
- If you could change one thing about your education, what would it be?
- How ambitious are you?

22 **Look at this picture and then discuss these questions:**

- What's happening in this picture?
- How do the people feel, do you think?
- What might the doctor and the woman be saying?
- Why do you think the little girl is having an injection?

- Do you usually consult a doctor if you're unwell, or do you let your body cure itself?
- How important is good health to you?
- How do you feel about injections?

23 **Speak for two minutes on this topic:**

> **What are your views on doctors and the medical profession?**
>
> ➢ keeping your teeth healthy and dentists
> ➢ the quality of health care in your community
> ➢ alternative medicine (acupuncture, homeopathy, etc.)

24

col·lo·ca·tion /ˌkɒləˈkeɪʃən‖ˌkɑː-/ *n tech* **1** [U] the way in which some words regularly collocate with others **2** [C] a habitual combination of words which sounds natural: *"Strong coffee"* is a typical collocation in English but *"powerful coffee"* is not. – see next page.

di·a·lect /ˈdaɪəlekt/ *n* [C,U] a variety of a language spoken only in one area, in which words or grammar are slightly different from other forms of the same language – compare ACCENT[1] (1), IDIOLECT

i·ron·y /ˈaɪərəni/ *n* **1** [U] use of words which are clearly opposite to one's meaning, usu. either in order to be amusing or to show annoyance (e.g. by saying "What charming behaviour" when someone has been rude) – compare SARCASM **2** [C;U] a course of events or a condition which has the opposite result from what is expected, usu. a bad result: *We went on holiday to Greece because we thought the weather was certain to be good, and it rained almost every day; the irony of it is, that at the same time there was a heat-wave back at home!* compare PARADOX; see also DRAMATIC IRONY

jar·gon /ˈdʒɑːgən‖-ɑːr- gɑːn/ *n* [C;U] *often derog* difficult or strange language which uses words known only to the members of a certain group; *computer jargon | the jargon of the advertising business*

plat·i·tude /ˈplætəˈtjuːd‖-tuːd/ *n derog* a statement that is true but not new, interesting, or clever; *a very uninspiring speech full of platitudes* – compare CLICHÉ, COMMONPLACE[2] – **-tudinous** /ˌplætəˈtjuːdənəs‖-ˈtuːdənəs‖-ˈtuː-/ *adj*

prov·erb /ˈprɒvɜːb‖ˈprɑːvɜːrb/ *n* a short well-known, supposedly wise, saying usu. in simple language: *"Don't put all your eggs in one basket"* is a proverb.

from *Longman Dictionary of Contemporary English*

25

Wilfred Owen (1893–1918) served for three years in Flanders as an officer.

He was killed by machine-gun fire on November 8th 1918, just a few days before the Armistice. Owen's poems exposing the futility and horror of war were not published until after the war had ended.

26

In your own words, tell your partners about the ideas in this paragraph:

Don't use aggressive behaviour

People will tend to see you as aggressive and overbearing if you stare at them, raise your eyebrows in disbelief, look at them over the top of your spectacles, or smile in a 'heard it all before' way; or if you point at them, thump your fist on the table, stride around or stand while they are seated; or, if you are seated, lean right back in your chair with your hands behind your head and your legs splayed.

from So you think you can cope with customers? – A Video Arts Guide

27

Retell this news story in your own words, beginning: *There was …*

One of the most determined and ultimately unsuccessful of all bank robbers was deaf German Klaus Schmidt, currently behind bars after being arrested because he couldn't hear the burglar alarm going off. Courageously refusing to allow his disability to get in the way of his criminal activities, Mr Schmidt, 41, had burst into a Berlin bank armed with a World War Two pistol and screamed, 'Hand over the money or I'll shoot.' Terrified staff had asked if he needed a bag, to which Mr Schmidt confidently replied, 'You're damn right it's a real gun!' 'We knew then that he was deaf as a doorpost,' explained the bank manager, 'so we set off the alarm. It was unbelievably loud, but he didn't seem to notice even when some people put their hands over their ears.' The hard-of-hearing robber waited patiently for five minutes, occasionally waving his gun in the air and crying, 'I'm a trained killer!' until eventually police burst in and arrested him. He is now suing the bank for 'exploiting my disability'.

28

Study these ideas and then ask your partners the questions:

Switches and knobs Think of the electrical equipment and gadgets you use:
- How easy was it for you (and other members of your family) to learn to use each piece of equipment?
- Can you remember how to make the gadgets do everything they're supposed to do?
  Or do you have to consult the instruction booklet?
- Do you have to look at the labels, or can you intuitively see which switch does what?
  Do they all follow these conventions:

increase/more   reduce/less

- And what about the ON switch: which way do you push it: IN or UP or DOWN?
  Does it make a helpful click or not?
- Have you ever used the wrong switch? Was it your fault or the designer's?

Sounds   Sounds can provide feedback:
- What noise does a zip make? If a zip was silent, what difference would it make?
- How can you tell if a car door isn't closed properly – can you hear it rattle?
- What other sounds can you think of that provide feedback when you're using a piece of equipment?

29 **In your own words, tell your partners about the ideas in this paragraph:**

Using body language

If you want to seem friendly and cooperative, look at the other person's face, smile and nod when they are talking, have open hands and uncrossed arms and legs, lean forward slightly or move closer to them. If you want to appear confident, look into their eyes, don't blink, keep your hands away from your face, stay still and don't make sudden movements. If you want to appear thoughtful, tilt your head to one side, stroke your chin or pinch the bridge of your nose, lean forward to speak and back to listen and keep your legs still.

from *So you think you can cope with customers? –* A Video Arts Guide

30

Siegfried Sassoon (1886–1967) served as an army officer on the Western Front in Flanders throughout the war. He survived the war and his collected poems include many written during the Second World War too. He collected and published his friend Wilfred Owen's poems in 1920.

31

ac·cent PRONUNCIATION /'æk·sᵊnt, -sent/ *n* [C] the way in which people in a particular area, country, social class, etc. pronounce words • *He's got a strong French/Scottish/Birmingham/upper-class accent.* • *He speaks with a* **broad/pronounced/thick** (=strong) *Yorkshire accent.* • *Although French is her native language, she* **speaks** *with an impeccable English accent.* • *I tried to get rid of my Coventry accent when I went to university.* • *I thought I could detect a slight West Country accent.* •⟨LP⟩ **Pronunciation, Varieties of English** ⓙ

cli·ché /£ 'kliː·ʃeɪ, $ -'-/ *n* a form of expression that has been so often used that its original effectiveness has been lost • *Every time I ask my dad for some money, he always comes out with the old cliché, "It doesn't grow on trees, you know."* [C] • *You should always try to avoid the use of cliché.* [U] • *His speeches tend to be boring and cliché-***ridden** (= contain a lot of clichés).

col·lo·cation/£ 'kɒl·əʊ'keɪ·ʃᵊn, $ 'kɑː·lə-/ *n specialized* • A collocation (also **collocate**) is a word or phrase which is frequently used with another word or phrase, in a way that sounds correct to people who have spoken the language all their lives, but might not be expected from the meaning: *In the phrase 'a hard frost', 'hard' is a collocation of 'frost' and 'strong' would not sound natural.* [C] • A collocation can also be the combination of words formed when two or more words are frequently used together in a way that sounds correct. *The phrase 'a hard frost' is a collocation.* [C] • Collocation is also the frequent use of some words and phrases with others, esp. in a way which is difficult to guess: *Awareness of collocation is essential for fluency in a foreign language.* [U].

jar·gon /£ 'dʒɑː·gən, $ 'dʒɑːr·/ *n* [U] *disapproving* special words and phrases which are used by particular groups of people, esp. in their work • *military/legal/computer jargon* • *Some school prospectuses contained jargon and unexplained acronyms which parents found hard to understand.* • Compare TERMINOLOGY.

plat·i·tude /£ 'plæt·ɪ·tjuːd, $ 'plæt̬·ə·tuːd/ *n* [C] *disapproving* a remark or statement about something that, although it might be true, is boring and meaningless because it has been said so many times before • *We'll get the usual politicians who'll* **mouth** *the usual platitudes about 'the glories of democracy.'*

sar·ca·sm /£ 'sɑː·kæz·ᵊm, $ 'sɑːr·/ *n* [U] (the use of) remarks which clearly mean the opposite of what they say, and which are made in order to hurt someone's feelings or to criticize something in an amusing way • *"You have been working hard", he said with* **heavy/biting** *sarcasm, as he looked at the empty page.* • *(saying)* 'Sarcasm is the lowest form of wit' means that sarcasm is the most unkind type of humour. • Compare IRONY ⟨FIGURATIVE SPEECH⟩.

slo·gan /£ 'sləʊ·gən, $ 'sloʊ-/ *n* [C] a short easily remembered phrase intended to bring an idea or a product to public notice • *'Coke, it's the real thing' is an example of a slogan.*

from *Cambridge International Dictionary of English*

Self-study introduction

Using the self-study notes

This part of the book contains:
- Self-study instructions on how to use the main part of the book on your own (where necessary)
- Answers and Model compositions
- Transcripts for the listening exercises

Follow this procedure when working on your own:
1 Read the self-study instructions for part A of the section
2 Do the exercise or activity in A in the main part of the book
3 Check your answers with the model answers (if these are given)
4 Follow the self-study instructions for part B of the section
5 Do part B in the main part of the book
6 Check your answers . . . and so on.

Compositions

If possible, ask another person (preferably an English-speaking person or a friend whose English is very good) to read and mark your work.

If this is not possible, compare your composition with the Model composition in the self-study notes.

If you can find someone to mark your work, this is the kind of feedback they should give you:
- the content in general
- the style and how easy the piece was for them to read
- information or ideas that seemed particularly interesting or amusing
- information which was missing from the piece
- sentences which were less easy to follow

Answers and models

The Answers and Model compositions will help you to check your answers and learn more. In some cases, where the questions are open-ended, Suggested answers are given and variations may be possible. When a model is given, you should compare your work with this – but you should ask a teacher or an English-speaking person to correct your work from time to time, so that you can find out what kind of mistakes you are making.

When you make mistakes or can't answer questions, make sure that you learn from your mistakes. In fact, it's impossible to learn if you don't make mistakes – if you got everything right it would mean you knew everything already!

Working without a teacher

Working alone using the self-study notes will help you to improve your reading, writing and listening skills, but you should try to get someone to read your written work and correct it. If you are using this book entirely on your own without a teacher or other students in a class, the self-study notes tell you how you can do the speaking activities using a cassette recorder with a microphone – but if possible, you should do some of these with another person.

Working regularly with a partner will give you a chance to discuss what you have been doing and read each other's work. You will find that you will learn a lot from each other and it will help you to feel that you are making progress. Perhaps arrange a regular session each week when you can work together.

Whenever you are doing an exercise in cooperation with another student, follow the instructions in the main part of the book. The self-study notes at the back of the book tell you how to use each exercise in the main part of the book when you are working alone.

There are a few exercises which you can only do with a partner. The self-study notes tell you which ones these are.

Working partly on your own

Parts of this book can be used in class and other parts can be done by you working alone. Your teacher will advise you which parts you should do on your own, depending on how much time is available for work in class – in this case you may be expected to check some of the answers yourself. You should try to work on your own through any exercises for which there is no time in class.

Students who are unable to follow a complete classroom course, through illness or other commitments, will find this book especially valuable. You will be able to catch up on work you miss and perhaps rejoin the class later – or go on working on your own if you are unable to continue attending classes.

What you need

- A piece of card, about the same size as this book, to cover up the model answers in this part of the book while you read the self-study notes. This will stop you seeing the answers by mistake.
- An exercise book in which to write your answers to the exercises and your compositions.
- A smaller pocket-size notebook for your vocabulary notes.
- A yellow highlighter, for highlighting the useful vocabulary and expressions in the reading passages and in the transcripts.
- ◀)) The set of three cassettes.
- A cassette recorder or CD player for listening to the recordings.
- A microphone for recording your own voice or a voice recorder (you can buy one of these in an office supplies shop, they use special mini-cassettes).
- A good English-to-English dictionary, such as one of the following:
  Cambridge International Dictionary of English
  Collins COBUILD Essential English Dictionary
  Longman Dictionary of Contemporary English
  Oxford Advanced Learner's Dictionary
- A good bilingual dictionary – but a tiny pocket-sized one is NOT good enough. Ask for advice on which one to choose if you don't already possess one.
- A good reference grammar book to answer your questions on English grammar, such as:
  Advanced Grammar in Use WITH ANSWERS by Martin Hewings (Cambridge University Press) or *Practical English Usage* by Michael Swan (Oxford University Press) are recommended.

As the exam approaches, you should work through the test papers in *Cambridge Proficiency Examination Practice 1* (Cambridge University Press) and you'll need the accompanying Teacher's Book, which contains the correct answers and transcripts.

Exam enrolment

If you are entering for the Proficiency exam (which is held in June and December), remember that you will need to enrol for it at least three months in advance. In some centres the latest date for enrolment is even earlier. If you are studying in your own country, the local British Council office can give you the address of your nearest centre.

Notes and answers for each unit

1 Leisure activities Hobbies Games Sport

Time to spare?

1.1 In my spare time . . .
TOPIC VOCABULARY

(A) Imagine that someone is asking you these questions: say your answers aloud softly to yourself. Use a dictionary to look up any words you need. You may prefer to write down your answers to some of the questions. Maybe record yourself on a blank cassette or voice recorder.

(B) 1 Imagine that someone is asking you these questions: say your answers aloud softly to yourself.

2 ◀)) Before you listen to the recording, look at the questions in the main part of the book.

The recordings are all unsimplified, natural conversations or interviews or radio programmes. The speakers talk at their normal speed. Don't worry if you can't understand every word that's spoken or if parts of a conversation seem very fast to you. No one, not even a native speaker of English, can (or needs to) catch every single word that's spoken in a conversation. So, just concentrate on understanding the main points given by the speakers.

In other words, don't panic if the voices seem very fast or if the speakers use some words you don't know. Just listen to the recording again a couple of times, looking at the questions in the main part of the book, and you'll soon find that you do understand all that you need to in each conversation. If necessary, pause the recording while you note down the answers.

There is a transcript for each listening exercise. Don't look at this until you have heard the recording at least twice through.

1 Look at the task first and try to anticipate (or guess) what the answers might be.
2 ◀)) Listen to the first 20 to 30 seconds of the recording so that you can get used to the unfamiliar voice. Don't try to answer the questions and don't look at the Transcript. (You may find it easier to concentrate if you close your eyes while you're doing this.)
3 ◀)) Listen to the recording all the way through and do the task. If necessary, PAUSE the recording during the conversation – this will give you time to think about the task.
4 ◀)) If you have only been able to do part of the task, listen to the whole conversation again and concentrate on finding the answers you missed or were unsure about. Again, PAUSE the recording where necessary.
5 Check your answers. If you have made any mistakes, it means you have misunderstood the speaker or the question.
6 ◀)) Listen to the recording again, but this time follow it in the transcript, checking any wrong answers as you go. Again, PAUSE the recording where necessary. Use a yellow highlighter to mark any useful new words or expressions.

7 ◀)) Listen to the whole recording all the way through. Sit back, close your eyes and listen – this will help you to appreciate and learn the sounds of English conversation, pronunciation and vocabulary.

Looking at the Transcript earlier would make the task much easier – but this will NOT help you to improve your listening skills.

➔ A low-pitched tone is recorded between each section on the cassette. When the tape is played forwards or backwards fast on CUE or REVIEW you will hear this as a high-pitched *beep* which makes it easy to find where each new section begins on the cassette.

Suggested answers:

Ruth:	a	Baking – cakes, tarts, cookies, etc.
	b	Being creative – almost like painting a picture
		Everybody enjoys the end product
		Watching a cake rise in the oven
Bill:	a	Scuba diving
	b	Like flying underwater
		Wonderful things to see
Sarah:	a	Surfing
	b	Satisfaction of doing what only the boys did
		'hanging ten' – standing with ten toes over the edge of the board
		Cruising the surf
Emma:	a	Looking after other people's children
	b	A warm feeling
		The smile she sees when they've had a good time
		Building a relationship
		Watching them grow up
Jonathan:	a	Going to the gym
	b	Not a lot – but it does keep him healthy

TRANSCRIPT *6 minutes*

INTERVIEWER: Ruth, what do you do in your spare time?
RUTH: I bake, actually. Uh...it's something I've done kind of for years and years. Er...I started off by making apple crumble, that was the first thing I ever made, but...um...I've kind of progressed a bit now and I really like...er...making things like a Bakewell tart, which...you know, a really massive one. And...er...I'll make it and kind of...er...call the family, and...er...the neighbours all call in or whatever, and it goes in about three seconds! Um...there's just something really creative about...about getting all these ingredients together. And...um...it's like sort of almost like painting a picture or something and you have this end product and everybody really enjoys it. And I like mak...making...um...scones and Welsh cakes and...um...and cookies for the children, because they really love those. Er...the...the sh...the only shame about it really is that...um...you put all this sort of hard work into it and they go really really quickly. Er...but it...there's nothing more satisfying than watching a Victoria sponge rise in the oven!
★★★

INTERVIEWER: Bill, what hobbies do you have?

BILL: Actually, er…I am a diver, a scuba diver. And that happened…er… . Strangely, when I was very young I did diving, when I lived in California, and I had an aqualung then for about a year. And then I went to college and sold it, and then years and years and years went by and I didn't dive, and then I went to holiday in Greece and I was…happened to be on a beach next to a diving school. And I thought, 'This is the best time. If I'm ever going to get my qualifications I will do it.' And I spent the week diving and studying diving and I got my certification, and now I dive whenever I can. I've dived on the Great Barrier Reef, I've dived on the islands off Santa Barbara in California, I've dived all around the Mediterranean. I love it, it's like flying through the water, and you have all those wonderful things to see.

★★★

INTERVIEWER: Sarah, do you have any hobbies?

SARAH: Yes, I do. I love surfing, I'm a typical Aussie [Australian] girl, and…er…when I was growing up my brother, because he was the boy, got the surfboard and I was saying, 'That's not fair! I got a boogie board,' which is the little foam thing, 'And he gets a proper surfboard. This is sexist, this is all wrong.' And I thought, 'No, I'm going to learn to surf.' And the next lesson I learnt is that the boys at high school don't want to let you have their board because they're convinced the girls will ding it up [damage it]. And they spend hours waxing their boards, but the girls aren't allowed to touch them. I thought, 'I'm going to save my money and I'm going to get one of these things and I'm going to be better than them all.' And…er…the next thing I know I…I saved my money and I got my own surfboard, which I said, 'Only girls can use.' So I got there…out there on the surfboard and I was terrible! I was absolutely terrible! I fell off every time I stood up, and it was the hardest thing I had ever done! But I kept at it, and eventually I got really cool, that I can now actually get to the front of the board and I can 'hang ten', which is where you get your ten little toes over the edge of the board. Then I fall off, I'm not that great, but…er…I am getting there. And whenever I go home I make sure I get my wetsuit on, so I don't get sunburnt, and I get out on that board and I just love cruising the surf.

★★★

INTERVIEWER: Emma, do you have any hobbies?

EMMA: It s not really a hobby, but…um…I like to look after children. Um…I think…I was the youngest of six, so I never had anybody younger than me to look after. Um…and so once I got old enough to look after other people's children, I…even if I didn't get paid, I used to always offer to help out. And anything ranging from babies to older children. I've worked at nursery schools. I know a friend who owned…who started a nursery school once and I spent my summer working for her for free. Um…and pretty much whenever anybody I know has a baby, I'm sort of the first one in going, 'I'll look after it! I'll baby-sit!' Um…which is a very bizarre thing but there's something…um…there's something quite warm when you . . . I mean it depends…depends on how big the child is, but even a bigger child when you've got them interested in something, or you've managed to do their homework with them, or…er…had a good day with them and they've really enjoyed themselves, and the smile they sort of give you at the end of the day when you say goodbye…or anything is…is…is very exciting. And can be also quite un…un…stressing. I looked after a…two children once, a four-year-old and a…and an eighteen-month-old for about…mm…five months…um…lived with their family. And when I had to go to the airport to say goodbye…um…the four-year-old started absolutely screaming and she wouldn't let go. It was absolutely heart-breaking. So it can be quite upsetting if you really get a bond with a child and then you have to say goodbye. But other…um…that's sort of a rare…you know, normally, don't have to say goodbye, so that's quite nice otherwise to have a relationship that lasts. You can watch them grow up.

★★★

INTERVIEWER: Jonathan, what do you do to fill your spare hours?

JONATHAN: Well, one of the things I try to do regularly is drag myself down to the gym, which I've only been doing for the last three or four years, really at my girlfriend's encouragement. Um…I find it deadly boring but it's good for me. So I try and go. I'm supposed…haha…I'm currently supposed to be going four times a week, which is the biggest joke you've ever heard. If I get down there twice a week it's a real achievement. And I do…what do I do? About twenty minutes on the running machines or the cycling or the rowing or something. And then all these weight-lifting machines. And it's supposed to be more each time and it's supposed to make me big and butch and look gori…look glori…gorgeous, but…um…I must say it's…er…I find it mind-numbingly dull.

INTERVIEWER: And…er…how long do you think you'll continue before you expect to see some serious results?

JONATHAN: Er…wh…Can you not see any serious results?

INTERVIEWER: Well, I mean, you know, you're looking fit and . . .

JONATHAN: I don't know it's something you never really complete.

INTERVIEWER: It's an ongoing process.

JONATHAN: I think so, yes. It's good for your overall health, keeps the heart healthy.

INTERVIEWER: And do you have a…a figure that you're aiming to replicate?

JONATHAN: Um…well, the trouble with the gym is that everyone else is more gorgeous than you are. So really anyone else's figure would be fine!

C **1** Suggested answers:

Hobbies:	painting playing the violin making model aircraft
Interests:	reading watching football computers
Indoor games:	draughts Scrabble bridge
Team sports:	baseball hockey basketball
Individual competitive sports:	badminton squash golf
Non-competitive sports:	water-skiing skiing sailing
Outdoor activities:	walking/hiking gardening riding

2 Imagine that someone is asking you these questions: say your answers aloud softly to yourself. Imagine also that you're being asked *Why?* and try to justify your opinions and explain your reasons. Maybe record yourself on a blank cassette or voice recorder.

1.2 **Comparing and contrasting**
GRAMMAR REVIEW

A Suggested answers:

1 Water-skiing is less difficult than sailing.
  = Sailing is harder than water-skiing.
Sailing is as difficult as water-skiing.
  = Both sports are equally hard.
2 Like you, I wish I could play the piano.
  = Neither of us can play the piano.
I wish I could play the piano like you.
  = You can play the piano, I can't.

211

3 Your essay was most interesting.
  = It was a very interesting essay.
  Your essay was the most interesting.
  = No one's essay was better than yours.
4 The cliff was too hard for us to climb.
  = We were unable to climb it.
  The cliff was very hard for us to climb.
  = We were able to climb it.
5 She is a much better pianist than her brother.
  = They both play quite well.
  Her brother is a much worse pianist than she is.
  = Neither of them play well.
6 She swims as well as she runs.
  = She is equally good at both sports.
  She swims as well as runs.
  = She takes part in both sports.
7 Bob isn't as bright as his father.
  Bob's father is bright, but Bob isn't that bright.
  = Bob is less intelligent than his father.
  = His father is more intelligent than Bob.
  Bob isn't all that bright, like his father.
  = Neither of them is particularly intelligent.

B Suggested answers – many alternatives are possible:

2 are far more strenuous than
  require a great deal more skill than
3 takes a lot longer than
  requires considerably more time and effort than
4 I'd rather go out for the evening
  I prefer to go to a club with my friends rather
5 as fast as anyone else in her class
  so fast that she invariably laps me
6 is a great deal less energetic than
  is not at all energetic – unlike
7 the least interesting hobby
  is one of the most expensive hobbies

C Corrections in **bold**:

1 It isn't true to say that London is **as large as** Tokyo / **larger than** Tokyo.
2 He's no expert on cars: to him a Mercedes and a BMW are **alike** / **the same**.
3 Her talk was most enjoyable and much more informative **than** we expected.
4 Don't you think that **the more difficult something is, the less enjoyable it is**?
5 **Fewer** people watched the last Olympics on TV than watched the soccer World Cup.
6 Who is the **least** popular political leader **in** the world?
7 My country is quite **different from** / **to** Britain.
8 She's such a **fast** runner **that** I can't keep up with her.

D Write your sentences, or say them softly to yourself. Maybe record yourself on a blank cassette or voice recorder.

1.3 Learning a musical instrument
READING

A Imagine that someone is asking you these questions: say your answers aloud softly to yourself. If possible, record your answers on a cassette recorder or voice recorder.

The instruments shown are:
piano   violin   maraca   harmonica   drums
French horn   accordion   guitar   saxophone

B Write your answers to the questions in note form – full sentences are not required in this case.

Suggested answers:

1 piano   violin   maraca   harmonica   drums   brass (e.g. French horn)   guitar
  electric accordion   saxophone
2 a sense of accomplishment   a creative outlet   an absorbing pastime
3 low back pain   shoulder strain   bleeding   unsightly swelling
4 You get depressed because you can't play it well enough – or you get depressed because you spend so long practising that there's no time for anything else
5 a piano: expensive, difficult to play, not sexy
  b violin: notoriously difficult
  c maraca: mildly entertaining but only to babies
  d harmonica: you quickly get bored with it
  e drums: very difficult to learn, but people think it's easy and fun
  f guitar: too popular, most people will play it better than you
  g electric accordion: anti-social
  h saxophone: playing it in public may destroy your credibility
6 Brass instruments (e.g. French horn) – if you like making rude noises. And the saxophone – if you really do learn to play well.
7 The drummer attacked someone who came up to him, and there was a fight.

C This exercise draws attention to some of the vocabulary in the passage. Take time to highlight the words, as only this can focus on the use of the words in context. Just matching the words and phrases is not enough.

Answers:

grudge	= *dislike*
syndrome	= *condition*
maudlin	= *self-pitying*
endeavour	= *effort*
be misled	= *get the wrong idea*
physical co-ordination	= *control of one's movements*
nuance	= *subtle variation*
unruffled equanimity	= *perfect calmness*
charisma	= *charm and magnetism*

D The passage is full of humour. It's important to be aware when a writer is not being serious, even if you don't share his/her sense of humour.

E 1 Suggested answers:

1 attention   2 meaning   3 writing
4 spelling   5 space/room   6 example

2 Everyone has their own methods of learning vocabulary items. There is, of course, no 'best way' of memorising vocabulary, and you may disagree with some of the ideas in this section.
  As time passes, if the highlighting ink fades, you can re-highlight the words you still want to be reminded of.

1.4 'You've got to be selfish'

LISTENING

A **1** Reading the questions through in advance and anticipating some of the answers will make it easier for you to follow the interview when you listen to it. It's also something you'll have to do in the exam, before you listen to the recordings.

2 🔊 Play the recording, pausing it at the places marked ★★★ in the Transcript.

This is an exercise in listening for specific information. The questions don't cover every point made. Even if you can't catch every word the speaker says (and she does speak rather fast some of the time), it won't stop you getting the answers to the questions.

Answers:

1 400 metres and 400 metre hurdles
2 1 to 1½ hours (but with warm-up and warm-down: from 9 to lunchtime)
3 She has to conserve her energy (for the training session the next day)
4 excited (not frightened, not nervous)
5 relieved (and proud to be there)
6 winning ✓ flying training ✓ travelling ✓ socialising ✓ standing on the winners' podium ✓ being applauded by the crowd
7 being injured (and not able to run)
8 confident, selfish (but never forget you're part of a team)

B This is an open-ended vocabulary exercise – the answers are a matter of opinion.

TRANSCRIPT *6 minutes 20 seconds*

NARRATOR: You'll hear an interview with Allison Curbishley. She's a professional athlete, and she's been a member of the British team at two Olympic Games.

ALLISON: My name is Allison Curbishley and I do 400 metres and 400 metre hurdles.

INTERVIEWER: What about, I mean…um…on a typical day, if you can have a typical day, what would…how would it start?

ALLISON: Um…well, if you take sort of at the moment, what we are now sort of coming into the season in…in… May…um…which is pretty much a hectic time for us, training is pretty intense. Um…I'd get up, I'd train round about…I go down to the track about nine. Um…we, you know, Coach would always, say, be at the track for about nine for ten, which would mean nine o'clock we'd be there to warm up, takes about an hour…um…and would be ready to run and start the session at ten, this is if we're on the track. And the session would usually take sort of somewhere in between half an hour and an hour and a half, depending on what we were doing. Um…and then it would be a…a gradual warm-down, stretch, have lunch straight away…um… replace all the…the lost energy, and then basically the rest of the day is pretty much…um . . . We might have another session to do later on in the evening, which would be a light circuit, or, you know, er…if we've done a heavy session in the morning we might just rest. Um…and it's a very easy-going lazy day for the rest of the day. Uh…we try, I mean, I try and keep myself busy. I read, I, you know, I love listening to music, and obviously TV and what . . . It just depends where we are, and you just keep yourself busy. And, you know, the group that I train with is very social, so we often spend time together, we love sitting around in coffee shops in Bath, you know, that's

what we do, that's what we spend our time doing most of the time.

INTERVIEWER: Work hard, play hard?

ALLISON: Well, this is it, you know, we've basically got to spend the afternoon…uh…doing very little, because you've got to conserve the energy for the training session the next day.
★★★

INTERVIEWER: Do you think there's still that attitude in Britain or overall that…um…it's the winning that counts, it's not the playing?

ALLISON: Yes, yeah, definitely, and I think…but I also think that, you know, as an athlete, you're in the wrong because, you know, I don't think any athlete would settle for silver if they had the chance of gold. Um…I think in general, yeah, the journalists do kind of take…they can't seem to see any good out of coming back with a silver medal from a…an Olympic Games. They don't see that as success they see it as a, you know, …pretty much a failure.

INTERVIEWER: From where I'm sitting even to be at the Olympic Games would be…er . . .

ALLISON: Oh, yeah, isn't it!

INTERVIEWER: . . . I mean, what was it like at…?

ALLISON: Oh, I mean, it was…er…it was very good for me because I'd gone as a…as a…um…relay member, and so there wasn't the pressure on me as an individual athlete, and I was sort of eighteen at the time. And…and, you know, you just I think just the feeling of stepping out onto the track on the sort of second last day just to compete in the . . . I'd been there the whole…I'd gone three weeks preparation with all the team, just to do that one relay leg at sort of pretty much the end of the Games. And it was quite…um…it…it was awesome, it really was. I never got frightened, which I thought I would, I thought I'd get very very nervous, but I just got excited. And you walk onto the track, and walk down the home straight and, you know, there's like a crowd of 80,000 people. Um…and the noise is…is just…just phenomenal, oh, it really was. And it's just, there's very little to describe…there are very few words that can describe the feeling that you, you know, you feel, just running down the back straight, and…um…you know, passing the baton on to the next . . . But I mean there was big relief…sigh of relief once you've passed the baton. But, you know, it was…and…and…it was just great for me to sort of experience that as a first major, then to go on to Athens sort of last year, and sort of pick up from there, you know, it was . . .
★★★

INTERVIEWER: What do you really love about your job?

ALLISON: Um…I love the feeling of a successful training session, I love the feeling of a successful race…um…and of achievement full stop. I mean, there's…um…last year, which was my most successful year…um…in which I gained two championship golds: um…one at European level and one at World Student level. And there's nothing like sort of standing on a podium watching the Union Jack going up, knowing it's for you, and listening to the National Anthem. You know, no matter whether you are patriotic or not you…you get a buzz from that. Um…you know, I…I love the travelling…um…although we don't see a lot of the countries that we go to. We see pretty much, you know, a 400-metre track looks the same wherever you are. Um…but it's nice having the opportunity to sort of taste different cultures and…and sort of . . . And, you know, I've been to so many more countries that I…at the age of sort of 21, 22 than I could ever have dreamed of. You know, and I…um…I just…I…I…I like coming back and relaying it to my parents, who haven't been able to travel with me, and have just been there on the other end of the phone, you know. And it's nice to be able to make them part of it. Um…I love the socialising, the social aspect of it. I've made some…you know, all my best friends are part of my sport now, although going through University and…and friends at home that I've grown up with, it's nice to have sort of the…the friends that bring you back down to reality, and. . .

INTERVIEWER: What do you not enjoy so much?

ALLISON: Um…obviously when you're injured, it can get you down, you know, you…you're not doing what you want to be doing. You…you know, somebody is actually stopping you from doing something that you love. Um…and there's the worry of now it's full time for me, you know…um…what do I do if I did get injured, you know?

INTERVIEWER: I'm just thinking of what att… human att… attributes would make a good sports person.

ALLISON: You've got to be confident, you've got to be selfish, you've got to be . . . Uh…but team work is just so important, and although, yeah, athletics is individual…um…you're constantly out for your team. You're constantly looking out for . . . A training group's a team, you know. Um…wherever you are, you know, you…you are part of a team, nobody ever neglects the fact that you are individual, and leaves you on your own, you know, there's always somebody there, just you yourself and your coach that…that partnership is a team.

Um…I keep saying selfish, you have to be very selfish. A lot of people don't like to admit that but you do. You are very very selfish and purely because, you know, if you're not getting sleep, the food that you need, the…you know, your training's going to fall to bits, you know, if you need to be in a perfect condition to turn up at the track for training, to turn up at the track to race.

1.5 Adjective + noun collocations
VOCABULARY DEVELOPMENT

A Suggested answers:

a **deep** lake   a **close/dear/great** friend
a **nearby/handy** shop   a **noisy** room overlooking the street   a **quiet/peaceful** room overlooking the garden
a **loud/deafening** noise
a **deep** silence   a **valuable** piece of advice
an **expensive/exorbitant** meal   a **profound/learned/difficult** book

B **1** Use a dictionary for inspiration if necessary.
As you can see from these **Suggested answers** there are very many possible combinations!

exciting/great/thrilling **adventure**
attractive/beautiful/delightful/ferocious **animal**
gifted/talented **athlete**
absorbing/entertaining/exciting/great/serious **book**
attractive/delightful/funny/gifted/hard-working/naughty/talented **boy**
exciting/great/serious/thrilling **game**
great/serious/slight **interest**
delicious/delightful/great **meal**
beautiful/great **painting**
gifted/great/talented **photographer**
attractive/beautiful/delightful **place**
great/serious/slight **problem**

beautiful/catchy/delightful/great **song**
absorbing/exciting/funny/thrilling **story**
delightful/gifted/hard-working/serious/talented **student**
entertaining/serious **talk**
attractive/beautiful/breathtaking/delightful/pretty **view**
attractive/beautiful/delightful/funny/gifted/hard-working/pretty/talented **woman**

2 Suggested answers:

amazing/incredible **adventure**
tame/rare/fierce **animal**
competitive/dedicated/trained/successful **athlete**
thrilling/boring/silly/old-fashioned/famous **book**
clever/silly/little **boy**
stupid/terrible **game**
enormous/huge **interest**
tasty/disgusting/dreadful **meal**
impressive/overrated/famous **painting**
famous/hopeless/brilliant **photographer**
fantastic/awful/dreary **place**
awkward/terrible/little **problem**
wonderful/nice/annoying **song**
incredible/improbable/long/short **story**
hard-up/lazy/diligent **student**
witty/stimulating/long-winded **talk**
fantastic/unforgettable/extensive/panoramic **view**
sensible/smart/intelligent/well-respected/successful **woman**

C There are many possible collocations in this exercise.
Suggested answers:

2 a famous **film star/writer**   a well-known **actor/politician**   a notorious **murderer/bigamist**   an infamous **tyrant/dictator**   a distinguished **professor/academic**
3 an extensive **vocabulary/choice**   a long **list/menu**   a wide **selection/variety**   a broad **education/range**
4 an old **car/tradition**   an elderly **gentleman/lady**   an ancient **castle/civilisation**   an old-fashioned **typewriter/attitude**
5 a new **fashion/idea**   a modern **building/design**   an up-to-date **dictionary/edition**   a recent **development/trip**   a fresh **egg/approach**
6 a major **disaster/influence**   a strong **influence/drink**   an important **point/decision**   a significant **number/amount**   a vital **ingredient/source**   an essential **precaution/member of staff**
7 an insignificant **amount/sum of money**   a minor **operation/injury**   a small **difference/shoe**   a little **girl/problem**   a trivial **mistake/matter**
8 a strange **dream/man**   an unusual **name/idea**   a rare **species/treat**   a peculiar **smell/suggestion**   an uncommon **occurrence/bird**

1.6 Tennis stars
READING

A **1** This exercise is similar to Part 1 of the Reading Paper.

Answers:

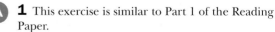

| 1 B | 2 C | 3 A | 4 B | 5 D | 6 B | 7 C |
| 8 A | 9 B | 10 D | | | | |

2 Highlighting or <u>underlining</u> quotations from the text helps when answering multiple-choice questions. This exercise is similar to Part 4 of the Reading Paper.

Answers:

> **1** C **2** C **3** A **4** D **5** B **6** C

B This exercise is similar to Part 3 of the Reading Paper – but in the exam there are more paragraphs missing, and one of the alternatives doesn't fit anywhere.

Answers:

> **1** B **2** A **3** E **4** D **5** C

C Decide how you would answer these questions, and say your answers softly to yourself (or under your breath). Maybe record yourself.

1.7 Using participles
ADVANCED GRAMMAR

A The contrasted sentences in this section illustrate some of the ways in which different structures are used to convey different meanings or a different emphasis.

Suggested answers:

> **1** Standing at the top of the hill, I could see my friends in the distance.
> **– I was at the top of the hill and my friends were in the distance.**
> I could see my friends in the distance standing at the top of the hill.
> **– My friends were at the top of a distant hill, and I could see them there.**
> **2** While preparing the meal, he listened to the radio.
> **– The radio was an accompaniment to the main task of cooking.**
> While listening to the radio, he prepared the meal.
> **– Cooking was an accompaniment to his main interest: listening to the radio.**
> **3** Finding the window broken, we realised someone had broken into the flat.
> **– We saw the broken window and this made us realise that there had been a break-in.**
> We realised someone had broken into the flat, finding the window broken.
> **– When the burglar found the broken window, he used it to make his entry. (This suggests that the window was already broken before he arrived and that made it easier for him to get in.)**
> **4** Before preparing the meal he consulted a recipe book.
> **– He couldn't start cooking until he had found the recipe.**
> After consulting a recipe book he prepared the meal.
> **– He looked for the recipe and then started cooking. (There is only a slight difference in emphasis between these two.)**
> **5** Crawling across the road, I saw a large green snake.
> **– (This sounds strange, and without a context could be understood to mean that the speaker was crawling across the road and came across a snake.)**
> I saw a large green snake crawling across the road.
> **– The snake was crawling across the road when I saw it.**

B Study the examples carefully.

C Answers:

> **1** arranged **2** arriving **3** reaching **4** shaken
> **5** finished **6** required **7** completing **8** lifting

D Suggested answers:

> **1** Not having a car, I usually travel by bus. /
> Not having a car means that I usually travel by bus.
> **2** Chanting loudly, the demonstrators marched into the square.
> **3** Finding their way blocked by the police, they turned back.
> **4** Having heard that he collects butterflies, I asked him to tell me about it.
> **5** Finding none of her friends (waiting) outside the cinema, she went home.
> **6** Not knowing much about art, I can't comment on your painting.
> **7** Drunk too quickly, coffee can give you hiccups.
> **8** Feeling a bit under the weather, I went to bed early.

E Corrections:

> **1** Looking out of my window, I saw a crowd of people in the street.
> **2** We thought he looked ridiculous wearing bright yellow trousers.
> **3** His father treats him like an adult because he is rather tall for his age.
> **4** Having been given such a warm welcome he felt very pleased.
> **5** I saw three old men sitting together playing cards.
> **6** If washed in hot water this garment will shrink.

F Suggested answers:

> **1** opening **2** Thinking **3** realising/realizing
> **4** shouting/yelling/trying **5** Going/Walking
> **6** opening **7** looking/peering **8** Faced
> **9** wondering **10** sitting **11** hearing

1.8 'Golden rules'
WRITING SKILLS AND COMPOSITION

A **1** These steps are not definitive, which is why the title is in inverted commas. Some people say:
The only golden rule is that there are no golden rules!

Suggested sequence:

> **1 Look carefully at the instructions.**
> **2** Discuss with someone else what you're going to write.
> **3** Do any necessary research.
> **4 Think about what you're going to write.**
> **5 Jot down all the points you might make.**
> **6 Analyse your notes, deciding which points to emphasise and which to omit.**
> **7** Use a dictionary to look up suitable words and expressions, and write them down.

8 **Write a plan, rearranging the points in the order you intend to make them.**

9 Write a first draft, perhaps in pencil.

10 Proof-read the first draft: eliminate errors in grammar, spelling and punctuation.

11 Show your first draft to someone else and get feedback from them.

12 Take a break.

13 **Look again at the instructions.**

14 Edit your first draft, noting any changes you want to make.

15 **Write your final version.**

16 **Proof-read your final version, eliminating any mistakes you spot.**

17 Have a rest.

18 Get feedback from other students on your final version (they are 'your readers').

2 Only the steps in **bold print** above might be feasible under exam conditions.

B **1** 🖉 If possible, ask another person (preferably an English-speaking person or a friend whose English is very good) to read and mark your work. If this is not possible, check your own composition through a week or two later. By then you will probably be able to find mistakes that you can correct yourself.

2 If you can find someone to mark your work, this is the kind of feedback they should give you:

- the content of the piece in general
- the style and how easy it was for them to read
- information or ideas that seemed particularly interesting or amusing
- information which was missing from the piece
- sentences which were less easy to follow

Model version:

You don't have to be rich to play squash: if you play at a public sports centre, rather than a private club, you soon discover that it's a game that everybody plays. Taking part in a league, you can meet people from all walks of life, and it's quite normal for men and women to play each other. However, unlike tennis, you can't play doubles, so it's not such a sociable game.

The reason why squash is such fun is that it's so easy to play. Beginners can have an enjoyable game right away and can get involved in the tactics and strategy of the game. With tennis, where it's a major achievement for a beginner even to hit the ball back over the net, you have to be quite proficient before you can do this. With squash, returning the ball is easy and you don't have to waste time retrieving all the balls that have been hit out. You only need one ball to play with and you can play at any time of the day or night and in all weathers. You don't even need to be strong to play: a soft, cunning service can be just as effective as a powerful, fast one. It does help to be fit and agile, though, because even though a game only lasts half an hour or so, during that time you're constantly using your energy and you don't have time for a rest while your opponent is off the court hunting for lost balls.

Perhaps it's because squash is such an energetic game that it's thought to be dangerous. Admittedly there is a risk of minor injuries like strains and sprains, or getting hit by your opponent's racket, because both players have to cover the whole court and sometimes get in each other's way. But if you're careful, and don't overdo it, it's no more dangerous than any other sport.

Finally . . .

Spend half an hour reading through the whole of this unit before moving on to Unit 2. This will help you to memorise the vocabulary and other points covered in the unit. Flipping through earlier units in the book regularly, recalling previous lessons, is a simple yet surprisingly effective revision technique.

2   Adventure   Exploration   Extreme sports

A sense of adventure

2.1   ## Eight Feet in the Andes
       TOPIC VOCABULARY AND READING

Background

The article is a review of one of Dervla Murphy's books. Most of her books concern travels she has made to exotic places, often in the company of her daughter Rachel. Among these are:

Full Tilt: Ireland to India with a Bicycle (1965)
On a Shoestring to Coorg: Experience of South India (1976)
Where the Indus is Young: A Winter in Baltistan (1977)
A Place Apart (1978) – a study of life in Northern Ireland
Eight Feet in the Andes: Travels on a Donkey from Ecuador to Cuzco (1985)
Muddling through in Madagascar (1985)
In Cameroon with Egbert (1989)

More recent journeys, not involving Rachel or any animals, have been in Africa on a bike:

The Ukimi Road (1993)
South From the Limpopo (1997)

A **1 & 2** Decide how you would answer these questions, and say your answers softly to yourself (or under your breath). Maybe record yourself on a blank cassette or voice recorder.

Among the qualities listed, the ones which are probably *least* important are:
arrogance   charisma   compassion   dignity
humility   intelligence   knowledge   modesty
– but clearly this is a matter of opinion.

B   **Answers:**

1 Juana (4 legs), Dervla and Rachel (2 legs each)
2 In the Murphys' eyes: Juana, the mule
   In the reviewer's eyes: 9-year-old Rachel
3 Three months (¶5) – one week less than the *conquistadores* (¶12)
4 In a tent (¶11)

C   **Answers:**

¶ 1 saunter = stroll
¶ 3 madcap schemes = crazy plans
¶ 4 frolic = amusing game
     heartening = encouraging
¶ 6 overenthusiastically = without restraint
     day one = the beginning
¶ 7 fretting = fussing and worrying
     coveted = envied and wanted

¶ 9 homespun = unsophisticated
¶ 12 sticky moments = dangerous incidents
¶ 13 trusting soul = someone who believes other
people are honest

D Answers:

1 She is sceptical and is sarcastic about their
unadventurousness and greed
2 Five (when they went to South India)
3 Rachel was going to go to school
4 She lost patience
She joined in with religious festivals too
enthusiastically
She wore unsuitable shoes which gave her blisters
5 It's pejorative – her views are considered to be
unoriginal or naive by the reviewer
6 Potatoes, tinned sardines, noodles
Juana ate alfalfa (a kind of grass)
7 She is stolen (and then presumably recovered
because '*all ends happily*')
8 Worst: Juana is nearly killed falling over a cliff
Best: the views and the kindnesses

E The ironic/sarcastic turns of phrase are underlined
here:

ONCE upon a time, with travel writing, the rewards
won related to the risks taken. No
longer. Travel writers travel by public transport; often
they just hop in the car. They travel round British
seaside resorts; they saunter up low mountains in the
Lake District. Greatly daring, they visit islands off the
coast. There is no point in travelling hopefully; far
better to arrive as quickly as possible and collect your
multinational publisher's advance.

F Maybe record yourself on a blank cassette or
voice recorder.

2.2 **Articles and determiners**
GRAMMAR REVIEW

A Answers:

1 What was the mule like? = Could you describe their
mule?
What are mules like? = What is a mule like?
2 Do you like tea now? = Have you overcome your
dislike of tea?
Do you like the tea now? = Is the tea all right for you
now?
3 Some of the difficulties were foreseen. = Not all of
the difficulties were foreseen.
Some difficulty was foreseen. = We expected a
certain amount of difficulty.
No difficulty was foreseen. = We didn't expect any
difficulty.
The difficulty was foreseen. = We expected a
particular difficulty.
All the difficulties were foreseen. = Every difficulty
was foreseen.
4 Would you like some coffee now? = Would you like a
coffee now?
Would you like your coffee now? = Would you like
the coffee now?

B Suggested answers:

COUNTABLE	UNCOUNTABLE
a piece of a hint a tip...........	advice
a round of	applause
an action	behaviour
an article of a coat a shirt....	clothing
a game a joke	fun
a fact a piece of	information
a chuckle a laugh	laughter
an item of a suitcase	luggage
a song a tune a piece of	music
an item of a piece of an article a report	news
an improvement	progress
a drop of a fall of	rain
a piece of an analysis research	
a fall of a flake of	snow
a dish of a piece of	spaghetti
a class a lesson	teaching
a means of a car a train	transport
a journey a trip	travel
an asset a fortune a possession	wealth

C Answers:

1 knowledge   2 experience/adventure   3 success/
experience   4 wood   5 adventure/experience/
thought   6 pleasure   7 imagination   8 failure
9 butter/soup/cheese   10 cheese   11 love/
knowledge   12 coffee

D Suggested answers:

The Murphys clearly see not Rachel but Juana,
their/the[1] beautiful glossy mule, as **the**[2] heroine of **the**
/their[3] story. She cost £130 and they fuss over her like
a[4] film star, fretting about **her**[5] diet, **her**[6] looks, **her**[7]
mood. Juana is coveted by all; as **the/their**[8] journey
proceeds it is shadowed by **their**[9] parting from her.
There is **a/the**[10] terrible moment when she falls over **a**[11]
precipice to Ø[12] certain death but for **a**[13] divinely
placed single eucalyptus tree in **her**[14] path.

She worries that Ø[15] religion is so little comfort to
the/a[16] Peruvian Indian, that **the/their**[17] babies chew
Ø[18] wads of Ø[19] coca, that **the**[20] boys Rachel plays Ø[21]
football with on Ø/**the**[22] sloping pitches have no future,
that she cannot repay **their/the**[23] kindnesses: **the/an**[24]
ancient shepherdess who shared **her**[25] picnic lunch of
Ø[26] cold potato stew on **a**[27] cabbage leaf, **the/an**[28] old
man who set **his**[29] dog to guard **their**[30] tent at night.

E Corrections:

1 Politics **doesn't** interest him, except when **an**
election takes place.
2 **Grapefruit** is my favourite **fruit**, but I don't like
bananas.
3 The news **is** depressing today: two **aircraft** have
crashed.
4 There **is a** crossroads at **the** top of **the** hill.
5 Mathematics **was the** most difficult subject at ~~the~~
school for me.
6 **The** Hague is **the** capital of **the** Netherlands, but
Amsterdam is **the** largest city.
7 ~~The~~ Women are usually safer drivers than ~~the~~ men.
8 We missed **the** bus and had to walk all the way home
– it was quite **an** adventure!

F Answers:

1 Travel broadens **the** mind.
2 Love makes **the** world go round.
3 **The** greatest adventure of all is life itself.
4 A friend in need is **a** friend indeed.
5 Absence makes **the** heart grow fonder.
6 While **the** cat's away, **the** mice will play.
7 Out of sight out of mind – as **the** saying goes.
8 **A** woman without **a** man is like **a** fish without **a** bicycle. (*feminist slogan*)

Extra information

Here are some nouns that tend to cause confusion:

Nouns that are singular but look plural:

athletics   economics   maths   measles   mumps news
physics   rabies   the Netherlands
the Philippines   the United States   the West Indies

Nouns that have irregular or unusual plurals:

analysis · analyses   crisis · crises   criterion · criteria
fungus · fungi   goose · geese   hypothesis · hypotheses ox ·
oxen   phenomenon · phenomena

Nouns with identical singular and plural forms:

aircraft   crossroads   data   deer   fish   grapefruit
rendezvous   salmon   series   sheep   species   trout

Nouns that are always plural:

binoculars   clothes   glasses/spectacles   handcuffs
headphones/earphones   headquarters   jeans   knickers
pants   pliers   police   premises   pyjamas   scales
scissors   shorts   sunglasses   tights   trousers
tweezers

2.3 Words easily confused
VOCABULARY DEVELOPMENT

A Consult a dictionary if you are in doubt about any of the meanings. (There isn't room to go into all the differences here.)

B **1** Suggested answers:

The words that do fit are given here, though some of the others might also fit if used humorously or imaginatively.

2 argument   fight   quarrel   row
3 sensitive   difficult   touchy   emotional   moody
4 attended
5 annoying   bothering   disturbing   harassing pestering
6 notebook   exercise book   diary
7 absent-minded   forgetful
8 benefits   advantages   rewards
9 exclusive   private
10 eventual   possible   imminent
11 course   training
12 further   farther

2 Here, as in other multiple-choice vocabulary exercises in this book, the distractors (i.e. the wrong answers) contain useful vocabulary which can be used in different contexts. In the exam you can ignore the distractors, but in *New Progress to Proficiency* they're there as a source of extra vocabulary.

2.4 Brazilian Adventure
READING

Most students find writing summaries one of the hardest parts of the Proficiency exam, but with adequate preparation it can become much less formidable. The work in this section, and similar sections in later units, helps you to prepare progressively for the summary-writing you will have to do in the exam.

Background

Peter Fleming (1907–1971) was the brother of Ian Fleming, creator of James Bond. He is best remembered for his entertaining travel writing.
Brazilian Adventure (1933) describes his experiences of an expedition to Brazil, which he joined after seeing this advertisement in *The Times*:

E XPLORING and sporting expedition, under experienced guidance, leaving England June, to explore rivers Central Brazil, if possible ascertain fate Colonel Fawcett; abundance game, big and small; exceptional fishing; ROOM TWO MORE GUNS; highest references expected and given.

Write Box X, *The Times* E.C.4.

(Colonel Fawcett disappeared on an expedition to find Eldorado and was never heard of again.)
Peter Fleming's other books include *One's Company: A Journey in China* (1934) and *News from Tartary* (1936).

A Answers:

1 Four people were directly involved in the expedition:
the leader (Bob), the Organizer, Major Pingle, Captain John Holman
And peripherally: Major Pingle's German partner
2 Bob, the leader — the Organizer
3 Not very
4 Yes, but that wasn't his real name

B In Part 5 of the Use of English Paper, the passages are shorter and there are fewer questions to answer.

Suggested answers:

2 Not a lot: at any rate, he had only shot one jaguar
3 To go by lorry instead of train OR To go by train instead of road
4 He was worried
5 A man who has had many adventurous experiences – or so he claimed
6 Captain John Holman
7 At his headquarters in Sao Paulo, Brazil
8 By telegram
9 None
10 Buying provisions, employing guides and making all the necessary arrangements
11 An entertaining fiasco, but probably not a disaster

C Suggested answers (some variations are possible):

1 kinds of expedition   2 actors   3 understatement
4 unwilling   5 up-to-date   6 you can't do without
7 very little information   8 untrue or exaggerated

D Decide how you would answer these questions, and say your answers softly to yourself (or under your breath). Maybe record yourself.

The book was published in 1933. The tone of the passage might be described as ironical, deadpan, humorous or amusing.

E 🖊 If possible, ask another person to read and mark your work.

Model summary:

> Although the Organizer was charming and had a beard, his vagueness didn't inspire confidence. He couldn't even commit himself on how they would get from Rio to Sao Paulo. He had given the responsibility for making the arrangements to someone called Major Pingle in Brazil, but it was unclear what arrangements he was making – if any – because only one message from Pingle had been received, and the Organizer had lost it.

2.5 'If something goes wrong . . .'
LISTENING

A Think about these questions before you listen to the recording.

B 🔊 **Suggested answers:**

1 a) physical exertion – he likes to be fit – mountaineering is a very good cardio-vascular exercise
   b) views   (no reason given, but presumably because they are spectacular)
   c) danger – the thrill of being at the end of a rope and having to 'do it right'
   d) company – he has made good friends with fellow-climbers
2 rock-climbing: acute terror
   mountaineering: worry, chronic anxiety
3 Alastair himself was unconscious – his partner had to save him
4 Because there was no evasive action they could take
5 Because there was a cable-car station at the top, where they knew they could shelter

TRANSCRIPT   *4 minutes 10 seconds*

NARRATOR: Part One
PRESENTER: Alastair Miller was a member of a recent British Combined Services expedition to Everest. We talked to him about climbing mountains and asked what he enjoys about mountaineering.

ALASTAIR: I enjoy the sh… the sheer physical exertion because I enjoy being fit anyway and I do a lot of sport and running and that sort of thing and I like just to be physically fit, and I find mountaineering is a nice way of doing that and probably that's one of the best ways because you're not actually running and pounding your knees and Achilles tendons and things. But if you're walking hard at altitude and uphill then that's probably as good a cardio-vascular exercise as anything. So I enjoy that aspect of it.

I enjoy the…the views, er…I enjoy the…the danger to a certain extent. I mean, I wouldn't go somewhere if I thought that I was going to kill myself, although I recognise that there is a risk of it. But I enjoy the…the thrill of being out on a…on the end of a rope knowing that if I don't do it right, then I am going to fall. Um…but hopefully that I'm going to get held and I'm not going to do a lot of damage, I…I wouldn't like to go climbing solo in a

situation where if I fell I was going to kill myself. I enjoy the…the company, because I think you…you make tremendous friends on these expeditions and I've got friends that I've climbed with who are amongst my…my best friends ever really and I've climbed with them on… numerous other times now.

PRESENTER: As he admits, climbing mountains can be dangerous. Has he ever been frightened?

ALASTAIR: Oh yes, I'm sure I have. Er…it's difficult to define specific instances but again I think there's a distinction between rock-climbing and…and mountaineering where…and the…the mode of being frightened is…is slightly different. In…in rock-climbing it's much more acute, if something goes wrong, you know you're going to fall off. And in fact the worst…my worst accident was…I didn't really have time to be frightened in, because it happened all so quickly, and that was…we were climbing…we were rock-climbing in…in Yosemite Valley in California, and the thing that I was tied onto on the cliff just pulled out and I fell the whole rope-length between myself and my partner. And as I fell past him I remember shouting, 'Stop me!' and I do have a vague recollection of falling but then I obviously hit something on the way down and was unconscious at the end of the rope, and so it was probably a lot more frightening for him than it…it was for me. So that's the sort of acute terror that you get from rock-climbing.

In mountaineering I think it's more the worry that you're going to get lost, the weather's going to come in, er…you're going to get hit by an avalanche, so there's the sort of more a chronic anxiety level there and I'm aware of that all the time. The weather…it never seems to be absolutely perfect conditions wherever you are, whether it's Himalayas or Alps, you're always aware there's that little wisp of cloud on the horizon which in a couple of hours could build up into a major storm.

And the other frightening experience was climbing a route called the Frendeau spur on the Aiguille du Midi in the French Alps, we came to the top of that in a…in an enormous thunderstorm and as we were climbing the final snow-slopes there was lightning literally striking the snow behind us, and setting off mini-avalanches and that was very frightening. But you just had to be philosophical because there was nothing you could do to avoid this lightning and if it hit you, well, then that was it. The only comfort about that was that it's a mountain that has a…has a cable-car station at the top, so although we were climbing up towards the top of the mountain, we were actually climbing towards safety and were able to scurry into the…into the cable-car station and…and shelter from the storm overnight and…er…get the first cable-car down the next day and have a beer to celebrate still being alive!

C 🔊 **Answers:**

> 1 pyramid   36   2 or 4   supplies and equipment
> 2 North   (local) porters   the members of the expedition
> 3 Camp 2   fixed   safe
> 4 wash   change their clothes   teeth
> 5 cramped   comfortable   safe

D Decide how you would answer these questions, and say your answers softly to yourself (or under your breath). Maybe record yourself on a blank cassette or voice recorder.

TRANSCRIPT   *3 minutes*

NARRATOR: Part Two
PRESENTER: What is it like taking part in an expedition to climb Everest?

ALASTAIR: A lot of it is boring, a lot of it's hard work, er… a little bit of it is frightening as we've discussed, and some of it is fantastically exciting and exhilarating and that's the bit that you remember and that makes up for everything else.

Then the major problem on any expedition, and certainly a large expedition climbed in the sort of style that we did, is…is the logistics of it. And to get all…it…as I'm sure people will know, it's what's called a 'pyramid effect': you've got 36 people at the bottom and you want to get two or four maybe at the top, so you slowly have to build up stores higher and higher up the mountain…er…to…to…in order to place your last four people on the summit. So you…there's an awful lot of carrying of stores and things. Now, on…on this particular side of Everest there are not a lot of local porters around, as there are on the south side, so on the south side you probably engage two hundred local porters who will carry your equipment up through the Khumbu Ice Fall into the area where you're going to be climbing from. On the north side you don't have that facility and you have to engage yaks. And so we had about 80 yaks loaded with kit, and they had to be looked after. The yaks would only go just a little bit above Camp One and from there on it was just expedition members doing all the carrying.

So that was how it worked. So you'd maybe do a week of carrying between One and Two, go down for a rest, and then come back up and find you'd be carrying between Camps Three and Four, or maybe eventually with luck, you'd actually get to be one of the lead teams and you'd be pushing the route out and of course that was when it became exciting and exhilarating to be places where nobody else had been. It was always exciting to…to…to be somewhere where you'd never been before, and I remember the first time I went up above Camp Two, I…it was absolutely brilliant: we were on fixed ropes which other people had put in so we were entirely safe, but for the first time we had crampons on and we were actually properly climbing rather than just walking.

A lot of it's uncomfortable, certainly above base camp, the facilities there . . . Camp One you might have, if you were feeling very brave, had a wash, but certainly above there you wouldn't do anything for a week or ten days, you would just not change your clothes, you'd only clean your teeth, but everything else was just in the same clothes crawling in and out of your tent and sleeping bag. Above Camp Two, which was at 20,000 feet [6,000 m] on the…on the very steep bit of the climb at Camps Three and Four we lived in snow holes, which we'd had to dig out ourselves and they were quite cramped and of course they…although they're comfortable and they're safe because if an avalanche falls across the top of a snow hole it might bury you in, you might have to dig yourself out, but it's less serious than being swept away if you're in a tent.

2.6   Keeping the reader's interest
WRITING SKILLS

A **1** The composition in the Student's Book is about 250 words long and seems to run out of steam after the first paragraph. The more effective features are in **bold print**, the less effective ones are <u>underlined</u>. However, this sort of thing is debatable because different readers are interested in different things.

It had been a long, tiring journey to S__. The ferry, which should have taken at most five hours, had had engine trouble and didn't arrive till 2 a.m. As the harbour itself was several miles from the main town – the only place where accommodation was available – and much too far to walk even by daylight, we **hoped against hope** that the local bus service would still be running. **Sure enough** one tiny, ancient blue bus was

waiting on the quayside but **imagine our dismay** when we saw that **about 98** other passengers were also disembarking with the same destination. We **fought** our way onto the bus and waited for the driver to appear. A man **staggered** out of the bar nearby and **groped** his way into the driving seat – **presumably** he'd been drinking since early evening when the ship was supposed to arrive.

We were <u>very frightened</u>. Most of the passengers hadn't seen the driver come out of the bar. The bus went <u>very slowly</u> up the steep road. On one side the cliffs **dropped vertically down to the sea hundreds of metres below**. We arrived in the town <u>at 3 a.m.</u>, but there was no accommodation. We found a taxi to take us to the other side of the island. We slept on the beach.

As it began to get light and the sun rose over the sea, **waking us from our dreams**, we realised that it had all really happened and that we were **lucky to be alive**.

2 Improved version:

> We were absolutely petrified and we knew that most of the other passengers hadn't spotted the driver coming out of the bar and were blissfully unaware of what might be in store. It was a nightmare journey: the bus was so full that it could hardly get up the steep, narrow hill that led from the port to the main town. On one side of the road we could see the cliffs dropping vertically down to the sea hundreds of metres below us, and we were afraid that at any moment we would all go crashing down to our deaths.
>
> But we survived. We arrived in one piece, and although the whole journey seemed to have taken days, by the time we arrived in the town it was still only 3 o'clock. To our dismay, though, there was no accommodation to be had for love or money. Fortunately, we found a taxi which took us to the other side of the island where there was a beach we could sleep on under the stars.
>
> The next morning, as it began to get light and the sun rose over the sea, waking us from our dreams, we realised that it had all really happened and that we really were lucky to be alive.

B **1** **Suggested answers** (many variations are possible):

1 There was nothing I could do but **sit there and wait for my friends to return**.
2 It was only after **unlocking the door** that I **realised I didn't know how to disarm the burglar alarm**.
3 My big mistake was to **throw everything into the dustbin without checking first**.
4 All I could do was **sit there watching the rain fall**.
5 You can imagine how I felt when **I found out what a big mistake I'd made**.
6 It all started when **my friends said I could borrow their house**.
7 To my utter amazement **nobody had noticed what I'd done**.
8 To our surprise **a total stranger was sitting in the bath**.
9 Slowly opening the door, **I shone my torch into the cellar**.
10 After a while **we heard some strange noises coming from the refrigerator**.
11 Without thinking I **slammed the car door, trapping my fingers**.
12 I held my breath as **the dog sniffed me up and down**.

2 & 3 🖊 If possible, do this exercise with a friend.

2.7 ## Position of adverbs
ADVANCED GRAMMAR

A It's impossible to lay down hard-and-fast rules about adverb position in English.

There is often a difference of emphasis achieved by placing adverbs in less usual positions, particularly at the very beginning or very end of a clause. Often, this is done using a comma (rather like a pause in speech) – or after a dash at the end of a sentence – as in these examples:

Adverb position usually causes students problems.
Usually, adverb position causes students problems.
Adverb position causes students problems – usually!

Suggested answers:

1 Tricia **only** wants to help.
  = **She's trying to be helpful, not interfere**
  Only Peter wants to help.
  = **Nobody else wants to help, only Peter**
2 Pam doesn't **really** feel well.
  = **She's slightly unwell**
  Anne doesn't feel **really** well.
  = **She's not totally well**
  Jack **really** doesn't feel well.
  = **I assure you that he's not well**
3 Tony and Jane **still** aren't married.
  = **Contrary to our expectations they haven't got married yet**
  Olivia and Paul aren't **still** married, are they?
  = **I know they used to be married, but I don't think/didn't think they are/were any more**
  Still, Sue and Bob aren't married.
  = **Nevertheless, they aren't married**
4 I don't **particularly** want to see Lisa.
  = **I've no special desire to see her**
  I **particularly** don't want to see Tim.
  = **He's the person I really don't want to see**
5 I enjoy eating **normally**.
  = **I like normal kinds of food, not unusual ones**
  Normally, I enjoy eating.
  = **I usually like eating, but in this case maybe not**
  I **normally** enjoy eating.
  = **I usually like eating**
  I enjoy eating – **normally**!
  = **I usually like eating, but in this case I don't**
6 **Carefully**, I lifted the lid.
  – *dramatic and emphatic*
  I **carefully** lifted the lid.
  – *not particularly dramatic*
  I lifted the lid **carefully**.
  – *not particularly dramatic*
7 Paul **just** doesn't like flying …
  = **He simply hates it**
  Olivia doesn't **just** like flying …
  = **She also likes lots of other things**

B Notice that, in formal style, *hardly ever, never, rarely* and *seldom* can be placed, for emphasis, at the beginning of a sentence, but that the word order changes:
Never have I been so insulted in my life.
Seldom have there been so many people at a concert before.

(This point is covered in **3.5 Using inversion for emphasis**.)

Suggested answers:

1 a) We have **nearly/practically/virtually** finished our work.
  b) I **utterly** disagree with what you said.
  c) It is **hardly ever/rarely/seldom** as cold as this usually.
2 a) I don't **altogether/entirely** agree with her.
  b) Your work has **greatly** improved.
  c) He isn't **exactly/altogether** brilliant.
  d) I enjoyed the show **enormously/greatly**.
3 a) The Olympic Games are held **once every four years**.
  b) I don't have the information **at the moment**, so I'll call you back **in the evening/within the hour**.
  c) **Most of the time** I agree with what she says, but **from time to time/once in a while** we don't see eye to eye.
  d) Although she had washed her hair **the previous day/before breakfast**, she washed it again **in the evening**.
4 a) I can't give you my answer **at once/immediately**, but I'll let you know **presently/eventually/later/shortly/soon**.
  b) Let me know **later/afterwards** what you thought of the film.
  c) It will **soon/presently** be time to go home, so you'll have to finish the work **afterwards/later**.
5 a) She was behaving very **foolishly/oddly/strangely**.
  b) He held up the prize **carefully/proudly** and thanked everyone **sincerely/warmly/thoughtfully**.
  c) She took his hand **gently/lovingly/reassuringly** and looked **lovingly/apprehensively/gloomily** into his eyes.
  d) I raised my hand **automatically/instinctively** to protect my face.
6 a) **Luckily**, I found my wallet in the car.
  b) **Strangely enough/Unfortunately**, she didn't get the job.
  c) **Hopefully**, I'll have finished the work soon.
  d) **Funnily enough/Amazingly**, they're getting married.

C Corrected sentences (some variations are possible):

1 I have **seldom** seen him so furious and I was **absolutely** shocked by his reaction.
2 He loses his temper **from time to time** but **most of the time** he is in a good mood.
  or **From time to time** he loses his temper but he is in a good mood **most of the time**.
3 All enquiries will be handled **discreetly** and you may write to us **in confidence**.
4 'Don't worry,' she said **quietly**, taking my hand and squeezing it reassuringly.
5 She told them **many times** to take care but they **repeatedly** ignored her advice.
6 The door **suddenly** burst open and we all looked up **in surprise**.
  or The door burst open **suddenly** . . .
7 I do my homework **every day** and it **usually** takes me an hour.
8 He doesn't **just** like ice cream, he loves it so much that he eats it **every day**.

D Suggested answers:

1 After a while they replied to my letter.
2 I'm afraid that's a mistake I make again and again.
3 I often eat out in the evenings.
4 I've practically finished writing this report.
5 They reluctantly helped me. / They helped me reluctantly.
6 I particularly don't want to go for a walk.
   (I don't particularly want to . . . *is less emphatic*)
7 Each branch of the company operates independently.
8 Presumably he will be feeling apprehensive.
9 You should always pay attention to your spelling.
10 She looked at me anxiously.

2.8 Be prepared!
LISTENING AND COMPOSITION

In this section the information and ideas given in the recording act as a basis for the composition.

A 1 Looking at the task before listening to the recording helps you to apply your previous knowledge and common sense to the task. Why not pencil in some of the answers you expect?

2 🔊 Answers:

PRECAUTIONS	
DO	DON'T
1 four	
2 careful	trained
3 deteriorate/get worse	weather forecasts (especially in the newspaper)
4 time	darkness
5 speed/pace slowest	behind
6 stop walking	
7 somewhere to shelter better/improved visibility	walk on/go on walking precipice

EQUIPMENT
1 plan   route
2 compass   landmarks   how to use it   your nose sense of direction
3 warm   waterproof
4 proper walking boots   sandals   trainers
5 rations   chocolate   raisins   sandwiches (*and something to drink!*)
6 torch/flashlight
7 survival bag   survival blanket

And . . .
let someone know where you're going
what time you expect to be back
report your safe arrival

TRANSCRIPT   *5 minutes 50 seconds*

PRESENTER: OK, so…um…it's…um…it's a lovely sunny day and you feel like going for a walk maybe up into the mountains. And off you go, hoping for a good trip. So far so good but according to Denis Rosser, you could be asking for trouble. Now what's all this about, Denis?

DENIS: Well, yes of course, most of the time, the majority of the time you'll have a marvellous day, you'll get back safely, maybe you're feeling a bit stiff the next day, but there'd be no problem. But…er…you should bear in mind that there are risks…er… in going walking in the mountains because they can be very dangerous places. First of all, you should

never ever head off into the mountains by yourself. That's very important. It's best to have at least four people actually in your party, and then if anything goes wrong, like someone breaks a leg, or sprains an ankle or something, one can stay with the injured person and two others can go off to get help. Er…so you should always be careful and not do anything you're not trained to do and take all the necessary precautions as well.

PRESENTER: What sort of precautions?

DENIS: Well, it's a good idea to expect weather conditions to deteriorate. You…you really mustn't rely on the accuracy of weather forecasts. But…er…but you should especially not…er…rely on ones in the paper, which are often at least twelve hours old before you…you read them. And mountains also have what we call their own micro-climate, which means that they have their own weather systems the…which can often differ considerably from…er…weather in the surrounding valleys or low-lying areas. I…in the mountains, the weather can change very very quickly as well, um… you can suddenly get thunderstorms developing and clouds come down quite suddenly.

   So…um…*cough*… Excuse me. When you…when you set out, you should also allow yourself plenty of time, er…because you don't want to let darkness catch up with you while you're still out. It's…er…it's better to arrive in the valley low down when it's, you know, three thirty, four o'clock in the afternoon rather than having to scramble down…down some path at the last minute when darkness is coming down. Another important thing is…er…not to leave anyone in your group behind. I mean, this might sound a bit silly but…um…the pace of the party really should…should…should be the same as the slowest member of the group and not the quickest.

   And if the…the visibility does worsen, if fog comes down or if you run into low-lying clouds or something, and you don't know where you are exactly, it's advisable to stop walking and find somewhere to shelter, and sit and wait for it to get better. Otherwise you might walk straight over a precipice or something, which wouldn't be too clever!

PRESENTER: Oh dear! But I suppose if you've got a map and a compass and things then, I mean, it's less likely to happen, isn't it?

DENIS: Er…well, yes I suppose so, but y…you must pr…you must plan your route first before you go really. I always mark my proposed route on the map with a…a yellow highlighter, which is a…a good tip, and you…you…then you know exactly where you are on the map all the time. And…er…and you must keep looking at your map, so…er…so you know while you're walking.

   And you're quite right: you should…should be carrying a compass with you…um…it really is the only way of knowing which way you're going if you can't see the sun and…er…there aren't any landmarks or anything. And make sure you know how to use it properly. It's a…it's amazing how many people wouldn't like to admit to the fact that they can't use a compass. And the important thing is: don't just follow your nose and rely on your sense of direction because often that will mislead you.

PRESENTER: And what should you wear, I mean, what sort of clothes should you wear and do you need…do you need other equipment at all?

DENIS: Well, you…you ought to take a rucksack with you really. Er…and even if it's hot and sunny when you set out, you've got to be prepared for…for wet and colder conditions to develop. So…um…er…you need waterproof clothing with you and…er…you'll also need warm clothing. Um…and of course proper footwear: it's not…not…there's no point in wearing sandals or trainers or something like that, you've got to have proper walking boots. If it's very hot then it's OK to wear shorts, but do take some trousers with you in your rucksack…um…and not jeans, because…er…they don't keep out the cold and…er…they'll make you feel even colder if they get wet, and in fact you'd be better off not hav…you know, having bare legs than jeans, jeans are really not…not good at all.

Also in your rucksack you'll need some…er…rations, emergency rations for…er…if you get stuck: chocolates, raisins, sandwiches, something to drink, things like that. And…er…a small torch is good…um…if…er…if you do get caught in the dark. Er…and you should also pack a survival blanket or a survival bag…er… they're very lightwake…um…weight and…er…they take up…er…very little room. They're indispensible.

PRESENTER: Oh really? I mean, what…what exactly are they?

DENIS: Well…um…a survival bag is a large plastic bag which you can climb into to protect you from the cold and wet, and…um…the survival blanket is a…a large plastic sheet that reflects the heat back to you. Um…either…either…either of them will save your life if you…if you have to spend the night in the open. Er…and…er…they're very good …good…er…things to take with you.

PRESENTER: It doesn't exactly sound like a barrel of laughs, this trip, does it?

DENIS: No…it…actually I shouldn't…er…I shouldn't panic people. The thing is if you take the precautions and you've got all this equipment and you know what you're doing, you're better prepared and therefore…er…you can walk all day long feeling confident and…and you'll enjoy yourself more. And one…one more thing that's vital: before you set out, let someone know where you're going and what time you expect to be back…er…and in that way…um… When you do get back as well, you know, you…you must report your safe arrival to them, otherwise they'll be worried and they might send out a search party…er…when it's not necessary. But…er…er…if you do get into difficulties and people know, then there will be a rescue party there if you need it.

PRESENTER: Yes, you're right. Well, Denis, thank you very very much. I mean, I'm sure you're absolutely right, it's better to be safe than sorry – or maybe possibly to stay at home? Haha. Thank you very much, Denis.

DENIS: Haha. Thanks a lot.

3 Two pieces of advice the speaker didn't mention:
Take plenty to drink – very important in hot weather
Take a mobile phone – a lifesaver if you get into difficulties

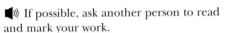 If possible, ask another person to read and mark your work.

Model summary:

Dear Hilary

I must tell you about my exciting holiday in the Alps. I went with a group of people from the university sailing club and we were staying on Lake Thun. In spite of being there for sailing we thought we couldn't miss the chance of a ride on a mountain railway or a walk in the mountains and the spectacular views you get from high up. None of us is a fitness freak, but I suppose we're quite fit — except for Tim who's really overweight.

We set off a bit late but when we got to the top of the cable car it was clear and bright and only 3 pm. None of us had walking boots as we had come equipped to sail but we had pretty sturdy trainers. We didn't have a map either and anyway the footpaths are well signposted. We planned to walk for about two hours on a circular route and then get the last cable car down at 6 pm. That was supposed to allow us plenty of time to dawdle and deal with blisters!

Well, after about half an hour Tim really began to drag. He found the path too steep and was quite

breathless. In the end, Jen said she'd stay with him and would meet us back at the cable car. That left me and Phoebe and Pete. We set up a good pace and reached the point where we thought we'd turn back at about 4.30. But then a mist descended and we were quite nervous of missing our turning or slipping as it had become rather wet. However we carried on. Phoebe did slip and she twisted her ankle so badly she couldn't walk anymore. Unfortunately we didn't have a first aid kit. Phoebe persuaded Pete and me to go on and get help at the cable car. We didn't like leaving her but it seemed the only thing to do. Well, we just about made it to the cable car before it was due to leave and told them about Phoebe. The staff phoned down to the village and they sent a rescue party up to get Phoebe. We met up with Tim and Jen and finally arrived back at our hotel somewhat frazzled but relieved.

2.9 *keep* and *hold*
VERBS, IDIOMS AND COLLOCATIONS

For more information on phrasal verbs and prepositional verbs, consult the *Cambridge International Dictionary of Phrasal Verbs*, or an English-English dictionary.

A This exercise covers collocations and some idiomatic phrases.

Answers:

KEEP	a diary a promise a straight face in touch with someone quiet someone company someone in the dark your eyes open your fingers crossed your temper yourself to yourself
HOLD	a meeting hands with someone someone responsible your breath your head high

B This exercise covers idiomatic phrases and some phrasal verbs.

Answers:

1 walk at the same speed as
2 compete with the neighbours in acquiring material possessions
3 maintain the same level of excellence/ progress
4 Don't tell anyone – it's a secret
5 be thinking of you and hoping that you have good luck
6 bear a grudge against me for it
7 stand up to logical examination
8 not revealing the whole truth/all the facts
9 delayed
10 Wait   stay at the other end of the line (on the phone) and not ring off

C This exercise covers phrasal verbs and some prepositional verbs.

Answers:

1	hold out	6	holding back
2	held out	7	keep in with
3	keep off	8	hold back
4	keep down	9	held out for
5	keep out of	10	hold on

3 People Friends and acquaintances Men and women

Everyone's different!

3.1 Getting away from it all
READING

A **1** Some of the reasons why the writer might be envied are:

living in a beautiful landscape   being cut off from phones and work   seeing whales

and some of the reasons why she might be pitied are:

constant interruptions   no entertainments   no shops

2 Decide how you would answer these questions, and say your answers softly to yourself (or under your breath). Maybe record yourself on a blank cassette or voice recorder.

B **1** Suggested answers:

Names	Who they were	Means of transportation
a *(not stated)*	depressed friend	float plane
b Dave, Diane & kids	her nearest neighbours	small boat
c Lise	lighthouse keeper's wife	Coast Guard helicopter
d Bob	lumberjack	on foot
e three men	Dept of Fisheries scientists	boat

2 Suggested answers:

Who they were	Why Margaret was relieved
a Frank and his spouse	Frank was recovering from an an operation and might have needed looking after
b A mother and her two sons	She couldn't have coped with the simple life and they were TV addicts who would have been bored, and annoying
c Guitar-playing friend	She wanted peace and quiet, not guitar music

3 Suggested answers:

a Local people she never met but who somehow knew she was alone and might need company, and who told Dave and Diane, Bob and the three men from the Department of Fisheries to visit her

b The writer is being ironic: she wants to show that she had been dreading the friend's visit and didn't want her to stay any longer

c There was so much that it's difficult to single out three aspects. But she certainly appreciated: watching the sea lions and whales   getting to know the people she met there learning about solitude and loneliness

C Answers:

foolproof · precarious   unassailable · vulnerable
outraged · unruffled   the bush · civilisation
unsolicited · invited   positively · not in the least
blissfully · unhappily   egged on · discouraged
abhors a vacuum · loves an empty space   came to
nothing · did happen   flagged · continued
tentatively · confidently   bustle · calm

D Decide how you would answer these questions, and say your answers softly to yourself (or under your breath). Maybe record yourself on a blank cassette or voice recorder.

3.2 Reporting – 1
GRAMMAR REVIEW

A Answers:

emphasise = stress   complain = grumble
confess = admit   disclose = reveal   forecast = predict
infer = gather   insinuate = imply   order = tell
promise = guarantee   reiterate = repeat
remember = recall   suppose = guess   yell = shout

B **1** Suggested answers:

They . . .
admitted agreed discovered didn't expect explained hoped imagined implied didn't know learned mentioned pretended never realised reckoned didn't remember didn't reveal didn't say shouted suggested wished
                                    . . . that we had done it.

advised asked explained implied mentioned reckoned didn't say shouted suggested
                                    . . . that we should do it.

agreed asked couldn't decide didn't expect hoped learned pretended promised refused didn't remember threatened wanted wished
                                    . . . to do it.

advised allowed asked didn't expect forbade persuaded reminded didn't tell wanted wished
                                    . . . us to do it.

advised asked couldn't decide discovered explained didn't know learned mentioned didn't remember didn't reveal didn't say suggested wondered   **. . . when to do it.**

advised asked couldn't decide explained implied didn't know mentioned didn't remember didn't reveal didn't say shouted suggested wondered   **. . . when we should do it.**

asked couldn't decide discovered didn't know didn't remember didn't reveal didn't say wondered   **. . . if we had done it.**

2 Answers:

The six verbs that don't fit are:

accused apologised blamed dissuaded forgave warned

You accuse someone . . .	of doing something wrong
You apologise . . .	for doing something
You blame someone . . .	for having done something wrong
You dissuade someone . . .	from doing something
You forgive someone . . .	for doing something
You warn someone . . .	about something *or* not to do something

C Suggested answers:

2 He refused to help me and told me that I would have to do it by myself.
3 She advised me not to write it all out in longhand.
4 He blamed me for our missing the bus, accusing me of misreading the timetable
5 He wondered if I knew when the performance started, not wishing to be late.
6 She suggested that I should telephone him to see if he was free that night.
She persuaded me to telephone him . . .
7 She warned me not to start giggling during the interview.
8 He persuaded me to type the letter out for him, promising to buy me a drink to thank me.
9 She accused me of borrowing her dictionary.
10 He threatened to call the police if I didn't move my car.
11 She agreed to accompany me.
I persuaded her to accompany me.
12 He forgave me for my rudeness, knowing that I was upset.
13 She implied that I should have finished writing the report.
14 She apologised for breaking my sunglasses by sitting on them.

D This activity can only be done with a partner.

9.8 Reporting – 2 is on page 103.

3.3 Punctuation and paragraphs
WRITING SKILLS

A Answers:

; semi-colon : colon ! exclamation mark
. . . ellipsis/dot dot dot - hyphen
— dash " " inverted commas/quotation marks
• bullet (point) ¶ paragraph number * asterisk
(brackets/parenthesis) [square brackets]
/ stroke/slash ' apostrophe . full stop/period

Some further points:

• *Quote . . . Unquote* is sometimes said instead of the cumbersome *Open inverted commas . . . Close inverted commas.*
• In handwriting it's more usual to use double quotes (" ") than single (' ').
• Dashes are more common in informal style than in formal writing – especially to add afterthoughts.
• Semi-colons are uncommon in informal style. Instead we tend to use a comma, or a full stop and a new sentence.
• Colons are used before explanations, and before a list, and also to introduce a quotation – but not to introduce direct speech, where a comma is more commonly used: He said, "Quotation marks are used to quote direct speech. Notice where the quotation marks and other punctuation marks are in relation to each other."
• Bullet points are also quite common these days – especially when listing ideas or points.

B Suggested answers (some variations are possible):

A rabbit goes into a butcher's shop and asks, "Have you got any lettuce?"
The butcher says, "We don't sell lettuce here. You need the greengrocer's across the road."
The next day the rabbit comes into the shop and asks for some lettuce again.
The butcher tells him, "Look, I told you yesterday. We don't sell lettuce. You need the greengrocer."
The rabbit comes in the next day and asks the butcher again, "Have you got any lettuce?"
The butcher goes mad. He says, "Look, I'm sick of this! How many times do I have to tell you I don't sell lettuce! If you come in here again asking for lettuce, I'm going to nail your ears to the floor!"
The next day the rabbit comes in and asks the butcher, "Have you got any nails?"
"Nails? No."
"Right," the rabbit says, "Have you got any lettuce?"

C Corrected version (some variations are possible):

I have known Jan Hall, both professionally and personally, for several years.
Since 1998, when she first joined my department, she has been a reliable, resourceful and conscientious member of my staff with a thoroughly professional attitude to her work. She has cheerfully taken on extra responsibilities and can be relied on to take over when other staff are absent or unavailable.
She particularly enjoys dealing with members of the public, and has a knack of putting people at their ease. She is particularly adept at defusing delicate situations with an appropriate word and a smile.
As her portfolio shows, she is also a very creative and talented person, and her work shows great promise.
During her time with us her attendance has been excellent.
She is an intelligent, thoughtful and imaginative person. I have no hesitation in recommending her for the post.

D Corrected sentences with comments:

1 **Sitting on the beach, we watched the windsurfers falling into the water.**
– Participle phrases usually require a comma unless they are the complement of verbs like *watch, see, hear, find, notice*, etc.
2 **The aspect of punctuation which is most tricky is the use of commas.**
– Commas are not used to separate identifying/defining relative clauses from the noun phrase. But commas ARE required before (and after) non-identifying relative clauses:
My best friend, who lives over the road, is rather shy.
3 **Could you tell me when to use a semi-colon?**
– Commas are not used in indirect speech after the reporting verb.

4 **Feeling completely baffled, we tried to solve
the problem with which we were faced.**
– Participle phrases usually require a comma.
Commas are not used in identifying/defining
relative clauses.

5 **He wouldn't dare say boo to a goose, he's so shy.**
A comma precedes a clause giving extra
information.

6 **There were, surprisingly, no punctuation mistakes in
his work.**
– Adverbs which 'comment' on the whole sentence
require commas. In this example, *Surprisingly, there
were no* . . . might be more usual. And *There were
surprisingly few punctuation mistakes* . . . would also be
possible.

3.4 Who's talking?

LISTENING

 Suggested answers:

FIRST SPEAKER
1 angry; at home
2 her husband (or older child?)
3 books or papers? (toys??)
4 the children (from school) or some people (from
the station?)
5 indifferent – or defiant?
6 he wants to avoid conflict?

SECOND SPEAKER
7 a female stranger
8 he mistakes her for a well-known TV actress
9 TV stars or characters in TV programmes
10 doesn't want to get involved? aloof?

THIRD SPEAKER
11 a friend
12 the team captain, the organiser
13 sports kit and equipment
14 the sports field
15 the match

FOURTH SPEAKER
16 the manager of a factory or power station
17 reporters
18 an accident, causing pollution or a radioactive leak
19 . . . any accident of this kind ever happening again?

FIFTH SPEAKER
20 a busybody
21 a child (a little girl?)
22 flowers
23 intimidated?
24 . . . to make you cry

TRANSCRIPTS *4 minutes 20 seconds*

FIRST SPEAKER: . . . Oh, look at this! They're all over the
place! I'm fed up with it, really I am. If I've
told you once, I've told you a thousand
times. Why should I have to do it for you?
You're the one who put them there and
they're yours not mine. Oh yes, I know,
you're 'going to do it later'. I wish I had a
pound for every time I'd heard that. Look,
I've got better things to do, all right? Oh,
don't look like that, of course it matters, it's
symptomatic of your whole attitude, this. Oh
God, it's almost time to pick them up now
and I've got nothing done at all this
afternoon, thanks to you. Yes, it is your fault

and don't pretend it's not and they're just as
bad. They think if you can get away with it,
so can they. It's just not fair. Look, I'm
warning you, if you don't make an effort to
change . . .
★★★

SECOND SPEAKER: Excuse me, um…aren't you…er…?
Oh…haha…no, course you're not, sorry.
Silly of me. It's just that…er…in this light,
but…er…now I can see I was wrong. Yeah.
And you're quite a bit taller too. Sorry
again. Has anyone mentioned the
resemblance before, I wonder? No, no, I
suppose not. Oh, don't you? Oh, you know,
Jane…um…Jane . . . whatsername, can't
remember her other name. She was in that
sitcom: you know, she played the daughter
and Geoffrey Palmer played the father. No,
not Geoffrey Palmer the other one,
um…the one who's in the coffee
commercial. What's he called? Er…oh, you
know, the mother was played by that blonde
actress, the one who was in that accident
recently. Miracle she wasn't killed,
apparently. Anyway, she was the mother and
this Jane was the daughter, and you look just
like her, you know. So…er… can I . . .? Oh.
★★★

THIRD SPEAKER: . . . Well, I said I was no good at it and I told
her not to include me but she insisted and
said I was 'just being modest'. So I had no
choice — well, I could have refused in *theory*,
but I didn't want to let everyone down and
she said it was too late to find anyone else.
So I called off my other arrangements and
got all the stuff you're supposed to have and
got the bus all the way out there, and there I
was all ready to go with all my things and just
as it was about to start the heavens opened!
Yes! So everyone took shelter and waited for
it to stop, but it just got worse and worse.
Anyway, after an hour or so of this, the
ground was just . . . well, you can imagine, so
they called it off and we all went to have a
drink, which was fun, seeing everyone again
after all that time. Still, I was a bit upset
because she told me they wouldn't be
needing me next time, and I'd taken the
trouble to get all the stuff, not to mention
the cost of it all, and now it looks as if I'm
never going to have a chance to use it.
★★★

FOURTH SPEAKER: No, no. There's absolutely no truth in the
rumour, none whatsoever. I've been assured
by my staff, that every possible precaution is
routinely taken and nothing like this could
possibly have happened. The odds against it
happening are literally thousands to one. So
well you see it couldn't have happened.
However, to set the public's mind to rest, the
whole area is to be closed to visitors for a
period of ten days while tests are made, I
m…thorough scientific tests by our own
team of experts. But, as I said, there's
absolutely no danger to the public at this
moment in time. Nor is there any likelihood
in the future of any . . .
★★★

FIFTH SPEAKER: . . . no, no, no, I don't think s…no, you
shouldn't. Look, I know there are lots of
them but…but it's wrong. Now, what if
everybody did it, there'd be none left, would
there? And…and…y…you've got so many of
them. It must have taken you ages . . . Look,
no, stop…stop please, you can't put them
back, not when… no, you can't put them
back now. Look…it…it's just not possible.
Please don't give them to me, I don't want
them. Look, the important thing is that you
don't do it again. They're…they're here for
everybody to enjoy, you see? I mean, how

would you like it if someone came into your garden and started taking yours? Quite honestly, you're a very, very . . . Oh, no, please, sorry, look don't get upset. I didn't . . .didn't mean to . . . Please don't. Look, I'm sorry, I didn't mean . . .

B **1** Suggested answers:

FIRST SPEAKER:	irritable, short-tempered, excitable
SECOND SPEAKER:	diffident, nervous, introverted
THIRD SPEAKER:	reasonable, pleasant
FOURTH SPEAKER:	self-important, assertive – or possibly: shifty, deceitful, corrupt, untrustworthy?
FIFTH SPEAKER:	officious, interfering, bossy

2 Describe each person softly to yourself (or under your breath). Maybe record yourself on a blank cassette or voice recorder. Here are some phrases you can use:

It seems to me that . . .
I'd say that . . .
This person sounded as if . . .
I wasn't sure whether this person was . . . or . . .

C 🖉 This exercise gives you more practice in reporting (see **3.2**). If possible, ask another person to read and mark your work.

Model reports:

> FIRST SPEAKER:
> She accused her husband of not tidying up the flat and reminded him that she didn't have time to do it herself. She suddenly realised that she had to leave to collect the children from school, but that didn't prevent her from warning him that he should mend his ways.
>
> SECOND SPEAKER:
> He had started talking to someone he thought was a well-known actress. When he realised he was mistaken he apologised, but he continued trying to make conversation with her. She ignored him and left him still talking.
>
> THIRD SPEAKER:
> She said she was upset because she had cancelled other arrangements and bought a lot of equipment in order to take part in a match of some kind. When the match was called off she was left with all the equipment, unused, and no prospect of being able to use it in the future. She had enjoyed meeting her friends again, though.
>
> FOURTH SPEAKER:
> He denied that there was any risk to the public, claiming that such an accident couldn't have arisen. However, he announced that the area would be closed to the public for the time being.
>
> FIFTH SPEAKER:
> The woman saw a little girl picking flowers and told her to stop. When she told the child not to do it again the girl started crying, which disconcerted the woman.

3.5 **Using inversion for emphasis**
ADVANCED GRAMMAR

A **1 & 2** The emphatic phrases are <u>underlined</u>:

1 <u>At no</u> level of society do women have equal rights with men.
 – *Emphasis on the word 'no' makes the sentence stand out and seem more dramatic.*
 Women do not have equal rights with men at any level of society.
 – *Straightforward and unemphatic, unless read aloud like this:*
 Women do not have equal rights with men at ANY level of society.

2 It occurred to me later that I had made a big mistake.
 – *Normal straightforward word order with the emphasis, as written, on the last phrase.*
 <u>Not until later did</u> it occur to me that I had made a big mistake.
 – *Emphasis on the time and the delayed reaction to what had happened.*

3 <u>At the top of the hill</u> stood a solitary pine tree.
 – *By saving up the pine tree to the end, suspense is created. By changing the word order from what is 'normal', both parts of the sentence are emphasised.*
 A solitary pine tree stood at the top of the hill.
 – *This is the 'normal' straightforward word order.*

4 <u>So lonely did</u> he feel that he went round to see his ex-wife for a chat.
 – *Emphasis on the depth of his loneliness.*
 He felt so lonely that he went round to see his ex-wife for a chat.
 – *As written, no particular emphasis, but when speaking this sentence we could give the same emphasis as the first sentence by means of stress:*
 He felt SO LONELY that he went . . .

5 <u>Little did they know</u> that the sheriff was about to draw his revolver.
 – *Emphasis on their unawareness, more dramatic than the second sentence.*
 They didn't know that the sheriff was about to draw his revolver.
 – *Unemphatic, matter-of-fact narrative.*

6 <u>Bang</u> went the door. <u>In</u> came Fred. <u>On</u> went all the lights. <u>Out</u> went the cat.
 – *The repeatedly 'unusual' word order makes this line more dramatic. However, this is rather overdone here and something like this might be preferable:*
 The door went bang as Fred came in. On went all the lights and out went the cat like a rocket.
 The door went bang. Fred came in. All the lights went on. The cat ran out.
 – *The sentences seem too short in this line, and it sounds rather lifeless.*

7 <u>Rarely are</u> shy people taken as seriously as assertive people.
 – *Emphasis on 'rarely'. This sentence sounds very formal or literary, and might sound pompous if spoken rather than written.*
 Shy people are rarely taken as seriously as assertive people.
 – *Straightforward and informal style.*

Note

There are no inverted verbs in 5 and 6, but there is a change in word order, with the subject coming after the verb. There are restrictions on the use of inversion, as these 'counter-examples' show:

*Bang went it.   *In came he.   *On went they.
*Out ran it.   *Out went we.   *Down came it.
*Up they put their umbrellas.   *Back went we.
*Out I threw them.

B   Suggested answers:

1 Little **did she/anyone realise** that she would win the competition.
2 Not only **does she play** the piano brilliantly but she **sings well/is an accomplished violinist** too.
3 Never in my life **have/had I been** so humiliated!
4 No sooner **had I got into the bath** than the phone **started ringing**.
5 Under no circumstances **should/must** the fire doors **be locked/blocked**.
6 Not until **everyone had** finished **were the rest of us** allowed to leave the room. (*many variations possible*)
7 Only after **a long search/chase were** the police able to catch the thieves.
8 Not once during her entire **life has she been** in trouble with the law.
9 Not only **is he** rather naive but he **also seems to be** very sensitive.
10 No sooner **had we started** our picnic than **it started to rain**. (*many variations possible*)

C   Suggested Answers:

2 Off drove the thieves with the police in hot pursuit.
3 Up went the umbrellas. Home we went, wet through.
4 Sitting beside her in the train was a tall dark stranger.
5 Lying under the table was a fat tabby cat, washing itself obliviously.
6 The edge of the cliff gave way and down she fell.
7 Behind the wall was a ferocious dog barking furiously.
8 Only /Not until then did I realise that I had made the biggest mistake of my life.

3.6 Long road to Utopia
READING AND SPEAKING

A   This is similar to Part 3 of the Reading Paper.

Answers:

1 D	2 A	3 F	4 B	5 C	6 E

B   Decide how you would answer these questions, and say your answers softly to yourself (or under your breath). Maybe record yourself on a blank cassette or voice recorder.

3.7 Opposites
VOCABULARY DEVELOPMENT

A   Answers:

1 sophisticated/worldly/crafty   2 cowardly/timid
3 unrepentant/unapologetic
4 accelerated/speeded up   5 innocent
6 hindered me/got in the way/obstructed me
7 saved it/put it by   8 pushed it closed/pushed it to
9 made me more worried/upset me
10 stayed calm/kept his cool   11 synonym
12 closed it quietly

B   **1**   Answers:

inadvisable inappropriate unaware unbearable
unclearly incompetent inconsiderate
inconsistent inconspicuous unconventional
unconvincing undecided indecisive undesirable
undignified indiscreet indistinct inefficient
uneventful unexpected inexplicable unfaithful
unforeseen unforgettable infrequent ungrateful
ingratitude unimaginative unmanageable
unpredictable unrewarding insincere insinceritiy
unsociable unsophisticated instability unstable
insufficient intolerant untrustworthy invisible
unwanted unwelcome

2   Answers:

disagreeable disapprove disarm disconnect
discontented disentangle illegible illegitimate
illogical disloyal immature disorganised
impatient impersonal impossible irrational
irregular irrelevant disrespectful irresponsible
dissatisfied dissimilar

3   Suggested answers:

clumsy · *careful*   fearless · *fearful/cowardly*
neat · *untidy/messy*   noisy · *quiet*
proud · *humble/modest*   rare · *common*
restless · *calm*   tactful · *tactless*
talkative · *quiet/taciturn*   trivial · *significant/serious*

C   Answers:

conceited · *modest*   deceitful · *truthful/trustworthy/open/frank*   fussy · *easy-going/laid back*   lazy · *hard-working*   malicious · *kindhearted*   mean · *generous/kindhearted*   narrow-minded · *liberal*
neurotic · *nonchalant*   pretentious · *unassuming*
secretive · *open/frank*   solitary · *sociable/gregarious*
sullen · *cheerful*   touchy · *easy-going*

(*imaginative*, *perceptive* and *talkative* aren't opposites of any words listed)

3.8 Not waving . . .
READING

 1 🔊 The two poems are recorded on the cassette (1 minute).

2 The answers given here are suggestions — your interpretation may differ slightly or considerably.

Suggested answers:

1 He drowned, presumably
2 *'I was much further out than you thought and not waving but drowning.'*
'Oh, no no no, it was too cold always, I was much too far out all my life and not waving but drowning.'
3 *'Poor chap, he always loved larking and now he's dead – it must have been too cold for him.*
His heart gave way.'
4 Having fun, playing pranks
5 line 7: the water
line 9: life
6 line 11: out of control, in despair
line 12: unable to cope
7 Not having fun, enjoying himself
8 the man: *lonely unappreciated unhappy solitary unnoticed doomed unlucky desperate sad sorrowful glum pessimistic*
the friends: *unappreciative uncaring laconic unmoved uninterested*

1 She is ambivalent: she wants a male friend but she is exasperated with men in general
2 They make it clear they are single, available and looking for a partner by making opening remarks and being friendly to her
3 She seems to be worried that time is running out: she may be 'left on the shelf'
4 Once you're committed to a relationship, breaking it off causes heartbreak
5 She's afraid she won't get another chance of finding a partner
6 All the other men she meets who aren't single, available or suitable as partners
7 *year · appear   ride · decide   gaze · days*
The rhyming adds humour to an otherwise pessimistic story
8 the poet: *lonely desperate witty humorous modest self-deprecating*
the men: *unreliable exasperating unpredictable attractive annoying desirable scarce*

B Decide how you would answer these questions, and say your answers softly to yourself (or under your breath). Maybe record yourself on a blank cassette or voice recorder.

3.9 It takes all sorts . . .
SPEAKING AND COMPOSITION

A **1** Suggested adjectives:

sympathetic, considerate, warm-hearted, intelligent, sensible, artistic

elderly, experienced, severe, sceptical, shrewd

sociable, sensitive, kind-hearted, blonde, stylish

solemn, serious, suspicious, miserable, shy, critical, reserved

funny, grey-haired, flamboyant, extrovert, energetic, lively, confident

amusing, humorous, affable, enthusiastic, genial, bald

dark-haired, youthful, charming, practical, unpretentious

sensitive, quiet, thoughtful, perceptive, modest, compassionate

2 Describe each person softly to yourself (or under your breath). Maybe record yourself on a blank cassette or voice recorder.

Clothes:	dress, blouse, suit, flowery shirt, t-shirt, sweater, tie, hat
Age:	middle-aged, thirty-ish, in his/her sixties, in his/her early twenties
Face:	oval, round, dark-skinned, black, pale, suntanned, wearing glasses, clean-shaven, with a moustache, wrinkled, laugh lines
Hair:	curly, frizzy, straight, pulled back

B **1–5** If possible, ask another person to read and mark your work.

Model version:

Dear Max,

I've written to Betty and Charlie to let them know when to expect you. They're both looking forward to seeing you and they've both offered to put you up for a few days. Just to prepare you, let me tell you something about them.

First of all: Betty. She's a single woman in her early forties and is passionate about music — she's a music teacher. Don't be deceived by her casual clothes into thinking she's easy-going — you should be aware that she is a tidiness fanatic. Everything in her flat has to be in exactly the right place and she's always cleaning. So make sure that you keep the guest room as tidy as possible and make your bed every morning. She has a quick temper, but she doesn't usually get cross with guests, only with her close friends! She's been a good friend of mine for a long time and you'll like her because she loves sitting up late at night talking about the world and telling funny stories. She has three cats, so try to be nice to them even if you aren't a cat-lover.

She'll meet you at the station, and you'll be able to recognise her because she's unusually tall and slim and has very curly red hair. She'll be tallest redhead at the station!

Charlie is a couple of years older than you and works for a firm of accountants. If he meets you on a weekday at the station, he'll be wearing a dark suit and he'll look like a typical businessman — but with no hair. He shaves his head and wears glasses, so look out for a skinhead businessman! (He's quite sensitive about losing his hair, so don't make any jokes about baldness!)

He has a small flat in the city centre, which he shares with a large black dog called Bruno, who looks very fierce but is actually a pussy-cat! If you offer to take him for walks while you're there, you'll be in Charlie's good books. There's a guest room which you'll be able to use for as long as you like. Charlie is pretty busy during the week but he and Bruno usually spend the weekend with friends in the country and he'll invite you to join them. They are a crazy bunch but really nice, so don't turn down this invitation!

Have a really good time and give Betty and Charlie all my love.
Send me a postcard!

Love,
Anna

P.S. Remember to phone them so they know when exactly you'll be arriving.

---

4 | Let's talk

Communication   Languages   Accents and dialects

4.1 Different ways of communicating

TOPIC VOCABULARY

A Decide how you would answer these questions, and say your answers softly to yourself (or under your breath). Maybe record yourself on a blank cassette or voice recorder.

Suggested answers:

He looks dangerous – intimidating and threatening.
> Now look here, if you do that again you're going to regret it.
> – Don't talk to me like that!
or – I think you're overreacting.

She looks delighted and triumphant – very pleased with herself.
> I've done it! I've passed!
> – Congratulations! Well done! I knew you'd do well.

He looks downhearted and depressed, very much down in the dumps.
> Oh God, I don't know what I'm going to do.
> – Cheer up! It's not as bad as all that. Try to look on the bright side.

B Answers:

2 mumbling   muttering   whispering
3 jot   note   scribble
4 glance at   scan   skim
5 chuckling   grinning   sniggering
6 frown   scowl   sneer
7 scream   shriek   yell
8 imply   intimate   suggest
9 expression   phrase   idiom
10 attitude   expression   tone

4.2 Meanings and translations

LISTENING AND SPEAKING

A **1** Some reasons why one might be tempted to buy the product:

It fits easily into your pocket or bag
It translates between six languages
It might be a good substitute for a dictionary
You can hear words spoken, not just see them printed

2 Answers:

1 at the airport ✗   at the chemist's ✓   at the railway station ✗   at the bank ✗   business ✓   camping ✗   complaining ✓   emergencies ✓   in the post office ✗   making friends ✓   motoring ✓   restaurants ✓   shopping ✓   sightseeing ✓
2 Spanish, German, English, French, Italian
3 'How much does it cost to get in?'
  'Please call the fire brigade.'
  'Is that your best price?'
  'We are still waiting to be served.'
4 'I have lost my voice.'
5 personal earphone (and the screen)
6 screen

TRANSCRIPT *6 minutes 15 seconds*

(The Voice was recorded from a real product: its intonation and stress patterns are sometimes rather eccentric!)

PRESENTER: As many of us who take our two weeks' holiday abroad will know, communication in a foreign language is often very difficult. Well, now there's a new gadget on the market for the tourist or businessperson, which can help to communicate in five different languages. It's called The Interpreter and it 'speaks' those languages. All you do is press the right buttons to find a word or phrase in, say, Spanish and it'll say aloud the same word or phrase in English and, if you prefer, German, French or Italian. Sarah Watts has been trying it out for us.

SARAH: The Interpreter has quite a wide vocabulary: over 13,000 words. It can say them all aloud and it can say them in phrases too. This means that all you have to do is press a button and either imitate what it says or just let The Interpreter speak to people on your behalf.

VOICE: *Hello.*

SARAH: Oh, hello, how are you?

VOICE: *I'm fine thank you.*

SARAH: (*fast*) Good. Now there are many situations that a traveller, whether he or she is on business or travelling for pleasure, may find themselves . . .

VOICE: *Excuse me.*

SARAH: Yes?

VOICE: *Please speak more slowly. I do not understand. I'm sorry.*

SARAH: Oh dear. I'm sorry too. (*as herself again*) Well, let's take for example the situation of someone alone in a foreign city, wanting to strike up an acquaintance with someone in a bar, for example. Let's see what opening gambits The Interpreter can suggest.

VOICE: *I am on holiday here.*

SARAH: (*responding*) Oh really?

VOICE: *Are you alone?*

SARAH: Yes . . .

VOICE: *Would you like a drink?*

SARAH: Thanks, I'll have an orange juice please.

VOICE: *Do you mind if I smoke?*

SARAH: No, go ahead.

VOICE: *What is your name?*

SARAH: Sarah. What's yours?

VOICE: *My name is . . .*

SARAH: (*as herself again*) But then the conversation might start to get rather more personal —

VOICE: *Are you married? Do you have any children? Are you busy tomorrow? Would you like to come out with me?*

SARAH: (*responding*) Er...
VOICE: *Please.*
SARAH: No thanks. But, perhaps if you have a free afternoon you would like to do some sightseeing?
VOICE: *What is there to see here?*
SARAH: Oh lots of things. There's a wonderful art gallery, and . . .
VOICE: *How much does it cost to get in? Is there a guided tour? How long does the tour take? Is there a reduction for children?*
SARAH: (*as herself again*) So much for culture. Of course the Interpreter's repertoire of phrases covers all eventualities, such as emergencies:
VOICE: *Please help me. I have been robbed. Get the police. Where is the nearest hospital? My child is missing. Please call the fire brigade.*
SARAH: Very polite! And shopping. Let's suppose you want to buy something unusual . . .
VOICE: *Where can I buy a bed?*
SARAH: Yes, that is unusual. Anyway, you go to a store and ask the assistant:
VOICE: *Have you got a bed? Show me a bed.*
SARAH: Or you might ask, rather more politely:
VOICE: *I would like a bed. I would like to see a bed. Which bed do you recommend?*
SARAH: So you select a particularly nice bed. And it might be worth checking if you can get a discount:
VOICE: *Is that your best price?*
SARAH: There's no discount, but you still want to make your purchase:
VOICE: *Can I buy this please? Do you take credit cards? May I have a receipt?*
SARAH: So your brand new bed is delivered to your . . . hotel? — no, you must have an apartment you want to furnish — But, oh dear, when you unwrap it:
VOICE: *The bed is broken.*
SARAH: So you go back to the store and say:
VOICE: *Can I exchange this bed?*
SARAH: This leads us on to the topic of Complaints. Let's suppose you're in a restaurant where the service is rather slow:
VOICE: *We are still waiting to be served.*
SARAH: And after your meal:
VOICE: *May I have the bill please? Is service included?*
SARAH: You examine the bill:
VOICE: *I think you have made a mistake. You have overcharged me. I want to see the manager.*
SARAH: So, there we are, the Interpreter covers a wide range of social situations, as well as business situations:
VOICE: *I am here on business. Where can I get some photocopying done? Can I send a fax from here?*
SARAH: And motoring:
VOICE: *My car won't start. Can you repair the car? I have run out of petrol. Where is the nearest petrol station? I have a flat tyre. Can you tow me to a garage?*
SARAH: And, finally, at the chemist's:
VOICE: *Have you anything for insect bites? Have you anything for sunburn? I want something for a headache. I want something for toothache. I have a cough.*
SARAH: Another useful one, which is not in the Interpreter's repertoire might be: (*hoarsely*) "I have lost my voice", perhaps!
The Interpreter comes with a personal earphone, and all the phrases appear on the screen as they are spoken, which is a great help in learning them and means that you can use it in complete privacy, without any of the people around you being able to hear it.
VOICE: *Excuse me.*
SARAH: (*responding*) Yes?
VOICE: *Is it safe for children?*
SARAH: Oh, yes I think so. And you can use it anytime you want to.
VOICE: *I am free tomorrow morning.*
SARAH: Oh good. Thank you for your help, by the way.
VOICE: *You're welcome.*

B Say your answers softly to yourself. Maybe record yourself.

C This activity can only be done with a partner, or preferably with two partners. If this isn't possible, look at the three Activities and decide for yourself which dictionary seems to be the most helpful and clear.

4.3 Attitudes to language
READING AND SUMMARY-WRITING

A Say your answers softly to yourself. Maybe record yourself.

B This exercise is similar to Part 1 of the Use of English Paper.

Answers:

1 A	2 A	3 D	4 B	5 A	6 D	7 C	8 B

C This exercise is rather similar to Part 2 of the Reading Paper.

Answers:

1 C	2 C	3 D	4 C	5 D

D **Answers:**

¶ 1 *objective* = impartial   *prejudice* = bias
instructive = revealing
¶ 2 *exhilarating* = stimulating   *euphoria* = happiness
mitigated = moderated
¶ 3 *associations* = connotations   *formulate* = devise
aesthetic = artistic   *pet* = favourite
¶ 4 *derisive* = contemptuous   *badge* = emblem
intrinsic = inherent   *the men* = workers
excite = arouse

E This discussion can only be done with a partner.

F This is similar to the kind of summary task that you will have to do in Part 5 of the Use of English Paper. The best way to approach this task is as follows:

1 First pick out the main points in the two halves of the text.
2 Make brief notes, attempting to rephrase some of the ideas in your own words.
3 Write your summary.
4 If possible, ask another person to read and mark your work.

Model summary:

> Prejudices in favour of or against regional, rural or city accents or individual words reflect the standpoint of the listener and have no absolute validity; that is to say that 'pretty' or 'ugly' or 'admirable' in relation to a Birmingham or Dorset accent, for example, are words which only say something about the listener's background and attitude. The idea that the 'Queen's English' means wealth, position and education is also based on this subjective view and merely reflects the historical connection of a local dialect, East Midland English, with the location of Oxford, Cambridge and London.

4.4 **–ing and to . . .**
GRAMMAR REVISION

A Continuations in bold print — meanings below *in italics:*

2 **a** We stopped to take photos but . . . **the light wasn't bright enough, so we went on walking.**
 – *We were walking along and then stopped in order to take photos*

 b We stopped taking photos but . . . **we went on watching what was going on.**
 – *We were taking photos and then we stopped taking them*

3 **a** Did you remember to send the fax or . . . **did you forget to send it?**
 – *You were supposed to do it: did you in fact do it?*

 b Do you remember sending the fax or . . . **have you forgotten all about it now?**
 – *Just think back for a moment: can you remember whether you did it or not?*

4 **a** I can't help you to feel better but . . . **I can sit by the bed to keep you company.**
 – *I'm unable to assist you*

 b I can't help feeling better, but . . . **I realise I ought to stay in bed today.**
 – *I'm unable to stop myself from feeling better*

5 **a** I'm not used to using a fountain pen but . . . **I'll try not to make a mess with it.**
 – *I'm not accustomed to using one*

 b I used to use a fountain pen but . . . **now I use a computer all the time.**
 – *I once used a fountain pen, but not now*

6 **a** She heard him scream, but . . . **she didn't take any notice.**
 – *He screamed once*

 b She heard him screaming, but . . . **there was nothing she could do to help.**
 – *He screamed repeatedly*

B **1** Collocations:

to call	– someone on the phone
to contact	– someone by phone / by post
to drop	– someone a line
to get	– through to someone on the phone
to give	– someone a ring
to keep	– in touch with someone
to reply	– to a letter
to tell	– someone a story
to write	– someone a letter

2 Suggested answers:

2 in contacting them
3 telling telling/giving it away to
4 to send them
5 tell the story
6 to reply to
7 keeping in touch with people/calling people
8 in getting through to her
9 giving me
10 to phone you
11 to leave a message on
12 to writing

C Suggested answers:

1 taking a taxi/going by underground if you've got a lot of luggage
2 to go there some day
3 taking any exercise/doing anything strenuous
4 staying up late/going out for the evening/staying up all night
5 trying to read the book
6 listening to listen to Mozart/listening to jazz
7 reading the book till I got to the end
8 walking in the hope that it might stop
9 working having a good rest/going out tonight
10 crying/screaming to listen/to stand by and do nothing
11 doing some extra homework/committing so much time to it
12 being/feeling to feel much better/to recover
13 to get through/to make contact again
14 to buy/to have to buy one
15 not to hear/to be deaf

4.5 **Paragraphs**
WRITING SKILLS

A Read the points through carefully.

B Say your answers softly to yourself. Maybe record yourself.

C **1** Read the analysis of paragraphs 1 to 6 first.

2 Suggested answers:

7 A different example is going to be given
8 A general point is now going to be made, after the example
9 A solution to the problem is going to be suggested
10 A new character or point of view is introduced, who works for one of the companies
11 Now other companies are going to be mentioned
12 Now here's an example of one of those companies
13 Another new character or point of view is introduced
14 Another new point of view is coming up
15 The final points are coming (though this is still part of the previous character's quote) – the new paragraph gives them prominence

D These were the breaks in the original article:

Mike Platt, commercial director of the business travel agency Hogg Robinson BTI, says: 'Our research among clients shows that they are increasingly using the train as an extension of the office, but they have two main concerns: one is the lack of privacy; the other is the poor signal they often get on their phone on the train.'

 Platt says he regards the ability to work for three hours as the second key advantage Eurostar has over the plane – the first being the ability to travel directly between city centres. Many companies take the opportunity to hold formal business meetings on Eurostar, calculating that if they book facing seats over a table, they can get away without their conversation being heard.

But he adds: 'People are split down the middle about mobile phones. Half want to use them, and the other half regard them as noise pollution and say that they can't do their own work if they are next to somebody who is barking down the phone.'

Last week saw the publication of yet another survey demonstrating that the British work longer hours than their European compatriots. Many of us clearly regard a train journey as an opportunity to do more work, rather than to relax and enjoy the journey. Maybe it is time we all let the train take the strain.

Extra activity

Look back at previous reading passages and count how many paragraphs there are in each of them:

Tinkling the ivories, jangling the nerves in 1.3 has 17
Hingis beaten by girl wonder from down under in 1.6 has 16
The ladies' man in 1.6 has 11
Eight Feet in the Andes in 2.1 has 13
Outlook Unsettled in 2.4 has 4
The great escape in 3.1 has 30
Attitudes to language in 4.3 has 4 paragraphs – each over 200 words long

In each case, why are there so many (or so few)? What is the effect of this?

Paragraphs in news articles tend to be very short, compared with books, perhaps because the typical reader's attention span is shorter. Also if there are longish quotes from people, each quote is usually a separate paragraph.

In the exam, where you have to squeeze a lot of different ideas into about 350 words, short paragraphs also seem better than long ones filled with complex sentences.

4.6 Wh- clauses
ADVANCED GRAMMAR

A **1** This is how each idea can be rephrased UNemphatically:

Intolerance annoys me.
I need a friend to lend a helping hand.
She always seems to succeed.
He may not get here in time, but it doesn't matter.

2 Suggested continuations:

2 One thing I like is **sitting at home with my feet up**.
3 All I want is **something cool and refreshing to drink**.
4 What I feel like doing **now is having a rest**.
5 What we need now **is an expert's advice**.
6 There's nothing I enjoy more than **going for a long walk in the country**.
7 I just don't want **to upset him by raising the subject of work**.
8 Something that often surprises me is **the way some people find it hard to learn a foreign language**.
9 What I want to do right now is **have lunch**.

3 Suggested answers:

2 I really do like sitting at home with my feet up.
3 What I want to drink is something cool and refreshing.
4 All I want to do now is have a rest.
5 All we need now is an expert's advice.
6 I really enjoy going for a long walk in the country.

7 What I don't want to do is to upset him by raising the subject of work.
8 The way some people find it hard to learn a foreign language is very surprising.
9 The only thing I want to do now is to have lunch.

B Matched sentences:

2 Say what you like. = Say whatever you want to.
Talk to anyone you want to. = Speak to whoever you want.
3 Whoever did you give it to? = Who in the world did you give it to?
To whom* did you give it? = Who did you give it to?
4 Why ever don't you phone him? = Why on earth don't you phone him?
Why don't you ever phone him? = Why do you never phone him?
5 All the sentences in 5 mean the same as each other!

* *To whom . . . ?* in 3 would sound very old-fashioned in present-day English.

C Answers:

1 Wherever **he goes, he takes a phrasebook with him.**
2 You can **arrive whenever you like.**
3 All **I did was stick out my tongue at her.**
4 What **you did was very rude.**
5 All **she needs is someone to tell her troubles to.**
6 I don't mind **where you put it.**
7 Whether **you write or phone doesn't really matter/ is immaterial.**
8 Whenever **you arrive, get in touch.**
9 What **he said made a big impression on me/ everyone.**
10 What **astonished me was her confidence.**

4.7 The English-speaking world
SPEAKING, LISTENING AND COMPOSITION

A Suggested answers (there are many possible examples besides the ones given here):

1 star leader butter
2 fat happy catch
3 hard dark drama
4 not · nought nod · gnawed sod · sawed tot · taught
5 shirt form term
6 hot want soft · grass laugh palm kitten bitter utterly attitude pass glance castle laughter

B 🔊 Answers:

1 AUS	2 USA	3 W	4 W	5 AUS	6 W
7 AUS	8 USA				

TRANSCRIPT *8 minutes   20 seconds*

BILL: Well what do you think accents...the...the...our own accents can tell us about...er...the differences in the social class and education of...er...er...where we are?

RUTH: I was brought up in a kind of a well-to-do South Wales town. Um...and...er...there certainly were judgements made on people, that they...if they had a very...a strong Valleys accent, I mean, it's wrong but that's...that is the case, yeah.

SARAH: It happens, yeah. And what about education, were you taught better grammar in school then, or is that just . . . ?

RUTH: Well, you know, you hear...sometimes you hear someone say...um...like a classic way to talk i...in the Valleys would be, 'I do go down to town on a Tuesday and I do buy my bread.' Well, now that's not correct English, is it?

BILL: That's not grammatically correct.

SARAH: No. I mean, in Australia you...you...we don't have accents as such like over here. I couldn't believe it when I came to Europe and this diversity of accents from moving one mile to the next. You either have one or the other, so you can't have a class system, because you don't know where people are from. Which I really like 'cause you again can't judge, like if I brought a boy home, my mum couldn't go, 'Ooh, he's not from a nice part of town!' you know, 'Don't go out with him!'

BILL: Well, I think i...it's interesting in America because, like Australia, we don't have the class thing so much, but we certainly have, in America a lot of different regional accents, I mean you've heard them in...in...on...in the movies and on television. But I think...er...this may be a silly generalisation, but I think, so far as I can tell, there is not a kind of value judgement that is levelled against the way people talk *per se*, it more depends on what they say.

SARAH: I mean, is there different accents from region to region?

BILL: Oh yeah. Sure. I mean, you...you...you've also heard...er...the New England accent, er...the Massachusetts accent of...er...J.F.K. remember, you heard the...you've heard the recordings of him, even though you weren't old enough to hear him yourself. And...er...real South, the Carolinas, and...and Georgia and that area, that kinda open...er...very soft Southern accent they have down there. And then there's the Mid-West, the kind of...er...I suppose the boring kind of long, nasal accent. And then there's New York and then there's West Coast where I come from. There's...I can't actually tell a lot of difference between Mid...Mid-West and my area of the West Coast, but there are lots of different ones.

RUTH: Yeah, it's interesting because, like, in Wales, it's a really tiny country, but there are such vast differences in accents, within kind of like miles, you know, apart.

SARAH: Yeah, and Australia's the same size as America and we've got two.

RUTH: Yeah, it's...it's incredible, I mean, it's like...um...in...in Cardiff, which is the capital of Wales, people talk like that and it's quite sort of nasal, you know and they says 'I go down the Arms Park, with my father and I has half a dark'. And then if you go, kind of just about ten miles away up to the Valleys, you've got, you know, people talking like that — oh I can't do it now, haha — 'I go down there...er...my...er...I've got a friend, you know, she says...um...I don't know, I...I'm finding it very difficult I am, you know'. And it's all...um...and then you go up to North Wales, which is...um...very 'sort of like that, you know, it's quite spiky, and...er...quite sort of...er...quite a difficult accent to understand'.

BILL: Well, this is very funny, that obviously there are certain areas that are funnier to listen to than others, now do people find them funnier? Inside Wales do they laugh at other people's accent?

RUTH: Defin...there's a...there is a North-South divide in Wales, I think, and it, you know, of course, we've got the added complication of the Welsh language, whereby people sort of in the North maybe will judge people in the South because the Southerners don't tend to speak Welsh as much as in the North or in the West...um...so they will, kind of, I've been called a half...a half Taff.

SARAH: See, it's the class system again, isn't it!

BILL: It is, yes.

RUTH: The Taff is the river that runs through . . .

SARAH: Like it's a bad thing.

BILL: Yeah.

SARAH: You know, it's amazing.

RUTH: But it's...it is. And then, you know, and we'll say, oh...um...there's a term in...in South Wales that refers to Welsh speakers as the 'Sharads'. *Sharad* is 'to speak' in Welsh. 'Oh yeah, he's a real Sharad, he's a real Welsh speaker.'

BILL: You mean he's pretentious about his speaking Welsh?

RUTH: Yeah, exactly.

SARAH: But do you know it's amazing, it's like when you...when I...when I first came over here, you sort of...you'd be scared of saying where people are from because you didn't want to insult them, because people take so much offence if you say they're wrong, you know, if you say they're from Bolton and they're from, you know, Denby, you know, 'Oooh!' You know, but, you can't tell that with Australia, and it's...a lot of people get confused between the New Zealand and Australian, I mean, I can't tell the difference between a Canadian and an American. Is there a difference?

BILL: Well, there is a slight difference, but you really have to be...you have to know the difference, I mean, Canadians...er...there's an 'ou' sound, when they say 'out', Americans say 'out' and the Canadians it's 'out', it's shorter, and 'about' and they also say 'Eh?' a lot. 'Eh?'

SARAH: Very, very similar like there's only a few little tiny things between New Zealand and Australia.

BILL: Very tiny little things.

SARAH: Like they say 'fush and chips' and we say 'fish and chips'.

BILL: Yeah, yeah.

SARAH: So it's only the close people that can...like we know the difference, but they don't. No one else do.

BILL: Now do you...do you find that some accents are easier on, and more pleasant on the ear than others?

SARAH: Oh, yeah.

RUTH: What, within Wales?

BILL: Within Wales and, well, and general of course as well.

RUTH: The...er...within...um...I...there is the classic Richard Burton, Port Talbot and Anthony Hopkins Welsh, which is beautiful . . .

SARAH: Which is lyrical isn't it?

RUTH: You know, and I would just...I would love to have that accent.

SARAH: But it's the same with American, isn't it? I mean, some of them, like you know, the Texas is sort of kind of cute to listen to, like everyone always says, 'Ooh, I'd love a Texas, you know, farmer guy!' As opposed to the New York, which is really crisp and sharp.

BILL: Yeah, yeah. When New York sounds like very nasal . . .

RUTH: Oh, but I love the New York!

SARAH: Yeah.

BILL: . . . and Texas is all very kind of round and slow everybody is different down there.

RUTH: But we went to New York last September and we just used to sit and listen. I mean, it was just fantastic listening to it.

SARAH: But the New York, it is a harsh, particularly the people, you know, the ones that are now native that are bringing accents in, that's what you find in Australia, there's actually only two accents, you've got the city accent and you've got the Outback, the Crocodile [Dundee]. Like, you know, 'G'day, mate!' Really slow, everything's like that. And then you've got the city one. But now, because we're a new country, we're getting so many immigrants, the second generations are now, think they've got an Australian accent, but it's mixed with their parents' accent.

BILL: Right yeah, you've got Greek-Australian, you got, you've got Irish-Australian . . .

★★★

SARAH: . . . and we realise we're all immigrants and you're pretty stupid if you start teasing someone else because you think, 'Well, where are you from originally?' It's only the Aboriginals who can really claim that they were there.

BILL: They were the originals.

RUTH: Do you think that...um...attitudes have...have changed towards accents over the years in the sense that, you know, were children encouraged when they were younger to lose their accents?

SARAH: I think the immigrants were and now they realise they don't have to, they're Australians and Australian is about being a multi-cultural society.

RUTH: Right. Yeah.

SARAH: But, yeah, I know my...I've got one very good friend who is Italian, and she used to get really teased because she sort of emphasised words differently and she really used to try but now she doesn't care.

RUTH: Doesn't care. I remember when I was growing up and I remember we had to...we were learning to sing...we were singing *Away in a Manger*, the Christmas carol, and I remember my teacher Mrs Sparks got really cross with us because we were singing...um...'Bless all the de-ar children' and it...and she used to say, 'It's not de-ar, it's dear' and we'd all be going 'Bless all the dear children' and it...and it was like, in some ways, if you had a strong accent it was discouraged, you know it was thought of as being common, whereas you know, now, it...if you...especially if you look at, you know, in broadcasting and things like that you get all sorts of accents from all over the country are encouraged.

SARAH: Yeah, well, what do you think of the Bri...you know when you hear a British P...you know, RP accent? I mean, I know if they came to Australia we'd go like 'Oooh, the Queen!' you know, we'd tease them. Is it the same in Wales, do you...are they looked upon as being . . .

BILL: Posh.

SARAH: . . . superior or posh?

RUTH: Yes, I mean, I think so. You'd get a posh Welsh accent, which would be somebody who'd speak sort of like that you know . . .

SARAH: Is that like English . . .?

RUTH: It's not, though, that's not RP.

SARAH: It's still not...it's still not RP.

RUTH: There's a posher version.

BILL: It's an equivalent.

RUTH: Yeah, an equivalent.

BILL: I think America has from the beginning . . . I mean, what Americans...when I was growing up, what people worried about was using incorrect grammar, it wasn't so much the accent you used, it was using, you know, using words that you shouldn't use or 'Don't say "ain't" ' used to be something you'd hear.

RUTH: Oh right, yeah.

BILL: Er...but it...but actually the accent itself, no, I mean, we all...Americans consider they talk with an American accent and there's an end, so there was no conscious . . .

C **1** Say your answers softly to yourself. Maybe record yourself.

2–4 Follow the steps in the Student's Book.

5 🖊 If possible, ask another person to read and mark your work.

Model version:

Throughout the world today there are an estimated 92 million German speakers, 76.5 million of whom live in Germany. The official German language, that is the one used in schools, academic institutions, in government and international dealings and above all in the written language, is called High German (Hochdeutsch) or standard German. This is the official language of Germany, Austria, Liechtenstein and one of the official languages of Switzerland. However there are quite a number of German dialects. These are generally spoken languages only and the people who use them are able to speak both dialect and High German but of course they write only in High German. The ability to function fluently and accurately in both written and spoken High German is vital to get a good job. There are also languages other than German and its dialects, spoken by minorities in certain areas.

There is a major historical language division between Northern and Southern Germany in terms of pronunciation and this is reflected in the dialects in

those areas. Some of the dialects in Germany are the following: East Prussian spoken by migrants from the former East Prussia (now part of Poland) in the Ruhr area; Low German (Plattdeutsch) spoken in parts of North Germany; Fränkisch, Swabian in southern Bavaria, Bavarian, Mecklenburgisch, Badisch (Baden-Wurttemburg), Alemannisch (near Lake Constance), Saxon, the dialect of Berlin etc. In fact nearly every area has its own dialect. Although dialects are undergoing a surge in popularity as people seek their identity in local and regional culture, at the same time they are under threat from the growing influence of the media.

The minority languages are often the results of the redrawing of borders as is the case with the language of the 50,000 Danish speaking people in Schleswig-Holstein. They call their language Frisk. Another minority language is Sorbian spoken by about 30,000 people who live in Brandenburg near the Polish border. Their settlement in Germany goes back to 600 AD when they moved from Poland or Czechoslovakia. Frisian is spoken by people in the north western lowlands of Germany. There are also minority languages spoken by the many refugees and foreign workers in Germany.

4.8 Forming adjectives
VOCABULARY DEVELOPMENT

A Answers (the verbs with two associated adjectives are in **bold print**):

-able	acceptable admirable advisable breakable **describable** **forgivable** obtainable predictable **preventable** recommendable
-ing	astonishing convincing distressing disturbing **forgiving** inspiring overwhelming promising upsetting
-ive	communicative cooperative deceptive **descriptive** informative instructive possessive **preventive** productive

B Answers:

-al	conventional educational **fictional** functional intentional musical personal professional proportional seasonal secretarial sensational
-ic	diplomatic enigmatic idealistic magnetic materialistic optimistic pessimistic realistic romantic
-ous	adventurous ambitious **fictitious** malicious religious spacious
-ly	fortnightly quarterly weekly yearly
-ed	curly-haired experienced long-legged pale-skinned

Notice also these suffixes:

-ed/-n	educated finished unknown satisfied
-ical	alphabetical historical
-ish	childish stylish boyish snobbish
-y	draughty funny airy brainy
-worthy	roadworthy noteworthy newsworthy seaworthy trustworthy

C Answers:

1 poisonous   2 astonished   3 automatic
4 idealised   5 stylish   6 economical
7 heartbroken   8 satisfactory   9 legible
10 childish

(There is more on *–ing* and *-ed/-en* in **5.5 Adjectives & participles**.)

4.9 *make* and *do*
VERBS AND IDIOMS

A Answers:

MAKE: an agreement with someone
          an appointment with someone
          an arrangement
          certain about something
          a comment about something
          an excuse   a good impression
          friends with someone   a lot of money   love
          a mistake   a profit or a loss   progress
          a reservation   sure about something
DO: your best   business with someone
          your duty   someone a favour
          harm to someone   a good turn
          the washing-up   wrong or right
          your own thing

NOTE *make* often refers to creative or productive processes, while *do* often refers to the performance of a service or work

B Answers:

1 manage to see
2 doomed
3 . . . how this concerns you
4 move up to allow me to sit there
5 invented
6 recompense/compensate
7 afford the necessities of life
8 repay you – I am very sorry and I can't compensate you
9 getting things out of proportion
10 have an embarrassing public argument
11 work harder/drive faster to catch up
12 show his good looks/personality well enough

C Answers:

1 made off with
2 done up
3 make up for
4 make up
5 made up
6 doing up
7 done away with
8 making for
9 done out of
10 made off

5
Food and drink   Cooking

Bon appetit!

5.1 To whet your appetite . . .
TOPIC VOCABULARY

In Britain, it's only waiters and waitresses who say 'Enjoy your meal'. Many British people don't say anything at the start of a meal, but some use the French expression: '*Bon appetit!*'

A 1 & 2 Say your answers softly to yourself. Maybe record yourself.

B 1 Suggested answers:

Appetisers/starters	melon salad soup prawn cocktail
Fish/shellfish	oysters mussels lobster prawn shrimp scampi sole swordfish clams octopus squid eel
Poultry	chicken turkey duck goose
Game	venison pheasant wild boar rabbit
Herbs	parsley basil rosemary tarragon bay leaf marjoram oregano dill
Spices	cinnamon nutmeg allspice pepper ginger paprika cloves
Dairy products	cheese yogurt butter cream buttermilk
Nuts	hazelnuts walnuts chestnuts cashews pistachios almonds Brazil nuts pine nuts
Desserts	apple pie chocolate mousse profiteroles rice pudding pancakes trifle fruit sorbet
Cakes and pastries	Christmas cake Victoria sponge Danish pastry almond croissant chocolate éclair blueberry muffin

2 Say your answers softly to yourself. Maybe record yourself. Here are some verbs you can use to talk about preparing and cooking food:

chop slice mix weigh knead beat whip
deep-fry pan-fry stir-fry grill roast steam
parboil sauté microwave bake *etc.*

5.2 Everything all right, sir?
READING AND SPEAKING

A This exercise is similar to Part 1 of the Reading Paper.

Answers:

1 D	2 A	3 C	4 B	5 D	6 C	7 C

B Say your answers softly to yourself. Maybe record yourself.

C 1 🔊 Here are some old 'Waiter, waiter!' jokes. Many of these depend on word-play.

TRANSCRIPT *1 minute*

PRESENTER: Listen to some 'Waiter, waiter!' jokes.
CUSTOMER: Waiter, there's a fly in my soup.
  WAITER: Shh, don't talk too loudly, everyone will want one.
CUSTOMER: Waiter, there's a dead fly in my soup.
  WAITER: It must be the hot liquid that killed it, madam.
CUSTOMER: Waiter, there's a fly in my soup.
  WAITER: Look, there's a spider on the bread, he'll catch it for you.
CUSTOMER: Waiter, what's this fly doing in my soup?
  WAITER: I think it's doing the breast stroke, sir.
CUSTOMER: Waiter, there's a dead fly swimming in my soup.
  WAITER: That's impossible, madam, dead flies can't swim.
CUSTOMER: Waiter, you've got your thumb in my soup.
  WAITER: Don't worry, sir, it's not hot.

2 This activity can only be done with a partner.

5.3 **Running a restaurant**
READING AND SPEAKING

A Say your answers softly to yourself. Maybe record yourself.

B Answers:

1 G	2 E	3 B	4 F	5 C	6 D	7 A

C Say your answers softly to yourself. Maybe record yourself.

5.4 **The passive – 1**
GRAMMAR REVIEW

A Suggested answers:

1 I'm afraid all the cakes have been eaten.
  – *Someone ate them, but I'm not saying who did*
I'm afraid I've eaten all the cakes.
  – *It was me that ate them, I confess*
2 Arsenal beat Chelsea in the final.
  – *We know both of the teams involved, no special emphasis*
Spurs were beaten in the semi-finals.
  – *We only know about the losing team, emphasis on their defeat*
Manchester United were beaten in the quarter-finals by Southampton.
  – *We know about both teams; the information about which side won is given emphasis when it is put at the end of the sentence*
3 He thinks people are plotting against him.
He thinks he's being plotted against.
  – *There is no particular difference in emphasis, but the active sentence seems easier to read*
4 The dough was rolled out and then cut into teddybear shapes.
  – *This seems like a report in impersonal style. The focus is on the action, not on who made it happen*
We rolled out the dough and then we cut it into teddybear shapes.
  – *Here it's us that did the work and it's more informal in style*
5 There was nothing to do.
  – *We were at a loose end, with nothing to occupy us*
There was nothing to be done.
  – *There was no solution to the problem, no remedy for it*

6 My wallet has been stolen!
I've had my wallet stolen!
Someone has stolen my wallet!
  – *These three mean the same: My wallet is missing and I don't know who's responsible*
That man stole my wallet!
  – *I accuse that man of stealing it*

B Comments on the examples in the text, <u>underlined</u> here:

. . . more than 230 steak houses <u>owned by</u> Grand Metropolitan.
– *This emphasises who the owners are: the active alternative* that Grand Metropolitan own *is a bit clumsy*
Nowadays if you don't like what <u>is provided</u> in your meal
– *The active alternative* what the restaurant provides in your meal *has to include the obvious information about who provides the meal*
. . . diners who complain . . . have their bill <u>torn up</u>.
– *The active alternative would take many words to explain:* they don't receive the bill because the manager or another member of the staff tears it up . . .
A poll <u>conducted by</u> Berni
– *Emphasis on who carried out the survey*
. . . the scheme <u>was initiated by</u> a group of Berni managers and tried out in the north of England
– *As the scheme is the subject of both verbs only one sentence is required and it is unnecessary to go into detail about exactly who tried out the scheme*
Other branches of the chain tried out the scheme after a group of Berni managers had initiated . . . *is clumsy*
<u>Armed</u> with this knowledge
– *This can only be used in the passive with this meaning unless we say* I armed myself with this knowledge . . .
Simon Smith, the manager, told me he <u>had been</u> pleasantly <u>pleased</u> at . . .
– *The active alternative would be* The lack of unscrupulous diners had pleasantly pleased him *which sounds awful*
Complaints <u>had</u> generally <u>been justified</u>.
– *There had generally been justification for the complaints would sound very clumsy*
. . . some people who did complain had to <u>be persuaded</u> to leave the bill to him.
– *Focus on the persuasion, not on the manager who did the persuading*

C Many of the original sentences are inelegant and clumsy: the passive rewritten ones are better, and easier to understand.

2 I was told by a friend that you have been awarded a scholarship.
3 Both cars were badly damaged in the crash, but no one was injured.
4 After the bather had been rescued, he was taken to hospital.
5 After he had been operated on, he was told to stay in bed for a week.
6 McDonald's hamburgers are sold all over the world.
7 Liverpool were held to a draw by Everton.
8 The square may be crowded with thousands of demonstrators tonight.

9 The plane was scheduled to land at noon, but it has been delayed.

10 The tennis match was rained off.

11 They were flooded with requests for free samples of the new product.

12 An escaped prisoner has been seen, who is believed to be dangerous.

(See also **12.5 The passive – 2**.)

5.5 Adjectives and participles
VOCABULARY DEVELOPMENT

A Suggested answers:

1 She has a talking parrot.
   – *a parrot that can speak*
   Have you heard her parrot talking?
   – *Have you heard it speak?*

2 She is an old friend.
   – *a friend I have had for a long time*
   My friend is quite old.
   – *not young*

3 All the people concerned were there.
   – *the people involved or who were affected*
   All the concerned people were there.
   – *the worried people*

4 It wasn't a proper meeting.
   – *it was only an informal meeting, no formal or binding decisions could be made*
   The meeting proper began at 9.
   – *the main part of the meeting; there had been an informal gathering before that perhaps*

5 The members of staff present.
   – *who are/were there*
   The present members of staff.
   – *current*

6 Is he the person responsible?
   – *the person who did whatever has just been mentioned or the person who is in charge*
   Is he a responsible person?
   – *someone who can be trusted*

7 I have a friend living in London.
   – *who lives in London*
   She has no living relatives.
   – *all her relatives are now dead*

8 He is a complete idiot.
   – *an utter idiot*
   the complete meal cost a mere £5.
   – *the whole meal, including drinks*

9 She has an elder brother.
   – *older than her (his exact age depends on her age)*
   Her brother is elderly.
   – *old, at least 70 years old*

10 The film had a very involved plot.
   – *complicated*
   The actors involved were unconvincing.
   – *involved in the circumstances described in a previous sentence*

B Remember that adjectival expressions can come in three positions in a sentence:

Before a noun A very **interesting** story.
After a noun We need the best ingredients **available**.
After a verb She is fast **asleep**.

Suggested completions:

1 That was a really **tasty** meal.
   Those buns look absolutely **delicious**!

2 The journey was an **utter** disaster.
   The meal was a **complete** success.

3 The fire isn't **alight** yet.
   Don't leave the baby **alone** all night.
   Shh! The baby's **asleep** in its cot.
   Her two sisters look **alike**.

4 The president **elect** takes office next month.

5 That was the most disgusting meal **imaginable**!

6 Work expands to take up the time **available**.
   Work expands to take up the **available** time.

7 I love the smell of cakes (which are) **baking** in the kitchen.
   The houses (which were) **damaged** in the storm have been repaired.
   A survey **conducted** by Berni revealed some unexpected information.

C Suggested answers:

1 Do you have all the **necessary** ingredients?
2 I object to his **downright** rudeness.
3 Don't forget to follow the **suggested** guidelines / the guidelines **suggested**.
4 The people **responsible** have all been arrested.
5 Never wake a **sleeping** baby.
6 In the sale there were bargains **galore**.
7 I'd love a **refreshing** glass of lemonade.
8 Can I try one of those **delicious-looking** cakes?
9 She is the nicest person **imaginable**.
10 It seems to me that he is an **utter** fool.
11 The meeting **proper** began promptly.
12 Some of the people **present** fell asleep.

5.6 Making notes
WRITING SKILLS

A **1–3** Each of the styles of note-making has its advantages.

The missing points are:

A packaging: environmentally damaging – plastic bottles in landfill sites

B distribution: transportation from overseas + water-short countries unnecessary + wasteful

C Water Companies Association say, '. . .
   British Soft Drinks Association say, '. . .

B **1** 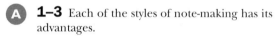 Some of the main points are **in bold** in the Transcript, but only the ones that are relevant to the topic of the article in **B2**.

2 Use only the points which are relevant to the topic of the article. If possible, ask another person to read and mark your work.

TRANSCRIPT *6 minutes 20 seconds*

LIZ: (Presenter) Do you start your day with a cup of coffee? I know that I do. Or maybe a cup of tea? Or hot chocolate? Or perhaps you have some fruit juice and a banana. Now you may not know, but all these **products come from developing countries in the South**, and one of the problems is that these products are often produced by **farmers** who are **not earning enough to support themselves and their families decently**. Craig Thomas reports.

CRAIG: Yep, that's right. These products are freely traded around the world and because there's a plentiful supply of these crops, the **prices paid to the growers are low**. And they're often paid by **middlemen, who buy at the lowest price** and have to make their own profits. Now, to make matters worse the **world price fluctuates**, depending on harvests around the world. And this means farmers never know how much their crop is going to earn them. And, of course, they depend on selling their crops to buy food for their families and to pay for their children's education. Uh…to take an example, let's look at bananas, and we can see how this works. Er…Sally Anderson has recently visited the Caribbean island of St Vincent and she's…she's with us today. Um…Sally, you've talked to farmers there.

SALLY: Yes, I have, and the problem that banana growers in many small Caribbean islands face is that a farmer and his or her family runs a small farm of one or two hectares. And their livelihood depends on **bananas**, it's often their only crop, and they **can't compete on price** with the giant plantations of Ecuador and Colombia, where workers are paid as little as one dollar a day. The quality of their bananas is superior, but the price is higher.

CRAIG: Right, well, one solution to this problem is the Fairtrade scheme, which was set up in 1992 by development agencies including Oxfam and Christian Aid. How does this work exactly?

SALLY: Well, the **Fairtrade scheme guarantees a decent fixed price to growers** who belong to a cooperative. This is a **guaranteed minimum price**, and this means that they don't suffer when the market price is low and therefore they **can afford to feed their families and educate their children**. They sign a long-c…term contract, which covers the cost of production, a basic living wage and when world prices rise above the minimum they get a little bit extra: **10 per cent is added as a social premium** which goes into a **social fund** to help **improve their working and living conditions**. And in return they undertake to produce high quality bananas and **refrain from using child labour** and to s… to **sustain the environment**.

LIZ: But it's not only bananas is it, Craig? Wh…what other kinds of Fairtrade food are available?

CRAIG: Well, best-known and most widely available is coffee. After oil, **coffee** is the most highly-valued commodity in the world. It's a huge market. And coffee is grown mostly in developing countries. And unfortunately most of the coffee growers around the world don't make a good living. Er…they often have to sell to…er…unscrupulous middlemen at very low prices. **Even when the world price rises, they don't benefit**. Now, Fairtrade can help them to improve their lives enormously. Coffee is the most widely marketed product under the Fairtrade brand. Er…the…the…the label on each pack of coffee may even inform you which community the coffee comes from and how buying it will help the local growers to improve their lives. Er…this pack of Cafédirect that I have here has a nice picture of Mario Hernandez in Nicaragua saying, "We have seen achievements. Now I have **money to buy clothes for my children, to build my house**. Day by day things are improving, because of the better price." So, there you are, the buyer feels a personal connection with the farmer.

LIZ: Mm, that's excellent. And how many producers belong to this Fairtrade scheme?

SALLY: Well, there are over half a million farmers in about 13 countries, and they all belong to **cooperatives**, as I said earlier. So their **communities share the benefits**. Now, to make this work, consumers in the North are being persuaded to support the scheme by paying a little bit extra for their bananas. But in return they get a high quality product and, more importantly, they get the warm feeling that they are playing the part in helping poorer people in the South.

LIZ: Mm, important, absolutely. Now, apart from coffee and bananas, Craig, are there any other products that come under this Fairtrade scheme?

CRAIG: Oh, yes, you can buy tea, chocolate and cocoa, er…honey, sugar, orange juice — all with the Fairtrade logo on the pack. Er…in fact, there are over 70 different food and drink products available now in the UK. Some of these are organics, some are not, but the Fairtrade Foundation monitors the standards of production and the quality of the products, all products. And almost all these products are grown by small growers who belong to co-operatives. Er…because this is one way to keep costs down. There's no middleman involved if the products are bought directly…er…from the cooperative. Small farms are not as cost-effective as larger plantations. So, sadly, the price has to be higher.

LIZ: Mm, so would you say the problem for consumers is the price?

CRAIG: Well, that's right. Um…on average Fairtrade products cost around 30 per cent more than the equivalent non-Fairtrade product. So they are more likely to be bought by better off shoppers. But still the number of products is growing all the time, and their popularity is growing too. Um…manufacturers who use the Fairtrade logo pay 2 per cent of the wholesale price to the Fairtrade Foundation, which uses…er…that money to monitor the scheme, and to find new sources and…er…raise awareness among both suppliers and consumers.

LIZ: But the big question is: Can you taste the difference?

SALLY: Yes, you can! Windward Island bananas taste absolutely wonderful.

CRAIG: Yeah, and the coffee is great too. Well worth the extra few pence.

SALLY: But best of all you know you are making a worthwhile contribution to the welfare of farmers *and* their families.

Model version:

The Fairtrade scheme was set up in 1992 by development agencies to try to make the life of the small producer in developing countries more secure. Most of the 70 products available in this scheme are grown by small farmers in the South who cannot compete with the big growers on price and, prior to the introduction of the scheme, were at the mercy of the world price and the middlemen for their survival. Usually they only produce one kind of crop and are thus more dependent on the vagaries of nature for success or failure. In many cases they do not earn enough to support their families or themselves and are never able to make long-term plans. Some cannot afford clothes for their children or the materials to build a house. The best known products in the scheme are coffee and bananas.

The Fairtrade scheme guarantees the farmers a minimum price however much the price fluctuates on the world market. When the world price goes above the minimum, the farmers receive extra. Fairtrade also cuts out the middleman who would always pay the lowest price possible even when the world price is high. In return the farmers organise themselves into collectives, agree to produce a high quality product, to sustain the environment and not to use child labour. In addition to the minimum price, they receive 10% extra when prices rise above the minimum and this goes into a social fund to benefit their whole community. The undertakings the farmers themselves make with regard to children and the environment also help to improve conditions in their community. Children are freed to go to school and their parents can provide them with books, and shoes for the walk to school. The scheme also raises awareness in the rich northern countries of the problems of the poorer south and gives them the opportunity to contribute effectively and to the long-term welfare of small farmers.

5.7 *should* and *be*
ADVANCED GRAMMAR

A Correct answers:

> 1 **is** – sounds more definite
> **be** – more formal
> **should be** – less definite, formal: should would normally be unstressed here
> 2 **am given** – straightforward, unmarked form
> **be given** – very formal
> **should be given** – quite formal
> 3 **should do** & **ought to do** – both mean the same here, asking for advice
> **can do** – asking for suggested alternative courses of action
> 4 **should arrive** – dramatic emphasis: cf . . .
> *when in walked Billy*
> 5 **feel** – normal, unmarked
> **do feel** – emphasising the verb
> **should feel** – more formal, less direct

B If you have difficulty with using *be* + past participle, which is actually the **subjunctive**, remember that its use is entirely optional. As long as you understand it and realise that it sounds rather formal, you may not actually need to use it.

In American English the subjunctive is used more frequently in informal language than it is in British English, where its use often sounds rather old-fashioned.

C **1** Many variations are possible – and should be encouraged in questions 6 to 9.

> 1 should make notes
> 2 should hand in
> 3 be done/should be done
> 4 should raise
> 5 should have to do
> 6 the environment should be protected
> 7 the weather should be so wet today
> 8 my friend should have lost her handbag
> 9 people should be so inconsiderate to each other
> 10 be elected/should be elected
> 11 should have any

(See also **13.4 Conditionals – 2**.)

5.8 Describing a process
LISTENING AND COMPOSITION

A **1** Do this before you listen and the listening task will be easier.

2 🔊 It's not necessary to understand all of the technical terms to do this exercise.

Answers:

Top row:	1	14	8	6
2nd row:	11	4	3	12
3rd row:	2	5	13	10
4th row:	9	7	15	

B **1 & 2** This exercise can only be done with a partner. But you'll need to look at the information in **Activity 2** or **15** for the composition task in **C.**

C 🖊 Write about wine or beer, then you can compare your work with the model version.

TRANSCRIPT *2 minutes 30 seconds*

JONATHAN: Everyone will tell you that margarine is natural and healthy.

JULIA: Yes.

JONATHAN: So it's made from vegetable oils like sunflower seed oil or corn oil, and vegetable fat is supposed to be better for you than animal fat.

JULIA: Mhm.

JONATHAN: Yes, it's supposed to contain less cholesterol, it's more healthy.

JULIA: Mm.

JONATHAN: And its sunny, natural taste seems attractive to people who care about their health, right?

JULIA: Yeah.

JONATHAN: But just how natural is it? Well, let me explain the process step by step.
First of all, the sunflower or other plant seeds are heated and then crushed to release the oil. This is a sort of crude plant oil which still contains impurities like resins and gums. So, what they have to do next is to add caustic soda.

JULIA: Oh!

JONATHAN: Yeah, this removes waste products which form the basic ingredients of soap.

JULIA: Oh, no.

JONATHAN: Yes, it may surprise you to know that quite a lot of the soap we use actually comes from this process.

JULIA: Right.

JONATHAN: So the next step is to add fullers earth, which bleaches the oil. And then they have pure, refined oil. Now, next, the oil has to be reacted with hydrogen using a catalyst, in this case nickel, and this process hardens the oils. All right?

JULIA: Mm.

JONATHAN: Now, after that the oils have to be neutralised, then they're bleached, and filtered to remove any waste products.

JULIA: Mm.

JONATHAN: Now...haha...at this stage there's often a rather nasty smell!

JULIA: Right.

JONATHAN: And this is removed by heating the hardened oils until they melt again.

JULIA: Mm.

JONATHAN: Not finished yet! Then the oils are mixed with small quantities of fish and animal oils . . .

JULIA: No!

JONATHAN: Yep, to create the right kind of blended oils. But there are more essential ingredients to be added. They have to add water, skimmed milk and some salt. And then they also have to put some flavour, artificial flavour, into this tasteless mixture and make it a nice yellow colour and put in some vitamins.

JULIA: Ohh!

JONATHAN: But even after this lengthy process the ingredients won't blend until they're emulsified. This is done by adding lecithin and monoglyceride to the mixture. Then the mixture is cooled and now, at last, it's ready to be extruded into a lovely plastic tub and a lid with pretty sunflowers is plonked on the top.

JULIA: Haha!

JONATHAN: So, that's how margarine is made. Butter, on the other hand, is simply made by churning cream. It's pure, it's natural and it tastes good too.

Model version:

```
225g plain wholemeal flour
1 tablespoon ground cinnamon
1 teaspoon ground nutmeg
½ teaspoon baking powder
110g butter
110g honey
110g sugar
1 large egg
handful sultanas
handful walnuts, chopped
225g carrots, peeled and grated
```

This is a description of how to make a carrot cake. First of all you need a medium size saucepan in which you put the butter, honey and sugar. Put the pan on a low heat and allow the butter and honey to melt and the sugar to dissolve in the resultant syrup. Remove the pan from the heat and allow the mixture to cool slightly. Then stir in the measured flour, baking powder, spices, nuts, sultanas, beaten egg and grated carrots. When all the ingredients are well combined, turn them into a greased and lined loaf tin. Pre-heat the oven to 170 degrees C. Bake for about an hour or until the cake feels firm to the touch and a skewer inserted into the centre comes out clean. Leave the cake in the tin for 10 minutes and then turn it out onto a cooling rack. The cake is best eaten within 3 to 4 days.

Travelling abroad   Tourism   Holidays   Transport

6

See the world!

6.1 Where would you like to go?
TOPIC VOCABULARY

A Say your answers softly to yourself. Maybe record yourself.

B Answers:

Soufrière is a small fishing port on the west **coast**[1] of the **island**[2] of St Lucia in the Caribbean. It lies at the centre of a sheltered **bay**[3] which forms a natural **harbour**[4]. The town is dominated by the Pitons: two mountain **peaks**[5] which were once **volcanoes**[6], covered in tropical **rainforest**[7]. If you travel **inland**[8] up the river **valley**[9] you come to a **plateau**[10] where there are plantations growing coconuts and tropical fruits, watered by little **streams**[11] flowing down from the hills. To the north there are impressive **cliffs**[12] plunging into the sea and around a **headland**[13] is a secluded hotel above a little **cove**[14], from where you can swim out to watch the fish around the coral **reef**[15]. The **view**[16] from the hotel is breathtaking.

Despite its wonderful **setting**[17], warm **climate**[18], friendly people and delicious local **seafood**[19], Soufrière isn't a popular tourist destination, perhaps because it lacks the sandy **beaches**[20] tourists expect in a Caribbean **resort**[21].

C After you've finished the exercise, look at the words you *didn't* choose. What situations would you use those words in?

Answers:

1 off the beaten track   out of the way   secluded
2 courteous   easygoing   hospitable
3 holidaymakers   pilgrims   travellers
4 drive   journey   trip
5 abroad   away from home   out of the country

D This may look easy, but even advanced students have difficulty in using English place names and nationality words – particularly when they are spelt similarly in your own language. Say your answers softly to yourself. Maybe record yourself.

6.2 Learning the language
READING AND SPEAKING

Background

Rose Macaulay's best-known novel *The Towers of Trebizond* (1956) is an amusing account of a young woman's travels in Turkey accompanying an eccentric aunt. Her other novels include *Dangerous Ages* and *Keeping Up Appearances*.

A These questions are similar to questions in Part 5 of the Use of English Paper. (In the exam, shorter answers than these are OK.) Finding the relevant information in the text is necessary in the Reading Paper too, of course.

Suggested answers:

1 They repeated things and spoke more loudly, believing that everyone can speak Turkish
2 Because she didn't expect them to ask questions when she said she didn't understand Turkish
3 Because a Mr Yorum was by then staying at the hotel
4 Because she had sent for him, he was saying 'I'm the person you sent for.'
5 She thought he might be offering to act as her interpreter
6 There was nothing to be done: there seemed to be so much confusion in Turkey that it didn't seem to matter.

B & C This activity can only be done with a partner. But do read the continuation of the passage in **Activities 4** and **16** to find out what happened next.

6.3 The future
GRAMMAR REVIEW

A Suggested answers:

1 I think I'm going to scream.
   – *I won't be able to stop myself from screaming (if I don't get out of here soon)*
   I think I'll scream.
   – *It might be a good idea for me to scream (it might attract someone's attention)*
2 It's still raining in Scotland.
   – *According to the weather report, the rain is still falling there*

It's still going to rain in Scotland.
– *According to the forecast, rain is expected once again in Scotland*
It will still be raining in Scotland.
– *(When you get there) the rain won't have stopped*
It still rains in Scotland.
– *The Scottish climate hasn't changed, it still tends to be quite rainy there*

3 I'll phone him after work.
– *Promise or offer: I undertake to phone him (maybe on your behalf, or because you want me to)*
I'm phoning him after work.
– *This is what I'm planning to do, I've set aside time to do it*
I'm going to phone him after work.
– *I intend to do it then – the normal 'uncoloured' future form*
I'll be phoning him after work.
– *Reassurance: I'm going to phone him (so don't worry) OR (While something else is going on, at the same time) I'm going phone him, and it may be a long call*

4 When are we having lunch?
& When are we going to have lunch?
– *What time is lunch?*
When do we have lunch?
– *What is the planned, arranged time for lunch?*
When shall we have lunch?
– *When would you like to eat?*

5 What time shall I get to your house?
– *What time would you like me to arrive?*
What time will I get to your house?
– *When will I arrive (if I leave town at ten)?*

6 I'll work hard tonight.
– *I promise to work hard*
I'll be working hard tonight.
– *(Please don't phone me because) I'm planning to spend the evening working and I'll be busy*

7 Will you be going shopping today?
& Are you going shopping today?
& Are you going to go shopping today?
– *Is this one of the things you're planning to do today?*
Will you go shopping today?
– *Request: I want you to go shopping*
Do you go shopping today?
– *Is today your regular day for shopping?*

B Suggested answers:

1 I'm going to   Will/Could/Can
2 Will you be   are in/go to/visit
3 Are you going to go   are you going to take/catch
4 breaks down   will you
  or broke down   would you
5 to land   will be/is going to be/might be
6 lands   will have been
7 has in store for/will bring
8 is going to be/is likely to be
9 are away on   'll be/ 'm going to be   'll send
10 'll have
11 get/receive   'll give you
12 decided/discussed   are going to do
13 phones/calls/needs/wants   'll   be having
14 will/is likely to   leave/have left
15 to reading   have

C 🖉 Say your answers softly to yourself. Maybe record yourself. Then write your two paragraphs.
If possible, ask another person to read and mark your work.

6.4 One word – different meanings
VOCABULARY DEVELOPMENT

In Part 3 of the Use of English Paper, candidates have to choose one word that will fit into a gap in three unrelated sentences. The missing words may be homonyms or words used in different senses in different contexts. (See also **16.10** for more about Part 3.)
Look at the examples before you do the exercises.

A Answers:

1 drive   2 left   3 show   4 article   5 second
6 faint   7 charge   8 funny

B Answers:

1 pound   2 appreciate   3 firm   4 case
5 will   6 cover

6.5 The friendly skies
READING

Background

Jonathan Raban's travel writing includes *Coasting*, an account of a journey by sea around the coast of Britain, *Old Glory* about a journey down the Mississippi River, and *Arabia through the Looking Glass* about a journey in the Arabian peninsula.
  His novel *Foreign Land* is about an old man who returns to a much-changed Britain after a lifetime spent overseas. *Passage to Juneau* is a wonderful account of a solo journey in a yacht from Seattle through the Inside Passage to Juneau in Alaska.
  In *Hunting Mister Heartbreak*, from which this passage comes, he tries to 'settle' in various parts of the United States, ending up in Seattle where he feels most at home.

A Say your answers softly to yourself. Maybe record yourself.

B Concentrate on enjoying the passage, and letting the sense carry you through despite the unfamiliar vocabulary and the 1,200-odd words.

C Answers:

1 D   2 D   3 B   4 B   5 C
6 B *or possibly*   D – *Oprah is Oprah Winfrey, the TV talk show host*   7 A

D Look back to the notes on vocabulary learning in **1.3 E**.

E Maybe the funny names at the end of paragraph 1?

6.6 Repetition
WRITING SKILLS

There is a big difference between deliberate repetition for effect, and the kind of unimaginative repetition of words, where the same words are repeated unimaginatively!

A **1 & 2** Saskatchewan is pronounced /sæsˈkætʃəwən/ or /səsˈkætʃəwən/.

The repeated words and structures are <u>underlined</u>:

---

10 Great Reasons to Visit Saskatchewan

Saskatchewan is a big province that constantly surprises. With <u>its</u> vast and changing landscapes, <u>its</u> colourful events and <u>its</u> rich heritage, it has a lot to offer. Covering it in a few words and photos is no easy task.

In the next 20 pages we present 10 great reasons <u>why</u> you should travel our province. <u>Why</u> Saskatchewan is special. <u>Why</u> it's a place where you belong.

We have thousands of reasons for you to see Saskatchewan – we're limited to 10 here. We're confident <u>you'll find</u> them reasons enough to visit. And that <u>you'll find</u> reasons more to return.

1. The Prairies

When people <u>think</u> Saskatchewan, they <u>think</u> prairies. <u>They think</u> fields of gold that stretch up against the horizon. <u>They think</u> bold, blue sky. <u>They think</u> vistas that seem flawlessly flat and that from the air resemble a patchwork quilt.

Prairie scenery can be breathtaking. Brilliant mustard and canola <u>waving</u> in the wind. Grain elevators <u>standing</u> like sentinels, <u>signalling</u> the approach of new towns. Sunsets <u>offering</u> their light shows of purple, orange and red.

The prairies are also rolling hills where you'd least expect them. Valleys full of wild flowers, prairie lilies and saskatoons. Plus plains and bush alive with prairie dogs, meadowlarks and white-tailed deer.

This year <u>stop</u> and <u>smell</u> the clover. <u>See</u> the images that have graced a thousand postcards. <u>Visit</u> the prairies.

2. The Parks

<u>Hike</u> a leafy aspen trail. <u>Zip</u> down a monster waterslide. <u>Join</u> a "wolf howl" under clear moonlight. Whatever your interests you can likely satisfy them in Saskatchewan's parks.

With nearly five million acres of Saskatchewan parkland, Mother Nature has plenty of places in which to work her spell on you. At our parks you can <u>sink</u> that championship putt, <u>watch</u> deer and elk by the roadside, <u>relax</u> at a four-season resort, or <u>pitch</u> your tent near a back country gurgling stream.

<u>Waskesiu</u>. <u>Grasslands</u>. <u>Moose Mountain</u>. <u>Cypress Hills</u>. Our parks are destinations, summer and winter. They put you in touch with a simpler, gentler <u>world</u> – a <u>world</u> where the sun shines bright and the deadlines and pressures of ordinary life are <u>far</u>, <u>far</u> away.

3. The Lakes

<u>Get</u> out your swimming trunks, <u>unfurl</u> those sails, <u>dust</u> off your water-skis, <u>take</u> the canoe and tackle box out of storage and <u>book</u> that cabin or resort. Saskatchewan's <u>100,000</u> – that's right <u>100,000</u>! – lakes await you.

4. The Fishing

Picture a lazy day on a crystal clear lake. Morning mist <u>comes</u> off the water. An evergreen shoreline <u>frames</u> your horizon. A bald eagle <u>circles</u> overhead. Then suddenly your line <u>tenses</u>, and everything <u>changes</u>. Your battle with a monster of the deep has begun.

and

---

10. The People

If there are 10 great <u>reasons</u> to visit Saskatchewan, then there are a million <u>reasons</u> to come back. Our <u>people</u>. <u>Superhearted</u>. <u>Lively</u>. <u>Famous</u> for their hospitality.

With a mosaic of cultures, Saskatchewan is truly the world in one place. Native Indians and <u>people</u> with British, French and east-European roots. <u>People</u> who celebrate their uniqueness at annual celebrations like Vesna and Folkfest in Sasktatoon, or Mosaic in Regina. Where the <u>food</u>, <u>fun</u> and <u>music</u> of the homelands trail long into the night.

When all is said and done, it's the <u>people</u> you meet who make a vacation unforgettable. We invite you to meet ours. Through them discover the place where you belong.

B **1–3** If possible, ask another person to read and mark your work.

6.7 Revision and exam practice
ADVANCED GRAMMAR

This exercise revises some of the advanced grammar points introduced in Units 1 to 5. The questions reflect some of the **HARDER** questions of this type that come up in Part 4 of the Use of English Paper.

Suggested answers:

2 We **were still waiting at midnight** for the plane to take off.
3 **Arriving at the airport, I was told** that my flight had been cancelled.
4 Never **having flown before,** I was very nervous.
5 The **only thing I want is to spend** the rest of my life with you.
   or The **only thing I want to do is spend** the rest of my life with you.
6 Not **only do they go on holiday** in the winter but in the summer too.
7 Little **did we realise that** our hotel was right beside the airport.
8 I propose **that he be sent a letter** explaining the situation.
9 She **never fails to get the** right answers.
10 Only after writing several letters of complaint **did we manage to get** our money back.

6.8 The impact of tourism
LISTENING AND COMPOSITION

A 🔊 Suggested answers:

1 200   2 about 75   3 off-limits   4 Europe (Germany, Italy, UK)   5a the underwater environment   5b the 'Robinson Crusoe' factor
6 imported   7 highly successful
8 get back home (unless they live in Malé)
9 beautiful/colourful   10 global warming

B Say your answers softly to yourself. Maybe record yourself.

C ✎ If possible, ask another person to read and mark your work.

TRANSCRIPT *5 minutes 30 seconds*

PRESENTER: The Maldives is a long chain of over a thousand tiny coral islands in the Indian Ocean. There are 26 atolls extending over 800 kilometres north-to-south and for 100 kilometres east-to-west. There are 300,000 Maldivians. Bob Allison has just returned from Malé, the capital. Bob, not all the islands are inhabited, are they?

BOB: No, Polly. Um...200 of the islands are inhabited and even these are very small. About 75 of these are developed as resorts and are off-limits to the general population. Likewise, *their* islands are generally off-limits to tourists so special permits or organised tours are the only way of visiting them. Tourism only came to the country in the 1970s. Until then the people lived from fishing and products of the coconut palm, as little else will grow in the poor soil.

PRESENTER: Right.

BOB: The people are all Muslims. A strict dress code applies and immodest dress is offensive to Maldivians. Maldivian staff are not allowed to serve alcohol, special staff from Sri Lanka or India have to do that.

PRESENTER: Right and what kind of people go there?

BOB: Well, the resorts in the Maldives attract tourists with promises of 'the last paradise on earth'. And if your idea of paradise is a pristine tropical island with swaying palm trees, pure white beaches and brilliant turquoise lagoons, then the Maldives will not disappoint. It's also a major destination for scuba divers, who come for the fabulous coral reefs and the wealth of marine life. Er...but it's not a place for low budget backpackers or for people who want to travel independently and live as the locals do. Most of the people who visit the Maldives are...are from Europe: mainly from Germany, Italy and the UK. It's a...a 12-hour flight from Europe and...er...500,000 tourists visit the Maldives each year.

PRESENTER: Mm, an...and what is unusual about tourism in the Maldives?

BOB: Well, the unique feature of tourism in the Maldives is that it is carefully managed. Er...the country's Tourism Master Plan identifies both the underwater environment and the 'Robinson Crusoe' factor as major attractions, but these are not seen as compatible with large-scale, low budget, mass tourism. The lack of local resources makes it necessary to import virtually everything a visitor needs, from furniture to fresh vegetables, so the Maldives cannot really compete on price. The strategy has been to develop a limited number of quality resorts, each on its own uninhabited island, free from traffic, crime and crass commercialism. The Maldivian tourism strategy also aims to minimise the adverse effects of tourism on traditional Muslim communities.

PRESENTER: Right.

BOB: Tourists can make short guided visits to local fishing villages, but must then return to their resort. Er...most are satisfied with this glimpse of local life and culture. But to stay longer or to travel to atolls outside the tourist zone requires a good reason, um...a special permit, and a...a local person to sponsor the visitor. Most tourists come to understand the restrictions after a short visit to an accessible island. Er...it's difficult to imagine how isolated Maldivian communities would benefit from extended stays by uncontrolled numbers of tourists.

PRESENTER: Mm, a...and how successful has this strategy been?

BOB: Well, like it or not, this highly regulated tourist industry has been enormously successful. There are more and better resorts, a steady increase in visitor numbers, and a minimal impact on the natural and social environment. The Maldives is internationally recognised as a model for sustainable, environment-friendly tourist development.

PRESENTER: But the...there must be some disadvantages?

BOB: Yes, there are. Um...most of the resort staff have to live on the resort islands. Their homes are often on distant islands, difficult to reach from the resort islands, and they can only go back there from time to time for short breaks. It's easier for staff who live in Malé who can get back to the capital more easily. Still, the work they do is not unpleasant. And may be preferable to emigration.

PRESENTER: Sure.

BOB: The country is heavily dependent on tourism — there are also small clothing factories and fishing. Almost everything the tourist needs has to be imported apart from coconuts and fish. Each resort island has its own diesel generator for electricity. Water is produced from sea water in desalination plants on each resort island. And these costs are sure to rise in the future. And will tourists be willing to pay more for holidays in the Maldives? That's the question. And there are probably more serious problems . . .

PRESENTER: What are they?

BOB: Well, first of all, *El Niño*. Coral is vulnerable to changes in sea temperature. When the sea temperature rises above 22 degrees, the coral turns white because it expels a minute...the minute organisms that live within its hard limestone core. These organisms cannot tolerate a rise in sea temperature of over 1 to 2 degrees Centigrade for more than a few weeks. The beautiful colours of the coral are no longer there and divers are disappointed.

PRESENTER: Oh, right.

BOB: And this is happening all over the Pacific and Indian Oceans, not just in the Maldives. And the other problem is global warming. The average height of the islands above sea level is only 1.6 metres. Coral islands are vulnerable to a rise in sea level. A big wall has been built around Malé to protect it from the sea, but that may only be a temporary solution. As the sea level rises, by the end of the century some islands will be under the sea.

PRESENTER: So go there while you still can?

BOB: Haha, yes, I think so. Start saving up now!

Model version:

Before tourism came to G__ it was truly a wild and beautiful place. Situated near a 10-kilometre stretch of sand on the northern coast of a Mediterranean island, with two rivers running clear and cold from the mountains, it was an obvious holiday destination. The scenery is breathtaking. The mountains which rise up in the centre of the island are snowcapped for most of the year and make a wonderful backdrop to the sparkling sea and the bamboo lined rivers. Fishing and small-holdings occupied the villagers before tourism. There was no natural harbour but a jetty had been built on rocks near the mouth of the larger river. Between the two rivers was a large area of marshland, home to many birds and mosquitoes! In the 19th century, when malaria was still a big problem, eucalyptus trees had been planted in an attempt to drain some of the water and reduce the number of mosquitoes. Those trees now tower majestically above the village square, providing shade from the hot sun. If you waded in the smaller river you could spot minuscule turtles, kingfishers darting along the water and herons and other water birds.

The first hotel was built about twenty years ago. It was small and seemed content not to be too busy. But in the last ten years tourism has really taken off here. A major trunk road was built from west to east along the northern coast which has made G__ accessible in an hour and a half from the nearest airport. Other hotels and self-catering apartments have popped up, some foolishly built very close to the marshes. There's a large and brash disco, a crop of chic souvenir shops and a wealth of simple restaurants. The village itself has improved in many ways and there's certainly enough work here between April and October to employ a good many locals and possibly incomers. The fishing fleet has been kept up and has impressive quays on both sides of the main river. The beach itself is so wide and long that it is quite possible to escape the cluster of sunbathers near the town and it could never be described as crowded.

The wild feel has gone, along with some of the wildlife, but the intrinsic beauty of the place still works its magic and has helped to keep the youngsters at home.

 6.9

come and *go*
VERBS AND IDIOMS

A Suggested answers:

1 accepted (with difficulty)
2 happen in the expected way   didn't succeed
3 made him too conceited   (*also*: made him drunk)
4 progressing   accompany
5 stopped liking   continue, complete
6 look at, discuss   occurs
7 Carry on, don't hesitate   be handy later
8 attacked
9 become independent   becomes successful   investigated, examined
10 was a great success   received a good reaction, was received gratefully

B Answers:

1 came up with
2 coming out
3 gone up   go down   (*also*: come down)
4 come across
5 went on at   go in for
6 went down with   (*also*: came down with)
7 goes off/goes in for
8 came round
9 comes up
10 came apart

---

 7   Money   Consumers   Shopping   Advertising

Spending your money

 7.1   ### Shop till you drop!
TOPIC VOCABULARY AND LISTENING

 A   Say your answers softly to yourself. Maybe record yourself.

B Answers:

2 mall   shopping centre   precinct
3 articles   goods   merchandise
4 a bargain   good value   value for money
5 manufacturer   supplier   wholesaler
6 retailer   trader   vendor
7 purchase   sale   transaction
8 make a down payment   pay cash down   pay a deposit
9 guarantee   twelve months old   warranty
10 courteous   helpful   knowledgeable
   – obsequious *and* subservient *are also possible, but only if used lightheartedly*

C ◀)) Suggested answers:

1 responsibility   independence   constant challenge   dealing with people (i.e. the customers and her team)   unpredictability   being busy all the time
2 watching what's going on in the department   ensuring that stock is on display   supervising the staff   intervening when there is a problem
3 hard work   standing all day   working on Saturday (not a disadvantage for Amanda herself)   working one late night every week
4 to manage a department in a larger branch   to stay in the selling side

TRANSCRIPT   *3 minutes 10 seconds*

PRESENTER: Amanda Hooper is twenty-six and is a department manager in a well-known department store. What does she enjoy about her job?

AMANDA: I think it's the responsibility that knowing that it's my department and that I can basically do what I like that, you know, that I think needs to be done to improve sales or to…um…have a more efficient team or to make my department look better and that's a constant challenge. Also you're always dealing with people, either customers or your own team, and people are very unpredictable, so one day is never the same as the next, it's always something different happening. And I like that, I like to be busy all the time.

PRESENTER: How much contact does she personally have with the customers?

AMANDA: Well, I mean I'm on the floor quite a lot because that's part of my job, to have a look at what's going on…um…see that stock's out, to see that everybody's doing what they should be. Um…but I don't actually serve customers as much as the sales assistants would do, I…I don't really go on the till and that's…sales assistants that's their job, and also to help and advise customers because they're the ones with the in-depth knowledge…um…you know, they know the ins and outs, what they can offer the customer, and they're better…perhaps better placed on a day-to-day basis to help a customer or choose something for them. Um…so…but I mean you do have to be on the floor, you have to hear what's going on, you have to check that they are being served correctly, that nobody's got a problem. So if you're about and there seems to be a situation developing, then you…you would go in and see everything was all right. But…um…my job isn't to stand around all day and help customers, that's…that's not what a manager's job is.

PRESENTER: What are the disadvantages of working in retailing?

AMANDA: It's hard work. You stand up all day, you don't sit down, as I've said. Um…it's hot, especially in this sort of weather. Sometimes some people would call the hours unsociable, I don't because I've never valued having a Saturday but I work a Tuesday to

Saturday week and my days off are Sunday and Monday. So if I was a great sport fanatic like my husband, who likes to watch the rugby, um…
I couldn't…I can't. Um…but that doesn't worry me because I hate sport anyway. Um…also we work a late night till half past seven on Wednesday…um… and that's…basically you should expect to work one every week.

PRESENTER: What are Amanda's ambitions?

AMANDA: Well, I've got one of the larger departments at the moment that…and that I look after and I'm responsible for, so really I'd probably be looking to move to a larger branch, still as a department manager…um…but perhaps with a more…bigger team and larger turnover…um…and also probably the extra pressures that working in a large branch brings. Um…but I think I always want to stay in the selling side…um…because that's, as far as I'm concerned, in retailing where it's at, retailing's all about selling…um…and without the selling side of it you can't do anything.

D This activity can only be done with a partner.

7.2 Prepositions – 1
GRAMMAR REVIEW

This is the original article – some variations are possible:

MONEY FIT TO LAUNDER

Great inventions rarely work first time. **In**[1] 1990 the Reserve Bank of Australia, the country's central bank, shipped an order **of**[2] commemorative banknotes, **among**[3] the first to be made **from**[4] plastic film rather than paper, **to**[5] Western Samoa. The Pacific islanders' excitement **at**[6] their new two-tala notes soon turned **to**[7] anger. Ink rubbed off the surface and smudged the portrait **of**[8] Malietoa Tanumafali, the revered head of state, **in**[9] whose honour the notes had been issued.

In[10] their early days, plastic banknotes shed ink, jammed **in**[11] note-counting machines and often refused to be refolded. But the Reserve Bank, which pioneered the technology, claims to have eradicated the sort of glitches that produced red (and smudged) faces **in**[12] Western Samoa. Australia issued its own plastic tender **for**[13] the first time in 1992. **By**[14] 1996, the country had taken the last **of**[15] its paper money **out of**[16] circulation. Now it is persuading other countries to follow its example.

The Australians say plastic cash has two main advantages **over**[17] the paper variety. First, it is hard to forge. As well as fancy inks and watermarks, it has a transparent window that makes life difficult **for**[18] counterfeiters. The second advantage is economic. Plastic notes are hard to rip and even survive washing machines. Although each note costs **around**[19] twice as much as a paper one to make, it lasts up to four times as long. The advantage is even greater **in**[20] humid climates, where paper notes can survive as little as four months.

Armed **with**[21] these selling points, the Reserve Bank's printing division is running a healthy export business. It makes plastic notes **for**[22] several countries, including Thailand, Brunei and a forgiving Western Samoa. DuraNote, an American company **with**[23] a plastic product, claims to be talking to central banks **in**[24] twenty-four countries. 'Until recently plastic cash was considered a novelty,' says Al McKay **of**[25] DuraNote. 'Now the central banks have become more cost-conscious they are taking it very seriously.'

Such scrimping **on**[26] costs even extends **to**[27] recycling, it seems. Australia plans to turn worn-out plastic notes **into**[28] wheelbarrows, compost bins and plumbing fittings. There may be money **in**[29] such products, **in**[30] more ways than one.

7.3 Something for everyone
READING

A Instead of making notes, maybe underline the appealing and unappealing aspects in the text with a cross or tick beside them in the margin.

B **1** Answers:

¶ **2** *parlance* = jargon ¶ **3** *avalanche* = plethora
¶ **4** *barmy* = crazy *mock-up* = replica
¶ **7** *meandered* = wandered *critical faculties* = ability to judge objectively ¶ **8** *oasis* = refuge ¶ **9** *blithely* = in a carefree manner *coughing up* = spending
¶ **10** *state-of-the-art* = ultra-modern *banal* = repetitive and dull ¶ **11** *proceeds* = profits
¶ **12** *pleasure dome* = palace of delights ¶ **13** *glorified* = seeming more important than in reality
¶ **14** *gratifyingly* = agreeably

2 Answers:

1 oasis **2** proceeds **3** gratifyingly banal critical faculties **4** meandered **5** cough up
6 parlance **7** avalanche glorified **8** mock-up
9 state-of-the-art **10** blithely barmy

C Some of these questions and the summary are similar to Part 5 of the Use of English Paper.

Suggested answers:

1 a tiepin, a woolly hat, a baseball pennant – and coffee and sandwiches
2 Albertan oil
3 pilgrims shrine
4 sarcastic, humorous
5 admiring scornful (i.e. ambivalent)
6 The model summary below shows just one person's personal reactions.

Model summary:

There are two things I hate in our wonderful consumer-friendly world: one is shopping and the other is theme parks (Disney in particular). So being captive in a giant mall, even if it does have its own waterworld, golf course and endless eateries, does not appeal. Come to think of it, I also hate air conditioning, muzak and fluorescent light. The sheer size would be another turn-off. I'm afraid I can't find anything about this mall which attracts to me.

7.4 Past and present
GRAMMAR REVIEW

A Suggested answers:

1 I didn't have time to read the paper this morning.
   – *The morning is over, it's now afternoon or evening (maybe I read it later in the day, or could read it later)*
   I haven't had time to read the paper this morning.
   – *It's still morning, so theoretically there's still time to read it this morning*

2 I had tea when Pam came in.
   – *I waited for her to come before starting*
   I was having tea when Pam came in.
   – *I started before she turned up*

3 By the time we had had lunch it was 2:30.
   – *We finished lunch at half past two*
   By the time we had lunch it was 2:30.
   – *We started lunch at about two thirty*

4 Where has Steve gone for his holiday?
   – *He's on holiday now, which place has he gone to?*
   Where is Steve going for his holiday?
   – *Where does he plan to go (in the future)?*
   Where has Steve been going for his holiday?
   – *In recent years which place has he usually visited?*
   Where does Steve go for his holiday?
   – *Generally or usually, what is his holiday destination?*
   Where did Steve go for his holiday?
   – *His holiday is over now*
   or, possibly: *he's on holiday still*

5 I had hoped you would invite me.
   – *I'm disappointed because you haven't invited me*
   I did hope you would invite me.
   – *. . . but you didn't*
   I was hoping you would invite me.
   – *I was looking forward to the invitation you have now given me and I'm glad you have invited me at last*
   or *I'm disappointed because you haven't invited me*
   I hoped you would invite me.
   – *I was looking forward to the invitation you have now given me*
   or *. . . but you're not going to invite me/haven't invited me*

6 What are you doing?
   – *What are you up to at the moment?*
   or *What is your current job?*
   What have you done?
   – *I know/suspect you've done something wrong or foolish*
   What do you do?
   – *What is your profession or job?*
   or *What action do you take (in a situation already or about to be described)?*
   What have you been doing?
   – *What activities have you been engaged in recently (since we last met)?*
   or *I know/suspect you've done something wrong or foolish*

B Suggested answers:

2 did you buy   suits
3 has been   has been/is
4 it had   started to   decided   wouldn't/might not came out
5 has   been   touch   'll get
6 went   hasn't had   since
7 have been   since   have you been   didn't   would be/were going to be   should have/could have   left wouldn't have missed
8 was   used to/would   haven't got such a sweet tooth/ don't eat sweets any more

---

C 1 & 2 🖉 Say your answers softly to yourself.
Maybe record yourself. Write a couple of paragraphs about your own view. If possible, ask another person to read and mark your work.

7.5 Enhancing customers' lives
LISTENING

A
Say your answers softly to yourself. Maybe record yourself.

B 🔊 Answers:

1 b	2 c	3 a	4 d	5 d	6 d	7 d	8 b

C 🔊 Answers:

1 lunchbox
2 dream
3 counters   fresh fish   cream cakes
4 restaurants   (and snack bars, tea rooms, coffee shops, etc.)
5 beer garden   breeze   view
6 June 1   September 1
7 store directory
8 bow   welcome
9 10 am   7 pm
10 railway   platform   commuter train
11 service   pleasure   range
12 customer loyalty

D
Say your answers softly to yourself. Maybe record yourself.

TRANSCRIPT   *8 minutes 15 seconds*

NARRATOR: You'll hear a broadcast about Japanese department stores.

PRESENTER: (Helen) Every country has its own department stores. There are some which are luxurious and cater for the very rich, like Harrods in London or Bloomingdales in New York, while some are more downmarket. But there's one country whose stores are totally unique, and that is Japan. In Tokyo, for example, visiting a department store does not necessarily mean going shopping. You might go there to see an art exhibition, or to amuse the children, you might want to drink beer in the roof garden, to have a meal, or just to relax and hang out with your friends. A Japanese department store doesn't really aim to sell things you need every day, like a supermarket might. It sets out to 'find ways of enhancing customers' lives'. Richard Green reports on Mitsukoshi, the oldest department store in Japan.

RICHARD: That's right, indeed, Helen. Um…Mitsukoshi started out as a kimono outlet in 1673. This was the first store where people could come in, browse around, and pay on the spot with cash for kimono cloth, rather than paying in…er…interest-bearing instalments as was the norm in those days. The merchandise then quickly diversified to include daily necessities and gift items, and Mitsukoshi grew to become the best-stocked and most prestigious department store in Asia by the 1960s. The store's reputation made it *the* place to buy gifts, and the Mits…Mitsukoshi logo continues to stand for quality. Um…for examples of the very best in Japanese customer service, Mitsukoshi is *the* place to go. And their flagship store in Nihonbashi is wonderful!

PRESENTER: So you reckon that it's worth a visit if you're in Tokyo?

RICHARD: Absolutely, it's a must! The subway stops right beneath the store — er...the station, by the way, is Mitsukosh...Mitsukoshi-mae, which means 'in front of Mitsukoshi' — and the best way in is via the grand entrance, especially if you can make it for...er...10 o'clock opening time. Being bowed to by all the assistants as you walk into the magnificent entrance makes you feel like royalty, I can tell you! You could spend all day walking round...er...and there are plenty of places to rest if you get tired of walking. It has a theatre, a cinema, a museum and an art gallery — and classrooms. It offers concerts, lectures and, ooh, all kinds of classes. They have a Ladies' Club with lectures and lessons in traditional arts and crafts, painting, flower arranging, calligraphy, and languages. They have art exhibitions too and lunchtime theatrical performances. Er...and the ticket, believe it or not, includes a lunchbox with *sushi*, wine, sandwiches and a magazine.

PRESENTER: Well, that certainly is a nice way to spend a lunchtime!

RICHARD: Yes. And there's a 'dream room for resting babies', where you can leave your baby while you...while you do your shopping. They can even arrange your wedding: Western or Japanese style.

PRESENTER: Are there other department stores that...er...that offer the same sort of services?

RICHARD: Well, er...the fact is all the department stores offer very similar services. Er...they don't all have a theatre, but most of them have exhibition areas and run classes in a 'community culture centre', er...where people can go to...to learn languages, for example. And down in the basement of every store, you'll find an enormous food department — not a supermarket but a huge area with hundreds of counters selling everything from...er...fresh fish to cream cakes. And many of them give you a...a free taste of their wares. So it's a sort of high-class market. And...er...near the top of the building there are usually several floors with dozens of little restaurants. Er...all sorts: Japanese, Western, Indian, Chinese, tea rooms, coffee shops, fast food, you name it. Places where you can have a big meal or...or just a snack, if that's what you're after.

Er...in the summer you can go up to the...to the very top floor, where there's a roof area with a beer garden, er...a play area for children, and you can sit in the open air, enjoy the breeze and...er...enjoy the view of the city. One store even has a golf school on the roof, ha, believe it or not! But at the end of the summer on September 1st all this is closed, even if the weather's still hot, because that's the official end of the summer in Japan and people start wearing their winter clothes then...er...as well. So...er...you have to wait till the next Summer, which starts on June 1st.

PRESENTER: Mm. As a...as a non-Japanese speaker, how does one cope with these places?

RICHARD: Well, at the main...at the main entrance you can...you can pick up a store directory and a brochure in English. Anywhere in the store, if you ask one of the assistants...er, 'Do you speak English?', they'll smile and rush off to find someone who does. It really couldn't be easier. The other thing is, every store has staff whose only duty is to welcome customers. So you find many lifts have a young female operator in a uniform wearing white gloves, who bows to you as you enter the lift and welcomes you to her lift, and she announces what's on each floor as the doors open and bows to you again as you leave. A...and when the store opens in the morning at 10 am, the staff stand at the edge of their department welcoming you. And at the close of business at 7 pm they're there again saying goodbye to everyone.

PRESENTER: And are those the shop hours? It's always 10 to 7?

RICHARD: Yes, usually. Oh, and they're all open six days a week. Er...they're always open on Saturdays and Sundays and on national holidays. They do close one day during the week — but different stores in the same district all close on different days. The floors with all the restaurants are open later, er...usually till 10.30. Some stores have their own railways too.

PRESENTER: Their own railways?

RICHARD: Yes, the...these are stores owned by one of the private railway companies: um...Od...Odakyu, er...Keio, Seibu and Tobu in Tokyo, for example. Er...you take the lift or escalator from the store all the way down to the station, and you step out onto the platform, where your commuter train is waiting to take you home. Er...the main store is the terminus of the line. Um...and some of these companies own baseball teams too: the Seibu Lions are one of the top teams.

PRESENTER: It sounds like these stores are all quite similar to each other.

RICHARD: Mm.

PRESENTER: So how do they...how do they go about...um...creating a difference between them, making their own mark, if you like?

RICHARD: Yeah, well, at one store, the assistants wear badges showing their hobby, such as, well, it could be 'Flower Arranger' or...er...'Veteran Golfer', so that customers can relate to them on a personal level. At another store they might wear bright yellow shirts, so that customers can identify them easily. Department stores in Japan don't compete on price but on the quality of their service, and the...and the range of choice they offer. All the stores are full of the latest gadgets, fashions and accessories from all over the world. Um...so above all it's...it's really to do with how much of a pleasure it is to spend time there.

PRESENTER: And...er...can you only find these Japanese stores in Japan?

RICHARD: No, there are big Japanese department stores in Singapore, Hong Kong and other Asian cities. Er...there is a Mitsukoshi branch in London but it's quite small. Um...a large number of its customers are Japanese people. One of the things assistants at the London store have to do is to help worried Japanese tourists find their lost luggage or passports, or...er...get in touch with relations – it's all part of the service they offer. And of course it encourages customers to be loyal to Mitsukoshi when they get back home again. Customer loyalty is very important.

PRESENTER: Mm, absolutely, if your customers are happy, they'll keep coming back again.

RICHARD: That's exactly right.

PRESENTER: Well, Richard, thank you very much indeed.

RICHARD: Thank you.

7.6 Dear Sir, ...
COMPOSITION

A This activity can only be done with a partner.

B 🖉 If possible, ask another person to read and mark your work.

Model version:

Dear Sir/Madam,

I am writing about the hi-fi system I purchased at your store six months ago. Since I bought the system I have moved house and am now living 150 kilometres away from your store. I have tried phoning you but the number has been constantly engaged or if I have been connected, I have been kept waiting in a queue and have not been able to continue hanging on. The last time I called, I waited for 35 minutes and still did not speak to anyone. So I have now resorted to writing.

Since I bought the system I have had nothing but trouble. First of all the CD player disc slot got stuck and wouldn't open or close. After three weeks you managed to provide me with a new system. Then the cassette player seized up and after a delay of six weeks you fixed it. Now the mini disk player will not function on record mode. One of my main reasons for buying this system was so that I could record my CDs on to MDs and listen to them on my car MD system. As I have a long drive to work it is important to me to have something entertaining to listen to instead of DJ chat.

Please can you suggest what I should do. As the system is under a year old you have a statutory obligation either to fix it or provide me with a satisfactory alternative. As I no longer live near your store I cannot deliver the system for repair in person. Nor am I willing to pay carriage on what would undoubtedly be an expensive delivery bill. I suggest that you arrange to collect it from my place of work (address enclosed) or nominate a store in my locality which will carry out the repairs on your behalf. Failing either of these options, I should like a refund of the full purchase price.

I enclose a copy of my original receipt with the details of the system on it.

I look forward to your early reply,

Yours faithfully,

7.7 Further uses of -ing
ADVANCED GRAMMAR

A Suggested answers:

1 receiving/dealing with/making   being/appearing
2 looking at/reading   discovering/finding out/seeing   buying
3 talking to/appealing to/speaking
4 reading
5 closing   (*This is really true.*)
6 taking/enrolling for/studying on/attending   doing   reading   keeping in touch   writing
7 to meeting
8 to being

B Answers:

1 their/them coming   their/them watching   their/them being/getting   reading
2 doing/'s doing   his/him making
3 them/their smoking   them/their asking
4 Tony falling   Jane/me/my trying

C Suggested answers:

1 It isn't worth travelling to London to do your shopping.
2 We were upset about his forgetting to inform us.
3 Instead of spending your money, it might be a better idea to save it.
4 Besides being a champion athlete, she speaks four languages fluently.
5 As well as having a job in an office, he works in a shop at weekends.
6 Without phoning them, you won't/can't find out if they're open.

---

7 Ever since first seeing her, he has been in love with her.
8 Your not consulting me beforehand was inconsiderate / Your failure to consult me beforehand . . .

7.8 Compound nouns
VOCABULARY DEVELOPMENT

A These are some of the compound nouns in the first six paragraphs:

¶1 West Edmonton Mall   flatlands
¶2 fluorescent lights   indoor plants service industries   department store
¶3 Empire State Building   jelly babies   cloakroom
¶4 consumer seductions   eating establishments bingo hall
¶5 wave machine   undersea life   skating rink golf course   financial service outlets
¶6 public relations   summer environment

B Suggested answers:

air conditioning   burglar alarm   common sense driving licence   fancy dress   estate agent generation gap   greenhouse effect   hay fever heart attack   hire purchase   income tax   junk food mail order   mother tongue   nervous breakdown package tour   paper clip   parking meter pedestrian crossing   pocket money   shopping mall show business   unemployment benefit weather forecast   window shopping

C Suggested answers (many variations are possible):

one-parent family   current account/affairs stainless steel   traveller's cheque   compact disc (player)   exclamation mark   swimming pool/costume/trunks   skating rink   delivery van/charge   chain store   clearance sale travel agent/agency   wastepaper basket

D Suggested answers:

1 shopping mall/shopping centre window shopping/bargain hunting
2 current account/bank account   credit card
3 charity shop   clearance sale/discount store
4 mail order   delivery charge
5 bar code
6 estate agent/real estate agent travel agent/travel agency/travel agent's
7 fancy dress   wastepaper basket
8 driving licence   traveller's cheques/pocket money

7.9 Advertising: Sequencing your ideas
WRITING SKILLS AND COMPOSITION

A This is the sequence of paragraphs in the original article:

1 e c b d g f a 9

Variations may be possible.

B Suggested answers:

¶ **a** . . . <u>our</u> German branches . . .
  Benetton's

¶ **b** . . . payments to <u>the fashion chain</u> . . .
  Benetton
  . . . saying <u>it</u> had no inclination . . .
  Benetton

¶ **c** . . . to sue <u>the company</u> . . .
  Benetton
  . . . which <u>they</u> claim . . .
  the group of German retailers

¶ **d** . . . if <u>they</u> wore . . .
  children of the parents who spoke to
  Mr Hartwich

¶ **e** . . . protested against <u>the advertisements</u> . . .
  the 'tasteless' ones mentioned in the headline

¶ **f** Several <u>similar</u> cases . . .
  similar to the proposed German lawsuits

C Say your answers softly to yourself. Maybe record yourself.

D **1–4** 🖉 If possible, ask another person to read and mark your work.

Model version:

> Advertising comes in many forms. There are TV commercials which are often as entertaining as the TV programmes themselves. There are huge, colourful posters on hoardings in the streets and ads in newspapers and magazines, which undoubtedly brighten our lives. Then there is the endless stream of mail-order catalogues, and junk mail which attempts to personalise the advertising process, by addressing you by name in every line of the text. The lowest form of advertising is "cold calling" when companies phone numbers in the telephone directory and try to get you interested in their product.
>
> The potency of advertising can be illustrated by two apparently unconnected facts: the huge budgets companies dedicate to funding their campaigns and the banning of tobacco advertising in Britain. Both underline the effectiveness of the process. But does it do us any good? Well, without advertising we wouldn't know about the many products on offer and the fact that we know there are several similar products means that competition flourishes and prices can be that bit cheaper. Advertising also provides a major source of income for newspapers and television companies. Without this income many newspapers would disappear.
>
> On the downside, advertising has helped to encourage rampant consumerism where demand is created for totally unnecessary goods and in many cases for goods which the purchaser cannot afford. This creates discontent among those unable to buy, a temptation to live beyond one's means and maybe even crime among those who feel it is their right to own as much as the next man. This increase in materialism and the throwaway society also contributes towards damage to the environment. Some ads, e.g. those for alcohol, may have a negative influence on the young who may associate glamour, social success etc. with drinking and feel that they have to drink to achieve status with their peers. Although the effect of competition is to drive prices down one cannot but wonder how much lower the prices would be without the costs of advertising.

8

Have I got news for you!

8.1 ## The media
TOPIC VOCABULARY

A Say your answers softly to yourself. Maybe record yourself.

(*Have I got news for you!* is something people say when they have something surprising to tell someone.)

B Answers:

> *article* = report   *circulation* = number of copies sold
> *editorial* = leader   *issue* = number   *magazines* =
> monthlies & weeklies   *main story* = lead story
> *newsreader* = newscaster   *the papers* = the dailies
> *reporter* = journalist   *reviewer* = critic
>
> Further useful vocabulary: *columnist   correspondent*
> *column   cover story   scoop*

C Brief explanations of the incongruities in each headline:

1 Dogs normally attack cats
2 *Actual meaning:* The staff of the hospital are guarding the victim of the stabbing
  Funny meaning: The guards at the hospital have stabbed a patient
3 *Actual meaning:* A drunk man was found by the police in a shop window
  Funny meaning: Police officers were found intoxicated in a shop window
4 Teachers are normally considered to be wonderful – this one was atypical
5 Controversy over the price of butter is increasing, but you spread butter on bread
6 Lighter means less heavy, but also cigarette lighter
7 *Actual meaning:* A mine is a kind of bomb
  Funny meaning: My . . . exploded . . .
8 *Actual meaning:* Negotiations about fish quotas . . .
  Funny meaning: A talking fish . . .

8.2 ## Modal verbs
GRAMMAR REVIEW

A Suggested answers:

1 Could you finish the article?
  – *Please finish reading or writing it*
  Were you able to finish the article?
  – *Did you manage to finish reading or writing it?*
2 Can you carry this box?
  – *Are you strong enough to carry it?*
  or *Please carry it for me.*
  Could you carry this box?
  – *Please carry it for me*
3 You can't leave yet.
  – *You're not allowed to leave / I won't allow you to leave*
  You needn't leave yet.
  – *You're not obliged to leave (but you can if you want)*

4 I don't need to read the paper today.
& I needn't read the paper today.
& I don't have to read the paper today.
& I haven't got to read the paper today.
– It isn't necessary for me to read it, I'm under no obligation to read it
I shouldn't read the paper today.
– It's wrong for me to read it, I'm not supposed to read it (but I may do so)
I haven't read the paper today.
– So far today I've had no chance to read it (but I may do later)

5 There could be an election this year.
– It's possible that there will be one
There has to be an election this year.
– This is the year when (by law) an election is held
or *The government are under a moral obligation to call an election*
There should be an election this year.
– It's likely that there will be one
or *There is supposed to be one, but it may not actually happen*
There will be an election this year.
– An election is going to be held this year, that's certain

6 That could be Tony at the door.
& That might be Tony at the door.
– It's possible that it's him at the door
That must be Tony at the door.
& That will be Tony at the door.
– I'm sure that he's at the door: no one else is expected
That can't be Tony at the door.
– Someone is at the door but I'm sure that it's not Tony
That should be Tony at the door.
– I'm fairly sure it's Tony

B Suggested answers:

2 They said that they might be able to help me.
They said that it was possible that they could help me.

3 He told me that I couldn't/mustn't use a dictionary in the exam.
He told me that I wasn't allowed/permitted to use a dictionary in the exam.

4 She asked me if I had to leave so soon.
She asked me if it was necessary for me to leave so soon.

5 He told us that we mustn't/shouldn't believe everything we read in the newspapers.
He told us that it was unwise to believe everything . . .
He told us not to believe everything . . .

6 She told us that she didn't dare to dive into the swimming pool.
She told us that she didn't have the courage to dive . . .

7 He told us that we needed to book a table.
He told us that it was necessary to book a table.

8 She wondered what time she had to arrive there.
She wondered what time it was necessary for her to arrive there.

C Suggested answers (more variations are possible):

1 The minister for sports said that fewer people can swim than in the past.
The sports minister has said that more people are unable to swim than in the past.

2 People mustn't smoke in any cinema.
Smoking is not allowed/permitted in cinemas.

3 Passengers (will) have to wear a seat belt in the rear seat of a car.
The wearing of seat belts in rear seats is (going) to be compulsory.

4 Drivers will no longer have to keep to 70 miles an hour.
Drivers will be able/allowed to drive over 70 miles per hour.

5 Thousands of people had to leave their homes after the earthquake.

6 There may well be another recession.
A recession is likely in the near future.

7 The socialists should win the election.
The socialists are likely to win the election.

8 Many commuters couldn't get home because of a railway strike.
A railway strike has prevented many commuters from getting home.

D 1 & 2 If possible, ask another person to read and mark your work.

8.3 Goodbye, England's Rose . . .
READING AND SPEAKING

A The title of this section refers to the 1997 Elton John/Bernie Taupin song, which has sold more copies worldwide than any other record in history. It was based on their original song, *Candle in the Wind* (1973) – same music, different words, which was a tribute to Marilyn Monroe.

B Answers:

¶ 1 *sideline* = unimportant event   *dignified* = shown respect

¶ 2 *reverberated* = echoed   *mythological status* = legendary position

¶ 3 *accelerated* = went faster   *unassailable* = invulnerable   *eroded* = damaged   *titillated and tantalised* = excited and fascinated   *spicy* = exciting   *alluring* = attractive

¶ 4 *gauche* = awkward   *chillingly* = frighteningly   *elusive* = mysterious   *alienation* = feeling of isolation

¶ 5 *unrelenting* = continuous   *causes* = charities

¶ 7 *hybrid* = mixed   *craved* = couldn't live without   *Establishment* = ruling classes   *dénouement* = ending

C Say your answers softly to yourself. Maybe record yourself.

8.4 '...that is part of the job'

LISTENING

 A 🔊 **Answers:**

1 off duty   **2a** ignore   **2b** calm
3 distressing/upsetting   4 part of the job
5 ridiculous   6 goats ate/nibbled her clothes
7 emergency   8 accurate

TRANSCRIPT   *7 minutes*

JAYNE: My name's Jayne Evans, and I'm a news journalist, which is a broad term for what I've been doing for the last fifteen years. I've been news anchoring, I've been news presenting, I've been news writing, newspaper writing, and producing.

INTERVIEWER: And jobs like that always seem so glamorous and so exciting, and would you say they actually are?

JAYNE: Yes, of course they are. They are exciting, they are glamorous, but, and there is a big but, they are hard work as well. Now, when I say that to people they say, 'Oh surely not, no, you must be joking!' But they are hard work because you don't stop. You may have the most gorgeous, glamorous hotel room, you may be eating the most delicious meals, but you're still working, you're still thinking about what you're doing, and you're still thinking about the piece of television that you're making. So you're never really off duty, but, hey, I'm not complaining.

INTERVIEWER: No, fair enough, fair enough. What about when you were a news anchor person?

JAYNE: Um...I must admit that when I first started doing it, I didn't enjoy it very much, because I was so nervous. Of course you're going to be nervous, you've either...when you're doing the radio news presenting, you know that there are possibly thousands, millions of people listening to you. When you're on television, they're also looking at you, and s...looking at how you look, and looking at what you're wearing, and they're also listening to what you're saying. Everything, you think, everything has got to be perfect.

INTERVIEWER: And have you ever had to...um...present any really difficult news cases, or things that have...um...where the news changes all the time, where you have to think on your feet?

JAYNE: Well, that is part of the job. You're live on air, you've got a little earpiece in your ear and you've got the people in the gallery talking to you all the time, at the same time you're reading the words on the autocue and if things change, you have to ignore the words that are in front of you on that autocue and listen to what someone's telling you in your ear, and speak those words. So...but that is part of the job, that's what you're paid to do, you're paid to look calm on the in...outside, while, of course, on the inside things are all scrambling and you're in a panic, but your job is to present things calmly to the public.

INTERVIEWER: What do you think are the most sensitive stories you've had to deal with?

JAYNE: Well, there have been plenty over the fifteen years of my journalistic career so far. Some that really stick in my mind are having to go to the scene of accidents, for example, the Paddington rail crash. That's very hard, because you're dealing with something that is very shocking, you're seeing something that shocks you personally, but you've still got to remain calm, and you've got to deliver the news very calmly and very sensibly, and very informatively. Another experience that sticks in my mind very vividly, one that I haven't been able to forget, is when I went to Romania, shortly after the overthrow of Ceaucescu, and I went to some of the hospitals there, and I saw cots with babies in them, all of whom had AIDS or hepatitis, and I knew those babies were going to die. So those stories that...that stick with me, they're... sometimes I think about them in the middle of the night, they're perhaps the downside of this profession, that sort of story, but even then, when you are covering that sort of story, there's a satisfaction in knowing that by covering it you're...you're telling the world what's going on, and what you're doing does actually matter.

INTERVIEWER: Yes, definitely. So do you have to develop a...a way of detaching yourself?

JAYNE: Ideally, you should. I think all of us are human, and I have to be honest that after covering stories like those stories, like...er...disasters, when you're dealing with bereaved people, I find it difficult to sleep for a few nights, and I'm only human, every journalist is only human, but in the end you have to try and put it to the back of your mind, because it is important that you tell the story properly and tell the story fairly, and do justice to the people who are bereaved or the people who are suffering. That's the most important thing. But yes, it does affect me, it does affect every journalist who covers stories like that, but that is part of the job.

INTERVIEWER: That's the darker side certainly, what are the funny bits?

JAYNE: Oh, there are so many funny bits, that's the great thing about this career. And I think what you have to develop is...um...a sense of the ridiculous, and enjoy the ridiculous, there are times when I've thought, 'What a silly way to make a living!' Times when I've been surrounded by herds of goats that are nibbling at my clothes, or times when I've been asked to deliver a piece to camera while hanging off the side of a boat, or I've been asked to jump out of an aeroplane and do a parachute jump for a report, and you think, 'Why am I doing this? I'm scared, or I'm dirty or I'm cold or I've got animals eating my clothes, why am I doing it?' But then you laugh and you think, 'Well, what a great...great way to make a living. And, hey, someone's paying me to do this'. It's ridiculous, but it's fun.

INTERVIEWER: Is there a typical day for a news journalist?

JAYNE: Well, no, there isn't and that is one of the most pleasing things about this profession, because you never know what's going to happen. If you're a news journalist, and you're sitting in the office, reading the newspaper, drinking coffee, you're waiting for something to happen, you're almost like another emergency service, in that when something does happen, you drop your newspaper, you drop your coffee, and you run out of the door with your notebook and your coat over your arm to the scene of whatever's happening. For example, I was sitting in Television Centre working for the BBC a couple of years ago, when the news came through that there was possibly a bomb planted at a race course, they said, 'Quick get out there'. So I got straight into a taxi, went to the...went to the race course and reported on what was happening, reported on the evacuation of the people coming out and filed my reports, my...mine was the first report to go on to the radio to say what was happening. It was a very exciting time. Another story I remember, again I was sitting there reading the newspaper, drinking coffee, and my news editor...editor said, 'Quickly get out there, apparently there's been a murder'. And I had to rush to the scene of a murder, where it was a very sad story, where...um...three children had been murdered, and again you get there first, you have to think on your feet, you have to broadcast almost immediately with the information that you have to hand, and then once you've done one broadcast, you gather some more information and you update your broadcast, and so the day goes on. It's very very busy, there's lots of adrenalin pumping, and while that adrenalin is pumping it's very important that also whatever you broadcast is accurate, so it's a very difficult combination of things. Your…inside your…your mind is racing, but you have to make sure that the words that come out of your mouth, or that come out of the end of your pen are accurate.

B Say your answers softly to yourself. Maybe record yourself.

8.5 ## Cream and punishment
READING

A **Answers:**

| 1 B | 2 F | 3 A | 4 E | 5 C | 6 D |

B Say your answers softly to yourself. Maybe record yourself.

C **1 & 2** 🖉 Making notes helps to bridge the gap between finding the relevant information in the text and writing a summary. The notes should be short. If time is short, though, and in the exam, it's probably OK to underline the relevant information in the text in pencil, or to highlight it.

The equivalent summary-writing task in the exam (Use of English Part 5) is based on two shorter texts, not a long one like this.

Model summary:

> Noël Godin believes that certain famous people who are full of their own self-importance and who lack humour should be deflated by a good dose of custard pie thrown in the face. His targets include big bosses and those who abuse their power. The pompous and those who restrict the freedom of others are also in line for a cream attack. He sees himself as a slightly mad terrorist who is making a political statement but who wounds only the self-esteem of his victims.

8.6 ## Prefixes
VOCABULARY DEVELOPMENT

The use of hyphens with prefixes is very hard to lay down rules about. The prefixes in **A** usually have a hyphen, the ones in **B** don't usually have one.

A **Answers** (the words with ? are possible but unusual):

anti-	anti-American anti-democracy? anti-federal anti-feminist anti-monarchy anti-test? anti-union
pro-	pro-American pro-democracy pro-federal pro-feminist pro-monarchy pro-union
pre-	pre-cooked pre-packed pre-test
super-	super-intelligent superstar superstore
half-	half-American? half-asleep half-brother half-cooked half-expect half-packed? half-time half-truth half-way

B **Answers** (the words with ? are possible but unusual):

re	reappear rebuild recapture refasten refillable regrow? reload renumber reprint reunited reusable revalue? rework?
un	unblock unfasten unload unusable
over	overbuild? overestimate overload oversimplify overvalue overwork (+ overgrown)
under	underestimate undervalue
out	outgrow outnumber outvote

Prefixes can also be used creatively or 'actively', as in these examples:
Once something is printed you can't **unprint** it.
This area has been **overbuilt**. (= there has been too much building)

C **Answers:**

self-	self-defeating self-educated self-employed self-explanatory self-governing self-preservation self-sufficient
co-	co-director co-exist co-owner
counter-	counter-measure
ex-	ex-director ex-official ex-owner ex-policeman ex-president
semi-	semi-automatic semi-circular semi-educated semi-employed? semi-official semi-productive?
sub	subheading substandard subtitle

D **Answers:**

1. oversimplification
2. overestimating
3. pro-strike outvoted
4. counter-productive over-react
5. subtitles
6. super-rich superstars outsell
7. self-explanatory
8. half-expected ex-wife
9. counter-attack pre-arranged
10. reappeared half-frozen

And here are some more prefixes:

ante-	(= before)	ante-natal anteroom
auto-	(= by itself)	auto-reverse auto-record auto-timer
fore	(= before)	forewarned is forearmed foretaste
post-	(= after)	post-war postgraduate
mega	(= large/great)	megastar megadollars
mono	(= one/single)	monosyllabic monochrome
bi	(= two/double)	bilateral bilingual bisexual bicentenary bi-annual
tri	(= three/triple)	trilateral trilogy triplet

8.7 There ...
ADVANCED GRAMMAR

A **1 & 2** Suggested answers:

1 There's somebody waiting to see you.
– *more informal*
2 There are no easy answers to most political problems.
– *more informal*
3 There's no point in trying to explain the problem to them.
– *no special difference in emphasis*
4 There is more coverage given to sport in some papers than others.
– *less emphasis on* some papers
5 Luckily for us there was a telephone box nearby.
– *no special difference*
6 There's no need to shout, I can hear you perfectly well.
– *more informal*
7 There are 14 branches of Mitsukoshi in Japan – and (there are) 14 associate stores too.
– *slightly more emphasis on the number*
8 Come quickly! There has been an accident! There may be some people hurt!
– *more informal*
9 There he stood with a sheepish grin on his face.
– *more amusing, narrative technique*
10 There were fifteen of us waiting in the lecture hall.
– *more emphasis on the number*

B Suggested answers:

1 will be/to be 2 must be no 3 comes
4 is a lot of 5 is just one 6 denying 7 being
8 seems

C Suggested answers:

1 The police say **that there were fewer than 5,000 people in the peace demonstration.**
2 The forecasters say **that there will be more sunshine next week.**
3 The England soccer manager says **that there is no doubt that his team will win tonight's international match.**
4 Environmentalists say **that there are too many cars causing pollution and accidents.**
5 According to the newspaper **there could/might be a general election this year.**
6 There **have been attempts to reconcile both sides in the teachers' strike/dispute.**
7 There **have been fewer road accidents this year.**
8 There **were no casualties when the ferry sank.**

D This activity can only be done with a partner.

8.8 Hitting the headlines
LISTENING AND SPEAKING

A Answers:

| 1 Japan | 2 USA | 3 Italy | 4 Italy |
| 5 Japan | 6 USA | 7 Italy | 8 Italy |

TRANSCRIPT   *5 minutes 30 seconds*

ANNOUNCER: And now it's time for 'Strange But True', introduced by Joanne Thomas.

JOANNE: Hello, and welcome to this week's collection of unusual stories which really happened this week, but did not hit the headlines. Today we hear about a Japanese boat made out of old beer cans, an office worker who pretended to be blind, and some very unsuccessful robbers in the USA. But first Sally Vincent in Rome, with news of an over-enthusiastic lifeguard. Sally?

SALLY: Thank you, Joanne. Well, for holidaymakers the sea can be a dangerous place, what with sharks and jellyfish and pollution and strong currents. But at the Italian resort of Ravenna these perils paled into insignificance alongside lifeguard Lorenzo Trippi, who was recently sacked for accidentally killing three people with lifebelts. Mr Trippi, a former discus-thrower, had been employed by Ravenna municipal council on account of his 'excellent physique and willingness to do good'. Things started to go wrong from the word go, however. A fellow lifeguard told reporters: 'Whenever he heard a cry he would rush into the sea and scream, "Don't panic!" And then he'd throw the life preserver at them.' Unfortunately, Mr Trippi couldn't shake off the habits of his discus-throwing days and would launch his lifebelts with just a little too much force and accuracy. Each time he hit his target square on the forehead and knocked them out — and they drowned. On several occasions he also threw lifebelts at people who were merely waving to relatives. One holidaymaker said: 'I was signalling my wife to get me an ice-cream with nuts, and the next thing I knew a lifebelt hit me in the face and broke my jaw.' So Mr Trippi is now looking for another job better suited to his talents!

JOANNE: Thank you, Sally. William Cosgrove in Tokyo was at the quayside to welcome home a Japanese folk hero.

WILLIAM: Four and a half months ago the Japanese adventurer Kenichi Horie set out from Salinas in Ecuador in a solar-powered boat with a difference — it's a cigar-shaped vessel made out of 27,000 recycled aluminium beer cans and driven by an electric motor. This week he sailed into Tokyo Bay after making the world's first solar-powered crossing of the Pacific Ocean. The 9.5 metre *Malt's Mermaid* has 12 square metres of solar cells that can generate one and a half kilowatts of electricity to recharge its two nickel-hydrogen batteries. One battery drives the boat's motor, the other the fridge, a radio, the lighting and a video recorder. He started out with 120 cans of Malt's beer, planning to enjoy one can of beer each evening while he was at sea, but one of his water purifiers broke so he had to conserve his stocks of liquid in case the other water purifier broke.

Mr Horie is a folk hero in Japan. He was the first person to sail solo across the Pacific – that was back in 1962. Since then he's made 7 more solo voyages, including crossing the Pacific in the world's shortest ocean-going sailing vessel, measuring just 2.8 metres – and sailing round the world both latitudinally (which is the normal way) and longitudinally (via the Arctic and Antarctic).

JOANNE: Amazing. Well, they do say that crime doesn't pay. This is what four men in the USA found out recently. Here's Philip Miller.

PHILIP: Henry Norton and his brother Billy were sent to prison yesterday in Oklahoma after being convicted of bank robbery. They broke into a bank in the middle of the night, emptied the safe of $100,000 and also stole the bank's video camera, which was recording their crime. Unfortunately for them the video recorder was located in another part of the bank, so they didn't get the videotape of them stealing the camera. The police were able to watch the video at their leisure and use it as evidence in their trial.

And in Kentucky last week two men tried to pull the front off a cash machine by running a chain to the bumper of their pick-up truck. But instead of pulling the front panel off the machine, they pulled the bumper off their truck, with the chain still attached to the machine. Also attached to the bumper was . . . their license plate! So the police had no difficulty in finding them early the next morning.

JOANNE: Duh! And finally here's Sally Vincent again from Rome.

SALLY: Some people will do anything to keep hold of their job. But there aren't many who can match the dedication of Claudio Ferro from Rovigo in Northern Italy. For 20 years he persuaded his fellow office workers he was blind. It all began when Mr Ferro applied for a job as a switchboard operator. This is what he said in an interview last week: 'I thought they'd be more sympathetic if I was blind, so I went to the interview with a white stick and dark glasses. They were extremely kind, especially when I pretended to fall down the stairs on my way out.' The ruse evidently worked because Mr Ferro landed the job, and spent the next two decades bumping into doors, knocking things off tables, and accidentally rubbing up against attractive women. He had no regrets and still says: 'It was wonderful. People got my shopping for me, and took me on holidays, and I always got a huge Christmas bonus.' His subterfuge was eventually discovered when fellow workers spotted his photo in a paper after he won a national cross-country roller-skating competition.

JOANNE: And with that from Sally Vincent, it's goodbye from us at 'Strange But True'. Join us again next week at the same time.

8.9 Freedom
SPEAKING

A & B Say your answers softly to yourself. Maybe record yourself on a blank cassette or voice recorder.

C This activity can only be done with a partner, or preferably with two partners.

8.10 Long and short sentences
WRITING SKILLS

A Suggested answers:

1 shortest sentence: 'These are bad times for talking.'
– an abrupt, intriguing opening, making you want to read more.
2 longest sentence: '[1] Early in the Seventies [2] Mr Weeds did break his silence [3] to ask his wife [4] if she wanted to go to Thailand, [5] and she broke hers [6] to say no, [7] but otherwise all has been mutual muteness, [8] a fact which, insists Mrs Weeds, in no way affects their love for each other.'
– the sentence contains eight different ideas (numbered in the quote above). Giving a lot of information in a single sentence is economical, but it's harder for the reader to take it all in, especially at the end of the sentence.
3 Direct speech is used three times by the writer (plus once by Mrs Weeds). This makes the whole article seem more immediate and authentic than if reported speech had been used, as it is in the longest sentence.

B The relevant sentences from the other articles:

Flying too close to the sun
1 She was 36.
2 As with Kennedy and with James Dean, John Lennon and Marilyn Monroe, she was a superstar who died young in violent circumstances, and as with them, it will guarantee her a mythological status.
3 'Unthinkable,' people said . . .

Cream and punishment
1 Gloup.
2 Meanwhile, 30 pie-throwers, who have been standing in groups of three, suddenly come together, and, in a whirlwind of cakes, they strike their target.
3 Lots – it's an interview.

C **1–3** This model version is the original article:

Possibly the worst day in the history of organised – or rather disorganised – crime was experienced by Miami thief Natron Fubble, 35, surely a prime candidate for the title of 'World's Most Inept Robber'. The day started with an early morning raid on a delicatessen which was cut short after the shop owner hit Mr Fubble in the face with a giant salami, breaking his nose. An attempted bank robbery ended before it had even begun when he met his mother in the same bank and was sent to do some shopping for her. The climax however came late in the afternoon, when pursued by irate customers after another failed hold-up, he took refuge in the boot of an empty car. Unbeknown to the clueless criminal, however, the car was in fact a police surveillance vehicle whose owners, returning from a cup of coffee, drove for five days across America tailing a suspicious lorry. His whimpers were eventually heard just south of Seattle where he was removed at gunpoint and arrested. He was sentenced to two years in prison, despite claiming he was on a top-secret undercover mission for the FBI.

8.11 Points of view
SPEAKING AND COMPOSITION

A **1 & 2** If you don't have a partner, look at the photographs and decide for yourself what you think is happening.

B **1–3** If possible, ask another person to read and mark your work.

Model version:

> <u>Before the incident</u>
> I was at Elements nightclub in town, having a night out with my friends and my brother. We danced a lot and I had had a few drinks. I don't mean I was drunk, just chilled, you know. Anyway, these guys started hassling us, making comments on our clothes, our hairstyles, our dancing. In fact they were being pretty rude about us altogether. In the end, I'd had enough and threw a punch at the one with the loudest mouth. One of the bouncers came up and warned us both. They backed off after that. They were out of their heads on something. I think it was booze. Anyway we stayed until the club shut. It was about 2.30 when we left.
>
> <u>The attack</u>
> Max and I started to walk back home. We had gone about 200 metres from the club when we were jumped on. We managed to throw them off and started running. We ran through the shopping precinct and car park and headed for home along the river. They seemed to be pretty fit and soon caught us. They threw me to the ground and Max ran off. There were three of them. They were extremely drunk and were yelling all kinds of abuse at me. The one I'd hit in the club started kicking me all over my body. I was trying to protect my head with my arms when another one pulled my arms away. The loudmouth then laid into my head. He kicked me on the left side of my head and cut my eye. My ear was very painful too. After that I lost consciousness. I was dimly aware of them talking; they sounded scared and I think they thought they might have gone too far.
>
> <u>After the attack</u>
> The next thing I remember is Max calling me. He was trying to make me stand up but I couldn't. The pain in my head and left ear was terrible. I kept fainting. I came to again in Casualty where a nurse and a policeman were asking me questions. I made a statement 3 days after I was attacked. I had to stay in hospital for 6 weeks. My hearing in my left ear is impaired and I'm terrified to go out.

8.12 *bring* and *get*
VERBS AND IDIOMS

B **Suggested answers:**

1 made me realise   raise   go unpunished for
2 caused   find a way round/find a way to manage in spite of
3 find a way of dealing with/recover from   asking for advice or help from
4 reveals/shows everyone my worst characteristics   be friendly with   making me feel depressed
5 made the whole audience laugh   understand the point of
6 criticising/poking fun at him   recovers from
7 get revenge   have my revenge on
8 nearly run out   come to the end of

9 make them understand
10 trying to communicate
11 make him less shy
12 fall asleep   not making enough progress with   got out of bed   started   completed/accomplished

B **Answers:**

1 get on with   2 get out of   3 got off with   got at (bribed or threatened)   4 get   down
5 brought about   6 get on   get in with
7 get on to/bring up   8 get round
9 get round to   10 get   up   11 bring up
12 getting up to

9   Education   Schools   Universities   Study skills
A learning curve

9.1 Happy days?
LISTENING AND TOPIC VOCABULARY

The 'three Rs' are **R**eading, w**R**iting and a**R**ithmetic. This term is used even in serious discussions about education.

A (steep) learning curve describes a skill that is hard for someone to master, particularly if they are being trained to do something or have to learn what to do in a new job. Some people also say that one's school days are *the happiest days of your life*!

A **Answers:**

1 geography   hate children   chemistry   beauty
2 Latin   subject
   enjoyed her pupils/what her pupils did
3 **a** good fun/interesting
   b beneath contempt
   c utterly contemptible
   d relationships and friendships
4 bully   victimised   English   heard   disapproved

TRANSCRIPTS   *6 minutes 40 seconds*

PRESENTER: Ruth you went to school in Wales. What kind of school did you go to?
RUTH: I went to a comprehensive school, um…which …er…was just around the corner from me, so it was really near. It took me five minutes to get to school every morning. I'd wake up at ten to…ten to nine and be in assembly at nine o'clock!
   What I didn't like about…er…our school…um…really, well it was one particular subject and that was geography. And I think the only reason I didn't like it was because of the teacher I had. And…er…his name was…um…Mr James, and he just seemed to really hate children. He…I don't even know why he was a teacher. He had no time at all for us, and he used to look at us with such scorn. And I can remember dreading his lessons so much because he was so nasty. I remember once going into the lesson and I just thought, 'I can't stick it here any longer!' So I pretended to faint, and even though I did a really good job, I think I was quite convincing, he…er…still had no sympathy for me whatsoever, and just said, 'Oh, get out of the classroom, Ruth Jones!' and was just really horrible.

Er...I really really didn't like chemistry. Um...all those symbols and...and formula and things like that, and I know some people...I remember one teacher saying, 'But chemistry is beautiful.' And I just thought he was mad. I mean, now that I'm older I can kind of see the beauty of science and all that, but...haha...when I was like fourteen I couldn't stand it. It used to make me physically ill to have to go to a chemistry lesson.

★★★

PRESENTER: Sarah, you went to school in England, is there one particular teacher that you remember from your school days?

SARAH: Well, my Latin teacher. I mean, I undoubtedly did Latin because of Mrs Marston, hahaha, who was a completely chaotic teacher. She...her passion for the subject overrode any lesson plan, so we were constantly taken off at tangents, and grammar was flung up on the blackboard, so I never understood Latin grammar. But I just adored it because of her complete passion for the subject. And also, she really enjoyed what we did, and that was...that was another hugely important element. Um...she wasn't...if she...if we'd done little Latin plays or something, she would roar with laughter at the back of the classroom, so there was a sense that she took genuine pleasure from what we did, as well as communicating something herself.

★★★

PRESENTER: Christine, you went to school in Scotland, what kind of school did you go to?

CHRISTINE: Well, it was a school which you went to at five and you stayed, all being well, until you were eighteen. And there were boys and girls, and it meant that you developed a really interesting view...er...of boys, which changed as you got older. So when I was very little the boys were good fun...um...and because I was a bit of a tomboy, they had...they did things and played with things in the classroom that I thought were much more interesting than the things the girls played with. And then we went through a phase of ignoring the boys strenuously because they were completely beneath contempt, and I suppose that was between the ages of about $10\frac{1}{2}$ and about 14 or 15. And then discovering that boys were awfully interesting but not the boys in your own year group which were...who were utterly contemptible...um...because girls and boys are so different in their development, aren't they? And a 14-year-old girl can see no merits whatsoever in a 14-year-old boy. And all the girls are...are gazing at the 16, 17 and 18-year-old 'big boys', who are much more interesting.

And then as we got to the end of our schooling...er...what in Scotland would be the fifth and the sixth year, in England would be the lower and the upper sixth years, the last two years. Of course things...the boys had caught up really and we became very good friends again all of us and so our last two years at school, um...I think we...we had lovely relationships and lovely friendships. And...er...we did lots of things together. And when we left school we had an amazingly tearful last evening, er...of...of...nearly fifty of us who'd been in the year group, of whom about thirty had grown up together since they were five. And leaving school was actually quite hard for us because having established good relationships with the boys around us in our last two years we all had long memories.

★★★

PRESENTER: What are your strongest memories of school?

CHRISTINE: Of hating some of it. My strongest memories are negative ones, of a period in my two last years in primary, as it would be, 11 and 12 where our class teacher . . . I just loathed her and so did almost everybody else in the class and she was a bully and she taught very traditionally and it was very much 'the three Rs' [*reading, writing and arithmetic*] and we were...we just had tests all the time, we were drilled in grammar.

And she also had an uncertain temper and was a great shouter, and her...the tip of her nose would go white when she was really angry and her whole face would go scarlet. And she also used the belt very freely, and I didn't approve of that, I thought it was wrong. And she used to belt people [*beat them with a leather belt on the hand*] for spelling mistakes. And I'll never forget, Anne Black and Alan Davidson who couldn't spell, and they used to make spelling mistakes and if by Friday you had twenty mistakes out of the hundred, twenty a day, you got the belt in front of the class and I just thought that was so wrong. And it never improved their spelling, I mean years later as sixth-formers they still couldn't spell. And Anne Black used to get it particularly badly because she was English, because her mother was English, and she used to spell as she sounded and she used to make...create the most awful offence by spelling *saw* S O R rather than S A W: *I sor it* because that's how she heard it. And she used to be victimised by Miss Rae, for her English spelling and so I...I really didn't like her. I just thought that the way she treated people was wrong, it wasn't with respect, it was...um...I don't quite know what she was doing when she bullied people, but she was a big bully. And I grew up very firmly disapproving of that way of treating children.

B Say your answers softly to yourself. Maybe record yourself.

C This is not an exam-style test and there are no 'right answers'.

A few words of justification about the examples:

1 award · grant · scholarship (all money that is given to finance someone's education)
grant · loan (the two most common ways of financing higher education)
trophy · prize · award (all honours that may be given for outstanding achievement)
award · scholarship is another possible combination: both are only given to the brightest or luckiest students, unlike a grant which all students are entitled to
✗ reward isn't connected with education, unless discussing its rewards or pleasures. Unlike a *prize* or *trophy* it is simply cash to pay someone back for doing something, like finding something that has been lost

In the suggested answers below, the words with similar meanings are connected with a dot: · .
The odd one out is at the end, after the cross: ✗. Other combinations may be possible:

2 certificate · degree · diploma · doctorate
certificate · diploma
recommendation · reference · testimonial
✗ licence (connected more with driving than with education, though it has something in common with a *certificate*)

3 assignment · composition · essay · paper · report
dissertation · thesis
✗ article (not usually written by a student, but by a journalist or an academic)

4 comprehensive school · grammar school · secondary school
junior school · primary school
kindergarten · nursery school
✗ gymnasium (= hall where pupils do PE: physical education)

5 BA · BSc · first degree   MA · master's · MSc
BSc · MSc   MA · BA   doctorate · PhD
✗ bachelor (unmarried man)

6 grades · marks · scores · credits
✗ numbers (the other words have something to do with assessment)
7 continuous assessment · evaluation
examination · test   study
✗ questionnaire (not a way of assessing, but a way of gathering information)
8 class · seminar · study group   seminar · lecture   study group
✗ conference (a gathering of people who attend a series of lectures and seminars)
9 apprentice · trainee · participant
freshman · student · undergraduate
graduate · post-graduate   pupil · schoolchild
✗ contestant (someone who enters a competition or game show)
10 associate professor · lecturer · don   coach · trainer
instructor · trainer   professor · teacher · tutor
✗ business associate (no connection with education)
11 correspondence course · distance learning course
evening course · part-time course · sandwich course
degree course
✗ race course (where horse races are held)
12 academic year   half-term · holiday · vacation
semester · term
✗ financial year (a term used in business)

D Say your answers softly to yourself. Maybe record yourself.

9.2 **Writing an application**
COMPOSITION

A This activity can only be done with a partner.

B **1–3** ✎ If possible, ask another person to read and mark your work.

Model version:

> My name is ___ and I am __ years old. I was born in ___ and am a ___ citizen. I live with my parents in a small village called ___.
>
> I attended my local elementary school before going to high school in ___, the regional capital. I finished my studies at high school two years ago. My favourite subjects at school were languages and history. Now I am studying English and Spanish at ___ University. When I finish my studies, I hope to take up a career in the travel industry, perhaps as an airline flight attendant or in a travel company. I love meeting new people from different countries, finding out about different cultures and sharing experiences with them.
>
> During the vacations I have a temporary job as tour guide and I have accompanied many groups of tourists from different countries around my city, showing them the sights. I particularly enjoy groups of Japanese people, because they are so interested in learning more about foreign cultures and ask such interesting questions. Although I can communicate with some of the younger Japanese visitors in English, the older ones find it hard to speak and understand me. I find it so disappointing and frustrating that we cannot communicate with each other.

> At my university, I have got to know a number of Japanese students. Talking to them has taught me a lot about Japan and its culture and history. I would really love to visit Japan and learn Japanese. But these are just dreams for me now because flights to Japan are more expensive than I can afford, and living where I do, it's not possible to attend any Japanese language courses.
>
> I know that Japanese is a difficult language to learn, but I enjoy challenges. Living in Japan for three months might be a difficult experience for some people, but I have heard so much about Kyoto from Japanese people, that I know I would instantly feel at home there. It would be the most marvellous place to be when learning Japanese.
>
> Being awarded a Sakura Scholarship would be a golden opportunity. It would make my dreams come true!

9.3 **My lessons in the classroom**
READING AND WRITING SKILLS

A **1–3** Suggested answers:

1 They had had no inkling that she was about to decide to give up teaching
2 She had become increasingly terrified and nervous at the prospect of teaching
3 Not particularly well
4 They became bossy, noisy and they had empty heads, thanks to the pressure of their peers
5 She would have had to stay behind after school herself (supervising detention)
6 The teaching staff of the school
7 They greet her and then carry on messing about
8 Having the stamina and a liking for teaching

B Answers:

beating loudly = pounding   incomplete = patchy
hungry = breakfast-less   tell off = remonstrate with
laughing disrespectfully = sniggering
way of putting things right = redress
unable to take action = incapacitated
exercise control = assert myself
laughing shrilly = cackling

C ✎ If possible, ask another person to read and mark your work.

Model summary:

> She believes that children have changed for the worse over the years and behave badly. Nowadays they are under pressure from advertising and from each other: the disruptive pupils dominate the hard-working pupils, which disturbs the whole class. Parents must also take their share of the blame, allowing their children to stay up late watching videos and not feeding them properly, so that when they come to school they are tired and hungry, and unable to concentrate on their work.

9.4 'It's just the most wonderful thing'

LISTENING

 A 🔊 **Answers:**

1 the long holidays ✓
  a good lesson ✓
  helping students to pass exams
  the funny things that happen ✓
  helping students to manage their work ✓
  working with people ✓
  making a contribution to students' lives ✓
  finding quick solutions to students' problems ✓
  communicating her passion for English literature
2 remember
3a subject   3b person
4a subject   4b people
5a law   5b gap year
6a friends   6b support
7a extra-curricular   7b workload
8a distractions   8b focus

TRANSCRIPTS *5 minutes 20 seconds*

SARAH: My name's Sarah Wilson, and I work in a girls' school in Cambridge, and I'm a teacher of English. And I'm also Head of Sixth Form, which means I look after the Sixth Form girls and look after all of their interests.

INTERVIEWER: And how big is the school?

SARAH: Um…there's about 500 girls in the school…um…and the Sixth Form's a relatively small one, there's about 80 girls.

INTERVIEWER: And…um…what do you most enjoy about your work?

SARAH: There's a whole range of things. Some things are really satisfying, because you can solve them quickly, so if somebody's upset because they can't, you know, their world seems to be caving in, you can usually take the pressure off them, and that's hugely gratifying. Um…another th…other times, you work with somebody for a long, long time, it might take them eighteen months to get round to being able to manage their work, or whatever. And that's also hugely gratifying, working with somebody over a long time. But also, I…when…when a lesson goes really well, it's just the most wonderful thing.

INTERVIEWER: I mean, did you imagine that you'd have endlessly long holidays when you went into teaching, which I'm sure is not the case at all?

SARAH: Oh, no, it is! Hahaha! I mean, the holidays are undoubtedly the most wonderful aspect of it, because when you…there's a curious thing, as the term progresses…um…you disappear into the school life…um…completely, and you need the holidays to remember who you are. Um…but I…but they are, and…and I would never dispute that, they are a great bonus, they…they're wonderful.

INTERVIEWER: So, besides the long holidays, what would you say you find most rewarding about teaching?

SARAH: Um…I think, working with people and the hilarity of things that can happen, just because human beings being what they are. And…and also the sense that you…you are contributing very profoundly to somebody's life.

INTERVIEWER: And…um…what do you not enjoy about your work?

SARAH: Um…I find…sometimes I find it very difficult coming from a pastoral point of view, so I very much see the girls as human beings, and sometimes…um…academic staff see the needs

of their subject, and I find, sometimes balancing that quite hard, and I find that quite distressing.

INTERVIEWER: And is it a job you'd recommend to people?

SARAH: Yes, definitely. If you love your subject, and you enjoy people, then…um…teaching would…would be an excellent profession. Um…but I think, people who go into it because they don't know what else to do, and don't like people, it is a disaster.

★★★

CLAUDINE: My name is Claudine Kouzel. I'm sixteen years old, and I'm a student at St Mary's School, here in Cambridge.

INTERVIEWER: And what sort of subjects are you studying?

CLAUDINE: I'm studying Spanish, English Literature, Biology and Chemistry.

INTERVIEWER: And this is for C . . .

CLAUDINE: For AS Level.

INTERVIEWER: A…yeah, AS level. And where do you…what do you think you'd like to study at university?

CLAUDINE: At this stage, I'm thinking of law, but I'm not entirely sure about that.

INTERVIEWER: And do you think you'll do a gap year?

CLAUDINE: Um…I don't think so. I think I'd just like to get started and . . . I mean, it depends. If I get a place that I can defer my entry and actually go to South America or something like that, but, you know, that's not really guaranteed so . . .

INTERVIEWER: No.

CLAUDINE: . . . I'm not sure.

INTERVIEWER: And what do you enjoy most about school?

CLAUDINE: It's mainly the people here. It's all…having all the friends around you, and I think the support of the teachers as well.

INTERVIEWER: What do you not enjoy so much about school?

CLAUDINE: I think, undoubtedly when you get into the Sixth Form, there is a lot of pressure. So…you've always got to think of the future, and try and balance…um…extra-curricular activities with, you know, the heavy workload that you've got on.

INTERVIEWER: And I suppose it could be…um…quite easy to just try and do too much?

CLAUDINE: Definitely. I think you can actually be pulled in so many directions, that you've got to be careful that your work doesn't slip as a result.

INTERVIEWER: And, what do you think you'll be doing in ten years' time? What would you like to be doing in ten years' time?

CLAUDINE: That's quite a hard question. Um…ten years' time? OK, I'm sixteen now, I'll be twenty-six. Um…I would like to have…have a successful career, I would like to travel as well. Um…I'm not actually thinking of having a family too early on. I'd like to kind of enjoy life and do all the things I want to do and then settle down, I think, and then have a family.

INTERVIEWER: This is a single sex school, so only girls. Do you think that's good?

CLAUDINE: I do actually, because I went to…um…a co-ed school before. Um…and I think, when you're doing your GCSEs and A Levels, you can have a lot of distractions, especially from boys, and I think having all girls really focuses you into what you want to do. So I mean, if I had kids I would definitely send them to a single sex school.

INTERVIEWER: They say it's better for girls to be at a single sex school than for boys, don't they?

CLAUDINE: Yeah.

INTERVIEWER: How do you sort of relax or forget about school? What do you do in . . .

CLAUDINE: My spare time?

INTERVIEWER: Yes.

CLAUDINE: Well, I haven't got much spare time, to be honest…um…but I like to read, watch some television. I like going to the theatre as well.

INTERVIEWER: Yeah, well you keep pretty busy at school, don't you?

CLAUDINE: Oh, definitely, yeah.

INTERVIEWER: Thank you very, very much.

CLAUDINE: Thank you.

SELF-STUDY UNIT 9

259

9.5 Question tags and negative questions

GRAMMAR REVIEW

A Suggested answers:

1 He didn't use to play squash, **did he?**
– *but now he does, and I'm a little surprised about it*
Didn't he use to play squash?
& He used to play squash, **didn't he?**
– *I'm fairly sure he did in the past*
He used to play squash, **did he?**
– *You told me he played once, but are you quite sure about that?*
Did he use to play squash?
– *I'd just like to know if he played once*
2 **Isn't** this a great party!
& This is a great party, **isn't it?**
& What a great party!
– *these mean the same and would be used in similar situations*
This is a great party!
– *This one seems a little lukewarm in comparison, but it means the same.*
3 So you enjoyed my talk, **did you?**
– *I know you enjoyed it, but I'd like you to say it again or tell me more*
So **you didn't** enjoy my talk?
– *I know you didn't like it, but I'd like you to tell me why*
So **didn't you** enjoy my talk?
– *I suspect you didn't like it, but I'd like you to confirm it or tell me I'm wrong*
So **did you** enjoy my talk?
– *I don't know if you liked it*
4 **Isn't** it strange that everyone thinks they are experts on education?
– *Don't you agree that it's strange?*
(I'm encouraging you to agree)
It's strange that everyone thinks they are experts on education.
– *I'm telling you this (you may or may not have an opinion on this matter)*
5 **Didn't** she do well in her exam!
– *this is an exclamation – she really did well!!*
She **did** very well in her exam.
– *I'm telling you: she got good marks*
Didn't she do well in her exam?
– *This is a question: I'd be rather surprised if she did badly, which is what I have just heard, but you seem to know more than I do*
Did she do well in her exam?
& How **did** she do in her exam?
– *both mean: Tell me what you know about her success*

B Answers:

1 hadn't we?
  Hadn't we better stop work soon?
2 aren't I?
  Aren't I right about this?
3 wouldn't you?
  Wouldn't you rather stay in bed than get up early?
4 can't they?
  Can't anyone apply for the scholarship?
5 will there?
6 shall we?
7 did they?
8 won't you/will you?
9 did he?
10 oughtn't they?

260

C 🔊 Answers:

sure:	1	3	7	8	10
unsure:	2	4	5	6	9

TRANSCRIPTS *2 minutes*

PRESENTER: Listen to the examples and then do the exercise in 9.5 C.
WOMAN: This is a great party, isn't it? ↘ *(falling)*
WOMAN *(aside)*: I'm sure, but I want you to agree.
MAN: He used to play squash, didn't he?
  ↗ *(rising)*
MAN *(aside)*: I'm unsure, but I think you know.
  1
MAN: We arranged to meet at 7:30, didn't we?
  ↘ *(falling)*
  2
WOMAN: Mm. But the film doesn't start till 8:30, does it?
  ↗ *(rising)*
  3
MAN: Yes, but there'll be time for us to have a drink beforehand, won't there? ↘ *(falling)*
  4
WOMAN: OK. You remember that film we saw last month, don't you? ↗ *(rising)*
MAN: Yes.
  5
WOMAN: It *was* Al Pacino, not Robert de Niro, in that film, wasn't it? ↗ *(rising)*
  6
MAN: I always get Al Pacino and Robert de Niro confused, don't you? ↗ *(rising)*
  7
WOMAN: Mm. You don't like Robert de Niro, do you?
  ↘ *(falling)*
  8
MAN: Not really . . . I think we both prefer Al Pacino, don't we? ↘ *(falling)*
  9
WOMAN: Mm, you do know it's Robert de Niro who's in tonight's film, don't you? ↗ *(rising)*
  10
MAN: Oh. In that case it might be better if we went to see something else, mightn't it? ↘ *(falling)*
WOMAN: Don't be so silly — you'll enjoy it!

D **1 & 2** Suggested answers:

2 All our work **will be done for us by robots and computers one day, won't it?**
  Won't all our work be done for us by robots and computers one day?
3 Computers **couldn't be installed in every classroom, could they?**
  Couldn't computers be installed in every classroom?
4 No robot teachers **have been invented yet, have they?**
  Haven't any robot teachers been invented yet?
5 Teachers **should be paid on results, shouldn't they?**
  Shouldn't teachers be paid on results?
6 Students **are often supported by their parents, aren't they?**
  Aren't students often supported by their parents?
7 The school-leaving age **might be raised to 19, mightn't it?**
  Mightn't the school-leaving age be raised to 19?
8 More **teachers would have to be employed, wouldn't they?**
  Wouldn't more teachers have to be employed?

9.6 Abstract nouns
VOCABULARY DEVELOPMENT

A **1** Answers:

-ation	cooperate administrate
-ion	destroy satisfy suspect
-ment	astonish enjoy punish

2 Answers (check your spelling carefully!):

-ation	application concentration explanation isolation justification negotiation pronunciation (pronouncement = solemn announcement) recommendation representation variation
-ion	contribution description invention objection opposition reception
-ment	achievement acknowledgement amusement embarrassment encouragement management

B **1** Answers:

-ty	humble senior
-ance	insignificant intolerant
-ence	absent present intelligent refer
-ism	real absent national/nationalistic/nation optimistic
-ness	clumsy fair happy rude
-ship	apprentice relate scholar sponsor

2 Answers:

-ty	authenticity availability creativity equality familiarity generosity honesty loyalty productivity reliability stability
-ance	extravagance relevance
-ence	diffidence incompetence inconvenience independence insolence self-confidence
-ism	favouritism professionalism symbolism
-ness	carelessness half-heartedness mischievousness (or mischief) narrow-mindedness selfishness
-ship	companionship friendship leadership

C Some suggestions:

-ation	imagination organisation realisation
-ion	alienation creation direction protection
-ment	replacement requirement retirement
-ty	informality normality instability eligibility
-ance	disappearance resemblance disturbance
-ence	reminiscence persistence disobedience
-ism	plagiarism journalism sexism extremism
-ness	helplessness aggressiveness mildness
-ship	membership ownership comradeship craftsmanship

D Answers:

-dom	bored free
-th	broad filthy healthy long stealthy strong warm wealthy wide
-cy	democratic bureaucratic delicate efficient fluent frequent inadequate inefficient redundant urgent
and	enthusiastic hysterical hungry proud sarcastic successful

E Suggested answers:

1 inconvenience
2 reliability/relevance/adequacy
3 enthusiasm description
4 bureaucracy inefficiency
5 favouritism fairness cooperation
6 relevance justification explanation
7 qualifications negotiation
8 references leadership
9 intolerance incompetence unreliability extravagance stubbornness *etc.*
10 loyalty professionalism self-assurance generosity reliability *etc.*

9.7 Managing your study time
READING

A Answers:

1 c	2 b	3 a	4 b	5 d	6 d

B Answers:

bluffing	= deceiving by pretending to be cleverer than he really was
assiduously	= painstakingly
blotted out	= made an effort not to think about
at sea	= confused
segments	= sections
strategically	= in a well-planned manner
dribble away	= gradually be lost
dipping into	= reading short passages, not the complete book
glazed over	= unfocused
prime	= best times for concentration, when you're on top form
swamp	= overcome, inundate

C Suggested key phrases:

¶ 4 organisation of time
time management
¶ 9 dividing big jobs into smaller sub-tasks
¶10 'investing' time
¶12 take control

9.8 Reporting – 2
ADVANCED GRAMMAR

A Suggested answers:

1 He told me that he would be arriving **tomorrow**.
– *His expected day of arrival is tomorrow (he may have said this yesterday or on a previous day)*
He told me that he would be arriving **the next day**.
– *His expected day of arrival was the day after he spoke to me (he didn't say this yesterday)*
2 She **advised** me to spend more time reading.
– *This is the gist of what she said and gives no special emphasis to the report*
She **urged** me to spend more time reading.
– *This gives special emphasis to the speaker's insistence*

3 He **dismissed** my plan as unrealistic.
  – *He rejected my plan*
  He **had doubts about** the effectiveness of my plan.
  – *This is more tactful: he disagreed with my plan, but didn't reject it completely*
4 He **promised** to make the call soon.
  – *Clearly a promise* **He said** that he would make the call soon
  – *This might be a promise, or just a statement of what he was going to do*
5 She **agreed**.
  – *She expressed her agreement*
  She **assured me** that I was right.
  – *This emphasises her wish to make me feel good*

The answers are in **bold print** below. Some of the interpretations are open to discussion.

TRANSCRIPT WITH ANSWERS

3 minutes

PRESENTER: Listen carefully to each speaker and select an appropriate adjective to describe their attitudes. ONE

1ST SPEAKER: Could I have a word with you? Yes. Well, you see, I've been looking at *your* work and comparing it with…with what the others have been doing and well, you know what I think about *everyone else's* work, don't you? I mean, it's improved a lot. Anyway, looking at yours in comparison I must say that you really are…I mean, yours is far and away the most . . . . **– angry**

PRESENTER: TWO

2ND SPEAKER: Could I have a word? Ah . . . yes, well . . . Look…um…I've been…I've been watching your work and I've been comparing it with…er…with [what] the others have been doing and well, er…I mean, you know what I think about everyone else's work, I mean that's…that's improved quite a bit. But…uh…looking at yours, I…I have to, I mean, you've you…you've really…you've just not…um…well, I mean, yours is just…
it's just . . . **– disappointed or diffident?**

PRESENTER: THREE

3RD SPEAKER: Could I have a word? Yes. Well, you see, I…I've been looking at your work and comparing it with…er…with what the others have been doing and…er…well, you know what I think about everyone else's work, don't you? I mean, w…it has improved a lot but . . . Anyway looking at yours in comparison I must say that you've really…I mean, yours is far and away the . . . **– impressed**

PRESENTER: FOUR

4TH SPEAKER: Could I have a word? Yes. Well, you see, I've been looking at your work and comparing it with…er…with what the others have been doing and…er…well, er…you know what I think about everyone else's work, don't you? I mean, *it* has improved a lot. Anyway looking at *yours* in comparison I must say that you've really, I…I mean, yours is far and away . . . **– sarcastic**

PRESENTER: FIVE

5TH SPEAKER: Could I have a word? Yes, yes. Well…um…you see, I've…I…I've been looking at your work and…um…comparing it with…er…with…er… with what the others have been doing and…um…well, um…you know…you know what I think about everyone else's work, er…I…I know you do. I mean, er…th…that's improved quite a bit, hasn't it?

Well…er…anyway, looking at yours in comparison I…I…I must say I…that you've really…er…I mean…er…yours is far and away the most . . . **– diffident or disappointed?**

2 **Suggested summaries:**

> 2 The second speaker regretted that my work hadn't improved in comparison with the others' work.
> 3 The third speaker congratulated me on my work and commented that it was much better than everyone else's.
> 4 The fourth speaker was unimpressed by my work and thought that everyone else's work had improved considerably.
> 5 The fifth speaker was unwilling to commit himself, but thought that my work had improved less than everyone else's.

C **Suggested answers:**

> 2 He promised to tell me when they arrived.
> 3 She reminded me to hand in my work (that evening).
> 4 He regretted that I couldn't make it to the party (the night before).
> 5 She congratulated me on passing.
> 6 He assured me that I would manage if I remained calm.
> 7 She insisted that I (should) visit them at the weekend.
> 8 He disagreed with me (politely).
> 9 She warned me not to park on the/that double yellow line.
> 10 He reproached me for behaving in that way / for my behaviour.
> 11 She claimed that she'd have helped me with my work if she had had more time.
> 12 He suggested that we (should) organise our time more efficiently
> He suggested organising our time more efficiently.

9.9 Progressive v. traditional methods
LISTENING AND COMPOSITION

A 1 Say your answers softly to yourself. Maybe record yourself.

2 The questions are similar to Part 2 of the Listening Paper.

Answers:

1 B	2 C	3 A	4 C	5 B	6 C	7 A	8 C

TRANSCRIPT   *7 minutes 40 seconds*

BETH: My name's Beth Titchener, I'm fifteen years old and I'm a pupil at Summerhill School.

INTERVIEWER: Tell me, what is…what…tell me about Summerhill School. How does it differ from other schools?

BETH: Well, the main difference is that the pupils don't have to go to lessons. And Summerhill's a democratic school, so everybody's equal and every…we have meetings, and everybody in the meeting has an equal say, where…in the meetings we discuss things like, oh, daily goings-on in…in the school and if someone's been making trouble or something, we discuss that in the meeting. And everybody has an equal vote, whether you're, you know, one of the youngest pupils or the Headteacher.

I can make my own choices about what I do, whereas in another school I'd be told what I have to do every day, and here I have much more responsibility over my own life. In a normal school you wouldn't be…you wouldn't be given any responsibilities. I think in most places children aren't seen as responsible enough, they don't think children are, you know, capable of holding any responsibilities.

INTERVIEWER: What made your family decide that this was the right school for you? Or you and presumably your family decide it was the right school?

BETH: Um…I don't know. I think it's because every…or quite often when I'd come home from my last school, because I went to a normal skate…state school before when I was about nine or something, and every time when I'd come home I'd be like, 'Why do I have to do what the teachers say all the time? Why do I have to always do what they say?' I'd have screaming fits on the way home, saying, 'I don't want to go back to school tomorrow, I don't want to go back!' And then my parents took me out of school for a while, but I just got really bored because I had no, you know, no people to socialise with or anything. And so, we came to look around at Summerhill and I really enjoyed visiting here, so I decided I wanted to be here, but I didn't fully understand the philosophy of the school or anything when I first came because I was only about ten or eleven, so . . .

INTERVIEWER: I think from the outside a lot of people, I imagine, you know, think, 'Oh, pupils don't have to go to lessons, that probably means no one would choose to go to lessons.'

BETH: I think when people are…when people don't go to lessons, I mean, because if you don't have to go to lessons, I mean, quite a lot of people when they first come to Summerhill, they've had to go to lessons for such a long time that as soon as they think, 'Oh, I don't have to go to lessons' they don't go to any lessons for ages, they just play, and after a while you start finding interests, like you discover what you're actually interested in, not what you're just made…been made to do, so like I had quite a lot of Japanese friends before and they'd be all talking in Japanese and I'd be like, 'Hang on a minute, I want to learn to understand them as well because this is really annoying me. I can't understand what these people are doing or what they're talking about and stuff.' So I decided, 'Yeah, I want to go to Japanese lessons.' And I went to every Japanese lesson I had, as much as possible until I could…had a kind of rough understanding of what they were talking about.

INTERVIEWER: If you had children would you send them here?

BETH: If they wanted to come here, yeah. I'd definitely, I'd ask them.

INTERVIEWER: And have you got brothers and sisters at home?

BETH: Yeah, I've got a younger brother, who came here for a while and then he…didn't really suit him and so.

INTERVIEWER: And what about friends…um…if you've been here five years, some of the…some of your friends must have left, I mean, do you still keep in touch with them?

BETH: Some…most of them, yeah. I mean, sometimes it's quite hard to keep in touch because most of them are from foreign countries and they, like, quite…some of my really good friends have gone off to school in Japan or New Zealand or somewhere, but we keep in touch a bit, yeah.

INTERVIEWER: I think that's wonderful. I mean, they're always going to be there wherever you travel, you'll be able to…um…touch base with them or you'll have a whole network of friends all over the world.

BETH: Yeah. There's so many people here from different cultures and different countries, you get to learn about lots of different…different peoples, different ways of living and stuff. It's what I also think is really good is there's hardly any racism in Summerhill, because there's so many foreign people that you kind of…everybody has to learn to live with people from other countries, and a person speak…coming from a strange country which you're not used to, speaking a strange language, generally in Summerhill people are more interested in them rather than…because they're used to everyone being different.

★★★

MICHAEL: My name's Michael Newman, I've worked at Summerhill for six years, and at the moment I'm teaching English, but…er…when…for my first four and a half years I taught Science here, and then for another year I've been a House Parent, so I've been very lucky, I've moved from one job to another within the school.

INTERVIEWER: And what do you really enjoy about your job?

MICHAEL: Um…I enjoy it…it's the only teaching job I've ever done where I can be myself, where I don't have to pretend or act, to have authority or to tell children what to do. You've kind of…you can be at the same level, you can have friends with the children and if you make a mistake or if you have a joke, you don't have to worry about losing control of the class, so you can just relax and be yourself.

INTERVIEWER: Do you think your teaching methods are different within this environment?

MICHAEL: It's very different in the sense that the children control what I do, so a child can interrupt me and say, 'No, I don't want to learn this!' and then I have to change it. So the very act of teaching becomes one of negotiation…um…if you were to see me, you wouldn't know that, unless you see…the children interrupted, if you were to see one of my lessons you'd think, 'No, this is a normal lesson,' because I…I, you know, I…I do lessons, GCSE [General Certificate of Secondary Education] English lessons, and the children will come and they have an expectation, they know it's a GCSE lesson, they'll probably have confidence because they've seen me teach already, that I'll be teaching them things that are relevant and that are interesting. But there will be moments in any of those lessons where someone could put their hand up and say, 'Well, I don't want to do this!' and…and we'd have to re-negotiate what's…what I was teaching and what they didn't like.

INTERVIEWER: But presumably if the rest of the group do want to do it, it's…they are outvoted.

MICHAEL: Oh yeah, yeah.

INTERVIEWER: Had you heard about Summerhill before…I mean, did you set out to teach here?

MICHAEL: No, I mean, um…if I look back, I mean, my whole life focuses on this place, but it was by chance that I worked here. I was in Italy teaching English as a foreign language for a year and a half and…er…and my mother was sending me the Guardian adverts, and I just saw it advertised, you know community school, democratic school. And I've always been interested in chil…how children learn ethics and values, and I just thought if I worked here I could see…see that happening, and actually…and see it happening without the authority of a parent or without the authority of a teacher. And I'm very interested in what happens in the meetings, and how the children here…they talk about what's right and wrong, they talk about, you know, 'Should we vote that way or not?' and 'Is it wrong to punish?', you know, 'What if you do fine someone, what should it be?' I mean, you have all these wonderful moral dilemmas, and there's a lot of discussion at the moment, in the meeting now in fact, about smoking and should you be allowed to smoke, what age should you be allowed to smoke, what should be the fines if you…you smoke? And you sh…you know, and you're not allowed to smoke, you know. Should the school be able to control your…your personal behaviour, should it…should the school show concern for the health of all its members? All those issues will be discussed by six-year-olds to sixteen and all the staff.

INTERVIEWER: That's fantastic!

MICHAEL: It is, yeah and it's affecting, and they're discussing it not as a role-play or as a debate, but actually, what they vote in the end's going to control the way they live.

3 Say your answers softly to yourself. Maybe record yourself.

B **1** ✏ If possible, ask another person to read and mark your work.

Model version:

> Most pupils in most countries don't have a choice of the kind of education they receive: they go to their local school and follow the courses that school provides, which is probably fairly traditional.
>
> In a traditional school, the assumption is that the teacher has knowledge which he or she shares with the pupils. This may involve 'chalk and talk' methods where the pupils sit in rows facing the teacher, who stands at the blackboard and lectures the pupils. A textbook is used, which contains all the information that the pupils require. Discipline is strict and misbehaviour is punished with detention or other sanctions. Examination success is the main purpose of this style of education.
>
> In a progressive school, the classes are often smaller, and the pupils work together in pairs or in groups under the guidance of the teacher, discovering information for themselves as they work together. Discipline is self-imposed, and in very progressive schools (such as Summerhill) pupils can choose to miss lessons and do nothing. Becoming a good person is the purpose of this style of education.
>
> Both methods have their critics and supporters. Supporters of traditional methods maintain that pupils need to be motivated by exams and are not mature enough to decide when to attend classes. Of course the teacher has more knowledge of the subject than the pupils and so it is his or her job to give them that knowledge, and to encourage them to learn and work hard and pass their exams.
>
> Supporters of progressive methods claim that each child is different, and may not be ready to learn at the same time. If they do choose to attend a particular class they are much more highly motivated than if they attend unwillingly. Self-imposed discipline is more effective than discipline imposed from above. Examinations are a curse, not a blessing.
>
> Different methods may suit different children. It is hard to reconcile the two sides to this argument, except by answering these questions: 'Which kinds of methods would I like to learn by?' and 'Would I send my child to a progressive school, or a traditional one?'

10

Fauna and flora   Natural history   The environment

Mother nature

10.1 Animals and plants

TOPIC VOCABULARY

A **1** Say your answers softly to yourself. Maybe record yourself.

People tend to refer to *mother nature* in a gently ironic way. The word *nature* is sometimes a feminine noun: 'Nature has her own way of maintaining a balance'.

2 Here are some suggested vocabulary items:

bird-watching   botany   budgerigar   cages   endangered
evolution   foliage   guard dog   habitat   hamster   kitten
pollution   puppy   recycling   roots

B **1** Answers:

1 endangered	2 breeding	3 accepted	
4 naturalist	5 worked up	6 wither	7 recycled
8 species	9 rodents	10 reptiles	11 prey
12 domesticated	13 vermin	14 claws	
15 plumage	16 feelers	17 flock	
18 endearing			

2 This is a good way of learning new words.

10.2 'Our cousins in the ocean'

LISTENING

A Say your answers softly to yourself.

B **1** 🔊 Pause the tape at the place marked with ★★★ in the Transcript, which is the end of **B1**.

Answers:

1 c   2 b   3 b (or a?)   4 a   5 c

2 🔊 Ticks beside the following reasons:

he feels an inexplicable affinity with them ✓
their brains are large ✓
they can move in spectacular ways ✓
some whales are impressively large ✓
they are perfectly suited to living in the sea ✓

TRANSCRIPT   *6 minutes 30 seconds*

PRESENTER: This week, we hear from zoologist, Ray Gamble.

RAY: My name is Ray Gamble, and I'm the Secretary of the International Whaling Commission. That's the body made up of 43 member governments who have responsibility for the management of the whaling industry, the regulation of that industry, and the conservation of the whale stocks throughout the world.

PRESENTER: Why isn't there a total world-wide ban on killing whales? Why can't whales be totally protected from being hunted?

RAY: We've had many problems in terms of management of whale stocks…er…because certain, particularly Arctic communities are very heavily dependent on the natural resources of a very severe environment. And so the…um…the Inuit people, the Eskimo peoples of Greenland and

...er...northern Canada an Alaska, have argued that they, in spite of a...a ban on commercial whaling, should be permitted to carry on catching for subsistence purposes. And so we have developed over the course of years, and...and with a great deal of...of heart-searching, a...a specific management regime for aboriginal subsistence whaling, which is much more heavily dependent, not on the number of whales in the ocean, but on the perceived need of the indigenous peoples who are hunting the animals. They need them for subsistence, for cultural purposes, er...social purposes. Um...many of these communities...um...feel bound together by the fact that they are hunters together. And so this has been a very important factor to build in on top of the...the basic biology of how many whales there are in the ocean.

And so I've had the chance of going out to...um...Alaska with the Eskimo whalers, standing on the frozen Arctic Ocean, and watching the bow-head whales swimming along the...the leads, the cracks in the ice that open up in the spring, and...and the hunters go out in their seal-skin boats and...and harpoon – hand harpoon, using the...the old...er...traditional techniques. Er...er...and that's a...a very interesting experience.

PRESENTER: But this may not be what enlightened people in Europe and North America want to hear, as Ray explains.

RAY: And of course many people now in the comfortable Western world...er...have a very different view of what a whale is...is there for. The aboriginal subsistence hunter sees it as part of his total environment: he's dependent on the animal and he feels a special relationship to the animal because it does sustain his life. But to the...the Western communities...er...which are not dependent on...on flesh for food now – there's a...a general movement against eating red meat – um...there's a...a preference to see the whale as a ...a beautiful animal, as a...an animal with a very large brain, an animal with...with great powers of being able to dive to...to great depths in the ocean and survive, and so on. Um...the whale is seen as a symbol of...of a...a...a life of freedom and...er...it evokes all kinds of...of non-culinary thoughts. So that the whale is...is now seen as something that has to be preserved an...and kept in respect in the ocean. And whether you go out on a whale-watching trip and see the whale for yourself or whether you just know that it's in the ocean, tha...that is what is important and...and the people who go out and hunt the whale for commercial purposes are very much seen to be...er...not the kind of people that you'd want to associate with any more.

So, it...the whale is no longer a...a renewable resource, but a...um...a...a figure to be seen as...as symbolising so much more for many people.

★★★

PRESENTER: Ray is obviously passionately involved with whales. What is it about the whale that stirs him?

RAY: They really are *very* exciting animals. Um...the large whales are very large. Er...to see a blue whale, which is the largest animal that...that has ever lived in the ocean...er...on...on this earth, and to see it turning and moving, twisting, so completely at home in the water, i...it's a very exciting sight. To see a...a large animal like a humpback whale leaping right out of the ocean is a very spectacular event to...to actually see this happen. So they...they are dramatic animals in that sense. And some of them are very big, yes, a blue whale is like a, you know, a couple of buses end to end, i...it's of that size, a hundred feet long, 150 tons perhaps of living, mobile animal.

And they do have very large brains. And so there is the sense that, you know, maybe they have a...a form of intelligence that...that . . . it's difficult enough to...to measure human intelligence,

measuring the intelligence in...in another species altogether is...is really quite difficult. But the fact of the...the very large brain suggests that there is...um...you know, a degree of...of affinity with man which has the large brain use o...on land. These have been described as 'our cousins in the ocean'. There...we feel a...an affinity of some kind.

When you've...um...have the chance to...to...to get close to a...a dolphin – I've been in a...a rubber dinghy with a wild but sociable dolphin swimming around – when it comes and...and peers at you out of the water, it's like looking into the eye of s...your pet dog, you think, 'There must be something in there, if only I could...could make contact with it.' It's the same with the dolphin, it's the same with the whale, that...that there is some kind of...of instinctive bond that you feel. They...they are impressive animals in terms of size and ability, and...and there is this sense that there's...there's more than...than we can grasp at the moment. There's something more that...that we may find out in the future. They...they really are very exciting animals.

C Say your answers softly to yourself. Maybe record yourself.

10.3 The Third Chimpanzee
READING

Background

This passage is from *The Rise and Fall of the Third Chimpanzee* by Jared Diamond, a well-known American ecologist and physiologist. He is also the author of *Guns, Germs and Steel (A Short History of Everybody for the last 13,000 Years)*, a marvellous account of human development and history from the first farmers to the present day. Both fascinating, thought-provoking – and funny too!

A Answers:

> 1 humans and pygmy chimps (if chimpanzees are 'the first chimpanzee')
> 2 humans depend completely on tools to make a living
> 3 none
> 4 lions
> 5 elephants (and others)
> 6 (see below)

Model summary:

> Anatomically humans and chimpanzees are very similar: the only differences are that chimpanzees have more hair and they don't walk upright – and they don't wear clothes. If the zoologist from outer space didn't notice (or couldn't understand) human speech he would think them to be very similar species. He would discover after doing genetic tests that humans and chimpanzees have over 98 per cent of their genes in common, which makes them more similar than closely related bird species.

B Answers:

> ¶1 minutest
> ¶2 gulf darker attributes rudimentary eclipse
> ¶3 intimated initially
> ¶4 affinities grunting
> ¶5 & 6 baggage
> ¶7 precursors
> ¶8 propensities

10.4 Conditionals – 1
GRAMMAR REVIEW

A Suggested answers:

1 I **feel** upset **when** I **think** about the destruction of the rainforests.
 – *Every time I think about them, I feel sad*
 I'**d feel** upset **when** I **thought** about people destroying the rainforests.
 – *I used to feel sad every time I used to think about them*
 I'**d feel** upset **if** I **thought** about the rainforests being destroyed.
 – *Sometimes I thought about them and I used to feel sad then*
 or *If I let myself think about it I would feel upset, so I don't let myself think about it*
 I **feel** upset **if** I **think** about the destruction of tropical rainforests.
 – *Sometimes I think about them and it makes me sad*
 I **felt** upset **when** I **thought** about jungles being destroyed.
 – *I felt sad every time I thought about them.*
 This is pretty much the same as *I'd feel upset when* . . . except that this suggests I didn't feel upset for quite so long. *When* suggests a more frequent occurrence than *if* in the above examples.

2 If you **don't leave** now, you'**ll** be late.
 & **Unless** you leave now, you'**ll** be late.
 – *You really ought to leave in case you're late*
 If you **left** now, you **wouldn't** be late.
 – *You probably don't intend to go now, so that means you will be late*
 If you **leave** now, you **won't** be late.
 – *You'll probably be going now, so that means you won't be late*
 If you **didn't leave** now, you'**d** be late.
 – *I'm fairly sure you're going, but supposing you stayed, you would be late*

3 If you'**re** interested I'**ll** tell you about my dream.
 – *Let me know if you're interested, and if you are, I'll tell you about my dream*
 If you **were** interested I'**d** tell you about my dream.
 – *I know you aren't interested, so I won't tell you*

4 **When** I **have** time, I'**ll** feed the cat.
 – *I'll open the tin later, when I'm not busy*
 If I **had** time, I'**d** feed the ducks.
 – *I'm very busy, so I can't/won't feed the ducks*
 If I'**d had** time, I'**d have fed** the dog.
 – *I was very busy, so I didn't feed it*
 If I **have** time, I'**ll** feed the goldfish.
 – *I may be too busy, but if I have a spare moment I'll feed them*
 If I **had** time, I'**d have fed** the birds.
 – *I'm very busy, so that explains why I didn't feed the birds*
 When I **had** time, I'**d feed** the rabbits.
 – *I used to feed the rabbits when I wasn't too busy*

B Suggested answers:

1 If you go too close to that dog it may/might/will bite you.
2 If I'd realised that you needed help, I could have given you a hand.
3 If the amount of carbon dioxide in the atmosphere is not reduced, the ozone layer will be permanently damaged.

4 If the forests hadn't been cut down, they might still cover most of Europe.
5 If people were less ignorant about the effects of pollution on the environment, there might be less of it.
6 If animals could speak in their own defence, we wouldn't have/need to speak up for them.
7 If everyone drove more slowly, there would be less pollution.
8 If there wasn't/weren't any acid rain these lakes would still have fish in them.
 If it weren't for acid rain, these lakes . . .

C Possible continuations:

1 If he hadn't been so generous, **he might still have some money left.**
2 If you aren't careful, **you'll fall off the ladder and break your neck.**
3 If she doesn't phone me by Friday, **I'll have to go round and see her.**
4 If everyone cared more about the environment, **they would do more to protect it.**
5 If any species becomes extinct, **it can never be replaced.**
6 If human beings became extinct, **there would be plenty of other species to take our place.**
7 Unless the governments of the world cooperate, **there is no chance of the global environment being adequately protected.**

D 1 Say your answers softly to yourself. Maybe record yourself.

2 If possible, ask another person to read and mark your work.

There's more in **13.4 Conditionals – 2**.

10.5 Showing your attitude
WRITING SKILLS

Background

Gerald Durrell (1925–95) ran his own zoo on the island of Jersey, and was a well-known broadcaster and zoologist. His books are mostly about his amusing encounters with animals and are full of anecdotes, notably: *The Overloaded Ark, The Bafut Beagles, The Drunken Forest, A Zoo in My Luggage. The Stationary Ark,* from which this extract is taken, is one of his more serious books.

His best-known book is *My Family and Other Animals,* the opening paragraphs of which are included in **13.3 Family life**.

A Suggested answers:

1 appalling 2 feel very strongly
3 rabid (= mad, raving) 4 far 5 just as
6 just as 7 ancient 8 obliterate

B Examples of emotive language:

It is odd how comforted people feel . . . purely to make money. No thought of science or conservation sullied their primary conception. . . . unpleasant fungus, . . . disgraceful . . . appalling. . . . I would like to stress that . . . totally impossible . . . rare beasts

I am not against . . . I am against . . . of immense
conservation value . . . animal abattoirs in a sylvan setting
I feel therefore . . . not simply clamour . . . acumen and
far-sightedness
. . . all of us . . . already too hard pressed by our
unbeatable competition . . . even the few good ones . . .

C **1** Make your own choices of phrases you want to
remember — preferably ones that you don't already
use in your own writing.

2 Suggested answers:

1 disgraceful
2 There is no doubt that
3 Quite frankly   appalling
4 am against   – in spite of this
5 Clearly   absurd
6 It seems to me that   but you must agree that absurd

D If possible, ask another person to read and
mark your two paragraphs.

10.6 Uses of the past
ADVANCED GRAMMAR

A Answers:

1 I wish that dog **would** stop barking.
– *It's barking and I don't like hearing it, but there's
nothing I can do about it*
I wish that dog **didn't** bark.
– *Whenever the dog barks I find it annoying*
I wish that dog **had stopped** barking.
– *It went on barking a long time (maybe all night),
which was very annoying*
I want that dog **to stop** barking.
– *It's barking and I don't like hearing it, but there's
nothing I can do about it*
or *You must order the dog to stop barking (said
threateningly to its owner, perhaps)*
2 It's time **for you to do** the washing-up.
– *You asked me to remind you of the time, that time has
now come*
It's time **you did** the washing-up.
– *You offered to wash up and you should have started
by now*
or *You never wash up but you ought to do it*
3 If only it were Friday!
– *I wish it were Friday*
Only if it was Friday . . .
– *This could only happen if today was Friday*
or *That could only happen on a Friday, not another day*
If it were only Friday . . .
– *If today was Friday, not a later day, then . . . (. . .
maybe the situation might be different)*
If it's only Friday . . .
– *As today is Friday, not a later day (we still have plenty
of time left)*
4 Would you rather I didn't help you?
& Would you prefer it if I didn't help you?
& Would you prefer me not to help you?
– *Do you want me to refrain from helping you?*
Would you rather not help me?
– *Do you want to do something else, rather than help
me?*

5 I **was going to** phone her tonight.
& I **intended to** phone her tonight.
& I **was to have** phoned her tonight.
– *I was planning to ring her this evening (but now the
plans have changed – maybe it's no longer necessary or
possible)*
I **am to** phone her tonight.
– *It's been arranged for me to ring her this evening*
6 I wish I **knew** the answer.
– *I don't know the answer unfortunately*
I wish **to know** the answer.
– *Please tell me the answer*

B Suggested answers:

1 wouldn't keep interrupting/disturbing
2 was done to stop/prevent
3 it if you arrived/you to arrive
4 had been more aware of
5 I was brave enough to / knew how to
6 were/was something we could do
7 were going to come
8 you played your saxophone / hifi
9 time we went / time for us to go
10 was fed / had its food

10.7 Biological diversity
READING

A Some of these questions are quite tricky – as they
will be in the exam!

Answers:

| 1 d | 2 a (research into DNA hybridisation) |
| 3 a | 4 b | 5 c | 6 b | 7 d | 8 a |

B Answers:

¶1 anathema   cook up   ¶2 argue   ¶4 thesis
¶5 reaper-man   permed   ¶7 yield

10.8 *put* and *set*
VERBS AND IDIOMS

A Answers:

put pressure on someone   two and two together
someone at their ease   a question to someone
a stop to something   someone in the picture
pen to paper
set a trap for someone   your teeth on edge
a good example   fire to something
your watch   the scene

B Answers:

1 said something thoughtless which embarrassed him
2 cost me   put an end to
3 depend on the success of one scheme or action
4 make him lose concentration and upset him
5 ascribed   discourage
6 asserted your authority
7 delayed

267

8 founded   intended/aimed
9 humiliating   put yourself in my place
  gives people an unfavorable impression of us both
10 wouldn't be surprised if / consider him capable of
   (making . . .)   trying to deceive me

C Answers:

1 put   up to
2 set up
3 putting   across/over
4 put   out   put   up
5 put up with
6 put in
7 putting aside/putting away/setting aside
8 sets out
9 put in
10 sets in

10.9 **Different styles**

VOCABULARY DEVELOPMENT AND WRITING SKILLS

This section deals with degrees of formality in vocabulary and also in grammatical structure. A 'neutral' style (one that is neither too colloquial, nor too formal) is likely to be appropriate in most types of composition that you will have to do in the exam – unless you choose to write a personal letter, for example.

A **1** Answers:

Different forms are more interesting to admire and study than lots of things that look the same.
　　　　　　　　　　　　　　　– neutral

It's a lot more interesting to admire and study different forms than lots of things that look the same.　　　　　　　　　**– informal**

Different forms are more interesting to admire and study than a large number of similar looking species.　　　　　　　　　**– formal**

I do like little kittens and puppies – they're ever so sweet, aren't they?　　　　**– informal/ colloquial**

I consider young kittens and puppies to be the most endearing creatures.　　　　**– formal**

Small kittens and puppies are delightful, I think.　　　　　　　　　　　**– neutral**

2 There are many examples of neutral style in the first half of **10.7**. Here are some of them:

The idea . . . gives most people a warm feeling inside.
. . . But what, exactly, is diversity?
. . . And which kind is most worth preserving?
. . . all species should not be equal.
. . . they suggest that preserving the rarest is not always the best approach.
. . . They reckon that if choices must be made . . .
. . . This makes sense from both a practical and an aesthetic point of view.
. . . saving one is nearly as good as saving both.
. . . Six species of crane are at some risk of extinction.
. . . Breeding in captivity might save them.

B Suggested answers (some variations are possible):

2 I hope your father has fully recovered (from his illness).
3 She was furious when she was told that she'd lost her job.
4 Organic fruit and vegetables are cultivated without the use of artificial fertiliser.
5 We were terrified when a large dog came bounding up to us.
6 Please be careful with the knife (you're using).
7 Testing cosmetics and shampoo on animals is not only pointless, it's also cruel.
8 You should have turned off the light when you left the room.
9 I think it's likely to rain fairly soon.
10 Instead of throwing your litter in the street, you ought to put it in a litter bin.

C Suggested answers (some variations are possible):

2 According to the experts, global warming is speeding up.
3 Even a small rise in temperature may have a big effect on the ice in polar regions.
4 Throwing cans and bottles away is an unnecessary waste of energy and materials. It's much better to recycle them.
5 Lunch is served from 12 o'clock.
6 Please be careful when getting off the train.
7 You're not allowed to use personal stereos or musical instruments here.
8 Although no vegetarians eat meat, vegans don't eat either fish or dairy products.

10.10 **Use of English Part 1**

EXAM PRACTICE

Background

This passage is from a book by Sir David Attenborough which accompanied the TV series *Life on Earth*.
David Attenborough is well-known as a TV presenter and enthusiastic naturalist. His other books, also accompanying TV series, include *The Living Planet, The First Eden: the Mediterranean World and Man, The Trials of Life* and *Life in the Freezer* about Antarctica.

A In the exam it's always advisable to read the passage quickly through for gist before filling in the gaps.

B **1 & 2** In the exam, usually, only one word is possible in each gap. The words used in the original text are in **bold**:

2 come across   **discover**   find
3 **shining**
4 **collect**   discover   gather
5 **disguised**
6 **enormous**   huge   immense
7 **creatures**   insects   types
8 experts   people   **specialists**
9 **concerned**   themselves
10 exactly   **just**   precisely   quite

11 biggest **richest** strangest
12 **exist** remain survive
13 **forms**
14 **careful** fortunate
15 attacked **bitten** stung

10.11 Save the Earth
SPEAKING AND COMPOSITION

A Say your answers softly to yourself. Maybe record yourself.

B ✍ If possible, ask another person to read and mark your work.

Model version:

> "The future of the planet looks bleak, but there's nothing I can do about it."
>
> Scientists and experts are continually warning us that our planet is doomed. Again and again, we hear the same depressing phrases: global warming, pollution, over-fishing, tropical rainforests . . . All because of what human beings have done and are still doing. Not enough people are worried about the future. Can anything be done? What can I do?
>
> Global warming is often cited as the most serious threat. Temperatures are rising and climate patterns are changing as the amount of carbon dioxide in the atmosphere rises. Greenhouse gases, which are emitted by burning fossil fuels in cars and power stations, are responsible for this. These emissions must be stopped if we want to stop global warming, and it's up to the politicians to enforce this. What can I do? Only vote for politicians who are going to be green. Every vote counts when a government has a narrow majority.
>
> Pollution is contaminating our rivers, lakes, seas and air. As more and more people are aware of this, there is going to be more pressure on polluters. Air pollution from traffic must be controlled if our cities are going to be places fit to live in. But if polluters themselves loathe pollution, it will stop. What can I do? Make more people aware. And technology is developing new ways of powering cars which we cannot imagine today. Before too long there may be new environmentally-friendly cars, eliminating the need for petrol and pollution.
>
> Fish stocks in every ocean are getting smaller all the time, due to over-fishing. Many fish never reach adulthood because of intensive fishing. We depend on fish as an important part of our diet. We need to control fishing, to conserve the stocks and allow them to regenerate. What can I do? Eat less fish and only eat fish that is caught by non-intensive methods.
>
> Once destroyed, a tropical rainforest cannot be replaced. But it can be managed by controlled forestry. What can I do? Only buy tropical hardwood from managed forests.
>
> If it was only me, as an individual, doing all the things I've suggested, it would have no effect. What I must do is persuade everyone else to share my views. What can I do? Support pressure groups like Friends of the Earth, who can influence the actions of governments and corporations. This may help our planet to survive a little longer for the benefit of our children and our children's children.

Reading Books Enjoying literature

11 Another world

11.1 Enjoying reading
LISTENING AND TOPIC VOCABULARY

A 🔊 **Answers:**

1 C	2 K + C	3 J + W	4 K	5 C	6 C
7 W	8 K	9 J	10 W + C + K		

TRANSCRIPTS *6 minutes 45 seconds*

INTERVIEWER: We talked to four people about reading. First here's Christine. What kind of books do you read?

CHRISTINE: I love detective fiction, I have to say. And I think that to me detective fiction has been a respite, it's been a treat, from serious grown-up reading. I learned to love books as a very little girl with my Dad who took me to the library twice a week, and I learned a great respect for plot...um...and for story-telling. And just loved the cliff-hanger story and still love it. Because I can get quite lost in one of those and I...I'm a very fast reader, and my desire to work out who did it and what happened next is so great that it overpowers everything else and I will disappear into a book for hours and not speak to a soul. But I get that from my father who is exactly the same, my Mum has never been a great reader and my Dad and I drive her mad, because we will sit for hours contentedly reading when we're together and she thinks this is awfully boring and...and unsocial. But my Dad is never not reading and that's where I got it from.
★★★

INTERVIEWER: Jonathan, what kind of books do you enjoy reading?

JONATHAN: Well, I always enjoy reading cook books. I'm quite a keen cook...um...so I get new ideas for recipes and things. But I just enjoy reading them as...as almost as fiction.

INTERVIEWER: Mhm. And...er...when...when do you read them?

JONATHAN: I will read them...mm...they're not books I tend to read at bedtime, they're more daytime books. If I have a...a few minutes to kill, I'll pull one on...off the shelf and have a browse.

INTERVIEWER: Mhm. And...er...what's your favourite book?

JONATHAN: Well, my favourite cook book would probably be Jane Grigson's Vegetable Book. She's a fantastic food writer anyway and I'm not a vegetarian, I love meat, um...but her Vegetable Book is fascinating because she covers each vegetable, each major vegetable in turn, gives you a bit of historical background and then all sorts of recipes involving the vegetable, and other ingredients as well. And it has a...a sense of history about it that I find very appealing.

INTERVIEWER: Mhm. And why do you enjoy reading?

JONATHAN: Well, I enjoy reading cook books, I think, largely because even if you're not cooking the recipes you're reading it conjures up a sense of other places, other flavours, other times in your life when you might have eaten something similar. And the promise of happy times in the future if you do cook this food for somebody else.
★★★

INTERVIEWER: Karen, how about you? What do you enjoy about reading?

KAREN: The immediate thing about a book is that is... just it takes you into a different world, you can immediately find yourself introduced to a whole set of behaviour or w...or ideas that, you know, you wouldn't easily come across in your own life. You can just shut the door and that's it. I mean, I think it's much more. I mean, it's much more pleasurable than television, although I mean, I'm interested in television and film as well, but you know obviously you can take it at your own pace, and you can read again and you can savour certain passages. And...um...I think it's just the idea...getting into one person's head, and sort of seeing how they see things. And just having... also, you know as I said before about readability, being caught up in a good story. I mean, you're lost for a few hours, aren't you? You're in a different world for a few hours. And that...and also just the tactile pleasure of holding a book, of a book as an object. I mean I like books as objects, I can never never throw them away ever, I could never give any even a scrappy old paperback I could never give it to a jumble sale.

★★★

INTERVIEWER: What kind of books do you enjoy reading, William?

WILLIAM: Er...I enjoy the classics. And...er...novels that are set in a different period of history. Um...I particularly like reading about periods of history I don't know anything about.

INTERVIEWER: And when do you read?

WILLIAM: Um...well, I'm a compulsive reader, um...so whenever I get the opportunity really, whether it's...er...on a journey, or when I'm at home with nothing to do, er...if I'm on holiday. Er...but any opportunity I get really I'll be into a book.

INTERVIEWER: And...um...what's your favourite book?

WILLIAM: Um...well, a book I've enjoyed recently was *Perfume* by Patrick Süsskind. Um...again a book set in a different period of history. Er...but this book in particular is fantastic because it is all about somebody...er...who notices the smells of things...um...much more than we would and...er...can actually tell what has happened in a...different areas of town by the smells that he can pick up there. Even things that have happened a long time beforehand. So it's a...it's a book that's written but has, you know, a great sort of sensual...er...feel to it.

INTERVIEWER: Mhm. And...um...what is it about reading that you enjoy?

WILLIAM: Um...I think it's just that, being able to transport yourself somewhere else...er...for whatever period you're reading for. Um...I think it's a great medium for creating...er...something that you don't know anything about and I'd actually rather read a book than watch a movie. I find it much easier to...er...escape somewhere else...um...when I don't have somebody's pictures showing me what it looks like. I can imagine it, a certain amount of it, myself and just enjoy the reading.

INTERVIEWER: Mhm, thank you.

★★★

INTERVIEWER: Finally, Christine again, why do you enjoy reading?

CHRISTINE: It's another world, it's going into a world...um...that somebody makes convincing, where there are characters in that world about whom you have a concern and you want to know what happens to them, and...um...it matters to know what is going to unfold and what happens next. And it's about expanding your picture of the world. It's taking you into bits of people's experience that you haven't got for yourself. Um...but the best book is one where you find the environment and the situation and the conflict if there is one, because most literature involves some kind of conflict. Er...the resolution of that conflict, or whatever, it...y...you just desperately want to know what it is. And it's that...um . . . it's that commitment to the creation the author has made that keeps you reading absolutely

desperately to the last page. Um...and it's about...er...magic as well, it's about being taken into a world that just transports you and you forget the here and now, you know, I...I could quite forget to feed the pussies if they didn't jump on my head if I were really engrossed in a book. And I regret the fact that I seem to have so little time to read these days. Um...one of my resolutions every year is to make more time to do it, and one of these days I will, you know, because I love reading.

B Say your answers softly to yourself. Maybe record yourself.

C Answers:

1 best-sellers thrillers whodunits
2 contents blurb dustjacket
3 dedication foreword preface
4 anthology book collection
5 complex intricate involved
6 get struggle wade
7 chapters sections units
8 figuratively metaphorically symbolically
9 message purpose side
10 readable thought-provoking well-written

D Answers (the Latin is given for your information only):

e.g. = **for example** (Latin: *exempli gratia*)
etc. = **and other things** (Latin: *et cetera*)
i.e. = **that is** (Latin: *id est*)   cf. = **compare** (Latin: *conferre*)   ff. = **and the following pages**   pp. = **pages**
ibid. = **from the book already mentioned** (Latin: *ibidem*)   viz. = **namely** (Latin: *videlicet*)   sic = **spelt in this way (probably misspelt) in the original work from which we are quoting** (Latin: thus)
N.B. = **note well** (Latin: *nota bene*)
© = **copyright**   ¶ = **paragraph number**

Most of the abbreviations can also be written without full stops: eg etc ie cf ff pp ibid viz NB

11.2 'My last novel is the best work I can do'

LISTENING

Background

William Boyd (b. 1952) is a writer whose early work deals humorously with the English abroad, but his later books are more serious and each one covers a quite different theme. Boyd's books are consistently well-written and thought-provoking.

His best-known books include: *A Good Man in Africa, An Ice Cream War, The New Confessions, Brazzaville Beach, The Blue Afternoon* and *Armadillo*.

The opening of *Brazzaville Beach* is in **11.3**.

A This activity can only be done with a partner.

B 🔊 Answers:

1 film and theatre
2 two to six in the afternoon
3 people he knows / his own life
4a masculinity and femininity / gender

4b personality
5 being autonomous   feeling free
   being self-sufficient
6 think themselves lucky / realise that others are
   worse off / stop moaning / not be so pathetic
7 university libraries / noisy, distracting places
8 first draft
9a second guess / anticipate
9b true
10 *Armadillo* (his most recent novel)

TRANSCRIPT   *12 minutes 50 seconds*

WILLIAM: My name is William Boyd, and I'm a novelist. Er…I also write short stories and scripts for films.

INTERVIEWER: And how did you start?

WILLIAM: I started…um…really when I went to University. Um…I did a lot of journalism, a lot of student journalism, I was a TV – er…not the TV critic, the film critic and the theatre critic of the university newspaper. Nice job! And…um…but I wrote a lot of stories and I actually wrote a…a novel while I was at university, which I never published or I never tried to publish, it was a…an autobiographical novel all about me and I had to get it out of my system. But…um…it was …er…really my university days that saw the beginning of my writing career.

I think also maybe deep down I realised I could never work for anybody! I was…I was…er…destined to be a freelance, and the wonderful thing about writing, I think, being a novelist, it is…it is the ultimate 'one man band', and…er…you are completely free and I think that i…if I had to sum up, you know, what does writing mean to me in one word, it would be 'freedom'.

INTERVIEWER: That's nice, that's lovely. And, I mean, on a typical day when you're actually writing, how do you…are you quite disciplined with yourself?

WILLIAM: Quite disciplined. I mean, er…when I'm writing a novel I try to write every day…um…but sometimes you can't because you've got a life to live, and…er…er…the central heating needs fixed, or you've got to go and do some shopping or something. But…um…I try to do, you know, is try to write every day as many days of the week as is possible, and…er…I don't have any rigid discipline, like I sit down at my desk at eight o'clock and rise from it at half past eleven for a cup of coffee. I …I can write for about three to four hours…um…and sometimes that's in the morning. And more recently I find that something's happened to my biorhythms or something, I find I'm writing more in the afternoon now after lunch from sort of…two to six is my normal stint. Um…but of course as the novel goes on and I get more and more caught up in it I begin to work longer days and seven days a week until by the end it's kind of a frantic sixteen-hour day going on.

★★★

INTERVIEWER: Now how do you come up on your characters?

WILLIAM: Well, sometimes they just s…suggest themselves to you. Um…sometimes they're maybe drawn from bits of life – I'm never…I'm not an autobiographical writer so I don't use my own life and the people I know as material for my fiction. Um…and sometimes you just have to sit down and invent them. Um…you know, I've…I've written from the point of view of a woman, and I…I knew that…er…I knew that was the first thing and then I had to think, 'Well, what kind of woman would she be?' And so I just…er…invented her, I invented her personality, and her…her physical appearance. And I think I am very much that type of writer,

I do use my imagination. I don't go to life for inspiration. I'm quite happy to sit and…and dream in a way, dream up things, and then there's another whole question of making it…them seem lifelike. But…er…a lot of it is…is a conscious act of…of choice and it's very much a question of…of me deciding and of…and of just setting my imagination to work.

INTERVIEWER: In *Brazzaville Beach* I…I loved the way that you were able to write as Hope Clearwater, and she was so real, she was just like it…um…she was, well, she was like a woman. I mean, was that difficult to write?

WILLIAM: Well, it was a difficult…er…process to…to get to the right method. And I think I have found the right method and I think it works both ways, I think if you are a woman wanting…wanting to write from the point of view of a man you should adopt the same method I did, which was to forget all questions of masculinity and femininity, to forget gender completely, and to concentrate entirely on personality.

And I think it's a kind of…we in a w…we're a bit knee jerk in the way we think, 'Oh, women are sensitive and warm and giving, and men…er…cannot commit and are cold and are frightened of their emotions'. Well, you know, that's a generalisation, um…you can't write a novel based on generalisations. So the more precise you are, the more idiosyncratic the character is, the more real he or she will appear in the…in the novel.

★★★

INTERVIEWER: What do you really enjoy about what you do?

WILLIAM: Well, I think the main thing I enjoy about it, or…is my complete and absolute self-sufficiency. Um…and I'm also deeply conscious of how lucky I am to be able to be, as Chekhov said, 'a free artist'. Um…I don't live in a country that's oppressed…um…I am uncensored. I can…I can earn a living…er…at what I want to do more than anything else in the world. I can decide not to work one day or work flat out for three months. And I think it's that absolute liberation, that absolute autonomy, that…er…is the thing I cherish most and which I would think I would feel most…er…um…unhappy about if it was removed. Um…and…um…as a result…um…I don't take it for granted, and then there's the compensation of…of being an artist practising your art form, which has its bad days and its exhilarating days, but I think it's really within the context of…of this…this absolute freedom and autonomy…um…that makes it…er…you know, so fulfilling.

INTERVIEWER: Is there anything you don't like about being a novelist?

WILLIAM: Well, I've got lots of grumbles and complaints but really…um…I think they're pathetic. [No, I'm sure they're not!] I…I…I…remember once being asked a question, when I was giving a reading and somebody said 'Er…do you suffer for your art?' And I immediately said, 'But of course I do'. And then I thought, 'Hang on a minute, what…what exactly do I suffer?' [Having to talk to such a bloody idiot!] 'What suffering are we talking about here?' So I really think it's a…a luxury…er…to complain. And…er…maybe if I was suffering from a terrible writer's block or if I was constantly being trashed by the critics and couldn't sell a copy, then I would be a more tormented soul. But…um…the little, you know, um…' slings and arrows of outrageous fortune' that you encounter in the writing life are…are…are as nothing beside the more serious injustices and grievances that…er…the world hands out. So I think those of us who…um…you know, moan and complain about, 'Oh, it's so hard and so difficult!' um…really don't know they're living.

★★★

INTERVIEWER: Can you write anywhere? Can you write here or do you prefer writing in a...um...particular location?

WILLIAM: No, I can write just about anywhere. And I think this is something because I started writing in universities and university libraries, people wandering around or whispering, and...so so I've never needed solitude and I still write in libraries, I still go to...um...a library to...er...to write sometimes. I also work in my house in my study but if the phone rings I'll answer it, if there...somebody knocks at the door I'll break off and go and answer the door. Um...and I've written on planes and in cafés and, you know, hotel rooms, all sorts of things. So I don't need the...those kind of, you know, special conditions which I think are actually a, well, an excuse for not working!

INTERVIEWER: Do you write...um...freehand or put it all on your...on a laptop or . . .?

WILLIAM: Well, I write...er...I write my novels...the first draft I write...I write in longhand, in pencil – it's very low tech! Um...because I think there's something...er...missing if there isn't a manuscript stage. I mean this is just for my case, I think that there's something about the head, the hand, the page link which is fundamental to writing prose, and I suspect, well, certainly for me, and I suspect it's to do with things like sentence length, and inner rhythm and cadence to a sentence. And also the act of crossing out and the act of inserting other words. Um...on the screen of a computer that's gone, it's always looks pretty much perfect, but you can see on a manuscript just from the scribblings and the second thoughts and the third thoughts the whole process of your fiction evolving and...er...it's a very curious indication about something that's going well, or something that's going badly. Um...if you've written five lines for example in longhand and you haven't put a full stop there's something at the back of your mind saying this sentence is getting far too long. You never get that feeling if you're typing it onto a screen on a computer because there's... everything is there but not there and endlessly malleable, but you've made those marks on the page and there's something about that act which I still feel is fundamental to my fiction writing. And so even though I've been using a computer now for seven years, and I write journalism on it and...and screenplays and so on, whenever I start a novel or a short story or a work of fiction I...er...always do the first draft in...in longhand and then I type it on to the screen, and edit it on the screen.

INTERVIEWER: And when you're writing, do you write in your head to an individual or are you writing...um...to the world?

WILLIAM: No, I think you...er...probably write for yourself, I think that you write the books you like to...would like to read. And I think it's always a mistake to try and second-guess your ideal reader...um...because...er...you will possibly not be true to yourself, your sincerity, your integrity. I think you have to really do what you want to do and not what you think you ought to do, and that way even if the book is, let's say, terrible and an awful failure, at least you will...will have been true to yourself, and you've got no one else to blame.

★★★

INTERVIEWER: Have you got...er...one of your novels that's your favourite?

WILLIAM: Um...I have sort of an answer to this which is a bit of a cop-out or it seems a bit of a . . . But I actually think . . .

INTERVIEWER: You don't mean you've been asked this before!

WILLIAM: I have been asked this before, but I always give the same answer, which is...sounds a bit of a . . . but I think that if you...if I had to choose one book to represent me, as it were, for posterity, it would always be my last book because I think that . . . Haha, I know! It's a . . . But it's true because in a writerly sense everything that's in your last book is as good as...as I can get at the moment. I mean, people have . . . I've...I've written seven novels now, and some people like my first novel better than any others, some people like my fourth novel better. But in my...from my point of view I know that my last novel *Armadillo* is the...is the best work I can do at the moment, though it's going to be supplanted by the novel I'm going to write next of course, which is going to be in writerly...in terms, better, more sophisticated, more mature. I'm more experienced, I've...I've learnt more, and that may not be evident in the success of the novel or the apparent perceived success of the novel, but it will be evident to me as the writer of it.

INTERVIEWER: Does it surprise you still that you have that ability?

WILLIAM: Sometimes it's amaz...you are amazed at what you have thought up, because it's spontaneous in the act of writing, something unplanned. You, you know, I do plan everything in advance, I sit down to write Chapter Five and I start writing it and I get an idea – out of the blue – and everything...everything changes. Um...so...er...it's almost functioning independently sometimes of me, and that's when I'm...er... astonished and I think, 'What on earth made me think of that?'

INTERVIEWER: Oh, it's exciting.

WILLIAM: Yes, it is, it is, and you hope it won't go away, that's the other thing, you hope this faculty will remain with you and...er...will in a way...er...continue to enrich what you write.

C Say your answers softly to yourself. Maybe record yourself.

11.3 Setting the scene . . .
READING AND SPEAKING

Background

We heard an interview with **William Boyd** in **11.2**.

The protagonist of *Brazzaville Beach* is a woman who, against the background of civil war in an African country, is studying chimpanzees and makes the alarming discovery that they engage in warlike activities with each other, just as humans do.

Barbara Vine is the pseudonym of the crime writer Ruth Rendell (b. 1930). Her books written under this name are more imaginative and strange than her more routine Inspector Wexford mysteries. She is a very accessible, stylish writer whose work dwells on life's losers and the darker side of human nature.

All of her Barbara Vine novels are highly recommendable: *A Dark Adapted Eye, A Fatal Inversion, The House of Stairs, Gallowglass, King Solomon's Carpet, Asta's Book, No Night is Too Long* and *The Brimstone Wedding*.

A Fatal Inversion concerns obsessive family relationships and a murder, the perpetrator of which is due to be executed as the book opens. During the rest of the book, the situation leading up to the murder slowly unfolds in flashbacks.

David Lodge (b. 1935) is a humorous writer whose work has a serious edge. Many of his works are concerned in some way with university life, and the worlds of game-playing, sexual intrigue and Catholicism.

His best-known books are: *Changing Places, Small World, Nice Work, Paradise News, Therapy* and *Thinks . . .*

The main characters of *Nice Work* are Vic Wilcox, the managing director of a struggling engineering firm, and Robyn Penrose, a feminist university lecturer. The book explores their different worlds and the developing relationship between two very different people.

Here and in **11.9** we have the opening paragraphs of some well-known novels, which I hope will whet your appetite, encouraging you to want to read more.

A Suggested answers:

1 She (or he) lives in a beach house somewhere in Africa, where she/he just happens to have landed up and is unlikely to stay for ever. She/he seems to be single.   [The reader discovers later that the narrator is a woman – some readers may recognise that the beach is in a Portuguese-speaking country.]

2 None (apart from '*some workmen*' and '*everyone else who lives round here*') – it gives a mood of isolation or self-containment

3 The narrator lives in a house on a beach: this is described in some detail in the last paragraph together with its garden – it is 'a few years' after 1964

4 Six: four of which are in the phrase '*Brazzaville Beach*', the title of the book – it seems that the beach is likely to be the main setting of the story

5 In ¶ 1 we find out where the narrator lives and we may be intrigued to know how she ended up there – the imagery of the *spar of driftwood* to which the narrator compares herself is striking
In ¶ 2 we find out the origins of the name of the beach, but without understanding what *Quadros* means in Portuguese or knowing about the conference in 1964, we are none the wiser. The style is very matter-of-fact
In ¶ 3 the reader is introduced to the political background of the story. The questions asked stand out stylistically
¶ 4 gives a detailed description of the house and its garden – the use of *I* and *my* emphasises that the house belongs to the narrator, she considers it to be her home. The style makes the place sound very attractive

B Suggested answers:

1 Very little: she is going to die at exactly 8 o'clock, her home is in the country, she is probably the narrator's aunt (her father's sister).
We don't know why she is going to die at 8 o'clock: it is a mystery [The reader later discovers that she is going to be executed.]

2 Four times – not all that many, but enough to set a mood of gloom

3 She reads poetry (Browning); she doesn't get on well with her father

4 The narrator awakes in her parents' house in a leafy suburb on a Thursday in August 30 years ago.

C Suggested answers:

1 He often wakes up early and can't go back to sleep, because of his worries at work; he works in industry in a senior position; he is married and has a son called Gary

2 She is Victor's wife: she is overweight, she takes sleeping pills, she reads in bed before going to sleep

3 Victor awakes in his bedroom very early on Monday January 13th 1986

4 Twelve: it makes us realise that he has a lot of problems – they attack him like alien spaceships in a video game. The technical terms (*fettling shop, core blowers,* etc.) are puzzling to the reader, but they mean a lot to Victor

5 ¶ 1 begins like a diary entry, followed by terse scene-setting sentences, and then we share Victor's thoughts and the questions in his mind
In ¶ 2 his worries are listed and made to seem like attackers in a video game
In ¶ 3 we are introduced to his wife – a series of actions are described, like a blow-by-blow account of a fight

D Say your answers softly to yourself. Maybe record yourself.

11.4 Describing a book
SPEAKING AND COMPOSITION

A Say your answers softly to yourself.

B 🖉 If possible, ask another person to read and mark your work.

Model version:

> *Leviathan* by Paul Auster
>
> *Leviathan* is a fascinating blend of detective story and literary novel by Paul Auster, an American writer whose other novels combine fantasy and realism, with an element of autobiography. The narrator of this story has a lot in common with Auster himself, but he is someone else.
>
> The story starts with an explosion on a remote roadside in Wisconsin, USA. A man is blown up by the side of a road and nobody knows who he is except Peter, the narrator of the novel. The rest of the story is about Peter's memories of his own encounters with former friend Benjamin Sachs and his journey across America meeting other people who knew Sachs. He is trying to piece together what happened to his former friend and what led to his death. What terrible things happened to him? Was his death an accident, suicide or murder?
>
> As we find out more about Sachs, we also find out about Peter himself. Peter tells us about his encounters with Sachs over the fifteen years of their intermittent friendship. Years pass and many things happen as they lose touch with each other for a couple of years, and then meet again. We meet Fanny, Lillian and Maria and find out about their different relationships with Sachs — and with Peter himself. Seen through the eyes of each of these women, Sachs seems to be different people. How can the same man be so different?
>
> The whole story is like a puzzle. Gradually, as we learn more about the characters, the pieces fit together and the whole picture starts to become visible. But the writer keeps us guessing until the very end. And the style of writing is clear, clever and thoughtful.
>
> One of the themes of the novel is that nobody is what they seem. We present different faces to different people, and as we grow older and move to different places we can become different people. We don't stay the same person.
>
> *Leviathan* is a thought-provoking and rewarding book. I can't wait to read it again.

11.5 Conjunctions and connectors – 1
GRAMMAR REVIEW

A 1 Don't highlight words you already use frequently.

Suggested answers:

2 Many blockbusters, such as James Mitchener's *Alaska*, are over 1,000 pages long.
3 He enjoys reading biographies, particularly ones about politicians.
4 Science fiction is an acquired taste – at least that's what sci-fi fans say.
5 She prefers reading non-fiction books, which means that she enjoys biographies, history books, as well as other similar books.
6 The reason why the book was a best-seller was that it contained a lot of explicit sex and violence.
7 He doesn't read much apart from thrillers.
8 Reading is not only an inexpensive hobby but it is also enjoyable.
Not only is reading an inexpensive hobby, it is also enjoyable.

B Suggested answers:

1 apart from / with the exception of
2 what is more
3 in particular / above all
4 even though / although   in other words
5 for example   consequently
6 nevertheless / however
7 at any rate / at least
8 above all / in particular / particularly / especially

11.6 Collocations: idioms
VOCABULARY DEVELOPMENT

A Answers:

1 pros and cons
2 facts and figures
3 ups and downs
4 swings and roundabouts
5 law and order
6 touch and go
7 thick and thin
8 wear and tear
9 over and above
10 few and far between
11 bread and butter
12 safe and sound

B Suggested answers:

a/an basket of fruit   bucket of water   bunch of flowers   carafe of wine/water   cup of tea   flight of stairs   flock of sheep   gust of wind   herd of cattle   item of luggage   jug of milk   loaf of bread   pack of cards   pair of tweezers   piece of equipment /cake   pot of honey   puff of smoke   range of hills   sack of potatoes   school of whales   slice of cake/bread   spoonful of sugar   spot of bother   team of helpers   tin or can of beans   tube of toothpaste

C Suggested answers (other humorous variations are possible):

1 a range of hills
2 a bunch of flowers
3 items of luggage
4 a pack of cards
5 gust of wind
6 a team of helpers
7 a spot of bother
8 a flock of sheep/swarm of bees, etc.
9 a flight of stairs
10 a pair of tweezers

D Answers:

She's as blind as a bat
The sea was as calm as a millpond
She's as free as the air
He's as cool as a cucumber
She's as hard as nails
He's as quiet as a mouse
She's as fit as a fiddle
He looked as white as a sheet
That story is as old as the hills
She looked as pretty as a picture
The children were as good as gold
She's as light as a feather
We were as warm as toast

11.7 A good beginning
WRITING SKILLS

A Read the article.

B Choose some 'nodders' and 'shakers'.

C 1 & 2 There are no suggested answers for these tasks. The extracts are genuine students' work.

D 1 & 2 ✐ If possible, ask another person to read and mark your improved opening lines.

11.8 It . . . constructions
ADVANCED GRAMMAR

A Answers:

1 Did Jane Austen write *Emma*?
– *slight emphasis on the last item mentioned: the book. However if a stress is put on different words in the sentence, the emphasis and implications change:*
Did Jane Austen write *Emma*? –
. . . I insist that you tell me
Did **Jane** Austen write *Emma*? –
. . . or was it <u>Anne</u> Austen?
Did Jane **Austen** write *Emma*? –
. . . or was it another author called Jane?
Did Jane Austen **write** *Emma*? –
. . . or did she edit it?
Did Jane Austen write ***Emma***? –
. . . or another book?
Was it Jane Austen who wrote *Emma*? –
– more emphasis on the author's name

Was Jane Austen the author of *Emma*?
– *emphasis on the author*
Was the author who wrote *Emma* Jane Austen?
– *emphasis on* the author. *(This structure sounds clumsy here with the two names juxtaposed)*
Was *Emma* written by Jane Austen?
– *emphasis on the author's name*
Was it *Emma* that Jane Austen wrote?
– *. . . or was it another book? Emphasis on the title, suggesting that this is the only book she was famous for (cf Was it* Wuthering Heights *that Emily Brontë wrote?)*
Was Jane Austen the author who wrote *Emma*?
– *emphasis on the author. (It seems unnecessary to use the term author here, and maybe woman might be more usual)*

2 What I enjoy reading is thrillers.
– *emphasis on* thrillers – *this structure helps to create suspense as we wait for the main point to be mentioned*
Thrillers are what I enjoy reading.
& It's thrillers that I enjoy reading.
– *emphasis on* thrillers
I enjoy reading thrillers.
– *no special emphasis, as written. In speech we might put stress on* enjoy *or on* thrillers

3 It was me who borrowed your book.
– *emphasis on* me *as the person responsible*
I borrowed your book.
– *no special emphasis*

B Suggested answers:

1 surprising/remarkable   get to the summit
2 wrote
3 a good job   warned/told
4 is unfriendly/unlikable   is very shy
5 long/too long   realised/discovered we had made
6 is it   never arrive anywhere
7 'll be/will be   who answers/picks up
8 to be   who was   is/'s me who reads

C Suggested answers:

1 It was only yesterday that she finished reading the book.
2 Is it the humour of her stories that you enjoy?
3 Was it *Emma* or *Persuasion* that you read recently?
4 It was because I was feeling worn out that I went to bed early.
5 It was a strange noise that woke me up in the early hours.
6 It was half past four in the morning when I heard the noise.
7 It was when I looked out of the window that I realised what had happened.
8 It was then that I found I couldn't get back to sleep.
9 It was about eight o'clock when I finally did get to sleep.
10 It wasn't until lunchtime that I woke up.

11.9 Three American novels
READING

Background

Ernest Hemingway (1899–1961), despite his image of being a hard-drinking, macho man of action, had a genius for evoking a time and a place in his writing, by means of a delightfully simple style. His prose is particularly accessible for foreign learners.

His best-known books include: *Fiesta (The Sun Also Rises), For Whom the Bell Tolls, The Old Man and the Sea, Men without Women* and *To Have and Have Not.*

A Farewell to Arms is a love story set against the background of the First World War.

John Steinbeck (1902–68) wrote about the lives of simple, ordinary people in America. His best-known books are: *Of Mice and Men, Cannery Row, Tortilla Flat* and *East of Eden* (the film of which starred James Dean).

The Grapes of Wrath is the story of dispossessed farmers driven off their land in Oklahoma, to search for a better life in California, which was 'the land of milk and honey'.

Paul Theroux (b. 1941) is a travel writer as well as novelist. His travels have taken him all over the world and are described in such books as: *The Great Railway Bazaar: By Train through Asia, The Old Patagonian Express, The Kingdom by the Sea, Riding the Iron Rooster, The Happy Isles of Oceania* and *The Pillars of Hercules.*

His novels are full of imaginative detail and exotic locations, each one quite different from the other. Particularly recommendable are: *Picture Palace, The Family Arsenal, O-Zone, My Secret History* (the first paragraphs of which are in **13.3 Family life**), *Milroy the Magician* and *Hotel Honolulu.*

The Mosquito Coast is the story of a family who abandon civilisation in the USA, and go to live in the jungle of Central America, hoping to build Utopia for themselves. But life becomes a nightmare. The novel is a compelling creation of an obsessive central character ('Father') and is told through the voice of his young son.

A Read the extracts.

B Suggested answers:

1 Extract 1 is from *A Farewell to Arms* by Ernest Hemingway (1929)
Extract 2 is from *The Grapes of Wrath* by John Steinbeck (1939)
Extract 3 is from *The Mosquito Coast* by Paul Theroux (1981)
2 Extract 2:   *May   day after day*
the changing weather   the growth of green weeds and their subsequent dying back
3 Extract 1:   *Troops went by the house and down the road   the leaves fell   troops marching along the road   the soldiers marching*   the use of prepositions and particles: *across, along,* etc.
4 Extract 3:   *savages   awfulness   dope-taking, door-locking, ulcerated danger-zone of rabid scavengers . . .*
a piling-up of words that suggest decay and violence
5 See the quotations in Answers 2–4 above
6 Extract 1 (Hemingway)
7 Extract 2 (Steinbeck) – or 1?
8 Extract 3 (Theroux)
9 Extract 2 – and 1?
10 *for discussion*

11.10 The future of reading?
SPEAKING AND COMPOSITION

A Say your answers softly to yourself. Maybe record yourself.

B 🖋 If possible, ask another person to read and mark your work.

Model version:

> I couldn't wait to try out my new eBook! It looked wonderful when I tried it out in the shop, but would I still love it when I used it at home?
>
> When I got home I plugged it in and left it to charge its battery while I went out to my evening class. When I got back it was ready to use.
>
> I began reading in the kitchen with the eBook resting on the table as I had a drink and a snack. The screen was easily visible, but not as clear and sharp as a page in a normal book. To change the page on an eBook you just press a button, or you can scroll the text if you prefer. You don't have to hold the pages open, like you do with a book, and you can change the font and font size to make it easier to read comfortably.
>
> I took my eBook to bed with me. This was when I discovered its best feature: you can read in bed in the dark! You don't need a light because the screen is bright. And if you fall asleep while reading (as I did!) the eBook turns itself off after a few minutes, keeping your place in the book till the next time you turn it on.
>
> The next day, I had a long train journey to make. I read my eBook with my Walkman playing, easily ignoring the other passengers' conversations and mobile phone calls. The time flew by and I was sorry when the journey was over.
>
> During the rest of the week and at the weekend, I read in public and in private. I read on the bus, in the park, in cafés, at home. But not in the bath and not at the beach — the eBook is splashproof but I didn't want to risk dropping it into water or getting it dirty or stolen.
>
> My verdict? Well, a paperback book is lighter, and a printed page is certainly easier to read than the eBook screen. The darker the surroundings, the easier it is to read. But you can store dozens of different books and magazines on one eBook. And you can also download newspapers, which makes reading on the train or on the bus easier than folding and unfolding a newspaper — and cleaner, because you don't get inky fingers.
>
> But technology is developing all the time with incredible rapidity. How long will it be before my lovely new eBook is superseded by something lighter, cheaper, more versatile and easier to read?

12
Science Technology Gadgets

The cutting edge

12.1 Science and technology
TOPIC VOCABULARY

A Say your answers softly to yourself. The photos show: the surface of a compact disc, a microchip and Velcro.

The *cutting edge* refers to the very latest technology.

B Answers:

1 application   2 meteorology   3 zoology
4 anthropology   5 computers   6 knob
7 generation   8 controlled   9 inspiration
10 impractical   11 equipment   12 patent
13 think up   14 socket (US outlet)
15 trial and error

12.2 The Freedom Ship
LISTENING AND SPEAKING

A 🔊 (For more information about the Freedom Ship, go to their website: www.freedomship.com)

Answers:

1 20,000   2 $138,000   3 $7 million   4 by ferry
5 75%   6 1,316 metres   7 220 metres   8 2 years
9 40-seater jets   10 mostly in warm climates
11 school and university   12 none   13 employee leasing services   14 it will be incinerated (burnt to produce energy)   15 diesel fuel
16 no worries: you'll hardly feel the waves

TRANSCRIPT   *5 minutes 20 seconds*

PRESENTER: Have you ever wanted to travel the world and still stay at home? It's soon going to be a possibility if Norman Nixon's plans work out. He's building a floating city and he's calling it the Freedom Ship. To tell us more about it, here's Sandy Harrison. So Sandy, tell us about the Freedom Ship.

SANDY: Yeah, well, the Freedom Ship is going to be nearly a mile long and it'll be home to 40,000 people. There will be 20,000 homes on board. The cheapest is going to be $138,000 for a 3 metre by 10 metre room with a fridge and microwave – that's bigger than the largest suite on a cruise liner! And the most expensive will be $7 million for a 450 square metre ocean-view residence. Most of the units will have a sea view, and the very cheapest ones will overlook a park or open courtyard. There'll be 10,000 staff, who run the ship and provide all the facilities.

PRESENTER: Right.

SANDY: Yeah, well, the idea is that it will slowly travel the world, pausing a few miles out from chosen destinations such as ports or exotic tropical islands that can only be reached by sea. It will be on the move for twenty-five per cent of the time and otherwise anchored off different ports. It won't go into the port because it's too large. There will be ferries to take people to and fro.

PRESENTER: And where is it going to be built?

SANDY: The ship will actually be built at Puerto Castilla in Honduras. It'll be five times larger than the largest cruise liner afloat. 1,316 metres long, 220 metres wide, 100 metres tall. But it's not a cruise liner, it's a city.

PRESENTER: Right, and…er…what will be on board?

SANDY: Well, there'll be a school and a university on board, a runway for planes, a fully equipped hospital, and hotels for people who want to spend a holiday on the Freedom Ship. The shopping mall, one of the world's largest, will also be one of the most beautiful. And per…in other words, it will be the first self-contained city that not only floats, but moves. The plan is for it to circumnavigate the globe every two years, going into port for the benefit of its residents and for tourists, who will come on board and shop at duty-free shops.

PRESENTER: What else?

SANDY: Well, let's think now. Um…a free public tramway will carry people around the ship. There will be small aircraft and hydrofoils to ferry people to and from shore. Also hangars, marinas, and repair and machine shops for private aircraft and boats. The runway won't be long enough to take a jumbo jet, or even a normal airliner, but it will be able to take 40-seat commuter jets and the runway can always be moved to face into the wind.

PRESENTER: Ha, of course!

SANDY: As the ship will spend most of its time in warm climates, people will want to enjoy the open air. It'll have 80 hectares of open space outside and this'll include tennis courts, parks and promenades with waterfalls, ponds, and extensive landscaping. Inside, most levels will feature large saltwater aquariums.

PRESENTER: Right.

SANDY: Entertainment facilities, including movies, theatres, clubs, casinos — also restaurants designed to appeal to a wide range of palates.

PRESENTER: So…um…what kind of people are going to live there?

SANDY: Well, Norman Nixon hopes that it'll become a 'global environment' with a…a large mixture of different nationalities and ages. It's not meant to be seen as a retirement cruise ship, but one where people could run their businesses and educate their children. And there will be no local taxes to pay.

PRESENTER: Ahh!

SANDY: Yeah, Freedom Ship may sound like a sort of resort city only for the rich. Yet there will be ample employment opportunities. Businesses can use the ship's 'employee leasing services' where workers will be trained, given uniforms, and provided with room and board on the lower decks.

PRESENTER: And all the latest technology I suppose?

SANDY: Oh, yeah, everything will be as environmentally-friendly as possible. Everything that can be recycled will be. And waste, sewage and non-recyclable materials will be incinerated and produce energy. Nixon plans for a pollution-free, energy-efficient and safe ship that will exceed current standards for both ships and land-bound cities. Standard cruise ships are, obviously, notorious polluters, but state-of-the-art technology will be used to make Freedom Ship as safe and environmentally-friendly and non-polluting as possible. The engines will use clean diesel fuel, not dirty marine fuel.

PRESENTER: Well, Sandy, it'd be no good for me. I get seasick when I go on a ship.

SANDY: Well, no worries there, apparently. Because of its size the Freedom Ship won't be vulnerable to hurricanes and storms. You'll hardly feel the movement of the ocean.

B This activity can only be done with a partner.

12.3 Design flaws
READING

Background

Bill Bryson was born in Des Moines, Iowa, in 1951. He settled in England in 1977. His books are often laugh-out-loud funny and describe his travels and experiences of everyday life. His best-known books are: *The Lost Continent* and *Notes from a Big Country* (about the USA), *Notes from a Small Island* (about Britain), *Neither Here Nor There* (about Europe) and *Down Under* (about Australia). He also writes about the English language and its history in *Mother Tongue* and *Made in America*.

Design flaws is one of the humorous articles in *Notes from a Big Country*. Another article from this is *Why no one walks in the USA*, which you can read in **17.4 A**.

A **1** (Humour is a matter of taste, and Bryson's humour is not to everyone's taste.)

Answers:

¶3 limitless	¶4 dress	¶5 font	¶6 imbecilic
¶7 blunder (on)	¶8 indentation		
¶9 spontaneously	¶10 manifold	¶10 envision	
¶11 moaning			

B Answers:

1 d	2 a	3 b	4 b	5 c	6 b

C 🖋 Say your answers softly to yourself. Maybe record yourself.

12.4 Verbs + prepositions
GRAMMAR REVIEW

A **1** Answers:

combine something **with**	
compare something **with**	
contrast something **with**	
depend **on**	
engage **in**	part **with**
invest **in**	reason **with**
lean **on**	rely **on**
mistake it/them **for**	separate something **from**

2 Suggested answers:

agree **with** someone **about** something
apologise **to** someone **for** something
approve **of**
bargain **with** someone **for** something
care **for/about**
decide **on/against**
experiment **on/with**
hope **for**

insist **on**
interfere **with/in**
intrude **on**
negotiate **with** someone **about/for** something
object **to**
quarrel **with** someone **over/about** something
resign **from/over**
retire **from**

smell **of/like**
struggle **with/against/for**
succeed **in**
suffer **from**
talk **to/with** someone **about** something
vote **for/against/on**
watch **for/over**
worry **about**

3 Answers:

admire him **for**	deliver it **to**
blame her **for**	punish him **for**
congratulate him **on**	rescue them **from**
consult her **on/about**	respect her **for**
convince them **of**	take it **from/to**

thank her **for**
threaten them **with**
use it **for**
warn him **against/about**

B   Answers:

1 through	2 in	3 through	4 for	5 with
6 of	7 through	8 of	9 from/at	
10 through	11 by	12 with	13 on	14 of/on
15 in	16 in/with	17 By	18 in/on	19 with
20 of	21 With	22 for	23 at	24 for

See also **14.4 Word order: phrasal verbs**, **15.3 Prepositions –2** and **17.5 Adjectives + prepositions**.

12.5   The passive – 2
ADVANCED GRAMMAR

A   **1** Answers:

1 c	2 i	3 d	4 a	5 e	6 b	7 g	8 h
9 e	10 f						

2 Sentences rephrased in the active (comments in *italics*):

1 Candidates may not use dictionaries in the examination.
– *Emphasis on* candidates *as the people who are involved*

2 His father criticised him but his mother praised him.
– *Emphasis on* father *and* mother

3 People have/Everybody has misunderstood him and made him feel inadequate all his life.
– *As the people involved are not important, this sounds strange in the active voice*

4 The college authorities have decided to restrict parking by students in the grounds.
– *Emphasis on the people who made the decision, rather than the decision itself*

5 Dangerous drivers (??) have injured several people in accidents at this junction.
– *We don't know who was responsible for the accidents (maybe the people themselves were partly responsible) so this sounds strange*

6 We heated the solution to boiling point and then allowed it to cool to 20°.
– *Emphasis on* we, *which is unusual in a report of a scientific experiment*

7 Although we arrived early, someone/the people in the office kept us waiting for an hour.
– *Emphasis on the people who caused the waiting*

8 We arrived late because bad weather/heavy air traffic delayed our flight.
– *Emphasis on the cause of the delay*

9 Someone/Sandy/My assistant (?) is photocopying the documents at the moment.
– *Emphasis on the person who is doing it*

10 Someone has/You have taken some money from my room.
– *Emphasis on the person, not the theft*

B   Answers:

1 She's fed up with being looked down on.
2 The children were looked after by their grandparents.
3 This matter is being dealt with by my assistant.
4 All breakages must be paid for.
5 Tony can't be relied on to finish the work on time.
6 The repairs will be seen to right away.
7 Her apartment had been broken into during the night.
8 Scientists are often looked on as experts.
9 It was pointed out to me that I was wearing odd socks.
10 He might be referred to as 'technophobic'.
11 Until permission is granted they can't expand the airport.
12 Some people might be intimidated by electronics, but not me.
13 How can all these old magazines be disposed of?
14 Those old magazines will have to be got rid of.
15 All the survivors of the accident have been accounted for.

12.6   give and take
VERBS AND IDIOMS

A   Answers:

give   advice to someone   an answer   an explanation   encouragement   evidence   permission   someone a kiss   someone a lift   someone a ring   someone a shock   someone some help

take   a liking to someone or something   a photograph   a pride in something   an interest in something   issue with someone   part in something   pity on someone   your time over something

B   Suggested answers:

1 assume   put up with hardships as well as easy times   start
2 be resentful   accepted it without resentment   put his side of the argument as well as I did
3 surprised   accepted
4 liked   (only used in the passive)
5 deceived   revealed what was supposed to be secret
6 raised an objection   be so familiar with him that she didn't appreciate him
7 show your feelings by attacking   raise the matter
8 invite out   help you stop thinking about your problems
9 imitate/mimic   removes   has no patience left
10 absorb

C   Answers:

1 took   away
2 taking down
3 given over to
4 take out
5 taken on   taking out   take off
6 have given   up   take up
7 taking over
8 take back

12.7 Suffixes
VOCABULARY DEVELOPMENT

A If in doubt about the definitions of any nouns, you should consult a dictionary. Say your answers softly to yourself.
Here are a few more examples:

An *administrator* is employed to run an organisation, but a *dictator* runs a country undemocratically.
They're both in control of other people.

A *chauvinist* believes that men are superior to women, or that his nation is superior to other nations.
A *feminist* believes that women should have the same rights as men.
They both have strong beliefs.

An *employer* is someone who employs people.
An *employee* is someone who is employed by an employer or a company.
They both work, but in different capacities.

Abstract nouns and verbs (Where no abstract noun or verb exists and a phrase or an unrelated word has to be used, these are *in italics*.)

administration · dictatorship
chauvinism · feminism
employ/employment
mine · *being under age*
persecute/persecution · prosecute/prosecution
research · search

attack · hijack
council · counsel/*advice*
fortune-telling/*tell fortunes* · storytelling/*tell stories*
pawn · *dealing in shares*
occupy the position before · *follow*
own/hold shares · *own a house*

serve drinks · moneylending/lend money
demonstrate · spectate
owning land · *like to be alone*
pay/payment
psychology · psychiatry
solve problems/deal with trouble · make trouble

B Answers:

deafen emphasise familiarise generalise
glamorise loosen moisten nationalise sharpen
straighten strengthen subsidise summarise
sweeten sympathise synthesise thicken tighten
victimise visualise widen

C **1** Highlight the words you want to remember.

2 This activity can only be done with a partner.

12.8 Thinking about the reader
READING AND WRITING SKILLS

A **1 & 2** Suggested answers:

1 'Humans do not always err. But they do when the things they use are badly conceived and designed.' (line 7)
'To me it sounds like equipment failure coupled with serious design error.' (line 20)
'While we all blame ourselves, the real culprit – faulty design – goes undetected.' (line 25)

2 Eighteen – it makes the text very personal
3 *we* three times
ourselves twice
4 None
5 Only once: *Consider the phrase . . .* (line 13)
6 Fifteen – it raises questions that the reader is encouraged to think about
7 The first five questions are answered, three of them with quotes:
'Pilot error . . . human error . . . Human error.'
The next questions are all unanswered, until *Human error?* in line 20.
The last three questions are answered with *While we all blame ourselves, the real culprit – faulty design – goes undetected*
8 Very well, by involving the reader in the questions to think about and by encouraging the reader to share the writer's personal experiences, as if in a diary or personal letter
9 *Perhaps:* A reader who might share his concern for accidents at nuclear power plants and the causes of airline crashes.
A reader who is sympathetic to his ideas, and is not an expert or a technologist.
An educated person
10 **a** He doesn't presuppose any technical knowledge and gives information that can be followed by any layperson. He is trying to interest and persuade the reader to share his views and not to give information.
b *Perhaps:* Using the first person frequently and having so many questions, makes a direct appeal to the reader, whom he assumes to be in sympathy
Or, perhaps? The overloading of first person pronouns and questions makes an assault on the reader, beating us into agreement

B **1 & 2** If possible, ask another person to read and mark your work.

Model paragraph:

Traffic has always ruled my life and restricted my enjoyment. When I was little I wanted to go and play in the park on the other side of the main road, but my mother wouldn't allow me to cross the road. Why? Because of the traffic. When I was older I wanted to go out with my friends on our bikes, but my father told me I mustn't ride on the main road. Why? Because of the traffic. Now I want to learn to drive and buy a second-hand car. But there's no point. Why? Because it's quicker to walk than drive and there's nowhere to park anyway.

12.9 User-friendly design
SPEAKING AND COMPOSITION

A **1** Say your answers softly to yourself. Maybe record yourself.

2 This activity can only be done with a partner.

B **1–3** If possible, ask another person to read and mark your work.

279

Model version:

Modern electronic devices like videos and televisions embody increasingly sophisticated technology. They're capable of performing multiple functions and there are numerous adjustments that can be made. But when you play a video do you use all the buttons on your remote control? No, you only use these: Play, Stop, Rewind, Fast Forward and Pause. Are they the most prominent or accessible controls? Probably not. Why can't those controls be bigger than the rest? And why can't all the other controls be underneath a plastic flap, which you can open when you *do* need to use them? And why do they all have black buttons which you have to examine closely to see which is which? Why can't the most frequently-used buttons be different colours, which light up when you press them, like mobile phones?

Even everyday non-technological equipment is badly designed. For example, going in or out of buildings can be quite hazardous. Some doors open inwards, some outwards — with a handle both sides. This means that doors have to say "Push" or "Pull" on them — and everyone has to read the sign before they can go in or out. How many times have you pulled when you should have pushed? Having a handle on the push side is totally unnecessary and confusing. There just needs to be a handle to pull on one side and no handle on the other side. Then every user would know what do and there would be no confusion.

Revolving doors are much more annoying. In supermarkets and airports they have to be large enough to accommodate trolleys as well as people. This is fine unless too many people and trolleys try to go through at the same time, and everyone gets stuck. Inside the door is a very small sign saying "Do not push". If you do push, which is what you intuitively do to make it go faster, the whole thing stops, trapping everyone inside. There are even doors at Heathrow Airport with built-in revolving shop windows showing products you can buy in the Duty Free shops, making even less room for people and their trolleys! Whose bright idea was that?

The problem is that designers are people who like things to look nice. If something looks elegant and attractive, they like it. But people need things to work properly and easily. Elegance is no substitute for user-friendliness.

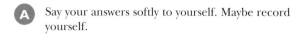

13

Relationships   Friendship   Families   Marriage

Just good friends?

13.1   Friends . . . and enemies
LISTENING AND TOPIC VOCABULARY

A Say your answers softly to yourself. Maybe record yourself.

B This activity can only be done with a partner.

 Answers:

1 R+S	2 W	3 W+S	4 R+W	5 R+W
6 W	7 S+R	8 S		

TRANSCRIPTS *8 minutes 10 seconds*

NARRATOR: Listen to Ruth, William and Sarah talking about friendship.

INTERVIEWER: Ruth, who is your best friend?

RUTH: My best friend is a girl called Kerry.

INTERVIEWER: When did you meet?

RUTH: Kerry moved to my home town when she was fifteen and I was fifteen and…er…her parents bought the hotel at the top of my road and so she used to walk to school…er…down my road every day and…er…one day I just caught up with her and…er…we started walking to school together.

INTERVIEWER: Why do you get on well?

RUTH: Um…we've definitely got the same sense of humour. We share the same sense of humour about a lot of things, I think that's really, you know, what it is that helps us to get on so well.

INTERVIEWER: How much time do you spend together and wh…what do you do?

RUTH: Well, I must be honest, er…we used to spend a lot more time together…er…before we got married and…er…had kids and stuff like that. Um…you know, we used to go to a lot of rugby matches together, er…rugby international matches. We used to go to Scotland and Ireland and…and stuff, and…um…just have a really good laugh. Er…but then, you know, marriage sets in and…um…children and things and so we don't actually see each other that often, but when we do, we just always have a really good time.

INTERVIEWER: What do you disagree or fall out about?

RUTH: Well, Kerry very much likes to stay in the past. And she loves to talk about the past, which I like doing as well. But she…she doesn't like changes very much and…um…you know, she likes to kind of…er…do things that we used to do when we were fifteen. So she'd still be happy to go…er…to Scotland to watch a rugby match, whereas that really has absolutely zero appeal to me now. Um…so I think maybe our kind of perspectives on life have changed and, you know, she'll say to me, 'Oh, you've become so boring, this, that and the other!' And I'll say, 'Well, you just live in the past.' So I think that…that's the only . . . We don't really disagree really badly over that, but that's certainly a difference between us now.

INTERVIEWER: Why is friendship important to you?

RUTH: Well, I think you go through life…um…and you have all these experiences, um…some good, some bad, and it's good to have people around you who have known you…er…for a long, long time, who can act as…um…a real support and…er…help you through good times…er…help you through bad times and share the good times with you. Um…and it's important to have people who understand you and who you can unload a lot of your feelings onto and…er…and ask opinions on, ask for help…er…about. Um…and just…er…have that kind of support network, and I think it's a very much a two-way system.

INTERVIEWER: How do you make new friends?

RUTH: Well, in the work I do I'm always meeting new people all the time and…um…I would say there's a difference between friends and acquaintances. Because I think it takes a long time to actually become close friends with somebody. Um…whereas you might make acquaintances, who you might kind of go out with and go to the cinema with or whatever, but

you won't have that same established history. Um…so I think as you get older, it's more difficult to make friends than it is when you're younger.
★★★

INTERVIEWER: William, who's your best friend?
WILLIAM: Er…my best mate is Geoff Buxton.
INTERVIEWER: When did you meet?
WILLIAM: Oh, we've known each other since we were kids. Er…our parents were friends together, we lived in the same street and we've known each other since we were about four.
INTERVIEWER: And why do you get on so well?
WILLIAM: Um…because of that really, I think. You know, we've…er…we've spent a lot of our lives together. We grew up in the same street and …er…grew up as kids, we went to the same school. Um…we went to the same secondary school, we even went to the same university. Um…we do quite similar things. We're, you know, different people but we have similar interests and stuff, so I think it's probably that.
INTERVIEWER: And how much time do you spend together and what do you do?
WILLIAM: Um…well, we both…er…live in the same area of town, um…so we see…er…each other, not every day but, you know, quite a few times during the week. Um…we play football together, um…we go out…er…with a similar group of friends. So…er…we socialise a lot together. So…um…you know, we go out to see the football and…er…watch films and go out drinking, stuff like that.
INTERVIEWER: And what do you disagree or fall out about?
WILLIAM: Um…ahh, that's difficult really. I mean we agree on most things. Er…I'm not too sure about his taste in music. Um…I'm not too sure about his taste in women sometimes. Um…I don't think we've really had too many girlfriends that the…either of us, you know has liked. Um…but we, you know, we're working on that.
INTERVIEWER: And why is friendship important to you?
WILLIAM: Um…I don't know, I think it's important to have someone who can…who's sort of fairly constant in your life, you know, who's there…er…no matter who you might have had an argument with, you know, someone who's…you can always run to and talk about things and…er…someone…er…who can tell you you're behaving like a bit of an idiot really, and you won't be offended by it.
INTERVIEWER: And how do you make new friends?
WILLIAM: Um…well, I suppose I meet people at work…um…or people that…er…Geoff might meet or . . . I quite enjoy meeting people that are complete strangers really on a night out or whatever.
★★★

INTERVIEWER: Sarah, who's your best friend?
SARAH: My best friend is a mad girl called Tonya.
INTERVIEWER: When did you meet?
SARAH: I met Tonya, I'd been in the UK for about two years and…er…we became sort of acquaintances and from there we worked on the friendship and now we're best of mates.
INTERVIEWER: Why do you get on well?
SARAH: Er…we've both got a warped sense of humour. And also we need people. I live on the other side of the world from my family, so I sort of need a new support system. And she has no mother or father any more, they passed away, so we understand about the same things. So for that we sort of have a common bond and from that we've grown.
INTERVIEWER: How much time do you spend together and what do you do?
SARAH: We can't actually spend that much time together because of our work schedules. She

now is in movie production so the…she's on set for hours, and of course I'm up and down the country or overseas, doing work. So…er…we spend a lot of time on e-mail and telephone. Um…it's a very expensive friendship! And…but whenever we get together we try to go away for weekends or even if it's just a girlie giggle over dinner, it's…we…we make an effort to do it when we're back in…both in the same place at the same time.
INTERVIEWER: What do you disagree or fall out about?
SARAH: What we actually fall out about is men. She's got the worst taste in men I have ever seen! And…er…she keeps falling for the same mistakes, so I end up going, 'Oh, my God, here we go again!' But you've got to be a friend and always be there when they do fall.
INTERVIEWER: Why is friendship important to you?
SARAH: Er…friendship's important because life can get so hectic and busy and…and…and you've got to put a lot of sort of energy into relationships, whether it be a personal relationship, you know, with a partner, or whether it be with friends, and if you have someone that knows you really well, you can just come home from a hard day and say, 'Ohh!' and you can rant and rave and you know that you don't have to explain why you're feeling that way. They can sort of go, 'Oh, here she goes again, yeah, yeah, yeah, yeah, yeah.' And…um…it makes you feel better that you're not bitching to the wrong people or you're…you've got confidence. As I said I live on the other side of the world, so friendship's very important, that I have a gr…a group of people, or even just one or two people around me to be there in the ups and downs.
INTERVIEWER: How do you make new friends?
SARAH: Making new friends is really hard as an adult. I think it's a lot easier as a child. But as an adult when you come to another country, people are already stuck in their little ways, they've got their partner, they've got their group of friends who know them, and they've got no need to make a new friend. They might like you as an acquaintance. But making friends with someone you really trust, and you want to open your soul and . . . That's tough! And it took me many years to get a very close group around me that I trusted, that I adored, that I had a lot in common with, that I felt safe with, and I wanted to make the effort with. Um…but as adults it's…it gets harder.

D Say your answers softly to yourself. Maybe record yourself.

E **1–3** Say your answers softly to yourself. Maybe record yourself. Some qualities that are missing from the first list are:

adaptability   communication   frankness   honesty   tolerance   trust

F **1** 🔊 **Answers:**

1 despondent *or* timid?
2 jaded
3 anxious
4 businesslike *or* impatient?
5 sarcastic *or* annoyed?

2 This activity can only be done with a partner.

3 Read the speech aloud and record yourself.

13.2 As the saying goes ...
GRAMMAR REVIEW

A These sentences contain structures that have been reviewed in previous Grammar Review sections. Questions based on proverbs like these are **NOT** likely to come up in the exam.

Suggested answers:

1 (unlike a *fair weather friend*)
2 When there **is a quarrel**, both parties **are responsible**.
3 What really **counts is what you** do, not **what you** say.
4 The world is **full of many different kinds of** people.
5 Be **tolerant** and **allow others to do** what they want to do.
6 You couldn't **have foreseen what would** happen.
7 Family **relationships are stronger than** other relationships.
8 A son tends **to behave in a similar way to his** father.
9 A remark **that is made jokingly may contain hidden truth**.
10 Absent friends **are quickly forgotten**.
11 When people **are parted from each other, they grow to appreciate each other more**.
12 After someone **has helped you, it's only fair to do something for them in return.**
13 If you **want something badly enough, you'll find a way of achieving it.**
14 Everyone **falls in love**, but they **recover from it** eventually.

B Do any of the proverbs have equivalents in your own language?

13.3 Family life
READING AND SPEAKING

Background

Gerald Durrell – see page 266.

Ian McEwan (b. 1948) is well-known for his short stories and novels which explore the slightly sinister and bizarre world of people who are leading seemingly normal lives. Particularly recommended are *The Child in Time, The Comfort of Strangers, The Innocent, Black Dogs, Enduring Love* and *Amsterdam*.
The Cement Garden is a disturbing story about a brother and his sisters who, after the death of their father, keep the death of their mother secret from the neighbours, and go on living as a family.

Paul Theroux – see page 275.

A The questions are intended to encourage you to look closely at the style of the extracts and discuss the content. They aren't exam-style questions.

Suggested answers:

1 The first is from *My Family and Other Animals*, the second from *The Cement Garden* and the third from *My Secret History*.
2 *Question for discussion* (The second seems to be the most intriguing – but the first is more amusing)
3 They are all told in the first person '*I . . .*'
They are about events that happened when the narrator was young (10, 13, 15)

The narrator seems to be an independent sort of child
4 The first extract is the only humorous one
The second extract is full of foreboding and menace, with its references to killing, death and ghostly faces
The third extract is more philosophical and the narrator is analysing his own character
5 In the first extract, the narrator was ten years old: he has a good sense of humour
In the second extract, the narrator was thirteen years old and though still a child in his ways, wished he could be more grown-up and fit in with adult male society
In the third extract, the narrator is a loner and an outsider, who up to the age of fifteen kept his second life concealed. He was a dreamer and, at fifteen, lonely
6 The family '*took over*' the book as he wrote it – their personalities were too strong for him to control, even when sitting alone writing
They behaved strangely
7 He probably had nothing else to do and was bored
He wanted to appear older so that he could relate to the driver and his mate
8 Poor people are not regarded as full members of society – they are outsiders
9 In the first extract he regards his mother and brothers (Leslie is a brother) and sister as amusing characters and as his equals, even though he was considerably younger than they were at the time
In the second extract, the narrator didn't like his father (perhaps feared him), describing him as '*irascible*' and '*obsessive*'. We don't know if his mother was living. We don't know about his relationship with his sisters
In the third extract, no members of his family are mentioned

B This activity can only be done with a partner.

C Even though there are no vocabulary questions in this section, the extracts should be treated as a potential source of new words.

13.4 Conditionals – 2
ADVANCED GRAMMAR

A **1** **Suggested answers:**

1 If it **weren't** for the children they would have split up by now.
– *fairly formal*
If it **wasn't** for the children they would have split up by now.
– *fairly informal*
Were it not for the children they would have split up by now.
– *very formal*
If they **didn't have** children they would have split up by now.
– *informal*
2 If you **should** see Terry could you give him my regards?
= You're not very likely to see him . . .
(rather formal style)

When you see Terry could you give him my regards?

= You probably will see him . . .

If you **happen to** see Terry could you give him my regards?

= You're not very likely to see him . . . *(informal style)*

If you **see** Terry could you give him my regards?

= You may see him . . .

Should you see Terry could you give him my regards?

= You're not very likely to see him . . .

(very formal style)

3 If you **wouldn't mind** waiting I'll let them know you're here.

= Please wait for a moment . . . *(very polite)*

If you **don't mind** waiting I'll let them know you're here.

= I know you have no objection to waiting (maybe because you just told me that you've got plenty of time) . . .

If you **wait** I'll let them know you're here.

= You have to wait (and not be impatient) . . . *(not polite)*

4 **Had** it not been for your help, I couldn't have done it.

– *very formal*

Without your help I couldn't have done it.

If it **hadn't** been for your help I couldn't have done it.

& If you **hadn't** been so helpful I couldn't have done it.

– *fairly informal*

I'm glad you helped me, **otherwise** I couldn't have done it.

– *very informal*

2 They would ALL be easier to understand with commas separating the clauses, except for the sentences using *but for . . .* and *without . . .*

B Suggested answers:

1 If you'd like to take a seat, I'll bring you some coffee.
2 Had they been more compatible, their relationship might have stood a better chance of surviving.
3 Should I miss my connection, I'll try to call you to let you know.
4 But for their parents' objections, they might have got married.
5 If you should have time, I'd like you to come and see us.
6 Had there been less traffic, we wouldn't have been (so) late.
7 If she were to tell him she is leaving, it would upset him.
8 Were it not for their wonderful relationship, they might not have decided to get married.
9 If it weren't for her patience and loyalty, she would have left him by now.
10 Without working hard at a relationship it's not likely to last.

C   If possible, ask another person to read and mark your sentences.

13.5 **. . . till death us do part?**
READING

" . . . to have and to hold from this day forward, for better for worse, for richer for poorer, in sickness and in health, to love and to cherish, till death us do part." (from the Church of England marriage ceremony)

Background

Tom Sharpe (b. 1928) is well-known for his comic novels, several of which are about the technical college lecturer, Henry Wilt. Sharpe himself used to teach at 'the Tech' in Cambridge. Among his other books are *Riotous Assembly*, *Porterhouse Blue* and *Blott on the Landscape*.

In *Wilt*, Henry Wilt is suspected of murdering his wife after she has mysteriously gone missing and he has been seen dumping a life-sized inflatable doll in a building site hole . . .

Nigel Williams (b. 1948), also a comic novelist, has written other novels set in the South London suburb of Wimbledon: *They Came from SW19* and *East of Wimbledon*.

The Wimbledon Poisoner humorously describes a series of murders which are committed in Henry Farr's suburban road – but not by him. Mrs Farr is not one of the victims.

Another amusing novel about wife-killing is **Michael Dibdin**'s *Dirty Tricks*, in which an EFL teacher marries a rich widow and tries to get his hands on her money.

A **2** Suggested answers:

1 Mrs Wilt
2 Clem, the dog
3 a small house (semi-detached)
4 Because he was a pedigree dog
5 Because he was not wealthy
6 He daydreamed
7 Losing his wife   becoming rich   becoming powerful and influential
8 He tended to lose them
9 He teaches (we can infer this from his wish to be Minister of Education – the Tech is the local Technical College)
10 A contrived accident – or murder
11 It seems to depersonalise her (making her seem less like a character in her own right, perhaps)
12 It emphasises his strange-sounding name (reminding us of *wilting flowers*, perhaps)

B **1 & 2** Say your answers softly to yourself. Maybe record yourself.

13.6 **Underlying meanings**
VOCABULARY DEVELOPMENT

Associations and underlying meanings are usually hard to explain, but they give some words richer meanings.

A Suggested answers:

yoga exercises	– middle-class? women rather than men? keeping fit? dieting?
Rovers and Mercedes	– better-off people? middle-class?
a semi	– less well-off people, suburbs, not as small as a terrace house or a flat but smaller than a detached house

an itinerary	– route provided by guide or travel agent, business travel, planned route
a pilgrimage	– religion, visiting religious sites
parried	– boxing, martial arts, fencing
the Tech	– further education? lower level than a university? students on sandwich courses? less motivated students?
fulfil his latent promise	– children or students who have so far underachieved, letters of reference for less able students

B **Suggested answers** (the words with more pejorative associations are underlined here):

cautious · prudent   cooperative · <u>obedient</u>
<u>difficult</u> · challenging   <u>dreamer</u> · idealist
<u>frank</u> · sincere   <u>gullible</u> · trusting
<u>humble</u> · modest   laid back · <u>lazy</u>
light-hearted · <u>frivolous</u>   <u>moody</u> · depressed
<u>naive</u> · innocent   optimistic · <u>impractical</u>
oversight · <u>mistake</u>   realistic · <u>pessimistic</u>
<u>solemn</u> · serious   stubborn · resolute
<u>studious</u> · hard-working   tease · <u>mock</u>

C This activity can only be done with a partner.

13.7 The narrator
WRITING SKILLS

Background

Margaret Drabble (b. 1939) is one of Britain's best-known writers. Her books, though touched with humour, seriously address the consequences of social change upon families and couples. Her best-known books include: *A Summer Bird-Cage, The Waterfall, The Needle's Eye, The Middle Ground, The Radiant Way, A Natural Curiosity, The Gates of Ivory* and *The Witch of Exmoor.*

The Millstone is about a young woman who has an illegitimate child, a poignant story which is both funny and sad.

A Suggested answers:

1 She seems to be very aware of her shortcomings, and doesn't take herself seriously
  She admires her own confidence and wishes she were braver
2 *. . . if I remember rightly . . . I do remember rightly . . .*
3 humorous self-mocking/self-deprecating literate, educated and possibly slightly pretentious (the use of words like *au fait, ascertain, our destined hotel,* etc.)
4 She presumably signed her own name in the hotel register: a puritanical receptionist may have refused to accommodate an unmarried couple, or at least asked embarrassing questions
  The fact that she is 'still not married' is a fact of some significance. The mixture of confidence and cowardice is going to play an important part in the story
  The story is probably going to contain a series of misfortunes, described with wry humour. *Having a millstone round your neck* means having a problem that won't go away. (Rosamund has an illegitimate child)

B **1** Using the first person means that the narrator can legitimately be expected to know everything about her own emotions. It makes the story more personal and is rather like a confession or diary. A third-person narrator wouldn't normally be expected to know so much. Compare this version – the details at the end of the first paragraph would almost certainly be omitted in a third-person narrative:

> Rosamund's career had always been marked by a strange mixture of confidence and cowardice: almost, one might say, made by it. Take, for instance, the first time she tried spending a night with a man in a hotel. She was nineteen at the time, an age appropriate for such adventures, and needless to say she was not married. She is still not married, a fact of some significance, but more of that later. The name of the boy was Hamish . . .
>   Hamish and Rosamund had just come down from Cambridge at the end of the Christmas term: they had conceived their plan well in advance, and had each informed their parents that term ended a day later than it actually did . . .

2 In **13.5**, it seems to be more amusing to view Wilt and Henry Farr through a third-person narrator's eyes, than to hear them speak for themselves. Compare these rewritten versions:

> Whenever I took the dog for a walk, or, to be more accurate, when the dog took me, or to be exact, when my wife told us both to go and take ourselves out of the house so that she could do her yoga exercises, I always took the same route. In fact the dog followed the route and I followed the dog. We went down past the Post Office . . .

> I did not, precisely, decide to murder my wife. It was simply that I could think of no other way of prolonging her absence from me indefinitely.

> I had quite often, in the past, when she was being more than usually irritating, had fantasies about her death. She hurtled over cliffs in flaming cars or was brutally murdered on her way to the dry cleaners. But I was never actually responsible for the event.

In the extracts in **13.3**, the use of the third person would make them sound less convincing, perhaps.

C **1 & 2** 🖉 If possible, ask another person to read and mark your work.

13.8 Writing a proposal
COMPOSITION

 A & **B** ✒ If possible, ask another person to read and mark your work.

Model version:

Lion Yard Student Centre

The need for a Student Centre
Research has shown that many students find it hard to make friends, particularly from different courses and faculties. A new Student Centre would encourage students from all faculties to meet in one central place, and make new friends.

Location
Lion Yard is a historic building, built 200 years ago as a warehouse. The building is derelict and is being offered to the community by its present owners for conversion into a Student Centre. The conversion would have to preserve the historic character of the building, as well as its façade. To achieve this, the interior walls would need to be demolished and new partitions erected to accommodate the facilities proposed below. There are three floors in the building, each of which would house different facilities.

Ground floor
The ground floor is an ideal location for a gym/fitness room and sports hall. The sports hall should be large enough for a basketball court or indoor soccer pitch. The gym/fitness room will need up-to-date equipment, but some of this could be obtained later. There will also be changing rooms and shower facilities. A staircase would lead from the main front door to the first floor.

First floor
This would be the main focus area of the centre, with a café, cafeteria and common room. Here students could meet over coffee, a meal or just sit together in the common room, which would be equipped only with sofas to encourage students to sit together. This would be a strictly non-smoking area. Smokers would be obliged to use the outside yard area in all weathers.

Second floor
For the moment this can remain empty. In the future this floor could accommodate study facilities or other social facilities, such as a bar or Internet café.

Cost
The cost of conversion and providing the facilities would be high, but I recommend that sponsors are found for each facility in the building. Thus each room would be named after its sponsor: the 'Cambridge University Press Café', the 'UCLES Cafeteria', etc. Former students of the University would also be invited to make contributions, and encouraged to donate equipment and furniture.

Staff costs would be relatively low, as all the staff would be students working part-time or even voluntarily.

14
Work Business Commerce

All in a day's work

14.1 Work and business
VOCABULARY AND LISTENING

A 1 Suggested answers:

Shazia enjoys working with people, being part of a team
Shazia doesn't enjoy the long hours, staying in the hospital overnight

James enjoys the variety, thinking on his feet, organising things, being left to his own devices, travelling, helping people to have a good life
James doesn't enjoy computers going wrong

Tessa enjoys the unpredictability, meeting interesting people, seeing her work in print
Tessa doesn't enjoy things going wrong: film, equipment, sometimes people

2 Say your answers softly to yourself. Maybe record yourself.

TRANSCRIPT   *9 minutes 15 seconds*

SHAZIA: My name is Dr Shazia Afridi...um...I live in London and I am a doctor. Um...I work as a neurologist...um...I work in...in a hospital in the centre of London...er...called Queens Square, which is part of the University College, London. Er...it's what's called a tertiary referral centre, which means that...um...it's...it deals with the very specialised cases of neurology and people come from all over the country.

INTERVIEWER: And what do you particularly like about your job?

SHAZIA: Um...I like...I like a number of things about my job, I like...I like working with people primarily, which is partly why I went into medicine. Er...I also like the fact that...um... I see new people every day...um...and I meet a wide...a variety of people and I like working in a team, which is something which is very important in medicine.

INTERVIEWER: Now is there anything you don't like about your job?

SHAZIA: Um...yes, I don't like the long hours. Er... unfortunately, being a doctor means you do have to work very long hours and you have to do what are called 'on called' which means you stay in the hospital overnight...um...and this affects your...your social life quite considerably and also means I'm away from my husband a lot of the time.

INTERVIEWER: If someone wanted to go into medicine, what advice would you give them?

SHAZIA: Um...I'll...well, I'd want them to know exactly what they're going in for. Um...so I think...er... working...work experience is a...is a very...er... beneficial thing to do. Er...they...they should probably attach themselves to a doctor and just follow them around for at least a week or...just to see exactly what the doctor does.
★★★

JAMES: I'm James Charles and I'm a butler and house-manager.

INTERVIEWER: And what happens on a typical day?

JAMES: Um...well, I...I open the post, I deal with...um...any post that's come in, anything that needs urgent attention gets done. I go on to the Net and check the e-mail and obviously check for faxes and things like that, that's the first…the first job really. Then there'll be a list of things to do, I mean, it maybe…um…anything, it may be that one of the cars needs to go in for service, it may be that…um…something has gone wrong with the telephones and I need to deal with that. I may have to go out, there may be something that I need to buy, so I, you know, I may take the car or one of the cars and go and…and do some shopping, and there may be research to do into a project that's going on at the moment, which…which can take some time…um . . .

INTERVIEWER: And can you tell me some of the things you enjoy about your work?

JAMES: Um…I like the variety, I like the fact that no day is the same as a different day. I like the…um…I like the reward that comes from thinking on my feet…um…organising things almost before the people that I work for know that they need things to be organised. I like the fact that I'm left quite a lot to work on my own devices. My boss works away or travels a lot, so I'm often there just on my own looking after the house or, you know, whatever goes on in the building…um…and I like the fact that occasionally I get to travel as well, not as often as I'd like probably, but…er . . .

INTERVIEWER: But you've been quite…to quite a few places with him, haven't you?

JAMES: Yeah, yeah, we have a…an associate company in California, where I…I go now and again. I've been involved in some business on his behalf in Australia…um . . .

INTERVIEWER: And has he got properties elsewhere?

JAMES: Yes, yeah, he has a holiday home in Jamaica and another holiday home in Italy in Umbria.

INTERVIEWER: And can you tell me some of the things you don't enjoy so much?

JAMES: Um…I don't like it particularly when computers go wrong. I'm not a great lover of…of technology and of course one has to use technology but it sometimes goes wrong in…er…in ways that are quite simple but beyond my brain.

INTERVIEWER: And does he expect you to be able to fix it as you're the butler/manager?

JAMES: Yeah, he has a habit of buying new technology and then not reading the book but expecting me to know how it works. Even though I haven't read the book either, of course.

INTERVIEWER: And if someone came to you and said, 'I've decided what I'd like to do is be a butler/house-manager', what advice would you give them?

JAMES: Be prepared to work very hard, be prepared to work long hours…um…and don't go into it unless you actually do care about helping people to…well, helping people to have a good life really. To…um…to make the path of their life as smooth as possible because that in itself is the major reward I think of this kind of job.

INTERVIEWER: What makes a good butler then?

JAMES: Lists, lists, lists. Very…you know you have to be very efficient. You can't afford to forget things so we all find a different way of doing it. I personally, you know, obviously I use computers and things but I make lists of things to do today and tick them off so that nothing as they say falls through the cracks. You have to be…you have to be cool, calm and collected too, you know. I mean, whether…whether people are annoying you or whether somebody's being over-demanding or whatever, you know, at the end of the day you are in a service position, if you like, and it's your job to…er…to do whatever, you know, somebody wants, you know, and if you don't like that then you're probably in the wrong business.

★★★

TESSA: I'm Tessa Holman, I'm a photographer…studio-based photographer.

INTERVIEWER: And can you tell me some of the things about your work that you really enjoy?

TESSA: I think probably the most enjoyable aspect is the…um…freedom of…of what I do, and also the lack of predictability. Um…I very much enjoy working with different people, meeting different types of people…um…having …er…a…a…different week every week, it's almost something different every day, never being able to predict what I might be photographing…um…from one week to the next really, and I've done some very interesting things and I've met an awful lot of interesting people.

INTERVIEWER: And are there any things about being a photographer that you don't like, or that you don't enjoy?

TESSA: The only thing that I…I s…find sometimes frustrating is that there's so many…um…things that can go wrong, from film to equipment to y…all the other variables that…um…er…human variables as well. Um…sometimes you feel that things are a little bit beyond your control when something happens that hasn't happened to you before…um…but other than that, no, I don't think there is. I think it's…um…a great job, a great job and I think I'm very privileged to do it. You know, it's…it's great to meet people, particularly if you…you admire them, you like them anyway, and then to…um…photograph them, I…I f…find incredibly exciting.

INTERVIEWER: And do you always photograph them not smiling, or not…er…you know, trying to look serious?

TESSA: It's very hard sometimes. The…the one person that I…I managed to photograph not smiling and looking very unlike herself was Julie Walters, who's a great…um…er…sort of comic actress, and…er…try as I might I couldn't raise a smile, she was not having a good day! One of the thing about…things about what I do is that…er…very often actors, actresses particularly sort of the…the very successful ones have to publicise a film, for example, that they've done and they'll be sent…um…seven photographers during the course of a day, to take their picture for various different magazines and newspapers. Um…and it's incredibly tiring for them, poor dears, but…um…you know, it…it's quite…it's quite difficult to…when you're only sort of number four or number five in the day when they really would like to go home, put their feet up and see their kids…um…to try and get them to be…um…original for you, is quite an uphill task…um…and that's why I think if you do manage to…to get something that's…that's really quite…er…other…as original as possible under the circumstances it's quite an achievement. And um…I think with Julie Walters, she was exhausted at the time that I met her, so that was…um . . .

INTERVIEWER: But you were still happy with the photos?

TESSA: Oh, very much, and she was incredibly pleasant and very, very nice, and…er…you know, expressed an interest in seeing the pictures, felt…er…felt herself that she was the best thing that she'd done that day.

INTERVIEWER: That's great.

TESSA: So that was…so that was nice that…er…to…to hear.

INTERVIEWER: Have you ever been surprised or disappointed by the results from a photo shoot?

TESSA: Um…I've been disappointed a couple of times…um…and yeah, also surprised. I think when you've gambled on…on a…on a…you're not quite sure if something's going to work, but you gamble on it, and it does come out and it does look very good, that's a…that's a really satisfying…um…you know, f…feeling. But also, because you have to hand your photographs over to a magazine or to a…to a newspaper…

um…they can do, ultimately really what they want with it, you know, they can make a layout look good or bad. Um…it's always very surprising when you get a…a magazine back that's got your photograph in it, and they've done a lovely job, or maybe given you a full page when you didn't expect that, and…and you sort of think, 'Yeah, I'm really proud of that, that looks great'.

B Answers:

1 D	2 C	3 D	4 A	5 C	6 B	7 B
8 A	9 C	10 B	11 D	12 D	13 B	14 D
15 C	16 B	17 A	18 C			

14.2 Collocations: verb phrases
VOCABULARY DEVELOPMENT

A **1** Suggested answers:

waves break   traffic lights change, but they can also break (stop working)   a boy's voice breaks (becomes deeper), but it can also change   a storm breaks   the weather can break (change for the worse), but it can also just change   your mood can change |day breaks

2 Suggested answers:

You can **break** . . .
a promise   a world record   an appointment (?)   crockery   someone's heart   a habit   the ice   the law   news to someone   the silence   your arm   your leg

You can **change** . . .
a promise (?)   a world record (?)   an appointment   a tablecloth   crockery   direction   gear   money   the bed or the sheets   a habit (?)   the law   the subject   trains   your clothes   your mind   your shoes

B Answers:

You can **follow** . . .
an argument   a line of argument   a route or directions   a story   a trade or profession   advice or instructions   someone's example or their lead   an idea   a football team
a football match   the fashion or a trend

You can **lose** . . .
an argument   control over something   face   heart   a football match   interest in something   the thread of a story   track of something   weight   your job   your nerve   your temper   your voice if you have a cold   your way or bearings

C Answers:

1 ask   lend   lifting
2 open   supply
3 cancel   placed   changed
4 pay   raise   collect
5 offered   resist   accept   lose
6 leads   running   strike
7 throw   drawing   bear
8 raised   reached   hold

14.3 A good ending
WRITING SKILLS

A Comments:

1 Not very appealing – it seems the applicant stands to get more from the arrangement than the employer. It's unwise to write this, even if it may be true
2 Seems fine, but maybe lacks a final punch
3 This is OK, though maybe rather dull
4 This is nice, though possibly rather pushy

B Comments:

9.3 ". . . And that is why I'm giving up."
– *short and punchy, sums up the whole of the article*
9.7 ". . . Once you start to think strategically, you begin to take control of your studies rather than letting them swamp you."
– *sums up the whole article, but rather wordy perhaps*
10.7 ". . . With clearer goals established, economic theory can tell environmentalists where to go."
– *a measured conclusion to the article, looking forward to further developments and progress*
12.3 " . . . In either case, it really isn't fair."
– *nice personal touch, encourages the reader to share the writer's feelings*
12.4B " . . . The scientists say the penguin is a better bet than human transport because it holds its body still as it swims."
–*some extra information is given which looks forward to further developments.*
A pleasantly colloquial final sentence
12.8 " . . . It is time for a change."
– *short and simple, looking forward to better things in the future*
14.5 "In fact that's not the case at all. Unfortunately, the only thing that seems to matter to some people is being better off than the next person."
– *rather disappointing as Prof Argyll's views on lottery winners only relate vaguely to the theme of happiness, and it's also a rather depressing ending*

The least effective seems to me to be **14.5**, but there are several contenders for 'most effective'.

C 🖉 If possible, ask another person to read and mark your work.

14.4 Word order: phrasal verbs
GRAMMAR REVIEW

A Answers:

1 a shop around
  b spoke up
  c had worn off
2 a pay it back / pay you back
  b won over
  c had left him behind
3 a saw them out
  b show her around
  c invite her/Pam out
4 a missing out on
  b checking up on you
5 a came up against
  b leading up to

B Answers:

1 tear it up   pay up
2 dream up   explain it away
3 hand in   talk him out of it   stay on
4 stick up for me / sort things out
5 caught out!
6 trade it in
7 wait up for me
8 climbed down
9 cracking down on
10 grew out of it

14.5 Learning to be happy
READING

A Say your answers softly to yourself. Maybe record yourself.

B Answers:

1 are passionate about
2 see eye to eye
3 some people
4 demanding jobs
5 reflecting on how they spend their time
6 not everyone can be happy
7 are less worried about being successful
8 become very unhappy

C Answers:

¶ 1	exercised	= kept busy
¶ 1	end	= goal
¶ 2	concludes	= judges
¶ 3	innocuous	= innocent
¶ 5	euphoria	= exhilaration
¶ 10	adrenalin-driven	= motivated by excitement
¶ 12	couch potatoes	= people who watch too much TV
¶ 17	mingling	= socialising
¶ 18	devout	= believing
¶ 23	inverting	= reversing
¶ 26	flipside	= less good side

D Say your answers softly to yourself. Maybe record yourself.

14.6 Beat the clock
READING

A Answers:

1 C   2 E   3 B   4 A   5 D

B **1** The 'most important' points are a matter of opinion. But generally, in this kind of article, the main point is likely to be in the last (or possibly the first) sentence of each paragraph.

2 This activity can only be done with a partner.

14.7 Looking for a job?
LISTENING AND COMPOSITION

A Answers:

1 Kerry   2 Neither   3 Neither   4 Neither   5 Anne
6 Anne   7 Kerry   8 Neither   9 Neither   10 Kerry
11 Both   12 Anne   11 Neither   12 Both
13 Anne   14 Neither   15 Anne   16 Neither
17 Neither   18 Kerry   19 Neither   20 Kerry

TRANSCRIPT *4 minutes 50 seconds*

CHAIRPERSON: . . . and...er...we've...er...we've discussed several ideas now and...and you've all had a chance to do some role-play of interviews, so I...I think it's time now for our two experts to give some final tips. Er...Kerry, let's take the application form first, because that's the first hurdle, isn't it?

KERRY: Yes, yes, that is the first hurdle. Um...now...er...my suggestion may sound silly but...er...it's not. Um...what you should do is...is actually photocopy the application form and practise filling in the copy so that you don't make any mistakes...er...when you do the final version. Um...and...er...always use the space provided, don't...you know, don't go on, don't exceed the space that you're...you're given, now this is important as well. Um...you may not know this but 95% of applicants are rejected on the basis...on the basis of the application form alone, it's very important. You see...um...people are so overworked, the selectors don't have time to...to read everything. Er...there...there may be 100 applicants for...for the job that...that you go after. Um...so they...they often skim the form, and they look for the important things...er...and the simple things: spelling, presentation and also vagueness, a lack of precision.

ANNE: Mm, yes. I agree with Kerry...um...but I would also stress that it is important to use words that actually show your interest in high achievement. Um...now, I'll explain what I mean: er...words like 'success', 'promotion'...er...'ambition', 'responsibility'. Er...it...it also helps if you've got something interesting or unusual to put on your form...um...this actually makes you stand out from the rest and it gives the interviewer something to talk to you about apart from anything else. Um...for instance, an adventurous holiday, er...a holiday job that you've done...um...an unusual interest you've got, as long as it's not too weird, you know, that sort of thing.

CHAIRPERSON: Mm, yes, I see, thanks. Now, about the interview itself...er...we've emphasised already the importance for the interviewee to ask plenty of questions, not just to sit there and be the passive partner. Um...Kerry, what do you have to say about that?

KERRY: Yes, that's...that's...that's very true. Always be positive, don't...um . . . Be confident, don't undersell yourself and always do lots of homework about the company that interviews you, find out about it, about...everything you can about it: it...its activities...er...its...if it has any policies...er...that...um...differ from other companies of that sort...er...and its subsidiaries...er...e...even its competitors.

ANNE: Mm, and the other thing to...to really be prepared for are some surprises at the interview. I've known all sorts of things happen, I've known applicants being asked to solve *The Times* crossword or sort through today's in-tray putting letters in order of priority. Er...the other thing that's quite common nowadays are group interviews with a few other applicants. Um...y...you might find that you're expected to spend a day with the personnel manager...er...having lunch with him, possibly even assisting him.

CHAIRPERSON: Another surprise technique that sometimes happens is…um…to provoke the candidate, the interviewer insults him or…or gets up starts shouting or something like that. And well wh…what should one do if that situation arises?

KERRY: Well, I mean, it…it's…it's pretty obvious: just don't lose your cool. You know, just…er…be…er…if you think about it, if…if you just keep it in your mind that that might happen, you'll prob…probably be all right but…er…with most surprise techniques it's…it's…it's impossible to be prepared for them, you just…um…have to learn to expect the unexpected.

ANNE: Yes, that's right, yes. And of course, don't panic. The…the best way to prepare yourself is just to practise being interviewed. A…and as…as Kerry said it's vital to present yourself positively as somebody who's socially sensitive, sparkling, has a sense of humour, adaptable and intelligent — if all those things are possible!

KERRY: But…haha…but if…er…if…er…in spite of all the…the advice we give you, you…you keep losing out…um…it's always good to try the technique of creative job searching.

CHAIRPERSON: Creative job searching? That's a new one on me!

KERRY: No well, it's…it's quite simple and you've probably done this sort of thing already. Decide on the kind of field that you want to work in and res…research it…er…do…do plenty of research and…and get in touch with the companies in that field and…er…oh, do…do everything you can: talk to people who work in…in these companies…um…an…anything to show your interest. If you can, um…get them to allow you to spend a day there to see what goes on and…um…who knows, in the end . . .

ANNE: They'll give you a job to keep you quiet?! Haha.

KERRY: Haha. No, but…er…if there's an opening, you'd be surprised, you'll be the person they think of to fill it.

CHAIRPERSON: Kerry and Anne, that's a great help, thanks a lot…er…I think it's about time for coffee now, don't you?

ANNE: Mm, good idea.

KERRY: Mm.

B Say your answers softly to yourself. Maybe record yourself.

C ✏ If you can't find a suitable advertisement, write an application for the job below.

If possible, ask another person to read and mark your work.

WORK IN
BERMUDA!

ACME Atlantic are a well-known and respected trading company. We handle imports directly from manufacturers in 35 different countries, often to our own specifications, and currently export to 46 different countries worldwide.

We are looking for enthusiastic people to work in our office in Bermuda on temporary 3-, 6- and 9-month contracts. Applicants must be able to speak and write at least one foreign language fluently and can be nationals of any country.

Experience in import/export will be an advantage, but as special training will be available this is not essential. The main requirements are a willingness to work as a member of a team, to cope with pressure, to use the telephone in a foreign language and in English and to be prepared occasionally to work long hours when necessary.

There are several posts available and long-term prospects are good, though initially all successful applicants will be contracted for a maximum of 9 months.

The salary we will offer is excellent. We will pay for your return air fare and provide adequate accommodation at a nominal rent.

Please apply in your own handwriting, enclosing your résumé, to Charles Fox, European Sales Office, ACME Atlantic Ltd, 45 Pentonville Road, London EC2 4AC.

Model version:

Dear Mr Fox,

I wish to apply for one of the temporary positions in your Bermuda office, as advertised in today's Daily Planet.

I am __ years of age and a citizen of __. I am at present in my second year studying __ at the University of __, which is a four-year course. When I finish my studies I am hoping to begin a career in the __ business, where I will be able to use my languages.

I speak English fluently, as well as Spanish and my own language. My written English is good. I am at present studying for the University of Cambridge Proficiency examination, which I will be sitting in June this year. My plans after this are to find work in another country before the new University semester begins in October.

I have worked during previous vacations in the local office of Acme Inc, where I was a member of a team dealing with enquiries from clients and suppliers from many different countries, using e-mail and the telephone. My line manager, Ms Muster, complimented me on my performance and would be happy to supply you with a reference regarding my character and suitability for a position with your company.

I am a hard worker, and I enjoy meeting people and dealing with people from different cultures. I enjoy work that is challenging and not routine, where each day presents new experiences and problems to deal with. I particularly enjoy working as a member of a team. The position you advertise seems exactly what I would be good at. I feel sure that my knowledge of __ as well as English would be a particularly useful contribution to the success of your team.

I am a calm, intelligent person and respond well to stress and pressure. I enjoy using the telephone and have plenty of experience in speaking to native speakers of English on the phone, as well as to other people who do not speak my language.

I am available from June 15 until October 15.

I enclose my CV which gives full details of my education, experience and background.

Looking forward to hearing from you,

Yours sincerely,

14.8 ## Use of English Parts 1 and 2
EXAM PRACTICE

Spelling is important here! A word spelt even slightly wrong loses a mark in the exam.

A These are the words in the original article, but several variations may be possible:

1 forced	2 approached	3 product	4 name
5 research	6 sale	7 exports	8 profits
9 hand	10 hope	11 developed	12 output
13 process	14 launched	15 benefit	

B Answers:

16 scientists	17 invention	18 technological
19 aromatic	20 production	21 consumption
22 dependence	23 uncertain	24 diversify
25 seller	26 continental	27 decaffeinated
28 striking	29 relationship	30 product

Music   Films   Paintings   Entertainment

15 Is it art or entertainment?

15.1 The tingle factor
READING

A Answers:

| 1 C | 2 D | 3 B | 4 C | 5 B | 6 A |

B Say your answers softly to yourself.

15.2 'You're being paid to be a child!'
LISTENING

Background

Simon Russell Beale (b. 1961 in Penang) is one of Britain's most famous actors. Since the interview was recorded, he has played Hamlet at the Royal National Theatre to great acclaim. His best-known TV performance was as Kenneth Widmerpool in Anthony Powell's *A Dance To The Music Of Time* on Channel 4.

Answers:

| 1 D | 2 C | 3 D | 4 D | 5 D | 6 C | 7 A |
| 8 C | | | | | | |

TRANSCRIPT *10 minutes*

SIMON: I'm Simon Russell Beale and I'm an actor.

INTERVIEWER: And you've just returned from a world tour of Shakespeare's *Othello*, er...where did you go?

SIMON: We went to Austria, Poland, the United States of America, er...Japan, Korea, China, Australia, New Zealand. It was an amazing experience.

INTERVIEWER: And what's it like playing Shakespeare to a non-British audience?

SIMON: Um...yes, that's quite a difficult question to answer because I don't...I mean, I...felt, after I'd played eight weeks in front of non-English speaking audiences, that...that my own performance, and indeed the whole show, was beginning to try too hard. It was...um...it's quite difficult to explain, but we were present...over-presenting it. Um . . .

INTERVIEWER: Were you aware then that the audiences were listening in a...to a language that wasn't their first language?

SIMON: Yes, although amazingly, and shamingly, the knowledge of Shakespeare in all those audiences was phenomenal and...um...er...they'd studied it, they knew exactly what Shakespeare was about, they knew exactly what *Othello* was about. So in that sense...er...the response was actually in some ways...er...quicker and faster than you find sometimes in...in...playing it in London. Um...but there was a diff...there were different reactions in different countries, um...and different things that made people laugh and different things that made people cry.

INTERVIEWER: And how do you think performing Shakespeare is different from performing more modern...er...plays?

SIMON: Well, it's a hugely disciplined thing to have to do because of course it's written in verse, and one must never forget that Shakespeare's a great poet, as well as a great playwright. Um . . .

it's to do with the...it's to do with the rhythm really. You have to, in a verse play, um...I...lull the audience in a way into this rhythmic heartbeat...er...that goes right the way through the play. And it...it's very interesting, it's...it's a...it should become a sort of subconscious thing in both the audience's ear and brain and indeed in the actor's...um...er...ear and brain as well. Um...but if it goes wrong you know it does. There's a sort of lurch, or there's a sudden break in the rhythm which you know is actually not what Shakespeare meant. He...he means a h...there's a th...a th...a gentle thud right the way through the play, it's just a heartbeat as I say right through the whole play. Um...and if you observe that, then oddly a lot of the emotional work that you have to do...er...as an actor is done for you by the playwright because he is so good.

INTERVIEWER: And how do you feel when Shakespeare's transported from Elizabethan times to modern day?

SIMON: Well, sometimes it works and sometimes it doesn't. I mean, one can't be prescriptive about these things. I...I think...um...certain people hate the idea of modern dress Shakespeare, and there are times even in our production of Othello when you think, 'Oh, hang on a minute, they...why do they use a gun when they...they're always talking about swords and things like that?' which is . . . I, in fact, in the end shoot somebody dead rather than stab them. Um...and I...I think in Othello actually, as...as it happens, it works extremely well because it's been very carefully done. I think that's the rule, if you're going to...if you're going to put it into a different era just...just be careful in the direction. Just make sure you don't make too many glaringly obvious er...mistakes or anachronisms, ...er...that ...er...that's going to jolt the audience out of concentrating on the play itself. But as a general principle I think there's no harm at all in...in setting it where you want to set it. You can set it on the moon if...if that's . . .

INTERVIEWER: Oh, I agree with that, I think audiences'll...will accept a convention...um . . .

SIMON: As long as it's clearly presented and as long as, yes, as long as, as I say, you're not jolted out of concentrating on the really important thing which is the words.

INTERVIEWER: Has anything surprised you about...um...during your time as an actor?

SIMON: Um...gosh! That's a tricky question. Um...I have to say there are things like I think actors and...um...people in the theatres that I've worked in, which is mostly Royal Shakespeare Company and the National Theatre, are...um... much kinder and much less insincere that the...than the popular image...er...portrays them as. And they're a...actors are essentially a very generous bunch of people. They're also a very bright bunch of people. Um...I've had to...had the luck to act with some, you know, extraordinarily bright and generous people. Um...so I suppose that, in a sense, is not a surprise but it's something that it would...I would like to be able to say is not the common perception.

INTERVIEWER: And how is performing on stage different from working in television or film?

SIMON: Um...somebody described it to me, a film director that I was working with...a television director said...er, 'Acting in film is like being a sprinter, and acting on stage is like being a...um...you know, a 400-metre runner'. There's a...there's a different type of energy needed in both. Um...there's long hours of waiting on film sets and then you suddenly have to do something extraordinary or emotional or funny or whatever...um...after hanging around for a whole day. Um...which I have to say I find difficult. Um...although I find the process of film-making intriguing and…and fascinating. Um…the…acting on stage is…is…requires a completely different energy…um…and it requires a different type of physicality. Um…again it's difficult to explain but there are certain actors who work very well on stage and don't work very well on film, and vice versa. And I think that's partly to do with their…the source of their energy which sounds very pretentious but I think stage actors…stage actors need a source of energy right down in their belly somehow, um…to produce the type of…of largeness of performance that can reach the back of an auditorium. Whereas film of course is a different…is…is much more internalised, and…er…and also you have…you have no responsibility in film on the pace of what you're doing. It's the…it's almost the first lesson I learnt when I first…er…started doing some serious filming which was only a couple of years ago, and…er…I suddenly realised I'd done a scene and the director came up and just said, you know, 'Just take your time. It's up to me as a…and my editor to make it pacey if that's what we want, but it's up to you to be as truthful as you can possibly be'.

INTERVIEWER: And…er…what do you really, really enjoy about being an actor?

SIMON: Oh, gosh! Um…well, I've been very lucky in that I've had to do…I've been asked to do great works of literature, which I have to say makes an enormous amount of difference, and that even includes the…the television that I did. Um…and exploring…exploring a…um…a character like Iago, you know, who's…borders on the psychopath. Er…it's just a fascinating journey. The other thing is, and this sounds very corny but it's true, is the camaraderie of the people that have met through the thirteen years that I've been working, and some of whom have remained friends for many, many years.

INTERVIEWER: And always will.

SIMON: And hopefully always will.

INTERVIEWER: And the fun, I always think it must be terrifically good…good fun.

SIMON: Oh gosh, yes! Yes, yes, also there is…there is a bit of a…a…a thing in…in every actor, isn't there, that . . . I talked about it as res… responsibility earlier, in a sort of odd way we never really have total responsibility and…and again that can be frustrating and sometimes you think, 'Oh I wish I could…I wish…I'd like to direct or I'd like to produce.' And lots of actors do that or write, where you have much more responsibility. But part of the fun of acting is the fact that it's still playing, isn't it? It's still being a child.

INTERVIEWER: But you're being paid to be a child.

SIMON: Yes, exactly, which is quite nice!

INTERVIEWER: And what do you not enjoy?

SIMON: Quite specifically learning lines, which is… it's . . . People ask, 'How do you learn lines?' It's just that that's a hard slog. That's just simply sitting down and like every job has a boring aspect, well that's the boring aspect of . . .

INTERVIEWER: Because Iago is the…one of the biggest Shakespeare characters?

SIMON: Yes, I think, well, I keep…I keep on being told it is the largest, that it's larger than Hamlet. I d…that might be…might very well be true in terms of number of words, um . . .

INTERVIEWER: And how on earth do you unwind after um…say, you've done two shows of *Othello*?

SIMON: You don't need to un…unwind after two shows of *Othello*, I'd fall over I think after two shows of *Othello*! Um…but I, you know, have a pint of beer in the…in the bar, you know, and there's usually people in, which is nice, friends…um…I'd always like to have a drink with them. Um…but I'm usually in bed within two hours of finishing a show. So I . . .

INTERVIEWER: That's because you . . .

SIMON: I…I don't find it particularly difficult to switch off.

INTERVIEWER: And lastly if…um…someone came to you and said they wanted to be an actor, is there anything…any advice you'd give them?

SIMON: Only to do it. I mean, I…I…I've been asked that a lot obviously and…and…and, you know, I used to think, 'Oh gosh, I ought to really… er…ad…advise them wisely and say, "Be wary, and it's a difficult business, and . . ." ' but eventually I…I…I've come round to the idea that if you…if you've got any idea that that's what you would like to do you've got to try it, and…um…for the…er…obvious and old reason that if you don't try it you'll regret that and it would be awful if you've…you know, you're 60 and you say, 'I wish I…I'd tried it.' So my only advice is: if the…if you want to do it, do it.

15.3 Prepositions – 2
GRAMMAR REVIEW

A Answers:

1 beside/next to   with
2 at   in   over   below
3 in   in   over
4 by   on/in   on
5 opposite   from   from   to   on
6 on   in   in
7 in   in front of   in   in   during/about
8 Besides   at
9 after   in   before
10 on   for   in/during
11 in   under   in   behind/in/on top of/under/ next to
12 into   in   in   by/beside/next to/under with   on

B Suggested answers (some variations are possible):

1 with   2 to   3 of   4 in   5 of   6 about
7 on   8 of   9 at   10 of   11 of   12 on
13 of   14 in   15 of   16 in   17 to

C Say your answers softly to yourself.

15.4 Conjunctions and connectors – 2
ADVANCED GRAMMAR

A Answers:

1 Despite my relative lack of knowledge of art, I know what I like.
2 Besides painting in oils, he (also) paints watercolours.
3 Without going to the box office today, you won't get seats for the show.
4 Due to the illness of both the tenor and soprano, the performance was cancelled.
5 Except for jazz, I like all kinds of music.
6 As well as missing his wife, he was missing his children (too).
7 Like you, I didn't enjoy the film.
8 But for the pianist's wonderful performance, I wouldn't have enjoyed the concert.

B **Suggested answers:**

1 Some people say that modern art is overrated, but **all the same I find the work of Pablo Picasso really fascinating.**
2 **It is sometimes said that** artists lead a good life: their hobby is their profession, but **they may have trouble making ends meet if they can't sell their work.**
3 **On the whole** Hollywood movies are ephemeral, **but every so often** you see one that you can't forget.
4 **To some extent** watching television is rather a waste of time, **but now and then you do see worthwhile, interesting programmes.**
5 **As a rule** politicians are honourable, dedicated people, **but there are exceptions to every rule and there are some who are corrupt or dishonest.**
6 **Many people believe that** reading is a wonderful source of pleasure; **however, some books are very badly written, and may not be worth reading at all.**
7 **To a certain extent,** people work because they have to, not because they want to, **but all the same many people do get a lot of satisfaction and pleasure from their work and their contact with people at work.**
8 **Generally speaking,** I enjoy all kinds of music **except for jazz.**

C **1–3** ✏ Look at **Activity 1** on page 199 before you write your composition. (This is not an exam-style task.)

Model version:

It is the end of a normal working day. In the foreground a farmer is still ploughing his field, half asleep, following his horse down a slope. Behind him a shepherd, with his dog and flock of sheep, is gazing up into the sky. However, we cannot see what he is looking at. Behind them both, stretching to the horizon, is the sea: an inlet or a bay surrounded by cliffs, with a magical city in the distance on the left, an island in the centre and castles and rocky mountain peaks on the right. A ship with its sails flapping in the strong wind is sailing close to the coast on its way to the open sea, sailing towards the west. The sun is just about to set. We notice, lit up by the last rays of the sun, the bare legs of a young man who is about to drown. Without knowing the title of the picture we would not realise this is Icarus, who has fallen out of the sky and splashed into the sea. No one has noticed except perhaps for one person: a man sitting alone on a grassy bank in the bottom right-hand corner. But there is nothing he can do apart from watch, powerless.

15.5 Use of English Part 5: *Guernica*
EXAM PRACTICE

A **1 & 2** Suggested answers:

1 Could make the general public talk about pictures or paintings
2 From the mass media
3 Because television is now most people's principal source of images
4 To emphasise that although political art exists, it is not effective
5 To emphasise the difference between the two meanings of value: price and worth
6 Wallpaper for the walls of the powerful: it is now completely without influence
7 He regrets it

B Say your answers softly to yourself. Maybe record yourself.

C Study the exam tips.

15.6 Two reviews
READING

A Answers:

1 c	2 a	3 c	4 c
5 c	6 d	7 c	8 a

B **1** Say your answers softly to yourself.
2 This activity can only be done with a partner, but look at **Activities 5** and **18** – they may amuse you!

15.7 Writing Part 2
EXAM PRACTICE

A The most crucial thing in the exam is to ANSWER THE QUESTION!

B **1 & 2** This activity can only be done with a partner.

C ✏ If possible, ask another person to read and mark your work. You can find reviews of recent movies at the Empire website: www.empireonline.co.uk.

15.8 Reading Part 1
EXAM PRACTICE

Answers:

7 B	8 A	9 D	10 B	11 C	12 A

15.9 Use of English Part 4
EXAM PRACTICE

Answers:

4 is expected to be poorly
5 is no question of me/my paying for
6 's previous film before *The Beach* was
7 was a fool to turn down the offer
8 never occurred to me to take up

15.10 good and bad
IDIOMS

A Answers:

1 can be used/in a satisfactory condition
2 That is a difficult/impossible question to answer – or one that I'm not willing to answer
3 reluctantly/unwillingly
4 in addition/extra
5 a favour
6 permanently

7 restless, sleepless night
8 considered to be impolite/rude
9 deteriorated even more
10 to my advantage
11 completely useless   dishonourable person
12 is valid

B Answers:

1 make good money
2 in good time   makes a good impression
3 as good as her word
4 as good as new
5 a bad leg/ankle/knee
6 in a bad way
7 've a good mind
8 put in a good word
9 gave it up as a bad job
10 while the going's good
11 in good faith
12 a good job

---

16 Health   Doctors   Psychiatrists   Keeping fit

Look after yourself!

16.1 A healthy life?
READING AND VOCABULARY

A Answers:

1 B   2 B   3 B   4 B   5 D

B Say your answers softly to yourself. Maybe record yourself.

C Answers:

1 flabby   plump   stout
2 a consultant   a specialist   his GP
3 skinny   slim   thin
4 stress   tension   worry
5 fainted   lost consciousness   passed out
6 twinges   ache   pain
7 vaccines   preventive medicine   healthy living
8 a sedative   a pain-killer   a tranquilliser
9 capsules   tablets   pills
10 pull through   get better   get well
11 rash   swelling   inflammation   (some people,
   particularly hypochondriacs, might go to the doctor about
   any of these problems)
12 catching   contagious   infectious
13 an examination   a check-up   a medical
14 pulled a muscle   sprained her ankle   fractured
   her wrist
15 alternative   complementary   fringe

D Answers (alternatives with incorrect spellings like 1 and 2 would NOT appear in the exam):

1 psychosomatic   2 anaesthetic   3 unbalanced
4 transmitted   5 gynaecologist   6 threw up
7 allergy   8 eradicated   9 stomach
10 agoraphobia

E Listen to the 'doctor, doctor' jokes, just for fun.

TRANSCRIPT   *1 minute*

PATIENT: Doctor, doctor, I keep thinking there's two of me.
DOCTOR: One at a time please.

PATIENT: Doctor, doctor, I've lost my memory.
DOCTOR: When did this happen?
PATIENT: When did what happen?

PATIENT: Doctor, doctor, my little boy's swallowed a bullet.
   What shall I do?
DOCTOR: Well, for a start, don't point him at me.

PATIENT: Doctor, doctor, I keep thinking I'm a pack of cards.
DOCTOR: Sit down. I'll deal with you later.

PATIENT: Doctor, doctor, I keep thinking I'm a dog.
DOCTOR: Lie down on the couch and I'll examine you.
PATIENT: I can't. I'm not allowed on the furniture.

PATIENT: Doctor, doctor, people keep ignoring me.
DOCTOR: Next please!

PATIENT: Doctor, doctor, I keep thinking I'm a spoon.
DOCTOR: Well, sit there and don't stir.

PATIENT: Doctor, doctor, I feel like a pair of curtains.
DOCTOR: Pull yourself together, man!

PATIENT: Doctor, doctor, my hair's coming out. Can you give
   me something to keep it in?
DOCTOR: Certainly. How about a paper bag?

PATIENT: Doctor, doctor, my wooden leg's giving me a lot of
   pain.
DOCTOR: Why is that?
PATIENT: My wife keeps hitting me over the head with it.

16.2 Speaking
EXAM PRACTICE

This section can only be done with a partner.

16.3 Relative clauses
GRAMMAR REVIEW

A Answers:

1 The doctor I spoke to yesterday told me not to
   worry.
   – I've talked to other doctors about my problem,
   but the one I consulted yesterday tried to reassure
   me (informal or neutral style)
   The doctor, **whom** I spoke to yesterday, told me not
   to worry.
   – I normally consult only one doctor and when I
   talked to him/her yesterday, I was reassured
   (formal style)
   The doctor, **who** I spoke to yesterday, told me not
   to worry.
   – I normally consult only one doctor and when I
   talked to him/her yesterday, I was reassured
   (informal or neutral style)
   The doctor **to whom** I spoke yesterday told me not
   to worry.

– I've talked to other doctors about my problem, but the one I consulted yesterday tried to reassure me (*formal style*)

2 He told us about the treatment, **which** made him feel better.

– Just telling us about the treatment improved his health, not necessarily the treatment itself

He told us about the treatment **that** made him feel better.

– It was the treatment itself that improved his health

3 They operated on the first patient **who** was seriously ill.

– Several other less sick patients were not operated on: the very ill one got preferential treatment

They operated on the first patient, **who** was seriously ill.

– Patient number one was very ill and he/she was operated on

B Answers (commas have been added where necessary):

The Californians have come up with a device for people **who**¹ have their own small swimming pool, **which**² should transform their lives as much as those indoor exercise bikes **which**³ were so popular in the 1970s did. Swimming, **which**⁴ is recognised to be one of the best ways of keeping fit, is impractical in pools **that/which**⁵ are too small for serious swimming. But the *Hydroflex* is a new device **which/that**⁶ can keep swimmers in the same spot and still allow them to do all the strokes. It consists of a plastic bar **which/that**⁷ is attached to the side of the pool by two lines and to the swimmer by a waist belt. The swimmer, **whose**⁸ legs are protected from the lines by the bar, remains stationary while swimming. It sounds like an activity **that/which**⁹ is only suitable for people **whose**¹⁰ desire to keep in shape helps them to ignore the taunts of neighbours **who**¹¹ happen to spot them in the pool.

C Answers (commas have been added where necessary):

1 He's the only person I know **who runs/swims/ walks** ten kilometres a day before breakfast.
2 I swam twenty lengths, **which took** me a long time.
3 He has two sisters both **of whom are** doctors. The younger of the two, **whose name is** Jane, qualified last year. He also has two brothers, neither **of whom** knows anything about medicine.
4 One of the children must have swallowed the pills **which had been/were** left in the bathroom.
5 All **of the things that/which** people say about hospitals is true.
6 She loves talking about her operation, **which made** us all feel ill.
7 The matron is the **person who** is in overall charge of the nursing staff.
8 Taking a degree in medicine, **which takes much** longer that most other university courses, is the only method **by which/by means of which** one can become a doctor.

16.4 ## Listening Part 1

EXAM PRACTICE

🔊 To simulate exam conditions, listen to each extract twice.

Answers:

Extract One	1 B	2 C	
Extract Two	3 B	4 A	
Extract Three	5 C	6 A	
Extract Four	7 B	8 C	

TRANSCRIPTS *5 minutes 40 seconds*

1

DOCTOR: Ah, Jim, good morning.
PATIENT: Morning, doctor.
DOCTOR: Have a seat. Right, now what seems to be the trouble?
PATIENT: Agh. Well, mm…I've got this awful pain in my chest. [Mhm.] I think I may have cracked a rib or something. It really hurts a lot, especially when I move. [Right.] I hoped it'd get better over the weekend, but on Monday it was even worse, and today if anything it's still worse again.
DOCTOR: Right, OK, well, let's have a look. [Thanks.] Does it hurt when I do this?
PATIENT: Aaah! Yes, it does.
DOCTOR: And this?
PATIENT: Oooh! Oh!
DOCTOR: Hmm. OK, well, when did you do this?
PATIENT: Oh, that's the funny thing. I'm not really sure when it happened. It just started hurting on Thursday when I woke up. [Mhm.] I…I thought I must have been lying awkwardly in bed, you know, like a crick in the neck. Th…then I thought back over the previous day and the only thing I can think of is that…what happened when I was in the supermarket. I was bending over the freezer and someone got me with the corner of their trolley. [Right.] It didn't really hurt at the time.
DOCTOR: OK, well, that must be it, I imagine. Well, there's not a lot I can do. Um…there's no point in…in…in going to have an X-ray. Er…I think you'll just have to let it get better by itself.
PATIENT: How long will that take?
DOCTOR: A couple of months.
PATIENT: A couple of months!!
DOCTOR: Yes, you just have to take it easy and rest. Take…you can take pain-killers if it gets too bad.
PATIENT: Mm. Oh, well, thanks a lot.
DOCTOR: That's all right. Er…come back and see me in a…in a month. OK?
★★★

2

REPORTER: Well, homeopathy was invented by a German chemist called Samuel Hahnemann. At that time it was already known that quinine, which is made from the bark of a tree that grows in South America, could be used to treat malaria. Hahnemann gave very strong doses of quinine to himself, his family and friends, who were all perfectly healthy people, and he found that they all developed exactly the same symptoms – it was as if they actually had malaria, which they didn't really, of course.

Then he carried out more experiments, using his friends and his pupils as guinea pigs, getting them to take doses of hundreds of other substances. [*actually only 100*] Including lots of different herbs and even metals like gold and copper, to find out what the effect of each one was – to…to find what symptoms developed. In this process of 'proving' the substances, he discovered that, for example, taking regular doses of arsenic caused vomiting and diarrhoea. So, in other words, he produced 'artificial' diseases.

Well, I suppose the crucial connection he made was between the cure and the illness, and this is one of the fundamental principles of homeopathy: treating like with like. He discovered that if patients suffering from the same symptoms, from natural diseases, were given minute doses of the same substance that caused the equivalent artificial disease, they actually got better. And he used the 'single blind' technique whereby none of the patients knew if they were taking an inert powder or the medicine itself – only he knew.

★★★

3

DOCTOR: Well, I'm a doctor and I've spent my life dealing with people who seek cures, and just want to get better. Er…they may find a…a…a smart office with framed diplomas on the wall reassuring, and enjoy being listened to sympathetically. But what counts for them is results. And the most impressive way to present results is in the form of testimonials from satisfied customers.

But anyone who's done any sort of…er…service job knows just how easy it is to acquire flattering testimonials. I mean, I have drawers full of grateful letters from patients who survived my treatment, thanks more to their luck than my judgement. And the fact is that anyone who treats patients can earn the same kinds of tributes, thanks to the body's vigorous powers of self-healing. And…um…I'm not suggesting that most of my patients are hypochondriacs!

★★★

4

MAN: I had a really strange dream last night.
WOMAN: Oh, don't tell me about it, please!
MAN: I wasn't going to. It just made me think about this piece I read the other day by J.B. Priestley. [Uh?] He says that he really likes dreaming, going to bed and lying still and then, oh, what did he say? Mm, 'By some strange magic, wandering into another kind of existence.' He said it was as if there were at least two extra continents added to the world . . .
WOMAN: What?
MAN: Uh… and, oh…er…'lightning excursions running to them at any moment between midnight and breakfast'. Then he wrote about 'huge mysterious anxieties, with…er…luggage that can't be packed and trains that refuse to be caught' and 'there are thick woods outside the bathroom door' [Bathroom!] and 'the dining-room is somehow part of a theatre'. And then, oh, what did he say? Oh, yeah, 'then there are moments of desolation and terror in the dream world, that are worse than anything we've known under the sun.'
WOMAN: Like?
MAN: Well, I'm not sure, but…but…ah, then on the other side of that the, you know, sometimes this other life can be very attractive and every now and then 'a serene glow or a sudden ecstasy, like glimpses of another form of existence altogether, that we can't match with open eyes'. Mm? I…I agree with him, dreams are wonderful. What do you think?

16.5 Use of English Part 2
EXAM PRACTICE

Answers (spelling must be correct for a mark in the exam!):

1 themselves   2 conference   3 loneliness
4 difficulty/difficulties   5 persistent
6 embarrassment   7 failure   8 outside
9 inadequate   10 conditioning   11 pre-disposition
12 psychologists   13 self-conscious   14 thought
15 partly

16.6 Listening Part 2: Was Freud a fraud?
EXAM PRACTICE

 To simulate exam conditions, listen to the recording twice.

A Suggested answers:

1 got worse   2 a good story / fiction
3 novelist/writer   4 slip of the tongue
5 disregarded / poorly reviewed   6 pleasure
7 not original / not invented by him
8 discouraged/restricted   9 fooled

B Say your answers softly to yourself. Maybe record yourself.

Suitable words to describe Professor Abrahams:

*vehement   sarcastic   scathing   brusque   urbane
malicious   energetic   erudite   quick-witted*

(A *psychologist* studies human behaviour, a *psychiatrist* treats people who have mental or emotional problems.)

TRANSCRIPT   *4 minutes 40 seconds*

PRESENTER: In most people's estimation the Viennese psycho-analyst Sigmund Freud ranks with Copernicus, Galileo, Darwin and Einstein as one of the greatest scientists of all time, in fact a true genius. Well, how true is this? Professor Carl Abrahams says we've all been fooled too long. Is that right, Professor Abrahams?

ABRAHAMS: Yes, the truth is that Freud is one of the most successful charlatans who ever lived. He pulled the wool over his contemporaries' eyes and his followers continue to pull the wool over people's eyes today. Now, just for a start: there's no evidence whatsoever that psycho-analysis has ever cured anyone of anything. Ha…it's become clear that Freudian psycho-analysis is pure hokum according to over 500 empirical studies of patients. Now, those who supposedly benefited from psychiatrists' treatment fared no better than those who were left to their own devices, indeed there's good evidence that it made some patients worse. Now, most professional psychiatrists know this very well, but the world is full of amateur psychiatrists like teachers, social workers, probation officers, and even parents, who attempt to apply misunderstood and speculative Freudian ideas.

PRESENTER: Speculative?
ABRAHAMS: Yes, yes. Freud's so-called apparatus for explaining human behaviour is pure speculation. Also there…there's no concrete evidence that his methods even worked for him. For example, the so-called 'wolf-man', this man who had dreams of wolves sitting in a tree outside of his house: now, he had exactly the same symptoms and the same problems for the rest of his life after supposedly being cured by Freud successfully. Freud concocted a beautifully literary story but he omitted certain factual details and he actually added his own imaginative content. Now, this has been proved by detective work in other patients he treated. Very often he clearly made an erroneous diagnosis and his treatment was unsuccessful but he chose to ignore these cases. In other words, Freud appears to have been a brilliant novelist but a lousy doctor.

PRESENTER: Now, Carl Jung's main criticism of Freud's work was that he placed excessive emphasis on sexuality and on childhood experiences as being the origins of neurotic disorders, wasn't it?

ABRAHAMS: Absolutely, his equation of pleasure with sexuality was unjustified. Now, it's caught the public's imagination and kept it for the whole of this century. Take the Freudian Slip that people refer to when they make a slip of the tongue…er…for instance: 'the breast thing to do' instead of 'the best thing to do', you see. Now this is popularly supposed to be due to a man's desire to return to his mother's body, like Oedipus, but it's…ha…it's all absolute rubbish of course.

PRESENTER: But how did Freud manage to fool people in the way you say he did?

ABRAHAMS: Ah, well, it's very interesting. Firstly he consciously set out to create a myth of himself as the misunderstood and persecuted hero, whose books were disregarded and poorly reviewed. Well, nothing could be further from the truth. Now, just look at the medical journals of the time and you will find long and enthusiastic reviews of every one of his publications. Some were even commenting back then on his genius. Indeed, the greatest myth of all is that Freud was a genius, that…that his was a truly original mind at work. He is popularly supposed to have invented the unconscious. Well…ha…again this is utter nonsense. People had been writing about the unconscious mind for 2,000 years before Freud, indeed it was being widely discussed by educated people long before Freud claimed it for his own.

For example, his so-called Freudian symbolism was common knowledge in Greek and Roman times and his supposedly new method of free association had been publicised by Sir Francis Galton years before Freud claims to have invented it. Now, other theories he claimed as original had been proposed by…er…Pierre Janet, for instance, and so on and so on.

PRESENTER: Well, all right, so Freud may have been a fraud, but how has his influence been harmful?

ABRAHAMS: Well…er…three instances. Number one: by encouraging speculation instead of experimental studies. Er…number two: by encouraging…er… nebulous philosophising and so on. And number three: by discouraging rigorous clinical trials. Now, although Freud is not taken seriously by any self-respecting professional any more, the psycho-analysts of the world are making a very good living from the gullibility of…er…the public, who still believe that Freud can not only explain their problems but even that he…that he knows how to cure them. In short, it'll be a long time before the myths, the utter myths, that Freud himself so…so artfully created can finally be expunged.

PRESENTER: Professor Abrahams, thank you.

ABRAHAMS: You're welcome.

16.7 Synonyms and homonyms
VOCABULARY DEVELOPMENT

A **1 & 2** 🔊 **Answers** (suitable synonyms and phrases which could also describe the tone of the speaker are given in *italics*):

1	furious	– *livid, vehement*
2	cross	– *annoyed, indignant, upset*
3	kind	– *sympathetic, amiable, affectionate*
4	bored	– *jaded, weary, fed up*
5	unemotional	– *phlegmatic, matter-of-fact*
6	friendly	– *cheerful, reassuring, welcoming, pleased, glad, positive*
7	sad	– *depressed, despondent, upset*
8	amused	– *delighted, enchanted, taking it as a big joke, finding the situation hilarious*

TRANSCRIPT *2 minutes 30 seconds*

PRESENTER: Listen to each speaker and select a suitable adjective to describe their mood or tone.

(The Presenter gives a number to introduce each speaker)

SPEAKERS: Ah there you are. I was wondering where you'd got to. Luckily I had some work to get on with so I wasn't bored. Anyway, even if the film has started by the time we get there, I don't think it'll matter – do you?

(The exact words used vary slightly from speaker to speaker)

B Answers:

amazed = *astonished*	annoyed = *indignant*	
clever = *talented*	confused = *bewildered*	
cured = *better*	depressed = *despondent*	
determined = *persistent*	different = *diverse*	
disappointed = *disillusioned*	dull = *dreary*	
encouraged = *heartened*	exciting = *thrilling*	
frightened = *scared*	glad = *delighted*	
respected = *admired*	revolting = *disgusting*	
shocked = *horrified*	upset = *distressed*	
worried = *anxious*	worrying = *disturbing*	

There are few *exact* equivalents when it comes to synonyms: near-synonyms are often used in different contexts.

C Suggested answers:

1 Surfing can be **risky**, but hang-gliding is **a far more hazardous pastime**.
2 There are many **effective** ways of keeping fit **and jogging is a particularly effective way of keeping in shape**.
3 I was **delighted** to meet my old friends again. It was **wonderful to have the chance to talk** about old times.
4 I'm sorry that you were **under the weather** yesterday. You look **as fit as a fiddle** today.
5 It was **very generous** of you to offer to help, but the work wasn't **particularly demanding**.
6 We went for **an invigorating** walk at the weekend, ending up at a **delightful** restaurant.
7 The original novel was **entertaining**, but the film they made of it was **dreary**.
8 The meal we had last night was **delicious**, but the wine **was disappointing**.

D Answers:

1 came up with
2 get through/across to them   got me down
3 take back
4 put up with
5 brings on
6 held up
7 made up   took in
8 came apart
9 go along with
10 put out

16.8 Writing Part 1
EXAM PRACTICE

A Make notes.

B **1** Do this under exam conditions, without a dictionary.

2 If possible, ask another person to read and mark your work.

Model version:

> Should we trust the experts when they tell us how to remain in good health and go on living for a long time? We all know that being overweight and unfit is detrimental to our health. The experts tell us what to eat, how to take exercise, how to avoid stress and not to drink or smoke. How can we possibly do everything they advise?
>
> Of course we should all try to eat a well-balanced diet with plenty of fruit and vegetables, fish and not too much red meat. Not too much fat and sugar and salt. And over-eating is clearly bad for us and will make us fat. We can follow expert advice on diet, but not too rigidly. Healthy food may be more expensive, and not everyone can afford it.
>
> We can keep fit by walking or cycling, but walking and cycling take time and, with the traffic and pollution in our city, they may be dangerous too. On the other hand, going to the gym or jogging can be too energetic. A more gentle form of exercise may be preferable: my recommendation is swimming regularly. Swimming is a wonderful way of exercising many muscle groups — and it helps you to relax. But not everyone has time to take exercise, if they have so much else to do.
>
> A certain amount of stress is necessary in modern life. People work harder and are more productive if they are under pressure. But if this stress is carried over into your leisure time and weekends, then it's certainly bad. We all need to learn how to deal with stress and then be able to "switch off" and relax by spending time alone and with friends. But not everyone can avoid stress, if it's caused by personal relationships and family life.
>
> We know that drinking heavily is bad for you and can lead to alcoholism. But, some experts say, a glass of wine helps to reduce heart disease. If we do drink, we should drink in moderation, and never get drunk.
>
> But if none of the recommendations fits in with your life-style, there's just one thing that will help you to stay healthy and live longer: don't smoke! Smoking is expensive, it's pointless, it's unhealthy and it's dirty. Anyone can stop smoking, if they have the will-power. And if they do, they'll save money and live longer.

16.9 Reading Part 3: Taking the waters
EXAM PRACTICE

Answers:

1 B   2 E   3 D   4 C   5 G   6 A
(F doesn't belong anywhere)

16.10 Use of English Part 3
EXAM PRACTICE

Answers:

1 count   2 operate   3 founder   4 exhausts
5 show   6 type

16.11 Use of English Part 5: Floating
EXAM PRACTICE

(A) Suggested answers:

1 To suggest stupid, senseless talk
2 Shabby and unfashionable
3 To evoke 'new age' music or hippies
4 To emphasise the non-sexual nature of the procedure
5 Drugs have a detrimental effect on your body; meditation is extremely boring
6 Because of the contrast between the tranquillity and serenity of floating, and the noise and commotion of going out into city streets
7 Loud recordings of waves breaking and whale noises are played to them
8 The effects of floating were discovered by an American scientist researching sensory deprivation. He found that spending time in salt water in complete darkness and silence enabled people to meditate, which induced feelings of extreme happiness. The craze swept across the USA after its appearance in a movie. In Britain, over forty have opened in the last six years, encouraged by recommendations from celebrities and doctors alike.

16.12 *mind, brain* and *word*
IDIOMS

(A) Suggested answers:

1 speaks frankly
2 freedom from anxiety
3 telling him off
4 promised
5 decide
6 couldn't decide
7 get a chance to speak
8 believe me
9 in my imagination
10 I forgot to do it
11 the ultimate
12 final decision

(B) Answers:

1 word perfect
2 picked your brains
3 go back on his word
4 brainwave
5 take your mind off
6 have a good mind to
7 word for word
8 it's their/his word against ours
9 had something on your mind
10 play on words
11 change your mind
12 racking my brains

17 The past is always with us

History Memories Changes

17.1 Use of English Part 1 and Reading Part 2

EXAM PRACTICE

A Say your answers softly to yourself. Maybe record yourself.

B Suggested answers:

1 style 2 name 3 made/woven/manufactured
4 native 5 emigrated 6 joined 7 business
8 idea/notion 9 reinforcing/strengthening
10 history 11 product 12 century
13 rest/whole 14 storm 15 example

C Answers:

1 D 2 D 3 C 4 B 5 D

D Say your answers softly to yourself. Maybe record yourself

17.2 War poetry

READING AND SPEAKING

A The poems are recorded.

B Suggested answers:

1 C 2 C (or A?) 3 C 4 C (though it is arguable that all the answers are true here)
5 B (again a case could be made for the other answers)
6 A 7 B 8 B (or A?) 9 B 10 A
11 C (or B?) 12 C (or A?)

C Find out more about the three poets by looking at **Activities 9, 25** and **30**.

17.3 Modifying adjectives and participles

VOCABULARY DEVELOPMENT

A **1** Suggested answers:

extremely pleased and *extremely important* are OK.
The others are wrong: it would be better to use *absolutely* instead

2 Suggested answers:

absurd ✗ preposterous ✗ improbable ✓
intelligent ✓ sensible ✓ brilliant ✗
amazed ✗ surprised ✓ astounded ✗
terrifying ✗ frightening ✓
fatal ✗ hazardous ✓ deadly ✗ harmful ✓
happy ✓ euphoric ✗
genuine ✗ believable ✓
identical ✗ similar ✓ priceless ✗ valuable ✓

interesting ✓ fascinating ✗
worthless ✗ futile ✗ inexpensive ✓
delightful ✗ pleasant ✓
essential ✗ important ✓

B Suggested answers:

1 He was **quite** determined to succeed, and he was **extraordinarily** disappointed when he didn't. We were **highly** amused, but pretended to be **really** sympathetic.
2 The amount of work that is required is **considerably** greater than we expected, and we'll have to make a(n) **really** great effort to finish it on time.
3 We were **absolutely** delighted to hear he was getting married, especially to such a(n) **exceptionally** nice woman.
4 He was feeling **thoroughly** depressed after his illness, but he made a **remarkably** quick recovery, and was **unexpectedly** cheerful after that.
5 We felt we had been **badly** let down when they told us our application had been rejected. We were **deeply** embarrassed because we'd told all our friends.
6 I'm sure her business will be **highly** successful, as she is a **remarkably** capable person, even though it's **perfectly** true that most new businesses don't succeed.
7 It was a(n) **absolutely** wonderful film and I thought the performances were **deeply** moving. It was **totally** different from any other film I've ever seen.
8 The role of women in history is not **fully** recognised by many historians, who tend to be **utterly** traditional in their attitudes.

C Suggested answers:

1 Some people find that it is quite impossible to remember historical dates.
2 We should be absolutely delighted to accept your invitation.
3 It happened so long ago that it has been completely forgotten.
4 It's quite futile to ask him to be tactful.
5 She was absolutely livid to find out about our plans.
6 It is totally improbable that he will succeed.
7 It is absolutely essential to remember to check your work through for mistakes.
8 We found the lecture quite fascinating.

17.4 The end of the war

READING

Background

Robert Graves (1895–1985) served in the First World War as an officer. *Goodbye to All That* (1929) is an autobiography describing his war experiences. Graves was nineteen when the war began, and many of his friends and fellow-officers died in the fighting. His prose works include *I, Claudius* and *The Greek Myths*, and his poems are to be found in any anthology of modern poetry.

A Answers:

1 C 2 C 3 C 4 C 5 D (the 'best' answer)
6 C

17.5 Adjectives + prepositions
GRAMMAR REVIEW

A **Answers** (one suggested meaning for *it* or *them* is in **bold italics**):

1 Drink up: it's good **for** you.
  – This **medicine** will have a good effect on you
  He was very good **about** it.
  – He behaved in a kind, calm way in spite of **the problem or difficulty** he had been caused
  She is very good **at** it.
  – She has a talent for a **particular sport or activity**
  She was very good **to** them.
  – She was kind to **the children**
2 She was angry **with** them.
  – Her anger was directed at **the people who had done wrong**
  He was angry **about** it.
  – He found **the situation** (of being passed over for promotion) annoying
3 I knew I was right **about** them.
  – My intuitions about **those people** were correct
  The choice was right **for** them.
  – **The people** who made the choice made the right one
4 We were pleased **with** them.
  – We were delighted that **the children** had performed well, which made us feel proud
  He sounded pleased **about** it.
  – He had been **promoted** and from his voice I gathered that he was glad
  We were pleased **for** them.
  – **The team** had done very well, and we tried to share their pleasure (even though it had done us no good)
5 She was sorry **for** them.
  – She felt sympathetic towards **the people who had suffered**
  He was sorry **about** it.
  – He regretted what he had done (**broken the window?**)

B **Answers:**

ahead ashamed aware capable conscious critical devoid envious guilty intolerant proud scared short unworthy wary weary	*of*
accustomed allergic comparable courteous cruel devoted equivalent hurtful identical impolite indifferent inferior irrelevant kind loyal preferable sensitive similar superior susceptible unfaithful	*to*

C **Answers** (the ones in *italics* can be used with more than one of the prepositions — see below):

annoyed apprehensive bewildered curious dubious fussy guilty *indignant* sceptical vague	*about*
absent famous responsible	*for*
absent far free	*from*
dependent intent keen	*on*
annoyed comparable compatible consistent conversant familiar *indignant* level patient	*with*

He was absent **from** class / **for** the test.
She was annoyed **with** me / **about** what I'd done.
They were indignant **with** us / **about** our behaviour.

D **Suggested answers:**

1 apprehensive sorry
2 kind proud annoyed impolite guilty good
3 critical accustomed responsible
4 indifferent sensitive sceptical aware hurtful
5 intent capable sorry wary

17.6 Listening Part 3: Emigration
EXAM PRACTICE

A 🔊 To simulate exam conditions, listen to the recording twice.

Answers:

1 D	2 D	3 C	4 D	5 B	6 B	7 A	8 C

TRANSCRIPT *7 minutes 15 seconds*

LECTURER: . . . and in the nineteenth century huge changes in population took place which affected the entire world. Er…the world population grew from 900 million in 1810 to 1600 million a hundred years later. So throughout the 19th century a pattern of voluntary and enforced emigration developed, reaching its peak…er…during the hundred years from 1830 to 1930.

Now, there were many reasons for this. Er…the famine caused by the failure of the potato crop in Ireland, and other harvest failures in agricultural regions all over Europe, er…religious persecution such as that suffered by the Jews in Russia, unemployment in urban areas and so on. But they all had one thing in common: the emigrants had nothing to lose. All right? So whatever happened to them at the end of their journey, it just couldn't be worse than what they were experiencing at home.

But there were also, of course, the advertised attractions of the New World, a place where, a…according to advertisements and rumour, cheap or even free agricultural land was on offer, where a…a…a penniless immigrant could 'become a millionaire'. [Haha!] Um…but, of course, as we know, the reality was different. The streets were not paved with gold, and reality for a poor immigrant could be…um…trying in vain to grow crops on semi-desert land in Montana, or…er…living ten to a room in New York and working for eight cents an hour in a clothing factory. [Oh!] Yes, really. Eight cents an hour. But…er…still there **were** opportunities, and it was probably better than the life they had left behind them in Europe. And the countries of the New World encouraged immigrants to come with promises of a better life. Yes, in the front there.

1ST STUDENT: Er…w…where did they come from and where did they go to?

LECTURER: Well, the largest number of emigrants in the nineteenth century was from Great Britain: eleven million went to the USA and Canada, two million to Australia and New Zealand. Ahh, the next largest . . . just give me one second . . . the next largest number was Germans: over six million emigrated mainly to the USA, but also to Canada and even Southern Brazil. Er…five million Italians emigrated to the United States and many more Italians went to Argentina. Four million Irish people went to the USA, many as a result of the Famine in the 1840s and its aftermath. Yes, that's…that…that…that was the…er…when a million people had died of starva…um…starvation when the potato crop failed. [Mm.] As I'm sure you know. Two million Russian emigrants, many of them Jewish, went to the United States. And then from Spain, most Spanish emigrants went to Argentina. Um...and from Portugal especially to Brazil. Oh, and large numbers of French people...um...emigrated, mainly to Canada and to North Africa, particularly Algeria.

2ND STUDENT: Er...excuse me.

LECTURER: Yes.

2ND STUDENT: Wh...what about Africans? Erm...the slaves weren't emigrants but they did settle in new countries too, didn't they?

LECTURER: Good point. Yes, we mustn't forget that the slave trade was still flourishing during the first half of the 19th century. Africans were still being shipped to the United States, to South America, and to the Caribbean – where their descendants now form the majority of the population on...on virtually every island if not all . . .

2ND STUDENT: Um...so . . .

LECTURER: Yes.

3RD STUDENT: So it was the USA which received the largest number of immigrants?

LECTURER: That's right, it was. Between 1830 and 1930, er...let me just get this right, yes, 35 million immigrants entered the United States. Proportionally, Australia certainly beats that: Australia's prop...population grew from a few thousand in 1800 to five million by 1900. Yes, on the left there.

4TH STUDENT: Um...er...so far you've...er...you've mentioned only...only the New World, but...um...I...I take it i...it wasn't just Europeans who emigrated?

LECTURER: No, by no means. Um...many people from India went to East Africa and South Africa, firstly to work temporarily as labourers on plantations. And...er...many of them never returned home. Er...the Chinese went all over the Pacific, particularly to the various countries of South-East Asia and also to the United States, where they...they hoped to make their fortunes in the Gold Rush and...and worked subsequently as labourers building the railroads — and...and most...um...stayed on afterwards.

5TH STUDENT: You're talking about what happened a hundred years ago. [Mmhm.] I was wondering what are the effects of all this on the countries today?

LECTURER: Ah, well that's an interesting...interesting question. Er...the number of second and subsequent generations grew and grew of course. There are well over thirty million Chinese people scattered around the world outside China and Taiwan. In the USA, because of the so-called 'melting pot' effect, the descendants of the early immigrants became English-speaking Americans. But more recent immigrants have retained their cultures and languages. Er...for example if you go to Argentina, there are districts in Buenos Aires where you can still hear Italian being spoken. Just as there are...er...German-speaking communities in...in Southern Brazil, where even second and third gener...generation immigrants still speak German as well as Portuguese.

Yes, in fact, almost every country has received immigrants at some time in its history. Some of this has happened more recently. Many Greeks, for instance, emigrated to Australia in the...in the fifties and sixties: the largest...er...the third largest, excuse me, the third largest Greek community in the world is in Melbourne.

And huge numbers of people from Mexico and Central America and the Caribbean have been emigrating to the USA since the 1940s. Cubans in Florida, Mexicans in California. And there was also a big influx of Koreans in the seventies and eighties: the world's second largest Korean community lives in Los Angeles. Yes?

1ST STUDENT: Um...but how can you tell what nationality someone is descended from? I mean, if they're Korean Americans they'll probably look different, but what about the Europeans?

LECTURER: Well, actually, a good way to find out the origins of people, if you go to a North or South American country, is to look in the...in the local phone book. [Oh? Haha!] Yes, strange but true! You see...you see Swedish surnames in the Mid-West of the USA, Italian surnames and Jewish names in cities like New York, er...Ukrainian names in Pennsylvania, Chinese and Korean names in California. In Canada there are many Scottish surnames. And all over North America you'll notice Irish names, Polish names, Hispanic names and so on in the phone book. And, interestingly, even if the grandchildren don't speak their grandparents' language, they often still do eat their national dishes at home or in restaurants. And this variety makes life for everyone in the country more diverse and interesting. Um...so, many people in North and South America can trace their ancestry back to another country – and, rightly, are proud of their origins.

B Say your answers softly to yourself. Maybe record yourself.

17.7 Listening Part 4: What if?
EXAM PRACTICE

To simulate exam conditions, listen to the recording twice.

Answers:

1 A	2 J	3 J	4 B	5 B	6 A

TRANSCRIPT *6 minutes*

PRESENTER: And in the studio today are Alan Forster and Jane Watson, both experts on early 20th century history. So, Alan and Jane, could the First World War have been avoided?

ALAN: Probably not. Er...John Keegan says 'the First World War was a tragic and unnecessary conflict' but I believe that the question in 1914 wasn't so much *if* a continental war would break out, so much as *when* it would happen, what form it would take and who would be the winners – and losers. But it could have been confined to a scale that wasn't worldwide in its events and influence.

JANE: I think it could have been avoided if things had turned out differently. At the very least it could have been much shorter by years, with the savings of millions of lives, if things had happened differently. And it could of course have turned out differently: Germany could have won.

ALAN: Also no one could have foreseen which nations would take part in the conflict. Nobody could foresee that the conflict would be so enormous or change so much or last so long. At the start of the war in August 1914, people said, 'It'll all be over by Christmas'.

PRESENTER: It all began when Austrian Archduke Franz Ferdinand and his wife were assassinated in Sarajevo on June 28th 1914, right?

ALAN: Yes, um...and on July 29th the Austrian army started to attack Belgrade, the capital of Serbia. On July 31st Austria, Russia, Turkey and France mobilised their armies – but Great Britain seemed ready to watch from the sidelines and remain neutral. It was a European affair, the British government thought. Relations between Britain and Germany were actually improving. Well, then Germany began to mobilise and declared war on Russia, Serbia's ally. France was Russia's ally, so they were committed to supporting Russia.

PRESENTER: And so that made France and Germany into official enemies, then?

JANE: Yes, and so what Germany did was to march through Belgium to attack France from the north. It was at this point that the British government joined the war knowing that this would bring the Germans a mere 30 kilometres from the English coast on the other side of the Channel.

ALAN: Yes, they could have put all their efforts into attacking Russia in the East, but this was considered to be the responsibility of the Austrian army.

PRESENTER: What if the British had delayed this decision by a week? And not started moving troops across the Channel when they did?

JANE: Well, the German army would have reached the coast but the French could still have prevented them from reaching Paris. It would have been too late by then for the British to move sufficient forces to France. This would have given Germany an overwhelming advantage. At this stage some sort of deal might have been reached.

ALAN: Yes, the Battle of the Marne was the major turning point. It was after this that semi-permanent trenches were dug and the Western Front was established – a front which would hardly change for four years.

JANE: Mm, in August 1914 the Germans should have won. The mistake they made was to remove men from the right wing (the western wing closest to the sea) and send them to the Eastern Front to protect Germany from Russian attack. They also strengthened the left wing – to protect Germany from attack from France. If they had maintained the strength of the right wing, their plan would have succeeded and the French army would have been contained inside a sort of sack with the German forces all around them. The right wing was too weak to complete this manoeuvre.

PRESENTER: And then there was a lost map, wasn't there?

ALAN: Ha, yes, on September 1st, a French patrol captured a German dispatch car, killing all their soldiers. They found a map which showed the German military plans for their next attack, which would bring the Germans to within 30 kilometres from Paris. This knowledge enabled the French to anticipate the next attack and stop it and to keep the Germans over 100 kilometres from Paris – a stalemate that would continue for another four years. The Front moved back and forth a few metres in various places, but in most places it never moved at all. Millions of lives were sacrificed for a gain of a few metres.

JANE: Mm, and the war might have been won by the Germans when on October 31st they attacked the British line at a place called Gheluvelt, near Lille in Northern France. They broke through the line and started to advance. But then they stopped for further orders. None came. 1,200 untrained Bavarian reservists waited for further orders instead of continuing the attack, which would have taken them to the sea, cutting the British army in half. An English Brigadier, Charles Fitzclarence, who was on the spot, made a swift decision. He sent all the men he had, a mere 370 men, in an attempt to stop the Bavarians. Against all odds they forced them to retreat and ended the German advance. Many of the Bavarians were killed, many were captured, but some managed to get away. One of those who escaped was a private from Austria – Adolf Hitler. What if he had been among the soldiers killed? Just one bullet would have changed . . .

ALAN: Well, also if the Germans had won – and they could have done this by reaching Paris – the war could have been over by Christmas. Millions of lives wouldn't have been wasted.

PRESENTER: What if the war had ended sooner? If Germany had made peace with France and Russia in 1914?

ALAN: Well, in Russia, peace would have allowed the Russian industrial economy to flourish, instead of being tied up in supporting the armies. And there would have been further moves towards democracy, which had been stopped by the war. There would have been no sealed train arranged by the Germans from Switzerland to St Petersburg to carry Lenin to start his Revolution.

PRESENTER: And if the war had ended sooner? So many lives would have been saved.

JANE: Mm, exactly, writers like Wilfred Owen and Rupert Brooke would have lived. There would have been an Ernest Hemingway but no *Farewell to Arms* and the most wonderful opening paragraph of the century: 'Troops went by the house and down the road and the dust they raised powdered the leaves of the trees.' [*See 11.9 for the continuation of this paragraph.*]

ALAN: Without the events of 1914 with its trench warfare, remorseless killing and disregard for human life, men like Adolf Hitler wouldn't have repeated this cult of death twenty years later.

PRESENTER: So, without the First World War, there would have been no Treaty of Versailles in 1919, no Second World War. And with no Bolshevik Revolution, there would have been no Soviet Union and no Cold War.

17.8 Writing Parts 1 and 2
EXAM PRACTICE

(A) & (B) ✎ Write both compositions under exam conditions (against the clock and without a dictionary). Ask another person to read and mark your work.

17.9 Speaking
EXAM PRACTICE

This section can only be done with a partner.

18

City life   Crime and punishment

Modern life

18.1 Reading Part 2
EXAM PRACTICE

(A) Answers:

1 D	2 D	3 D	4 C	5 B	6 D	7 D	8 C

18.2 Use of English Part 3
EXAM PRACTICE

(A) Answers:

1 sound   2 sharp   3 notices   4 fair   5 land   6 square

18.3 Use of English Part 4
EXAM PRACTICE

A Answers:

1 of crime prevention depends on
2 didn't/did not scream for fear of waking
3 a gradual increase in the
4 had their flat broken into / break-ins at their flat
5 journey to work takes an/one hour
6 is some doubt about the exact
7 not be able to rely on
8 of modern life are what I

18.4 Reading Part 3
EXAM PRACTICE

A Answers:

1 F   2 H   3 G   4 A   5 B   6 E   7 C

18.5 Use of English Part 5
EXAM PRACTICE

A Suggested answers:

1 She has no real friends
2 Destructive, causes a lot of damage progressively
3 There is something for everyone to enjoy in a healthy city
4 A small amount attaches itself

5 For people who find it hard to make friends, life in a city can be terribly lonely. The more people there are around, the more a lack of companionship leads to their feeling of isolation. But cities are thrilling places, full of so many different things to do which appeal to so many different tastes. Some excitement is dangerous and even unhealthy, however.

18.6 Writing Parts 1 and 2
EXAM PRACTICE

A 🖉 If possible, ask another person to read and mark your work.

Good luck!
Goodbye!

Leo Jones

Index

Grammar review and Advanced grammar

Vocabulary development

Writing skills and Composition

Verbs, idioms and collocations

Exam practice

Reading

Listening